Material Culture Studies in America

Material Culture Studies in America

Compiled and edited

with introductions and bibliography

by

Thomas J. Schlereth

The American Association for State and Local History

Nashville, Tennessee

Library of Congress Cataloguing-in-Publication Data
Main entry under title:

Material culture studies in America.

Bibliography: p.
Includes index.
1. Material culture—United States—Study and teaching—Addresses, essays, lectures. 2. Material culture—United States—Addresses, essays, lectures. 3. Archaeology and history—United States—Addresses, essays, lectures. 4. United States—Civilization—Study and teaching—Addresses, essays, lectures. 5. United States—Social life and customs—Study and teaching—Addresses, essays, lectures. 6. United States—Civilization—Addresses, essays, lectures. 7. United States—Social life and customs—Addresses, essays, lectures. 8. United States—Industries—Addresses, essays, lectures. I. Schlereth, Thomas J.
E169.1.M416   1982   306'.0973   82-8812
ISBN 0-910050-61-9   AACR2
ISBN 0-910050-67-8 (pbk.)

Publication of this book was made possible in part by funds from the sale of the Bicentennial State Histories, which were supported by the National Endowment for the Humanities.

Designed by Gary Gore

To
makers of American things
writ and wrought, past and present

Contents

Tables

Acknowledgments

Author and publisher make grateful acknowledgement to the following, for permission to use in this book the materials credited to them:

The University of Pennsylvania Press, Philadelphia, Pennsylvania, for "American Studies: Words or Things?" by John Kouwenhoven, in *American Studies in Transition,* edited by Marshall W. Fishwick, pp. 15–35. Copyright 1964 by the University of Pennsylvania Press.

The American Archivist, Society of American Archivists, for "Manuscripts and Manufacts," by Wilcomb E. Washburn, in *The American Archivist* 27 (April 1964): 245–250.

Agricultural History, American Agricultural Society, for "The Use of Objects in Historical Research," by John T. Schlebecker, in *Agricultural History* 51 (January 1977): 200–208.

Gazette, Canadian Museums Association, for "Culture, History, and Artifact," by Steven M. Beckow, and "On the Nature of the Artifact," by Steven M. Beckow, in the *Gazette* 8 (Fall 1975): 13–15, and the *Gazette* 9 (Winter 1976): 24–27.

The University of Chicago Press, for "Folk Art," by Henry Glassie, in *Folklore and Folklife: An Introduction,* edited by Richard M. Dorson (Chicago: University of Chicago Press, 1972), pp. 253–280.

Richard M. Dorson, Indiana University, and the University of Chicago Press, for "Folk Art," by Henry Glassie, in *Folklore and Folklife: An Introduction,* edited by Richard M. Dorson (Chicago: University of Chicago Press, 1972), pp. 253–280.

Henry Glassie, University of Pennsylvania, and the University of Chicago Press, for "Folk Art," in *Folklore and Folklife: An Introduction,* edited by Richard M. Dorson (Chicago: University of Chicago Press, 1972), pp. 253–280.

Augustus Peabody Loring, Chairman, American Walpole Society, for "Some Remarks on the Practice and Science of Connoisseurship," by Charles F. Montgomery, in the *American Walpole Society Notebook* (1961):7–20.

Mrs. Florence Montgomery, New Haven, Connecticut, for "Some Remarks on the Practice and Science of Connoisseurship," by Charles F. Montgomery, in the *American Walpole Society Notebook* (1961): 7–20.

The State Historical Society of Wisconsin, for "The Challenge of the Artifact," by William Hesseltine, in *The Present World of History* (Madison: State Historical Society of Wisconsin, 1959), pp. 64–70.

Mills Lane IV, editor, the *American Walpole Society Notebook,* for "Some Remarks on the Practice and Science of Connoisseurship," by Charles F. Montgomery, in the *American Walpole Society Notebook* (1961), pp. 7–20.

Studio Vista and Van Nostrand Reinhold Publishers, London, England, and New York, for "The Six Requirements of Design," by David Pye, in *The Nature of Design,* by David Pye (1972), pp. 21–29.

David Pye, Royal College of Art, for "The Six Requirements of Design," in *The Nature of Design,* by David Pye (London and New York: Studio Vista and Van Nostrand Reinhold, 1972), pp. 21–39.

Winterthur Portfolio, Winterthur Museum and the University of Chicago Press, for "Artifact Study: A Proposed Model," by E. McClung Fleming, in *Winterthur Portfolio* 9 (June 1974):153–161.

Oxford University Press, for "Axioms for Reading the Landscape: Some Guides to the American Scene," by Peirce F. Lewis, in *The Interpretation of Ordinary Landscapes,* edited by D. W. Meinig (New York: Oxford University Press, 1979), pp. 11–32.

The *Journal of Architectural Education,* Association of Collegiate Schools of Architecture, "Axioms for Reading the Landscape: Some Guides to the American Scene," by Peirce F. Lewis, in the *Journal of Architectural Education* (September 1976): 6–9.

Museum News, the American Association of Museums, for "Pop Pedagogy: Looking at the Coke Bottle," by Craig Gilborn, in *Museum News* 47 (December 1968): 13–18.

Natural History, the American Museum of Natural History, for "Death's Head, Cherub, Urn and Willow," by James Deetz and Edwin S. Dethlefsen, in *Natural History* 76 (March 1967): 29–37.

Journal of Interdisciplinary History and the M.I.T. Press, for "Meaning in Artifacts: Hall Furnishings in Victorian America," by Kenneth L. Ames, in *Journal of Interdisciplinary History* 9 (Summer 1978): 19–46.

Technology and Culture, Society for the History of Technology, and the University of Chicago Press, for "The 'Industrial Revolution' in the Home: Household Technology and Social Change in the Twentieth Century," by Ruth Schwartz Cowan, in *Technology and Culture* 7 (January 1976): 1–23.

Ruth Schwartz Cowan, State University of New York at Stony Brook, for "The 'Industrial Revolution' in the Home: Household Technology and Social Change in the Twentieth Century," by Ruth Schwartz Cowan, in *Technology and Culture* 7 (January 1976): 1–23.

Geographical Review, American Geography Society, for "Building in Wood in the Eastern United States: A Time-Place Perspective," by Fred Kniffen and Henry Glassie, in *Geographical Review* 56 (1966): 40–66.

Industrial Archaeology, for "The Service Station in America: The Evolution of a Vernacular Form," by Bruce Lohof, in *Industrial Archaeology* 11 (Spring 1974): 1–13.

Pioneer America: The Journal of Historic American Material Culture, and the Pioneer America Society, for "An Indiana Subsistence Craftsman," by Willard B. Moore, in *Pioneer America* 8 (July 1976): 107–118.

English News, Houghton Mifflin Company, for "Monuments and Myths: Three American Arches," by Joseph F. Trimmer, in *English News* 1 (March 1976): 1, 6–7.

Chicago History, Chicago Historical Society, for "Chicago through a Camera Lens: An Essay on Photography as History," by Glen E. Holt, in *Chicago History* 1 (Spring 1971): 158–169.

Journal of American Culture, The Popular Press, for "Embellishing a Life of Labor: An Interpretation of the Material Culture of American Working-Class Homes, 1885–1915," by Lizabeth A. Cohen, in *Journal of American Culture* 3 (Winter 1980): 752–775.

Lizabeth A. Cohen, University of California at Berkeley, for "Embellishing a Life of Labor: An Interpretation of the Material Culture of American Working-Class Homes, 1885–1915," in *Journal of American Culture* 3 (Winter 1980): 752–775.

Keystone Folklore, for "Immaterial Material Culture: The Implications of Experimental Research for Folklife Museums," by Jay A. Anderson, in *Keystone Folklore* 21 (1976–1977): 1–11.

Society for Historical Archaeology, for "In Praise of Archaeology: Le Projet du Garbage," by William L. Rathje, in *Historical Archaeology and the Importance of Material Things,* edited by Leland Ferguson (Columbia, S.C.: Society for Historical Archaeology, 1977), pp. 36–42.

William L. Rathje, University of Arizona, for "In Praise of Archaeology: Le Projet du Garbage," in *Historical Archaeology and the Importance of Material Things,* edited by Leland Ferguson (Columbia, S.C.: Society for Historical Archaeology, 1977), pp. 36–42.

Historical Archaeology, Society for Historical Archaeology, for "Tin*Can Archaeology," by Robert Ascher, in *Historical Archaeology* 8 (1974): 1–16.

Robert Ascher, Cornell University, for "Tin*Can Archaeology," in *Historical Archaeology* 8 (1974): 1–16.

The moment just past is extinguished forever save for the things made by it.
—George Kubler, *The Shape of Time*

I dedicate this book to Australopithecus, who first caught a glimpse of the human soul in a piece of rock.
—Miles Richardson, *The Human Mirror*

Material culture is not merely a reflection of human behavior; material culture is a part of human behavior.
—William Rathje, ''In Praise of Archaeology''

Preface:
On Studying the Things They Left Behind

This book, like many other American artifacts, came into existence out of necessity. In teaching introductory seminars in American material culture over the past several years and in talking with colleagues engaged in the same task, I suddenly realized how accurate was Lucius Ellsworth's lament, over a decade ago, that when "the historian seeks information about the theory of material culture . . . he quickly discovers the lack of readily available information." [1] Ellsworth and coauthor Maureen O'Brien sought to mitigate this problem with their collection of reprints titled *Material Culture: Historical Agencies and the Historian* published in 1969 and now out of print. As teachers of courses on historical agency administration in a program jointly sponsored by the Hagley Museum and the University of Delaware, Ellsworth and O'Brien understandably concentrated their anthology on providing readers with a "knowledge of the types and functions of contemporary historical agencies in the United States." Thus, although their title might suggest otherwise, the actual contents of their book was primarily devoted to the relationships between historical institutions and historians, and only secondarily to material culture research.

As will be evident, I am in debt to the Ellsworth-O'Brien collection (two of its articles are reprinted here), but in this volume I have endeavored to expand its scope and content. [2] Those who currently teach material culture studies in American universities, museums, and historical societies are still without an introductory Baedeker to the field's classic and contemporary research. Hence my rationale and emphasis in assembling this anthology has been to collect previously published material culture scholarship, which often appeared in specialized journals and hence was frequently difficult to secure, that I consider to have the greatest utility for teachers and students in all types of educational programs where artifacts are used as meaningful evidence in cultural studies. In searching for such essays, I came upon several useful works in many of the subfields of material culture studies, such as history of technology, folklife studies, [3] cultural anthropology, historical archaeology, cultural geography, and art history, [4] but I found no single work that would provide the beginning student with a brief overview of the history, theory, and practice of the subject.

Several other related objectives inform this volume. For instance, I have concentrated on finding essays that contain a historical orientation because I, a cultural historian, am a firm believer in material culture studies as one of the more underrated avenues to historical awareness and understanding. In my judgment, material culture studies are done best when they are done from a historical perspective. The scholars I have chosen to present the current state of the art, I believe, share that perspective. Also I would be less than candid if I did not admit here that one not so "hidden" agenda behind the making of the anthology was to persuade other historians of the enormous validity, in some cases absolute necessity, of consulting a domain of evidence that they have heretofore largely ignored.[5] In this missionary effort, I by no means wish to suggest that documentary, oral, and statistical evidence are not to be used in historical research. I merely wish to claim that objects can provide us with numerous and valuable insights into the past. To neglect such data in any modern historical inquiry is to overlook a significant body of research evidence.

Authors included in this volume have taken such a methodological injunction seriously. Taken as a group, their work forms an eclectic reader, eclectic in the nineteenth-century usage of that term—that is, a selection of the best work that is available. I think their essays represent the common core of American material culture scholarship in the past three decades.

In Part I: Statement of History, I have attempted to provide a brief historical context in which the reader can evaluate work of past and present researchers in the field. By a curious irony, material culture historians have paid little attention to their own history. Not unlike many American anthropologists who have sought out subjects farthest from themselves to study, material culturists have been reluctant to analyze themselves. I have tried to do so from the perspective of an intellectual and cultural historian. In my historical survey, I have proposed an interpretive model of American material culture studies. I have also suggested an outline of where the movement is at present. My purpose in this undertaking has been twofold: first, to encourage historical self-conciousness about American material culture studies and second, to stimulate further dialogue within the movement—on its past, present and future. In this second endeavor, I have been particularly motivated by Simon J. Bronner's remark that "a conceptual understanding of the approaches to the study of objects is a prerequisite for future theoretical formulations." [6]

With such a rationale in mind, I have organized the volume around the manifestos and polemics of the movement (Part II: Statements of Theory), followed by a brief selection of its classic techniques and models (Part III: Statements of Method). A diverse, although by no means comprehensive, collection of recent innovative and experimental research (Part IV: Statements of Practice) concludes those parts of the book that I have borrowed from other scholars. In order to alert the reader to other important material culture research not reprinted here,[7] I have added a bibliographical essay (Part V: Statement of the Field) knowing, however, that it, too, will inadvertently neglect important persons and publications.

As editor, I must assume all responsibilities for such oversights. I must also apologize to authors of the book's essays where I have had, on occasion, to abridge certain articles or slightly alter original titles. My most serious intervention, however, has been to omit most visual materials, such as cartography and photography, that originally accompanied some studies. I finally succumbed to this regrettable but unavoidable decision after encountering innumerable difficulties in both locating the original illustrations and in securing the appropriate editoral permissions to reproduce them. (In a few articles, some passages have been slightly rewritten to incorporate a description of an illustration, but only where absolutely necessary for comprehension.)

Inasmuch as I have titled this primer *Material Culture Studies in America,* I deliberately restricted its scope largely to research dealing with American material culture and to American scholars pursuing such research in America.[8] Moreover, scholars pursuing formal academic study of American artifacts in universities and museums are emphasized to the neglect of an extensive corpus of material culture literature generated by private collectors, amateur researchers, and avocational historians. As final disclaimer, I would also readily acknowledge that this anthology neither purports to cover all regions of this country, nor all types of artifactual evidence and, certainly, not all theories, methods, and practices of material culture studies.

Although this volume has no pretentions to being encyclopedic, it assuredly aspires to be educational. I hope it will be both a benchmark and a blueprint for the next generation of material culture scholars who face the challenge of what I and others have called "the age of interpretation" in contemporary artifact research. This book attempts to document the historical development of previous generations as well as to provide a survey of current products, practices, and practitioners.

To these last-named individuals, the men and women who generously consented to allow reproduction of their scholarship and whose work constitutes the bulk of this volume, I am most grateful. I have learned much from each of them. In my introductory headnotes to each of their studies, I hope I have accurately represented their assumptions and arguments as well as prompted new readers to examine their theories and techniques with the critical analysis such work deserves.

I am likewise indebted to editors and editorial boards without number. A complete list of all those who gave permission to reproduce the twenty-three articles reprinted here appears in the volume's acknowledgments. The editorial staff of the American Association for State and Local History has conscientiously assisted me during this project, beginning with my first proposal of it to Gary Gore, then publications director, through to its final printing under Joan Cash and Betty Doak Elder. Two editors—one abroad, Martha I. Strayhorn in the publications offices of the AASLH; one at home, Wendy Clauson Schlereth in her upstairs study—have consistently improved my prose. Those who have patiently deciphered it, typed it, retyped it, corrected it, and retyped it again and again—Barbara Thompson, Margaret Jasiewicz, Cheryl Reed, Amy Kizer, Janet Wright, and Sandy DeWulf—have been faithful friends indeed. So have those scholars cited in the first footnote of my introductory essay on the history of material culture studies. These friends read various drafts of that essay and offered gentle but firm and discriminating critique and counsel. Others such as Kenneth Ames, Howard Wight Marshall, Simon Bronner, John Mannion, Michael Owen Jones, and Joanna Schneider Zangando have generously given me advice and assistance with all the other components of the volume.

These colleagues believe, as do I and the other authors in this book, that, within disciplines as varied as historical archaeology, art history, cultural geography, American Studies, environmental psychology, cultural anthropology, folklife studies, and the history of technology, there is increasing credibility being given to scholarship based on the "identification and interpretation of [material culture] data reflecting patterned human behavior." The success of these scholarly enterprises, remarks Leland Ferguson, "in isolating regularities within the material remains of historical American culture continually reinforces our awareness that perhaps as important as the ideas people happen to write down are the things they leave behind." [9]

"The Things They Leave Behind"—such might have been the title of this volume, for contemporary students of American material culture are becoming equally fascinated with both the "they" and the "things" of the past. We recognize more clearly now the validity of Henry Thoreau's reason for calling an arrowhead a "fossil thought" or Henry Glassie's admonition that "the only reason to study artifacts is to get at the people behind them." [10] I would also add a final reason for artifact study: to help us understand ourselves, or, to turn Glassie's injunction around, to help get at those people who now stand in *front* of the enormous cache of artifacts that have survived to our own time. I trust that this primer will demonstrate that material culture study, in addition to all else it aspires to accomplish, enlarges our individual understanding of both personal identity and contemporary culture.

THOMAS J. SCHLERETH

Part I

Statement of History

We have many Chairs of History but few historians of chairs.
—Marie Elwood, *Material History Bulletin*

Voltaire to the contrary, history is a bag of tricks which the dead have played upon historians. The most remarkable of these illusions is the belief that the surviving written records provide us with a reasonably accurate facsimile of past human activity. . . . In medieval Europe until the end of the eleventh century we learned of the feudal aristocracy largely from clerical sources which naturally reflect ecclesiastical attitudes; the knights do not speak for themselves. . . . If historians are to attempt to write the history of mankind, and not simply the history of mankind as it was viewed by the elite and specialized segments of the race who had the habit of scribbling, they must take a fresh view of the records.
—Lynn White, *Medieval Technology and Social Change*

If I could say it, I would not have to dance it.
—Isadora Duncan, *My Life*

1

Material Culture Studies in America, 1876–1976

Thomas J. Schlereth

Charting and assessing the complicated history of the American interest in material culture since 1876 might be compared to writing a brief guidebook to a continent.[1] All one can hope for is to indicate the major landmarks and lines of development and interaction—the larger contours of an immensely complex intellectual and cultural landscape. Inevitably some of the most interesting features will be omitted and, inevitably, the description of the landscape will depend, in part, upon the author's vantage point.

As I assembled this anthology of American material culture studies, I became cognizant of the lack of any historical research on an intellectual activity that was primarily historical. While certain segments of the history of material culture studies in America had been adumbrated by isolated historiographers in American archaeology, folklore, anthropology, folklife, art, and the history of technology,[2] no one had attempted a synoptic historical overview that might try to answer these questions: When did a serious scholarly interest in material culture studies begin in this country and how was it nurtured by individuals, institutions, and events? How and why did this intellectual activity grow in terms of research, publication, teaching, and public outreach? What was the historical relationship between formal material culture scholarship and a wider public interest in the extant artifacts of the American past?

Definitions and Nomenclature

Before undertaking to answer these broad questions, it is necessary to define, inasmuch as that is possible, what is meant by "material culture." Scholars in the field are continually expanding and contracting the definition,[3] but one by

1

anthropologist Melville Herskovits that I find most useful simply suggests that material culture can be considered to be the totality of artifacts in a culture, the vast universe of objects used by humankind to cope with the physical world, to facilitate social intercourse, to delight our fancy, and to create symbols of meaning.[4] Other researchers have continually amended or abridged such a working definition (a topic worth investigating as an unresearched subject in the American history of ideas,[5] but most are agreed that physical objects are crucial to what constitutes material culture. Hence, Leland Ferguson argues that material culture includes all "the things that people leave behind. . . . all of the things people make from the physical world—farm tools, ceramics, houses, furniture, toys, buttons, roads, cities."[6]

The word "material" in material culture typically refers to a broad but usually not unrestricted range of objects. It comprehends the class of objects known as artifacts—objects made or modified by humans. Hence many material culture scholars exclude natural objects such as trees, rocks, fossils or skeletons from definitions of their subject. However, when natural objects are encountered in a pattern that suggests human activity—a stone wall or an Osage orange hedgerow in an otherwise random forest, a concentration of pig bones in a pit or a pile of oyster shells, a tattooed body or a prepared meal—these natural materials become material culture.

Most scholars are also quick to point out that in one sense the concept of material culture is something of a contradiction in terms, since material culture is not culture but its product. *Material culture* properly connotes physical manifestations of culture and therefore embraces those segments of human learning and behavior which provide a person with plans, methods, and reasons for producing and using things that can be seen and touched. In this sense, material culture constitutes an abbreviation for artifacts in a cultural context. To put it still another way, material culture entails cultural statements that can take the form of plowshares, hallstands, political campaign buttons, service stations, funerary art, electric washing machines, short gowns, or dog-trot houses.

Material culture studies, I would suggest, are an equally diverse lot. Elsewhere I have defined this multi-faceted endeavor by comparing it to a gigantic Barnum and Bailey circus tent under which a variety of acts takes place simultaneously.[7] The eclectic endeavor has often been identified by several roughly synonymous labels: "artifact studies," "physical history," "museum studies," "pots-and-pans history," "material history," "above-ground archaeology," and "hardware history."[8] Increasingly, the rubric material culture studies is being used as the most generic name to describe the research, writing, teaching, and publication done by individuals who interpret past human activity largely through extant physical evidence. I prefer the term material culture studies over a label such as artifact studies or physical history because, given its origins in archaeology and anthropology, the name connotes a strong interest among its practitioners in studying human behavior. To quote Ferguson again, most material culture researchers have "a firm conviction that material data has a potential to contribute fundamentally to the understanding of human behavior." For "material culture is not merely a reflection of human behavior; material culture is a part of human behavior." [9]

Material culture study is, therefore, the study through artifacts (and other pertinent historical evidence) of the belief systems—the values, ideas, attitudes, and assumptions—of a particular community or society, usually across time. As a study, it is based upon the obvious premise that the existence of a man-made object is concrete evidence of presence of a human mind operating at the time of fabrication. The common assumption underlying material culture research is that objects made or modified by humans, consciously or unconsciously, directly or indirectly, reflect the belief patterns of individuals who made, commissioned, purchased, or used them, and, by extension, the belief patterns of the larger society of which they are a part. In the enterprise of material culture studies, suggests art historian Jules Prown, "the term *material culture* thus refers both to the subject matter of the study, *material,* and to its purpose, the understanding of *culture.*" [10]

Two American scholarly journals now carry the term *material culture* on their mastheads. In 1978, *Pioneer America,* a quarterly that publishes the research of scholars and amateurs alike, assumed the subtitle *The Journal of Historic American Material Culture;* in 1979, the *Winterthur Portfolio* (begun in 1964 as a clothbound annual devoted primarily to the specialized research of professionals in the American decorative arts) became a quarterly emphasizing the research of several disciplines that seek "to integrate artifacts into their cultural context." [11] Significantly, *Winterthur Portfolio* has also acquired the subtitle *A Journal of American Material Culture.* In the United States, the label material culture frequently appears as the disciplinary specialty of scholars,[12] in the titles of monographs, scholarly papers, fellowships, and conferences,[13] and as the subject of college and university courses.[14] At Yale University, the Center for the Study of American Arts and Material Culture was established in 1977 in conjunction with that institution's American Studies Program. An extensive material culture studies program has existed at the Smithsonian Institution since 1965 in conjunction with the George Washington University, the institution that appears to be the first to have awarded a graduate fellowship specifically for interdisciplinary material culture research.[15] Finally, James Deetz has proposed that departments of material culture be established in American universities, departments "open to many people currently in other academic Balkan countries." [16]

To what do we attribute this surge of scholarly interest in the study of American things? A partial explanation for some of the current academic fascination or flirtation with material culture is probably related to the current employment crisis in many institutions of higher learning. The federal government's funding emphasis on American social history, particularly through an agency such as the National Endowment for the Humanities, has also heightened interest in the heretofore neglected artifacts of social interaction, domesticity, minorities, women, ethnicity, and the like.[17] Administrators and researchers at a relatively new federal agency, the American Folklife Center (established by an act of Congress in 1976 and located at the Library of Congress), have taken the mandate of Public Law 94–20, H.R. 6673 "to preserve and present American folklife" as a directive to concern themselves with all types of artifactual evidence. An excellent example of the American Folklife Center's strong emphasis on using American material culture in interpreting the broader understandings of folk culture in the United States was the agency's exhibition with the Smithsonian Institution titled "Buckaroos in Paradise: Cowboy Life in Northern Nevada" (1980–1981) and catalog of the same name prepared by Howard Wight Marshall.[18] An enormous proliferation of museums, the principal repositories for the collection, preservation, and exhibition of moveable material culture in the United States, is a third factor in the expansion of scholarly activity in which individuals seek to document and interpret human behavior primarily through physical remains, whether apart from or in conjunction with written records.

In any working definition of material culture studies, there exists a crucial evidential emphasis on physical remains or artifacts, an emphasis shared by each of the major fields of inquiry—archaeology, anthropology, art history, cultural geography, history of technology, and folklife studies—that are usually included under the material culture studies umbrella. Thus, although they may ask different questions in different ways of the same mode of material culture (a New Orleans shotgun house, for instance), each of these disciplines has common cause in the interrogation of such an artifact as primary evidence. Most material culture study usually involves fieldwork research where artifacts are collected, identified, compared, and categorized either *in situ* or in the assorted museums, private and public collections, and historical agencies where they are currently housed.[19] A historical perspective also characterizes material culture studies since, as most of their names indicate (history of technology, art and architectural history, and so forth), they seek to measure and understand change over time. Finally, perhaps the hallmark of the current emphasis in American material culture studies is an increased quest for a truly interdisciplinary focus, conceptually and methodologically, in the concern to analyze the artifact as a concrete manifestation of cultural history.[20] "Wherever it is being studied today," observes John Mannion, "material history is not the preserve of any single traditional discipline. Work in this field is shared by a number of specialized subfields in the social sciences and the humanities, notably art and architectural history, cultural geography, historical archaeology, museum anthropology, folklore and folklife, and, to a limited degree, by dialectologists and social historians." Mannion goes on to note that the "multidisciplinary nature of the study of material culture is hardly surprising considering the ubiquity and centrality of the artifact in the cultural milieu, its relative stability, its complexity, its multifunctional features, and broad range of factors, ecological, economic, and sociocultural, involved in its production, diffusion, acceptance, longevity, and use." [21]

An interest in interdisciplinary cooperation and the recognition of the usefulness of artifacts in historical research has only emerged slowly among those who specifically define themselves as material culturists.[22] In the past, the formal study of American material culture remained largely the province of the single investigator, the professional or avocational researcher, who considered himself strictly an art historian or archaeologist, an architectural historian, or a historian of technology.[23] Material culturists now openly advocate a convergence of disciplines and argue, with George Kubler, that in order to secure meaningful cultural historical interpretations, the objects used as evidence can no longer be parceled out as the special preserve of the different disciplines.[24]

Material Culture Studies and Americana Movements

In addition to the assorted activities that I have defined as material culture studies in America, there is a larger and interrelated cultural phenomenon that can only be vaguely characterized by an amorphous label such as the "Americana movement." While not a dominant cultural trait of the future-oriented, throw-away American society that many historians also consider deeply ahistorical, this periodic and sometimes pecuniary interest on the part of the American people in American objects as collectibles, national icons, status symbols, or local totems stretches back into the nineteenth century. By the Americana movement, I simply mean the multiplicity of individuals and institutions that, because of their involvement with one or more types of American objects, could also be said to be interested, in their various fashions, in American material culture.[25] All of them have shared, and continue to share, a common concern with the identification or preservation of American artifacts as a source of information, insight, profit, or enjoyment.

Thus, for example, the Americana movement involves, in part, local historical societies, private and public museums, and community organizations in this country as well as parallel repositories in areas of art, natural history, and technology. As Neil Harris has suggested, the movement has also entailed popular exhibitions, such as world's fairs and international trade expositions;[26] likewise, it has offshoots in the entertainment, recreational, tourist, and publishing industries. The historic preservation movement, the most adequately studied component of the Americana coalition's various constituencies, has assuredly nurtured both professional and avocational interest in the nation's architecture.[27] Finally, there is the American collector, naturally an extremely important force in the general American fascination with American objects.

Ranging from wealthy businessmen, like Henry Ford and Henry Francis duPont, who amassed hordes of artifacts as parts of their personal fortunes, to private antique collectors with acute research interests, like Nina Fletcher Little and Jean Lipman, to thousands of anonymous antiquarians infatuated with accumulating everything from silver spoons to Jim Beam bottles, the collector has influenced American material culture studies.[28] So too have all the ancillary enterprises and entrepreneurs surrounding the collection of artifacts: hobbyists, dealers, appraisers, curators, craftsmen, and festival organizers and fair promoters. One way to begin measuring the potential impact of these important influences on material culture research is simply to ask questions such as: What type of Americana has been collected? How was it collected? Why was it collected? How was it displayed? How has it been interpreted?

To date there is a paucity of historiography on the development of the Americana movement in general,[29] and little has been written on the history of American material culture studies in particular.[30] Obviously, both have had some reciprocal and even symbiotic impact upon each other, thereby making it exceedingly difficult for the historian to sort out direct causal influences. Intersection and interaction assuredly took place, and, where I have been able to document the influence of the Americana movement on the material culture studies movement, I have so argued. For the purposes of this study, however, I have focused my principal attention on the smaller, more specialized segment of the story: the historical development of material culture studies in America, 1876–1976. The history of the Americana movement needs to be written, but I have chosen not to relate it here. In order to sample its current flavor and diversity, I might suggest glancing at an appropriately named popular magazine, *Americana,* a monthly publication of the American Heritage Foundation. In the remainder of this essay, I do explore several components of that larger story—the expansion (in number and type) of American museums, the tremendous growth of historic preservation activities, the democratization of antique collecting, and the renewed interest in local history and community heritage— but I do so only as the historical context for a more circumscribed story.[31] Hence my primary objective here is simply to outline the intellectual history of those individuals and institutions who nurtured and were nourished by scholarly activity in an area of inquiry that has come to be called material culture studies. This area of inquiry has been less a formal school of thought than a way of focusing the mind. It is a way of focusing teaching and research that is frequently interdisciplinary and usually historical, often involves fieldwork, and nearly always uses objects as a primary evidential data base.

In order to understand the history of American material culture as a scholarly enterprise, I have divided it into three chronological phases: (1) the collecting or classifying period (1876–1948); (2) the descriptive or historical period (1948–1965); and (3) the analytical or explanatory period (1965–present). (See table 1.1.) Each period has a dominant attitude toward material culture, an attitude I have sought to make clear by its name. To be sure, the three periods overlap. In historical reality, of course, they do not break as evenly or as neatly as my Procrustian outline would suggest; there are interstices among them, and they do not always apply to all scholars or to all institutions. To formulate them at all, I have to operate at a rather abstract level and consequently run the risk of oversimplifying and overgeneralizing. For example, the earlier interest in collecting artifacts and arranging them in appropriate typologies by no means ceased in the late 1940s; it continues with vigor in the present. Likewise, there were occasional efforts by such men as R. H. Halsey and L. V. Lockwood at careful historical description of material culture evidence prior to the post-World War II years. Important analytical studies by J. Kouwenhoven, C. M. Watkins, and J. B. Jackson can also be found before the

TABLE 1.1
The Shifting Paradigms:
A Brief Historical Overview of Material Culture Studies in America

Characteristics	Age of Collecting (1876–1948)	Age of Description (1948–1965)	Age of Analysis (1965–)	
	I	II	III	IV
Pioneering Scholars	J. Henry C. Dana C. Wilcomb W. Nutting G. Goode W. Appleton L. Lockwood I. Phelps Stokes H. Cahill S. Clark H. DuPont R. Halsey H. Mercer	J. C. Harrington L. Jones C. Watkins J. Kouwenhoven T. J. Wertenbaker F. Kniffen J. B. Jackson C. Peterson J. Cotter J. Downs E. Ferguson W. Whitehill C. Montgomery	B. Hindle C. Hummel I. Noël Hume D. Yoder P. Lewis W. Roberts G. Kubler J. Schlebecker E. Dethlefsen A. Gowans A. Garvan A. Ludwig J. Deetz	D. Kelsey H. Marshall C. Carson S. Bronner M. Jones J. Prown M. Leone J. Vlach J. Anderson P. Marzio C. Gilborn K. Ames R. Cowan C. Kidwell R. Trent H. Glassie
Typical Intellectual Emphases	Historical associationism; primacy fascination; search for artistic uniqueness	Cult of connoisseurship; taxonomy fascination; search for American uniqueness	Vernacularism, typicality, methodology fascination; search for artifact's evidential uniqueness	
Principal Research Concerns	Collecting, salvaging, preserving, hoarding high-style, unique, or elite artifacts	Preparing descriptive typologies, chronologies, classification systems of artifacts	Seeking to use artifacts to analyze human behavior in societal context	
Interests in Artifacts and Artifact-Makers	Objets d'art: An artiste creating art	Results of craft processes: A technician working in a tradition of artisanry	Consumer goods and services: a citizen involved in community life	
Main Disciplinary Specialties	Art history, architectural history; anthropology, archaeology	History of technology; folk art and folklife studies; cultural and historical geography; cultural history; historical archaeology	Social history; industrial, commercial, experimental archaeology; museum studies; social and environmental psychology; folkloristics; cognitive anthropology	

TABLE 1.1 (PART II):
The Shifting Paradigms

Professional Institutions	The Walpole Society; College Art Association; Society of Architectural Historians	Society for History of Technology; Decorative Arts Society; American Association for State and Local History	Pioneer America Society; Society for Industrial Archaeology; Society for a North American Cultural Survey
Research Centers Established	Smithsonian Institution; Colonial Williamsburg; Index of American Design; Henry Ford Museum	Winterthur Museum-University of Delaware; Cooperstown Program SUNY–Oneonta; National Park Service Index of Early American Culture	George Washington University; University of Pennsylvania; American Folklife Center; Boston University; Indiana University
Typical Serial Publications	*Antiques; The Antiquarian; Art in America*	*Technology and Culture; Winterthur Portfolio* (annual); *Pennsylvania Folklife; Contributions from MHT*	*Material History Bulletin; Winterthur Portfolio* (quarterly); *ALHFAM Bulletin; Journal of Interdisciplinary History; Journal of American Culture*
Historiographical Assessments	W. Kaplan, "R. H. Halsey: An Ideology of Collecting American Decorative Arts" (1980)	C. Montgomery, "Classics and Collectibles" (1977)	S. Bronner, "Concepts in the Study of Material Aspects of American Folk Culture" (1979)
Representative Publications	I. Lyon, *Colonial Furniture of New England* (1891); C. Wissler, "Material Cultures of North American Indians" (1914); H. Mercer, *Ancient Carpenter Tools* (1929); F. Kimball, *Domestic Architecture of the American Colonies* (1922); R. Burlingame, *March of the Iron Men* (1938)	J. Kouwenhoven, *Made in America* (1948); J. Lipman, *American Folk Art* (1948); S. Giedion, *Mechanization Takes Command* (1948); C. Montgomery, *American Furniture: The Federal Period* (1966); A. Gowans, *Images of American Living* (1964)	H. Glassie, *Folk Housing in Middle Virginia* (1975); L. Ferguson, *Historical Archaeology and the Importance of Material Things* (1977); K. Ames, *Beyond Necessity* (1977); M. Jones, *The Hand-Made Object* (1975); P. Benes, *The Masks of Orthodoxy* (1977); J. Fitchen, *The New World Dutch Barn* (1968)

mid-1960s. But, as I hope will be evident, a discernible shift in conceptual and methodological emphasis in the scholarly approaches to American material culture can be fairly clearly traced over these three time segments.[32] The following tripartite analysis attempts to document how and why this historical development occurred.

The Age of Collection:
Pioneer Studies and Early Trends, 1876–1948

The American interest in material culture originated in the assorted borderlands and hinterlands of the nineteenth century's universe of knowledge. It began in the pioneering and often overlapping eclecticism of museum founders, curators, and benefactors, as well as early antique collectors, historic preservationists, antiquarians, and local history enthusiasts.

Founders and First Achievements

Harold Skramstad and Charles Coleman Sellers have argued a convincing case for Charles Willson Peale as perhaps the first serious collector-student of American artifacts in this period.[33] Another Philadelphian, John F. Watson, sometimes acclaimed as the "first historian of the American decorative arts, along with William Bentley and Cummings F. Davis of Salem and Concord, Massachusetts, respectively, were other antiquarians seriously concerned with the collection and preservation of historical relics.[34] To cite still other examples, Alan Gowans has proposed we considered Louisa Caroline Huggins Tuthill as the first historian of American architecture, while James Deetz has suggested James Hall might merit a similar distinction in United States historical archaeology.[35]

No matter who was "first," there was scattered activity, antiquarian and academic, among a few mavericks intrigued with American things. Charles Willson Peale can appropriately serve as a representative type. Peale, who in 1784 founded one of the first great collections of material culture in America, known variously as "The American Museum," "The Philadelphia Museum," or simply "Peale's Museum," had an early impact upon embryonic research in American natural history, cultural anthropology, the history of technology, and art history. In Charles Sellers' estimation, the Peale Museum inspired numerous American amateur collectors and much intelligent collecting, particularly that of Joseph Henry, the first executive secretary (1846–1878) of the Smithsonian Institution.[36]

With the creation of the U.S. National Museum as the first of the so-called bureaus of the Smithsonian in 1838 and the institution's subsequent growth under the leadership of Henry and his successor, S. F. Baird, the country came to have its first national museum that would eventually become a major depository of the material, documentary, and graphic record of the nation's history, culture, and technology.[37] Publications concerning this record issued forth from the Smithsonian in a variety of formats: the *Annual Reports* commencing in 1846; the *Contributions to Knowledge* from 1848; and the *Miscellaneous Collections* from 1862. *Ancient Monuments of the Mississippi Valley* (1848), the Smithsonian's first publication and often catalogued as volume one of the *Contributions* series, is a classic in American archaeology and an early benchmark in the literature of material culture studies.[38]

Only a few other monographs prior to 1876 have achieved similar status in the material culture bibliographical canon. These would include: William Dunlap, *History of the Rise and Progress of the Arts of Design in the United States* (1834); Robert Dale Owen, *Hints on Public Architecture* (1849); Owen Jones, *The Grammar of Ornament* (1856); the *Transactions* (1771–present) of the American Philosophical Society; J. Leander Bishop, *A History of American Manufactures from 1608–1860*, 3 volumes (1861–168); and Horace Bushnell's essays, "The Age of Homespun" (1851) and "The Day of Roads" (1846).

Authors of the majority of these nineteenth-century studies of material culture confronted their data in terms of what Kenneth Ames has called "centripetal patterns" of inquiry rather than in "centrifugal patterns." [39] By the centripetal pattern, Ames means the type of researcher who "starts with an object or an artisan and spirals inward, comprising smaller, tighter, and more specific questions" about the artifact or its maker. The centrifugal pattern marks the work of conceptualizers and theoreticians whose questions of material evidence "move outward from small issues to larger, more encompassing, and more fundamental concerns." Such questions prompt the researcher to be concerned with "the study of man in the broadest sense." To conclude his appraisal of these two mental styles and methodological penchants, Ames notes: "With centripetal questions, point of view is taken for granted, underlying assumptions are usually ignored and untested. Centrifugal patterns may bring point of view into an examination of the nature of questions asked and the motives behind them." [40]

Much of the American scholarship on artifacts done prior to World War II by avocational researchers falls into Ames's centripetal pattern, a perspective he sees as almost congenital to the antiquarian, the curator, and the collector. So it was. This initial generation of American material culture enthusiasts, with the exception of a few with a strong anthropological perspective, saw their task as primarily one of "find and save"; their main objectives were the collecting and preserving of historical materials. Hence their major legacies are the valuable collections now housed in the country's art, natural history, and technology museums as well as in its historical societies.

Although the writing of a comprehensive cultural history of the American historical society still awaits its historian, it is apparent that the founding of such organizations, often for filio-pietistic reasons, occurred in two waves. Interestingly enough, the two innundations roughly correspond to the nineteeth-century periods of massive European immigration to this country. In the first era, roughly 1820–1850, founding members of the earliest historical societies were absorbed in genealogical records (especially the records of family dynasties), the collection of documentary material, and, to a limited extent, the collection of graphic and artifactual data.[41] In the second period, beginning in the late 1870s, these collecting interests came to include artifacts on a much wider scale. J. B. Jackson, Dianne Pilgrim, and Elizabeth Stillinger have pointed out that while there were individual historical buildings saved (such as Mount Vernon) and collections of Americana gathered (like those of William Bentley) before the 1870s, the awareness and appreciation of American artifacts greatly expanded in the last three decades of the nineteenth century.[42]

Historians of the Arts and Anthropologists

Architectural historians and historians of the American decorative arts, however, disagree about when, specifically, in that particular post-Civil War decade this expanded interest in American artifacts actually occurred. The Centennial Exposition held in Philadelphia in 1876, a seemingly obvious occasion to prompt an increased American sensitivity to the nation's historical material culture, actually contained very few pre- or post-Revolutionary era artifacts. The furnishings of "A New England Log House and Modern Kitchen" and a tawdry exhibition of memorabilia associated with George Washington constituted the majority of historic artifacts on display. The thrust of the Centennial Exposition was on the present and the future, not the past.[43] One characteristic of that future, however, was the Colonial Revival, a design style, aesthetic, and value system that did not go out of style for a century. The Colonial Revival was an important catalyst to the material culture studies movement, particularly in the research fields of American architectural history and the decorative arts.

While modern architectural historians contest whether or not certain buildings at the 1876 exposition specifically sparked this interest in American colonial buildings,[44] there is little doubt that the celebrated trip by architects McKim, Mead, and White, along with William Bigelow, in search of seventeenth- and eighteenth-century prototypes for new buildings for their clients prompted an awareness of colonial housing.[45] Publications on the topic quickly followed as the colonial vogue gained momentum: Arthur Little's *Early New England Interiors* (1878), William M. Woollett's *Old Homes Made New* (1878), and James Corner's *Examples of Domestic Colonial Architecture in New England* (1892). A functional interest in one area of material culture research (architecture) spilled over into another (decorative arts) where work ranged from Frank E. Wallis, *Old Colonial Architecture and Furniture* (1887), a grab-bag collection of sketches and measured drawings of varying quality and subject matter, to Irving Whitehall Lyon's impressive work, *The Colonial Furniture of New England* (1891), a pioneering study employing most of the basic techniques of modern decorative arts research—formal analysis, history of styles and forms, investigation of documentary materials (including use of probate inventories), and comparison with European prototypes.[46]

Lyon's scholarly approach to domestic artifacts was, in part, indebted to the growing methodological sophistication among European art historians who, along with the anthropologists and archaeologists, were the veterans among academic material culture practitioners. Erwin Panofsky and James Ackerman have traced the development of art history in the United States in three stages corresponding roughly to three generations.[47] An initial group of researchers was active at the end of the nineteenth century when the perspective of a scholar like Charles Eliot Norton of Harvard, ofttimes acclaimed as "the father of art history in America," held sway. In Norton's view, the art object was ethical, worth collecting, and the desirable accoutrement of a cultivated person but not something on which one would do original research. Norton, however, unlike Lyon but like the majority of his generation, did not specifically study American art. This state of affairs changed in the succeeding two generations of art historians writing in America, one working from World War I to 1930 and the other from 1930 until after World War II.

While a few American amateur anthropologists and archaeologists applied a Nortonian art history perspective to New World artifacts (viewing the material "antiquities" of the Americas principally as highly prized objects of aesthetic contemplation), other scholars in these emerging fields took a more social scientific approach. For example, Otis T. Mason, of the U.S. National Museum, expended much effort in extensive fieldwork bent on the discovery of the material culture of Native American peoples. Indian technology and its artifacts and inventions comprised much of these early anthropological studies using material culture evidence. W. H. Holmes, Clark Wissler, and Frank H. Cushing, for instance, contributed important papers to the *American Anthropologist* on Indian decorative arts, the origins of inventions, basketry, and weapons.[48] Between 1894 and 1904 Mason churned out several landmark monographs: "North American Bows, Arrows, and Quivers" (1893); *The Origins of Invention* (1905); and "Aboriginal American Basketry" (1902). As William Fenton points out, Mason's approach to artifacts was fairly systematic in that he foresaw the idea of the culture area, an explanatory concept which was later used by Franz Boas in arranging exhibitions of material culture, first at the Columbian Exposition in Chicago in 1893 and afterward at the American Museum of Natural History in New York.[49]

While it is difficult to pinpoint exactly what role a major world's fair such as the Chicago Columbian extravaganza had on contemporary material culture studies, some of its influence on the Americana movement can be documented.[50] Unlike the 1876 centennial, the 1893 "White City" was abundantly blessed with artifacts of historic popular culture. Pennsylvania sent the Liberty Bell along with a reproduction of the Independence Hall clock tower atop its exhibition building; Massachusetts built a full-scale replica of the Hancock house (a structure that had been torn down thirty years before); and Virginia modeled its state pavilion after Mount Vernon. Exhibits of historical artifacts abounded in these and other state buildings as well as in the United States Government Building. A monograph on the historic material culture assembled in the government displays was eventually published under the title "Colonial and Revolutionary Objects." [51] A group called the Chicago Folk-Lore Society also mounted an exhibition at the exposition, displaying its material culture collections and publications (e.g., *The Folk-Lorist*) and hosting the Third International Folk-Lore Congress held in conjunction with the 1893 fair. Several papers dealing with material culture research were presented.

Concurrent with the popular historicism of the nine major American world fairs (Chicago, St. Louis, Buffalo, Nashville, San Francisco, San Diego, Seattle, Omaha, and Portland) between 1893 and World War I came the second wave of new historical societies, museums, and patriotic organizations. Simply to enumerate a few of the organizations and their dates of origin provides persuasive evidence that a large part of the institutional matrix of material culture studies, particularly in its collecting phase, was established prior to 1920: the Association for Preservation of Virginia (1889); the New York State Historical Association (1899); and the Society for the Perservation of New England Antiquities (1910), particularly under the leadership of William Sumner Appleton.[52] There were, as well, a host of pioneer associations, genealogical groups, "oldest inhabitant" clubs, and local historical societies newly founded during these years, and several historical agencies established before the Civil War underwent reorganization and revitalization under new executives, demonstrating a new interest in the visual as well as the verbal dimension of the American past. One sees in particular both the Americana and material culture movements augmented by the work of George Francis Dow, secretary of the Essex Institute of Salem (1899–1936); Solon J. Buck, superintendent of the Minnesota Historical Society (1914–1931); John Cotton Dana, director of the Newark Museum Association (1913–1939); and Charles P. Wilcomb, founder of the Oakland Museum (1910–1915) in California.

Historians' Disdain; Collectors' Delight

Academic historians also underwent institutionalization during this period, both in their founding of the American Historical Association (1884) and in their increasing presence on college and university faculties. During the time of professionalization and institutionalization, many American historians found their methodological orientation being defined by such German-trained scholars as Henry Baxter Adams at Johns Hopkins University, established in 1876. Adams, along with his like-minded and like-named contemporary George Burton Adams, indoctrinated a generation of researchers with the acclaimed "scientific method of history" and its total dependence upon exhaustive documentary (verbal) sources.[53]

While the increased objectivity, internal criticism of sources, and scholarly precision that the "scientific" historians brought to their task infused the discipline with an increased intellectual rigor and a heightened respect for appropriate evidential documentation of scholarly writing, the long-range ramifications for historical material culture studies were disastrous. In their celebration of the textual data of American history, the scientific historians chose to ignore completely the artifactual evidence of the national past. As they became ensconced in the universities, the professional historians of the late-nineteenth and early-twentieth century abandoned their former affiliations with various local and state historical associations, where an assortment of material culture studies were being done by collectors, curators, and amateur researchers. Soon museum historians, avocational historians, and gentleman-scholars like James Ford Rhodes came to feel, largely because they lacked the credential of a doctorate in history and did not teach history in a college or university, that they were excluded from the emerging national forum of scholarly activity and camaraderie that became the American academic historical profession.[54]

Since American academic historians took little professional or personal interest in the growing effort to collect and classify the artifactual record of the American past, the continuing (albeit nascent by modern standards) work in material culture studies in other disciplines, principally anthropology and art history, had little impact on American historical interpretation. The work, nonetheless, continued and was soon institutionalized in several formats: new national organizations, major exhibitions of American artifacts (particularly in the decorative arts), professional journals, and an array of publications, some of which continue to be reprinted because of their significance to subsequent scholars. For example, 1909 and 1910 were watershed years for material culture studies in the American decorative arts and for the future of American museums. In 1909, after four years of preparation, the Metropolitan Museum of Art in New York City opened the Hudson-Fulton celebration exhibition of early American fine and decorative arts. Occasioned by a dual historical anniversary (discovery of the Hudson River in 1609 and the first successful application of steam technology to its navigation by Robert Fulton in 1807), this "first nationally recognized exhibition to present American furnishings to the public" was largely an outgrowth of the efforts of eastern establishment collectors such as Robert De Forest, Eugene Bolles, and R. T. H. Halsey. De Forest, then president of the Metropolitan Museum of Art, considered the decision to exhibit American artifacts a bold departure: "It seemed to me and to my friend, Henry W. Kent, an opportunity to test out the question whether American domestic art was worthy of a place in an art museum, and to test it out not theoretically but visually." [55]

Exhibitions perform several functions in material culture scholarsnip. They act as a basic display case of evidence often inaccessible to many students. They can also serve as the analytical vehicle whereby material remains are arranged in a new relationship so as to prompt a new interpretation about the past. Exhibits, unlike books, also bring like-minded students of the object together physically in one place to compare notes, to gossip, to exchange ideas, and to meet each other.

Charles Montgomery saw this as one of the most important legacies of the 1909 exhibition along with its new method of classification of objects by period and by form.[56] At the Hudson-Fulton show, many collectors, dealers, antiquarians, curators, and authors met for the first time. This proved such a rewarding experience for a select few, including Henry Kent, Eugene Bolles, and Luke Vincent Lockwood, that they met again at the Union Club in Boston and founded an elite organization, patterned after a British prototype, known as the American Walpole Society. During the following seventy years, the Walpoleans were among the major private collectors and philantrophic donors to the major museums of the northeastern United States of high-style, sophisticated American artifacts.[57]

New Museums: Indoor and Outdoor

Several of these collectors contributed to two other major art and decorative art exhibitions that occurred in the 1920s: the opening of the American Wing of the Metropolitan Museum of Art in 1924, particularly in its use of the period room (an exhibition technique pioneered in this country by Charles P. Wilcomb at the Golden Gate Park Museum in San Francisco in 1895) and the Girl Scouts Loan Exhibition at the American Art Association's New York galleries in 1929.[58] Wendy Cooper has traced the influence the latter show had on subsequent research in furniture history, providing a historiographical study of "a generation of collectors of American objects," including Francis P. Garvan, Louis G. Meyers, and Henry Francis DuPont, many of whom eventually converted their private collections of American material culture into public institutions for research in the field.[59]

The institutionalization of American material culture collecting assumed a new form in the 1920s. In addition to a rash of historic preservation projects, such as the preservation of historic architecture in cities like San Antonio, Philadelphia, New Orleans, and Charleston, two major historical museums were launched by multimillionaires. In 1924, while restoring the South Sudbury, Massachusetts, Red Horse Tavern, known since the publication of Longfellow's 1863 Tales as the Wayside Inn, Henry Ford began to entertain the idea of creating a museum (ultimately the Edison Institute) containing the artifacts of "the common man, the material culture of the middling sort, not the arts of the elite." [60] In 1927 John D. Rockefeller, Jr., initiated his financial support of the organization that would evolve into Colonial Williamsburg, Virginia.

Ford, who in 1905 had begun collecting the artifacts of American invention (particularly Thomas Edison's experimental phonographic apparatus), first considered reconstructing an early New England village on the more than 2,500 acres he had acquired surrounding the Wayside Inn. In 1924, the city of Williamsburg offered itself to Ford for five million dollars, hoping he would establish his museum on their eighteenth-century site. Had he accepted the proposal of the city, the institutional and intellectual history of Williamsburg and its important role in both the Americana movement and in material culture studies would have been quite different. The major museum complex that Ford did erect, however, at Dearborn, Michigan, and the collections that he and those curator-collectors who followed in his wake amassed in the mechanical arts, transportation, communications, lighting, shop machinery, power sources, agriculture equipment, and home arts were (and are) unsurpassed resources for material culture study. In the judgment of current historians, Ford's view of history, of research, and of artifactual evidence is now seen to be fraught with cultural paradox and ideological myopia, but his highly influential role in the formation of one of the important centers for material culture research in the United States cannot be denied or underestimated.[61] "He was a collector with a vision," writes one associate, "a man who established collecting patterns for others. His efforts in the field of Americana predate those of the Rockefellers, the duPonts, the Garvans. He recovered those common, everyday artifacts that no one else considered or would consider. His work in archaeology and the conservation of artifacts launched the exacting sciences we know today. He made mistakes, of course, for he traveled an uncharted course." [62]

John D. Rockefeller's sponsorship of the rebirth of Williamsburg, while not the first outdoor museum village restoration, captured the public imagination in a fashion similar to Ford's Greenfield Village.[63] Whereas the automotive entre-preneur had reconstructed a town site, the petroleum giant endeavored to restore a sleepy, provincial, colonial capital to its former physical form. The competition between these two historical philanthropists created institutions that eventually ac-quired extensive curatorial and research staffs. As they grew over the decades, these two institutions became prototypes for similar outdoor history museums that were established immediately after World War II.

Williamsburg, given its restoration imperative, understandably made contribu-tions to material culture research in the areas of historical archaeology and Amer-ican architectural history. Pioneer investigators sought out "the evidence of the spade" in their attempt to fill in the gaps left amid documentary evidence of seventeenth- and eighteenth-century Virginia, a region that subsequent archaeolo-gists, such as John Cotter and Ivor Noel-Hume, continued to excavate for another half century.[64] When the firm of Perry, Shaw, and Hepburn undertook the massive Williamsburg architectural restoration project, they sought to reproduce, insofar as extant evidence permitted, accurate historical structures. This quest for authenticity, while by no means always achieved, sparked renewed interest in American architectural research and historical restoration.[65] The Williamsburg "look" has probably influenced more restoration practices of the historic preservation move-ment, more interpretive techniques of innumerable historic house museums, and more tract-development landscapes of post-World War II suburbia than is com-monly imagined. Williamsburg also contributed to the material culture literature through the volumes it published as the "Williamsburg Architectural Studies," a publication series that parallels its monographs, "Williamsburg Archaeological Studies," in historical archaeology fieldwork.

While anthropological research using extensive material culture evidence waned in the 1920s,[66] work in art history and its progeny, architectural history and the history of the decorative arts, enjoyed a revival. The early generation of Lyon, Singleton, and Earle was joined by a younger cadre of collectors, authors, and curators such as Henry Mercer, Wallace Nutting, John Hill Morgan, R. T. Halsey,

I. N. Phelps Stokes, and Fiske Kimball. Like the late-nineteenth-century collectors, most of this generation of wealthy or middle-class businessmen (Mercer, Nutting, Morgan), stockbrokers (Halsey), and attorneys (Lockwood), were self-taught hobbyists. Halsey, Lockwood, Mercer, and Kimball, however, became so absorbed in working with American artifacts that by the end of their lives their avocational involvement had ultimately eclipsed their professional business interests.

In addition to engaging in more sophisticated material culture research than had earlier private collectors, this coterie (see table 1.1, column I) wrote much more: Mercer extensively on tools, Nutting and Lockwood on furniture, Kimball on architecture, and Morgan on painting.[67] Besides their monographs and exhibition catalogs, these gentlemen scholars contributed to new journals such as *Antiques* and *The Antiquarian*. *Antiques*, founded in 1922 by Homer Eaton Keyes and edited by him until 1938 (when Alice Winchester took over for an equally influential tenure as editor), has been viewed by some scholars as "without a doubt the most valuable single repository of published material on the American arts, particularly the decorative arts, that exists." [68]

As its name suggests, *Antiques,* like its early contributors, tended to foster one of the two major perspectives that permeated much of the Americana movement and subsequently the work of many material culture students. Both attitudes can be found, however, in the late-nineteenth century and, as Wendy Cooper has noted, they still exist today. On the one hand there are those who wish to view objects purely aesthetically, outside of their societal context, much as the "new critics" evaluate a single piece of prose or poetry, without regard to historical milieu and solely as creations of art. On the other hand, many students and scholars find it foolhardy to isolate the object from the society that produced it for a specific function at a specific time.[69] The early antiquarian collectors, Cummings Davis, Ben Peerley Moore, George Sheldon, and Henry Davis Steeper, tended to acquire American artifacts not so much for aesthetic reasons, but for what they took to be primarily cultural or historical purposes.[70] The next generation, however, the men and women who opened the American Wing of the Metropolitan, who mounted the early exhibitions there, and who contributed to *Antiques,* had a quite different focus in their approach to material culture evidence. Their concern focused primarily on the aesthetic quality and connoisseurship of objects. Their approach, strongly reinforced by the critical canons and methodological approaches of the fine arts that were emerging in the 1920s, in turn, greatly influenced the American art history component of the material culture studies movement until well into the 1960s.

Had academic historians, however, shown any interest whatsoever in the early-twentieth-century material culture research going on in museums, historical societies, and among private collectors, this often ahistorical perspective might not have developed as it did. With their primary allegiance to the written document, supposedly the only historical data possessing "scientific" historical veracity, professional historians in early-twentieth-century universities and colleges showed comparatively little interest in working out a methodology for interpreting nonverbal documents or in helping to collect or preserve such data. Moreover, American historians knew little of developments in anthropology or archaeological research,[71] and the disciplines dealing with the history of technology and folklife had yet to appear on the academic scene. No significant response was forthcoming from professional historians to James Harvey Robinson's 1912 call for a "New History" concerned with "every trace and vestige of everything that man had done or thought since he first appeared on the earth" and based on "not only the written records but the remains of buildings, pictures, clothing, tools and ornaments." [72]

One might have had good reason to expect a promising response to Robinson's injunction in the thirteen-volume series *History of American Life* (1927–1948) edited by social historians Arthur M. Schlesinger, Sr., and Dixon Ryan Fox. Occasional attention was paid to what the authors called "nonliterary remains," and many of the illustrations were of important artifacts. The "Critical Essay on Authorities" at the end of each volume began with a short section on "Physical Survivals" that listed historic houses and collections of smaller artifacts. However, the citations for the illustrations, the simplistic comments on the actual physical survivals, and the textual references showed no systematic use of this material culture data. Interestingly enough, the author who appears to have demonstrated the greatest sensitivity to material culture as historical evidence in the series was the one scholar who was not a university historian—James Truslow Adams. His volume *Provincial Society* came out in 1927.[73]

With the advent of Franklin D. Roosevelt's New Deal in the 1930s, the documenting and interpreting of American material culture supported by governmental funding expanded enormously. With the assistance of several federal agencies, a series of projects was begun that not only expanded the resources available for artifact study in the United States but also introduced and provided early training for a generation who went on to careers involving them in material culture research as museum and university historians.[74]

The Federal Arts Project's Index of American Design, begun under the direction of Constance Rourke, employed artists to render 20,000 examples of native objects—furniture, textiles, pottery, glassware, and other utilitarian artifacts. Over the years, Rourke argued in various publications that America had a rich native tradition not only in formal letters and fine arts, but also in the ordinary, everyday objects made and used by the common folk. Influenced by the concept of culture developed by anthropologists such as Ruth Benedict and George Murdock,[75] Rourke maintained that culture was not just the sum of national contributions in the arts and crafts but also a configuration, an intricate whole of diverse parts. In other words, objects had to be studied in a cultural context and *all* objects were worth studying. These ideas received the enthusiastic endorsement of Holger Cahill, former curator at the Newark Museum, self-taught collector of American folk art, and head of the overall Federal Arts Project. With Cahill's support, Rourke and her Index of American Design set out to discover and illustrate the nation's vernacular artifacts. The result was a compendium of over 20,000 plates, selected from the many more precise drawings by Arts Project employees around the country, which illustrated everything from duck decoys to interior wall decorations and kitchen utensils to cigar-store Indians.[76]

Cahill's and Rourke's interest in what has come to be called American folk art was, as Beatrix Rumford has carefully documented, part of an important collecting vogue that had gathered momentum in the 1920s. In fact, the first exhibition of this genre of material culture in the United States took place at the Whitney Studio in 1924, the same year as the opening of the American Wing at the Metropolitan.[77] The first scholarship that accompanied this twentieth-century discovery of a seemingly new type of artifact not surprisingly focused on collecting and classifying. Despite the fact that most folk objects were created by their users primarily for functional purposes, the early research followed the pattern established in other fields imbued with an art history approach considering only aesthetic beauty or so-called unique "American design." [78]

The Index of American Design was but one of the 1930s' manifestations of American democratic nationalism that has periodically permeated both the Americana and the material culture studies movements. Workers employed under the Federal Writers Project of the Works Progress Administration prepared state and city guides containing valuable geographical, historical, and often artifactual data for communities across the United States.[79] The Historic Sites Survey of the National Park Service, the first systematic classification of the nation's historic and archaeological monuments, was initiated in 1937; this collecting enterprise lead to a number of historical renovations, restorations, and reconstructions of various National Park Service properties (Historic National Parks, Historic Sites, and National Monuments) over which the Park Service had jurisdiction.[80] Architects working on another Park Service project, the Historic American Buildings Survey, undertook the beginnings of a national collection of measured drawings, photographs, and written data on early American architecture. Finally, federal agencies such as the Farm Security Administration underwrote extensive documentary photography programs that later became an important material culture resource when scholars in the 1970s rediscovered the value of photographs as historical documents.[81] With the exception of the underwriting of the Smithsonian Institution and a few other sporadic federal projects, these New Deal activities and agencies of the 1930s marked the United States government's first major, comprehensive involvement in American material culture studies. That role continually increased over the following half century.

In Depression America, academic historians remained largely indifferent to this expanding interest in the nation's artifacts. In the proceedings of the American Historical Association for 1939, later edited by Caroline F. Ware as a book, *The Cultural Approach to History*, there is hardly a word in the volume's introduction or thirty-six essays describing the new tools of the cultural historian as applied to extant physical remains. The single exception was one pioneering essay, "Documentary Photographs," by Roy Stryker and Paul Johnstone.[82] Yet three

scholarly landmarks using the material evidence of American technology to interpret the American past were produced during the 1930s: *The Great Plains* (1931) by
Walter P. Webb; *The March of the Iron Men* (1938) by Roger Burlingame; and
Technics and Civilization (1934) by Lewis Mumford. Webb, Burlingame, and
Mumford, were mavericks within a history profession that remained primarily
interested in past politics, economics, and diplomacy. An upstart, interdisciplinary
academic field began in the mid-1930s, however, that would offer material culturists more professional respect and scholarly attention. Usually called American
Civilization or American Studies, academic recognition came with the establishment of the first comprehensive Ph.D program in History of American Civilization
at Harvard in 1936. In the immediate post-World War II era, the numerous other
American Studies departments and programs that sprang up in other colleges and
universities came to be among the most hospitable of academic homes for material
culture studies by the 1970s.[83]

The Age of Description:
Proliferation and Professionalization, 1948–1965

As an interdisciplinary enterprise, the American Studies movement had an
affinity with the diverse scholarship being done in the several disciplines comprising
American material culture studies. For example, as early as 1948, George Tremaine
McDowell, a professor of English in the Program in American Studies at the
University of Minnesota, issued a seminal statement attempting to define the nature
of American Studies as an academic discipline. McDowell argued for a multidisciplinary approach to American culture and recognized the role that material culture
evidence should play in such study.[84] In 1951, he, along with Americanists Ralph
Gabriel, Roy Nichols, F. O. Matthiessen, Robert Spiller, and John Kouwenhoven,
formed the American Studies Association. Its official journal, the *American
Quarterly,* even in its early years published an occasional essay dealing with artifacts as indices to American culture. Introductory courses in material culture began
to appear in American Studies curricula and discussions were generated on the
respective merits of literary, artistic, and material evidence. For instance, an established American Studies teacher-scholar such as Kouwenhoven quickly became an
ardent proponent of the academic study of material culture in his own scholarship
and in methodological jeremiads such as his now oft-quoted manifesto, *American
Studies: Words or Things?* [85]

Through the mid-1940s, despite the extensive collecting and assorted research
that had been done, no established bibliographical canon and few truly interdisciplinary models of material culture scholarship existed. Hence, in retrospect, the
year 1948 looms as something of an unprecedented milestone to later scholars. That
year, for example, Kouwenhoven brought out the enormously influential book
Made in America.[86] Dealing with artifacts that ranged from clipper ships to

balloon-frame houses and from jazz to skyscrapers, Kouwenhoven argued the case for a distinctive American vernacular aesthetic in the nation's material culture.

Most artifacts "made in America," argued Kouwenhoven, were not elite, high-style objects but rather vernacular, folk creations, owing as much of their identity to cultural context as to stylistic tradition. Such a perspective was echoed in Edgar Richardson's biography of *Washington Allston* (1948), which was an attempt to study an American artist in the light of his intellectual milieu. This theme was echoed a year later when Oliver Larkin published his *Art and Life in America.*[87]

Indicative of the typically descriptive (rather than consciously analytical or interpretive) orientation of most American material culture studies in the post-war era were the 1948 publications of James Flexner's history of American painting, *The First Flowers of Our Wilderness* and Jean Lipman's *American Folk Art in Wood, Metal and Stone,* a work that gave renewed and probably exaggerated emphasis to the "art historical" focus in the study of such artifacts.[88] (See table 1.2, part I.)

A similar methodological perspective colored much of American architectural history, despite the subdiscipline's new self-identify within a professional organization, the Society for Architectural Historians, founded in 1940. Descriptive compendiums like Henry Chandless Forman's *The Architecture of the Old South* (1948) characterized the state of the art, rather than the occasional innovative monograph such as George Kubler's *Mexican Architecture of the Sixteenth Century* published that same year or Anthony N. B. Garvan's *Architecture and Town Planning in Colonial Connecticut* (1951).

All this publishing activity occurring around 1948, the same year that Bernard Baruch, in a speech before the Senate War Investigating Committee, coined the phrase "the Cold War," suggests the possible political ramifications of American material culture studies within the wider cultural history of the nation in the postwar decade. The publishing renaissance also paralleled the sudden expansion of the history of technology and of folklife studies, two areas of material culture research that grew rapidly throughout the 1950s. Scholars in both areas, however, labored independently of each other as well as somewhat in isolation from the more established disciplines, such as art history, archaeology, and anthropology, that employed artifacts as evidence. Although both new fields expanded almost simultaneously, I will discuss the rise of folklore and folklife studies first.

Emergence of Folklore/Folklife Studies

American folklorists with a bent for studying Indiana barn types, Afro-American coil basketry, or Louisiana log pirogues as folk-cultural evidence have had an almost century-long fight on their hands simply to win recognition of their research from their fellow folklorists. In fact, as Don Yoder has shown, a number even felt they had to change their name.[89] Most American students of folk artifacts came to call their study "folklife" or *"Volkskunde"* (to use the older German term) instead of "folklore." [90] The creator of the term "folk-lore," English antiquarian W. J. Thoms, described the word's meaning in 1846 as "that department of the study of antiquities and archaeology which embraces everything relating to ancient observances and customs, to the notions, traditions, superstitions and prejudices of the common people." [91] The emphasis on the literary and oral quality of past folk experience—the folktale, the folksong, the proverb, and other oral literature, that is to say, the "lore" in folklore—strongly influenced those Americans (e.g., William Wells Newell, T. F. Crane, Franz Boas, J. Owen Dorsey, and F. J. Child) who founded the American Folkore Society in 1888. As recurring definitions of American folklore illustrate, traditional American folklore research, like most academic historical research in this country, never escaped this addiction to written and oral data. [92]

Early academic folklorists such as Stith Thompson, the founder of the first graduate degree program in American folklore in 1948 at Indiana University, tended to emphasize "the dances, songs, tales, legends, and traditions, the beliefs, and superstitions, and the proverbial sayings of peoples everywhere" rather than the "materials of culture." [93] Thompson's own research never delved deeply into what he called "physical folklore." His magnus opus was *The Folktale* (1946), but his students and several of his colleagues at Indiana University began to argue for the inclusion of American artifacts as well as oral forms and social customs in folklore research. [94]

The institutionalization of material folk culture research among professional folklorists occurred in 1949 when three young scholars, Alfred L. Shoemaker, J. William Fry, and Don Yoder, organized the Pennsylvania Dutch Folklore Center with headquarters at Franklin and Marshall College in Pennsylvania. As in much other American material folk culture work, European precedents, particularly the Irish Folklore Commission in Dublin and the Folk Archives at the Universities of Uppsala and Lund in Sweden, exerted a strong influence on the Pennsylvania Center. [95] The center became a research institute with a library and folklife archive. It also sponsored an annual regional folk festival and began publishing a journal, initially called *The Pennsylvania Dutchman* and later known as *Pennsylvania Folklife*. By 1957, the same year the center's journal underwent a name change, Yoder and his colleagues decided to change their name to the Pennsylvania Folklife Society (the first official use of the term "folklife" in the United States). Over the following two decades, folklife studies contributed to both the popular national interest in artifacts, largely through an association with living history museums such as the Pennsylvania Farm Museum at Landis Valley and regional folk festivals like the Mennonite Folk Festival at North Newton, Kansas, as well as to the expanding material cultural studies movement of the 1970s through teaching and research programs like those at the University of Pennslyvania and SUNY–Oneonta at Cooperstown, New York.

Don Yoder, an advocate and historian of the folklife movement, defined the folklife movement as "the 20th century re-discovery of the total range of the folk culture. Folklore is not so much its parent as is anthropology, especially what Americans call cultural anthropology and Europeans ethnology or ethnography. The cultural anthropologist studies *all* aspects of a culture—farming, cooking, dress, ornament, houses, settlements, handicraft, trade, transportation, amusements, arts, marriage, family, religion—to name a few of the subjects included as chapter headings in any basic recent text.'' In another statement on the history of folklife studies in American scholarship, Yoder noted that ''in the American academic world, folklife studies shares subject matter not only with cultural anthropology but also with the two historical disciplines, the older American history and the new American civilization or, as it is frequently called, American studies.'' [96]

Consequently, one way that anthropological scholarship, which was somewhat taken with using objects as research evidence before the turn of the twentieth century but which lost interest in that approach prior to World War I, reasserted its influence in material culture studies was through folklife studies and American Studies.[97] In universities like the University of Pennsylvania, museums like the Smithsonian Institution, and agencies such as the Library of Congress, where folklife, anthropology, and American Studies were conjoined, material culture teaching, research, and interpretation took on an strong anthropological cast.[98]

Role of the History of Technology

Cultural anthropology, however, had almost no discernable impact at all on the history of technology, a second new area of material culture studies to emerge within the post-World War II era. Less than a generation ago, the history of technology was pursued almost entirely by museum curators, engineers, technologists, and amateur writers of popular volumes on the history of American inventions. As Brooke Hindle has carefully catalogued, the bulk of the nineteenth- and twentieth-century work prior to 1950 can be categorized as collective biographies, encyclopedias and dictionaries of the mechanical arts, local histories, and general surveys.[99] With the possible exception of Constance McLaughlin Green's early attempt to pay some attention to urban material culture, few early studies took seriously the technological artifact as actual historical evidence. Most were marred by chauvinistic excess, an unsophisticated understanding of technical creativity, and an overly optimistic view of historical change induced primarily by technological innovation.[100] The best of them, however, remain useful sources of information, many containing storehouses of valuable statistical data. They were, like the efforts of the early generations of researchers in other areas of material culture studies, largely an enterprise of collecting and cataloguing. By the mid-twentieth century, however, the task of the historian of technology became one of precise and scientific description of how an artifact or a class of artifacts, for example, the internal combustion engines or land transportation vehicles, originated and developed. Throughout the 1950s, a series of pioneering monographs surfaced demonstrating the sophistication of these internal histories of technology.[101]

The organizing principle of many of these histories was often a recital of the increasing technical success of the material culture being investigated. Around this basic assumption, three explanatory models emerged in the early historiography of American technology. One interpretation of the supposedly "progressive" nature of the history of American technology was decidedly economic. Working from the premise that American technology developed in direct response to capital accumulation and labor scarcity, scholars of this persuasion confined their research to how capital was amassed and why it was invested in this or that mechanical improvement. Another research perspective, nicely summarized by John Sawyer, took a mildly behavioral approach to technology,[102] and a third centered on proving or disproving the "Americanness" of American technology—a methodological and ideological preoccupation of many researchers in the subfield since its institutional origins in the Cold War decade of the 1950s.[103]

This "national character" debate, an issue that permeates other disciplines that investigate American material culture, has two basic sides. The least popular and yet certainly not the least plausible is the argument that Americans borrowed their artifactual innovations from Europe in general and from Great Britain in particular. In the concept of interchangeable parts in manufacturing, for instance, historian Robert Woodbury disputed the long standing claim that Eli Whitney originated this idea by simply calling attention to earlier engineering development by Jeremy Bentham and Marc Isambard Brunel in England and Louis Blanc in France.[104] Another school of interpreters attribute American technology primarily to indigenous, not imported, mechanical genius. They have tended to depict the American past on large canvasses, tracing the roots of American technological genius back into the physical or geographical aspects of the national experience. While their historical panoramas have given considerable emphasis to technological artifacts, these metahistorians of material culture, such as Roger Burlingame, Walter P. Webb, Lewis Mumford, John Kouwenhoven, and Daniel Boorstin, have sometimes also endeavored to synthesize the role of the arts and architecture in their quest for an answer to the question "what is American about American things?" Understandably, their typical intellectual mentors were also men of the long view: Henry Adams and Frederick Jackson Turner. For example, Adams's writings on technology strongly influenced Mumford's *Technics and Civilization* (1934); the Turner thesis had a profound impact on Burlingame's *March of the Iron Men: A Social History of Union through Invention* (1938) and his *Engines of Democracy: Invention and Society in Mature America* (1940), as well as on Webb's *The Great Plains* (1931).

Burlingame and Mumford were among the first serious thinkers to speculate about what historian George Daniels calls "the big questions" of the history of American technology.[105] Burlingame, following W. G. Ogburn's concept of "cultural lag," and Mumford, borrowing from Patrick Geddes' typology of cultural-technological evolution, sought to investigate technology as a social phenomenon.[106] The interaction between technology and society fascinated these searchers for an American *Zeitgeist*; the "culture" behind technology's material culture especially intrigued these scholars in their quest for a comprehensive explanatory concept by which to chart the direction of American history. Such an external interpretive approach to the artifacts of American technology found favor with other cultural historians interested in identifying what was exceptional about American material culture, including John Kouwenhoven, J. L. Burn, Frank W. Fox, and Daniel Boorstin.[107]

Institutionalization and Specialization

Such an interest in movement beyond mere descriptive chronologies of technical material culture to analytical models and interpretive frameworks received some impetus from the rapid institutionalization that the history of technology, like several other areas of material culture study, underwent in the late 1950s. Eugene Ferguson, the movement's veteran historiographer, dates the beginning of the history of technology as a separate academic discipline to the precise year of the appearance of a novel artifact destined to alter modern American history. In 1958, "while Sputnik was yet in orbit," recalls Ferguson, the Advisory Committee for Technology and Society met at the Case Institute of Technology in Cleveland. The advisory committee had grown out of the Humanistic-Social Research Project of the American Society for Engineering Education. Its prime mover had been Melvin Kranzberg, a professor of history at Case, who argued the need for a national organization to foster the study of technological material culture. Such a group, the Society for the History of Technology, developed out of the advisory committee, with Kranzberg emerging as the "chief architect and builder" of the organization's journal, *Technology and Culture*. Significantly, the quarterly aspired to be concerned not only with "the history of technological devices and processes, but also with the relations of technology to science, politics, social change, economics and the arts and humanities." [108]

In the following decade, a segment of the Society for the History of Technology (usually known as SHOT) membership, strongly influenced by developments in Great Britain and anxious to claim a particular sector of technology as their own province, formed the Society for Industrial Archaeology. Such specialization was a portent of things to come. Several other professional organizations that dealt with particular branches of material culture evidence grew out of or broke away from parent organizations during the 1950s and early 1960s. Out of the College Art Association, for instance, came the Society of Architectural Historians in 1940, from which the Decorative Arts Chapter (later the Society of Decorative Arts) was organized in 1975. All three groups issue publications in which material culture research is reported and reviewed.[109]

In American anthropology and archaeology another similar evolution took place. Archaeologists within the American Anthropological Association argued for the intrinsic validity of their profession as a distinct scholarly discipline; some of them also insisted on the equal importance of studying artifacts of literate societies as well as the material culture of preliterate or prehistoric societies that archaeologists had traditionally investigated. One outcome of this intramural debate was the formation of the Society for Historical Archaeology in 1967. A number of interpreters trace this trend in American archaeology's approach to material culture back to Walter W. Taylor's *A Study of Archaeology* (1948).[110]

In the years immediately after World War II, the general avocational interest in American artifacts also underwent institutionalization. In 1947 the Early American Industries Association (founded 1936) began publication of a quarterly, *The Chronicle of the Early American Industries Association*. In that year the National Council for Historic Sites and Buildings was organized in the United States. Following an institutional evolution that became increasingly commonplace in the boom years of historical agency expansion, the private-public National Council for Historic Sites and Buildings became the National Trust for Historic Preservation two years later. The Trust, a private agency chartered by Congress, grew to number over 100,000 individuals and organizations and became a strong force in architectural and decorative arts preservation.[111]

In the fulcrum year of 1948, the New York State Historical Association at Cooperstown began a ten-day summer adult education program where, with considerable attention to artifacts, an attempt was made "to explore and utilize a wide variety of disciplines concerned with the past and its relation to the present."[112] The next summer, Cooperstown's seminars on American culture were expanded to ten Chautauqua-like courses extending over two weeks. The following year Colonial Williamsburg and *Antiques* magazine joined together to implement the Cooperstown concept in a format that came to be known as the Williamsburg Antiques Forum. Gathering speakers from around the country, many of whom had not met and exchanged ideas before, this week-long forum became an annual event for both the connoisseur and the general collector. Other American museums (e.g., Henry Ford Museum, Old Sturbridge Village, and Pennsbury Manor), began sponsoring similar antique forums, seminars, and week-ends as the collecting of American objects grew from an antiquarian hobby of an economic elite to a popular pasttime of middle-class enthusiasts who frequented the innumerable flea markets, study groups, and garage sales that occurred every weekend in the United States. One sociologist has described this intriguing phenomenon as "the democratization of the antique." [113] Unfortunately, however, this significant dimension of the Americana movement and its impact upon material culture studies in the United States has not been thoroughly described, much less carefully analyzed.

Nor do we know enough about another historical trend that enormously influenced both the quantity and quality of American material culture studies in the post-World War II era: the unprecedented expansion of history museums, a phenomenon anticipated in 1948 by Laurence Vail Coleman in his three-volume *The Museum in America*.[114] Several new outdoor historical villages, some in the planning stages in the 1930s, came into reality in the late 1940s because of the personal interest and financial largesse of individual underwriters: Old Sturbridge Village, Massachusetts, largely the creation of Albert Wells and Cheney Wells, opened in 1946; Plimoth Plantation, Massachusetts, the dream of businessman-amateur archaeologist Henry Hornblower, was incorporated in 1947; in that same year Electra Havemeyer Webb, a long-time collector of American furniture, toys, china, and quilts, along with her husband James Watson Webb, an avid devotee of early American buildings, established the Shelburne Museum in Vermont.[115]

Earlier in the decade, Stephen C. Clark, wealthy heir to part of the Singer Sewing Machine fortune, founded the Farmers' Museum located at Cooperstown, New York and, significantly, it was in 1947 that Louis C. Jones assumed the directorship of the Farmer's Museum, a post he held for the next quarter century, and prepared its first comprehensive collection and interpretation policy statement.[116] At the same time that Jones introduced a new scholarly orientation at the Farmer's Museum, a more veteran historical agency, the National Museum of the Smithsonian Institution, experienced a marked shift in its historical methodology of using artifacts when C. Malcolm Watkins was appointed head of the Division of Cultural History, also in 1948. Watkins, an anthropologist who, like Jones, also exerted a pervasive influence over his institution for the next twenty years, introduced the cultural history orientation that lay behind such Smithsonian exhibits as the original "Hall of Everyday Life" galleries. In 1952, largely at Henry H. Flynt's urging, Historic Deerfield, Massachusetts, came into the existence; also in 1952, Henry Francis Du Pont opened his private collection of American decorative arts to the public as the Winterthur Museum in Delaware which, while not an outdoor museum, played a major role in material culture scholarship.[117]

Practically all of these new history museums eventually developed a research component where material culture study was further institutionalized in an academic setting. Begun in 1952, the Winterthur program, as an interinstitutional (jointly sponsored by the Winterthur Museum and the University of Delaware), interdepartmental (comprising the departments of art, history, and English), and interdisciplinary (art history, social-cultural history, and intellectual history) enterprise, served as the prototype for many of the other museum-university related programs that followed.[118] Initially called "The Winterthur Program in American Decorative Arts and Cultural History" (changed in 1955 to "Early American Culture"), the curriculum was a pioneering endeavor in material culture studies on three fronts: as an early example of university-museum collaboration at the graduate level; as an effort to offer graduate preparation for scholar-curators seeking careers in museums that emphasized the "work of the artist and artisan"; and as an educational experiment directly allied with the new discipline of American Studies.

Scholars and Scholarly Apparatus

In addition to new professional associations, such as the Society of Architectural Historians and the Society for the History of Technology, and museum-university programs such as at the Winterthur Museum and the Cooperstown Graduate Programs (begun in 1964),[119] American material culture studies underwent institutionalization through the founding of new journals and newsletters, the establishment of new types of scholarly apparatus, and the publication of the first "classics" by individuals who were later heralded as among the founders of material culture studies in postwar America.

Besides the serial publications already mentioned, one should note the appearance of the Smithsonian's *Contributions by the Museum of History and Technology* (1966), the *Winterthur Portfolio* (1964), *History News* (1945), *Furniture History* (1965), *Winterthur Conference Reports* (1969), *Landscape* (1952), and *Pioneer America* (1968). Certain university presses, such as those at Yale, Wesleyan, Princeton, and Virginia, also became receptive to publishing monographs on American material culture as did a handful of commercial houses, including W. W. Norton, Charles Tuttle, Stackpole, and E. P. Dutton.

An early experiment in providing material culture studies with a comprehensive methodology for describing and cataloging the enormous number of artifacts that had been collected by various individuals and institutions over the past century was the Index of Early American Culture. In creating this data bank, Anthony Garvan and Frank Sommer sought to apply the principles of the Human Relations Area Files developed by George Murdock and codified in the *Outline of Cultural Materials* (1950).[120] The Index of Early American Culture attempted to organize all human culture—intellectual, social, and material—into eighty-eight major topics. One such file that catalogued data for Boston, 1676–1725, was established at the Winterthur Museum; another bank that surveyed Philadelphia, 1725–1775, was begun at the University of Pennsylvania.[121]

Although the index never succeeded to the degree that its originators had hoped, its aspirations are illustrative of the several characteristics that I have termed the "Age of Description" in material culture historiography. (See table 1.1, col. II.) These characteristics include a quest for systematic, comprehensive reference tools; an attempt to widen the realm of material culture investigations beyond the confines of traditional art history, particularly to include the more holistic approach of anthropology; a concern to unite both the museum and the academy in the common cause of artifact scholarship; and, finally, to aid in the professionalization process of a discipline that, in its aspiration to be interdisciplinary, constantly suffered from the want of any discipline at all!

The Index of Early American Culture engaged the enthusiasm and the energies of several representatives (Charles Montgomery, in addition to Garvan and Sommer) of the first, self-conscious cadre of professional material culture scholars in the United States. This small but diversified group, working in museums, historical agencies, and universities, and composed of men such as John Kouwenhoven, Louis C. Jones, James Marston Fitch, Fred Kniffen, Charles Peterson, Joseph Downs, C. Malcolm Watkins, Edward Alexander, Eugene Ferguson, J. B. Jackson, George Kubler, E. McClung Fleming, Walter Muir Whitehill, John Cotter, Anthony Garvan, and Charles Montgomery, did much of their most creative work in the first two and one half decades of post-World War II America.[122] Their intellectual heroes were as varied as their original disciplinary affiliations: many had geographical interests borrowed from Carl Sauer; Fiske Kimball's early American architectural studies inspired some; Constance Rourke's work on American folk art motivated others. The anthropology of Franz Boaz, the decorative arts scholarship of R. T. H. Halsey, and the sweeping cultural analyses of Lewis Mumford stimulated still others.[123]

Only a few professional academic historians appear to have had an impact on this generation of material culturists. Dixon Ryan Fox, Arthur Schlesinger, Sr., and John Krout had a slight influence on men trained at Columbia or Harvard. Several, however, acknowledge Thomas J. Wertenbaker as the one historian who both preached a brand of material culture history in his classroom at Princeton and practiced it in his books on colonial America. In 1947 Wertenbaker completed his series, *The Founding of American Civilization,* a trilogy begun in 1938 that demonstrated an impressive knowledge of Anglo-American artifacts of the seventeenth and eighteenth centuries. In documenting his research, Wertenbaker was the first established university historian to make extensive use of the Historic American Buildings Survey records, the Pictorial Archives of Early American Architecture at the Library of Congress, and the fieldwork research reports, particularly archaeological, prepared at Colonial Williamsburg.[124]

The work of Wertenbaker deserves mention not only because he was practically alone among American historians in recognizing the value of material culture as resource material for American history, but also because his professional odyssey is almost archetypal of the generation of material culture scholars that followed him. (See table 1.1, col. II.) That next generation shared several common characteristics. Almost all had come to material culture research by some other discipline or vocational route. Few, with the exception of those with anthropological training, such as Kniffen or Watkins, or those with a familial interest in antiques, such as Garvan, were specifically trained in interpreting the artifactual record of a literate society. If any common denominator existed as to their formal academic training, it would have to be art and architectural history. One would still be forced to say, however, that this generation of material culture scholars was largely self-taught in the task of working with artifacts, self-taught, usually, through their personal research in the history, art, or technology museum collections with which many of them came to be affiliated and, of course, through years of their own extensive fieldwork. Their major published research resulted in a significant corpus of scholarship that, in turn, became the textbooks of the next generation of material culture researchers.[125]

An Americana Resurgence

In the 1950s and 1960s, the multifaceted Americana movement in the United States expanded on all of its many levels. Some historians see the folksong revival of the early 1960s as one manifestation of a new popular interest in folklore and folk art; others have taken note of a "new romanticism" in the counter-culture's fascination with a more simple, rural existence where rugged, individualistic artisans pursue crafts such as leather-working or basket-weaving. Cold War tensions and anxieties about the American identity in an age of affluence have also been suggested as possible factors in fostering patriotic reverence for historic American things as totems of national character and superiority.[126]

No matter what the exact causes for this widespread resurgence of interest in Americana, few observers dispute the fact that the revival was assuredly the most populist in American cultural history. Historic preservation in America, for example, gradually widened its scope beyond the task of salvaging the mansions of "famous American men," a task usually undertaken by a few, wealthy, socialite matrons.[127] Preservationists in the 1960s, for instance, sought the restoration of factories, slave quarters, and even entire urban areas as important artifacts of the American past. Widespread interest in practically the entire built-environment indirectly pressured a shift in architectural history, a discipline that in this country had focused its attention almost exclusively on the classic structures of antiquity and of Europe up to the Renaissance, with only an occasional nod to American Georgian structures and possibly the classical revivals of the early-nineteenth century.[128] It was, for example, only in 1948 that the first major historical scholarship by an American on the skyscraper, a building type indigenous to America, was published.[129] Despite this shift in topical emphasis, most American architectural scholarship still concentrated on collection, classification, and particularly, description.

The expanded teaching and research in American architectural history, like that in American art history, was bolstered by the enormous strides made in the postwar technology of graphic reproduction. Artifactual evidence could be reproduced more easily and in color on 35mm slides, in books, and in magazines. No doubt in the near future some student of the material culture of America at the midpoint of the twentieth century will research the full implications of this "graphics revolution," without which the now ubiquitous slide-lecture on any material culture topic would not be possible. We would also be without publications such as *American Heritage* (first published in 1949); the numerous, lavishly-illustrated museum catalogs describing all manner of American artifacts; as well as the Carnegie Study of the Arts which, when finally completed in 1960, made available to teachers and students a textbook of essays and slide transparencies of some 2,500 objects in eighteen categories of American material culture.[130]

Increased tourism in the recent decades also expanded the visibility of artifacts to both the scholarly and the general public. Although the dimensions and ramifications of this relationship are only beginning to be explored by sociologists, social psychologists, and anthropologists,[131] it is an important chapter in the historiography of material culture research, especially as carried out in museums and historical societies.

Unlike material culture scholars in the academy who communicate their research primarily through journal literature or monographs, the material culturist working within the institutional context of a museum or historical agency is frequently required to communicate his or her research through various three-dimensional media, such as the temporary display, the permanent exhibition gallery, a period room, a historic house, an outdoor historic site, or even a re-created outdoor historical community or village. The "reader" of these research efforts can be quite different than the reader of material culture scholarship as presented in articles and books; frequently he or she is a tourist. The economic reality of what tourists want to see and are willing to pay to see has often influenced material culture research in many American museums. In what ways and with what long-range effects such an influence exists remains another unexplored research topic of the profession's intellectual history.

In a similar vein, a book-length study should also be done on how major historical anniversaries, such as the 1961–1965 centennial of the Civil War or the bicentennial of 1976, have prompted new directions in material culture study. The bicentennial understandably generated an interest in the artifactual remains of the 1876 centennial and the entire second half of the nineteenth century.[132] Charles Montgomery argued that the major exhibitions of the 1976 celebration gave evidence of increased professionalism and the higher level of scholarship in material culture studies that had been building over the past thirty years.[133]

Montgomery rightly pointed to several other factors that help explain the increased interest in American artifacts. The federal government, for instance, has played a fairly active role since the early 1960s. The National Endowments for the Arts and the Humanities, the Smithsonian Institution programs, as well as specific federal legislation, such as the National Arts and Cultural Development Act of 1964, the National Museum Act of 1966, and the Folklife Preservation Act of 1976 supported scholarship and exhibitions involving American material culture.[134]

Expanded Professionalization

An increasingly better-trained network of museum personnel (curators, exhibit designers, researchers, and administrators) sought increased professionalization through national meetings, journals, and special conferences of the American Association of Museums and the American Association for State and Local History.[135] Local history, in particular, has undergone a dramatic renaissance in recent years and, in turn, has sparked the collection, classification, and description of the artifactual records of many local American communities on the neighborhood and small-town level.[136]

Simultaneously with the growing professionalism among material culture scholars in museums came an awareness among a few academicians of the possibilities of interinstitutional, interdepartmental, and interdisciplinary programs such as those pioneered by the Winterthur Museum and the University of Delaware in 1952. For example, two years after the Winterthur-Delaware program began, the com-

bined Hagley Museum-University of Delaware program opened. The real proliferation of institutions where formal material culture studies could be pursued came in
the second half of the 1960s: the Cooperstown Graduate Programs (New York State
Historical Association-State University College of New York at Oneonta, 1964);
Shelburne Museum-University of Vermont (1965); University of Michigan-Henry
Ford Museum (1967); Old Sturbridge Village-University of Connecticut (1970);
and Boston University-Boston Museum of Fine Arts (1970). In addition to complete
degree programs with various emphases in material culture studies, single course
offerings in the field were to be found in art, architecture, and American Studies
departments.[137] Very few, however, were in history departments.

By the 1960s, yet another generation of material culture researchers had come
into their scholarly majority. (See table 1.1, col. III.) As with the preceding generation, most in this group had not been formally trained in anything called "material
culture studies" but rather in one of the three academic enterprises that had struggled for identity and independence throughout the 1950s: the history of American
decorative arts, the history of American technology, or American historical
archeaology. As before, there were exceptions, such as Carl Condit (who earned a
Ph.D in literature) or Wilcomb Washburn (who was initially trained as a political
historian and took his doctorate in American Studies).

The corpus of work done by this generation of scholars provided the expanding
material culture studies movement with another seminal bookshelf of scholarly
literature.[138] These important books, mostly researched and written in the 1960s,
functioned as stimuli to further research, as methodological models for subsequent
scholars to imitate or challenge, and, as before, as the textbooks for the next
generation of students who would take up material culture study. Indebted to these
scholarly efforts, a fourth generation (see table 1.1, col. IV), the first to be specifically trained for their varied careers in material culture research (university
teaching, museum curatorship, historic preservation, and so forth), has begun, in
turn, to publish its own research in the collection, description, and, in a few
instances, interpretation of American artifacts.[139]

Age of Interpretation: A Quest for New Methods, New Subjects, and New Syntheses, 1965–Present

What can be expected of this fourth generation? Where might American material culture studies go next? Perhaps one direction will be the continuation and
possibly the intensification of the quest for appropriate research designs, methods,
models, or paradigms (to use the term currently fashionable in social science) in
artifact research. As we have seen, the more intellectually audacious individuals in
the earlier generations had struggled with the nettlesome issues of appropriate
methods and adequate explanation. They realized that if the movement was to
achieve intellectual substance and the academic respectability that many in the

second generation eagerly sought, they must find defensible techniques for analyzing the material culture evidence that earlier laborers had collected and classified. The major task of the third generation entailed moving beyond the simplistic assertion that artifacts are important and are somehow related to the people who produced them.[140] The crucial task remaining for contemporary material culturists is to expand the emphasis of the discipline from the description of artifacts to the interpretation of them.

Recent proposals offered for artifact analysis suggest the currency and urgency of this vital task. Not before the 1960s did any serious discussion surface as to the evidential potential of the artifact for historical research,[141] and not until 1974 did the movement see an attempt at using a systematic procedure whereby a single artifact might be comprehensively analyzed.[142] Only in the 1970s have methodological issues begun to be explored, via conferences, book reviews, and journal articles, with the seriousness and sophistication they deserve.

During this time, the important activities of collecting and describing material culture data continued apace. Surveys of the built environment of the United States by the Historic American Building Survey, as well as by state, local, and private historic preservation organizations, multiplied throughout the 1970. Private and professional artifact collectors organized their efforts though new organizations, some having national appeal, such as the Victorian Society in America, founded in 1969 and publisher of the monthly *Nineteenth Century* since 1975, and others catering to highly specialized interests, such as the Association for Gravestone Studies, founded in 1976 and since 1979 the publisher of an annual called *Markings*. Still others, in organizations such as the Dunlap Society (named for William Dunlap, who is often credited as being the first American art historian), have set out to document on microfiche the corpus of American art and architecture. American historical museums increased in numbers and also in total holdings. During the years from 1950 to 1980, the number of American historical museums practically doubled.

Many scholars, recognizing that modern America continues to destroy the context, sequence, and embodiments of its historic material culture at an alarming rate, have tried to collect as much of such data as possible before it disappears completely. It was this concern that motivated the coalition of cultural and historical geographers, folklife researchers, and ethnographers who started the Society for the North American Cultural Survey.[143] The work of this survey, as with those conducted by government agencies such as the Historic American Buildings Survey, the Index of American Design, the American Folklife Center, and similar organizations at the regional, state, or local level points out a crucial fallacy about the artifact as evidence: that artifacts are the most ubiquitous, durable, and comprehensive manifestations of past culture.

"Antiquarians in their romanticism extol the longevity of artifacts compared to the written word," John Mannion reminds us, "but material culture is a highly perishable phenomenon, and examples of longevity are all too rare. Entire traditional cultural landscapes can be obliterated or transformed by a new wave of immigrants, as in the case of Indian imprints with the advent of Europeans in North America, or by economic forces such as the impact of the Industrial Revolution on the medieval material culture of Britian, or by the urbanization of the countryside, as in contemporary Canada." Mannion concludes, therefore, that "the student of material culture should focus more on the dynamic nature of the artifact, its changeability and adaptability, displacement and replacement, rather than its longevity." [144]

To get at Mannion's "dynamic nature of the artifact," some modern researchers have turned to material culture "collections," such as probate records and household inventories, in order to expand the range and comprehensiveness of their analyses. The spade work in this approach was done by dedicated collectors in the 1920 and 1930s who painstakingly copied statistical data piecemeal out of census records, newspapers, and family papers. Henry W. Belknap's *Trades and Tradesmen of Essex County, Massachusetts* (1929) and George F. Dow's *The Arts and Crafts in New England* (1928) were pioneering compendiums. [145] Although the initial collection of such information is always a laborious process, with the aid of computers the data can now be sorted, recollected, compared with and contrasted to similar data from other material culture statistical collections in ways hardly thought possible previously.

Demography, political behavior, and social structure were the historical topics to which quantitative methods were first applied by American scholars. Now the techniques developed in these analyses have been employed by material culture scholars investigating the social and economic status of typical colonial men and women in Plymouth, Massachusetts; Sleepy Hollow, New York; Essex County, Massachusetts; St. Mary's, Maryland; and Williamsburg, Virginia. [146] For example, Brown University and Plimoth Plantation have received a major "research tools" grant from the National Endowment for the Humanities to collect and publish the seventeenth-century probate records of the Plymouth colony. In such studies, artifacts of a highly technological society, such as computers, may help us better understand the material culture of a largely pretechnological one.

Computerization techniques are also being used in the collection, identification, registration, and storage of the abundant material culture presently housed in American museums and historical societies. Fred Rath, Jr., and Merrilyn Rogers O'Connell have compiled an annotated guide, the *Documentation of Collections: A Bibliography on Historical Organization Practices* (1979), and Robert Chenall has proposed a schema, *Nomenclature for Museum Cataloging: A System for Classifying Man-Made Objects* (1978), that is easily adaptable to computerization. Information storage and retrieval technology has also been suggested as a panacea to several pressing research needs in the field, including the lack of adequate finding aids to material culture collections in various institutions around the country (no National Union Catalog of Material Objects exists in the United States comparable, say, to the National Union Catalogs of Books, Serials, and Manuscripts); the lack of up-to-date material culture bibliographies;[147] and the lack of adequate identification and promulgation of graduate research as it appears in theses and dissertations.[148] Such basic aids to research, many argue, would provide American material culture studies with greater organizational visibility, particularly in the nation's universities, where the movement must still struggle for academic respectibility. For this to happen, however, more extensive peer review of published monographs and of museum exhibitions—two major forums whereby material culturists communicate their research—remains an absolute necessity.[149]

The journals in which such peer review could occur have multiplied during the past decade. Prior to 1965 (the beginning of the *Winterthur Portfolio*), the periodical literature with which the serious material culture scholar had to keep current entailed no more than a half dozen serials. Now the list numbers over two dozen: *Pioneer America: The Journal of Historic American Material Culture* (1965); *Material History Bulletin* (1971); *Journal of Early Southern Decorative Arts* (1975); *Studies in Traditional American Crafts* (1978); *Environmental Review* (1976); *Furniture History* (1965); *Association for Preservation Technology Bulletin* (1969); *Bulletin of Glass Studies* (1977); *Classical America* (1972); *Industrial Archaeology: The Journal of the Society for Industrial Archaeology* (1968); *Journal of American Culture* (1978); *Textile History* (1968); *Nineteenth Century* (1975); *ALHFAM Proceedings* (1974); *Historical Archaeology* (1966); *Decorative Arts Newsletter* (1975); *Journal of Popular Culture* (1967); *Southern Exposure* (1972); and *Folklore Forum* (1967).

Within the pages of these new journals, as well as in the established forums such as *Technology and Culture, Pennsylvania Folklife,* or *Antiques,* one finds meticulous, exhaustive, often comparative and descriptive scholarship of a single object or a genre of objects. In such detailed and invaluable works, the age of description can be seen to have truly come of age.

Other evidences of this trend are recent museum exhibition catalogs. Although a thorough scholarly study of the catalog as a device for the communication of material culture research information and insight has yet to be written, there is little doubt the genre has matured as a standard vehicle for disseminating scholarly descriptions of artifacts. In this sense, certain catalogs have become helpful reports of work in progress or, where their data has been fairly comprehensive, useful reference tools for the material culturist's library.[150] A few daring scholars have even used the medium to speculate about the interpretive messages of artifacts in a wider cultural context.[151]

The majority of these innovative studies are in the area of the decorative arts, broadly defined, and this may mean that the most innovative interpretive exhibition techniques have concentrated on using such material culture as evidence. A more easily demonstrable observation about them, however, is that they have been influenced by what many professional historians are calling "the new social history." In the past decade this trend toward increased sensitivity to the history of commonplace activities, particularly those of large aggregates of common people (e.g., workers, slaves, women, and children) heretofore generally neglected by historians, has captured the imagination of a major academic wing of the American historical profession. Variously described as "history from the bottom up," "grass-roots history," "popular history," "history of the common man/woman," "non-elite history," and "underside history," the new social history hopes to qualify as the main cynosure of historical scholarship in our own time.[152]

The recent work in social history has many sources; in one sense it is not new at all, since it draws on the labors of assorted late-nineteenth century antiquarians, many of them anonymous and many of them nascent material culture collectors, who gathered, preserved, and often reconstructed genealogical and community records of their families and localities. Moreover, current social history draws on the work of the first flowering of professionally trained economic historians around the turn of the century who, like John R. Commons at the University of Wisconsin or Arthur Schlesinger, Sr., at Harvard University, wrote careful historical accounts of labor and business associations and of public and educational institutions. The current social history harkens back, also, to scholars like Theodore Blegen at the Minnesota Historical Society and to Carl Bridenbaugh at Brown University who helped interject into academic historical inquiry the themes of immigration, folk history, urban growth, and industrial development. Finally, it should also be remembered that Henry Ford established the museums at his Edison Institute in 1929 because he "wanted to preserve what he appreciated as the contributions of the plain men who never got into history." [153]

While it would be enticing to claim that the rise of material culture studies has had a significant influence upon social historians who have investigated the past lives of ordinary people, the truth is more the reverse. American social historians have only recently begun to consider material culture evidence as crucial data in their analyses of the social structure, life processes, or social behavior of large aggregates of historic populations. In the recent development of the social history approach, other formative influences were at work. In the 1960s, American historians with a strong social science orientation (and a few material culturists with disciplinary bases in cultural anthropology and folklife studies) became aware of the new social history being done abroad. For example, British social historians such as E. J. Hobsbawn and E. P. Thompson influenced American thinking about the socioeconomic impact of industrialization. Scandivanian scholars like Sigurd Erixon drastically shifted the theoretical assumptions of cultural geography and regional ethnology.[154]

A cadre of French scholars, beginning their work prior to World War II and publishing their findings in the *Annales d'historie économique et social,* have also had an impact on social historians in the United States. Usually referred to in American historiography as the *Annales* school, these researchers, led by scholars such as Marc Bloch, Fernand Braudel, and Philippe Ariès, sought to investigate society as a whole, to write what they called "total history." This research coterie took particular note of extant material culture evidence in rural France and sought to integrate its interpretation into their attempts to recreate holistic views of the *mentalité* of past society.[155]

The combined influence of the *Annales* school, the British labor historians, and several indigenous developments in American historiography has meant at least two things for American material culture studies. First, since many of the major innovations in social history methodology have had a strong social science orientation, this has had the effect of prompting a greater willingness to entertain this mode of scholarly inquiry in the material culture studies camp. Such a shift has understandably widened the scope of data to include such things as popular culture artifacts, industrial sites, and funerary art previously ignored by earlier material culturists. Second, in the task of investigating artifacts of the past having a strong bearing upon social structure, social status, and social institutions, a subtle transformation has begun to take place among some material culture researchers. Whereas the first and second generations of scholars in the field were staunch humanists, trained in the humanities, schooled in their social and cultural values, and dedicated to their preservation and promulgation, the current generation has drunk (some more deeply than others) of the acclaimed "new" wine of the social sciences, particularly of social history in its various vintages. Understandably, the imbibing has affected their speech (to read them one must know the meaning of regression coefficients, prosopography, and the Guttman scale), their social outlook (many were socialized during the turbulent 1960s), and their way of asking questions about the past. Because of the steady imperialism of social history, a number of material culture scholars have now begun to work out of a different intellectual paradigm. Whereas once the scholarly paradigm for the bulk of material culture studies was that of art history, now that pervasive mode of analysis has lost some of its explanatory power. Social history now clamors to be the heir apparent.[156]

Whether or not the social history perspective will capture the place that art history and its allied fields, architecture and decorative arts, once held remains to be seen. Perhaps social history's more enduring legacy to American material culture studies will be its heightened (critics would say exaggerated) sense of methodological awareness. The central message of social history scholarship appears to be the pressing need for every historian to remain ever concerned with a single, paramount question: "How representative is this or that piece of evidence?" Social historians currently argue this issue in the proliferation of new journals that emphasize methodology,[157] in books and essays that demand greater self-consciousness on the part of historians about their assumptions and procedures,[158] and in appeals made by some that historical methodology itself be recognized as a crucial subdiscipline.[159]

Nothing like this debate has occurred yet among material culture scholars. The discussion has assuredly begun within the field's particular disciplines, but there have been few calls for a full-scale revisionist stocktaking of artifact scholarship as a whole.[160] If one were to take such an inventory, even as a most introductory survey, what would one find in the 1980s? What are the scholarly goals of the men and women currently pursuing material culture studies in the United States? What are their guiding intellectual frameworks? How would one identify their methods of explanation regarding artifactual evidence? Do their methods, purposes, and theories of material culture study fall into any particular "school" or "trend"?

In raising such questions, I think one can discern a number of conceptual positions that currently inform material culture research. (See table 1.2, parts I, II, and III.) I enumerate them as the art history, symbolist, cultural history, environmentalist, functionalist, structuralist, behavioralistic, national character, and social history approaches. Their diversity suggests that an age of interpretation in American material culture studies has perhaps truly begun.[161]

One might discuss the intellectual configurations of material culture study in any number of ways—by artifact genre (e.g., vernacular building or photography), by disciplinary focus (e.g., folklife or archaeology), or by traditional divisions of knowledge (e.g., arts, humanities, sciences). Instead, I have endeavored to explore them as ways of thinking that transcend each of these categories; I have sought to explore them as communal and individual epistemologies about the historical past and how scholars go about collecting, describing, and, particularly, *interpreting* that past with special attention to material culture evidence.

Eschewing categories based primarily on artifact genre or disciplinary affiliation, I have resorted to another set of labels (symbolist, functionalist, structuralist, and so forth) in order to identify contemporary material culture scholars and their current work. I hope this effort helps to characterize recent scholarly trends without caricaturing them. Every good intellectual historian recognizes that inevitably an enormous range of epistemological diversity exists within any single group of supposedly like-minded thinkers. I fully recognize that my categories tend to homogenize the work of various individuals, placing them, as I do, in certain categories. I am well aware that in a comprehensive historiographical analysis, individuals should be differentiated more carefully one from another within the grouping in which I have placed them and recognized as possibly holding different methodological positions at various stages in their respective scholarly careers.

For instance, I have characterized the work of Michael Owen Jones as exemplifying the behavioralistic approach to modern material culture studies. Although Jones himself uses the term "behavioralist" frequently in his recent work, he is not particularly comfortable with it because of certain associations it evokes, particularly that of the strict behaviorism of B. F. Skinner or of the less deterministic behavioral approaches of anthropologist Edward Hall or sociologists Edward O. Laumann and James Morris. Since Jones is presently interested primarily in human cognition and behavioral interaction as prompted by the manufacture or use of artifacts, and not in the objects *per se*, his behavioralistic (my term, not his) perspective differs substantially from that of fellow folklorists such as John Vlach or Henry Glassie.

Mention of Glassie's prolific work prompts me to suggest that he could be included in several of my categories (environmentalist, functionalist, and behavioralistic) in addition to the one I have assigned him—structuralist. Similarly, the informed reader will quickly recognize many other scholars included in my cast of characters who could and do play several parts in the *dramatis personae* of contemporary American material culture research.[162] In fact, almost all of the truly innovative thinkers in each of my heuristic categories has frequently borrowed methods and concepts from any number of the other perspectives.

Hence I hope that the reader will remember several caveats that I have tried to keep in mind as I sought to choreograph what Gene Wise, in another context, has called "the paradigm dramas" of modern work in material culture studies. First, one should remember that even if various scholars share a common name and general perspective, they do not necessarily agree on how they should proceed in the name of that perspective. Second, it should also be noted that while there may be a generally consistent position within a category of seemingly like-minded thinkers, individual scholars within that grouping will frequently exhibit inconsistencies, or, to put it more positively, are willing to experiment in their work as they try one assumptive framework or methodological perspective and then another, perhaps combining various elements of several approaches.[163]

In discussing nine approaches to American material culture studies, I have ordered them as a reflection of what I see the current intellectual state of the field. Never monolithic, it was initially dominated by historians of the arts. Now contributions are increasingly being made by scholars from many disciplines, especially from social history, the social sciences, folklife studies, and historical archaeology. I am also persuaded that the significant contours of modern American material culture scholarship can be separated, for purpose of analysis, into three major historiographical configurations, depending upon what dimension of artifact study the researcher decides to give primary emphasis in his research methodology, in his interpretation of his data, and in his mode of communicating that data's significance to others.

In brief, these three general approaches consider: first, the artifact as an identifiable object of art created by an artiste; second, the artifact as primarily the result of a mental and manual process often called craftsmanship; and third, the artifact as a significant manifestation of the economic and social status of an individual in society. (See category *Interests in Artifacts and Artifact Makers,* Table 1.1.) For example, applying this typology to current research on the craftsmen in early America would suggest that in the craftsman-as-artiste tradition, it is the *works* of the craftsman that the historian primarily chronicles, in the craftsman-and-his-artisanry tradition it is principally the *working* of the craftsman that is studied, and in the craftsman-as-historical-actor tradition it is the craftsman *as a worker* that primarily concerns the researcher.[164] In the scholarship on the historical import of the craftsman in early America, this focus on either the work, the working, or the worker can be traced through three fairly distinct historiographical traditions that, over the past half century, have either concentrated on the craftsman and his product, his process, or his person. These three artifact orientations—towards the object as an individual creation, as a technical achievement, or as the work of a social class—have colored, to varying degrees, each of the conceptual positions in current American material culture studies.

The Art History Paradigm

Within the field of traditional art history and its handmaidens, architectural history and the history of decorative arts, the emphasis on the singular object still dominates the discipline's current philosophy and practice. Called "object fetishism" by its critics, "object primacy" by its advocates, this approach to material culture study remains content to "let the object speak for itself." [165] From this perspective, the main purpose of studying an artifact is its intrinsic merit as an object or more specifically as an art object, a position argued, for instance, by John Kirk in his detailed studies of early American furniture. [166] Ken Ames points out that this basic research objective of understanding and appreciating each individual object more fully usually leads traditional art historians to three other tendencies that color their approach to artifact study: creator worship (concern for who made it or an exhaustive study of an object's maker as intrinsically worthy of research), primacy fascination (concern for who made it first or a valuation being automatically assigned to an artifact's novelty or innovative elements), and normative evaluation (what it is worth as art as opposed to its possible social cultural, or political significance). [167] In architectural history, these traits similarly manifest themselves in a methodology that concentrates on an area's few classic homes and public buildings and on the decorative elements of their facades, neglecting the quantitatively dominant vernacular buildings and the economic, cultural, and social functions of the internal spaces of such buildings.

By creator worship, Ames means that practitioners of a strict art historical approach often contend that the most trivial details of a painter's or an artisan's life are *ipso facto* worth recovering, even though no attempt is made to justify or to explain how such details have any interpretive or conceptual value. Ames's complaint about the overly normative focus of much American art and decorative art scholarship stems from the tendency he finds in such work to judge artifacts deemed to be art (e.g., painting, sculpture, architecture, and photography) largely in terms of twentieth-century art trends and aesthetic canons. A faculty member in the Winterthur Museum-University of Delaware graduate program, Ames has presented his critique of the traditional art history approach most comprehensively in a publication devoted to American folk art that served as a Winterthur exhibition catalog, *Beyond Tradition: Art in the Folk Tradition*. Interestingly enough, the Winterthur Museum, long a bastion of high art and decorative arts scholarship, has also recently been the institutional setting for a spirited discussion on the viability of art objects as historical evidence. Folklorists John Vlach and Simon Bronner, writing in the *Winterthur Portfolio*, have allied themselves, although for different reasons, with the general thrust of Ames's argument, while Jules Prown has marshalled an impressive defense of the art historical approach. [168]

Well established in graduate programs like those at the University of Delaware (first to award a doctorate specifically in American art history in 1968), nurtured by profusely illustrated commercial magazines retailing art and antiques (such as *Art and Antiques*), and bolstered by block-buster art exhibitions (such as Jean Lipman's and Alice Winchester's 1973 show "The Flowering of American Folk Art" at the Whitney Museum), the art history methodology continues to exert considerable influence as an interpretive focus in American artifact study. (See table 1.2, part I.) The continuity of the art historical approach is evidenced by the fact that visitors to the Lipman-Winchester extravaganza at the Whitney Museum understandably compared it, in research design, evidential base, and explanatory technique, to Holger Cahill's similar show in 1932 at the Museum of Modern Art.[169]

To draw the conclusion, however, that no new methodological challenges or innovations in American art history have occurred during the last forty years would be false. Perhaps some of the most exciting work that has emerged recently among those current scholars still strongly wedded to the artistic approach is being done by a cadre of "new" decorative arts historians. Ken Ames, Robert Trent, Susan Myers, Robert St. George, and others have been pushing and pulling at the traditional art history paradigm from different directions for the past decade.

Recognizing that much art history scholarship follows a "top-down diffusionist theory," in which the antecedents and prototypes of artifacts are usually traced to the highest socioeconomic levels of society, often to urban centers, and frequently to Europe which, for American art, is often seen as the fountain of creative ideas and good design, these scholars have sought to overcome the excessive "object fetishism" so seemingly endemic to their traditional approach to material culture. For example, Robert Trent, in his analysis of Connecticut chairs may have fashioned a new approach that permits qualitative art historical judgments without denying the relevance of anthropological theory in regard to the quantitative patterning of artifacts. In his quest for a feasible synthesis of Henri Focillon, George Kubler, and Henry Glassie, Trent postulates the following:

(1) that an object's significance derives more from its position on a continuum of preceding and subsequent work than from its own uniqueness;

(2) that folk art craftsmen work according to their own systems of compositional logic which may or may not have a direct relationship to "high-style" influences;

(3) that the "masterpiece" theory of decorative arts scholarship has prevented serious aesthetic consideration of folk artifacts because that theory assumes a model of "correctness" based on neo-Palladian ideals and a "fine arts aesthetic;" and,

(4) that to be fully understood aesthetically each object must be compared to all the art forms of its culture and yet be simultaneously recognized as an independent composition on that continuum, one which responds to the stylistic and market impulses and the compositional logic which the craftsman has brought to it. This continuum approach helps to avoid placing value judgments on the concepts expressed by the words "high," "fine,"

TABLE 1.2 (PART I)

The Current Research Trends in American Material Culture Scholarship

	Art History	Symbolist	Cultural History
Main disciplinary perspectives	Architectural history; decorative arts history	American Studies, American literature	Historical archaeology; cultural anthropology; experimental archeology; folklore
Usual artifact interest	Masterpieces of art and decorative arts	Public monuments, civic totems, icons, popular culture	Preindustiral, agrarian material culture of communities
Definition of history	Biography of individuals and their works	History of ideas, myths, symbols, and the imagination	Past is real; it can be recreated, rebuilt, reassessed, in the present
Interpretive objectives	Depict the historical development and intrinsic merit of art objects	Portray the abstract as well as the concrete meanings of past artifacts	Muster all empirical resources in the recovery of certain historic pasts
Frequent research methods	Analysis of the established canon of Western art	Discover dual life of objects as both facts and symbols	Fieldwork; historical archaeology; folklife interviewing
Publication and Presentation formats	Museum exhibit catalog; single artifact exhibit; biography; period room	Monograph; historic battlefield site; temporary exhibits	Field work report; historic house restoration; outdoor historic museum village/community recreation
Typical scholarship	J. Kirk, *American Chairs: Queen Anne and Chippendale* (1972) C. Montgomery, *American Furniture: The Federal Period* (1966) J. Lippman and A. Winchester, *The Flowering of America Folk Art* (1973) J. Prown, "Style As Evidence," *Winterthur Portfolio* (1980)	A. Tractenberg, *The Brooklyn Bridge: Fact and Symbol* (1965) A. Ludwig, *Graven Images: New England Stonecarving and Its Symbols, 1650–1815* (1966) R. Rudsill, *Mirror Images: Influence of the Daguerreotype* (1971) R. Venturi, *Learning From Las Vegas* (1972)	J. Cotter, *Archaeological Excavations at Jamestown* (1957) I. Noël-Hume, *Here Lies Virginia: An Archaeologist's View of Colonial Life and History* (1973) J. Deetz, *In Small Things Forgotten* (1977) R. Schuyler, *Historical Archaeology* (1978)

and "folk," recognizing that folk and elite art are parallel systems of aesthetic experience or alternative systems of compositional logic.[170]

Trent sought to explore the relationship of a particular form to other forms fulfilling similar functions. Following Focillon's principle that "objects must be set in a series, not in discontinuity," Trent painstakingly analyzed the components of the form of folk chairs from one region. By carefully measuring each object and computing the mathematical ratios of one part to another, he was able to establish that more than a visual and bilateral-symmetrical quality existed in the form. The equations suggested production principles which guided the chairmaker and ultimately dictated the visual end-product.

As Trent has re-evaulated formal analysis in contemporary art history research, Jules David Prown has sought to reinvigorate a more sophisticated use of stylistic analysis. Prown maintains that style is inescapably culturally expressive, that the formal data embodied in artifacts is therefore of value as cultural evidence, and that the analysis of style can be useful for other than purely art historical studies.

In several provocative essays, Prown has argued that two testable hypotheses follow from his general premise that a society, in a particular time and place, deposits a cultural fingerprint, as it were, on the artifacts it produces. First, he suggests that we can "expect to find shared stylistic elements in the objects—furniture, silver, architecture—produced in the same place and at the same time." Second, we can also "expect to find a change in style concurrent with a shift in cultural values." [171]

To demonstrate this use of style as an investigative tool, Prown proceeds to examine the stylistic commonalities on either side of the striking instance of marked stylistic change in the arts of America that occurred between the third and the fourth quarters of the eighteenth century over what he considers "the watershed years of the Revolutionary War when America made the transition from colony to nation." Using largely elite material culture evidence (John S. Copley's paintings, Samuel McIntire's side chairs, Abraham Dubois's silver tea service, Christopher Gore's neoclassical mansion in Waltham, Massachusetts), he first extracts the stylistic significance of this varied artifactual data and then proceeds to extrapolate its cultural meaning.

Analysis of the stylistic features of objects, concludes Prown, qualitatively alters our understanding of the time and place, the culture, that produced them. "Although analysis of style does not usually provide new factual information about the engendering culture, it does provide a different, more subjective, more visceral mode of understanding, an affective mode triggered by sensory perceptions." [172]

The Symbolist Perspective

The aesthetic as well as the social, political, and cultural experience produced by an artifact, particularly if it is a singular mode of material culture, such as a Statue of Liberty or a Brooklyn Bridge, concerns another small contingent of

American material culturists. Although by no means as tied to the specific object for
their evidence as traditional art historians, these symbolists share with the artistic
approach an intense humanistic perspective on artifact research, a belief in the
qualitative rather than the quantitive measurement of evidence, and a conviction
that specific forms of material culture reflect an age's climate of opinion. (See table
1.2, part I.) For this reason the symbolist perspective is discussed here rather than
later with several other approaches with which it could be argued to have equal
affinities.

Symbolist material culture studies share a curious genealogy. Having deep
roots in American literary and intellectual history as well as in American ethnographic scholarship, particularly on foodways,[173] the approach has achieved its
greatest visibility and exerted its widest influence through the "myth-and-symbol
school" of American Studies research. Monographs such as Leo Marx's *The
Machine in the Garden: Technology and the Pastoral Ideal in America* (1965), John
Kasson's *Civilizing the Machine: Technology and Republican Values in America,
1776–1900* (1976), and Alan Tractenberg's *Brooklyn Bridge: Fact and Symbol*
(1965) sought to establish artifacts as powerful "cultural symbols" capable of
yielding special insight into the worldview of a people at a particular time in a way
unmatched by most other historical sources of the period. By distinguishing between the "fact" and the "symbol" components of a material culture form, such as
Tractenberg attempted with the Brooklyn Bridge, the symbolist designates "two
separate modes of existence: one [having] a specific location in time and space; the
other, its place in the mind, or in the collective imagination of Americans." [174]
Thus, in his interpretation of John Roebling's and Washington Roebling's magnificent structure, Tractenberg first ascertained the facts of the bridge's political,
economic, and construction history to 1883 when the span was opened; then he
proceeded to analyze its various symbolic meanings as well as its symbolic impact
on later "high-culture" artifacts, such as the paintings of Joseph Stella and John
Marin, and literary creations such as Hart Crane's epic poem, *The Bridge*. As one of
the main connections with American literature that contemporary material culture
studies possesses (many of its practitioners are professors of English in American
Studies departments), the symbolist approach has also been tried on other American
monuments, historic markers, gravestones, popular cultural artifacts like
MacDonald's fastfood restaurants, as well as on machines, and even on entire
cities.[175]

Scholars have even begun to apply the perspective to the topic of electoral
politics, those quadrennial rites that produce a mindboggling quantity of
documentary evidence. Yet, as these historians are discovering, every presidential
race since 1820 has also generated, used, and then discarded countless campaign
artifacts—from the "Old Hickory Forever" thread boxes and "Hero of New
Orleans" tokens of Andrew Jackson through the buttons, bumperstickers, and
plastic peanuts of Jimmy Carter—that deserve material culture study. Properly

understood, such artifacts add a dimension to our understanding of the electoral process that cannot be gleaned from the written record alone.

In what he calls "a study in inferential reconstruction," Roger Fischer has examined the thousands of different objects manufactured and used in 1896 (the year the celluloid campaign button made its debut into presidential politics) for the national campaigns of William McKinley and William Jennings Bryan in order to understand their possible symbolic importance in American politics. Fischer evaluated the nearly one hundred different types of badges, stickpins, and mechanical gadgets that were used; he looked at banners, pillows, plaques, tapestries, belt buckles, bandannas, shirts, watch fobs, canes, paperweights, ashtrays, cigar holders, match safes, mugs, plates, trays, bracelet charms, spoons, rings, razors, mirrors, and innumerable other items bearing the likenesses of the Republican and Democratic standardbearers.[176]

Edith Mayo, in a parallel series of investigations, has explored similar material culture data in an attempt to document women's involvement in American political life. Her study of the symbolism behind campaign artifacts shows how widespread women's participation in political activities was, long before their organized drive to obtain the vote. Democrats, Whigs, and Republicans all produced and distributed campaign items that had special appeal to women. The historian's use of this data has been helpful in both women's studies and in the psychological history of American political behavior.[177]

The symbolist technique received additional endorsement in E. McClung Fleming's 1975 manifesto calling for the systematic study of a single artifact. Fleming insisted that material culture could, along with its obvious "concrete" functions, also perform important "abstract" functions; that is to say, material culture data could be examined for unconscious beliefs, ideas, taboos, fantasies, projections, values, and hidden meanings. Such abstract or symbolic meanings might emerge at the time of the artifact's construction or at various other junctures in the object's existence. It is also possible that the original creators or users of such symbolic artifacts might not always fully articulate the more abstract cultural meanings latent in such objects. Therefore, maintains Fleming, the material culture student's responsibility is to ferret out the latent symbolic content manifest in the manufacture, usage, and survival of material forms and, where possible, to infer broad cultural patterns from such symbols.[178] In a spirit somewhat akin to the art history approach, symbolist researchers tend to award objects a life of their own, distinct from their creator's original intentions for them, and sometimes more revealing to later generations seeking to interpret them as uniquely representative of a certain historical end.

Simon Bronner points out that a number of symbolist studies, including one by Fleming, have been analyses of the material symbols of American patriotism.[179] Bronner has also identified some of the difficulties of this method of material culture interpretation: "In historical analysis one assumes that symbolic artifacts can be identified by connecting them to themes of American history. Themes presumably affect American cultural behavior although causation is difficult to prove. Because the identification of themes from symbolic evidence is the analyst's subjective prerogative, a problem of fallaciously fitting the data to supply the theme exists." Furthermore, argues Bronner, "arbitrary identification of symbols without supportive evidence for their validity seems especially counterproductive to research particularly if *a priori* assumptions are applied to the data." [180] In many cases, symbolic researchers are guilty of a complaint frequently made about literary critics, namely that they read too much into a text.

The Cultural History Orientation

A number of scholars in cultural anthropology, folklife studies, and historical archaeology would concur in Bronner's critique of the symbolists. These other investigators, while concerned with depicting the character of past cultures, argue that research must be based upon much broader data than certain symbolic artifacts.

Strictly for the purposes of discussion, this diverse cadre of material culturists can be called cultural historians, even though some of them might disclaim the label as a bit misleading (see Table 1.2, part I). Until recently, the majority of this group sought, via an assortment of methods, to recapture and understand vanished historical periods for which scant evidence, literary as well as material, existed; they saw their research task as the reconstruction of the origins and development of local and regional cultures in time and place.

In folklife studies, such scholars have been labelled as historical reconstructionists; in anthropology and archaeology, they have often been called cultural historians. [181] I have found it useful to make a further distinction, dividing cultural historians into two categories: *static* reconstructionists and *process* reconstructionists. Static reconstructionsits include those anthropologists, archaeologists, and historic preservationists primarily concerned with viewing material culture data as the function and result of unique events. Such researchers see their task as the collection of past cultural activity and bygone life ways. Implicit in this cultural history approach is a definition of culture (and hence of material culture) as a normative phenomenon—that is, a consensus of shared ideas, values, and beliefs. By contrast, process reconstructionists are especially anxious to decipher the complex dimensions of cultural change and to sort out the intricate dynamics of cultural transformations in the past. Such theorists usually regard material culture data as expressions of recurring cultural processes; they view their research as an emerging "science," a mode of inquiry seeking to establish general laws of behavior based upon the evidence of documented events and extant objects. Culture, and hence material culture, is defined as "man's extrasomatic adaption to his total sociological and ecological environment." [182]

Unlike the process reconstructionists, the static reconstructionists tend to study the past primarily for its own sake. Scholars such as Jared Van Wagener and Iorweth Peate, for example, took seriously the historian's fundamental imperative to document, to interpret, and to communicate a total sense of the past. If the past is real, it can be resurrected, often physically rebuilt, through patient empirical research. As the art history approach to material culture study tends to contemplate the artifact as an aesthetic end in and of itself, this brand of cultural history, when pushed to its extreme, tends to view the whole past as an end in itself. Historical reconstructionists muster every resource available in their recovery and restoration process. Often artifactual evidence must serve as the principal evidential base, because that is the only resource available when little or no other type of documentation survives.

American historical reconstructionists have found certain pasts more in need of rebuilding than others. The majority of their work has focused on America's preindustrial craft villages or its rural agricultural communities. Industrialization or urbanization have not been major research interests of these material culturists; the artifacts of ethnicity, communitarian organizations, and the everyday life of agrarian people within a regional framework have, however, attracted their attention.[183]

Before a historical reconstruction of such societies can be done, either in the format of a scholarly book or, more likely, as a museum site such as Connor Prairie Pioneer Settlement, Indiana, or Old Sturbridge Village, Massachusetts, much data must be collected and classified. Extensive fieldwork, therefore, is demanded as the appropriate research strategy for the material culturists working in the outdoor living history museums movement and in historical site archaeology.[184] Folklife scholarship has greatly influenced the former. Examples of historical reconstruction study with a folklife orientation include Henry Glassie's "The Wedderspoon Farm" (1966) and John T. Schlebecker's "Stockmen and Drovers during the Revolution" (1973) and his compendium *Living History Farms* (1968). Instances of historical reconstructionism within the context of historical site archaeology are Ivor Noël Hume's *Here Lies Virginia* (1963); and John Cotter's *New Discoveries at Jamestown* (1957) and *Archaeological Excavations at Jamestown* (1959).[185]

Inasmuch as the outdoor living history museums movement will be discussed in a later context, historical sites archaeology can serve here to represent another facet of culture history—the "process" school of American archaeology. While there have been isolated excavations of Euroamerican archaeological sites undertaken at various times in the course of our national history, for example, by Thomas Wright (a French settlement on St. Croix Island in Maine in 1797) and by James Hall (Miles Standish's house in Duxbury, Massachusetts, in 1853), it was not until the 1930s that the National Park Service under the stimulus of the Great Depression initiated a continuous tradition of comprehensive investigations of North American historic sites. Although efforts were somewhat disrupted by World War II, the field has expanded to the degree that the number of new sites doubles every decade. The Society for Historical Archaeology, founded in 1967 and joining the earlier and more localized Conference on Historic Sites Archaeology, lists in its *Newsletter* over two hundred excavations underway in 1980, and these are only those reported to the editors.

Historical archaeology in the service of historical reconstruction initially prided itself in establishing the total authenticity of a reconstructed site—authenticity as to chronology, physical features (especially architectural), and site layout. While many historical archaeologists are still content to confine their research to reconstructing chronologies (proving, for instance that a certain ceramic style preceded another), a new breed of historical archaeologist is emerging who demands from material culture information about sexual divisions of labor, sociocultural activity areas within a site, demographic and paleonutritional problems, technological semantics, and even the intricacies of kinship.

American archaeologist Mark Leone and others see this conceptual and methodological shift largely centered around the issue of cultural change rather than cultural homogeniety. Process reconstructionists, Leone suggests, hope "to contribute general knowledge about how culture, not specific cultures, changes." [186] In this endeavor, process theorists by no means reject history, for they admit it is only in the unfolding of long sequences that some cultural processes become visible. They are, however, anxious to discredit the assumption that the total reconstruction of past lifeways can be accomplished.

Instead they advocate, through the use of the contemporary conceptual models of evolutionism, cultural ecology, and systems theory, the comprehensive study of how culture changes. In this brand of cultural history, material culture plays a significant role. Addressing fellow archaeologists in 1972, Leone argued: "Were archaeology to become the science of material culture or material objects, past and present, the entire field would be revolutionized. At the moment, material culture as a category of phenomena is unaccounted for. It is scattered between interior decorators, advertising firms, and historians of technology. But when one considers how little we know about how material culture articulates with other cultural subsystems, one begins to see the potential. There exists a completely empty niche, and it is neither small nor irrelevant." [187]

The recent work of James Deetz can serve as an exemplary response to Leone's call for using material culture as cultural historical evidence. Deetz, an anthropologist and archaeologist long associated with the historical reconstruction of Plimoth Plantation and with work on artifacts excavated and collected there and in various areas of New England, has proposed a tripartite evolutionary model for interpreting all of New England society in the colonial period. Deetz initially argued his theory and method in a research working paper, ("A Cognitive Historical Model for American Material Culture") published in a significantly titled anthology (*Reconstructing Complex Societies*), which he subsequently elaborated in a small volume called *In Small Things Forgotten: The Archaeology of North American History* (1980). [188] Extant documentary and material culture evidence suggested to Deetz that New England evolved through three phases: a Stuart yeoman phase (1620–

1660), a localized Anglo-American era (1660–1760), and a Georgian period (1760–1830). Although Deetz used all the evidence available, including census records, cartography, probate inventories, and other assorted documentary data, he made a special attempt to employ "aspects of the material culture record which represented universals in the lives of people of early Anglo-America: ceramics, since everyone ate; housing, since everyone lived in some kind of a building; gravestones, since everyone died, although not all were commemorated by a memorial." [189] To a lesser extent, musical forms, trash disposal, and foodways were also used in the Deetz analysis. Of particular interest is that Deetz's paradigm challenged the traditional political and diplomatic history interpretation of the American independence movement as the major cultural watershed—the major cultural change, if you will—of American colonial history. The documentary and material data that Deetz assembled and integrated suggested that the revolution actually had little impact on American cultural history; in fact, the general American cultural pattern before and after the war was of a greater involvement with English material culture than had previously been believed. Throughout his study, Deetz emphasized that what he wanted was to understand "the process by which English people became Americans, and what profound changes were worked on their world view in the process of the transformation." [190]

Deetz's pioneering work is paralleled by that of historical archaeologists such as Cary Carson, Robert Schuyler, Stanley South, Bernard Fontana, and Edwin Dethlefsen, who have all gone well beyond James C. Harrington's 1957 position that archaeological use of material culture could only contribute chronological control data to our understanding of the past.[191] The aim of these cultural historians of cultural process, as stated by Dethlefsen in a provocative essay, "Material Culture and Human Beings" (1980), is to understand how "human beings, like all beings, survive through a system of organized and integrated structure and behavior that is not only constantly adjusting to constantly changing circumstances but whose parts must be constantly adjusting to changes in the nature of their integration." If successful, claims Dethlefsen, this approach to material culture studies should help "develop our capacity to see better into the *future*, by pursuing the systemic trends we shall have observed in the past. We shall learn to extend them forward in the form of predictive models, and thereby *anticipate* some of the pleasures and pains of ongoing human adjustment." [192]

While still challenged by the task of producing as accurate and comprehensive historical reconstructions as is humanly possible, the process reconstructionists are well aware of the methodological pitfalls of their technique. They recognize, for instance, that the attempt to re-create in either a monograph or a museum the historicity of traditional life is always subject to the charge of presenting the past as a static rather than a dynamic phenomenon—as an isolated event rather than a contextual narrative. While they are far less willing to accept a consensus model of reconstructed culture, their interpretations are still prone to stress uniformity and homogeneity.[193] Finally, because of the romantic notions of early historical reconstructionists, such as Jared Van Wagener and Henry Chanlee Forman, who tended to view the past as primarily a harmonious, agrarian existence that was supposedly destroyed by technology and urbanization, the approach has never been applied, in any systematic way, to the material culture of the rural-urban continuum on the American city.[194]

The Environmentalist Preoccupation

With the exception of recent work done by cultural geographers such as James E. Vance and David Ward,[195] a similar antiurban charge could be leveled at another group of material culture researchers whose preoccupation with the artifacts of the American landscape prompts one to label them as environmentalists. (See table 1.2, part II.) Not all of them are environmental preservationists or determinists, but they do believe "any sign of human action in the landscape implies a culture, recalls a history, and demands an ecological interpretation; the history of any people evokes its setting in a landscape, its ecological problems and its cultural commitments; and the recognition of a culture calls for the discovery of traces it has left on the earth." [196]

Such a definition, while written by a cultural geographer for cultural geographers, would also find considerable support among many contemporary historical geographers, like Peirce Lewis and John Stilgoe, regional ethnologists, such as Henry Glassie and Howard Marshall, and landscape analysts, including J. B. Jackson and Grady Clay, who seek to follow "cultural traces" primarily in the material culture evidence left on the American land.[197] Objects, argue many material culture environmentalists, are crucial to understanding the interplay between an environment and its inhabitants. Consequently, researchers are particularly interested in questions as: What is the origin of humanity's material culture? By what means are the ideas that generate such material culture disseminated? Or to use their terminology, how are such mental templates diffused across time and space in a geographical area such as a region?

Scholarship relating artifacts and environments extends back at least three generations. Many contemporary environmentalists, preoccupied with the migration and diffusion of objects such as fences, barns, field patterns, and houses, are indebted to the early work of Carl O. Sauer who, in turn, had been highly influenced by the cultural anthropologist A. L. Kroeber, a fellow faculty member at the University of California in the 1930s.[198] The interpretations of *The Great Plains* (1936), by metahistorian Walter Prescott Webb, or of *The Grasslands of North America* (1947), by historical geographer James Malin, are other examples of the environmentalist approach. Perhaps the greatest influence on the current generation of cultural and historical geographers has been the teaching and publishing career of Fred B. Kniffen at Louisiana State University. Many contemporary advocates of the environmentalist approach—geographers, folklorists, and anthropologists—were trained by Kniffen and now promulgate his interests and his methods.[199]

TABLE 1.2 (PART II)
Current Research Trends in American Material Culture Scholarship

	Environmentalist	Functionalist	Structuralist
Main disciplinary perspectives	Cultural and historical geography; regional ecology; cultural anthropology;	History of technology; cultural anthropology; folklife studies; experimental archaeology	Folklife studies; ethnography/linguistics; cultural anthropology
Usual artifact interest	All landscape features, especially housing	All components of a technological system	Vernacular folk housing; popular culture data
Definition of history	Cultural change revealed in cultural landscape	Rational development, adaptation, transmission and function of artifacts as "tools"	Past behavior discovered in previous communication systems
Interpretive objectives	To depict cultural adaptations across space	To explain the evolution of human technologies over time	To ascertain basic universal patterns that structure human consciousness
Frequent research	Fieldwork to test the concept of diffusion of artifacts in a region	Fieldwork and experimentation to test "usefulness" and "practicality" of objects	Comparative fieldwork to find the "artifactual grammar" of physical data
Publication formats	Folklife/anthropology museums; monographs; cultural atlases	Craft demonstrations; technology museum exhibits; experimental archaeology	Monographs; single-genre artifact exhibits
Typical scholarship	F. Kniffen, "Folk Housing: A Key to Diffusion" (1963) J. B. Jackson, "The Westward-Moving House," (1957) P. Lewis, "Common Houses Cultural Spoor" (1975) *North American Cultural Survey Atlas* (1982)	W. Roberts, "Folk Architecture in Context," *Pioneer American Society Proceedings* (1973) J. Anderson, "Immaterial Material Culture," *Keystone Folklore* (1977) R. Howard, "Interchangeable Parts, Re-Examined," *Technology & Culture* (1978) E. N. Anderson, "Folk Art of Landscaping," *Western Folklore* (1972)	H. Glassie, *Folk Housing in Middle Virginia: A Structure Analysis of Historic Artifacts* (1975) H. White, "Structuralism and Popular Culture," *Journal of Popular Culture* (1974) E. Wilson, "Form Changes in Folk Houses," *Geoscience and Man* (1974) B. Herman, "The Whole Cloth of Ethnography," *American Material Culture and Folklore* (1982)

To study material culture, Kniffen proposed five methodological procedures: identification, classification, arrangement, interpretation, and presentation. The identification of cultural features in the form of artifacts on a particular landscape and, where possible, limited to a specific historical time framework constitutes the first step toward deriving what he terms a "cultural taxonomy." [200] Classification follows and entails division of the objects into types. Arrangement of the types into complexes enables the analyst to plot the diffusion of a culture through time and space. The interpretation step requires examination of the diffusion process in order to determine origin, dissemination routes, and the distribution of culture. Conclusions are to be presented via some appropriate communication medium.

Among folklife scholars and cultural geographers, the Kniffen model of reconstituted diffusion routes of material culture data has been enormously influential: there is hardly an article or monograph in American landscape studies that does not cite either Kniffen's now classic methodological essay, "Folk Housing: A Key To Diffusion" (1965) or the practical applications of his theory. [201]

The environmentalist approach to material culture research rests on several assumptions. To begin with, it accepts as axiomatic the belief that culture diffuses across space and acquires and looses elements through the effects of the environment. A particular penchant for vernacular or folk material culture, especially housing, exists because, as Henry Glassie claims, folk artifacts supposedly remain stable through time but are variable over space. [202] Belief in such stability often invests artifacts with a superorganic existence, minimizing the individual's role in their creation. Implicit also is the ascription of an "innate cultural conservatism" to groups producing such objects. [203] A more doctrinaire diffusionist in his first major publication, *Pattern in Material Folk Culture of Eastern U.S.* (1969), Glassie has recognized the inherent determinism in this perspective in his more recent work, *Folk Housing in Middle Virginia* (1976). He, like several other contemporary environmentalists, now seeks to avoid interpretations of material culture evidence made strictly in terms of ecological forces to which individuals must conform or explanations in which the individual's singular creativity and personal cognition play no significant role.

Environmental material culturists work with at least three other presuppositions related to the concept of diffusion: rural, preindustrial landscapes presumably best preserve artifactual survivals of culture; such a landscape provides the material culturist with superior data for ascertaining a succession of regional cultures across time; and a region's diverse material culture is, at its core, integrative. That is to say, all the culture manifested in a region's material culture can be considered to be an integrated whole. Thus, if one artifact, such as a dog-trot house type, spreads (diffuses) across a region, it is assumed other artifacts, (e.g., smokehouses, fence rows) related to the house type, will also diffuse. [204]

In order to monitor and to interpret such movement, contemporary scholars working with material folk culture have resorted to an assortment of techniques.

John Moe, for example, has employed the work of the cognitive anthropologists in an oral history approach to informant fieldwork.[205] Others have turned to quantification, particularly when attempting to deal with the classification and arrangement procedures in the Kniffen model.

The Functionalist Rationale

Another contingent of material culture scholars with topical interests in the history of technology and in folklife studies have been labeled functionalists. Like the environmentalists, they maintain that culture is integrative. However, functionalists also hold that culture is primarily a means of adaptation to environment, with technology being the primary adaptive mechanism. (See table 1.2, part II.) Thus, instead of accepting the diffusion processes as adequate explanations for cultural change, they seek to find rationales in the "usefulness" of objects in their adaptive relations to their environments. The utility of an artifact within the context of a technological system, whether it be a saddle-bag house, a Corliss steam engine, or an interstate highway system, provides the key to understanding transmission and adaptation in this approach to material culture research. With only a secondary concern for the origins of artifacts, the functionalists are primarily interested in the process, change, adaption, and the cultural impact of objects. In this quest, they aspire to a more dynamic interpretation of material culture than the somewhat static approaches of the symbolists and the environmentalists.

Bronislaw Malinowski's and A. R. Radcliffe-Brown's approaches to anthropological research provide part of the theoretical base for the functionalist approach to material culture. Lewis H. Morgan, Melville Herskovits, Emile Durkheim, and especially William Bascom were also among the first anthropological functionalists. Within the history of technology, the work of Siegfried Giedeon, Lynn White, and Carl Condit bear the stamp of a functional interpretation.[206] Other researchers have come to adopt a functionalist perspective out of their own trial-and-error field work and from frequent association with certain artifact genres, such as technology.

One sees shifts in methodological emphases in scholars such as Warren Roberts, previously a strong advocate of the environmentalist perspective in material folklife studies who has begun to argue for a more functionalist technique in several recent publications.[207] Diffusion, he has claimed, fails to provide a total explanation for the shaping of artifacts. Instead, criteria of "practicality" in a "local context" are more important determinations. But when defining context, functionalists like Roberts tend to sound somewhat like diffusionists in that they usually include factors such as available materials, weather conditions, technical competencies, support services, family structures, and economic systems that affect the selection, use, and transmission of material culture.

In truth, the functionalist school in material culture research is equally concerned with the maker of an object as with his or her milieu. Material culture functionalists try to explain both how an object was "worked" (how its maker acted in order to make it), as well as how the object itself "works" (how it actually functions in a socio-cultural context).

Refinement of the term "function" began with the early writings of Ralph Linton and various other anthropologists and some folklorists. The distinction was made between "use" (an object's strict and obvious purpose) and "function" (a more complex meaning that transcends use and often must be inferred by the researcher). Thus when folklorist E. N. Anderson attempted to decipher the functions of twentieth-century landscaping as folk art, he sought to demonstrate how such behavior not only fulfilled the purposes of erosion prevention and climate control, but also was a response to the deep sociocultural and even psychological needs of modern American homeowners.[208] On a more detailed and complex level, Petr Bogatyrev's highly influential 1937 monograph, *The Functions of Folk Costume in Moravian Slovakia* (first translated into English in 1971), categorizes the magical, religious, regional, national, erotic, and everyday functions of traditional attire.[209]

Those who espouse the functionalist approach are anxious to demonstrate that material culture is, at its core, a reflection of the rationality and practicality of the participants in a culture.[210] A participant's description of his own motives often helps the researcher establish a functional explanation. Thus oral history fieldwork is a frequently employed research tool in this approach. But often such information is not available or the informant is only cognizant of an object's purpose and not its function. Then the researcher is left with his own conjectures as to the functional sequence that originally existed in the manufacture and use of an artifact. Such a fascination with the "mind of the maker" often allies the functionalist with the structuralist and the behavioralist.

An interest in the cognitive processes involved in the production of past material culture likewise intrigues a group of scholars who now call themselves "experimental archaeologists." The history of their approach has been summarized by Jay Anderson and Robert Asher, and elaborated by John Coles in his book *Archaeology by Experiment*. Anderson stated, "experimental archaeology was developed as a means of 1) practically testing theories of past cultural behavior, especially technological processes involving the use of tools and 2) obtaining data not readily available for more traditional artifact analysis and historical sources." [211] Since experimental archaeology seeks to "imitate or replicate" the original functions or processes involved in using certain artifacts, the technique has also been called "imitative archaeology."

Perhaps the most spectacular and most publicized application of the approach has been the *Kon Tiki* expedition of Thor Heyerdahl. Heyerdahl sought to test his hypothesis that people, with certain contemporary technologies available to them, could have sailed the 4,000 miles between South America and the Polynesian Islands, transplanting themselves and their culture before 1100 A.D. Other topics of particular interest to experimental archaeology include research on tool manufacture, house-building, and especially foodways. In each case, a key research objective is to discover how artifacts originally functioned in the society that made and used them.[212]

The Structuralist View

Functionalist research bears at least a family resemblance to a habit of mind that claims all cultural systems can be viewed as languages. That is to say, every aspect of culture (e.g., kinship, social organizations, art) has a functional role and also a sign value. An axe is not just a tool designed for a particular use, but also a sign which can be juxtaposed to other signs, constructing complex systems of communication. In itself this notion of the sign value of objects, words, or behavior is not new. However, a group of twentieth-century French thinkers—anthropologist Claude Lévi-Strauss, literary critic Roland Barthes, and historian Michael Foucault, following upon a linguistic conceptual revolution initiated by Ferdinand de Saussure's *Course in General Linguistics* (1916), have elaborated the idea, developing a method of cultural analysis often called structuralism. They hope this method of analysis will yield nothing less than "the basic and universal patterns that structure—however, unconsciously—human consciousness." [213]

Despite this laudable aspiration, there is no agreed upon definition of terms or methods in structuralist theory and no simple canon of precepts that one can memorize in order to apply the theory to material culture research. The approach has, however, attracted historiographers and exegetes, hagiographers, and enemies.[214] Many material culturists seem to be drawn to structuralism because of the perspective's basic premise that all cultural systems should be treated as languages and, as such, can be systematically analyzed as to their structure through methods borrowed from linguistics. In their analyses, structuralists hope ultimately to uncover the covert as well as the overt meanings of cultural systems. Such hope is possible because they believe that the activities, products, and institutions of humankind are largely expressions of the unconscious and that a careful structural decoding of these signs will yield a full understanding of human culture. Finally, in what John Blair calls "mainline structuralism," there are also three recurrent premises: binary oppositions are considered basic to the conceptualization of any subject; primary emphasis is on the synchronic functioning of systems as opposed to their diachronic unfolding through time; and paradigms are more important than syntagms.[215]

What has this type of thinking meant to the current generation of American students of material culture? While it has yet to have any sweeping impact on the movement as a whole, some anticipate it will become one of the major philosphies of interpretation. Moreover, its partial endorsement by Henry Glassie, a current leader in the field, will undoubtedly ensure continued debate about structuralism's theory and, perhaps, its application to artifactual data.

Structuralism's application in American material culture studies has been primarily confined to two subfields: American popular culture and vernacular folk housing. In these two areas, Barthes and Lévi-Strauss strongly influenced the American research. In *Elements of Semiology* (1968), Barthes analyzed cultural systems, such as clothing, automobile design, and furniture, and proposed that the different products of human culture can be conceptualized as the intersection of a vast number of different "languages." [216] Lévi-Strauss, in works such as *The Savage Mind* (1966), has also developed techniques for applying linguistic models to material culture data, such as the masks of the Indians of the American Northwest. [217] Barthes's work, although not always strictly structuralist, has also influenced the popular culture research of Hayden White, R. E. Johnson, and Bruce A. Lohof, whereas Lévi-Strauss's impact has been primarily on scholars such as Tom Carter, Bernard Herman, and Henry Glassie. [218]

American folklorists have mounted the most extensive effort to date in applying structuralism to artifact analysis. While all are intent on analyzing objects primarily through the relationship of their forms in order to find their cultural meaning, this cadre of researchers can be subdivided into biological structuralists and linguistic structuralists. Edna Scofield in her early work on Tennessee houses serves as an illustration of the former; Glassie in his more recent study of middle Virginia housing can be considered as an apt model of the latter. [219]

Biological structuralists, like Scofield, assume that material culture evidence contains a natural order of "families," "species," and "varieties" analogous to plant and animal classification systems developed by the natural sciences. "The original structure of a given species," Scofield writes of Tennessee house types, "is generally simple, and the more complicated structure develops gradually as the organism assumes more complicated functions, or as environmental conditions become more favorable." [220] With this premise, Scofield surveyed all varieties of housing types in Tennessee, seeking out the typical, rather than the unique, shapes (e.g., square, rectangular, circular) of residential buildings. She concluded that all southern houses developed from the square "one-room log cabin." By interpreting the rectangular double-pen house as two connected square units, she assumed that this growth resulted because of a predetermined evolutionary development. She further explained the additions of an open hallway, a second story, and an extra wing as but the natural structural evolution or genetic succession from the primordial square unit. What the material culture, by itself, does not explain, however, is the rationale for changes in each stage of structural development. If objects follow the biological process that simplicity will always evolve into complexity, what role do the makers of such objects play in the process? Who determines the original structural concept, such as the square floor plan in Scofield's houses? The final question, of course, is, can all cultural data be ultimately reduced to such abstract formulations? [221]

Many strict structuralists believe so. Few, however, have followed the biological model of Scofield; most have turned to linguistic models, as has Glassie. From the linguist Noam Chomsky, Glassie borrowed the concept that "culture is pattern in mind, the ability to make things like sentences or houses." [222] Rejecting the concept that objects are the simple products of passive minds, Glassie attempted to develop a systematic model that would account for and help analyze the design abilities of an idealized maker of artifacts. As a case study, he investigated the builders of 156 houses constructed between the middle of the eighteenth century and World War I in a seventy square-mile area of middle Virginia. HIs research objective, using almost exclusively the material culture data left behind by the anonymous builders, was to discover the unwritten boundaries or "artifactual grammar" of the creative process as it was exercised in that particular region's vernacular architecture.

Glassie began his "structural analysis of historic artifacts" with a geometric base structure similar to Scofield's—the square. Instead of arguing that houses evolve, however, he proposed that it was the ability to design houses that did. That design competency he found in seventeen extant structural types and subtypes of middle Virginia houses accurately reflected, in his estimate, numerous conscious and unconscious individual decisions among the builders of the houses. Combining the basic structuralist techniques with intense localized fieldwork (documenting housing plans, decorative motifs, and building hardware), he sought to articulate "rule sets" for forming the base structure's extension, the massing and piercing of the base structure; expansion backward, the massing and piercing of the backward expansion; upward expansion, the massing and piercing of that section; and the roofing. Replete with elaborate tables and charts that seek to plot "the paradigmatic structure of mind in the middle Virginia architect," Glassie used his artifactual grammar to classify an assortment of material culture evidence, such as bricks, hinges, woodwork, and window placement, in order to understand the rationale for the creation of house types.[223]

American material culture structuralism, as personified by Glassie's *Folk Housing in Middle Virginia*, understandably has drawn criticism from various camps. Historians claim that despite its token gestures to tracing a change in minds, the approach, by definition, tends only to work in areas of relative cultural stasis. Fellow folklorists have complained that Glassie's subjective system of binary mental opposites (intellect-emotion, internal-external, complex-simple, and twelve others) borrowed from Gaston Bachelard, Christian Norberg-Schulz, and, of course, Lévi-Strauss, merely substitutes one kind of ideological arbitrariness for another. Others remark that the results of such structural analysis are not adequately comparative to other analyses and hence not verifiable. Still others argue that structuralism is really a tool of description, not analysis, for it does not adequately account for behavioral processes.[224]

The Behavioralistic Concept

In attempting to establish the relationship between cognitive processes and structural manifestations, Glassie's experiment represents another tendency in current American material culture studies: the gradual shift within the last decade from a primary concentration on the historical artifact to an emphasis on the historical artificer. Or, to recall the change in focus suggested at the beginning of this discussion of the fourth generation's theories and methods, it marks a shift in concern in artifactual research from emphasis on the work to emphasis on the worker.

In the 1970s, a small group of material culture researchers emerged who were more intrigued with the producer than his or her products. (See table 1.2, part III.) Although they usually began their analyses with artifacts, American things were but the means to another end: understanding specific individual behavior defined, for example, by Michael Owen Jones as "those activities and expressive structures manifested principally in situations of first-hand interaction." [225] This approach tends, naturally, to focus on the individual creator of objects, proceeding on the assumption that each individual is unique in his or her beliefs, values, skills, and motivations. In the study of what an individual makes, the researcher aspires to understand and explain cognitive and behavioral processes, personal creativity, and aesthetic impulses.

The behavioristic orientation, which Jones usually refers to as "folkloristic," is not to be confused with the behaviorism of certain methodologies in the social sciences influenced by the theories of B. F. Skinner. Nor should Jones's approach be directly grouped with folklife scholars such as Yoder, Anderson, Roberts, since he does not subscribe to the culture construct as an organizing or explanatory principle as they do. Jones states his interests as "studying the continuities and consistencies in behavior, manifested primarily in first-hand interaction, through personal observation or by means of records composed by others in order to understand better and appreciate more fully what people make and do and how they think." [226]

Unlike the environmentalist or the cultural historian, the behavioralist is not likely to be concerned with the geographical-historical determinants of objects and their features. Instead, the behavioral approach to objects and their manufacture emphasizes the diversity of human creative expression and motivation. Although much in debt to the social and behavioral sciences, this perspective also shares a degree of kinship with the art history focus in its concentration on an object's creator and how his individual beliefs, values, and aspirations shape his creations.

Folk art and foodways, understandably, have been the material culture genres most thoroughly studied by behavioralists. While there has been some investigation of the creative imagination involved in early native American pottery and gravestone carving,[227] the majority of the published behavioral research has been on twentieth-century objects and their makers. Most behavioralists want to understand the modern context instead of reconstructing past societies.

Michael Owen Jones, a folklorist, has been both proponent and practitioner of this orientation in contemporary material culture studies. Beginning with his dissertation at Indiana University, "Chairmaking in Appalachia: A Study in Style and Creative Imagination in Folk Art" (1970), and extending through publications such as *The Handmade Object and Its Maker* (1975) and *People Studying People* (1980),

TABLE 1.2 (PART III)
Current Research Trends in American Material Culture Scholarship

	Behavioralistic	National Character	Social History
Main disciplinary perspectives	Folkloristics; folk-life science; psychohistory; cognitive anthropology; environmental and social psychology	Philosophy of history; history of technology; Whig history/Marxist history	Family history; women's history; labor history; black history; urban history
Usual artifact interest	Folk art; foodways; spatial constructs; domestic artifacts; photographs;	Entire material culture corpus but especially technology	Artifactual remains of non-elite groups; probate data; inventories, wills
Definition of history	Biography; contemporary activity	National character; ideology	Evolution of collective biographies within social structures
Interpretive Objective	To investigate the life stages and the social processes of behavior	To understand the ideological configurations of any national culture	To investigate the common activities of common people in social groups, classes, institutions
Frequent research methods	Fieldwork observation; oral history interviewing; historical psychoanalysis; hypothesis testing	Synthesize previous scholarship (documentary, graphic and artifact evidence) into a broad, interpretive overview	Statistical articulation of quantitative data; test explanatory concepts such as modernization
Publication and presentation formats	Folk art demonstrations; informant interviews; social/psychological statistics	Multi-volume history textbooks; block-buster museum exhibits; permanent gallery installations	Monographs; living history farms; historic house museums
Typical scholarship	M. Jones, *The Hand-Made Object* (1975) E. Hall, *The Hidden Dimension* (1966) D. Upton, "Toward A Performance Theory in Vernacular Architecture," *Folklore Forum* (1979) S. Bronner, "Investigating Identity and Expression in Folk Art," *Winterthur Portfolio* (1981)	J. Kouwenhoven, *Made in America* (1948) A. Gowans, *Images of American Living* (1964) D. Boorstin, *The Americans,* (1958–1973) R. Burlingame, *March of the Iron Men* (1938)	J. Demos, *A Little Commonwealth* (1970) P. Benes, *Masks of Orthodoxy* (1977) C. Clifford, "Domestic Architecture," *J. Interdisciplinary History* (1976) K. Ames, "Meaning In Artifacts," *J. Interdisciplinary History* (1978)

Jones has consistently sought to analyze the creation and consumption of objects and all the behavioral expressions (plans, preparations, processes, and so forth) surrounding them.[228] Limiting himself largely to contemporary evidence, (e.g., furniture made in the Cumberland mountains of southeastern Kentucky, "add-ons and re-dos" in southern California), Jones has sought "to discover a way to account for the nature of an object made by hand" in order "to understand more fully human behavior." Furthermore, Jones maintains that "research into human behavior must begin as well as end with human beings and should focus on the individual." [229] Following his own injunction in his major book, *The Handmade Object and Its Maker,* he concentrated his research primarily on one man, a upland southern chairmaker named "Charley." Jones did this for two reasons. First, he insists that "an object cannot be fully understood or appreciated without knowledge of the man who made it, and the traits of one object cannot be explained by reference only to antecedent works of an earlier period from which later qualities allegedly evolved. Second, much of what has been called art, especially what has been labeled folk and primitive art, is useful in some way, which means that the object produced is as much an instument to achieve some practical result as it is an end in itself (including not only drums and chairs but also masks, bis poles, and divination tapers)." As a consequence, Jones maintains that "the researcher cannot divorce what he calls artistic or creative processes from technological ones; the outputs of production serve not only what some people refer to as aesthetic ends but also practical purposes; and the evaluations of products admit considerations of both appearance and fitness for use." It is for this reason that Jones insists that terms such as "artist," "craftsman," "producer," "creator," and "chairmaker" be used interchangeably, that no artificial distinction be made between "art" and "craft," and that "to create" be used as a synonym for "to build" and "to construct." [230]

In Jones's behavioral analysis, each individual maker of objects possesses a novel configuration of skills. His approach tends to stress the diversity of human creativity rather than the uniformity sought by the structuralists in their quest for universal patterns structuring human consciousness.[231] While both perspectives hope to enter the "mind of an object's maker," in order to get at the "mental template" of *homo faber*, the structuralists tend to investigate large aggregates of data (for example, Glassie's 156 Middle Virginia houses) and the Jonesian behavioralists such as Thomas Adler and Simon Bronner concentrate on a few craftsmen and their products.[232]

Mention of housing recalls another type of artifactual data in which other behavioralists have been interested. Edward T. Hall, in works such as *The Hidden Dimension* (1966) and *The Silent Language* (1959), has explored how spatial constructs, such as the arrangement of rooms, the size of rooms, or the arrangement of objects in rooms, influence human behavior. Hall's research into proxemics parallels work by sociologists Edward O. Laumann and James S. Morris in their study of living room styles and social attributes. Still other examples of the behavioral analysis applied to domestic artifacts include Michael Lesy's and Robert Akeret's highly controversial interpretations of family photographs.[233]

In a recent manifesto subtitled "Toward a Behavioral History," Jones singled out Allan Ludwig's *Graven Images* (1966) as one application of the behavioralist perspective to early American material culture evidence.[234] Ludwig's research into the symbolism, rituals, and forms of funerary art in Massachusetts and Connecticut reveals a different story than conventional histories of New England Puritanism based solely on written sources. The strictly verbal evidence depicted the Puritans as an iconophobic, nonmystical people whose piety, while once pronounced, declined dramatically near the end of the seventeenth century. Not so, suggests the cross-section of New England gravestones that Ludwig documented, analyzed, and interpreted. The material culture evidence yields at least three contrary conclusions: 1) that symbols on gravestones demonstrated the flourishing of a very strong religious sentiment in New England until well into the nineteenth century; 2) that America has had an art tradition which emphasized abstraction, simplicity, and purity of line and warrants serious attention for its excellence as well as its relationship to modern aesthetics; and 3) that the Puritans in America created much figural as well as religious art, despite the inference that has usually been drawn from official written sources that they were highly iconophobic culture.

In Jones's estimate, Ludwig's careful examination of the visual imagery of funerary artifacts, creations not officially controlled by church authorities, reveals an iconographic tradition that evolved in the day-to-day interactions of the people. "This iconography in stone," claims Jones, "was understood by, and was meaningful to, many individuals regardless of educational level, social status, or personal achievement. For the forms created by New England stonecarvers were largely universal patterns, continuous through time and thus basic to human expression regardless of national or religious identity, the principal 'Americanism in style' being 'the eccentricities of individual hands' discernable in particular local areas." [235]

Using material culture data from the distant American past, though, remains the exception rather than the rule among advocates of the behavioral model. Most research deals with contemporary persons, processes, and products and fieldwork is a *sine qua non*. With this in mind, Jones, along with Robert A. Georges, published a primer, *People Studying People* (1980). This research guide attempts to show the beginning student how to gather data about human behavior and culture, and alerts the student to the active role he or she plays in the process of gathering this data.

Fieldwork, as espoused by Jones and other behavioralists, seeks to identify the impact of a craftsman's beliefs, values, and aspirations upon the manufacture, use, and sale of his products. As research technique, it has a certain affinity with scholarly trends now variously labeled "the new ethnography," "ethnosemantics," or "cognitive anthropology," [236] A mere listing of book titles provides a shorthand review of this related approach: *Ask The Fellows Who Cut the Hay*, by folklorist G. Ewart Evans; *You Owe Yourself a Drunk: An Ethnography of Urban*

Nomads, by anthropologist James Spradley; and *Anthropology toward History: Culture and Work in a 19th-Century Maine Town*, by American Studies scholar Richard Horwitz.[237] Unlike Jones's focus on the individual, these studies concentrate on a much larger number of subjects. Yet their ultimate research objective is the same: explaining the diversity of human behavior through an understanding of individual cognition systems.

The behavioralistic research orientation has spawned a corollary approach to material culture study frequently called *performance theory* by its advocates, who can also be found in the structuralist and functionalist camps. Intrigued by the many unexplored interconnections between material and the mind, these scholars apply a "performance" or "phenomenological" mode of analysis to artifacts.[238] For example, researchers such as Dell Upton and Thomas Adler argue that the human process involved in conceiving, making, perceiving, using, adapting, decorating, exhalting, loathing, and eliminating objects are intrinsic elements of human experience and such experience, not just the object, is what the material culture student should strive to comprehend. To performance theorists, the human processes of creation, communication, and conduct are the important features of material culture research.[239]

In his attempt to get into the minds of the makers of artifacts, Upton has pursued the validity of performance theory in his investigation of vernacular architecture of early Tidewater Virginia. By studying the "performance" extant in traditional houses, he has attempted to recreate the shapes of patterned behavior within such buildings. In the enterprise, he sought answers to questions such as: From whom does a builder of a house get his ideas? What does he do with such ideas between the time he learns them and the time that he produces a structure? The intention behind creation also determines *ex post facto* reconstruction of performances. Material culture scholars, using this technique, share a degree of affinity with the experimental archaeologists described earlier (as a dimension of the functionalist perspective) and with the process reconstructionists (discussed in the cultural history approach).

Adler also suggests that performance theory should be applied to the contemporary material culture researcher as well as to the topics he researches. Making specific reference to bluegrass banjos and traditional woodworking tools, Adler suggests the necessity of personal experience with the artifacts that the researcher studies in order to understand more fully how earlier people actually experienced such objects. Thus, in addition to the usual referential knowledge (e.g., seeing a banjo in a mail-order catalog or reading a description of it in a nineteenth-century diary) and mediated knowledge (e.g., hearing banjo music played over a radio or by a person at a folk music concert), a material culture student must also, whenever possible, acquire experiential knowledge (e.g., by playing the banjo). In order to understand performers of the past, we must become performers in the present. In summary, Adler argues that "a scholarly interpreter who would speak of bluegrass banjos or traditional woodworking tools or any other traditional instruments is on the strongest possible ground if he can bolster his referential and mediated knowledge with the knowledge gained from actually trying to engage instruments in expressive acts. He needs to do not only fieldwork, but artifactually involved fieldwork. It is certainly not necessary that we all become great performers, but it is essential that we pay attention to the importance of experience as a force operating on tradition. That can best be accomplished by recognizing our inevitable personal involvement with our objects of study." [240]

The research strategy of fieldwork, as advocated by the various proponents of the behavioralistic approach to material culture studies, is a demanding one. Because many elements of an individual's life are considered highly significant in reference to the artifacts he makes or uses, the investigator must decide what factors are most significant. In making such decisions, the researcher may find himself making subjective statements about the relative importance of one set of factors over another set. "Ideally, analytical perceptions of unconscious aspirations or projections would be checked with the informant," writes Simon Bronner, "but the folk artist may not be able to recognize such inferences or he may acquiesce to the researcher's interpretation. Thus, the behavioral approach presents serious fieldwork problems, not only because an extraordinary amount of observation is required but because rationales for behavior often are the most difficult information to elicit." [241]

Bronner himself has suggested one way around the difficulties of the behavioralistic approach via what he calls a "praxic perspective." In something of a departure from the different but behavioristic perspectives of Jones and Vlach,[242] Bronner argues that a praxic perspective, which he acknowledges is indebted to the philosophies of Aristotle, Karl Marx, John Dewey, and George Herbert Mead, attempts to "consider the philosophical underpinnings of a researcher's concern for objects in a cognitive-behavioral frame." In studying any form of material culture, Bronner proposes we evaluate it in terms of "praxis," which may be defined as "customary ways of doing, making, and using things shaped by a dialectic between self and society, individual and environment, reality and artificiality. Praxis thus incorporates emphases on behaviors, processes, and thoughts that generate objects and culture, but adds an important consideration of the dynamic and complex relations between thought and action, conduct and communication, motivation and meaning." [243]

The National Character Focus

If a key concern of many behavioristic researchers is to bring the study of objects down to its least common denominator—the individual's interaction with others resulting in the making and using of objects, then another coterie of scholars takes a quite opposite tack in using artifacts to explain the collective *Weltanschauung* of an entire nation. This approach shares many of the assumptions of both the cultural history and the functionalist perspectives, but its practitioners possess a sufficient number of other unique characteristics for it to merit a separate identity in this taxonomy of contemporary material culture research strategies. I have labelled it the "national character" school, in part because of its relation to a similarly named and oriented trend in American Studies scholarship and, in part, because its adherents have sought nothing less than an explanation of the totality of the national experience.[244] In undertaking this epic enterprise, a number of American scholars have used assorted material culture evidence in their sweeping, interpretive surveys of the American national ethos.

Many material culturists of the national experience variety might also be called metahistorians because of their ambitious efforts to synthesize all historical evidence, including documentary, oral, and material, in order to go on to formulate broad characterizations of the mentality and behavior of a whole society. Syntheses do not come small, and in order to do justice to such colossal undertakings, these historians have frequently found that the articulation of their visions required multivolume publication formats, like Daniel Boorstin's *The Americans* (1958–1973); single volume surveys of amazing historical scope, such as Alan Gowans, *Images of American Living* (1964); block-buster museum exhibits, exemplified by the Yale University Art Gallery's, "American Arts and the American Experience" by C. F. Montgomery, P. E. Kane, and Chermayeff and Geismar Associates (1975); permanent museum gallery installations, such as the Smithsonian Institution's "A Nation of Nations" (1976); or popular culture reviews, like Tom Wolfe's *The Kandy-Kolored Tangerine-Flake Streamline Baby* (1965).

In the most successful of these attempts to write or to mount a national epic, material culture data has been blended with a philosophy of history. Generality, breadth, synthesizing, and interpretive daring distinguish the best work of metahistorians who seek to read from objects not only their visual meaning but also the motivations and cultural forces which produced them and which they, in turn, stimulated. Critics of the national character approach to material culture evidence point out, however, that a major flaw in the less successful studies is their tendency to use objects, such as Currier and Ives prints, the steam engine, or the Kodak camera, as mere illustrations of generalizations gleaned from more traditional written sources rather than as the foundations of new interpretations based upon careful analysis of the actual artifacts themselves. Others complain that scholars seeking to paint the national portrait, with the broad brush strokes of a Crèvecoeur, a Tocqueville, a Whitman, or a Turner, too often fall victim to the beguiling but treacherous temptation of believing they can unlock the secrets of a distinctively American character by viewing that character through a particular ideological prism refracting one object.[245]

Unlike some European material culture scholars, few Americans have turned to the giant modern ideologues, such as Georg Hegel, Karl Marx, Sigmund Freud, or Jean-Paul Sartre, for a single unifying, if often controverted, explanatory perspective.[246] Surprisingly few American Marxist scholars (Gordon V. Childe being a notable exception) have sought to examine American material culture in order to explain the country's national character and historical development. For example, Eugene Genovese, perhaps currently the most well-known American Marxist historian,[247] paid only token attention to black material culture in his analysis of slavery, *Roll, Jordon, Roll: The World the Slaves Made* (1974). Socialists, likewise, have not offered any holistic explanation of United States material history from their political perspective. Random articles appear in journals such as *Catalyst: A Socialist Journal of the Social Services* and the *Radical History Review* published by MARHO: The Radical Historians Organization, but no one, with the possible exception of David Noble in his *America by Design*, has yet produced a comprehensive interpretation of American material culture along clearly delineated economic, class, and political divisions.[248]

Interestingly enough, the scholars who have produced the most wide-ranging interpretations of American civilization through American material culture have professed to be completely nonideological in their approach. In answer to Langdon Winner's query, "Do Artifacts Have Politics?" metahistorians like Walter Prescott Webb, David Potter, Roger Burlingame, and Daniel Boorstin have preferred to answer "No," unless, of course, one means democratic politics.[249] In fact, if there is a dominant trait in the genetic make-up of the American national character, as described by material culturists from Horace Bushnell to Alan Gowans, it is how the pragmatic, vernacular, and progressive forces of democracy have shaped and been shaped by American things.[250] Students following this perspective have proclaimed their interest in the entire American material culture corpus but, in their books and exhibits, they have tended to focus on technology as the artifactual data most revelatory of the nation's ideology. Lewis Mumford's classic statement in *Technology and Culture* (1964) still characterizes contemporary scholarship. He argues that "from late neo-lithic times in the Near East, right down to our own day, two technologies have recurrently existed side by side: one authoritarian, the other democratic, the first system-centered, immensely powerful, but inherently unstable, the other man-centered, relatively weak, but resourceful and durable." [251] In his own prolific writing on American technology, Mumford has steadfastly maintained that machines, architecture, even whole cities can be accurately judged not only for their contributions to efficiency and productivity, not only for their positive and negative side effects, but also for the ways in which they embody specific forces of power, authority, and ideology.

An eagerness to interpret technical artifacts in the language of a nation's character, while often found in nineteenth-century promotional tracts and business histories, traces its modern scholarly roots to Roger Burlingame's two surveys of technology's impact on American life and thought. Applying the thesis of the unifying and democratizing effect of technology to American material culture, Burlingame found the sewing machine, the factory system, railroads, steel mills, the automobile, mass-produced tools, and numerous other artifacts to be liberating, egalitarian forces. His book titles aptly summarize his position: *March of the Iron Men: A Social History of Union through Invention* (1938); and the sequel, *Engines of Democracy: Inventions and Society in Mature America* (1940).

Other scholars have similarly extrapolated the ideological configurations of American history from American artifacts. For example, John Kouwenhoven's glorification of what is uniquely "Made in America"—assembly lines, clipper ships, balloon-frame houses, skyscrapers, bridges, jazz, and films—attributed their significance to the fact that they were made by "the first people in history who, disinherited of a great cultural tradition, found themselves living under democratic traditions in an expanding machine economy." [252] J. C. Furnas' social history trilogy, *The Americans* (1969), *Great Times* (1974), and *Stormy Weather* (1977), parallels many of Kouwenhoven's themes, as does Gilman M. Ostrander's *American Civilization in the First Machine Age, 1890–1940* (1972), Christopher Tunnard's and Henry Hope Reed's *American Skyline* (1956), and Elting E. Morison's *From Know-How to Nowhere* (1974). [253]

The quest for a novel American identity, born either out of national pride, a sense of cultural or artistic inferiority, or the concern over lost unities and purposes that characterized some American scholarship since the Korean War, has often led these metahistorians far beyond the artifacts with which they began their studies. However, their synoptic approach to material culture study has received much support from American Studies programs and as such the approach is usually included in that discipline's historiography. [254]

Alan Gowans and Daniel Boorstin, two American Studies scholars intrigued by the search for the definitive traits of the American character, have also been major contributors to this phase of the material culture studies movement. Unlike many of the national character theorists mentioned thus far, Gowans concentrated his research on architecture and the decorative arts, especially furniture, rather than technology. In a model study of its genre, his *Images of American Living* sought to explore the national ethos by investigating architecture and furniture as "cultural expressions." Assuring the material culture student that only in "knowing the patterns, [do] we know history," he went on to fit American artifacts into four major patterns (medieval, classical, Victorian, and twentieth-century America), each roughly coinciding with a century of development. Throughout this odyssey, however, the material culture evidence yielded proof of various cultural patterns familiar to other historians of the national experience. For example, suggested Gowans:

the pattern of progressive conquest over nature can be seen, from the time men first faced this wilderness with primitive iron tools to the age of jet travel and electronic computers. There is the pattern of social change, from homestead and self-contained plantation to megalopolis. There is the pattern of changing concepts of the nature of art and architecture, from the idea that the artists's proper concern is with beauty (however that may be defined) to the dogma that he ought to express the reality of himself and his work (whatever that may be). Finally, the history of architecture and furniture reflects a pattern of evolving democracy, political and economic—both the ideal of raising the whole cultural level of a population en masse, to create a society like none seen in the world before, a nation without peasants or hereditary aristocrats, whose every citizen would be a responsible and contributing member; and something of the cost in folly, perversity, and vulgarity that the pursuit of life, liberty, and happiness by the common man has often entailed.[255]

Beginning with the basic point of view of an art historian who also became quite interested in cultural anthropology, Gowans attempted to read from objects not only their artistic meanings but also the cultural forces that produced them. His scale was enormous—the architecture and furniture of the entire continental United States, and his scope was extensive, covering 1550 to 1950. One critic remarked, however, "he tends to use objects studied primarily by art historians as the basis for his generalizations: fine chairs, architect-designed houses, et cetera. He transfers artistic judgements into cultural judgements too easily and thus we see a 'decadent' work of art quickly become a causal factor in a decadent society. Such generalizations raise the question of whether Gowans' judgements are formed from the objects themselves or whether the objects are merely illustrative of generalizations gleaned from more traditional written sources." [256]

Such a charge might assuredly be levelled at the prolific work of Daniel Boorstin, perhaps the best American representative of the national character approach to material culture studies. Boorstin's principal research method is to synthesize all extant scholarship on documentary, graphic, and artifact evidence into a sweeping, interpretive overview. His famous trilogy, *The Americans*, especially its final volume subtitled *The Democratic Experience*, exemplifies the Boorstin approach. Drawing upon an enormous array of research in the history of technology, communications, architectural history, and popular culture, Boorstin demonstrates what he calls the "democratization of democracy in America." [257] Proof is found in a cornucopia of material culture, as diverse as any inventory of consumer goods in twentieth-century America: plate-glass windows, ready-made clothing, telephones and television, the assembly-line, food packaging, photography, mail-order catalogs, and department stores. In charting the personality development of the Americans from their "colonial experience" (volume I) through their "national experience" (volume II) and then to their culminating "democratic experience" (volume III), Boorstin says he wants "to rediscover America," particularly in the evolution of certain American institutions, ways of life, and artifacts. Two volumes tell how American ways became different from European; the last relates how those new "democratic ways" became standardized or homogenized. In this final volume, American things and the ways of making or getting them are clearly the focus of the interpretation. Certain things, however, nurture Boorstin's democracy better than others, and technology emerges as the key to the American nation's character. For example, in a recent essay whose title, "The Republic of Technology," aptly summarizes his entire thesis, Boorstin extolled television for its "power to disband armies, to cashier presidents, to create a whole new democratic world—democratic in ways never before imagined, even in America." [258] In *The*

Americans, similar exegeses on Model-T Fords, Polaroid cameras, Pullman Palace cars, and Decca records argue the case that American ideology is experimental, pragmatic, egalitarian, nonideological, and novel.

Boorstin's claim for an American exceptionalism, based upon certain exceptional American artifacts, might be seen to parallel the functionalist and symbolist approaches to material culture studies discussed earlier. His technique has certainly drawn similar opposition.[259] Critics claim that the national character approach begs several methodological questions: Have all Americans or even most Americans actually shared common beliefs or values over their entire history? Do not most surveys of the national character turn out to be homogenized, progressive histories of "winners," of those attitudes and artifacts that prevailed and succeeded? Why would material culture data be more representative of the national ideology than documentary or graphic evidence? Is such a holistic attempt to chart the dominant worldview of a entire society past and present, possible in a pluralistic or geographically diverse country such as the United States?

The Social History Paradigm

Parallel research aspirations that sought to look at the whole of history can be seen among the European historians of the *Annales* school. In the early 1930s, French scholars Marc Bloch and Lucien Febvre set out to examine the entire compass of society, including its social groups, social institutions, and social structures, through a sociohistorical perspective. Perhaps most important of all, they wanted to widen the conventional of perimeters historical study to include the day-to-day experiences (working, child-rearing, schooling, play, social and economic mobility, marrying, dying) of large aggregates of the population (e.g., peasants, minorities, women, and ethnic groups), that had previously been excluded in most traditional French history texts. In works such as *Centuries of Childhood* (1963) and *Capitalism and Material Life, 1400–1800* (1973), Philippe Ariès and Fernand Braudel have continued the *Annales* tradition into the 1970s.[260] Their work provided the stimulus for a final approach to material culture studies that can be labelled social history. This perspective deserves additional clarification here because it may prove to be the most influential research orientation among contemporary American material culture scholars.[261]

In addition to the French historians, British labor and economic historians such as E. P. Thompson have shown American researchers that they can conceive of history "in terms of the processes affecting the great majority of people alive at any given time, with special attention to the anonymously downtrodden, those whose standard of living and prestige are lowest." [262] Like these British social historians, American scholars also adopted the premise that historians should be intensely skeptical of literary sources of evidence (always the product of a small elite) and should use quantitative data, whenever possible, to assure that their conclusions are truly representative of the social aggregate they are investigating. To certain material culture historians long accustomed to working with nonliterary sources—tools, furniture, structures, and archaeological shards—these basic canons of the acclaimed "new" social history only reinforced their own methodological perspective. A convergence of interests might also be seen in a mutual attraction to nonunique and nonliterary sources of past human activity. Finally, it might be noted that both modern material culture studies and the new social history have strong interdisciplinary roots, the former in the arts and humanities, the latter in the social sciences.

What scholarship has this seemingly obvious coalition of similar interests, data, and origins produced over the past two decades? Unfortunately, not nearly the quantity of monographic literature or museum exhibitions that one might have expected. Several reasons have been suggested. Academic social historians have tended to write only for other fellow specialists, showing little interest in disseminating their data, methods, and conclusions even to other historians. By a curious irony, an elite that has sought to study the history of the masses has been reluctant to translate their research to a wider professional audience, much less the general populace. Material culturists have, in their turn, only begun to grasp the full implications of the social history perspective. Traditionally content to collect and describe objects, they have resisted the task of analyzing and extracting social behavior from such data. Finally, whereas the new social history has been preoccupied with methodological issues and the representativeness of evidence, material culture researchers have only begun to recognize such questions in their scholarship. This recent work can be roughly grouped into a half-dozen or so categories whose identity is derived from the type of artifactual evidence in which its researchers have been most interested: housing, domestic artifacts and furnishings, foodways, costume, photography, tools and technology, work, social institutions, and social behavior.

Housing, along with consideration of its interior spaces and artifacts, has been of particular interest to American social historians ever since John Demos suggested the interpretive possibilities of seventeenth-century vernacular buildings. In his attempt to reconstruct family life in the Plymouth colony, Demos employed dwellings and dwelling foundations to raise vital questions concerning housing types and how they might have influenced behavior and validated social status.[263] Demos also turned to domestic artifacts: fireplaces, cooking utensils, chests, tables, chairs, and bedsteads. Investigation of these artifacts, in their extant three-dimensional forms and as they were recorded in seventeenth-century probate inventories, prompted Demos to ask questions about what he called "the more intangible aspects of family life," issues such as personal privacy, social segregation (by age, sex, race, and class), repression of familial anger and aggression (displacing it, via the civil and criminal courts, toward one's neighbors), and child-rearing practices.

In an analysis of Pilgrim clothing, he discovered additional proof of Philippe Aries's thesis that, prior to the eighteenth century, children were clothed very much in the manner of their parents.[264] To Demos, "these are facts whose significance extends well beyond the immediate sartorial context,'' for such material culture data suggests that "childhood as such was barely recognized in the period spanned by the Plymouth Colony. There was little sense that children might somehow be a special group, with their own needs and capacities." [265]

Demos repeatedly cautioned that his social history analysis of the material culture of a single seventeenth-century New England colony was inferential, speculative, and, at best, only a case study. Yet *A Little Commonwealth* turned out to be a benchmark monograph, possessing many of the traits that characterize the social history approach to material culture. In addition to making use of demographic data (e.g., census records) and probate inventories, a practice now being widely followed by material culture historians at research centers such as St. Mary's City, Historic Deerfield, and Colonial Williamsburg, [266] Demos unhesitatingly borrowed models and methods from the social sciences. For example, from social psychology he applied the theory of "displacement" to help explain crowded living spaces and the amazing lack of familial conflict within such areas; from cultural anthropology and sociology he used the concept of "primary and secondary institutions" to explain the family, its structure, its personnel, and its material culture within a network of kinship patterns; finally, from developmental psychology he adapted Erik Erikson's "eight stages of man" model to measure the life-processes of individuals from infancy and childhood through old age and death.

Since Demos first ventured into social history, via the subfield of family history, other scholars have used the approach to investigate the artifacts of domesticity in other contexts and in other historical periods. The current vernacular architecture movement, now sponsoring a newsletter and an annual professional meeting, has been heavily influenced by the social history perspective. [267] So have scholars such as Kenneth Ames, Clifford Clark, and Harvey Green, whose seminal articles on Victorian hall furnishings, Gothic revival residences, and domestic artifacts stand as model essays in the application of social history to material culture studies. [268] Monographs about women and by women, such as Gwendolyn Wright, *Moralism and the Model Home* (1980); Dolores Hayden, *Seven American Utopias* (1976); and Martha Moore Trescott's anthology, *Dynamos and Virgins Revisited* (1979), are additional examples of current work that contributes to women studies, often subsumed under social history's umbrella, as well as to material culture research. [269]

Following up on Demos's early interest in life cycles, other historians have begun to study the material culture of birthing and burying. For example, the enormous literature seeking the social and cultural meaning of gravestones, cemeteries, and burial practices can now be found in a journal, aptly labelled *Markings*, devoted exclusively to this topic. [270] Interest also has been institutionalized in the Association for Gravestone Studies. In this context, perhaps the best integration of careful social history and detailed material culture research, using some analytical techniques borrowed from both traditional art history and anthropological structuralism, is Peter Benes, *The Masks of Orthodoxy* (1977). Attendant upon this interest in death is the fascination with the experience of mourning and its historical meanings. *The Puritan Way of Death* (1977) by David Stannard represents this trend which has also manifested itself in several museum exhibitions and catalogs.[271] Finally, attempts to understand the history of death in America have had parallels to investigations of old age as a historical phenomenon. In David Hackett Fisher's study of old age in New England, artifactual evidence, such as eighteenth-century family portraits, meeting house seating arrangements, and men's clothing, form a significant evidential base for his conclusions.[272] To date, surprisingly little work has been done with the artifacts of childbirth and early child-rearing practices. One rich area of future material culture research would appear to be in the social and cultural history of children's toys.[273]

Social historians, whether interested in material culture as evidence or not, have also paid scant attention to eating, assuredly one of humankind's universal necessities. Despite the enormous material culture that surrounds this essential experience, it has been largely ignored by serious material culturists, with the exception of foodways scholars such as Jay Anderson, Charles Camp, Roger Welsch, Don Yoder, and the contributors to the January 1981 special issue of *Western Folklore*, "Foodways and Eating Habits: Directions For Research." [274] The geographical and chronological focus of most this research has been primarily on rural and preindustrial communities. Only recently has attention been given to the artifacts of twentieth-century food preparation, service, and disposal. In the latter instance, William Rathje has employed the long-established archaeological techniques of midden analysis to the household trash cans of Tucson, Arizona, in order to determine food consumption and food waste and the correlation of such factors to food price levels.[275]

In addition to examining the artifacts of what and how Americans eat, some social historians have begun to analyze the artifactual evidence of Americans at work. Spurred on by the "new" labor histories of E. P. Thompson and Herbert Gutman, these researchers have set out "to capture the total historical experience of the American working people rather than only that part expressed through the labor movement." [276] Such an objective requires looking beyond the familiar topics of traditional labor history, such as strikes, union leaders, and politics, and attempting instead the reconstruction of the earlier worlds of the working people, including their personal habits, customs, habitats, and tools. In a few instances, such as in the studies of Quebec artisan culture by Jean-Pierre Hardy, scholars have made extensive use of material culture data in researching the social history of working class life. In other work, like Bruce Laurie's investigations of Philadelphia working people, artifactual evidence merely supplements documentary and statistical data.[277] To date, social histories of the American makers of "American things" have focussed primarily on the colonial craftsmen and on mechanics or artisans caught in the transition from a preindustrial economy to an industrial one. For instance, the shoemakers of Lynn, Masschusetts, have received fairly extensive attention in articles and monographs, as well as in a material culture exhibition,

"Life and Times in Shoe City: The Shoe Workers of Lynn," mounted by the Essex Institute in 1979–1980. A related use of artifacts, particularly historical photography, is found in Tamara K. Hareven's and Randolph Langenbach's *Amoskeag* (1978).[278]

The Hareven-Langenbach collaboration points up two final directions taken by modern material culturists in following the social history perspective: urban history and ethnic history. Use of housing, transportation networks, public buildings, and commercial, industrial, and manufacturing structures as crucial evidence to interpret American urban life is a research tradition at least as old as I. N. Phelps Stokes' six-volume study, *Iconography of Manhattan Island* (1915–1928). Numerous contemporary scholars make extensive use of the extant physical fabric of the city as their primary evidence.[279] Ethnicity and race, long considered important factors in folk artifacts, are now seen by material culturists as significant issues in the life experiences of certain social groups. Here one thinks of the pioneering work of William Ferris, John Vlach, Charles Fairbanks, and Robert Schuyler on black material culture,[280] Margaret Hobbie and Charles van Ravensway on the Germans,[281] as well as the efforts of Roberta Greenwood and others on Asian-American material culture.[282] Numerous other examples might also be cited that suggest the range of the social history approach in artifactual study of ethnic groups in this country.[283]

Current Trends and Future Aspirations

I hope it is evident from the preceding discussion that an increasing eclecticism characterizes the contemporary material culture studies movement, embracing as it does almost all American artifacts in one huge Whitmanish hug. As Kenneth Ames points out, "the diversity of questions being asked and the variety of disciplines generating them indicate that material culture is perceived as a new frontier for scholarship." [284] Pluralism will undoubtedly continue to characterize the movement in a proliferation of periodicals, newsletters, societies, and organizations devoted to the study of American artifacts.[285]

Current American material culture scholarship is also promoting another trend in its changing the definition of what constitutes a historical artifact, first as to its antiquity and, second, as to its provenance. The old prescript coined by dealers, collectors, and the U.S. Customs Office, "one hundred years doth an antique make," no longer holds among those who now work with American artifacts. Instead there has been a drift away from the older fascination with the colonial material culture of the seventeenth and eighteenth centuries, particularly of revolutionary America, to artifacts of the recent past. In addition to a new interest in the post-Civil War era, there is developing a great interest in art deco and art moderne decorative arts and architecture, in documentary photography since 1900, and in the material culture of roadside America. Now, for example, a Society for Commercial Archaeology studies artifacts of the highway strip.[286] All of this "professional" collecting of the contemporary is paralleled on the amateur level by the growth of flea markets and innumerable house, lawn, and garage sales where objects of every kind are offered, traded, and bought by an ever-widening public. Nearly everything is fair game today.

Along with the collapse of the once rather rigid chronological perimeters of what might be deemed "an historical artifact" has come the absorbing interest in the material culture of the American Everyman. As Fred Kniffen put it, "There must be, for example, less concern for a house because some famous character lived in it and more concern that it is or that it is not typical of the houses of its time and place. The study of the unique normally adds little to the sum of understanding of human behavior. The study of the kinds of *things* used by people during a given historical period reveals a great deal about them." [287] This emphasis helps explain the expanding vogue of the social history approach among material culturists as well as why there has been a slight shift in research interest from the public sector to what Carroll Smith-Rosenberg has called "private places," that is, the household, the bedroom, the nursery, kinship systems, and voluntary associations. [288]

The new populist emphasis of artifact studies that focuses on vernacular, commonplace, and mass-style objects as opposed to that which is unique, elite, or high-style, has had analogs in other dimensions of the American material culture movement. The historical preservation cause in the United States now seeks more aggressively to save whole "historical districts" (even industrial or commercial ones) instead of simply the "Old Manse" of the town founder; American museums now mount more exhibitions devoted to the material culture of varied ethnic groups, of workers, of dissidents, and even of people who were the counter-culturists of yesteryear. [289] A blossoming popular culture movement has also added to the democratization of American objects studied, arguing that mass-produced lawn ornaments and suburban garden plots are as crucial indices to the American experience as are a Tiffany lamp or a Duncan Phyfe chair. [290]

Although the historical profession as represented by the American Historical Association has been laggard in recognizing material culture scholarship in its journals and at its professional conclaves, there are a few signs that more collaboration is ongoing between those whom E. M. Fleming calls "university historians and museum historians." [291] Organizations such as the American Association for State and Local History have, on occasion, united both groups in programs and seminars dealing with their mutual interest in artifacts. Local conferences and symposia such as those sponsored by the Cooperstown Graduate Program, the Winterthur Museum, the Connor Prairie Pioneer Settlement, and the North Carolina Department of Natural Resources have also nurtured interdisciplinary and interinstitutional cooperation. [292] Unfortunately, the official history establishment, the American Historical Association and its membership residing in college and university departments of history, remains largely indifferent to this scholarly activity. A sample of the major texts used to survey the current interpretative trends and methodological perspectives in the writing of American history reveals a complete ignorance of the type of contemporary scholarship included in this anthology.[293] Perhaps material culture studies will only enter the formal historical academy through a postern gate, possibly left open by the social historians, when traditional historians become less preoccupied with "words" ("the curious obsession of historians," suggests Roger Burlingame) and become more intrigued with "things" and what a careful study of them might reveal about the past.[294]

Why should historians employ artifactual evidence in their efforts to research, document, analyze, and communicate the past? As this abridged survey of the material culture studies in America suggests, and as the following essays will further demonstrate, at least three answers can be offered in response to this fundamental question. First, material culture evidence should obviously be used in historical research when it is the only evidence available. For example, in the case of Dutch barns in America and the cultural history surrounding them, no significant documentary, statistical, or oral data survives; only material culture evidence remains extant for the historian to interpret.[295] A second argument to be made for the general historian's use of artifacts would be as supplementary evidence in research case-studies when the available documentary and statistical data for a topic is limited or seriously flawed. In such instances, material culture evidence verifies the historian's interpretations initially based upon other extant data. Examples of this methodological usage are frequent in the fields of architectural history, the history of technology, and cultural anthropology.[296]

Finally, the third major research strategy in which material culture evidence can be deployed by the general historian would be to test already established interpretations or newly argued hypotheses about the past based strictly on documentary and statistical data. This revisionist perspective, a common practice in general historiography, subjects long-accepted historical generalizations, such as the importance of the fall line in American historical geography or the superiority of nineteenth-century American agricultural machinery, to close scrutiny from another angle and with aid of different evidence.[297] Typical revisions of our understanding of the American past that have been made by comparing material evidence with previously established documentary and statistical data include James Deetz's rewriting of the cultural history of the American revolutionary period and Merrit Roe Smith's and Robert Howard's reversals of the standard explanation for nineteenth-century American technological creativity and progress.[298]

To the extent that material culture scholars can subject the standard interpretations of the past in history and other academic fields to fruitful reassessment, the movement will gain increasing attention and will establish additional links with a wider circle of disciplines that nurture and, in turn, are nurtured by its pluralistic approach to historical inquiry. Fortunately, material culture study has emerged in contemporary scholarship not as a formal discipline or a doctrinaire school, but rather as an arena for disciplinary encounter, a staging ground for fresh intellectual adventure using artifacts as crucial evidence for the interpretation of the American past.[299] As a clearing house of interdisciplinary effort, the movement needs to remain experimental and exploratory in fashioning its contributions to the task of documenting, explaining, and communicating the kaleidoscopic nature of past American culture. Of course, it must be acknowledged that any variegated and vigorous intellectual enterprise generates dross as well as gold. Hence in American material culture studies, past and present, there have been writers too quick to formulate loose hypotheses based on inadequate data and too eager to exaggerate the explanatory potential of extant artifacts.

The challenge of material culture research, however, remains one of the more exciting tasks ahead of contemporary American historians. "The mission," notes Brooke Hindle, "is a great one. Even the beginnings registered so far are exciting. They point to the fulfillment of the deep-running need of this generation and those to come for a better history of their past which is both true and useful. It will be truer and more useful than the present histories," concludes Hindle, "precisely because its abstractions will be tied by an intricate web to the real world of material culture." [300] While the verdict may not be in on the total achievement of material culture research, the individual contributions of scholars in this anthology assuredly demonstrate the legitimacy of Hindle's, and my own belief, in the viability and versatility of the material culture approach contributing to a more comprehensive, more true, and more useful understanding of the American historical experience.

Part II

Statements of Theory

Truth is a ratio between the mind and things.
—Marshall McLuhan, *The Gutenberg Galaxy*

What intellect restores to us under the name of the past is not the past. In reality as soon as each hour of one's life has died, it embodies itself in some material object, as do the souls of the dead in certain folk-stories, and hides there. There it remains captive, captive forever, unless we should happen upon the object, recognize what lies within, call it by its name and so set it free.
—Marcel Proust, *Remembrance of Things Past*

2

American Studies: Words or Things?

John A. Kouwenhoven

Introduction

Every scholarly trend has its manifestoes. Prior to the publication of the following essay in 1964, only a handful of occasional theoretical arguments for material culture studies had appeared. The majority of such defenses had been issued within the disciplines traditionally associated with using objects as evidence, disciplines such as archaeology, art history, and architectural history. No attempts had been made to argue the case from a cross-disciplinary perspective for a cross-disciplinary audience. It was significant, therefore, when Marshall Fishwick initiated a new publication series sponsored by the Wemyss Foundation on "theory and methodology in American Studies" that John Kouwenhoven was chosen to launch the endeavor with this proposal for greater emphasis on American material culture studies in both the American Studies movement and in American education.

Kouwenhoven has been a pioneer practitioner of both American Studies and material culture research for the past three decades. He has long been interested in probing the totality of the American culture or, to use his terms, discovering "how common our common culture is." His own answer to that inquiry, briefly alluded to here in his two-paragraph discussion of the "vernacular arts," has been explicated in great detail in his essays and books, particularly his classic Made in America (1948).

The following essay is admittedly a polemic desirous of redressing an imbalance that the author sees resulting from an overdependence on verbal evidence in our thinking processes, in our educational system, and in our study of the past. Kouwenhoven insists that we tend to interpret reality almost solely by words instead of interpreting words by the specific reality of which they are but symbols. He cautions against the inevitable bias in such a preoccupation with verbal evidence, particularly its "averaging-out quality" that reduces human experience (past and present) to overly abstract formulas. Instead, he argues—as does this entire anthology—for greater attention to object evidence in personal knowing as well as in historical studies.

Kouwenhoven's claims for the validity of analyzing "American things" in order to be able to "formulate useful verbal generalizations about American culture" is an appropriate opening statement for this anthology. First, the essay is one of the classics in the methodology of American Studies, the discipline in which material culture studies appear to have found their most receptive interdisciplinary academic niche; second, it suggests how several other fields, including cultural anthropology, archaeology, history of technology, folk art, and museology studies, use material culture evidence—another objective of this anthology; third, and perhaps most important, the essay argues that anyone interested in doing artifactual analysis and interpretation must be guided by a simple imperative: "See the object first." In order to perform the type of multifaceted "sensory thinking" that Kouwenhoven urges, one must encounter the object firsthand. If possible, one must tramp across the Brooklyn Bridge or handle a Pennsylvania Dutch fraktur, not just read about it or consult a photograph of it. A final caveat for students of material culture is also raised by this selection: it should not be forgotten that while the authors in this collection write of "things," they do so, as we all do, with "words." Language, despite its many limitations, continues to be a key vehicle by which we communicate what we know through and about objects.

The Kouwenhoven selection was first published as a nineteen-page booklet underwritten by the Wemyss Foundation of Wilmington, Delaware, in 1964. It has been reprinted in Marshall Fishwick, ed., American Studies in Transition (Philadelphia: University of Pennsylvania Press, 1964) and in Lucius Ellsworth and Maureen O'Brien, eds., Material Culture: Historical Agencies and the Historian (Philadelphia: Book Reprint Service, 1969). The essay is invariably found on every course syllabus dealing with American material culture studies. It is reprinted here, complete, from the original Wemyss Foundation publication.

In addition to numerous articles, John Kouwenhoven has written several seminal works, the titles of which reveal the scope and originality of their author: Adventures of America, 1857–1900 (1938); Made in America: The Arts in Modern Civilization (1948); The Columbia Historical Protrait of New York (1953); The Beer Can by the Highway: Essays on What's American about America (1961); and (with Janice Farrar Thaddeus) When Women Look at Men–An Anthology (1963). John Kouwenhoven is completing a cultural history of the Eads Bridge in St. Louis.

The discovery and exploration of America has been going on for roughly five hundred years. That is a long time on any scale except the geological. One would think that by now we would know pretty well what America is, even if we disagreed about its merits and demerits.

Perhaps we do know, but you would never guess it from reading the books its discoverers write about it or from attending the conferences where they gather to discuss it. Conferences and symposia on American civilization are, I believe, commonly thought of, even by their most enthusiastic promoters, less as ways to settle things than as ways to unsettle them. They are set up to facilitate what is called "an exchange of ideas"—a curious phrase that suggests swapping notions as we might swap cigarette lighters, each of us pocketing and going home with the other fellow's instead of his own. Maybe some are exchanged, but very few are changed, apparently. The symposia and conferences I know about seem, at least, to have contributed very little to any agreement about what American culture is, let alone what it is worth.

In this essay I shall contend that part, at least, of our difficulty results from a fatal imbalance in the techniques we employ as explorers and discoverers in the field of American Studies. I shall suggest, as forcefully as I can, that we have been too ready to accept verbal evidence as if it were the equivalent of the evidence of our senses. I shall argue that we have been so preoccupied with words that we have neglected things; that we have, in fact, based our ideas of America primarily upon ingenious verbal generalizations that are sometimes laughably and sometimes tragically unrelated to actualities.

You may remember reading about Sir John Hawkins, the tough-minded and vigorous Elizabethan seaman who visited the French colony in Florida, at the mouth of the St. John's River, in the 1560s, in the course of one of his slave-trading voyages in Queen Elizabeth's good, but ironically named, ship *Jesus*. Hawkins reported, on his return to England, that there were unicorns and lions in Florida. The unicorns he knew about because some of his crew got pieces of unicorn horn from the French, who said they got them straight from the Florida Indians. So there was no doubt about the unicorns. As for the lions, Hawkins had not actually seen any of them, but there was no doubt about them either. Lions, as everyone knew, are the natural enemies of unicorns. It was therefore obvious, as Hawkins put it, that "whereas the one is, the other cannot be missing."

It is easy enough to see how absurdly funny Hawkins's report on Florida becomes when he accepts, as he does here, his own verbal ingenuity as the equivalent of reality. But I wonder if those of us who report nowadays on America are not as likely as Hawkins to be bewitched by our own verbal ingenuities. In any event, I shall ask you to follow me, along a somewhat circuitous route, through some speculations about the verbal traps we lay for ourselves and about a possible way to avoid them.

A few years ago there was a trial in the New York Court of General Sessions that the newspapers referred to as "The Circus." It was a fantastic affair in which at one point a defense lawyer called the prosecuting attorney as a defense witness; at another the prosecuting attorney cross-examined himself; and everybody on both sides repeatedly lost his temper. Once, when the exhausted and frustrated judge was trying to follow the rapid-fire argument of one of the lawyers, he interrupted with a plaintive comment that has haunted me ever since. "The only things you say," expostulated the judge, "that I don't understand are your words."

Perhaps the judge's remark is especially haunting because we hear so much these days about the need for greater speed in coping with words. Speed reading is getting to be the rage. Children in school, suburban matrons, and businessmen are taking speed-reading courses. One wonders if they are bent on becoming participants in some sort of cosmic Court of General Sessions where, like the plaintive judge, the only thing said to them that they do not understand will be the words.

For words are deceptive enough, even if we take them slowly, as the recent studies in semantics have shown. And is it not curious that the science of semantics—the systematic study of the relation between verbal symbols and what they denote and connote, and of the way these word symbols affect human behavior—should be flourishing at the same moment in our history when we are energetically learning how to hasten over those verbal symbols? The more we are aware that words can be treacherously misleading, the more we want to race through them, lest we be misled. Perhaps we are doing so in justifiable self-defense.

For words are, in fact, deceptive and misleading, not just because they are ambiguous, as we all know they are, but because of an inherent limitation of language itself. That limitation was pointed out a hundred and thirty-four years ago by a banker in Utica, New York, who made a hobby of the study of language. His name was Alexander Bryan Johnson. In 1828 he published a small volume entitled *The Philosophy of Human Knowledge, or A Treatise on Language*, made up of lectures he had given at the local lyceum. Eight years later he published an expanded version with the title *A Treatise on Language, or The Relation Which Words Bear to Things*, and eighteen years later, in 1854, a third and more fully developed version.

In none of its versions did the book make any impression upon learned circles at the time, since Johnson had no university connections and was unknown to the intelligentsia of Boston, New York, or Philadelphia. He sent copies to eminent men, such as Professor Benjamin Silliman at Yale and August Comte in Paris; but why would such people be interested in the ideas of a banker in Utica? As Comte said, in a curt letter of acknowledgement: "Although the question which you have broached may be one of the most fundamental which we can agitate, I cannot promise to read such an essay. For my part, I read nothing except the great poets ancient and modern . . . in order to maintain the originality of my peculiar meditations." The only serious review any of the three versions received was a long and favorable discussion of the first in Timothy Flint's *Western Review*, published in the frontier city of Cincinnati in 1829. Not until 1947—more than a century later—was the book rediscovered and republished by Professor David Rynin of the University of California.

Since its rediscovery, Johnson's book has come to be acknowledged as a pioneering study in semantics and one of the most original philosophical works ever written by an American. I take both these evaluations on faith, since I am neither a student of semantics nor a philosopher. All I can say on my own authority is that Alexander Johnson's ideas have profoundly impressed me and that the objections brought against them by Professor Rynin himself, in his introduction to the reprint, and by other semantics scholars seem to me irrelevant. I mention this only because I intend to use and develop some of Johnson's perceptions, and because I want it to be clear that I know my comments do not find support in current semantic theory.

As Johnson saw it, the radical limitation of words (their radical "defect") is that they are general terms of names, referring to things that are individual and particular. Even though we know, for example, that no two blades of grass are alike, the word *grass* suggests an identity. This suggestion of identity encourages us to disregard the different looks, feels, tastes, and smells of the uncounted blades that comprise the actuality of grass as we experience it.

Since words have this generalizing characteristic it is inevitable, Johnson argues, that if we contemplate the created universe through the medium of words, we will impute to it a generalized unity that our senses cannot discover in it. In our writing, thinking, and speaking, we habitually "disregard the individuality of nature and substitute for it a generality which belongs to language."

One result of the delusive generality of verbal symbols is that two people can be in verbal agreement without meaning the same thing. You can say to me that television commercials are sometimes revolting, and I may reply "yes, they certainly are revolting sometimes." We are in complete verbal agreement. But the particular commercials you had in mind may not be the ones I was thinking of. Perhaps, indeed, I have never seen commercials like those you were referring to; perhaps if I had seen them, I would not have thought them revolting. I might have enjoyed them. The less our direct, first hand experience of television commercials coincides, the less chance there is that any verbal agreement—or disagreement—we arrive at in discussing them will have any significance whatever.

Verbal symbols, then, are inherently "defective." They are at best a sort of generalized, averaged-out substitute for a complex reality comprising an infinite number of individual particularities. We can say that a pane of glass is square, oblong, round, or a half-dozen other shapes, and that when it is shattered the pieces are fragments or slivers. But for the infinite variety of forms which those slivers in reality assume, we have no words. The multiple reality we generalize as "slivers of glass" can never be known through words. We can know that reality only through our senses, the way we experience blades of grass in lawns or commercials on television.

This generalizing characteristic of language is, of course, its great value. It is what makes human communication possible. A language consisting of separate words for each of the particularities in the created universe would be bulky beyond reckoning. No one could ever master its vocabulary. We have good reason to be thankful for the ingenious symbol system that averages out reality into the mere ten thousand words that are necessary for ordering meals, writing love poems, and composing essays on American civilization. And no harm would come of it if we did not fall into the habit of assuming that reality corresponds to the words we have invented to represent it.

More often than not, however, we do fall into that habit. "What is this?" our child asks us, showing us what he has in his hand. "A stone," we reply—or, if we have had Geology I, "a hunk of quartz." Long practice has habituated us to this device for eliminating all those particularities of texture, of color and form, of smell and taste, that were the very things that interested the child. The averaged-out concept inherent in the word *stones* is admirably efficient for many purposes of communication, as when we are admonishing people who live in glass houses. But it does not tell your child what he has in his hand.

His senses tell him that. If he has learned anything from your words it is only that he must disregard the evidence of his senses. For the thing he has in his hand is not at all the same shape, or color, or feel as the one he asked about yesterday, which you also said was a stone (or a hunk of quartz). You have begun to teach him to interpret reality by words, instead of interpreting words by the specific realities of which they are the symbols. You have given him an effective lesson in the convenient but deceptive process by which we habitually translate the individual particulars of existence into the generalized abstractions of language. Unless he talks about stones only with people who are familiar with hunks of quartz more or less like the one he has examined, he is on his way, like the rest of us, to the Court of General Sessions.

I have magnified the difficulties he faces in order to emphasize an important point. People who have not experienced similar particularities cannot receive from one another's words the meaning those words were intended to convey. For meaning is not a property of words, a static entity which words somehow embody. Meaning is a process that words sometimes facilitate: a process in which awareness passes from one consciousness to another. Words do not *have* meaning; they *convey* it. But they can convey it only if the receiving consciousness can complete the current of meaning by grounding it in comparable particulars of experience.

A man who has never been out of the American Southwest—who grew up in and has never left Santa Fe, New Mexico, for instance—and a man born and brought up in the Hebrides, off the western coast of Scotland, could not conceivably mean the same thing by the word *sunlight*. The less our cluster of experienced particulars corresponds to that of people by whom our words are heard or read, the less chance there is that those people will understand what we are saying.

What makes language function as satisfactorily as it generally does, despite its limitations, is that we use it chiefly to communicate with those who share the set of experienced particulars we call our common culture. One way and another we acquire some shared familiarity with a tremendous number of things. We get around, vicariously or otherwise. Even in the Hebrides there are no doubt people who have visited Santa Fe, or Las Vegas, whose sunlight will pass for Santa Fe's except among the finicky. And if our words are heard or read by those with whom we share a significant accumulation of experiences, they *can* convey our meaning well enough for all practical purposes—and even for some impractical ones as well. They can do so, that is, provided neither we nor those to whom we speak abandon our allegiance to the particulars we have experienced.

So far, my argument adds up to something like this: Our words can convey meaning only to those who share with us a community of experienced particulars and to them only if we and they scrupulously refer the generalized verbal symbols to concrete particulars we are talking about. Your translation of an experience into words can be understood only by someone who can interpret those words by referring them to a similar experience of his own. If he cannot do that, the current of meaning is short-circuited. A Santa Fe experience that might be adequately translated by the words "My wife has a smile like sunlight" cannot be the experience into which those words would be translated by a habitual Hebridean.

It seems obvious, therefore, that we must determine the limits of our community of experienced particulars. This is another way of saying that we need to discover how common our common culture is. Otherwise we will waste a great deal of energy and time in feckless attempts to communicate with people who cannot make sense of what we say.

To some extent our common culture is limited by geography. There are many places in the world where particulars, like those we experience in New York, or Wichita, or Walla Walla, are simply unavailable. To be sure, it would be naive to assume that geographical or political boundaries are the bounds of our common culture. A turret-lathe operator in Wichita might share a more significant community of experienced particulars with a turret-lathe operator in Bombay than with a professor of American literature who lived two blocks away. An economics student in New York or Walla Walla might share a more significant community of experienced particulars with a student of economics in Heidelberg than with a fine arts major at his own college. But the particulars that constitute American culture are by and large available in New York and Wichita and Walla Walla, whether or not the professor and machine operator, or the economics major and fine arts major, are aware of them; whereas in many areas of the world those constituent particulars are not available at all.

No doubt it is with some awareness of this problem that those of us concerned with American culture devote our efforts to programs like the international exchange of students and teachers, the encouragement of foreign tourism in this country, and the sending abroad of such cultural emissaries as Peace Corps groups, theatrical troupes, musical performers, and exhibitions of arts and crafts. Unwilling to trust to such routine agencies of international contact as commerce and the armed forces, we are deliberately making available to those in other lands certain particulars of our culture that we hope will serve to ground the current of meaning when we talk to them about ourselves. The only trouble is that we disagree among ourselves about which particulars we should make available. The State Department has its own ideas; some Senate committees have others; and private agencies like the

American Legion, the Hollywood film exporters, and the Institute for International Education have others still.

The lack of general agreement about which clusters of particulars constitute the distinctively "American" experience emerged clearly from a symposium entitled *American Perspectives*, published by Harvard University Press in 1961 as one of the Library of Congress's series on twentieth-century American civilization. Ten distinguished authorities contributed essays to that symposium, discussing such "clusters of particulars" as American literature, American business, American philosophy, and American popular culture. The volume was edited for the American Studies Association by Professor Robert E. Spiller (a past president of the association) and Eric Larrabee (then managing editor of *American Heritage*). The auspices were impressive.

But despite a good deal of preliminary consultation and planning, and the best of intentions, the symposium admittedly failed in its purpose. As the editors ruefully acknowledge in their preface, "the hoped-for unity of the book did not materialize"; the contributors "found themselves in no firm agreement" either in their premises or in their conclusions.

I refer you to this book as one of the particulars I have in mind when I say that, up to now, we have not determined the limits of the community of experienced particulars we call "American culture." To put it bluntly, our verbal attempts to discover America fail because we do not know what we are talking about.

It is my conviction that part of our difficulty stems from an excessive preoccupation with verbal evidence. The particulars to which we refer, whether we are talking about politics or mass production, painting or social behavior, are too exclusively literary. Historians and social scientists are almost as bad as the literary critics in this respect. And so are the nonspecialists.

I do not mean to suggest that novels, poems, plays, and other writings are not significant particulars of our culture. I think they are, and I earn my living as a teacher of courses in literature. But as I have tried to suggest, we have a weakness for mistaking words for things. We tend to forget that a novel about life in the slums of Chicago is not life in the slums of Chicago.

The novel is a cluster of verbal symbols whose arrangement conveys to us, with more or less precision, the emotions and ideas aroused in the writer by those particulars of Chicago slum life that he happened to experience. The writer's emotional responses to Chicago slum life, and his ideas about it, may be in themselves significant facts of American culture, especially if the novel communicates them to many readers, or even to a few who act in response to them. But these emotions and ideas, and the novel that conveys them, are not Chicago slum life. That is something that can be known only by direct sensory experience; and if you or I experienced it, its particulars might arouse in us emotions and ideas very unlike those we acquire from the novel.

If we can accept some such view as this of the significance of literature and other verbal documents (including "case histories" and other data of the social sciences), we will realize how necessary it is to consider other kinds of evidence in our speculations about American civilization and culture. Verbal evidence is, plainly, not enough, especially if we remember that not all civilizations have found, in literature, the most complete or significant expression of their vital energies. It may be true that the creative genius of England has been most fully expressed in literature, and that we can more or less ignore English music, painting, and architecture without seriously distorting our image of England's achievement. But other cultures have obviously expressed themselves most significantly in other forms. One thinks, for instance, of Roman building, of Dutch painting, and of German music. The fact that we are heirs to much of England's culture, including its language, does not necessarily mean, as Constance Rourke long ago pointed out, that we have, like the English, expressed ourselves most fully in literature.

In all of our studies of the past we probably rely, far more than we should, on verbal evidence, wherever it is available. As Lynn White, Jr., says in the preface to his book, *Medieval Technology and Social Change:*

Voltaire to the contrary, history is a bag of tricks which the dead have played upon historians. The most remarkable of these illusions is the belief that the surviving written records provide us with a reasonably accurate facsimile of past human activity. . . . In medieval Europe until the end of the eleventh century we learn of the feudal aristocracy largely from clerical sources which naturally reflect ecclesiastical attitudes: the knights do not speak for themselves. . . . If historians are to attempt to write the history of mankind, and not simply the history of mankind as it was viewed by the small and specialized segments of the race which have had the habit of scribbling, they must take a fresh view of the records.

The general pertinence of Lynn White's words to the problem of discussing American culture will, I hope, be clear. But I want to apply them in a special way.

It is important to recognize that, as White indicates, major segments of the population do not speak for themselves. Not everyone has the habit of scribbling (though it sometimes seems so). And I think it is true that in American civilization—and perhaps in what we call modern civilization elsewhere in the world—men and women whose work has most creatively expressed the energies of their times have often been nonscribblers. All of us, insofar as we rely upon our senses rather than upon verbal preconceptions, would acknowledge that American culture is expressed more adequately in the Brooklyn Bridge than in the poem Hart Crane wrote about it.

I have talked a good deal about words, rather than about things. I have done so in an effort to call attention to the limitations of words as evidence of the realities that constitute our culture, hoping thereby to remove the chief obstacle to the consideration of things. If we can get rid of those verbal lions and unicorns, we may be able to see and hear and touch and smell and taste the things that are really here.

Archaeologists and anthropologists have long known how important things are as testimony. And historians in some areas have learned a good deal from nonverbal evidence. Lynn White's book rescues the nonscribbling knights and other medieval people from oblivion by examining things such as the stirrups that gave the knights unprecedented control over horses and the cranks that gave medieval mechanics new control over power. Similarly, museums of folk art, and museums like the Smithsonian Institution, acknowledge the importance of tangible objects as evidence of the culture of large numbers of people who did not have "the habit of scribbling."

It is chiefly from the archaeologists and anthropologists that we might learn techniques that we can adapt to the recognition, appreciation, and evaluation of the nonverbal elements of American culture. We must, I am convinced, learn to perceive and savor with our five senses the things nonscribbling Americans have made, in somewhat the same way that the archaeologist or anthropologist approaches the artifacts and folk arts of other times and places.

A good deal of attention has been devoted recently to the study of what are called American folk arts; but those engaged in such study can contribute little to our understanding of American civilization for the simple reason that we really do not have any folk arts, properly so called. Those we have are other people's. For the term folk arts is properly applied to artifacts made in traditional forms and patterns that originated, and survive, among groups cut off, in one way or another, from the main stream of contemporary life. The things we call folk arts are things like Navaho sand-paintings or Pennsylvania Dutch fraktur.

Surviving remnants of traditional folk arts can still be found in isolated communities of even this highly industrialized and urbanized nation. And many are the collectors and students who cherish them. So many, in fact, that the folk arts will soon be, if they are not already, a big business. But delightful and interesting as these hand-crafted variants of traditional forms and patterns may be, they cannot tell anything much about American culture. The love of them, or the faddish popularity of them, can tell us a good deal. But the objects themselves cannot.

The nearest thing to folk arts that American culture has produced are those artifacts that I once labelled "the vernacular arts." The term has its limitations, but I meant it to serve as a generalized label for nontraditional forms and patterns of many sorts. By it I referred to objects shaped empirically by ordinary people in unselfconscious and uninhibited response to the challenges of an unprecedented cultural environment.

The principal novelties in that environment, in nineteenth-century America, were, it seems to me, a technology based upon power-driven machines rather than handcrafts, and a social and political system based upon the mobility-oriented institutions of democracy rather than the status-oriented institutions of aristocracy. Specifically, the products of the vernacular arts were the tools, toys, buildings, books, machines, and other artifacts whose texture, shape, and so on were evolved in direct, untutored response to the materials, needs, attitudes, and preoccupations of a society being shaped by the twin forces of democracy and technology.

It is my contention that direct sensory awareness of such vernacular objects provides an important kind of knowledge about American culture. Perhaps, indeed, the most necessary kind if we are searching for a community of experienced particulars that embodies the dynamic energies of an emergent American culture.

Up until very recently these important constituents of our culture were entirely overlooked by scholars and critics, and even now they are known chiefly through verbal accounts of them. It is no wonder that our verbal theories about American culture have seemed so irrelevant to people who know its everyday vernacular realities at first hand in factories and filling stations, on farms and in offices. If we are ever going to formulate useful verbal generalizations about our culture, we are going to have to look at, and handle, and contemplate the particulars of this vernacular tradition.

Ideally, of course, we should experience these particulars in the cultural context that produced them, not isolated from that context as displays in museums or world's fairs or exhibitions. But wherever we encounter them, let us respect the things themselves and test whatever is said about them against our first-hand sensory awareness. It will not be enough to approach these vernacular things as we customarily approach the fine arts and folk arts displayed in museums. Go to any museum and you will observe how ready people are to permit words to usurp the dignity and authority of things. Some unfamiliar object on display catches our eyes because of its form or color. We go over to examine it more closely, but before we have done more than glance at it we notice the label that the museum's curators have supplied in their ardor to educate us. The label probably provides valuable knowledge about the object—what it was made for; when, where, and by whom it was made; and so on—knowledge that might well sharpen our sensory awareness of the object if we returned to the contemplation of its form and color and texture. But more often than not the label replaces the thing as the center of our attention; having mastered the words we are satisfied that we have mastered the thing. So we pass on to the next display and read its label.

As Joyce Cary says, in his little book *Art and Reality*, there is a good deal of truth in the notion that "when you give a child the name of a bird, it loses the bird. It never *sees* the bird again, but only a sparrow, a thrush, a swan." In all phases of our lives the primitive magic of words still works its spell among us, and we think that we have mastered creation by naming it. Like the child who is attracted by the form and color and feel of a particular stone or bird and asks "What is it?," we ask the label what it is that caught our eye. And like the child, we have been educated to accept the verbal reply as a substitute for the thing itself.

This is, of course, only one of many ways in which we have taught ourselves to accept translations of reality for the original. Even in nonverbal realms we increasingly encounter reality at one remove. More and more of us know the game of baseball not as a cluster of directly experienced sensations, including the mixed smells of cold beer and hot franks and peanuts and cigars, but as sights and sounds only, as selected and translated by television cameras and microphones. Fewer and fewer of us know the taste of tobacco on the tongue, or the taste and feel of tobacco smoke, now that cigarettes have filter tips, some with the filters recessed a quarter inch away so you can't even touch your tongue to them. More and more of us experience the arts—literature, painting, sculpture, and music—filtered through some translating device. Many of us know painting and sculpture primarily through two-dimensional photographic translations that either distort the colors or average them out into tones. Most of the music we hear has been translated, with higher or lower fidelity, by microphones and electronic tubes or transistors.

These various forms of translation all differ in an important way from the sort of translation that occurs when we translate the particulars of experience into words. They all alter some aspects of the thing, but they do not generalize it or average-out its uniqueness. A photograph of a scene on some Main Street translates a three-dimensional reality that we experience only with our eyes; but the pictorial image, like the original, is a specific and individual thing, not a generalization. Any verbal description of the scene would, on the other hand, be composed of words that are generalized symbols, each capable of standing for (or referring to) many different particulars of the same general class.

To discover America, to become aware of American culture as a community of experienced particulars about which we can effectively communicate our perceptions to one another, we must first of all be aware of the limitations of verbal translations of reality. Then we can set about the job of training our young people and ourselves to think with our senses as well as with words.

At present our educational system is almost exclusively concerned with training our capacity to think verbally. What this means is that we learn to think words such as "bridge" or "beer can." We then think about those words and link them with others to form verbal concepts. These concepts are articulations and juxtapositions of words that have properties we call syntax, logic, and so on. And they can be recorded, memorized, and easily made available to others in identical copies.

The ease with which verbal concepts can be recorded and repeated is a great and powerful advantage. Word-thinking has become the basis of our educational system—except in those areas (notably the exact sciences) where vagueness and generalization are intolerable. In those areas, apprenticeship, laboratory or studio work, or some other system of acquiring first-hand familiarity with specific particulars, has necessarily been retained. But so impressive are the properties of language that subjects to which its generalizing properties are appropriate, subjects like philosophy, sociology, theology, and history (including literary history and art history), dominate the academic curriculum, to say nothing of the American Studies Association. I do not wish to belittle such subjects or to depreciate the wonderful powers of language. But we must not permit our admiration of word-thinking, and our respect for its achievements, to blind us to its limitations—limitations that derive from the inescapable limitation of words themselves: that is, their averaging-out tendency.

The danger is not that we will underestimate the importance of word-thinking in education, but that we will overlook the importance of what might be called sensory thinking. I do not know if there is a better word for it, but I know that just as we can think the words bridge and beer can, we can also think the appearance of a bridge, or the apperance of a beer can. That is sight-thinking. As Alexander Bryan Johnson remarked, the properties and limitations of sight-thinking differ from those of word-thinking. A sight-thought of a bridge is evanescent; it flashes on our consciousness, then fades. Also, it is comprehensive, including all visible aspects of the bridge at one and the same instant, whereas a word-thought about a bridge has to be accumulated gradually by adding words together. Finally, and most importantly, the sight-thought of a bridge is specific, not generalized. We can sight-think an individual bridge, or even a group of individual bridges; but we cannot sight-think a generalized abstraction of bridges.

Just as there are sight-thoughts, there are also feel-thoughts, smell-thoughts, taste-thoughts, and sound-thoughts. The terms may sound odd and unfamiliar, but we all know the realities to which they refer. With a little effort we can think the feel of a cold beer can in our hand, and think the taste of the metal as we drink from it. And we know that these other sense-thoughts, like sight-thoughts, are evanescent, comprehensive, and specific.

These sense-thoughts share, then, a significant property that differentiates them from word-thoughts. They are specific, not generalized.

They also share a significant limitation, as compared to word-thoughts. They cannot be arranged in logical or syntactical patterns. The kind of direct and specific awareness we derive from sensory thoughts, unlike the awareness we derive from word-thinking, cannot be communicated symbolically to others in conventional forms that can be easily recorded, memorized, and reproduced in identical copies.

Yet, if we trained our capacities for sensory thinking, instead of discouraging them as our educational system customarily does, it would be clear that this limitation is an asset, rather than a liability, if only because the nondiscursive properties of sense-thoughts can serve as a check on the discursive thinking we do with words. The editors of that scholarly symposium on American civilization mentioned earlier concluded their preface with a wistful reference to the possibility that ''if there were more unity in modern man's total view of himself and his world,'' the symposium itself might have produced a more consistent and unified image of our culture as one part of that world. What interests me in that conclusion is the implied assumption that there could be (or should be) a unified total view of the sort described. The very idea of such a unified and consistent view is, I suspect, a verbal illusion. It is an illusion we could not entertain if we had not become habituated, by our schooling and long practice, to accept words, unhitched from particulars, as the ultimate realities. Such terms as ''modern man himself'' and ''modern man's world'' are only remotely affiliated, if at all, with any of the infinitely diverse individual existences to which the terms pretend to refer. Who on earth, the reader should ask, is ''modern man himself''? To what, if any, specific reality do the words refer?

But that is the very question we do not ask. Because we are educated as we are, we expect to find in actuality the unity and consistency that verbal symbols can be arranged to express, forgetting that the unity and consistency are properties of a system of verbal symbols, not of the multifarious particularities that are averaged-out in our nominative generalizations. Because we are educated as we are, we too readily assume that in the realm of speculative discussion, as in the realm of faith, "in the beginning was the word."

In American Studies, as in the humanities generally, we have been largely preoccupied with records left by those "who had the habit of scribbling" (and more recently, thanks to the "oral history" projects, by those who had the habit of prattling). And it is chiefly from this verbal evidence that we have happily or gloomily deduced the lions and unicorns (as logically demonstrable and as nonexistent as Sir John Hawkins's) about which we theorize and argue. If there are no unicorns hereabouts, let's stop arguing about them. Our primary allegiance, as sentient creatures, is surely not to the creations of our verbal ingenuity, but to the particular sights, tastes, feels, sounds, and smells that constitute the American world we are trying to discover.

3

The Challenge of the Artifact

William B. Hesseltine

Introduction

If John Kouwenhoven looms as one of the earliest and most vociferous advocates of material culture studies, then the late William Hesseltine, a distinguished historian of the American Civil War, is often depicted as the most provocative devil's advocate of the movement. The brief selection below is often cited as the best early example of the historian's traditional hostility toward artifacts as historical evidence. In fact, at least three studies have been written to refute it: John Chavis, "The Artifact and the Study of History" (1964); Holman Swinney, "The Artifact as a Historical Source" (1965); and Charles T. Lyle, "The Artifact and American History" (1970).[1]

Hesseltine, a feisty, argumentative, immensely literate political historian, was, above all, a man of the word. In his highly touted history graduate seminars at the University of Wisconsin, he demanded close textual analyses of documents and cogent, graceful narrative exposition in writing history from them. He delighted in playing the role of the bete noire, a position he assumes in the following essay with typical gusto, occasionally overextending his own case or exaggerating the position of his opponents.

Historians have repeatedly either ignored artifacts altogether, as in a recent assessment of the current state of the profession by eleven leading historians (in Charles F. Delzell, ed., The Future of History [1977]), or they have dismissed them, in Hesseltine's estimate, as being "illustrative rather than instructive." He bases his argument on the claim that historians cannot subject artifacts to the internal criticism normally applied to documentary sources.[2] To Hesseltine the political historian, material culture evidence seems at best applicable, and only in a minor way, to social history. He insists that objects in and of themselves are mute and inanimate in answering the supposedly "big" questions of history.

*Moreover, the historian cannot extract meaning from objects by themselves nor
can they be used as evidential building blocks whereby a narrative explanation of
past human activity can be written.*

*The Hesseltine position, deliberately overstated for its didactic impact, raises
several questions of which readers might be mindful as they evaluate other studies
in this anthology, particularly those included in Parts III and IV. Are documents
or objects ever really studied in the unlikely vacuum that the author establishes by
his canons of internal criticism? Are not both types of historical evidence
interpreted in comparison with other related evidence? For instance, is not Colonel
Chaillé-Long's diary, which Hesseltine cites, only comprehensible when evaluated
in terms of other verifiable literary evidence such as the colonel's correspondence,
newspaper clippings, and so forth? Are there not examples of research where
careful historical investigation of the artifactual remains has expanded or even
revised the explanations that historians had previously formulated strictly on the
evidence of literary remains? Have not archaeologists, particularly the current
cadre of historical archaeologists, gone well beyond the simplistic, circumscribed
use of artifacts that Hesseltine and the sources he cites attribute to this discipline?*

*The context of this article was a panel discussion titled "The Artifact in
History," held at a national meeting of the American Association for State and
Local History at Columbus, Ohio, in 1957. In addition to Hesseltine's remarks,
opening statements were also made by panelists J. C. Harrington of the National
Park Service and Anthony N. B. Garvan, then at the Smithsonian Institution. A
spirited discussion followed the opening presentations, both among the panelists
and with conference participants who raised questions from the floor. A transcript
of all the talks and the discussion was published in The Present World of History
(Madison, Wisc.: American Association for State and Local History, 1959) and is
a recommended supplementary reading. The Hesseltine excerpt, reprinted here in
full, has been taken from pages 64–70 of this volume.*

*William Hesseltine published in nineteenth-century American military,
political, and diplomatic history, particularly the Civil War era. His major books
included: Lincoln and the War Governors (1948); Third-Party Movements in the
United States (1962); and The Blue and Grey on the Nile (1961).*

In the common idiom, accepted alike by the professional historian and the
layman, the history of mankind is marked and measured by artifacts. The artifacts
are the tangible evidences of man's ingenuity, his craftsmanship, and his art. The
houses in which men lived, the tools they used, the materials which they mastered
and bent to their service are the conventional measures of civilization and progress.
We may classify the tools with which men met and mastered the problems of the
material universe, and from the classification identify the ages of man—the Stone
Age, the Bronze Age, the Ages of Iron and Steam, the Age of Electricity, and the

Atomic Age. The classification of "ages" and "eras" is, in fact, infinite. We may make the classification according to architecture, running the listings from the cave dwellings of Mesa Verde, through Romanesque and Gothic and Late General Grant to the complex and apparently insubstantial sheds of Frank Lloyd Wright. We may classify the "ages" of man by his means of transportation—the footpath era, the ox-cart age, the turnpike years, the canal boat period, the railroad age, the automobile era, and the airplane age. And not only do we classify, but we also measure civilizations in terms of the artifacts which they have used. By definition, "civilized" man has more, and more complex, artifacts than does the barbarian.

The universal acceptance of the artifact as the evidence of superiority or, at least, of greater desirability, has become an instrument in political and social progress. Commodore Perry leveled the artifacts of a "superior" civilization at the houses and palaces of Tokyo, "opened" Japan, and prepared the way for that train of events which led to the greatest of all demonstrations of the greatest of all artifacts at Hiroshima. History and legend are filled with stories of the "civilized" man displaying the superior artifacts of his culture—a watch, a compass, a spyglass—to primitive people and winning sometimes his own life and sometimes a moral, or even a material, victory.

One such case might serve to illustrate the point. It was in 1875 that an American officer, a youthful veteran of the great war between the states and then in the service of the Khedive of Egypt, set out from Gondokoro to journey to the capital of M'Tesa, the "king" of Uganda, far up toward the headwaters of the Nile. Lieutenant Colonel Chaillé-Long's expedition has been forgotten to history, and his record and deeds ignored through international rivalries. British interests in Africa preferred, for reasons of their own, to discount and to discredit Chaillé-Long, and to give the honor of visiting M'Tesa to their own man, Henry M. Stanley. Yet a full year before Stanley got into Uganda, Colonel Chaillé-Long had visited M'Tesa, had persuaded the monarch of Uganda to recognize the suzerainty of the Egyptian Khedive, had traveled on the waters of Lake Victoria, had explored an unknown section of the Nile River, and had discovered one of the lakes from which the great river flowed. It was an achievement of far-reaching consequences, and its significance for this discussion lies in the fact that it was accomplished largely by impressing the savage M'Tesa with the superior artifacts of a superior civilization.

Chaillé-Long prepared himself for the expedition by acquiring a music box which played "Dixie" and an instrument which he described as a "battery"—a shocking machine, which, turned by hand, was capable of delivering a slight electric shock to anyone holding its two metal terminals. In addition, he rode a horse, an animal unknown in Uganda, and for this purpose clearly as much an "artifact" as the battery and the music box, which could jangle a highly inappropriate tune. The instruments, properly displayed, did their work. Four thousand people swept the road over which the Great White Prince traveled from the borders of Uganda to the capital and gasped in astonishment when Chaillé-Long dismounted from his horse and proved that he was not a centaur. M'Tesa was pleased with the music box and properly shocked by the battery. Recognizing the superiority of a state which could command such artifacts, M'Tesa made a treaty acknowledging fealty to Ismail, the Khedive of Egypt, and promising full cooperation in opening his country, his lake, and his river to the trade and commerce of his powerful overlord.

But such a case, primitive though it may be in its setting, is not essentially different from the situation which prevails in the world today. The United States maintains "Amerika Hauser" in Germany, supports "cultural centers" in Latin America, and sends technical advisers to the lands of the Orient to demonstrate the superiority of American artifacts and, by implication, to assert the superiority of American civilization over that of American rivals and competitors.

Whatever might be the utility of such material competition in the political struggle, and however convenient it may be to classify the "ages" of man by the relics and remains of past civilizations, the objective historian might well wonder whether artifacts, whether ancient or modern, represent anything fundamental in the development of mankind. Did the transition from the Old to the New Stone Age or from the Stone Age to the Bronze Age—or, for that matter, from the Age of Steam to the Atomic Age—mark any basic transition in the mind of man? One can, of course, arrange the collected artifacts in a museum from the earlier to the later in date, from the simpler to the more complex, but does that amount to anything more than the imposition of the museum-keeper's concepts upon the inanimate objects in his custody? Or, to put the question another way and to bring the question into focus on the problem of the historian, is the artifact a useful, viable source for the understanding of the human past?

The consensus seems to be that it is not. Repeatedly writers on the subject of historical methodology have dismissed the artifact as "illustrative" rather than instructive. For the most part, be it admitted, they have done so regretfully, spending more time on the discussion of the meaning of artifacts than their conclusions would seem to warrant. Years ago Lucy M. Salmon scolded the historians for their failure to use the "sources" which surrounded them. In her *Historical Methodology* (1933) she devoted chapters to the "Record of Nature," the "Record of Archaeology," the "Record of Monuments," and the "Record of Language," but in the end she found that these various "records" were of little moment or significance. She quoted, with apparent qualms but nonetheless with approval, the conclusions of David G. Hogarth who wrote *Authority and Archaeology* in 1899. According to Hogarth, archaeology had distinct limits. It stopped "short of any possibility of truly reconstituting the picture of the human past: for to that end the literary documents are all essential." The desert sands, said Hogarth, "have given us specimens of almost every product of the ancient life of the Nile Valley, as readily to be recognized as on the day they were buried. We have all the material and circumstance of its life: only the life is wanting. . . . Unaided by any record of contemporary human intelligence which may inform him, not so much of what was, but of what seemed, the student of archaeology occupies a position not less external to the object of his studies than an astronomer observing a star. For the relation of the circumstances of life to life itself he can only draw on his subjective experience acquired beyond a gulf of time or space.''

Still later in the list of those writing on historical methodology is Allan Nevins. In his *Gateway to History*, Nevins discusses material remains and such ''representational material'' as chiseled stones, stamped coins, woven tapestries, vases, and sculptures. For these things, and for restorations like Old Salem and Williamsburg, he has words of praise, but his commendations are weakened by his conclusion that material remains throw more light on social and economic history than on political history and are ''more valuable for the descriptive than for the analytical elements in history.'' As for coins, Nevins thinks that they might correct or supply a date, or furnish a conventional portrait of an ancient ruler or a divine creature, but their value to history ''lies simply in illustrating it.'' In the end, Nevins concludes that artifacts—the material remains of the past—are ''essential parts of the mass of evidence upon which historians must rely. They are important elements in the immense flood-system which drains the past for the benefit of the present, not to be ignored because they flow apart from what is today the great central stream of historical evidence, the written or printed word.'' Thereupon, Nevins ignores the minor stream.

Even more recently, Louis Gottschalk, writing under the rubric *Understanding History* (1950), came to essentially the same conclusions and with the same veiled reluctance. ''To be sure,'' says Gottschalk, ''certain historical truths can be derived immediately'' from artifacts. ''The historian can discover that a piece of pottery was handwrought, that a building was made of mortared brick, that a manuscript was written in a cursive hand . . . that sanitary plumbing was known in an old city, and many other such data from direct observation of artifacts surviving from the past. But such facts, important as they are, are not the essence of the study of history. . . . A historical context can be given to them only if they can be placed in a human setting. . . . Without futher evidence the human context can never be recaptured with any degree of certainty.''

Yet in each case, the writers on historical methodology have shown reluctance to conclude that artifacts are of minor significance. Artifacts, after all, are facts, and facts are the raw material out of which the historian constructs a narrative of the past. Moreover, artifacts have many things in common with the literary relics of the past. The documents, the letters, the manuscripts, the articles, and the printed books, which Nevins calls ''the great central stream of historical evidence,'' are also artifacts. They, too, are the handiwork of man. The paper upon which they are written, the ink marks upon them, even the conventional symbols which represent sounds and are combined into words, are as much artifacts as peace pipes, arrowheads, or war bonnets. On matters of external evidence, the area of identification which the historian has learned to call external criticism, the literary and the material relic go hand in hand. The historian may establish the fact of an artifact as readily and by much the same procedure as he can establish the external fact of the written word. He can reject the spurious document as readily as he can repudiate the "authentic" reproduction in an antique shop. He can detect forgery in literary and artistic form and establish, with reasonable certainty, the date and sometimes the maker of either a pothook or a postsherd.

It is, however, in the realm of internal criticism that the artifact differs from the fact derived from the literary remain. In external criticism, the historian "tells" things to the document or to the relic. He tells the age, the nature, the use of the artifact. He compares it with known relics, establishes its authenticity, and, when he cannot possibly imagine what function it served, he can accept the archaeologists' catch-all explanation that it had "religious significance." Then, having "told" things to the document, the historian "asks" it questions, and the literary relic, unlike the material artifact, replies. This, in the formal language of historical methodology, is internal criticism, and by it the historian extracts meaning from a document. He determines time and place and persons. He learns facts and opinions about a specific event. Out of the "answers" which the literary document gives, the historian may attempt a description and an evaluation of a past event. A series of documents furnishes information about causes and consequences, permitting the construction of a narrative of a historical process.

But the artifact, in contrast to the literary remain, gives no answers to the historian's queries. It contains no information which the historian may extract by the process of internal criticism. The battery which Chaillé-Long carried to M'Tesa of Uganda may still exist in the Ugandan National Museum. Some mechanically-minded curator may have restored it to working condition and safely locked it in a glass case where bus loads of Ugandan school children, slyly munching peanuts, may glance at it when a half-trained girl guide identifies it as the prehistoric ancestor of the Lake Victoria Power Plant. The music box may still, with only slight repairs, be capable of jangling the notes of "Dixie," but it appears, no doubt, in the musical exhibit to illustrate some phase in the evolution of the grand piano. The leopard skin mantle which M'Tesa gave Chaillé-Long may hang, behind glass, in the African room of some Baltimore museum, its spots changed by moths, its luster gone, and nothing about it conveying the sense of glory which once it gave to a proud beast of the jungle or to the Great White Prince who represented the majesty of the Khedive of Egypt.

On the other hand, in the Abdin Palace in Cairo there is Chaillé-Long's report on his mission to M'Tesa, and in the publications of the general staff of the Egyptian army it appears in printed form. In the Library of Congress and in the files of the *New York Times* are Chaillé-Long's contemporary letters. In two books and in numerous articles Chaillé-Long told the story, with sundry variations, of his trip to Uganda and of how his manipulation of the artifacts of a superior civilization brought M'Tesa to acknowledge the suzerainty of Egypt over Uganda. The literary remains enable the historian to construct a viable, probable account of an episode in what Chaillé-Long called "Central African Diplomacy." They give meaning and significance to the artifacts. But the artifacts alone convey no information, answer no question for the historian, carry with them no traces of the once important roles they played. The leopard skin on the museum wall and the battery and the music box in the show cases are as sterile and meaningless as the chords of "Dixie" once were in the Ugandan jungle. We have no technique of internal criticism which will extract meaning and significance from these mute and inanimate objects.

Herein lies the challenge of the artifact, a challenge which it offers to the archaeologists, the curators of museums, the keepers of the kitchenmiddens of civilization. By what means, by what processes of internal criticism, can these remains be made to divulge the parts they have shared in mankind's past? What questions can these walls answer? What, in fact, are the questions which they should be asked?

Perhaps, indeed, there are no questions which the artifact can answer. There are people masquerading as historians who contend that the human past is so complex, so inexplicable, so inflicted with innumerable factors, that its reconstruction is impossible. These people deny the possibility of determining causation or assessing consequences. They are content to establish facts, or a reasonable facsimile thereof, and to arrange them to illustrate some particular concept. For the most part their concepts are partisan, and they arrange their facts to illustrate a political bias. Insisting that all historical writing is selective, they select on the basis of moral or political preconceptions and arrange their facts with an eye to the imagined future instead of to the probable past.

Although such people arrogate to themselves the label of "intellectuals," they are essentially anti-intellectual. Fundamentally they are denying the capacity of the human intellect to penetrate the mysteries of human experience. Confused by the complexities of causation, they deny the possibility of assessing causes. Yet, to render their anti-intellectualism complete, they allege that they can influence the future by pressing their biased versions of the past. They are presentists, concerned with present issues and problems, selecting facts to illustrate their desired solutions, and fixing their eyes upon a future dream-world as improbable as their concepts of the historic past.

If the collectors and custodians of relics, the curators of the museums, the diggers into ancient mounds and once-inhabited caves are content to classify themselves with the anti-intellectuals, then they will continue to display their sterile artifacts in the showcases and to arrange their exhibits in such an order that they may advance some preconceptions, some bias, or some partisan point of view. If so, they will be like keepers of old car graveyards who supply parts to hot-rodders but make no contributions to the development of mechanics.

If, in other words, the artifacts of man's past serve only as illustrations, then they might as well be reduced to the conventional form of illustrative material— pictures. One could save building space and custodial care by taking stereopticon views of the objects in museums, tabulating the dimensions and other data on computer cards, filing the pictures and the cards, and discarding the junk to antique dealers or depositing it on the city dump. If objects have only illustrative value—serve only to enable bus loads of school children and station-wagon loads of picnickers to "visualize" some irrelevant fragment of the past—then historians can make no use of them and historical agencies, whose primary purpose is to advance the study of history, should cease wasting money and manpower on them. If the museum performs merely a "teaching" function, then the custodians of what used to be called the "cabinets" should assemble with the educationalists and form themselves into a branch of the National Education Association.

There is, however, another alternative—the alternative of meeting the intellectual challenge of the artifact. Artifacts are historical facts, and as facts they should be as meaningful to the historian as the facts derived by the internal criticism of literary remains. It is in this meaningful relation that the facts of the historian differ from the facts of the antiquarian. The antiquarian collects facts much as the museum curator collects artifacts—for themselves. He displays them, much as the suburban housewife displays her antique furniture—for their patina, their lines, or their design. The historian, however, gathers facts for their meaning and for their utility in reconstructing a viable narrative of mankind's past. The facts which he gathers have relationships with one another; they present cause and effect, event and consequence, situation and response. They are not sterile items displayed in showcases, but useful tools by which he can recapture some meaningful portion of human life on the earth.

It is because he seeks meaning that the historian looks longingly at the artifact, wishing that the processes of internal criticism would enable him to extract meaningful information from it. Reluctantly he turns away. The relics—the batteries, the music boxes, the leopard skins, the peace pipes, even Daniel Webster's very own two-horse carriage or the glistening 1913 Ford that will still run under its own power—are merely illustrative material suitable for school children, teaching devices of dubious merit that properly belong in the Department of Methods, School of Education, two-credit course numbered 174.

But plaintively the historian turns to the curators of the cabinet with his query: how can these artifacts be made into historical facts? By what critical method can they be examined? What internal evidence can they produce to aid in the search for historical truth? It is the essence of anti-intellectualism to say that these walls cannot talk. Of course they can talk. It is only that we cannot talk to them, cannot ask them questions, and cannot understand the answers. But until artifacts can be subjected to internal criticism and made to bear their witness, the task of historical methodology is unfinished.

4

Manuscripts and Manufacts

by Wilcomb E. Washburn

Introduction

To the question "American studies—words or things?" John Kouwenhoven answered objects. William Hesseltine championed words. In the following essay, Wilcomb Washburn, an American historian who has worked at the Smithsonian Institution in many capacities, insists on both as "the companion keys to the past." Washburn's thesis is simple, yet persuasively argued: in order to understand a manuscript one must have knowledge and patience; in order to comprehend a manufact (his term for material culture evidence that aptly illustrates the common etymological ancestry of artifacts and manuscripts), the same demands must be met.

Washburn's observations were initially directed to archivists, collectors, and scholars particularly interested in gathering, identifying, and preserving past verbal evidence. In fact, this essay has been excerpted from a longer study that was first read before the Manuscript Society in 1963 and published in the official journal of the Society of American Archivists, The American Archivist 27 (April 1964): 245–250. Washburn rightly blames his fellow historians for using material culture only marginally in their research and teaching, thereby causing libraries and even museums to neglect collecting such data in any truly systematic, scholarly fashion. He is also anxious to break down the barriers that have existed between museum personnel, who superintend the majority of artifact collections in this country but are often not conversant with the most recent trends in historical research, and university-trained scholars, who, more often than not, have no understanding of standard museological practice or curatorial perspectives on artifacts. Curiously, a similar tension does not appear to exist between archivists, who deal primarily with verbal documents, and traditional historians, who base most of their studies on such written sources.

The essay below also seeks answers to some of Hesseltine's reservations about the use of artifacts by historians. To the latter's inability to see the applicability of material culture evidence to political history, Washburn suggests several genres of objects (presidential china, election campaign buttons, and so on) that might be deployed and even offers an example of his own historical scholarship on the topic. He likewise reiterates a theme proposed earlier by Kouwenhoven that artifact study is one way of overcoming the inherent elitist bias of most literary remains that are the product of that small minority of people in the past who could write. A parallel observation is that material culture evidence is the historian's earliest evidence, predating the invention of writing, and therefore possesses the oldest historical pedigree as data.

The essay, moreover, briefly alludes to two approaches within the broad range of artifact studies that have surfaced since World War II: experimental archaeology and cultural symbolization. One is reminded by Washburn's allusion to the impact of reconstructed artifacts at Jamestown, Virginia, of the current archaeological technique, cogently summarized by John Coles in Archaeology by Experiment (1973), where material culture evidence from archaeological remains can be amplified and historical insights can be gained by reconstructing and testing models of equipment and work processes formerly used in transport, in food preparation, and in technology. American Studies scholarship has long been interested in a "myth and symbol" approach to American cultural history. A selection reprinted below in Part IV by Joseph Trimmer shows how Washburn's claims for the use of artifacts in this methodological context are viable.

Wilcomb E. Washburn is the author of The Governor and the Rebel: A History of Bacon's Rebellion (1958), the editor of a documentary volume, The Indian and the White Man (1964), as well as editor of the Proceedings of the Vineland Map Conference (1971) and The Indian in America (1974). As this volume's bibliographical essay shows, he has also written extensively in scholarly journals on museology and material culture. He currently serves as director of the Office of American Studies at the Smithsonian Institution in Washington.

I should like to discuss what I regard as the unjustifiable theoretical distinction between manuscripts and museum objects. This distinction is made primarily by university scholars in the humanities and in some of the social sciences, but unfortunately it is reinforced by some in the museum world who speak of a dichotomy between "idea-oriented" scholars and "object-oriented" scholars.

I would challenge the concept because I think it confuses the particular vehicle of an idea with the idea itself. The important distinction is not between the written word and the material object but between the specific fact and the general idea. The specific fact may be either in the form of a written document—a manuscript—or a material artifact or "manufact" (if I may be permitted to use an archaic term to demonstrate the close relationship of the artifact and the manuscript). The historian has an obligation to the specific before he plunges into the general, and it is this responsibility that unifies the manuscript and the manufact. Too often the historian wishes to skip the process of establishing the specific fact before he explains the general meaning. It is here that the real conflict exists.

Too often the university-trained scholar assumes that the manuscript in the library can tell him what happened, whereas the object in the museum can merely illustrate the fact. Let us remember, however, that the written word is the Johnny-come-lately of scholarship. The greater part of the history of mankind is "written" in the tools with which man worked and in the objects that he constructed. The manufact is the expression of the culture and activities of most of the world's early history and the archaeologist is its prime interpreter.

Manufacts have continued to be produced since the invention of writing and can be "read" in the absence of, or in conjunction with, manuscripts. Not only archaeologists, but historians, anthropologists, technologists, and others are interpreters of manufacts. These individuals often know many nonwritten "languages" (which are nevertheless means of expression) through their knowledge of the different classes, properties, and histories of manufacts, just as the traditional scholar knows many written languages that lead to an understanding of the varied manuscripts with which he deals.

The understanding of phenomena often depends upon a competence in handling both of these vehicles of expression—manuscripts and manufacts. Often, manuscripts must play a role subordinate to manufacts in the process of gaining and communicating knowledge. A manuscript describing the dimensions and price of a certain object can be invaluable to the museum scholar attempting to document a piece in his collection, but it can never express in its own right the beauty or ugliness of the piece. This can be "read" only in the piece itself by a mind trained to discriminate in these matters.

The few manuscript remains concerning the three ships that brought the first settlers to Virginia have none of the power to *represent* that experience that the reconstructed ships have, despite the imaginative assumptions made in building them. Anyone who has seen the Virginia ships at Jamestown or, better still, sailed in them on the Chesapeake Bay knows how forceful an expression of the meaning of a seventeenth-century sea voyage these objects are.

How forceful in revealing the tastes and characters of the presidents and their wives is the china selected for use in the White House! One has only to glance at the examples in the Smithsonian's collection to perceive the grace and dignity of the china of President Washington and some other early presidents, the unabashed experimentation of some of the late nineteenth-century china, and the cold formality of most of the twentieth-century china. Words cannot tell the story so well as the mute plates do.

Many other manufacts have a greater power to express meaning than their closest equivalents in the manuscript field. In the Division of Political History we are avid collectors of political campaign paraphernalia because we think that such objects are often more effective documents in the history of American political life than are political expressions conveyed through the medium of the written or printed word. Some of the banners in our collection evoke a more immediate political response than many reams of inscribed paper.[1] Our knowledge of the communication process is still too sketchy to enable us to judge with precision what is effective and what is not, but the power of symbolic representation—the field in which objects rather than words provide the means of communication—is vast and compelling. One need only think of some outstanding American political symbols—the log cabin, the rail-splitter, the full dinner pail—to become aware of the fact.

If the manuscript and the manufact are equivalent in meaningfulness, why has the manufact been comparatively ignored and slighted in the intellectual world? I suggest that it may be the *use* to which the two sources of knowledge have been put. In the one case, manuscripts have been carefully collected by individuals and institutions for eventual use by the scholar, by whom they may be edited and published or otherwise used in the standard tradition of scholarship. In the other case, manufacts have too frequently been collected primarily for their public display value, not for scholarly use. Sometimes the distinction is not perceived by museum officials. Intent on filling museum exhibit halls, concerned with meeting what it conceives to be its responsibility to educate the public, the museum may often find a more ready justification for purchasing a specimen that will fill an exhibit need than for supporting a research project the scholarly results of which cannot be foreseen. I do not speak of specific museums in this connection but only of a subtle shift in emphasis—in some museums in this country—from a primary concern with uncovering new knowledge to an attempt to communicate existing knowledge directly to the general public. Of course, some museums both increase knowledge and communicate existing knowledge, but not all.

We can all remember the old days of manuscript collecting, when a signature would be neatly cut out and preserved although the body of a letter would often be discarded. Something of the same spirit is evident when one continues an archaeological excavation only to the point at which sufficient "show" objects have been obtained. Few reputable institutions would impose such limitations, but the gap between reputable institutions and irresponsible "pot hunters" is not completely void. Both the manuscript and the manufact have their public or "show" function, whether in the form of a quotation from an original document in a popular secondary work or in the form of an object in a museum display case; but to serve also for scholarly purposes these objects must be collected fully, examined thoroughly, and interpreted accurately before they are allowed to reach the general public.

It has always been possible to confuse the outward form of a fact with its essential meaning. The student confuses the passing of an examination with the acquisition of knowledge. The advertising man concentrates on the external indications of success rather than upon the internal components. When the museum has sought to acquire and to satisfy a mass market, it has sometimes confused the ends its manufacts were meant to serve with their external, publicly perceived form. While the manuscript has remained the building block of the literary historian who has conveyed its meaning to the public in a second step, the manufact has too frequently been placed in the hands of the display artist for direct transmittal to the public. True, these objects have been "interpreted" by carefully prepared labels, but these labels are frequently ignored or casually sampled.

To understand a manuscript one must have knowledge and time; to understand a manufact demands the same requirements. Neither knowledge nor time, however, is necessary to see a manufact. The museum visitor is encouraged to see and to understand, but little concern is shown when he fails to understand. The negative effects of misunderstanding are not usually assessed. Shortening labels, making exhibit cases more attractive, and creating special lighting effects may bring more visitors to see an exhibit, but whether these measures create more understanding is often difficult to know. The total amount of understanding in a crowd of a thousand spectators at a new exhibit may be less than that in a handful of people viewing an old exhibit. It is easy to confuse the symbols of success with success itself.

It may be that the curator of manuscripts has been saved from the problems facing the curator of manufacts through no virtue of his own. But whether or not credit should adhere to him personally, his rigid concern with seeing that the written record of our past is used for scholarly purposes as well as for popular purposes should be an example to curators of those companion keys to the past—manufacts.

5

The Use of Objects
in Historical Research

John T. Schlebecker

Introduction

A question posed early in the following essay—do objects make any real difference in the study of history?–haunts much of the theoretical literature on material culture research. John T. Schlebecker's answer to this perennial concern is modest: "Sometimes," is all he will claim. As did Washburn and Kouwenhoven, he calls our attention to the many ways by which literary evidence can be extremely misleading to historians and how objects can sometimes disprove historical interpretations based solely on documentary data.

Artifacts, like documents, he rightly insists, can likewise be misleading and even bogus. Schlebecker aptly illustrates this important point with a cogent discussion of how replicas, fakes, and two-dimensional representations of objects (35mm slide transparencies, photography, and Xerography) can distort the meaning of three-dimensional objects. He also cautions anyone trying to do historical research with artifacts to remember two major research problems still facing the material culture studies field.

First, artifact collections are scattered all over the world in all types of institutions, museums, historical societies, and archives, and yet accurate material culture research usually requires a comparative approach to the subject, such as Schlebecker has done in his analysis of farming implements in both eighteenth-century England and America. Second, in addition to artifact collections being scattered everywhere, the objects that they contain are filed or classified in many different ways, and many are not categorized at all. As yet no commonly accepted scholarly apparatus is widely used for identifying an artifact within a collection so that another scholar can quickly find it and thereby evaluate the research done by a colleague who used it as historical evidence.

Go to the original source! Lift it! Hold it! Inspect it! Try it out on your own!
These imperatives about studying artifacts echo throughout the Schlebecker
argument for seeing, touching, testing, and using objects as historical data.
Impressive scholarly precedents exist for such an approach, he suggests, including
the admonitions of Polybius and Herodotus. Persuaded as he is that the study of
history is simply the adding of vicarious experience to actual experience and
thereby expanding and enriching it, Schlebecker sees artifact study as helping
historians do this more accurately and effectively.

It is no accident that the examples we find demonstrating this point (such as
using objects to investigate the way early agrarian implements worked, which manual
labor farm tasks were most difficult, and so forth) are from agricultural history. In
addition to this historical subfield, Schlebecker's research interests include an area
of material culture study—particularly as institutionalized by the Association for
Living History Farms and Agricultural Museums (ALHFAM) and its annual
publication, ALHFAM Proceedings—that has pioneered in involving visitors in
hands-on, direct contact with objects in historical museum environments as well as
careful research in experimental archaeology and replicate agrarian work
processes.

Schlebecker, a past president of ALHFAM, urges the material culture student
to see objects in a larger cultural context as well. For example, having empirically
compared American and European farm implements, he notes that Americans
always made a tool as strong as it had to be but no stronger, as heavy as it had to
be but no heavier. This technological tradition partially accounts for the way that
Americans came to pre-eminence in the invention and development of much
aerospace engineering, from the airplane to the spaceship.

The following essay appeared originally in Agricultural History 51 (January
1977): 200–208. In addition to being an extremely active member of the American
Agricultural History Society, publishers of Agricultural History, and ALHFAM,
John T. Schlebecker has contributed numerous monographs to American material
culture studies including: Cattle Raising on the Plains, 1900–1961 (1963); History
of the American Dairying Industry (1967); an excellent survey, Whereby We Live: A
History of American Farming, 1607–1972 (1975); and a standard reference work,
A Bibliography of Books and Pamphlets on the History of Agriculture in the
United States, 1607–1967 (1969). He is currently chairman of the Department of
Industries at the Smithsonian Institution, Washington, D.C.

When the old farmer first saw the giraffe, he declared, "There ain't no such
animal." Historians tend to a similar cast of mind. They seem willing to believe
almost anything as long as it is not three-dimensional.[1] One prominent agricultural
historian, while holding an authenticated Roman scythe, asserted that the ancient
Romans did not have scythes. He pointed out that he had never encountered refer-

ences to scythes in the literature. A thing could not exist unless it had been written about.

Most professional historians not only do not use, but do not know how to use, three-dimensional evidence. Historians disagree with this statement—visions flit through their minds of Grecian urns, fallen statues in antique lands, and stone sickles from Jarmo in Iraq. Most scholars have only seen pictures of these things. Furthermore, few of them value simple things nearer to the present and to home. A John Deere plow of 1838 also has its secrets to reveal, especially when tested metallurgically.[2]

On the other hand, expertise in archaeology and metallurgy requires more training than historians can usually achieve. Some, of course, specialize in these fields, but most do not. Most importantly, historians should be able to use artifacts and objects while employing only those skills which ordinary people have. Regardless of the field of history, scholars can make important use of things in addition to their use of documents.

Obviously, historical evidence must be used critically, and objects are evidence. People who would never think of using Arthur Young's *Travels* as evidence of farming methods in South Carolina will cheerfully accept a seventeenth-century Welsh plow as evidence of the kinds of plows used in America a century later. The object, like the document, must be of the right time and place.

A replica, if properly made, can sometimes substitute for the real thing. John Froelich's tractor, which the Deere Company reconstructed from plans and descriptions, provides impressive evidence about the tractor, even though the real machine disappeared years ago. The same may be said of the many replicas of Cyrus Hall McCormick's 1831 reaper. In 1931 International Harvester had many of these replicas made, and they seem to have spread all over the face of the earth. As antiques they are worthless, but as working machines of true proportion and detail, these replicas are nearly as good as the real thing. The use of replicas presents no more problems than using the Force Transcripts or the Sparks Transcripts for documents which have subsequently disappeared. In fact, full-scale replicas, or even small models, are probably less objectionable than microfilm or Xerox copies of documents.

Microfilm gives no accurate idea of the size of the documents; the Elephant Folio of Audubon and a drugstore sales slip can show up as roughly the same size. Both microfilm and Xerox fail to show changes in the color of ink, which may be important in corrected or altered manuscripts. This failure can be especially dangerous when the changes were made in the same handwriting, but possibly at different dates.

Small models of objects have some advantages in that complicated details of operation or construction appear clearly, while the student encounters no great danger of losing fingers, legs, or life.

Objects, like documents, can be fraudulent. The Donation of Constantine, or the recent Vinland Map, have their three-dimensional counterparts. People keep finding stone moldboard plows which turn up from time to time. They bring them to the Smithsonian convinced they have evidence that pre-Columbian Indians used plows.

Any successful fraud must fit into all the other known facts. The fraud cannot drastically alter our understanding of the past because it will receive exhaustive scrutiny. Real evidence can usually stand close examination. The Vinland Map seemed plausible because it fitted fairly well with the Norse and Icelandic sagas, and with some certified archaeological evidence. The map was neither here nor there as evidence; it merely made the perpetrator a little money. Similarly, any plow purported to have belonged to George Washington must closely resemble other eighteenth-century Virginia plows. In short, there is not much to fear about fraudulent objects, because they are either very nearly correct or are obviously fakes. Since homely objects have only low monetary value, fakers have few incentives to manufacture false implements.[3]

The question arises, however, why use objects at all? Why, particularly, if the historian has an abundance of documents? Well, why study the past? Many reasons for studying history have been advanced since Herodotus. Doubtless even beginners have reasons which satisfy them, and most reasons have something to recommend them. For one thing, the study of history can help add vicarious experience to actual experience. The student of history can land at Jamestown without fear of starving and visit Ford's theater without danger of being shot. To the experience of our brief lives we can add the discoveries made by countless people across centuries.

So with the use of objects. What the student can learn depends to a great extent on what experiences the examiner brings to the object, and also on what the observer wants to learn. Thus, individual reactions to things vary, but all can learn something from objects, just as all can learn something from history. When historians studiously ignore three-dimensional documents, they seem to do so because they cannot tell in advance what they might learn. They act as though the search for objects will lead to less certain results than the search for pieces of paper.

Do objects then make any real difference in the study of history? Sometimes. Seeing ordinary things often reveals a conceit historians find uncomfortable. Who has not said when visiting a museum, "I didn't know they had those things back then." Hardly any description of the Franklin stove leaves a correct impression of the invention.[4]

Seeing is not enough, however, and if at all possible the object should be touched, handled, and lifted. Clearly, a photograph will not serve because no one can manipulate a picture in the same way they can manhandle a thing. To know that a grain cradle weighs eleven pounds is not really as useful as lifting it and walking with it. Even dimension appears clearer when the object is seen. Other intangibles, such as balance and feel, which only muscles can really convey to the brain, require handling of the object. A shoe may look fine, and it may be the right size, but it still may not fit. The only way to tell is to try it on. Historical objects also reveal something in this way.

Verbal descriptions often fail to convey much of anything. Anyone who has assembled Christmas toys knows the problem, even when a drawing accompanies the words. A verbal description of how to tie a shoelace is virtually useless, although a diagram might make it clear. Patent specifications used to include drawings. Inventors apparently could not often accurately describe their contraptions. From the patent specifications for a cotton picker issued in March 1916:

> I claim as my invention:—
> 1. In combination in a cotton picker, the chains of slats carrying the picker, each slat having a vertical shaft with gearing thereon, picker spindles mounted on the arm and driven from the said gearing, a gear on the shaft on each slat, and a fixed rack meshing with the gear on its inner side adjacent the pathway for the plant, a fixed rack mesh with said gears on their outer side for reversing the picker spindles and discharges the cotton, rollers on the vertical shafts and a guard rail on the opposite side of the rollers from which the rack is located for holding the gears in mesh with the rack adjacent the plant pathway, substantially as described.[5]

Thereafter follow four more similar paragraphs. The machine so described is at one of the Smithsonian warehouses at Silver Hill, Maryland. Most people who see it can pretty well figure out how it worked.

Objects may make a difference as to how the story is told. Without profundities, consider a few of these discoveries which may yet make their way into historical literature. Eli Whitney supposedly began making interchangeable parts for guns at his factory in Connecticut. Edwin Battison of the Smithsonian brought together four of these guns and the parts were not interchangeable. So much for that. In the Nordiska Museet in Stockholm they have, or used to have, the stuffed remains of Gustavus Adolphus's horse. The horse and its furnishings allow something to be surmised about horse power in seventeenth-century Sweden. This can also be learned from the examination of horse skeletons, but most historians do not relate to bones as well as they relate to stuffed horses.

Horse power and effectiveness can be perceived to some extent by the examination of harness, especially if the harness is put on a horse. This requires the help of someone who can do this, but such help is not impossible to find. The Swedes disbanded their horse artillery after World War I, but they saved the harness. In World War II they decided to bring the horse artillery back, and they found that horses had increased in size very remarkably, because the old harness would not fit.

In this vein, ox yokes present interesting changes in oxen. The Iowa Living History Farm found that old yokes would not fit modern oxen, which suggested something about the comparative strength of the animals. Strange things happen in this matter, so caution is called for. In America, farmers usually trained draft oxen from calfhood, and they used training yokes to do this. The yokes increased in size as the oxen grew. If someone mistakes a training yoke for a work yoke, serious misjudgments about the size of old oxen would result.

Scythes, sickles, and cradles not only give an impression of weight, but if used a bit, give a clearer idea of farm drudgery. He who swings a cradle will learn why cradlers received more per day than ordinary reapers. In all of these implements, it is extremely informative to handle the implements made and used in America, and those made and used in Europe. More of this later.

Very often things have field modifications which the user added to the machine to do what was wanted. How can anyone truly grasp the changes that users made in machines without seeing the modified machines—the Fordson with a winch on the front and reapers with small changes from the original? In this sort of study it is possible to understand how changes in design and new inventions came about, and what these changes came to.

Plows tell a great deal about social attitudes and do this rather better than they show differences in soil or in the mechanic arts. A close comparison of plows of European and American manufacture shows some things which can be discovered no other way. Pictures will not do, nor descriptions; if they could do the job, historians would have discovered more sooner. In these matters, no one needs any expertise. The plow, lifted by its handles and rolled from side to side, tells its own story.

Objects deteriorate and disappear. Some things last almost forever. Fences come and go, but if possible, all agricultural historians should see a hedgerow. The plants in it live and die, but the hedgerow goes on forever, if undisturbed and occasionally renewed. So also do forests and prairies. No description really does a hedgerow, or a prairie, justice; they must be seen.[6]

Anyone trying to use objects in historical research faces three difficulties at once. First, one obvious impediment is that the objects are spread all over creation. The scholar has to travel thousands of miles to find objects. Still, Polybius (203–120 B.C.) noted that in olden times, when travel was difficult and dangerous, there might have been an excuse for not visiting the site of Hannibal's camp. But, he argued, nowadays when travel is easy and safe, serious historians should go where things are. It is asking a lot to ask an American agricultural historian to travel to the Frilandsmuseet in Denmark to see an 1857 McCormick reaper. It is asking a lot, but it is not, however, asking too much.

Second, as Herodotus and Marco Polo discovered, it is so very difficult to cite museum collections. Herodotus apparently visited museums and used what he discovered in them, but he just about gave up on trying to tell what he had done. Marco Polo did better on citations (in the text) but because even he had only a hazy idea of geography, he could not always say exactly where he saw something. He also faced the other common difficulty of this type of research: people tended not to believe him.[7]

Third, memory does play tricks, especially when we deal with objects. Selecting a bookcase or a coffee table for a special place without measuring can result in unbelievable errors. Words, written or spoken, can more often be remembered better than objects, or even events through which we have lived. As Dylan Thomas recalled, "I can never remember whether it snowed for six days and six nights when I was twelve or whether it snowed for twelve days and twelve nights when I was six." [8]

If memory has not played tricks, and if documentation is roughly possible, what do the objects reveal in any wide sense? They may throw more than a little light on larger events. At the outbreak of the American Revolution, for example, Europeans generally considered American farmers and farming to be inferior to European in technology and methodology. This value judgment may be suspended for a moment. American farmers, however, were unquestionably different, as a survey of their surviving implements suggests.

In general, American farmers used implements and tools which were less substantial and rather lighter than their European counterparts. However, American implements seem to have been adequate to the work imposed on them. American farmers usually had fewer and less specialized implements than did European farmers. Inventories of estates rarely showed more than two plows on an American farm, but often showed many shares and other plow parts. The American farmer usually wanted the least cumbersome implement that could be devised which would still do the job. Sturdiness and long life of the implement was of little or no consequence. In this casual attitude toward capital goods, the American farmer had already adopted a view of life which later generations made into a precept of behavior. It amounted to a lack of materialism in one sense: a farmer had better things to do with his life than to manhandle indestructible plows or construct everlasting fences.[9]

For the harvest, cradles, scythes, sickles, and hooks did the job, and by 1774 these were, to a surprising extent, already manufactured in volume to a standard pattern for a wide sale. It is difficult to say where the bulk of the items were made, but Pennsylvania seems to have been one source for most of America.[10] Mass production seemed to require standard forms, and variety took the form of farm-made handles and other wooden parts of the implements. The same was roughly true of plows, harrows, and various sorts of cultivators. Thomas Jefferson intended his plow design to serve as a guide for farmers. He aimed at uniformity, ease of manufacture, and maximum strength with the least possible weight and drag.[11] The metal parts were of heavy wrought iron, generally, rather than light, high-grade steel. Even so, the American implement was no heavier than it absolutely had to be.[12]

On the side, it may be that this tradition, already apparent on the farms during the American Revolution, carried on into other areas of endeavor. The Americans made a thing as strong as it had to be, but no stronger; as heavy as it had to be, but no heavier. This tradition may partly explain how Americans came to be pre-eminent in the invention and development of the airplane, and how Americans quickly outdistanced all others in space exploration.

Of course, the tradition also had its concomitant side of quick obsolescence and waste of resources. Anything which is only as strong as it must be for the task in hand will not be strong enough to last very long. Such a tradition, however, had the advantage of not producing those useless ruins and piles of junk by which the past strangles the present. Quick obsolescence also facilitates quick adoption of newer and more efficient devices.

For historians, actually trying out some tool, or replica, opens new insights because it is possible to discover how a tool was actually used.[13] A flail, for example, does not work as someone might think who just saw it. The rail-splitting contest held annually at Belle Grove, Middletown, Virginia, permits participants to discover how tools were used, and also allows them to see what the product was like. Such efforts also suggest what tools had to be used, or were likely to be used. Wedges, for example, rarely appear in inventories of estates and not often in the literature. Yet experience in woodworking indicates they had to be present in fairly decent numbers on every farm, and surely made up part of every pioneer's equipment.

One perplexing aspect of research is to come upon literary evidence which adequately describes a long-vanished device. Various sources offer evidence that eighteenth-century New England farmers pressed and baled hay, possibly before the Revolution. Yet, so far as I know, we have no idea of how the press worked, or what its final product was, except that it may have been bales of hay. Such bales apparently made up part of the American line at Dorchester Heights. How useful it would be if we knew what the press was like, because then we could figure what the product was like, and from that estimate its utility in the fortifications at Dorchester.[14]

Sometimes only the object can tell how it was made, and by inference, something of the maker. If the object was mass-made, and the object alone can usually reveal that, then a commerce can be assumed at both ends. A considerable commerce means there was money, if only of account. The quality of an object appears from the object; the quantity may appear in the records. Commercial farming on a considerable scale may be revealed by the quality and quantity of tools and household equipment.[15]

In the category of objects I might also mention the place. In general, whatever the field, seeing the places marvelously enhances understanding of the men and events. Bill Mauldin drew a cartoon showing Willie and Joe looking down from the heights after the battle of the Anzio beachhead. The caption reads: ''My God! Here they wuz an' there we wuz.'' [16] This sort of discovery should not by any means be confined to military or agricultural history.

After serving on many committees, I visited Independence Hall, and got, I thought, a better idea of what must have gone on at the Constitutional Convention. The visit convinced me that the work of committees is influenced by the environment where they meet. Old Polybius was probably right. Visiting the place of historical interest is not simply something that would be nice to do. Those who have had experience in these matters know that travel is, as Polybius insisted, absolutely necessary.

6

Culture, History, and Artifact

Steven M. Beckow

Introduction

This article cogently summarizes several of the themes that have reverberated throughout the previous arguments for artifact study as well as in the assorted models for material culture analysis discussed thus far. Its author, Steven M. Beckow, a cultural anthropologist who worked for a number of years at Canada's National Museum of Man in Ottawa, is exactly the type of museum professional that E. McClung Fleming had in mind when calling for new contributions on the theory of artifact study.

As will be quickly evident, Beckow prefers the term "artifact" to "material culture" in describing "the works of man." He does so not only because, like a good historian, he knows that the term "artifact" predates that of "material culture," but also because he finds the latter term bulky and subject to much misunderstanding unless precisely defined. Suffice it to note here that this debate over nomenclature has characterized, and no doubt will continue to characterize, scholarship using nonverbal sources as historical evidence. As argued in this anthology's preface, "material culture" currently appears to be the most frequently used label by English-speaking scholars, principally because it is a generic term, a collective noun that covers all of the disciplines involved in using physical remains of the past. Nonetheless, in reading any research in the field, the reader is well advised to seek out the author's definition of terms. Many scholars use the terms artifact and material culture as synonymous and interchangeable. Others, such as Beckow, do not.

He does, however, offer a succinct evaluation of the way material culture study should go on in history museums. In the first part of his analysis, he uses three concepts basic to anthropological research (culture, history, and artifact) and shows their applicability to museums, the major depositories (rather than libraries or archives) of much extant artifactual evidence other than architecture. Beckow then suggests and explicates a four-fold typology for classifying "the regularities and variations in human ideas, acts, and artifacts." In short, there are the four dimensions of human culture by which past cultural remains can be arranged: the formal, the functional, the temporal, and the spatial.

In the second part of his essay, Beckow further expands his thesis that material culturists, especially those in museums, should read and implement in their own writing and exhibitions the work of the major twentieth-century anthropologists (he calls them "cultural scholars"), including individuals such as A. L. Kroeber, Clyde Kluckhohn, Clifford Geertz, and Bronislaw Malinowski. In the author's estimate, the scholarship done by these thinkers is ranked among the major contributions to the corpus of material culture's theoretical literature. To demonstrate this point, he offers five axiomatic statements concerning artifacts and their significance for the historian be he or she a museum curator, a classroom teacher, or an undergraduate student. In advocating stronger intellectual ties between museum-based and and academy-based scholars, Beckow joins an increasingly vocal chorus in both types of institutions arguing for greater collaboration in artifact research. The reader will note that the selections throughout this anthology, especially in next sections on method and practice, are invariably from one of these two major constituencies of material culture research. Hence often it is useful to compare and contrast the different perspectives when both are used to research and interpret common material cultural evidence.

Steven M. Beckow's article first appeared in two parts in the Canadian Museums Association Gazette, the quarterly journal of the Canadian Museums Association, a major museum professional organization in Canada. The two parts were "Culture, History, and Artifact," Gazette 8 (Fall 1975): 13–15; and "On the Nature of the Artifact," ibid., 9 (Winter 1976): 24–27. Beckow is currently completing his doctorate in cultural history at the University of Toronto. At the National Museum of Man in Ottawa, he worked in the History Division, as both a cultural historian and as a research associate; he has also taught history and anthropology at a number of Canadian junior colleges and universities.

The intent of this paper is to look at the relation of cultural studies to museum work, examine the relation of museum work to the general welfare of the community at large, and discuss a number of broad approaches to certain museum functions. My point of departure will be to examine three concepts basic to research carried on in all human history museums—the concepts of culture, history, and artifact.

All Scholars in Human History Museums Study Culture

For those who feel uncertain about the nature of culture, the following interpretation may prove heuristic. Culture, whether considered as a continuum or a class of phenomena, may be seen as an organization of ideas, manifest in act and artifact (though consisting of neither), by means of which man experiences his world and takes purposive action. Of all the animals, only man experiences his world through his conceptualizations of it. The evidence of these material conceptualizations is the products (or objectifications) which he fashions by applying his ideas to his actions. Men create two products with culture: cultural behavior and artifacts. Culture is neither act nor artifact, but we can discover information about culture by working back from the acts and artifacts which are available for our scrutiny.

We say that culture consists of ideas alone because we are aware of certain constraints upon culture which only an ideological conception of it meets. For instance, culture must be transmissible from one human agent to another. The transmission process must leave the receiver with the knowledge to make, use, and value either the behavior or the artifact involved. We know that it is impossible to transmit behavior and artifacts from one generation to another, apart from the ideas which give them context and meaning; all that can be conveyed or communicated are ideas through which behavior patterns and artifacts can be manufactured, employed, or valued. Thus human culture consists simply of the ideas that men possess and use to understand their world. Only man demonstrates the capacity to fashion a cultural system; only man can manufacture meaning, or, as a team of scholars phrased it, "make sense". He organizes his ideas into categories like etiquette, technology, politics, medicine, religion, and philosophy. When we at museums engage in the interpretation of either acts or artifacts, our reason for engaging in the task is to illuminate culture—that is, to illuminate the ways of thinking and designs for living which men brought to bear on their total round of life.

In carrying out this type of examination, museum scholars undertake a historical inquiry. History has been defined as the study of human actions in the past, carried on by the interpretation of evidence, for the sake of human self-knowledge. That definition is so wide that it could be considered to take in areas of study like anthropology, folklore, linguistics, and so on. If we were to define anthropology broadly as the study of man, we might have used this alternate term as conveniently to describe the focus of museum scholarship. It matters little what general term we employ to indicate that human history museums are concerned with human actions in the past. Perhaps the phrase "cultural history," which has been widely accepted in both history and anthropology, will prove acceptable as a covering phrase to scholars in both disciplines. Whatever term we choose, it should be fairly clear that human history museums focus their attention on actions which have actually been completed or the products of these actions. For many years, anthropologists have had a conception of history which leaves outside its domain much which is undoubtedly historical. Many anthropologists feel history to be concerned with events through time; a study of events at one point in time has been deemed other than an historical undertaking. On the contrary, the sole constraint upon a historical study is that it concern itself with events which have actually occurred. Thus the historian would not concern himself with the metaphysical or the futuristic, except insofar as to study the thought and behavior of metaphysicians and futurists, or to examine the impact they had on their society and times. In all that he does, then, the historian restricts himself to things which have actually occurred.

Thus all scholars in human history museums are engaged in a form of cultural inquiry whose context is historical. Their purpose is to illuminate aspects of human culture—the ideas man brings to the experiencing of his world. This description applies to the museum-based linguist, genealogist, aesthetician, archivist, popular culturist, folklorist, archaeologist, ethnologist, or historian. Their study proceeds through the interpretation of a particular kind of evidence.

Cultural History Should Be Artifactual History

While it is true that much scholarly research is carried out by museums by means of direct observation of the behavior of certain human groups, the largest single task of museums will continue to be the preservation and interpretation of artifacts. Artifacts, quite simply, are the works of man. We are accustomed to think of artifacts as solid and conspicuous objects, but an artifact could be a beam of light aimed at a distant point in space, or a cloud of strontium-90 atoms raining down on the earth. Artifacts are produced, reduced, or reassociated by men acting in a purposeful fashion. A radio is an example of an artifact wholly produced by man. A gold ingot is an example of an artifact reduced through a process of refinement by man. And a circle of prehistoric hearth stones is an example of a group of objects simply reassociated by man. Each gives evidence of the human presence; each testifies to the existence of certain human skills and intentions. It is these skills and intentions which the museum scholars seek to recover through an interpretation of the artifact.

In the past artifacts have been regarded as "material culture." The phrase, however, obscures certain relationships if we consider culture to be an organization of ideas. The term "artifact," which predates the term "material culture," testifies with less equivocation to the fact that the object is an evidence or a material embodiment of human *artifice*, art technique, technology, or skill. Culture itself is ideological; it has no material component. Its products, however, are material. The fact has led certain theoreticians consistently to point out that artifacts are, not "material culture," but "material traces of culture." The obvious way to sidestep such a bulky term, nonetheless, is to employ the term which so effectively captures the very nature of the object, the term "artifact."

Thus we can now refashion our earlier statement, making it more precise, by saying that what unites museum scholars in human history institutions is the study of cultural history through the interpretation of artifacts. Whether we use photographs or maps, oil paintings or television transmissions, decorated easter eggs or stovepipe hats, we take the artifact in hand and oblige it to yield its meaning, context, and associations. And it is these aspects of the artifact which we communicate to the general museum-going public or the scholarly community in our displays and publications.

Cultural scholars, moreover, look at culture from a number of vantage points. Before discussing why, we should consider how. All cultural scholars ponder the regularities and variations in ideas, acts, and artifacts. When they search for regularities and variations, they are said to be looking at the formal aspect of culture. When they search for particular kinds of regularities and variations which are arranged according to purpose, end, or function, they are said to be looking at the functional aspect of culture. When they arrange their regularities according to time, they are examining the temporal aspect of culture; according to space, the spatial aspect. These matters may seem of little significance to us until we consider how various types of museums concentrate on one or two aspects of culture only. For example, a science and technology museum may focus only on those ideas under the functional heading which relate to man's attempts to control the environment. A ski museum may focus only on those ideas which have gone into the manufacture, use, and valuation of certain recreational objects; again the focus is dictated by considerations of end or function. There are other museums which concentrate on the temporal aspect of things: if they preserve evidence of fads (nonpersistent ideas), they are termed popular-cultural museums; if they preserve evidence of traditions (persistent ideas), they are termed folk-cultural institutions. Finally, all museums have some sense of territorial relevance; demarcating the boundaries of interest involves spatial considerations. There are local, regional, provincial, and national museums. All have definite spatial conceptions of their responsibilities.

Moreover, museum scholars, when designing exhibits through which to disseminate information to the general public, make extensive use of approaches founded upon these four ways of viewing culture. We communicate information about culture either through temporal-spatial, formal-functional, or temporal-formal displays. Temporal-spatial displays look at discrete events through recognizable time and space. They might be histories of a particular settlement in a discrete epoch, or biographies of individuals, or genealogies of clans. Whatever their particular subject, they are specific as to personalities, places, and time.

Formal-functional exhibits, on the other hand, stop the clock and look at the varieties of phenomena either at a single point in time or else through timeless dimensions. Such an exhibit does not focus on events as unique phenomena but as instances of a general type: they display forms or classes of events. An exhibition of the types of weapons used by man throughout human history, a display of all the things one can do with maple sugar, or a display of the varieties of decorative beadwork would be examples of formal-functional displays.

A temporal-formal display combines aspects of the first two. It looks neither at a single point in time nor at a timeless dimension. Nonetheless, though it follows events through time, the time dimension is not discrete as in temporal-spatial displays, but nondiscrete. We do not discuss the history or biography of an individual entity, but the progress or evolution of a form or class of events. That this type of display deals with forms reveals its relation to the formal-functional display. The elucidation of the evolution of steam power in Canada, the discussion of the progress of banking and finance in the last two centuries, or the treatment of the development of shipping on the West Coast would all be examples of temporal-formal exhibits. Each of these approaches involved different aims and methods. It is enough for us here to be clear on the nature of the differences among them and to be able to develop our exhibit methodology in accordance with the strengths and purposes of each approach.

These then are some of the general conceptual foundations of human history museum scholarship. The museum scholar has a particular and vital role to play vis-á-vis the public he serves. I might best suggest what that role is by comparing him to a therapist who works not with the individual but with the community. It is the museum scholar's task to give the community a sense of well-being and social-relatedness. The museum worker accomplishes this by illuminating the community's collective consciousness, its sense of shared identity. Just as the individual feels secure when he is aware of his antecedents and capabilities, so the community feels reassured when it is aware of its history and potential. The museum scholar contributes this reassurance through the displays and exhibitions setting out the facts of national development and common experience.

Museum scholars, however, serve not only the collective memory, but also the collective conscience. They generate not only an appreciation of certain events, they also argue for certain courses of action. Some museums increase an awareness of our multicultural heritage; others instill a sense of local, civic, or regional pride. Some remind Canadians of the necessity to protect the environment; others to look out for the interests of disadvantaged members of the community. The challenge is stimulating, but the responsibility onerous.

The Culture of Generations Long Since Vanished Is Manifest in Their Artifacts

Above I defined culture as an organization of ideas, manifest in act and artifact (though consisting of neither), by means of which man experiences his world and takes purposive action. Man generates culture by virtue of a power he has which is unique in the animal world. Man alone, in a continuous and accumulative fashion, bestows meaning freely and arbitrarily on things and events. When man bestows meaning on some thing or event, we call that meaningful thing a symbol. A symbol is something which stands for something else, and the connection is inherent neither in its form nor in its function. Man has arbitrarily bestowed that meaning upon it, and we must be able to find out about that meaning for the symbol's connection to man to be apparent. An example would perhaps make this clear. If we were strolling about the streets of Rome at the time of the Christian persecutions, would we be aware of anything unusual were we to see, chalked on the walls of a building, the outline of a fish? Would we say to ourselves simply that a rude artist had decorated walls with it, or would we know ourselves to be in the presence of Christian refugees thereby? To know that we were in the presence of Christians would require us to know the symbolic meaning of the drawing. The Greek word *ichthus* is made up of five letters which in Greek were used by early Christians to denote "Jesus Christ, Son of God, Saviour." A fish symbol alerted those *in the know* that Christians were about, that they were resolute and defiant in their determination to worship freely, and that they declared their presence boldly to those who wished them well or ill.

Thus the fish-drawing in that context served as a symbol—a vehicle of meaning, an evidence of human ideas or culture. The symbolic meanings by which men experience their world and take purposive action constitute an era's culture. When we study artifacts, then, we are studying what one anthropologist called "the symbolic transmutation of physical objects and environment into cultural artifacts." When we work with artifacts, we are not attempting to know them in their physical fullness, but in their cultural meaningfulness. The late Clyde Kluckhohn reminded us that a watch and lawbook "in themselves, are nothing but metals, paper and ink. What makes them important is that some men know how to make them, others set a value on them, are unhappy without them, direct their activities in relation to them, or disregard them."

Thus artifacts have a place in the world of man; they are simply part of the physical world of being, but also of the human world of meaning. When we look upon a human construction like the cathedral at Chartres, we know ourselves to be in the presence of human intentions and values given objective form. Chartres is made of stone and glass, to be sure, but, as Clifford Geertz points out: "It is not just stone and glass; it is a cathedral, and not only a cathedral, but a particular cathedral built at a particular time by certain members of a particular society."

Explaining artifacts exclusively by their composition and form has been termed by anthropologists the fallacy of reductionism. In committing it, we are saying that higher-level reality (in this case, the cultural) can be explained simply and fully in terms of lower-level reality (the physical). But this is clearly not so. A watch cannot be explained without references to ideas of time, converted motion, scheduling, and so on. Ideas are not physical but cultural realities, invented by men, exclusive to the human world, and used by men to understand things around them.

The function of a museum scholar or curator is to recover the ideas used by men to understand their world by preserving human artifacts and then by unlocking their meaning within their original contexts and with their original associations. Without cultural repositories to carry on this work, there would be in time no knowledge of human achievements and philosophies. All human scholarship, in the end, is traceable to information provided by materials stored in cultural repositories, whether museums in the narrow sense of specialized museums like archives, libraries, galleries, and the like.

Artifacts Form Man's Answer to the Problem of the Inaccessibility of Energy

Were man in Eden still, as the song goes, he probably would not have invented artifacts. In Eden, energy was universally accessible. Man had only to reach up to procure the pleasing fruits of the garden; spoilage, containment, and transportation were not problems; moreover man had no need to build an artificial environment to protect himself from the elements, whether that second skin was in the form of clothing or of shelter. Thus man's survival was guaranteed by a benevolent regime and his own efforts were superfluous.

But Eden is metaphorical. It suggests a state of grace where man is a perfect and natural animal, rather than a human and cultural animal. Outside Eden, energy is not universally and effortlessly available. Foods must be gathered or grown; they must be stored and transported; they must be prepared and served up. In all these processes, artifactual tools, containers, and implements are essential. Moreover, man himself must create a second, artificial environment to protect himself from inclement weather; his clothing and buildings are such a man-made outer wrapping. Bronislaw Malinowski put the human condition succinctly:

Man in order to live continually alters his surroundings. On all points of contact with the outer world he creates an artificial, secondary environment. He makes houses or constructs shelters; he prepares his food more or less elaborately, procuring it by means of weapons and implements; he makes roads and uses means of transport. Were man to rely on his anatomical equipment exclusively, he would soon be destroyed, or perish from hunger and exposure. Defense, feeding, movement in space, all physiological and spiritual needs, are satisfied indirectly by means of artifacts even in the most primitive modes of human life.

Obliged to solve problems of conserving the energy within him and procuring more energy from without, man invented tools and machines to give him more capabilities than his physical human inheritance allowed. This brings me to my next point.

Artifacts Extend Human Capabilities

Marshall McLuhan defined artifacts, or media, as "the extensions of man." The manner in which man solves his energy problems is to extend his natural powers by artifactual means through time and space. He extends his memory through time and space by means of computer memory banks, books, tape recordings, and photographs. He extends his eyesight through time and space by telescopes, x-ray plates, stellar photography, electron microphotography, radar, and sonar. He extends the range of his voice with drums, radios, telegraphy, telephones, microwave relays, and satellite relays. He extends the reach of his teeth and hands with spears, guns, harpoons, knives, saws, vice grips, arrows, lariats, and laser beams.

With this array of extensions, man can stand on the earth and look into space, listen to long-dead relatives he has never met, gaze on the visage of Egyptian pharaohs, or ponder his future with predictions and projections. No other animal is capable of such extension of its natural endowments. Museums, by preserving artifacts, record the ways in which man has extended himself through time and space.

Artifacts Serve Not Simply Human Needs but Also Human Values

Man is a being, but he is a human being. He is an animal, with the same needs as all animals, but his ways of solving these need-related problems are human or cultural ways. Man does not simply eat; he eats at appropriate times, in appropriate ways, and feeds on appropriate foods. What constitutes the appropriate is what is valued as being appropriate. Ultimately human values may override human needs, and the animal, fasting unto death or riding into the Valley of Death, may choose to kill itself. Thus our descriptions of various artifacts are double-barrelled, describing both need and value sides of the artifact. For example, we talk of a ceremonial cup, fancy dress, robe of state, or formal tea service, part of the label referring to need-related and part to value-related aspects of the artifact. When we illuminate the human skills, intentions, and values which are evident in the artifact, we are relating conceptions which have to do both with human needs and also with human values.

Artifacts Reveal Information about Human Culture in Their Forms and in Their Functions

The shape, size, color, mass, design, or form of an artifact is the aspect of it which our senses perceive first and immediately. We describe the composition of a tool, the settings of jewelry, the shape of a container, or the design of a stained-glass window. We know more about Greek culture if the amphora we are researching carries upon it inscriptions and drawings instead of simply a solid-color finish. We thus describe dimensions of embellishment or decoration as well. These formal aspects are one of our major sources of interpretive data. We know about the artifact, even in the absence of any accompanying explanation of it, by inferring things from its form.

We also know things about it by inferences we make from an appreciation of its function. Form is related to pattern; function to process. Form describes constant aspects of an artifact; function, variable aspects. A clay pot is a certain fixed structure (relatively speaking); it is sometimes filled with something, sometimes not. Its form is that of a pot; its function is to contain. Since the dawn of civilization, men have in general created artifacts with increasingly sophisticated forms and increasingly complex functions. This reflects, of course, the fact that man's predicament has become increasingly complex. He must now not only scratch furrows in the earth to grow his crops; he must also explore new areas of food growing and gathering, extending his reach to the bottom of the sea and into the atmosphere as well. He seeds clouds; he detects storms by use of satellites; he harnesses the energy in algaes; and he extracts petroleum from the sea and converts it also into food. His circle of life is constantly widening, and his call for more and more complex extensions of less and less adequate human capabilities is continually called for. Our task as museum scholars then is to match our vision of preservables with that of mankind in general of extendables. Nothing small or large is undeserving of a place in a museum somewhere. Computers, abacuses, and notched sticks are all problem-solving devices; each merits a place in the human memory.

Thus underlying the idea of an artifact is the idea of culture. We are all students of human culture, and our source of information is almost exclusively the human artifact. Artifact interpretation is one of our prime skills, hand-in-hand with skills of artifact preservation and display. When the dances all are danced and the problems all are pondered, we enter to gather up artifactual traces of human activity, and preserve the memory of what we did and how we did it in other ages. When we think on this, and consider the narrow range of artifactual repositories in the country, we might turn to assessing how well we are carrying out our responsibility to keep a record of the human presence and mind in our areas of competence or jurisdictions.

7

Folk Art

Henry Glassie

Introduction

Definitions are crucial to systematic thinking about any complex subject. Without precision in meaning and exactness in nomenclature, widespread misunderstanding often occurs in both the conceptualization and the investigation of a subject. Folk art, a major component of material culture study, has long been beset by such confusion. In the following essay, Henry Glassie sets out to bring clarity to this semantic morass and to offer his own definition of folk art.

In this extended attempt at a thorough definition of terms, Glassie reviews an assortment of labels frequently used to describe folk art: popular, naive, provincial, crude, primitive, unsophisticated, kitsch, and nonacademic. He finds all of them unacceptable in the task of ascertaining "the meaning behind the assertion that an object is 'folk art.' " Glassie rejects these notions about folk art because he maintains that folk art is not confined to a particular historical period, nor is it inevitably rural, nor is it without its own sophisticated structural and aesthetic principles.

Having suggested what it is not, Glassie proceeds to expand an initial working definition of folk art, "the traditional aesthetic philosophy that governs the selection, production, treatment and use of forms," in two ways: first, by tracing the historical development of folk art study and, second, by a detailed exegesis of the terms "folk" and "art." In his brief history of the awareness of Western folk art, William Morris is singled out as an appropriate role model for the modern material culturist studying folk art. In Glassie's estimate, Morris, more than any other nineteenth-century individual, originated and stimulated the interest in folk art and craft in English-speaking countries. To be sure, other people and events influenced the field, and he also cites twentieth-century activities such as the work of the Works Progress Administration's Rural Arts

Exhibitions, Holger Cahill's books and museum shows, and the writings of American folk art curators and collectors.

In Glassie's judgment, folk art collectors and curators have especially mistreated the terms *folk* and *art*. He consequently devotes the major thrust of his revisionist critique to showing how these interpreters fail to realize the true creativity of the folk artist and the role he and his art play in society. In order to demonstrate that the folk artist is neither naive, unsophisticated, nor crude, Glassie focuses on two related but separate propositions. He first defines the "art that is folk" and then explains the "folk culture that is art." Quoting aestheticians ranging from Sir Joshua Reynolds to Claude Lévi-Strauss, students of material culture from Franz Boas to Bernie Wise (a lower-Potomac waterman in Maryland), Glassie offers a pluralistic, culturally-based definition of American folk art that includes everything from New England gravestones to Puerto Rican santos, from hex signs on Pennsylvania barns to central-hall **I**-houses in southern Indiana.

By insisting that we must not study folk art on a museum's walls but rather in the historical-cultural context in which it originated, Glassie also offers the material culture student a conceptual framework for artifact interpretation. He maintains, for example, that since "the folk aesthetic can rarely be elicited directly, analysis of artifacts, behavioral observation, and ethnoscientific questioning are the means for its determination." One method of ethnoscientific questioning he has employed in his later material culture research on folk housing is structuralism. Adumbrated here in his discussion of Western folk art ornamentation and its repetitive usage of binary sets, he has made extensive use of the structuralist approach in a landmark study, *Folk Housing in Middle Virginia: A Structural Analysis of Historic Artifacts* (1975). Glassie's recognition of the simultaneity of the artifact's aesthetic and practical functioning in the work of industrial designers and folk craftspeople parallels a similar claim of Bruce Lohof, whose essay "The Service Station in America: The Evolution of a Vernacular Form" (see chapter seventeen) also operates from a structuralist perspective. Willard Moore's study "An Indiana Subsistence Craftsman" (see chapter eighteen) also supports Glassie's concern to relate folk art and folk craft.

Glassie concludes his essay in material culture theory with a practical injunction. If we tend to think that folk art has failed to survive into the modern world of mass production and mass consumption, he enjoins us to "search your room for artifacts that do not seem to be artistic but that, nonetheless, exhibit the repetitive and symmetrical aesthetic" that he maintains to be a universal principle of Western folk design. This repetitive-symmetrical aesthetic underlying such "modern" objects is actually a concrete manifestation of a traditional folk aesthetic.

Any serious student of American material culture must become familiar with the enormously insightful scholarship of Henry Glassie. Trained as a folklorist with special interests in cultural geography and the history of art, Glassie has *greatly influenced the training of others in the folklore departments at Indiana University and the University of Pennsylvania, where he currently teaches. His published work in the field of material culture studies has been equally important and includes: Pattern in the Material Folk Culture of the Eastern United States (1969); Forms Upon the Frontier: Folklife and Folk Art in the United States (1969), coauthored with Austin Fife and Alta Fife; and All Silver and No Brass: An Irish Christmas Mumming (1976). In addition to the essay reprinted here from Folklore and Folklife: An Introduction, ed. Richard M. Dorson (Chicago: University of Chicago Press, 1972), pp. 253–380, and the studies noted in the editor's introduction to Glassie's essay "Building Wood in the Eastern United States: A Time-Place Perspective" coauthored with Fred Kniffen (see chapter sixteen), two others deserve special notice: "Structure and Function, Folklore and the Artifact," Semiotica (1973): 313–351, and "The Types of Southern Mountain Cabin," in Jan H. Brunvard, ed., The Study of American Folklore (New York: Norton, 1978), pp. 391–420.*

The artifact, the object of material culture such as the crucifix or plow, simultaneously gives pleasure and serves some practical, social, or economic end. If a pleasure-giving function predominates, the artifact is called art; if a practical function predominates, it is called craft. These simplifications are less important than the complicated truth that all artifacts have more than one function, whether a single function is clearly dominant or not. The interior of a house is designed primarily to be used, and its function may be classed primarily as economic; its exterior is designed primarily to be seen, and its function may be classed as primarily aesthetic. The artifact is art to the extent that it is an expression of an intention to give and take pleasure, and it is folk art to the extent that the intention was esoteric and traditional. The artistic nature of a folk artifact is generally subordinate to its utilitarian nature so that most folk art exists within the immediate context of folk craft. The problem of folk art (as opposed to folk craft) scholarship, then, lies less in identifying specific forms and technics than it does in identifying the characteristics of the traditional aesthetic philosophy that governs the selection, production, treatment, and use of forms.

A History of the Awareness of Folk Art

Young William Morris saw the skies and streams running black. Agriculture had given way to industry: the cities, packed with rural immigrants, were becoming slums, shunned by middle-class suburbanites. Each Sunday found fewer people in church; each day found a bellicose government more committed to an anti-Russian stance. They were times of prosperity and intolerance. William Morris hated the times: he looked at the sky blanked with soot; he looked into the milky faces of the workers, locked into a mechanical routine; he saw the waste of labor and life, and looked for an alternative. In 1853, Morris, a child of romanticism who was reading Scott's Waverley novels by the age of four, began his studies at Oxford where he quickly became part of a brotherhood of artists who were comforted in mutual conversation on neomonastic possibilities and socialism, on the decline of art and being. In that year, John Ruskin published the second volume of *The Stones of Venice*, and its chapter, "The Nature of Gothic," provided Morris with the idea he needed to organize conversation into concept and action. Medieval Gothic art, Ruskin wrote, is seen as savage, but unlike the great styles that came before and after, it was not based on slavery: imperfect, it was noble and moral. The artist was laborer, the laborer artist, and the lesson holds for the present:

If you will make a man of the working creature, you cannot make him a tool. Let him but begin to imagine, to think, to try to do anything worth doing; and the engine-turned precision is lost at once. Out come all his roughness, all his dullness, and his incapability . . . but out comes the whole majesty of him also. . . . . It would be well if all of us were good handicraftsmen in some kind, and the dishonour of manual labour done away with altogether. . . . There should be less pride felt in peculiarity of employment, and more in excellence of achievement. And yet more, in each several profession, no master should be too proud to do its hardest work. The painter should grind his own colours; the architect work in the mason's yard with his men.[1]

The Middle Ages provided the alternative. Morris's friends, the painters of the Pre-Raphaelite Brotherhood, leapt the worldly and rationalistic High Renaissance to find stimulus in the spiritual intensity of Botticelli and Fra Angelico. Like his contemporaries who were similarly infused with the new romantic spirit and spent their leisure in the collection of ballads and Märchen, Morris became aware of the aesthetic energies of the Middle Ages found in works by Chaucer and the architect of Amiens cathedral—an awareness followed by the recognition of the local survival of humble medieval monuments and a hazy comprehension of the (somewhat degenerated) persistence of medieval sensibilities and talents among rural folksingers and craftsmen. In the same half decade that the Chaucerian scholar, Francis James Child, published *English and Scottish Popular Ballads* in the British Poets Series and that the analytical 1856 edition of the Grimms' *Kinder- und Hausmärchen* appeared, Morris and Company opened its doors. The craftsmen at The Company labored tediously by hand to produce works in the modern medieval taste: stained glass and oak furniture, embroidery, wallpaper, metalwork, tiles, carpets, jewelry, and tapestries. Morris called himself a designer, but his gentle upbringing did not keep him from the loom and dye vat; often mistaken for a laborer, Topsy Morris was the kind of artist Ruskin called for. His involvement with medieval art led him to study as well as practice; he was both a weaver and a museum consultant on antique textiles. In 1879, when the movement for folk museums was gaining momentum on the Continent,[2] William Morris founded the Society for the Protection of Ancient Buildings in England.

Whether composing poetry in the style of the ballad or marching in a Socialist demonstration, translating Icelandic sagas, complaining about urban sprawl, or designing the Kelmscott Chaucer, Morris provides us with an exquisite exemplar of the Victorian intellectual's rearview medievalism.[3] Product and producer of romantic radicalism, Morris was but one among many advocates of medieval revival (and he was no more influential than his friends John Ruskin and Dante Gabriel Rossetti), but more than any other he originated and stimulated the interest in "the lesser arts," in folk craft and art. Morris's scholarly inclinations limited the freedom of his creative practice, but his ambiguity of role allowed others, stimulated by the arts and crafts movement that flowed from his genius, to move in either an artistic or a scholastic direction. On the Continent, the progressive artists rejected the arts and crafts historicism, but accepted its emphasis on craft and naturalistic decoration; as a result art nouveau is the only movement in western art since before the Renaissance noted as much for its furniture and jewelry as for its painting and sculpture. The serious interests of the personalities of the arts and crafts movement were compatible with other antiquarian aspects of the romantic nationalism of the period. In different western countries collectors rummaged through the countryside, and the museum became a repository for collections of old folk artifacts, a source for revivalistic designers, an escape for careworn workers and, on the Continent and especially in Scandinavia, where the folk museum idea was born, a center for research on the history of artifacts. Before the end of the nineteenth century, nationalistic pride in old things as mirrors of a country's development had jelled and had become the dominant motive for the collection, preservation, and reproduction of folk artifacts. In the late 1880s, at the time that the American Folklore Society was founded, the American authors of popular books on architectural design, though still inveighing against the old-fashioned "barnesque style of Architecture" and still recommending elaborately ornate English, French, and Swiss folkishly romantic designs, were beginning to accept the "Colonial"—American romantic— as an important modern style.[4]

The interest in the folk artifact developed apace with romantic nationalism, receiving official sanction in the 1930s—in Nazi Germany and depression America. While Thomas Hart Benton and Ben Shahn were celebrating folklife in paint and the Works Progress Administration was funding ballad collectors,[5] artifacts were being assembled for the Rural Arts Exhibition held at the Department of Agriculture in 1937. The interest of the governmental handicrafters was more in therapeutic and economically rehabilitory utilization than in scholarship, and, like the English arts and crafts movement, it involved the invention, diffusion, and alteration—"improvement"—of crafts as well as their preservation; still, the exhibit was a major impetus for the spread of interest to contemporary craft. At the same time that the New Deal's "rural-handicraft movement" was endeavoring to democratize the concept of art, exhibiting new quilts and baskets as if they were Old Masters,[6] others were hunting for lower-class art that paralleled that of the wealthy—in short, for paintings and sculpture. Serious American collectors had been producing books on the "decorative arts," such as furniture and silver, since the turn of the century, but it took the egalitarian 1930s to produce the seminal book on American "folk art," Holger Cahill's *American Folk Art: The Art of the Common Man in America, 1750–1900.*[7]

There are now many museum exhibits and many big books devoted to "folk art." There is material to study, but no theories have been developed to enable that study. Neither the Congrès international des arts populaires held at Prague in 1928, nor the symposium on folk art in *Antiques* magazine in 1950 came near a satisfactory definition of folk art. One of the most knowledgeable scholars on folk art, Robert Wildhaber, director of the Museum für Vokerkunde and Schweizerisches Museum für Volkskunde, could state recently that for the field of folk art (unlike many other areas of folk cultural research) "a definitive scientific study still remains to be written." [8] The concepts useful in determining what folk art is do exist, but they exist outside the thinking of the compilers of most folk art collections. They exist in writings on art by art critics and historians, aesthetic philosophers, and artists; they exist in writings on the means and manners of cultural expression by folklorists, anthropologists, and linguists.

It would be easy to dismiss the writings of "folk art" collectors with exactly the adjectives they apply to the materials they study: naive, provincial, primitive, crude, unsophisticated, and nonacademic.[9] Some of their notions must be discarded because "folk" is not one "style" of art, folk art is not confined to a certain historical period, folk art is not inevitably rural, and the subjective evaluation of an alien academic is of no worth in a scientific study. If, however, we assume a compassionate, cultural-relativist posture, we will discover in the vague writings on "folk art," and its conceptual companion "country furniture," [10] a set of notions that are consistent with more rigorous thinking.

Both of the words, folk and art, have been mistreated. The adjective "folk" when applied to an object provides specific information about the source of the ideas that were used to produce the object. Saying of an object that it is "art" provides information about the intentions of its producer. In order to expose the meaning behind the assertion that an object is "folk art," the words will be treated serially below.

Art That Is Folk

The ideas that the artist puts into action to create an object can be classified by the relationships they bear to the cultural norm that receives overt and massive support from the agents for economic, religious, and political stability. With regard to this public culture, some of the ideas in the artist's mind may be considered conservative, some normative, some progressive, or, in the usual terms of the folklorist, folk, popular, and elite (or academic). If the idea was, when expressed, conservative, the resultant object, the song, story, or sculpture, can be called folk. Saying that a thing is "folk," then, implies that the idea of which it was an expression was old within the culture of its producer and that it differed from comparable, contemporaneous ideas explicitly advocated as the popular culture of the dominant society. That means that the folk object is like the elite object but unlike the popular object in depending for its existence upon local or individual patronage (although the time depth of the networks linking localities can enable a folk idea to achieve numerical dominance). It means also and most significantly that the folk object, unlike the popular and elite object, is not part of rapidly changing fashions; the establishment of the folk nature of an idea is the demonstration of its persistence through time. The artist may or may not be aware of the fact that his idea is folk; his conservatism might be self-consciously archaic and nativistic, or it might be the only way he knows: the folk artist's usual answer to an inquiry about the logic of his *métier* is, ''Well, how else would you do it?''

The division of culture into folk (conservative), popular (normative), and elite (progressive) is often treated as if it carried socioeconomical validity. Although considered to be ''levels of society,'' these abstract distinctions are most useful when thought of as opposing forces having simultaneous existence in the mind of every individual, though one or another of the modes of thinking may predominate in certain individuals or in the groups they combine to form.

Against this background, we may examine the ''folk art'' collectors' adjective, ''naive.'' In getting at their meaning it is useful to recognize that their studies have been tempered by historical concepts of connoisseurship and style. By style they mean a subjectively determined assemblage of artistic features that fits into a chronological sequence, or, more or less, the elite and popular aesthetic of a distinct period. The works displayed in a ''folk art'' gallery are called ''naive'' because (1) they do not fit into a ''style''; (2) they represent a single ''style'' incompletely; (3) they represent a mixture of ''styles''; (4) they represent an apparent imperfection of execution within a ''style.''

These distinct connotations of ''naive'' provide a series of possible relationships between folk and nonfolk impulses. The first case is the object produced out of ideas that are unrelated to those of the contemporary popular and elite dominant cultures. These ideas may have originated in primitive, nonliterate cultures. Primitive art was once easily separable from western folk or elite art; today most art is produced within the socioeconomic frame of the West and phenomena like African airport sculpture and modern Navaho rugs are folk art. Of the ideas within western folk art, some are of such ancient origin—an antiquity provable via archaeology—that there is no way to relate them except within the folk tradition, while others are ideas of elite origin and popular dissemination that thrive within the folk tradition, although they are outmoded and have lost their mass support.

The action of the western folk artist usually results in a new artifact that closely resembles an old one, since the artist who deviates from known and accepted sources can jeopardize his status.[11] While the elite artist may be willing to risk his standing to appear ahead of his times, it is only a rare folk artist who strives for innovation; his replication is an affirmation of a tradition. This does not mean that the folk artist is an exacting copyist or that there is no margin for variation within folk tradition. From his perceptions of a number of similar artifacts, the folk artist abstracts a structural concept that is a minimal description of the form of an object, containing a specific relationship of components without which the object would not be the object—without which a bench would not be a bench. From his perceptions he abstracts, as well, a small set of rules that define the limits within which he can modify the concept according to his taste and talent and the taste and pocketbook of his client. The long benches in the kitchens and on the porches of Pennsylvania German farmhouses, for example, are basically the same, except that there is a traditional tolerance for the elaboration of the ornamentation of the legs, the fronts of which vary from straight to complex combinations of C-scrolls. The mental process of abstraction not only enables variation within a tradition, it facilitates creativity. When a new idea is presented to the artist he does not have to reject or accept it completely. Through the process called *bricolage* by Claude Lévi-Strauss,[12] the new idea is broken down and compared with old ones, and a composite idea is developed to suit the artist's psychobiological nature and his social and physical environment. The novel synthetic idea may be a compromise of fashionable and unfashionable ideas; its result may be seen by the folklorist as partially folk and by the art historian as an incomplete expression of a "style" or as a mixture of "styles." In mid-eighteenth-century Lancashire, for example, a common piece of furniture was an oak settle with up-to-date "Queen Anne" cabriole legs and padded seat and outmoded "Jacobean" arms and wainscot back.[13] A horizontal line imagined through the settle would separate it neatly into its seventeenth-century upper half and eighteenth-century lower half. Since pieces of the kind were made later than the date of origin of their newest elements, their older elements were out of style and traditional—they were folk. While the settle is a simple example, the mental dynamics of *bricolage* allowed for very complicated synthesis of old and new ideas.

Most of the "naive" paintings hanging in "folk art" galleries are there because the curator considers them to be "untrained" but "expressive" attempts at illusionistic representation. Generally the curator distinguishes only between academic and nonacademic art;[14] "folk art" becomes then a category for art works that are substandard but charming. These "folk paintings" are either good expressions of a popular style that has limited appeal to the modern curator because it lacks elite analogues, or poor expressions of a popular style that are appealing because of an accidental similarity to modern art, or they may even be folk art.

Huck Finn at the Grangerfords' provides the modern reader with a flood-lit view into the home of a mid-nineteenth-century carrier of the popular culture. Huck was impressed with the mass-produced hardware and clock, but the art in the neoclassical-maudlin mode gave him "the fan-tods." One picture was of "a woman in a slim black dress, belted small under the arm-pits . . . and she was leaning pensive on a tombstone on her right elbow, under a weeping willow, and her other hand hanging down her side holding a white handkerchief and a reticule."[15] Such pictures were painted and stitched by girls under the watchful scowl of a teacher. Schoolgirl exercises of the sort are found in most "folk art" collections,[16] although they are clearly examples of popular rather than folk art.

The gallery's walls are lined with portrait and genre scene, landscape and still life. Using the same kind of thinking that generated the communal theory of ballad origins, the "folk art" curator occasionally supposes that the untutored geniuses of his imagination independently invented the varieties of realistic painting. It took centuries of labor by the best of western minds to isolate landscape and still life as distinct pictorial types, and, as the critic Clement Greenberg has pointed out, "it is highly unlikely that a 'naive' artist would have ventured upon pure landscape or still life without being encouraged by precedents." [17] The precedent for the naive painter was the same as that for the sophisticated painter; they had the same sources, produced the same popular art. The difference was that naive painters were people who, in Joyce Cary's term, had difficulty closing the mind-body gap—they were children or adults of limited talent.[18] Most of the naive paintings produced by middle-class daubers in the late-eighteenth and early-nineteenth century in Latin America,[19] as well as in Europe and the United States, were the same kind of Sunday painting that is popular among today's hobbyists. They copied landscapes from books like *Views in America, Great Britain, Switzerland, Turkey, Italy, The Holy Land, Etc.,*[20] and simply did not copy them very well. Their portraits and especially their genre representations of workaday life are valuable records, often, of folk behavior but no more valuable than the popular genre paintings of more talented people, like William Sidney Mount in America or William Powell Frith in England, from whom the genre concept came to the naive painter. Whether naive or sophisticated in execution, a mid-nineteenth-century Chippendale highboy is part of the mainstream aesthetic and can be considered folk only if we class clumsy rendi-tions of the latest hit tunes as folksongs—and we do not.

In his third discourse, Sir Joshua Reynolds marshaled ancient authority to define the artist as the person who corrects the imperfections in nature.[21] Figurative folk art is not crude popular art; it is the improvement of reality. It is the result of drawing the real world or the illusionistic popular artwork through a traditional filter that improves the figure, that is, renders it more in keeping with the folk aesthetic philosophy held by the artist and his audience. The most significant attribute of the filter is that it yields works that are impressionistically low in specific information and that can be, therefore (as an individual folktale, ballad, or artwork would be), repeatedly experienced by the same audience. The walls of houses in southern Sweden were decorated in the eighteenth and nineteenth century with paintings compatible with the aesthetic that scholars are accustomed to find in the ballad.[22] The painted people, like the protagonists in a ballad, are minimally identified as individuals (most have the same face) and are unemotional (the faces have the same expression). The characters are ambiguously familiar: their dress is anachronis-tically modern and local, but they are engaged in foreign activities of biblical or historical origin; farmers do not sing about the agricultural round, and it is a city person, not a peasant from Småland or Halland, who wants a landscape or a painting of farming. The ballad does not limit the imagination by supplying psychological motivations or descriptive details, and the singer does not histrionically highlight the ballad's drama; similarly, the Swedish folk painter does not dictate the audience's perceptions and reactions with illusionary space. The artist's unmodeled figures exist flatly without a hint at the third dimension; they are quietly focused with only the amount of action and setting absolutely required for identification; they do not tell a story so much as refer to a known story. The ballad and the paintings exhibit the traditional horror of the vacuum; the ballad when heard presents no aural lacunae, and in the Swedish paintings the blank spaces are similarly stopped with spots and dots and flowers. The ballad is an oral expression, the wall painting a material expression of the same folk aesthetic.

The selection and treatment of the content in the Swedish wall paintings were conditioned by the filter that had been developed to make the naturalistic art of the post-Renaissance period suit folk taste. The formalistic aspects of the filter caused a drive to frontality and symmetry. These characteristics can be found in the Swedish paintings, but the filter's best test came during Spanish colonialism. In the areas into which the Spanish religious adventurers introduced ecstatic baroque art—the Philippines, the Caribbean, Central and Latin America, and the southwestern United States—the folk carvers stilled the supercharged gesticulations of the baroque into symmetry. The image faces forward, the nose of its face perpendicular to its shoulders. It was designed to be viewed from the front—a two-dimensional denial of its three-dimensional actuality. Passionate realism had given way to geometric design. But the design was not mere decoration. The religious power of baroque sculpture was clearly signified by the actions of the figures, but as with African sculpture, the Spanish colonial *bulto* was not manifestly potent. In Africa, the power may be conserved tensely inside the figure,[23] but in western religious folk art power is brought to the placid figure by the believer. The power of the polychromed wooden saint is apparent only when the carving stands as an icon within its sacred context, when a human being is using it as a mediator with God. Superficial realism had given way to transcendent symbolism.

The symbolizing nature of the folk filter led to the establishment and repetition of conventional designs. Just as people were drawn from the front, tulips were drawn from the side, sunflowers from the top, and four-legged beasts from the side, spread into a flying gallop. A characteristic motif in Europe and European America was the angel reduced to its cherubic essence: a winged head. The expressionless visage faces forward; on each side is a wing of equal size. The motif is a characteristic piece of western folk design; a bilaterally symmetrical whole, composed of three distinct units, the outside two being mirror images of each other, the central one—the focus of attention—being different but internally symmetrical.

Figurative paintings and sculpture that postdate the Renaissance and seem to be naive may be stabs at realism that failed, or they may be the products of an aesthetic flourishing outside the mimetic progression. Given their cultural milieux and the intentions of their artists, they may be bad or they may be good, and it is not always possible to tell which is which from the work alone. But representational folk art is not a failure at illusionary art; it is, like European fine art before Giotto and after Cezanne, like most primitive art, abstract.[24] The beginning of Renaissance art was marked by a move from convention to realism. Folk art is characterized constantly by moves from realism to convention.

Folk Culture That Is Art

The person with an idea to express can choose from among communicating media with different potentials for permanence and semantic clarity. Bodily action leaves a gesture, a word, or an artifact in the air. These media affect different sets of senses. Any medium, affecting any sense, can be the conveyer of an aesthetic, and art, therefore, can be either gestural or verbal or material, although art is generally considered to be only those parts of an event that the anthropologist has termed material culture: the artist produces a material object that is perceived visually. Other kinds of sensory perception, though often ignored, are important in material folk culture, especially taste and smell, in the case of the folk art that is food, and touch. The academic critic may restrict his appreciation to observation, but the folk critic wishes to "feel of it," to gauge the artifact's surface and balance with his hands. It is the peculiar property of material culture that its expressions can be touched and that exactly the same object, not merely a representation of it as in a recording of a tale, can be repeatedly re-experienced.

The artifact produced out of the maker's aesthetic, out of, essentially, his desire to please himself and his audience, is art. With centuries of art criticism behind us, it is often surprising that the folk artist has no articulation for his aesthetic other than production. But as recently as the sixteenth century, the aesthetic vocabulary was quite limited. By reading the words of Giorgio Vasari, the painter and friend of Michaelangelo who spent his leisure writing the biographies of artists and examining the works he admired, his aesthetic can be understood, but nowhere in his *Vite*, first published in 1550, can one find that aesthetic rigorously and lucidly outlined. Similarly, the folk aesthetic can rarely be elicited directly; analysis of artifacts, behavioral observation, and ethnoscientific questioning are the means for its determination. Modern Papago Indian potters were shown alien kinds of pottery; quietly they listened to suggestions for innovation; then, silently they continued to make pottery of the old kind, thus materially stating their taste.[25] Bernie Wise, a lower Potomac waterman and old-time market hunter, could readily separate good duck decoys from bad, good workboats from bad, but only rarely did he bother with verbalized rationalizations for his selections.[26] Cruising through the harbor of River Springs, Bernie easily classified the workboats docked there. Most were old and accepted types of craft used in tonging for oysters and trot-lining for crabs. There were also two new types, both combinations of a bow from one tradition and a stern from another. One of these, the "flare-bow"—its bow copied from a police boat that had come from up the Chesapeake Bay—had proved popular and its maker, Perry Gibson, was kept busy supplying the demand for boats of the kind. The other boat with its "dory bow" and "box stern" looked "pretty funny" to Bernie; he grinned, nearly chuckling, and said that he did not guess there would ever be another like it. Bernie Wise and his friends have an aesthetic. The lack of an aesthetic vocabulary does not prevent aesthetic operation.

The modern designer,[27] anticipated by John Ruskin,[28] recognizes the simultaneity of the artifact's aesthetic and practical functioning. Like the industrial engineer, the folk artist often denies his aesthetic, defending his choices and actions solely on the basis of utility. Though he lavished great care on the form and finish of the baskets he made, John O. Livingston, a proud central Pennsylvania craftsman, discussed their virtues only in terms of their strength and usefulness.[29] But man does not make an artifact without applying or communicating his aesthetic; there is no artifact totally lacking in art. In working to establish valid distinctions among artifacts, the art historian George Kubler identified the useless object—the thing that is not a tool—as the work of art.[30] Useless objects—objects of art—do, however, fit into large structures as components in objects combining aesthetic and practical functions: a painting, itself "useless," is hung on the walls of a house, a useful tool in environmental modification, or in a museum, a useful educational tool.

In folk tradition there are few material objects that can be legitimately separated from their contexts as objects of art, and the only common one is the garden, the product of the aesthetic application of the farmer's tools, techniques, and expertise. The medieval philosopher, for whom art was not a reality independent of other realities, viewed the garden as the supreme worldly delight; for Dante it was the pinnacle of Purgatory. Francis Bacon wrote, "God Almighty first planted a garden. And indeed it is the purest of human pleasures." [31] The dooryard's traditional plots of flowers, whose existence is owed alone to the desire to participate in the creation of beauty and live in its presence, are folk art. But they exist not in a vacuum, but as the decorative elements in traditional landscaping plans—plans that include the location of the woodshed and dungheap as well as the flower garden.

The garden decorates the land as the painting decorates the wall. The art historian has often made the error of equating art and decorative ornament,[32] and most writers on folk art consider art to be the independently movable ornament, such as a framed painting, or the conceptually separable surface ornament of a tool, such as a painting on the sides of a cart, and they have generally failed to recognize art unless there is an obviously applied decoration. However, some, like Herbert Cescinsky, an unacknowledged disciple of Morris and one of the earliest serious students of furniture, have been aware that a utilitarian artifact, "destitute of ornament," can still be artistic in "shape, proportion or otherwise." [33]

On a utilitarian object, the most obvious art is the applied ornament. Folk ornamentation may be classified into human and animal forms, vegetable forms, geometric (nonnaturalistic) forms, and surface treatment. These kinds of ornament are listed in the order in which they are most obviously distinct from utilitarian intent. This is the reverse order of their commonness as folk decoration, and it is the chronological order in which Western artists isolated them for representation and appreciation. The landscape developed as an independent pictorial type long after the portrayal of the human being, and only very recently have artists created works from which all figures have been eliminated, leaving only a solid color or the texture of the surface. In the mid-1960s in New York, Ad Rinehart explored the minimal limits of art with his rollered black canvases.[34] Many folk cultures have no tradition of human representation, fewer lack naturalistic designs of any sort (consider the Oriental rug), fewer still have no kind of nonnaturalistic geometric decorative design, and there are no folk cultures that lack traditional proclivities for surface treatment, for certain colors or textures. The stern Old Order Amish, who express a rejection of decoration, are attentive to surfaces. The women wear dresses without "patterns," but they may be bright blue or purple. The expensive suits of the men have been reduced to the flat black of an Ad Rinehart painting.[35]

The degree of ornamentation varies from culture to culture. In some folk cultures, such as the Irish, the aesthetic drive is channeled more through oral than material media and there is little ornamental folk art. In other folk cultures, especially those that thrived in the glow of baroque high art in Holland, Scandinavia, France, and Germany, the amount of ornamental elaboration is great. Most of the folk cultures of North America are closer to the Irish than the Central European pattern.

In most of western folk decoration there are two major laws operative: the dominance of form and the desire for repetition. In some fine art, such as Gothic architecture, impressionist painting, or progressive jazz, basic forms are confused under decoration, but no matter how many curls or swirls the folksinger employs, the skeleton of the melody remains apparent, and the basic form of folk artifacts is never obscured by ornamentation. Rather, ornament serves frequently to reinforce the visual effect of form; its elements may be outlined or their shapes echoed in lines drawn on them. The interior decoration of the usual room in an American folk house, for instance, consists of the color of the walls, the shapes of which, determined by openings, are outlined in woodwork, the edges being emphasized with a beaded moulding. The ornamental turning on the usual folk chair is restricted to its peripheries: the tops and bottoms of its posts. Over-all patterns are generally bound to formal areas of the object: each drawer of a bureau, each panel of a chest, is likely to have a self-contained ornament.

Folk ornamentation is repetitive, and repetitive in the ways Paul Klee described as simplest in his *Pedagogical Sketchbook*.[36] Western folk ornamentation almost never reaches the sophistication of the nonsymmetrical balance of elite art or the rhythmic complexity of much of primitive art.[37] Often it consists of the continual repetition of the same motif, d: dddd. Most folk thinking involves the possibilities of binary sets. The ornamentation might consist of pairs of the same motif, *dd: dd dd dd*. The motif might be mirrored to form a symmetrical whole: *db: db db db* or *dddbbb*. A second motif might be introduced to form a pair, *de: de de*.

But the thinking only rarely becomes so complex as to include three different motifs: *d e r*. Triplets usually involve the repetition of the same motif—*d: ddd ddd*—or the insertion of a different motif in the center—*ded* or *dbd*—but most usually the tripartite motif consists of the symmetrical pair—*db*—separated by a second element that is bilaterally symmetrical, so that the resulting unit still exhibits symmetrical halves: *dAb: dAb dAb* or *dddAbbb*. Through the use of different patterns in a single artifact, a complex, over-all design can be accomplished, but the thinking in the design of folk ornamentation (or in the performance of folksong or tale) does not often go beyond repetition, with bilateral symmetry being a special case of repetition. And it does not often go beyond variation in terms of the number two, with three being a special case of two when two of the three elements form a pair. Within folk cultures, naturalistic and asymmetrical forms, such as the human body, were accepted, but they were geometrically reworked so they could be used within the decorative tradition of binary repetitiveness.

The artist's idea, his plan for production, includes an invariable structure. The components that the structure serves to organize are nonessential—removable—or they are essential—those that, if removed, would cause the structure's destruction. A person's choice and handling of the components in a structure is his style, and his product is art at least insofar as his feeling for beauty determines his style. Given the same structure and the same components, an artist can create a symmetrical or an asymmetrical artifact; the folk artist typically chooses the former, and his choice is the mobilization of his aesthetic. His artifact can be art, in part, even without decoration, although the art in simple forms is often difficult to see. If one were to look at traditional American jugs, the artistic nature of the decorated jug would prove obvious: a jug might have applied modeling, incising, painting, or a special glaze. If such ornamentation were the jug's only art, then the basic jug forms, given the identity of clays, techniques, volume, and use, would be the same, but they are not. There are distinct, contemporaneous preferences for very different basic forms that can be explained only on the basis of a folk aesthetic.

In arranging an artifact's essential components (the elements of its basic shape), the folk artist works with the same laws that he employs in working with the nonessential components (ornamentation). In especially complex forms, such as the town, the symmetry may be confined to individual elements rather than to the entire form, but the ideal in even complicated western folk designs was to form a symmetrical whole through the repetition of individually symmetrical units.

Any folk artifact could be chosen to illustrate the operation of the mechanics of the western folk aesthetic. The facades of most Anglo-American folk house and barn types are examples of the bilaterally symmetrical tripartite design, *dAb*, that is found in innumerable decorative motifs—for example, the angelic head with wings found on early gravestones. The Anglo-American folk house front has three elements, the central one of which differs (it has a door) from the identical side elements that have one or two windows aligned per floor. In selective and adaptive response to the nineteenth-century introduction of the Gothic and Italianate architectural styles—confusingly asymmetrical in grander examples, though available, too, in easier to swallow, more symmetrical versions—a folk Victorian decorative repertoire was developed: the Gothic tower was reduced to a gable and added at the top of the facade's central element.[38] Italianate brackets were lined repetitiously under the eaves, marking a natural joint in the form. Carpenter Gothic gingerbread, the rococo scroll-sawed answer to the gentry's gargoyles, was complexly curvaceous, but it was composed of symmetrical elements, symmetrically applied to places, the corners and tops and bottoms of porches mostly, where they did not disguise the house's basic form—its floor plan and facade, both possible to represent formulaically as dAb.[39]

Most folk artifacts are basically utilitarian in nature. They are also artistic, but usually artistic only to a degree that does not hinder their practical effect. The Kentucky rifle was often carved and inlaid;[40] to its maker, its user, and its modern collector, it was beautiful, but it was mainly a tool for the acquisition of protein: it could be beautiful, but it had to kill. If writers on the subject have overemphasized the artistic nature of utilitarian objects, they have also overemphasized the utilitarian nature of aesthetic objects. The folk artist is regularly denied his aesthetic on the assumption that his products served some specific, often magical, purpose. If the ornament of artifacts is isolated, some of it can be seen as directly and some of it as indirectly operational. Johnnie Brendel, whose granddad was a painter of "hex signs" on Pennsylvania barns, laughs at those who have accepted the piece of urban apocrypha, perpetrated by pop writers, that the "hex signs"—John and his Pennsylvania German neighbors call them "barn stars" or "barn flowers"—are apotropaic.[41] He can gloss the colors in the dominant local design, the "Cocalico star": the green is the early fields, the yellow the ripe grain, and the white signifies the purity of the Virgin. But while the Cocalico star (like all conventions) might be considered vaguely good luck, it is painted high on the barn to beautify it. This does not mean that the barn, thus aesthetically embellished, was left vulnerable to witches and lightning, for Bible verses were secreted within, and a tiny, five-pointed star—exactly the pentangle that Sir Gawain wore on his shield when he sallied off to keep his appointment with the Green Knight—was scratched in a continuous line on beams, on trough and manger, on plow or harrow.[42] The pentangle is an operational design, considered to have direct influence in the world of confusing cause and effect. Biblical scenes on Swedish walls and Spanish-American santos,[43] like most representational folk art, are part of a sacred system. They are examples of informational art designed partially to affect behavior and facilitate control over events; they are indirectly operational. The art of the folk artifact when isolated—the shape of a jug, the shallow carving on a chest—is mostly abstract, and it exists as a result of a response to a culturally nurtured impulse that is, while weaker, as real and as basic to man as hunger.[44] Most folk art, though subdued by utilitarian ends and restricted narrowly by tradition, exists to allow man to explore his innovative nature. It exists to delight.

Conclusions

William Morris's quarrels with the art of his era came out of his recognition of the rationalistic fragmentation of the aesthetic experience: art had lost its place in life. In the setting of Morris's observation, two major conclusions about folk art can be offered, one on the relationship of art to other aspects of culture, the other on the relationship of art to the individual's psychology.

In the fifteenth century, Bruelleschi raised the dome of Santa Maria del Fiore into the Florentine sky and declared the separation of architect and builder. By the next century, artists like Raphael and Brueghel had separated painting from its dependence on religious function. Since the Renaissance, a spiral of self-consciousness, energized by the interaction of critic and practitioner, has left the artist and his work utterly isolated; the modern artist can state that "the new art outstrips life and shuts the door on 'practical utility.' " [45] But the artifacts of folk art exist as complementary syntheses of the practical and aesthetic. Even things for which no practical use is envisioned are often designed as if they were utilitarian objects; the sgraffito plates of England, Germany, and Pennsylvania provide an example.[46] The folk artist is sensitive to his audience's needs and pleasures. The artist and his client collaborate, mutually influencing each other's decisions, sharing an unspoken aesthetic, and discussing artifacts from the angle of practicality. In folk culture, art and labor are blended in the way William Morris wished them to be.

As part of his romantic legacy, the folklorist often imputes to the singer or tale teller the kind of expressive and variable, free flowing and organic aesthetic that Morris ascribed to the medieval craftsman. But western folk art, whether oral or material, is characterized by repetition, by forms that are composed of repeated motifs, by forms that exhibit over-all symmetry, and by forms that are memorized and repeated. Repetition proves the absence of mistake and presence of control— control over perception and expression, control over concept, technique, and material. As Herbert Read has pointed out, symmetry as a proof of mastery has characterized Western artistic consciousness since Neolithic times.

If folk art seems dead, it need only be realized that the engineer who denies art has internalized the repetitive-symmetrical aesthetic, and when he creates a "purely functional" object, he usually activates not the organic functionalist philosophy but the same traditional aesthetic as did his great-grandfather, the house carpenter or wheelwright. An automobile need not be bilaterally symmetrical, like a wagon, or a horse, when viewed from the front; an office building's facade need not be composed of repetitive units of equal size. But if they were not, the designer and his audience would think they looked odd or were the result of a mistake (a lack of control). The artifact of the modern engineer or the puttering do-it-yourselfer might not be folk from the standpoint of its dominant practical intent or the discrete elements of its form or its technological processing, but from the standpoint of the aesthetics of its design it probably is. So, if folk art seems dead, search your room for artifacts that do not seem to be artistic but that, nonetheless, exhibit the repetitive and symmetrical aesthetic (there are probably none that do not). Their designer will defend their symmetry on solely practical grounds, but the appearance they presented to him and his client, whose unverbalized aesthetic is folk, was a major cause for their existing in the shape they do.

If folk art seems insignificant, ponder the reinforcing effect on the western child raised in an immediate environment where most things—the furniture, the windows and doors, the houses along the street—are symmetrical. He will grow into a man who will place great value on repetition, control, and equilibrium. He will, as farmer or city planner, try to draw nature into symmetry. He will, as old-time craftsman or industrial engineer, create objects that are apparently artless but that are actually—as if Mondrain and Klee never existed—products of the traditional repetitive-symmetrical aesthetic.

Part III

STATEMENTS OF METHOD

A method based on the document is prejudiced; fated to neglect the majority of people, for they were nonliterate and, within the boundaries of literacy, to neglect the majority of people, for they did not write. Even today, in societies of almost universal literacy, it is a rare soul who bequeaths to future historians a written account of his thought. . . . How can you study a society if you attend only to the expressions of a small and deviant class within the whole?
—Henry Glassie, *Folk Housing in Middle Virginia*

Perhaps more than anything else a museum's exhibition environment is an accurate index of its attitudes toward material culture.
—Harold Skramsrad, *Material Culture and the Study of American Life*

8

The Connoisseurship of Artifacts

Charles F. Montgomery

Introduction

Webster's Third International Dictionary defines the connoisseur as *"one who is expert in a subject; one who understands the details, techniques or principles of an art and is competent to act as a critical judge."* Connoisseurship, as a way of looking at and appraising objects, began as one of the cultural hallmarks of the Renaissance gentleman who came to be expected to exhibit a knowledge and appreciation of the fine arts. Jonathan Richardson, an English collector of paintings and drawings, summarized these *"Qualifications of a Connoisseur"* in his *Two Discourses (1719),* the first book on the subject published in English, and distinctly equated the exercise of them with the process of *"Becoming a Gentleman."* In common parlance, connoisseurship still retains this association with a self-proclaimed, discriminating gentility, with a special, almost secretive, artistic sensitivity possessed only by a privileged elite of curators and collectors of *objets d'art.*

When art came to be studied systematically in twentieth-century university art departments, classes in connoisseurship also developed. In such courses (usually small seminars), advanced students were repeatedly drilled in the exercises of how-to-look-at and what-to-look-for in their examination of art works. Largely within the emerging field of decorative arts, this method of study was expanded from two-dimensional objects (primarily paintings) to a range of three-dimensional artifacts such as furniture, silver, textiles, and ceramics. Charles Montgomery, one of the acknowledged connoisseurs of American art, was a pioneer teacher, scholar, and writer in this important approach to material culture. After many years as a dealer in antiques, he came to the Henry Francis Du Pont Winterthur Museum in 1949 and continued as director and senior research fellow until 1970. Beginning in 1952, he taught courses in the Winterthur Program in Early

American Culture, an innovative and novel graduate program conjoined with the University of Delaware, that he, along with E. McClung Fleming, largely conceived and implemented.

Although the following essay was originally intended for his fellow collectors in the American Walpole Society, it bears the imprint of the "homework of study" that Montgomery sought to implant in each of his students of the American decorative arts: his injunction "to approach every object with an inquiring mind as well as with an inquiring eye." As will be evident from his format and his examples, he devised his fourteen-point analysis primarily for the study of the decorative arts. Nonetheless, the rudimentary questions that he raises are, in fact, applicable to any form of material cultural evidence. They are included here as a primer of the beginning inquiries that must be made of any artifact.

If Montgomery's "subjective exercise" (as he labeled this essay) rides a particular hobby horse, it is his concern with chronology and its absolute necessity in artifactual study. In one sense, the step-by-step format of the study can be said to culminate in his tenth axiom. To be a connoisseur requires, among other things, learning certain chronologies, just as to be a mathematician requires mastery of certain tables and formulae. For example, the succession of high historic art styles (mannerism, baroque, rococo, classical revival, and so on), the development of paint pigments, the history of technological and industrial processes, and the sequence of excise and tariff legislation are but a few of the obvious chronologies that the student of material culture must know.

Charles Montgomery sought to widen the traditional questions of connoisseurship beyond merely aesthetic concerns. If his approach to material culture evidence is not as functional or cultural as that proposed by scholars in Part III, his analysis is strikingly prescient of several of the more anthropological inquiries now concerning the students of American artifacts. For instance, as early as 1961, he was anxious to explain regional, even subregional, vernacular characteristics in American material culture patterns. He was also asking important questions about anonymous craftsmen—the unknown independent workmen or makers of specialized parts. Likewise he presses the reader to question how much "mass production" of artifacts may have actually taken place rather routinely in so-called preindustrial societies.

The excerpt below originally appeared under the title "Some Remarks on the Practice and Science of Connoisseurship," in the American Walpole Society Notebook, 1961, pp. 7–20. This journal, along with its English prototype, The Volume of the Walpole Society, is an important resource for Anglo-American material culture studies, particularly in the Anglo-American decorative arts of the seventeenth and eighteenth centuries. Montgomery served on its editorial board for many years and published several major studies in its pages that have become minor classics in their fields. His most important books include A Guide to the Winterthur Collections (1962); American Furniture: The Federal Period (1966); and The History of American Pewter (1973). Montgomery also wrote the essay

"Design and Decorative Arts of the Seventeenth and Eighteenth Centuries," in
the Carnegie study, *Arts of the United States (1960).* When he died in 1978 he
was a Professor of Art History and Curator of American Art at Yale University.

🦅

Each connoisseur probably consciously or unconsciously looks at an object
from many points of view and probably finds it necessary to take all or part of the
series of steps or exercises which are set out below. These steps are the prosaic
homework of study and observation that provide the data for rational judgment. The
goal is to determine the date and place of manufacture; the author, if possible; and
where within the range of its fellows the object stands in terms of its condition,
excellence of execution, and success as a work of art.

I. Over-All Appearance

Three-dimensional objects

When first looking at an object, it is important to let oneself go and try to
get a sensual reaction to it. I ask myself: Do I enjoy it? Does it automatically
ring true? Does it sing to me?

Sometimes I look at it with half-closed eyes from various angles to sense
the sweep of line and massing of form. I ask myself: Are the lines clean and the
masses in accord with its style? Is the stance one of grace? Does the object
have unity? Is it sculpturesque in the relationship of masses and voids? What
about the harmony of the whole and the integration of the parts? Did the author
deviate from the norm to such a degree that this is a new conception and more
interesting than the norm?

Two-dimensional objects

Prints, drawings, watercolors, and textiles, including needlework, also
demand harmony and integration of design. Quality of line and unity is a thing
of subtlety, yet more often than not, a prime factor in differentiating the work
of the master from that of the follower.

II. Form

Form, more than any other quality, distinguishes a work of art. Conception and
proportion give it nobility and distinction. Study of the orders of architecture to
instill a sense of proportion was basic in the education of the sixteenth-, seven-
teenth-, and eighteenth-century designer and craftsman.

Overall measurements, and in some cases those of individual parts, are necessary to establish the norm and general proportions. They are vital as a part of the record and for making comparisons with related pieces, especially through photographs.

Some measurements help in determining authenticity. Often the weighing of a piece of silver provides a basis for comparison of the present weight with the original weight (frequently scratched on the bottom of early pieces by the silversmith). A difference of more than an ounce (from wear and polishing) puts one immediately on guard against repairs or alterations of form.

Measurements of individual parts may also reveal information concerning age. For instance, the difference of diameter of turned chair stretchers or round table tops is indicative of age because wood, as it grows older, continues to shrink across the grain more than with the grain.

III. Ornament

The range to be considered here is very broad. Obviously, to evaluate the effectiveness and quality of ornament, one must be well acquainted with (1) the types of ornament employed, and the heights of technical excellence achieved by artists and artisans in a variety of times and places, working in the style of the object in question; (2) the attitude of the artist or artisan toward ornament; and (3) what the ornament was intended to accomplish. I ask myself: Was the ornament used to cover up structural features that might otherwise be unattractive? Or was it used to highlight and emphasize certain elements or features? Ornament provides punctuation and, at its best, gives not only pattern and rhythm, but also unity to the composition. Color, figure (as in wood), texture, turning, carving, engraving, enameling, painting, appliqués, printed design, and a hundred other means may have been employed to attain ornamental effects. But for each, I ask myself: Why is it there? Does it accomplish its purpose? Is the over-all effect the better for its presence? Basically, ornament is secondary to form and ought to heighten its effect rather than obscure it.

IV. Color

Art historians have sought for many years to arrive at a uniform color vocabulary for describing and analyzing paintings, and today there are several complex methods and theories for color analysis. Whereas the student of paintings must learn to chart value, hue, and intensity in order to evaluate color effect, the problem seems less difficult for the student of the decorative arts. Here the ideal is to find objects with original color showing as little fading or discoloration as possible. On this point it must be noted that most colors used prior to the Revolution were strong colors, more often than not the primary colors of red, blue, and yellow used in such a way as to provide vivid contrasts. I can well remember the anguish of some antiquarians over the colors of original unfaded eighteenth-century wallpaper when it was first hung in a Brooklyn Museum room. The colors were called harsh, violent, and vulgar; and so they may seem to our taste today.

Equally shocking is a brilliant unfaded American needlework picture in the Boston Museum of Fine Arts. Although such examples document color usage that seems strident to us, such unfaded examples, whether painted cottons, patterned silks, embroidered pictures, wallpaper, or printed furniture are, I believe, the prizes to be sought just as one seeks jewel-like clarity in the color of porcelains or pottery. Many facts concerning color achievement offer clues to dating. For instance, it was impossible to print green on textiles until the nineteenth century. Prior to that time green was obtained by applying yellow over blue.

V. Analysis of Materials

In this step, the goal is to gather and assess information on the individual constituents, such as woods, textile fibers, pigments, metals, and fasteners (whenever possible, I make observations in direct sunlight). Instruments ought to be used to heighten the powers of perception so that one may make the most accurate possible observations. These may include the magnifying glass, the camera (for a permanent record and enlarged details, as of silver marks), the microscope, X-ray, and ultraviolet light. The connoisseur on occasion may resort to the laboratory for identification. Increasingly, analysis of materials is being used by museum curators and connoisseurs as an aide in dating. The carbon-14 process, widely publicized for dating ancient objects within comparatively broad limits of time, is of little use to most connoisseurs, whereas accurate information on the exact constituents of an object (combined with knowledge of the history of technology) often provides definitive evidence about the object. For instance, the Prussian blue in the pigments of a painting clearly establishes that that layer of paint could not possibly have been applied prior to 1704, the date of discovery of this artificial pigment. Not long ago the presence of titanium in the decoration of a group of purportedly ancient Chinese vases led to the exposure of the entire group as forgeries, titanium being a twentieth-century discovery. Today the microscopic identification of woods, particularly of secondary woods in furniture, is a tremendous aid in determining the origin of furniture, since cabinetmakers were accustomed to using woods native to their locality for the interior parts of their cabinetwork.

VI. Techniques Employed by the Craftsman

Here the goal is to evaluate (1) the quality of craftsmanship; (2) the techniques and practices employed (and through this study to determine whether they are typical of a period, locale, and culture); (3) the personal idiosyncrasies of workmanship of the author of signed or documented pieces; (4) the congruency of the parts and whether the whole is by one author or is made up at a later date of two or more antique parts. This study often reveals restorations.

Although excellence of craftsmanship may seem self-explanatory, it is important to keep in mind that quality of workmanship within a craft varies widely with
time and place. Some men worked with a high degree of naturalism, their product
revealing nature in fluidity and artistry; others sometimes achieved equally successful results with less skill, utilizing abstract ornament and simplified form. Contrast,
for example, the sinuous lines of a Philadelphia Queen Anne armchair and the
abstract ship-carved ornament of a four-square Hadley chest.

The phenomenon of regional and national characteristics of objects is widely
recognized and is one with which every connoisseur must be thoroughly familiar.
Characteristics for most objects fall into a pattern, more often than not, peculiar to a
particular area. Strangely enough, the reasons behind most of these phenomena are
as yet little understood to us. Why, for instance, did the cabinetmakers of Philadelphia favor the stump rear leg and the mortising through of the stile so that the
end of the side-rail tenon shows on the back? Or why did the New York silversmith
favor the cocoon-shaped thumbpiece and the foliated applied band about the base of
tankards? It is easy to accept the idea that every individual has personal traits and
that the work of an individual artist or craftsman may have highly individualistic
characteristics, but it is much harder to ascertain the reason why a group of artists or
artisans in a given area worked in the same vernacular.

Since consistency is the hallmark of method and work of any craftsman,
congruency of the parts of an authentic object can be considered axiomatic. Hence,
one expects that the dovetails of drawers within a section or in upper and lower
sections will be similar in concept and execution.

VII. Trade Practices

Trade practices often reveal valuable information. The branded name of the
maker, while common in French furniture, is, like the label, seldom encountered in
English cabinet wares; yet both are quite occasionally met in the American product.
Therefore, one would be much more wary about a labeled piece of English furniture
than he would about an American piece.

Whereas by law the wares of the English silversmith must be stamped with
letters indicating date of manufacture, quality, and maker's mark, in the colonies no
mark was required. Hence, even though most silversmiths in America used either
their name or initials to identify their product, an unmarked example is more likely
American-made than English.

Excise and tariff laws also result in practices which are of assistance in dating.
For instance, the presence of the word "England," "Japan," or "China" on an
object usually indicates that it was made after the enactment of the McKinley Act of
1891, requiring the presence of the name of the country of origin on a newly made
article before it could be imported into the United States. More obscure, but equally
valuable, is an English law in effect between 1776 and 1811 offering tax relief to

English cotton manufacturers if they but wove three blue threads into the selvage of their white goods. The presence of these threads offers inconvertible proof that white cloth is English in origin and woven between these years, and one may assume that printed textiles with such threads in the selvage were made during this period and are English in origin. For years these blue threads went unnoticed in block- or copperplate-printed textiles simply because no one had come across this obscure English law. I am sure that, as further study is carried on, many more such aids to identification can be discovered if each of us approaches every object with an inquiring mind as well as an inquiring eye.

VIII. Function

The study of function ought to lead us to the understanding of basic character as well as give us the reason for an object's existence. One of the most widely used dictums of the twentieth-century art historian and designer is "form follows function." This is, of course, as true of decorative arts as of architecture. Exploration of either function or form leads to such questions as: Why was this object made? What were the limiting conditions imposed by materials, techniques, and skills? What was the intent of the artist?

Sometimes important clues to authenticity may be gleaned from observation of functional qualities. Can the object have adequately performed the uses for which it was intended? Does the evidence of wear and tear occur where one would expect it if the object had been used as designed? For instance, does the dent made by the thumbpiece on a tankard lid come at just the right spot on the tankard handle? Does the wear on the rung of a chair occur at the point where it was natural to rest the feet?

IX. Style

The analysis of style involves the study of form, ornament, color, and craft techniques, and the weighing of data gained through virtually each of the preceding steps; but it particularly involves a knowledge of function, since, in the decorative arts, most objects were made for useful purposes. This knowledge of function enables the connoisseur to better understand the objects with which he is working. As is well known, there was a succession of historic art styles, such as mannerism, baroque, rococo, and classical revival, to name but four. Through a knowledge of the history of art, the connoisseur will be well aware of these broad movements so that he can analyze the object within a frame of reference of such styles in their broadcast dimensions. Perhaps the greatest shortcoming of the American connoisseur up to now is his failure to attempt an evaluation of the American product against these standards.

X. Date

To arrive at a date for an object requires not only consideration of all the preceding data, but also mental or actual comparison with documented objects. Appearance, form, and particularly a knowledge of its evolution, ornament, and style all play an important part in arriving at an approximate date.

In American arts, one of the greatest handicaps to the connoisseur is the lack of files of dated objects which have been validated and can be relied upon. Because of the obvious importance of dated objects, one must be constantly on the alert, when dealing with them, that the dates are genuine and not apocryphal. There are numerous examples of dates which, because they were added at a later time through misinformation or intent to deceive by the person who added them, are inaccurate. In the preceding steps, many clues to dating have been noted, such as the value of information to be derived from technology, date of discovery of man-made constituents (as Prussian blue), trade practices, and so on.

In cases where the author is definitely known through signature, stamp, or other mark, it is essential that the biography of the author be noted to establish beginning and end dates of the period within which an object by him could fall. A knowledge of his career and works will yield information as to where this particular piece falls within his overall production.

Obviously, no piece can be earlier than its earliest feature, nor later than its latest part. The connoisseur will have at his fingertips the general periods in which a particular style flourished and the particular methods of workmanship then in vogue.

Sometimes the interpretation of the intellectual meaning—that is, the iconography (devices, arms, and allegories)—of the object will lend helpful clues to dating. For instance, the number of stars (signifying states) around the eagle may yield quite precise dates, and obviously no piece bearing the eagle and arms of the United States could have been decorated before 1783, the date of their adoption.

XI. Attribution

Signature of the Author

For signatures of any type, the observer determines whether the signature is actually that of the author applied at the time of manufacture; or an authentic label or mark (stamped with an old die) applied at a later date to an unmarked piece; or a fraudulent inscription or signature of some type applied to an unmarked example by the forger.

Types of signature include: (1) engraved inscription; handwritten signature in ink, chalk, or pencil; and enameled on glass (signatures could also of course be scratched, engraved, or otherwise imposed); (2) printed or engraved labels; and (3) a device, name, or initials stenciled, printed, punched, stamped, or burned. In the case of initial marks, I constantly ask myself: What proof is there that these initials are the mark of the craftsman to whom they are attributed? This is of particular significance in the case of pewter and silver marks in differentiating between the pewter made in America and that made in England, and between the silver made in the Channel Islands, the West Indies, or other British colonies and that of colonial America.

Stylistic Attribution

One of the most difficult aspects of connoisseurship is to make sound attributions on the basis of style. The problem is widely recognized in the case of unsigned paintings. Are they by a particular hand? Or are they copies or adaptations from his atelier? Or are they the work of a forger? Since it was comparatively easy to imitate another man's style without achieving his virtuosity, long familiarity with an artist's work—particularly his details of execution—is necessary to enable the connoisseur to make reliable stylistic attributions. It is virtually impossible to differentiate with absolute certainty the work of the master and that of his shop. How can one be absolutely certain that an example bearing the label of Duncan Phyfe was actually made by him, when one remembers that he had more than one hundred journeymen and apprentices working for him at times.

Another case in point is that of the journeyman glass blower, who moved from factory to factory, taking his models with him. For this reason, no piece of glass can be said positively to have been made in the Stiegel factory, although from fragments excavated from the factory site in Manheim, Pennsylvania, patterns such as the diamond daisy produced there are well documented, as is also the fact that, after Stiegel's bankruptcy, his workers moved on to other glasshouses.

Another problem, of which we know little as yet, is the contribution and influence of the independent carver, inlay maker, turner, or parts maker. It is already established that many cabinetmakers bought strips of inlay, turnings, carved legs, or chair backs from other shops, and that silversmiths sent out works for engraving and may indeed have purchased thumbpieces, handle terminals, foliated bands, and other embellishments from specialists. Such problems as these make stylistic attribution complicated and highly conjectural in many cases.

XII. History of the Object and Its Ownership

Documentation through sales and exhibition catalogues or family history is a well-known method and device for authentication. Such history can provide valuable information as well as an aura of authenticity, but here skepticism should be the byword. I constantly ask myself: Is such documentation logical? Are there gaps in the history? Are there implausible assumptions? As in all attribution, I must ask: Is this history or attribution possible? plausible? probable? certain or positive?

I prefer to regard the history of an object and its ownership as supporting data, rather than primary data. True, there are certain exceptions, such as in the case of books, where signatures, early bookplates, shelf marks, and other indication of early ownership may be regarded as virtually irrefutable.

XIII. Condition

Evidences of natural aging and wear, such as coloration, patina, and softening of edges, corners, and contour, are but a few of the attributes of the antique that add fascination to any object. But the thing with which the connoisseur must come to grips is the demerit to be attached to wear, tear, and accidents. The older, the rarer, the less obtainable, and the finer the object, the more restoration, repairs, or blemishes the connoisseur is prepared to accept. Here each man must be his own judge and set his own criteria. But it goes without saying that the higher the standards of the connoisseur in this respect, the finer the quality of the individual objects in his collection is likely to be, and, by the same token, the less likely the great rarities.

XIV. Appraisal or Evaluation

As an initial comment on this subjective exercise, one must begin with a highly debatable point, namely, the weighing of importance versus rarity. In some categories, the bigger the piece, the more important it is or was, inasmuch as more material and normally more labor were involved in its making, and hence its initial expense was probably greater.

It may follow that, because of its initial cost, its incidence was lower, and thus it may well be more important, as well as rarer, today. On the other hand, some large pieces, particularly paintings and furniture, are difficult to house or to display, and consequently the market price is lower. But the connoisseur, who is always pitting his judgment against that of the marketplace in the hope or expectation that the history of taste will swing to prove him right, must make his own decision. It must be noted that, in all ages, while the public has been fascinated by the large, the imposing, and the grandiose, more often than not the connoisseur has delighted in the miniature, the jewel-like, and the exquisite. The ultimate goal in studying any object, as mentioned before, is to answer the question, how good or how bad is it in terms of beauty or aesthetic value, intrinsic value in terms of materials and long hours of skillful fashioning, and extrinsic value in terms of association, ownership, or competition? The connoisseur must ask himself: Is it important as a thing of beauty? Is it rare, typical, or illustrative of the culture that produced it? Is it worthy of purchase? And, if so, at what price?

9

The Six Requirements
for Design

David Pye

Introduction

*Material culture students frequently employ the term "design" in the
identification, classification, and interpretation of objects. Without the idea of
design, one cannot build or make anything. A child constructing a sand castle has
some kind of picture in his head that is telling him what to do next. The designer
of the first bow and arrow had somehow stumbled on the design (perhaps, in part,
through observation) that a bent piece of wood with a string in tension attached to
both ends will propel an arrow. So it is with bridges, bungalows, barges, and
beer cans. All, having been designed, have design. Hence, in order to analyze such
material culture, the anthropologist, art historian, archaeologist, or historian of
technology must understand the fundamentals of design and the design process.
As Fred B. Kniffen and Henry Glassie insist in a later selection (see chapter
sixteen), all artifacts are the result of a series of mental and manual processes,
each object represents the externalization of an inner template that is both personal
and cultural.*

*David Pye rests his summary of the six requirements of design on these
premises. His primary objective is to distinguish design as a philosophical concept
from solely sociological considerations. In doing so, he raises important questions
about those interpreters of artifacts who see an object's design conditioned only by
its function. Pye proposes that it is more complicated than that; hence he has us
consider questions such as: What does function mean in scientific terms? Can
design, even theoretically, be "purely functional," purely utilitarian, leaving
nothing free to choice, to art? Is an object's appearance or its ornament only
"useless work?" If so, does that necessarily make it "worthless" as well?*

As will be evident, Pye answers these difficult questions in a language that

*beginning students may find terse and abstract. His prose is not punctuated
with as many apt examples and concrete illustrations as one might wish, but there
are pithy one-liners (such as ''it is a fair guess that arrows were the first things
ever designed for a minimum of weight'') and each of his general maxims
eventually becomes clearer as he offers his exegesis of them. Much like
geometrical theorems, Pye's six requirements of design are best understood once
one knows their corollaries and their proofs. In short, the excerpt that follows is
not easy reading; each sentence is like an epigram, pregnant with many layers of
meaning and often requiring rereading. It is well worth the effort, however, for
here is a philosophy of workmanship, a brilliant, succinct condensation of the ways
that, in Pye's words, use, ease, economy, and appearance effect design. As
Benno Foreman suggests in his introductory comments on this Pye selection in his
seminar manual,[1] this essay ''should play the same role for the decorative arts
historian that the Sayings of Chairman Mao plays to the dedicated Chinese.''*

*David Pye has expanded his theory of design merely sketched here in two
small handbooks, unfortunately little known in the United States: The Nature of
Design (London: Studio Vista and Van Nostrand Reinhold, 1972), from which the
following selection (pp. 21–39) has been excerpted, and The Nature and Art of
Workmanship (London: Studio Vista, and Van Nostrand Reinhold, 1971). Both
should be considered as required reading for the serious student of American
material culture. David Pye, a professor of furniture design at the Royal College
of Art, London, has himself designed a wide range of objects, including
buildings, furniture, jigs, tools, and disguises for warships.*

When a device embodying some known essential principle of arrangement is to
be adapted so as to achieve a particular result, there are six requirements to be
satisfied:

1. It must correctly embody the essential principle of arrangement.
2. The components of the device must be geometrically related—in extent and
   position—to each other and to the objects, in whatever particular ways suit
   these particular objects and this particular result.
3. The components must be strong enough to transmit and resist forces as the
   intended result requires.
4. Access must be provided (this is a special case of 2 above).

These four together will be referred to as *the requirements of use*.

5. The cost of the result must be acceptable. This is *the requirement for ease
   and economy*.
6. The appearance of the device must be acceptable. This is *the requirement of
   appearance*.

Design, in all its fields, is the profession of satisfying these requirements. The question we have to consider is: how far, if at all, does each of these requirements limit the designer's freedom of choice?

Various aspects of the arrangements of mechanisms are dealt with in the science of kinematics, which concerns motion or stillness without reference to force and mass; that is to say, it concerns itself with the movements of the components of devices but not with their strength or substance. It is a first principle of kinematics that mechanisms which are kinematically identical may be dissimilar in appearance, which amounts to saying that although the mechanisms are of different shapes they may share the same essential principle of arrangement. The functionalists presumably did not hold with kinematics, or perhaps considered the function of a mechanism to be independent of its motion!

Neither in textbooks of kinematics nor in patent specifications are essential principles of arrangement stated in very general terms. The essential principle is ultimately concerned only with the capability of the things in the system to transmit forces of as yet unknown strength to the desired places and in the desired directions and to modify them as desired. This capability depends on the arrangement of the things. Any statement of the essential principle is above all a general statement and must therefore be concerned not with the arrangement of particular things but rather of things of certain classes. The second requirement of those we enumerated, that the geometry shall be what the particular result entails, sets limits to the designer's choice of shape. It will be seen that the limits leave still an infinitely wide freedom of choice in the matter of shape.

It is worth noting that the essential principle of arrangement of every device was abstracted from, and is a generalization based on, the first embodiment of the invention, an embodiment which, being real, had a particular geometry entailed by particular objects and a particular result. It is not always easy to make a true generalization, separating the essential arrangement from the incidental geometry. This fact may have contributed to support the belief in ''functional'' design. Because we visualize particular things, and can never visualize anything but what is particular, we fail to realize what an enormous latitude in choice of shapes we normally enjoy.

It would be most interesting to know the history of the idea that any device embodies an essential principle and so can be adapted to other results and objects than those in the first invention. There can be little doubt that this idea has sometimes been repugnant.

The third requirement is that the components must be strong enough to transmit the forces or resist them. The forces involved will originate both from the intentional input of energy, in particular gravitation. This requirement obviously affects the size of each component, and in combination with the first two conditions, the essential principle and the geometry, it may begin to shove the designer in the direction of one shape rather than another. But in these days we are apt to forget what a very slight restriction on shape the calculation of structures does actually impose. This is because we take it for granted first of all that the minimum amount of material ought to be used (a cheese-paring attitude which fortunately did not hold in, for instance, Rome, Athens, Venice, Chartres, and a few other places), and because we habitually use standard prefabricated components when making structures. The fact that you have calculated the minimum cross section necessary to a member, such as a column, need not often prevent you from making it any shape you like.

Until very recent times, experience and rule of thumb based on it were the only things which could help a designer to decide what sizes the components of a system would need to be in order to give them adequate strength. In many trades, still, no other aids are used. Since exact methods of measuring changes have been evolved, it has been possible to predict accurately what sizes will be adequate. The train of thought is of this form: "We know that one unit of this stuff will support two tons. We want to support eight tons. How many units do we need? Four."

Wise after the event, we may feel that our ancestors were rather slow not to have thought of this. But even if they had wished for something more trustworthy than their own experience as a basis for prediction, which doubtless they did not, the train of thought described above is not the whole story. You have first to establish that one unit of the stuff supports two tons.

Suppose that you take a one-inch cube of some material and increase the load until your cube begins to crush, and suppose that when it does you find that the load is two tons. You may quite possibly then expect a two-inch cube, containing eight cubic inches, to support eight times as much, namely sixteen tons. But you find to your surprise that it supports only eight tons, or four times as much. You may then conclude that what matters is the area of the stuff in contact with the load: load eight tons, area four square inches, eight divided by four equals two tons per square inch of area in contact. Of course you are still wrong. The area in contact has very little to do with it. It is easy for us to see this, but it was not easy for the first man who did that kind of experiment. He had to think it out, or perhaps, poor man, find it out. Moreover the strength of timber is not a thing one can be sure of even now, however carefully it is graded. Experience or caution will influence decisions in which it is involved.

In order to take the design of any structure even to the stage of a sketch the designer must first assume, roughly, the sizes which each part will need. Nowadays we shall verify these by calculation. In old days we should have been obliged to do so by trial. But we, like our ancestors, can only design if we are capable of making reasonable preliminary assumptions based on experience. There is no other way. The difference between their proceedings and ours is in the method of verification of the assumed sizes, not, at this stage, in the method of designing. Design always involves making trial assumptions based on experience. These may appear on paper or be carried in the designer's head. The process is essentially a process of trial and error however the assumptions are verified, and this applies to many other assumptions besides those we make about strength.

It must be emphasized that design, of every kind, is a matter of trial *and error*. There are always some trial assumptions which no calculation or drawing can verify. Men cannot foresee the future. Design, like war, is an uncertain trade, and we have to make the things we have designed before we can find out whether our assumptions are right or wrong. There is no other way to find out. When we modify our prototype, it is, quite flatly, because we guessed wrong. It is eminently true of design that if you are not prepared to make mistakes, you will never make anything at all. "Research" is very often a euphemism for trying the wrong ways first, as we all must do.

Science has enabled us to make a few of the advances in technique which are obviously desirable, and these we shall presently discuss. It has not enabled us to predict the behavior of people, which very many designers urgently need to be able to do. It has not enabled us to foretell what will actually happen in any particular case. It has enabled us to make better predictions about responses than our fore-fathers could make, but our predictions are still pretty shaky. We cannot design a new spacecraft or a railway train which does not rock and get it right the first time, nor yet the second time. We design failures because we cannot make reliable predictions about responses. Nor do we in fact rely on them. We rely only on trial and error, or as we euphemistically say, on experience. If scientists had as much foresight as is sometimes believed, we should no longer have to rely on experience and could rely on them instead!

When a device is so designed that its component parts are only just strong enough to get the intended result without danger of failure, we may say it is in its minimum condition. This condition may be sought for other reasons than direct economy of material. In a large bridge, for example, the main problem may well be to make it carry its own weight. The traffic will be a mere flea on its back. Consequently every part of the bridge must be as small as possible consistent with its doing its work. The bridge must stand up, but only just. It is the small bridges which are massively built. The larger they are the lighter they usually seem, and are, relative to their size. It is a fair guess that arrows were the first things ever designed for a minimum of weight.

I suspect that the functionalists sometimes meant by functional design simply design aimed at the minimum condition for a device. In that case, "form should follow function" would mean that every system should be in its minimum condition, thus having certain limitations imposed on its form.

To say of most buildings that they shall be in their minimum condition is no more and no less arbitrary than saying that they shall be in the Corinthian order. Neither *diktat* has any bearing on how well or ill they do their job. If the system is in any adequate condition—and one adequate condition is the minimum condition—then it produces its intended result whether in the Corinthian order or not. It may be argued that the minimum condition is more economical. In houses it most certainly is not. The workmanship, research, and calculation needed to design and achieve it will cost far more than the material saved.

In engineering, on the other hand, the minimum condition may really be worth having for the sake of economy in cost or in energy at work. What applies to it does not apply to houses.

Among the shapes most often called ''functional'' are those streamlined shapes which appear in parts of devices which penetrate things; for example, a ship's hull under water, an aircraft, a spearhead, some projectiles, or an axe.

It is not easy to penetrate solids and fluids at any considerable speed. There are too many unwanted resistances in the response. When a minimum of resistance is required, the geometry becomes very exacting and imposes very close limits to the designer's freedom of choice. There is not too much difficulty in getting any old shape of ship through the water at one knot, but some kind of immense washtub propelled at thirty knots will produce a very awkward response and take a vast amount of energy. If high speed or easy penetration is required, then the unwanted parts of the response must be reduced to a minimum.

In these designs, as in all others, compromises are invariably made. The visible shape of a streamlined craft depends as much on what you have chosen to streamline, that is, to put inside it, as on the laws of nature. Every make of aircraft differs in shape from every other.

These ''functional'' shapes designed for a minimum of change in the way of shifting air or water are as much chosen shapes as any other, and a minimum condition is as much a chosen condition as any other adequate condition. The reasons for the choice may be economic or aesthetic or defensive or silly or doubt-less of many other kinds.

The fourth requirement of use is that for access. We think of a device as a self-contained system, but of course no system is self-contained. Every device is a subsidiary part of a more extended system (which must contain among its other components, man). Since any device will have to become a component of a larger system or of several in turn, its geometry must be suited not only to its own proper result but also to the result of the extended system or systems. It follows that a prime requirement in the design of many devices is accessibility. The quay must allow the crane access to the ship's hold. The ship must draw no more water than covers the sill of the dock. The engines and their accessory devices must be disposed so as to allow easy access for the engineer's hands when he is maintaining them. The most familiar requirements for accessibility occur in buildings, and the art of planning them in its utilitarian aspect is largely concerned with affording the users of the building easy access to the several parts of it. Things do not invariably get in each other's way and access is sometimes so easily provided that the requirement is never noticed; but it can in other cases be most difficult to satisfy, for the most characteris-tic quality of modern devices is their complexity. Where there is complexity, requirements for access become difficult to satisfy and impose distinct limitations on the designer's freedom of choice (or, in some motor cars, evidently defeat him altogether). The ultimate causes of complexity in devices nearly all lie in the requirement for ease and economy, but to trace the immediate causes and distinguish in principle the various very different ways in which they take effect would be a considerable undertaking. There is, for example, a clear distinction in principle between a mechanism and a mere aggregation of systems. A mechanism is a combination of distinct systems, but the result of each entails that of another. A thing like a stove is also a combination of distinct systems, but here although the result of one may or may not affect that of another, the result of one entails the result of another. One could remove the entire system for riddling the ashes and the entire system for regulating the draught, and still one could get the intended result somehow. There is no essential principle of arrangement for the systems *inter se* in an aggregation like a stove; but in a mechanism there is. A mechanism is one system built up of systems. Most mechanisms, however, show an accretion of palliating systems also, such as antifriction bearings and lubricating systems which could be omitted without affecting the essential arrangement of the system.

The fifth requirement, that for ease and economy, has very wide implications. Theoretically it is possible to design for a result without the design being influenced in any degree, either directly or indirectly, by economy. In practice this does not happen. The most lavish and magnificent buildings show the mark of economy in, literally, every stone. The influence of economy in design is universal. Economy here implies something more than saving money.

Any change originated by man exacts a cost from him. The cost is reckoned in effort, trouble, and time, often in running risk and enduring discomfort also. Adam found this out. "Economy," as used in this essay, must be understood as referring primarily to this unpleasant catalogue and only secondarily to the money which we pay to avoid enduring it; for when we pay a price in money for a device, as a rule we are paying directly or indirectly to escape the natural cost in effort or discomfort, trouble, time, or risk of the result which the device gives.

The great majority of devices simply enable us to get cut-price results. There are really rather few devices which make it possible to get results which without them would be unattainable. The only such devices in the realm of transport, for instance, are the vessel, the raft, the aircraft, the hovercraft, and the rocket. No form of land transport qualifies; all are merely palliative. One can walk.

Economy is the mother of most inventions, not necessity, unless in the sense of poverty and hardship. A requirement for convenience is simply a diluted requirement for ease and economy. It is true that much convenience is an idiotic sort of economy, but it is quite impossible to draw a line between saving labor, sensible convenience, and the idiotic "convenience" catered for by the waste-making economy which Vance Packard has so well and horrifyingly dissected in *The Waste Makers.*

The consequences of the search for "improvement" in devices are manifold. Perhaps the most obvious consequence is seen in the engineer's preoccupation with producing machines of higher efficiency with less waste of power in friction and in the importance in most manually driven machines of a high mechanical advantage, for we would all rather use a long lever than a short one. Such good engineering in the service of economy does impose limitations on the designer's freedom of choice of shape, but only very loose ones, for they mostly affect size alone. The lever is a fair example. The fact that you must make it long prevents you only from designing something short and thick while it leaves you an infinitely wide choice in other directions.

The more remote consequences of the search for cheaper results exert much more effective limitations than these, but the limitations which result from cheapening the manufacture of a device are far and away the most stringent of any. A low retail price in the shop often overrides every other consideration in design.

The requirements of use are imperative. If they are not complied with, the device does not give the result. The requirements of economy are on a different footing, for the amount of weight given to them is a matter of choice.

All possible useful results except transformations of energy are shifts—shifts of particular things, large or minute, over particular distances in particular directions. The things, the distances, and the directions are legislated for by the requirements of use. The speed of shift, the energy needed to produce it, the amount of energy wasted in the process, the unwanted changes which accompany the shift, and the labor or distress exacted from people, are all legislated for by the requirement for ease and economy.

It seems to be invariably true that those characteristics which lead people to call a design functional are derived from the requirements of economy and not of use. I have found no exception. Streamlining, omission of ornament, exposure of structural members, and "stark simplicity" all derive directly or indirectly from requirements of economy (which is not to say that they do in fact give economy!). A result, though not always at an acceptable cost, can always be got without these characteristics. They are inessential. In some cases indeed they are as much features of style as any overt system of ornament.

A thing may be called "purely utilitarian" if it is designed so as to comply with the requirements of use, and of ease and economy, but ignoring the requirement of appearance. No such thing really exists, for nothing can be made without some concession, however slight and unwitting, to the requirement of appearance any more than a human being can be entirely amoral. Work done solely for the satisfying of the requirement of appearance may be called "useless work." Useless, of course, does not mean worthless.

The sixth condition is that the appearance of the device must be acceptable. This conflicts headlong with the requirements of economy, and it is heartening to see how so many designers and manufacturers consistently expend useless work on satisfying it. Smoothness and all the qualities of surface finish, flatness, straightness, fairness of curves, neat fitting, and neat detailing at junctions—all the qualities of appearance which decent workmanship produces—are to be seen still in immense numbers of the things of all sorts which men make. Almost all of these graces could be omitted or made worse without any loss of effectiveness in the devices which exhibit them. They are taken so much for granted that one would think people supposed that they were achieved automatically. No credit for them is given where credit is due. There is no realization that they are an affair of art and not less important than design in the large, for without them the best of design is entirely wasted so far as appearance goes. A surprisingly large proportion of manufacturing time in nearly every field is in fact taken up with useless work catering for the requirements of appearance.

The requirement of appearance imposes very distinct limitations on the designer's freedom of choice of shape in the large. This is done through the medium of styles of design, which confine him to a fairly narrow canon of shapes. It can be argued that design has invariably exhibited styles because some clear limitations on freedom of choice are psychologically necessary to nearly all designers. When design gets too easy it becomes difficult. Styles provide these desired limitations when, as so often, the requirements of use and economy do not impose limitations which are close enough.

10

Artifact Study: A Proposed Model

E. McClung Fleming

Introduction

E. McClung Fleming's five-fold classification of the basic properties of an artifact (history, material, construction, design, and function) and set of four operations (identification, evaluation, cultural analysis, and interpretation) to be performed on these properties share an obvious kinship with the previous analytical schema of Charles Montgomery and David Pye. However, Fleming's model for artifact study presses the investigator to go beyond the perspective of the connoisseur or of the student of design and workmanship. His aspiration is to provide a holistic framework that identifies the many possible approaches to the subject, thereby "relating them to each other and thus suggesting the outlines of a program of collaborative research for all who are engaged in the study of the artifact."

As noted in this volume's introduction, the Fleming model was developed in the context of the study of the early American decorative arts and the discipline of American Studies, specifically in the seminar "The Artifact in American History," which he taught in the Winterthur Museum-University of Delaware Program in Early American Culture. His argument here, in part a humanistic manifesto ("to know man we must study the things he has made") and in part a technical checklist (a comprehensive exercise whereby the material culturist can systematically tally up an object's evidential potential), is easily followed. It contains a helpful summary of typical primary and secondary verbal sources–probate records, bills of sale, family records, newspaper advertisements, design books, emblem books, travel accounts, city registers, and so forth—that are vital for serious research in nonverbal sources. In this context, the author offers another answer to William Hesseltine's claim that most artifacts remain largely unintelligible to the historian. Fleming's counter-claim is that, in fact, the procedures used in reading the content of a nonverbal document parallel those used in the reading of a verbal document. In each case, the would-be reader must start by being literate. Consequently, Fleming proposes a vocabulary for deciphering material culture evidence on four different levels.

Within his model, Fleming gives new definitions to familiar terms (e.g., contrast his use of design with that of Pye's), borrows useful concepts from other disciplines (such as George Kubler's methodology involving "real and virtual intersections" in art history), as well as contributes his own perspective (for instance, his definition of "product analysis" and "content analysis").

Nestled among the step-by-step quartet of operations involving a quintet of properties are two simple but important observations of which the reader should be aware, since they tell much about the present state of material culture study in the United States. Fleming, like John T. Schlebecker, urges "the adoption of a more uniform and exact classification system for artifacts" if material culture research is to become a respected academic discipline. Fleming's second agenda for the field's future is a plea for material culturists to test and improve on his model as well as to propose other paradigms.

He muses that one could reasonably expect substantial methodological contributions to artifact scholarship to have come from the staff professionals at the 3,600 cultural history museums in the United States. To a certain extent, museum professionals have pioneered in the techniques of identification, preservation, and display of objects, but they have been reluctant to move on to the more theoretical levels of cultural analysis and interpretation as proposed by Fleming's model. Where methodological issues have been debated, often they are buried in staff reports, museum catalogs, and in memos regarding the installation of gallery displays. In order to press museum curators to think more systematically about the theoretical concepts that should undergird artifact research and the communication of that research, Fleming and others have argued that museum exhibitions be considered as "curatorial publications" where the epistemology of the exhibition is tested and reviewed. [1]

Another alternative is, of course, for curators and scholars to apply Fleming's own model. Following the article from which this selection is excerpted in Winterthur Portfolio 9 (June 1974): 153–161, Fleming offered a specific instance of his theory put into practice. The reader should consult this impressive, detailed analysis of a 1680 American court cupboard from Salem, Massachusetts, and see the cupboard in the collections of the Winterthur Museum. This analysis is found on pages 161–173 of this Portfolio issue.

E. McClung Fleming, a seminal influence in shaping the educational component of the Winterthur Museum-University of Delaware Program in Early American Culture for over two decades, began his career as an American political historian, writing his first book on R. R. Bowker: Militant Liberal (1952). His articles, "Early American Decorative Arts as Social Documents," Mississippi Valley Historical Review 9 (1958); "The American Image as Indian Princess, 1765–1783," Winterthur Portfolio 2 (1965); and "From Indian Princess to Greek

Goddess: The American Image, 1783–1815,'' ibid. 3 (1967) have been important
studies in iconographic analysis. Fleming, now Professor Emeritus, continues to
do research on a new book in American material culture at the Winterthur
Museum.

Every culture, however primitive or advanced, is absolutely dependent on its
artifacts for its survival and self-realization.[2] The earliest records of man include
objects made to satisfy his many needs—to extend his physical and psychic power
over nature and his fellow man, delight his fancy, affirm his sense of form, and
create symbols of meaning. If a basic wonder about man is his capacity for building
culture, certainly the next wonder is his astounding capacity for making things as
part of his culture. In this he surpasses the animal a thousand times in cunning,
power, imaginativeness, beauty, destructiveness, and grandeur. To know man we
must study the things he has made—the Parthenon, the Panama Canal, Stonehenge,
the computer, the Taj Mahal, the space capsule, Michelangelo's *Pietà*, the highway
cloverleaf, the Great Pyramid, and Rembrandt's self-portraits. The artifacts made
and used by a people are not only a basic expression of that people; they are, like
culture itself, a necessary means of man's self-fulfillment.

Study of artifacts is therefore a primary humanistic study. Along with the study
of man's physical constitution, his ideas and institutions, the physical settings in
which he has lived, and the records of his actions in time, there is an obvious,
natural, universal fascination with the things man has made. Kenneth Clark has
popularized a dictum of John Ruskin's: "Great nations write their autobiographies
in three manuscripts, the book of their deeds, the book of their words, and the book
of their art. Not one of these books can be understood unless we read the two others,
but of the three the only trustworthy one is the last." [3] Nevertheless, the exploration
of the things man has made may be one of the least developed of our humanistic
studies. Using Leslie A. White's three main subdivisions of culture—material,
social, and mental—it can be argued that material culture has received less systematic attention than the other two.[4]

Certain academic disciplines do, to be sure, center their attention on artifacts.
First in popularity is art history, with its study of those works of man having a
relatively high aesthetic component—architecture, sculpture, painting, graphics,
and decorative arts. Second, perhaps, is archaeology—prehistoric and historic—
with its examination and analysis of the entire spectrum of man-made objects
recovered from the earth. A more recently organized discipline is the history of
technology, which gives serious attention to artifacts made to perform work. Far
less organized than these three disciplines in its approach to artifacts is cultural
history, which in many instances has made effective use of both practical and
artistic objects, but which has not, as yet, developed either models or a methodology for the analysis and interpretation of this kind of primary source material. The

first and only session devoted to material culture as such by the American Historical Association was at its 1964 annual meeting and by the Organization of American Historians at its 1972 annual meeting. Other disciplines analyzing and interpreting material culture include cultural geography and folk culture.

Related loosely to the preceding disciplines, but concentrating on specific types of material culture, are museums. Of the 6,000 museums in the United States and Canada, some 2,200 might be classified as natural history museums. The latter include museums of science and technology, art, and history, though more and more museums—such as historic house museums and outdoor "living" museums—cannot be neatly classified under these headings. The American Association of Museums defines these institutions chiefly by their collections of artifacts. Their mission is the acquisition, cataloging, conservation, exhibition, study, and interpretation of artifacts. It would be logical to assume that a substantial contribution to the study of material culture should come from the community of numerous and rapidly growing cultural history museums in this country.

Important progress has been made in analysis of the physical properties of museum objects and in methods of preventing their physical deterioration. Important progress, also, has been made in exploring the different ways in which the encounter of observer and object can be promoted through imaginative attention to angles of vision, lighting, and use of multimedia communication. At the information level, techniques are constantly being improved for identifying and cataloging objects in museum collections, moving toward more standardized methods of classification, better methods of material analysis, and devices for faster information retrieval. There has not been equivalent progress in differentiating the information level from the conceptual level in the museum scholar's research with collections, and it is especially on these conceptual levels, which this paper will call cultural analysis and interpretation, that more work remains to be done. For example, the interrelationship of the artifact and its culture is implicit in all that museums say and write about their collections, but relatively few contributions have been made to a theoretical understanding of the ways in which the artifact explicitly implements, expresses, and documents a particular way of life. In short, museums have paid relatively little attention to developing a discipline of artifact study.

A Proposed Model for Artifact Study

This paper is an attempt to present a model for artifact study.[5] It is a model that can, I hope, identify many of the possible approaches to the subject, provide a framework relating them to each other, and thus suggest the outlines of a program of collaborative research for all who are engaged in study of the artifact. The model has been developed in the context of the study of early American decorative arts. With this background it doubtless bears the special impress of thinking oriented toward cultural history, but it should be equally applicable in other areas of study. The model uses two conceptual tools—a five-fold classification of the basic properties of an artifact and a set of four operations to be performed on these properties. (See table 10.1.)

The five basic properties provide a formula for including and interrelating all the significant facts about an artifact. These properties of an artifact are its history, material, construction, design, and function. History includes where and when it was made, by whom and for whom and why, and successive changes in ownership, condition, and function. Material involves what the object is made of—woods, fibers, ceramic bodies, metals, glass, and so on. Construction has to do with the techniques of manufacture employed, workmanship, and the way parts are organized to bring about the object's function. Design includes the structure, form, style, ornament, and iconography of the object. Function embraces both the uses (intended functions) and the roles (unintended functions) of the object in its culture, including utility, delight, and communication.

The four operations to be performed on the five properties yield answers to

TABLE 10.1
Diagram of a Model of Artifact Study

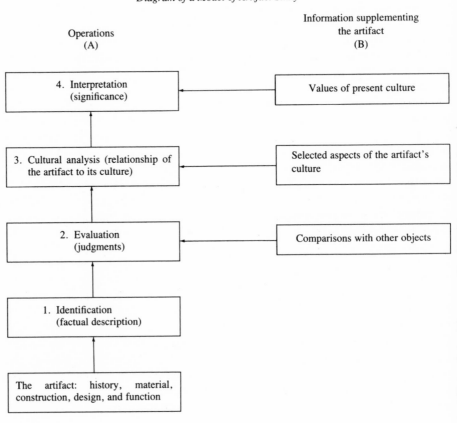

most of the important questions we want to ask about an artifact. These operations are identification (including classification, authentication, and description), which results in a body of distinctive facts about the artifact; evaluation, which results in a set of judgments about the artifact, usually based on comparisons with other examples of its kind; cultural analysis, which examines the various interrelationships of an artifact and its contemporary culture; and interpretation, which suggests the meaning and significance of the artifact in relation to aspects of our own culture. Each of these operations may involve each of the five properties of the artifact, and each successive operation is dependent upon those preceding it. Identification is the foundation for everything that follows; interpretation is the crown. A further word about each of these four operations is in order.

Identification: Identification should begin with the question, what is it? The answer is classification—specification of the general class to which the particular object under consideration belongs. Most current systems of classification are unsystematic. Many are based on function (chair, floor covering, coffeepot, or firearm), some on material (textile or glassware), others on construction (painting or print), or on iconography and subject matter (map). The adoption of a more uniform and exact classification scheme for artifacts should be considered a major item of unfinished business in the development of a rigorous discipline of material culture study.

The second step in identification is authentication to determine whether the object is genuine.[6] Is it actually what it purports to be in date, provenance, authorship, material, and construction? Is it a fake or forgery made with a deliberate intent to deceive or a reproduction made without intent to deceive? Is this log cabin the one in which Daniel Boone actually lived? Is this sword truly the one worn by George Washington at Yorktown? Was this silver tankard, with its Paul Revere mark, really made by Revere? The skills of connoisseurship or laboratory analysis, or both, may be used in authentication, which is sometimes referred to as "external criticism." Authentication is the precondition for accurate identification. Another element in identification is description, possibly by both words and images. Description often begins with measurements that specify the dimensions and sometimes the weight of the object. The essence of description is the concise and orderly delineation of the physical aspects of the object.

The chief objective of identification is to provide accurate information about the five properties of the artifact. This information must obviously be based on authentication and will either precede or follow description. Since it is the rare artifact that fully identifies itself with a maker's mark or label, a date, and an owner's initials and that remains (like a building or a gravestone) in the place of its origin, this information must be hunted out. Finding it can involve a combination of connoisseurship and extensive, painstaking research using not only a number of primary and secondary verbal sources (probate records, family records, bills of sale, newspaper advertisements, design books, emblem books, travel accounts, city registers, and so forth), but also a growing range of sophisticated technical hardware.

The tools of the scientist are increasingly employed by museums to reveal physical and chemical properties not apparent to the naked eye. Authentication can hinge on the results of these investigations, which necessarily require a knowledge of what was technologically feasible in various historical periods.

Identification can be simple and brief, as in the case of picture captions, exhibit labels, and catalog cards, or it can be extended and detailed. Extended identification might involve discovering biographical details about the maker, the purchaser, or the owner of the artifact; the cultural geography of its place of origin; the sources and characteristics of the material; the origins and antecedents of the techniques of construction or the design motifs employed; the history of the functional form; or the meaning of the iconography. An important type of extended identification contributed by art historians is the location of a center from which the style or ornament of an artifact was originally diffused and the modifications this style underwent.[7] It is obvious that the amount of extended identification that can be undertaken is unlimited. The fruits of this research can be embodied in monographs that are not artifact studies in themselves, but can form part of, or contribute to, the identification operation in artifact studies. One property of the artifact—function— so obviously involves the whole artifact, rather than its details, and so uniquely relates the artifact to its culture that the extended identification of function is considered to be part of the operation of cultural analysis discussed below.

Evaluation: Although our understanding of an artifact must begin with the identification of its properties, it can be greatly extended by the evaluation of those properties in terms of our culture's value standards. There are two kinds of evaluation. One has to do with judgments of aesthetic quality and workmanship, for instance, the appropriateness of material and texture, skill and taste of craftsmanship, effectiveness of overall design (proportion, balance, and unity), and expressiveness of form, style, and ornament. Such judgments result in a ranking of the artifact's qualities—for example, excellent or poor—and depend on a subjective exercise of the observer's taste and discrimination. The other kind of evaluation consists of factual comparisons of one object with others of its kind in quantifiable terms, such as relative size, cost, rarity, or temporal primacy, as determined through objective research. If extensive, this research may become the operation of cultural analysis as defined below. Evaluation can result in applying to the object such adjectives as similar, unique, early example, avant-garde, *retardataire*, and so on. Evaluation might compare the given artifact with other artifacts made by the same craftsman, or it might compare the given artifact with similar ones made by other craftsmen in the same subculture. An artifact made in one region might be compared with a similar one made in another region.[8]

Identification and evaluation constitute the special province of connoisseurship and curatorship. When these operations are accomplished through direct perception—the trained eye and knowing touch matured by the special kind of artifact expertise resulting from extensive experience in examining and comparing objects—and the findings are interpreted by a well-stocked memory bank of precise images, we are in the presence of the connoisseur.[9] When connoisseurship is supplemented by additional skills in the cataloging, care, conservation, exhibition of objects, and scientific examination, we are in the presence of the curator. Identification, and to a lesser extent evaluation, provide the essential building blocks for conceptual generalization about the artifact. These generalizations represent the fruit of the third and fourth operations, cultural analysis and interpretation.

Cultural analysis: The third operation, cultural analysis, begins where identification and evaluation leave off. It is found in any one of a dozen different kinds of artifact study that seek to examine in depth the relation of the artifact to aspects of its own culture. Certainly it embraces the largest potential of artifact study.

One important form of cultural analysis deals with the functions performed by the artifact in its culture. Unlike the other artifact properties of material, construction, and design, function involves both the concrete and the abstract aspects of the artifacts, the reasons for its initial manufacture, its various intended uses, and its unintended roles. Functional analysis, indeed, reveals the essential importance and meaning of the things man has made. Ordinarily, the most obvious and simplest function of an artifact is its utility as a tool. Discussion of the utility function will necessarily involve discussion of the human behavior associated with the artifact and the social groups of structures engaging in that behavior. The artifact also functions as a vehicle of delight through its form and decoration. Finally, by means of its materials, construction, design, and use of signs and symbols, the artifact functions as a vehicle of communication conveying status, ideas, values, feelings, and meaning. In some cases functional analysis will indicate the ways in which the artifact became an agent of major change within its culture.[10]

Related to functional analysis are several kinds of historical analysis that further seek to indicate the place of the artifact in its culture. For example, the esteem in which an object was held by its culture might be determined from learning the quantity produced or imported, prices paid, and allusions to the particular form in both pictorial and verbal documents of the period. Research in these areas would suggest the social function of the artifact and whether its use was confined to one class or subculture or was more widespread.[11] Whatever meaning it held for its culture and how it conveyed that meaning is an essential part of cultural analysis.

Other forms of cultural analysis that may yield significant conceptual generalizations are sampling operations involving a body of related artifacts. For purposes of cultural analysis, artifacts may, for example, be grouped according to one or more of the following criteria: their identification with a specific culture or subculture, geographical area, a single maker, or a group of makers, a unique set of physical and aesthetic characteristics, and so on. The purpose in cultural analysis is to isolate characteristics common to the group that enable the researcher to make inferences of a general nature about the society that produced and/or used the body of artifacts. On the basis of one type of sample, cultural analysis might establish a chronology of construction techniques or design traits. The chronology might focus on whether design traits found in one region predated or followed similar design traits found in other regions. Relationships determined from a sample could be graphed to indicate chronological sequences, expressed in tabular form to clarify types and subtypes, or subjected to statistical analysis.[12]

Cultural analysis can carry artifact study beyond description toward explanation by "the explication of those critical links that exist between human behavior and its material products." [13] Some of these links, termed "real intersections," were discussed by George Kubler in a passage in which he underlined the importance in art history of going beyond identification to cultural analysis:

In the history of art, which is a young discipline, it has long been necessary to restrict attention to manageable questions like artistic biography and catalogues and iconography. It is now apparent that those tasks have been accomplished and that we need not repeat them over and over. . . . Many more new tasks lie in connecting the history of art with other fields of thought, by finding intersecting lines of investigation where thought renews both itself and the fields it illuminates. In other words, the history of art can look beyond its own well-worn road to intersections with other roads. These intersections, however, are of two kinds. There are real intersections, as when economic history and silversmithing connect in the use of coin silver. But there are also virtual intersections which exist only in the beholder's mind. . . . They exist as possibilities, and it is in them that we can hope to discover some latent system of relations far more instructive than those revealed by the study of real problems.[14]

Kubler's real intersections between the component subsystems of a culture suggest a host of interesting and important research possibilities, most of them of an interdisciplinary nature. This interdisciplinary approach to cultural analysis explores parallels or relationships between the expressive products of one cultural subsystem and similar patterns in other subsystems, such as how an artifact relates to the religious beliefs, ideas, standard of living, and politics of its subculture. Erwin Panofsky regarded this comparison of the "intrinsic meaning or content" discovered in different cultural subsystems as the ideal meeting ground of the various humanistic disciplines.[15]

Research along these lines, which Richard Sykes argues could be the unifying theme of American Studies, is beginning to appear. The intersections between the old silver of American churches and denomination, type of piece, church location, and so on, have been explored by Anthony Garvan with the aid of a computer. He has also traced relationships between the iconography of New England porringers and Puritan ideas of love and marriage. Intersections between the iconography of Edward Winslow's silver sugar boxes and concepts of courtly love, marriage, and fertility have been suggested by Edward J. Nygren. Barbara Teller has examined intersections between ownership of four types of imported ceramic forms and three income levels in eighteenth-century Providence. Henry Glassie has studied Anglo-American material culture of the eighteenth century in relation to the Georgian mind-set, and Alan Gowans has pointed out connections between Federal-Adamesque architecture, Federalist politics, and new mercantile wealth. Other real intersections throw light on "the dynamics of change in material objects as a function of changes in the society which produced them," as in the investigation of changes in gravestone iconography in relation to changes in religion, population, social values, and social organization in early New England by Edwin Dethlefsen and James Deetz.[16]

Kubler's virtual intersections, which can throw a brilliant light on the larger character of the artifact, consist of noncausal, unprovable, but possible correspondences and conformities between artifacts and cultural constructs. Examples are studies correlating the pattern of ceramic usage in early Plymouth with that of the Stuart yeoman foodways subsystem; relating living room styles to intergenerational mobility, frequency of church attendance, and political party preference; and hypothesizing that the development of eighteenth-century American Georgian architecture conforms to six principles of maturation.[17]

Two reciprocal methods of procedure in discovering the real and virtual intersections of an artifact with its culture are product analysis (the ways in which a culture leaves its mark on a particular artifact) and content analysis (the ways in which a particular artifact reflects its culture). From the standpoint of product analysis, every artifact—in its history, material, construction, design, and function—is a product of its culture. "Every epoch, everywhere," Edgar Kaufman asserted, "creates the objects it needs in its own spirit, its individual character unmistakably stamped on them." From the standpoint of content analysis, every artifact is a document bearing some content of evidence about its culture, and in this role it can serve as primary source material for the cultural historian. "It is easy to overlook the data afforded by physical survivals and objects of material culture," warns the *Harvard Guide to American History*, "yet such vestiges of the past may be quite as revealing as written records." Artifacts are not only natural facts in themselves, but the evidence they contain can be read to establish historical facts on which the structure of historical interpretation can be raised. These historical facts may indicate the technological level of a culture, the materials at its command, its taste and form preference, quality of craftsmanship, trade relations, standard of living, social usage, popular enthusiasms, and life-style.[18] When the scholar's research subject is a particular artifact, he will probably concentrate on explaining how the shaping influence of the culture made the artifact what it is. When the scholar's subject is a particular culture, he will probably concentrate on extracting evidence from the artifact about the character of its culture.

It is evident that both product and content analysis equally involve the interrelationship of artifacts and culture. Of the two, the former is the more readily accepted and carried out. Content analysis, on the other hand, is a less familiar concept. The general proposition that the structures, tools, dress, jewelry, settlement patterns, and art of a people help us to understand that people is universally accepted; it is the chief basis of all foreign travel and museum visitation. But when the specific question is raised as to just what these objects tell us, the proposition often seems less clear. Little has been written on the specific question as to whether and how artifacts (nonverbal documents) constitute evidence of a culture in the same way as written texts (verbal documents).[19] In fact, procedures in reading the content of a nonverbal document parallel those in reading the content of a verbal document. In each case the would-be reader must start by being literate. In the case of the verbal document, he must understand the vocabulary of nouns, adjectives, verbs, and prepositions and how they are put together. In the case of the nonverbal document, he must understand the vocabulary of material, construction, design, and function and how they are put together.

Assuming one is literate in the language of the document to be read, it is necessary to begin with identification. The unidentified document is worthless as evidence. Sometimes a document carries its own identification. A letter may indicate where and when it was written, by whom, and to whom; a silver tankard may bear a maker's mark that gives a good clue as to who, where, and when, or a coat of arms that indicates for whom. At other times the document does not identify itself, and extrinsic aids must be used—a comparison of the unidentified item with identified ones, the resort to handwriting experts and connoisseurs of craft construction, and the consultation of calendars, atlases, dictionaries, encyclopedias, and handbooks of heraldry. Moreover, not only the general character of the document, but its terms will have to be identified—proper names, place names, reference to events, ornament, and iconography that can be clarified only with the help of outside references. If sound identification is finally made, it does not matter whether it was made by the use of reference tools or not. Certainly no assumption is implied, with either the verbal or the nonverbal document, that the document must "speak for itself" and be self-identifying.

Once validated as authentic and identified, the document can be read for content. The content of each document will be formulated in a series of statements. The artifact is actually a bundle of facts, and its content is, in theory, the sum total of all the statements that result from combining what we know about its properties with what we know about its history. In practice, content is only those statements that seem relevant to our investigation.

Once the content is available, it will normally be evaluated for its importance. Does it constitute new evidence? Does it confirm or contradict existing evidence? In all these steps in reading the content of the artifact, the scholar using the nonverbal document is proceeding through the same operations employed by the scholar using the verbal document. He stands under the same imperative to be objective, to be skeptical, to use public standards, and to use intuition with caution. The conclusions of the one need be no more impressionistic than those of the other.

Interpretation: The last of the four basic operations involved in artifact research is interpretation. Whereas cultural analysis was concerned with the relations of the artifact to its culture, interpretation is concerned with the relations of the artifact to our culture. More specifically, interpretation focuses on the relation between some fact learned about the artifact and some key aspect of our current value system, and relation must be sufficiently intense or rich to have self-evident meaning, significance, or relevance. Interpretation does not result in a statement of fact that can be documented, but a statement of relationship born of what Panofsky calls "synthetic intuition" and imagination that goes beyond documentation. As in content analysis, an artifact is not subject to just one "correct" interpretation, but many. Interpretation will vary as the personal, class, ideological, and national interests of interpreters and their audiences vary. Whatever the audience aimed at, interpretation will suggest the particular values held by it that are represented by the object under consideration. The study of the artifact is not complete until an interpretation of its significance has been offered.

The particular facts about the artifact that interpretation singles out for our attention may have come from the operations of identification, evaluation, or cultural analysis. It might be an association with some famous person or event in history; the use of some costly, rare, or novel material; some innovative technological principle embodied in construction; the superlative quality of design; the strategic character of symbolic function; the cultural changes effected by use; or the way the artifact expresses the lifestyle of the age or culture in which it originated. The value to which an object relates may be our love of statistical "firsts." Thus the significance of an artifact might be interpreted as the fact that it was the largest or tallest or costliest or first one of its kind. For an American audience, other relevant values to which facts about an artifact might be related are upward social mobility, American nationalism, American superiority or uniqueness, urbanization, ecology, democracy, mechanization, black power, or women's liberation. One might interpret the significance of the Model T Ford to be the pioneering application of the assembly line to mass production, its improvements on the internal combustion engine, or its provision of cheap transportation. On the other hand, its significance might be found in the fact that it was a particular instance of the general democratization of technological benefits or that it created a revolution in the lifestyle of rural America. Or its significance might be found in its effects and consequences, such as the increased mobility of the American people, the liberalized sexual ethics of the middle class, or air pollution.

11

Axioms for Reading the Landscape: Some Guides to the American Scene

Peirce F. Lewis

Introduction

While decorative arts historians such as Charles Montgomery have developed elaborate methods for understanding single objects, another cadre of researchers have explored techniques for identifying, classifying, and interpreting huge aggregates of diverse material culture. Within the latter group of interpreters we find cultural and historical geographers and landscape historians. While such researchers are sometimes intrigued by single genres of artifacts (e.g., Pennsylvania bank barns or Indiana covered bridges) often they work with a multiplicity of material culture, especially as it appears (or appeared) on the American landscape.

The titles of Peirce F. Lewis's six "axioms" for reading the cultural landscape verify this point. He proposes a simple set of guidelines by which to read the material culture still extant on the land. In his words, these techniques are like "the rules of grammar [that] sometimes help guide us through some particularly convoluted bit of syntax." Other scholars, such as Henry Glassie and Richard Latham, have noted the aptness of the linguistic analogy when speaking of "reading" artifacts; it may ultimately prove to be the most useful metaphor in the quest for a fairly comprehensive material culture studies methodology of object interrogation and interpretation.

In this essay, Lewis only hopes to prompt initial questioning that entails cultural, historic, geographic (or ecologic), and environmental inquiry into the physical data one finds scattered about both on the countryside and in the cityscape.

Two major assumptions underline his axioms: first, all human cultural landscapes have cultural meaning; and, second, culture is integrative, having a unity and wholeness. To explore these two premises fully, Lewis recommends (as does Craig Gilborn in the succeeding essay) that the material culture student pay attention to "common things" and "common landscapes": billboards and bomb shelters, motels and mobile homes, city parks and city dumps. Such a claim for a democracy of artifacts—all are equal because all reflect culture—can be contrasted with other approaches that tend only to investigate elite objects, such as Gorham silver or Sheraton chairs.

The approach of a cultural and historical geographer such as Lewis derives some of its techniques from geomorphology, plant ecology, and traditional geography, as well as from maverick landscape historians like J. B. Jackson and Grady Clay. Hence, one will find the nomenclature (for example, "diffusion," "region," and "convergence") of these disciplines intermingled with language (such as "taste," "fashion," "fad," "camp," and "kitsch") that Lewis also borrows from general cultural historians' discourse. He also offers some neat terms of his own devising, for example, his "corollary of historical lumpiness."

Perhaps the key questions that his essay raises for material culture study are: How do we keep from studying artifacts in vacuo? What precautions must be taken in order to insure adequate cultural context in any material culture analysis? One might also ask how many of the landscape axioms are applicable to investigating data that has been already disturbed from its original cultural context? Do the axioms have appropriate explanatory power when tested on artifacts housed in museum collections or historical societies?

Lewis has indirectly reflected on this issue in a useful essay, "The Future of the Past: Our Clouded Vision of Historic Preservation," Pioneer America (July 1975), and he has also done a seminal article, "Common Houses, Cultural Spoor," Landscape (January 1976), on the cultural and historical diffusion of the vernacular house type known as the upright-and-wing. In addition to being a major contributor to the landscape-reading exercises in The Local Community (New York: Macmillan, 1972), he has also authored the cultural geography case-study New Orleans: The Making of an Urban Landscape (Cambridge, Mass.: Ballinger, 1976) for the Association of American Geographers' Comparative Metropolitan Analyses Project.

The "axioms" essay, like those authored by Charles Montgomery and E. McClung Fleming in this section on method, was first a classroom exercise, in this case a geography course on the American landscape that Lewis teaches at the Pennsylvania State University. It appeared in a slightly abbreviated format in the Journal of Architectural Education (September 1976) and in the form reprinted here in The Interpretation of Ordinary Landscapes edited by D. W. Meinig (New York: Oxford University Press: 1979), pp. 11–32.

For most Americans, ordinary landscape is something to be looked at, but seldom thought about. I refer to man-made landscape or what geographers call "cultural landscape," not "natural landscape." It rarely occurs to most Americans to think of landscape as including everything from city skylines to farmers' silos, from golfers' putting greens to municipal garbage dumps, from ski slopes to manure piles, from the mansions of millionaires to the tract houses of Levittown and the immobile "mobile homes" of the ordinary rural trailer "park"—in fact, whole countrysides and whole cities. Although the term is seldom so used, it is proper and important to think of cultural landscape as nearly everything that we can see.

At first that idea sounds odd. The noun "landscape" evokes images of snow-capped mountains and waves beating on a rock-bound coast. But the fact remains that nearly every square millimeter of the United States has been altered by human-kind somehow—at some time. "Natural landscapes" are as rare as unclimbed mountains and for similar reasons. George H. L. Mallory expressed a very American sentiment when he said he wanted to climb Mt. Everest because it was there. Americans tinker with landscape as if pursued by some inner demon, and they have been doing so ever since their ancestors landed at Jamestown and Plymouth and began chopping down trees. They continue today—the sound of the power lawn mower is heard throughout the land.

All of this is obvious, but the implications are less obvious, though very simple and very important to our understanding of the United States. The basic principle is this: *all human landscape has cultural meaning*—no matter how ordinary that landscape may be. It follows, as Mae Thielgaard Watts has remarked, that we can "read the landscape" as we might read a book.[1] Our human landscape is our unwitting autobiography, reflecting our tastes, our values, and our ideas, in tangible, visible form. We rarely think of landscape that way, and so the cultural record we have "written" in the landscape is liable to be more truthful than most autobiographies because we are less self-conscious about how we describe ourselves. Grady Clay has said it well: "there are no secrets in the landscape."[2] All our cultural warts and blemishes are there and our glories too, but above all, our ordinary day-to-day qualities are exhibited for anybody who wants to find them and who knows how to look for them.

Very few academic disciplines teach their students how to read landscapes or encourage them to try. Traditional geomorphology and traditional plant ecology are two happy exceptions, they are disciplines which insist that their practitioners use their eyes and think about what they see. It is no accident that some of America's most accomplished landscape readers derive from those fields, the very fields that encourage students to view the world as a whole. A few—a very few (other academics, cultural geographers, and folklorists)—can do it too. The distinguished folklorist Henry Glassie and his equally distinguished geographic mentor, Fred Kniffen, come immediately to mind.[3] David Lowenthal and John Fraser Hart are leaders in the small company of American geographers who read landscape well.[4] Once in a long while, you run across an accomplished landscape reader in an unexpected place, and the result can be dazzling. George Stewart, for example, hung his academic hat in the English department at the University of California, Berkeley,[5] and we are all the richer for it. But it remains a sad fact that most academics who should be our most expert landscape readers are egregiously inept. To be sure, there are glorious exceptions: people like Alan Gowans, Reyner Banham, and Grady Clay, but they remain exceptions nevertheless.[6]

So unless one is lucky enough to have studied with a plant ecologist like Pierre Dansereau, a geomorphologist like J. Hoover Mackin, or a man like J. B. Jackson, who simply has kept his eyes and mind open all his adult life, one is likely to need guidance.[7] To "read landscape," that is, to make cultural sense of the ordinary things that constitute the workaday world of things we see, most of us need help.

What we needed, I concluded, were some guides to help us read the landscape, just as the rules of grammar sometimes help guide us through some particularly convoluted bit of syntax. Little by little, I began to write down some of the rules that I found helped me understand what I saw over the years of looking and learning and teaching about American landscapes. I call these rules "axioms," because they seem basic and self-evident, as any proper axiom must be.

The Axiom of Landscape as Clue to Culture

The man-made landscape—the ordinary run-of-the-mill things that humans have created and put upon the earth—provide strong evidence of the kind of people we are, were, and are in the process of becoming. In other words, the culture of any nation is unintentionally reflected in its ordinary vernacular landscape.

The corollary of cultural change. Our human landscape—our houses, roads, cities, farms, and so on—represents an enormous investment of money, time, and emotions. People will not change that landscape unless they are under very heavy pressure to do so. But there is evidence of change all around us, and we must conclude that the pressures are (and have been) very strong.

The regional corollary. If one part of the country (or even one part of a city) looks substantially different than some other part of the country (or city), then the chances are very good that the cultures of the two places are different also. Thus, much of the South looks different than the rest of the country, not only because the climate is different, but also because some important parts of southern culture really are different from the rest of the country, although not necessarily in the way that some propagandists would like us to think. So also, Negro ghettos in northern cities look different than adjacent white areas, because the culture of ghettos remains distinctive.

The corollary of convergence. To the degree that the looks of two areas come to be more and more alike, one may surmise that the cultures are converging also. Thus many small southern towns look quite different from their northern counterparts; while meantime, Atlanta looks more and more like the "standard" northern city, and some of it looks still more like Phoenix, perhaps America's most super-

American city. One may properly conclude that the cultural rift between North and South is growing narrower, but that the process of reunion is taking place faster in urban places than in rural ones.

The corollary of diffusion. The look of a landscape often is changed by imitation. That is, people in one place see what is happening elsewhere, like it, and imitate it if possible. The timing and location of such imitative changes are governed by various forms of geographic and social diffusion, which are surprisingly predictable, and which tell us a good deal about the way that cultural ideas spread and change. For example, Greek Revival architecture spread from Virginia into upstate New York in the early nineteenth century, thence, in debased form, to other parts of the country. Both the spread and the debasement took nearly a century to complete.[8] In the 1970s, California landscape tastes were widely and wildly imitated in most parts of the country. The delay between California invention and eastern imitation is extremely small, sometimes almost instantaneous.

The corollary of taste. Different cultures possess different tastes in cultural landscape; to understand the roots of taste is to understand much of the culture itself.

While most people admit they have "taste" in landscape, and in fact would insist they do, they often claim that their tastes are based on "practical" grounds. That is ludicrously untrue in most instances. A huge amount of our day-to-day behavior and the landscapes created by that behavior is dictated by the vagaries of "fashion" or "taste" or "fad." And when we speak of "taste," we are talking about culture, not about practicality.[9]

At first glance, some fads seem trivial, like hula-hooping or skate-boarding, apparent eccentricities that sweep the country and then are gone. But what guides those fads? Are they really so different from deep-seated cultural biases that anthropologists and cultural geographers take so seriously, like dietary "laws" that encourage us to eat the meat of steers and chickens and produce nausea at the thought of eating cats and dogs? Why do we build domes and spires on public buildings but rarely on our houses? Why did lightning rods suddenly appear on the American scene and then disappear except as antiques? (Climatic change, perhaps?) Why do we plant our front yards in grass, water it to make it grow, mow it to keep it from growing too much, and impose fines on those who fail to mow often enough?

The Axiom of Cultural Unity and Landscape Equality

Nearly all items in human landscapes reflect culture in some way. There are almost no exceptions. It follows that most items in the human landscape are no more and no less important than other items in terms of their role as clues to culture.

Thus, the McDonald's hamburger stand is just as important a cultural symbol (or clue) as the Empire State Building, and the change in McDonald's building design may signal an important change in cultural attitudes, just as the rash of Seagrams's shoebox skyscrapers heralds the arrival of a new kind of American city—and a new variant of American culture. The painted cement jockey-boy on the front lawn in lower-middle-class suburbia is just as important a symbol as the Brooklyn Bridge, and the California skateboard is as important as the Washington Monument, no more, no less.

The axiom parallels an equally basic proposition: that culture is whole—a unity—like an iceberg with many tips protruding above the surface of the water. Each tip looks like a different iceberg, but each is in fact part of the same object.

But note these caveats: (1) If an item is unique (like the only elephant-shaped hotel south of the 40th parallel, located in Margate, New Jersey), it may not seem to mean much, except that its creator was rich and crazy. (2) One should not be too hasty, however, in judging something "unique." That elephant-shaped hotel has many very close relatives, such as giant artichokes in Castroville, California, and billboards that blow smoke rings in Times Square. In some circles, such things are called "camp," "pop," or "kitsch." (3) The fact that all items are equally important emphatically does not mean that they are equally easy to study and understand. Sometimes the commonest things are the hardest to study.

The Axiom of Common Things

Common landscapes, however important they may be, are by their nature hard to study by conventional academic means. The reason is negligence combined with snobbery. One has no trouble finding excellent books about famous buildings like Monticello or famous symbolic structures like the Brooklyn Bridge.[10] Curious antique objects get a lot of attention too: olde spinning wheels and Olde Williamsburg. But it is hard to find intelligent, nonpolemical writing about mobile homes, motels, gas stations, shopping centers, billboards, suburban tract housing design, the look of fundamentalist churches, water towers, city dumps, or garages and carports, yet such things are found nearly everywhere Americans have set foot, and they obviously reflect the way ordinary Americans behave most of the time.

The corollary of pop literature. Happily, not all American writers, nor foreign visitors, are as snotty as American scholars. Even though there is little written about motels and fast-food eateries in the "standard" scholarly literature, the country is awash with fascinating and useful material about these common items. One merely has to look in the right place. Some of the "right places" include the writings of the "new journalists," like Tom Wolfe, who reflects with devastating accuracy on such things as the landscape of drag-racing, Las Vegas billboards, the architecture of surfing (including surfers' arcane haircuts) and above all, the cultural contexts from which such landscapes spring.[11]

Trade journals written for people who make money from vernacular landscapes are also such places. If, for example, you want to know why your local franchised hamburger joint looks the way it does, start with the journal *Fast Food*, published (not surprisingly) for managers of fast-food restaurants, among others. There is remarkably candid advice on restaurant design that has been road-tested to catch the traveler's eye: outdoor signs and landscaping formulae that are based on cool, even chilly appraisals of American popular taste—a matter which lies at the very roots of culture. Journals like *Fast Food* can usually be trusted for their business judgment.[12]

Other "right places" include literature, often in the form of slick brochures that tell you not very subtly what you are supposed to see when you go to certain places. Recent changes in the landscape of the Pocono Plateau, for example, are much more easily understood after one has seen the marginal eroticism in brochures that beckon newlyweds to any of several Pocono "Honeymoon retreats." Old photographs and prints are obvious sources of historic information about landscape. Old advertisements are thought quaint and used to decorate suburban bathroom walls, but those old ads speak volumes about past technology, past taste, and past cultures.

The rare, oh, so very rare, book by a perceptive person who has really looked at a real landscape and discovered what it means is also valuable. If one really wants to understand what Americans are doing and thinking and aspiring to, sample the glories of George Stewart's *US 40: Cross-section of the United States of America* (1953) or Grady Clay's superb *Closeup: How to Read the American City* (1973). Almost anything by J. B. Jackson will do the job nicely, although "The Stranger's Path" is especially perceptive. Some of Jackson's greatest coups appear as un-signed "Notes and Comments" in *Landscape* during Jackson's editorship in the 1950s and 1960s.

The Historic Axiom

In trying to unravel the meaning of contemporary landscapes and what they have to "say" about us as Americans, history matters. That is, we do what we do and make what we make because our doings and our makings are inherited from the past. (We are a good deal more conservative than many of us would like to admit.) Furthermore, a huge part of the common American landscape was built by people in the past, whose tastes, habits, technology, wealth, and ambitions were different than ours today.

The corollary of historical lumpiness. Most major cultural change does not occur gradually but instead in great sudden historic leaps—commonly provoked by great events like wars, depressions, major inventions, and the like. After these leaps, landscape is likely to look very different than it did before the leap occurred. Inevitably, however, a lot of "pre-leap" landscape will be left lying aroung, even though its reason for being has disappeared. Thus, the southern landscape is littered with sharecroppers' houses, even though the institution of sharecropping has nearly disappeared—a victim of the boll weevil and a concatenation of other forces that combined to destroy the old Cotton Belt in the early 1900s and provoked a migration of black farmers northward, eventually to change the entire urban landscape of industrial America. Most small towns in America, at least of the Norman Rockwell ilk, are like the Cotton Belt: obsolete relics of a different age. There are no more being built today, and unless things in America change radically, there will be no more.

The mechanical (or technological) corollary. To understand the cultural significance of a landscape, or an element of the landscape, it is helpful (and often essential) to know how the landscape originated, not just in general, but in particular about the mechanics of technology and communications that made the element possible.

For example, we can speculate endlessly (and often pointlessly) about the "symbolism" of, say, the American front lawn, made of mown green grass— perhaps as a status symbol or perhaps reflecting a borrowing from England and thus a subliminal reflection of our admiration for things English. But much of that "symbolic speculation" is likely to be hot air unless we really know how a lawn works—in a very mechanical way. The fact that most of us have direct experience with lawns—planting and mowing and fertilizing and irrigating and cursing them— obscures two important facts: First, that we do many mechanical things to establish and maintain a lawn that we take for granted (such as getting the lawnmower serviced) but are nonetheless essential. Second, that we need to know who invented the machinery to make the lawn possible; who took that invention and engineered the machinery so that it came within the financial reach of every man (invention and engineering are emphatically not the same thing); who adopted the machinery; how the idea spread; and, above all, when all this happened, in what order, where these events took place, and how they spread, often in direct defiance of environmental good sense.[13]

All that, of course, is a big order for something so commonplace as the American lawn. Yet pause and consider what we are really discussing. Every step of the way we are investigating the evolution of American culture: where things started, when, and how. The key word is how, for unless one knows about the technology behind the landscape element we are concerned with, the fact remains that we really know very little about it. Speculation about symbolism will remain unprofitable.[14]

The Geographic (or Ecologic) Axiom

Elements of a cultural landscape make little cultural sense if they are studied outside their geographic (locational) context. To a large degree, cultures dictate that certain activities should occur in certain places and only in those places. Thus, all modern American cities are segregated: streetwalkers are not found throughout the city, nor are green lawns, trees, high buildings, or black people. This axiom is so obvious that it need not be mentioned, except that so many scholars and "practical" people persistently flout it. Architectural historians publish books, full of handsome photographs of "important buildings," artfully composed so that the viewer will not see the "less important" building next door, much less the telephone wires overhead or the gas station across the street. The "important building" is disembodied, as if on an architect's easel in a windowless studio somewhere. So also, planners make grand schemes to improve sections of existing cities—plans drawn on large blank sheets of paper, with adjacent areas shown in vague shades of gray or not shown at all—as if the planning district existed *in vacuo*.

Again and again, historic preservationists throw up white picket fences around "historic buildings," while adjacent neighborhoods go to ruin. Inside is "history"; outside is not history. (Then preservationists wonder why the general public equates historic preservation with Disneyland!)

One can, of course, claim too much for the virtues of landscape reading. It is not a panacea—not the key to an understanding of culture and sometimes it is not even a key. Indeed, it can be a dangerous game, because it is pleasant to go outdoors and let your eyes roam idly across some nice bit of scenery and tell yourself that you are engaged in research. (Landscape reading will not put libraries out of business.)

One can, however, quite literally teach oneself how to see, and that is something that most Americans have not done and should do.[15] To be sure, neither looking by itself nor reading by itself is likely to give us very satisfactory answers to the basic cultural questions that landscape poses. But the alternation of looking, reading, thinking, and then looking and reading again can yield remarkable results, if only to raise questions we had not asked before. That alternation may not only teach us more than we had ever dreamed. It may save our sanity.

12

Pop Pedagogy: Looking at the Coke Bottle

Craig Gilborn

Introduction

In the lexicon of modern commercial and industrial design, Americans have contributed several classics: for example, the Dixie cup, the Willys Jeep automobile, and the Eames plywood chair. Craig Gilborn maintains that the Coca-Cola bottle also deserves "classic" status because of its form, durability, powerful sculptural and optical aesthetic, and its ubiquity. In his judgment, it also merits the title of an American cultural symbol par excellence and thus deserves careful study by students of historic American material culture.

To do such a study, Gilborn suggests a series of techniques not unlike E. McClung Fleming's proposed model but involving three (rather than Fleming's four) operations that can be performed on any type of artifact. In addition to demonstrating how to submit ordinary Coke bottles to the basic research steps of description, classification, and interpretation, Gilborn also enumerates the methodological and learning objectives that underlie each operation as a teaching exercise. Suggestions are made as to how objects (e.g., the Christian cross, the American flag) might be assessed using the Gilborn approach.

Gilborn's essay shares common ground with several others in this anthology. Much like John Kouwenhoven, Gilborn is concerned by the lack of "object education" in the American school curriculum; he hopes more museum-based educational programs would work to overcome this deficiency. In addition to paralleling Fleming's methodology (Gilborn took a degree from the Winterthur Program and served there for six years as director of education), his detailed analysis of the Coke bottle's diagnostic attributes, temporal sequence and duration, and stylistic evolution, can be compared to the investigation of New England gravestones reported on by archaeologists James Deetz and Edwin Dethlefsen in chapter thirteen. Finally, Gilborn recognizes, as does Ruth Schwartz

Cowan in her analysis of changing household technology (chapter fifteen), that the student of American material culture must always be aware of the marketplace; that is to say, that buying habits, economic depressions, and especially advertising play major roles in the history and interpretation of objects. As Gilborn succinctly puts it: "When the product cannot adapt to the changing pattern of buying habits, it will fail or become obsolete—the artifactual equivalent of extinction in the natural world."

Gilborn has been a consistent advocate of establishing stronger institutional and intellectual ties between historical studies in museum galleries and in academic classrooms. This article first appeared, appropriately enough, in Museum News (December 1968). Two years later, the Bowling Green University Popular Press reprinted it in an anthology of popular culture studies, Marshall Fishwick and Ray B. Brown, eds., Icons of Popular Culture (Bowling Green, Ohio: Bowling Green University Popular Press, 1970). Craig Gilborn is currently the director of the Adirondack Museum in New York State.

The redoubtable Samuel Johnson was citing a condition, and not offering a choice, when he wrote in the preface to his *Dictionary* (1755), "I am not yet so lost in lexicography as to forget that words are the daughters of earth, and that things are the sons of heaven." Dr. Johnson did not elaborate about the two realms of words and things, but he may have been acknowledging that words are not capable of translating all of those attributes of an object that are available to, and integrated by, the human senses. The cliché about a picture being worth a thousand words should be enlarged to include things: *Any thing is worth a thousand words.*

Knowledge of an object means that we have had some experience with it, either directly or on some previous occasion with an object that is similar or identical to it. In an article in *Museum News* I tried to convey the complexity and cultivation of this nonverbal knowledge as it is revealed in the performance of such object-centered specialists as the museum curator, the primitive hunter, and the preindustrial men and women whose daily tasks presupposed a vast body of informed, first-hand experience. Narrowing the scope of this article, I will pick up the discussion at the point in which recent educational theory and practice were said to be seeking to provide students with the kinds of first-hand experiences that challenge and motivate the scholar and scientist in their pursuit of knowledge.[1]

Objects are capable of yielding a considerable amount of information about themselves and the conditions in which they were formed or fashioned. Scholars and scientists in fields such as art history and criticism, archaeology, paleontology, and the life and earth sciences use terms and methodologies appropriate to their study of primary, nonverbal data. Without minimizing the differences that exist among those disciplines which take objects for their main source of evidence, it is worth asking whether the analysis of objects may not involve common modes of perception and organization, and, if so, whether this residuum may not be applied, in schematic form, in schools and museums where an introductory exercise in the study and handling of objects is both desirable and proper.

The "classic" Coca-Cola bottle is admirably studied for such an exercise. The Coke bottle has been manufactured for more than fifty years, a long history by modern standards. The bottle has maintained a continuity of form during this period but with discernible modifications from which relative and absolute chronologies can be obtained without resorting to any evidence but that presented by a sample of the bottles. Coke bottles are found in large quantities throughout the United States (and in most nations of the world); they are inexpensive, expendable, durable, and possess sculptural and optical qualities of great complexity. Accompanying the Coke bottle is an extensive lore consisting of anecdotes, personal associations, and behavior traits (for instance, the "Coke break") that amount to a "folk" tradition that is truly national in scope. Hence, the bottle is, by any practical educational standard, a model vehicle for the performance of those operations which are basic to the systematic analysis of objects.

A number of operations are involved in the study of objects.[2] Three broad operations, each capable of further subdivision, are identified in the sequence in which, generally, they are carried out: description, classification, and interpretation. The discussion that follows is based upon these operations as they apply to a study of the classic Coca-Cola bottle.

Several cautionary remarks are in order. First, the exercise outlined below cannot provide all the experiences that are part of the work that is performed in the field. For instance, description for the archaeologist frequently includes an entire site, not simply the objects uncovered in the site. Second, different disciplines place different emphasis upon the operations. Art historians seldom work out classifications, partly because the differences seem so much greater than similarities and partly because it is presumed that previous scholarship has established classifications that are still useful. Finally, this project is aimed at providing instructors with information and suggestions that can help them introduce students to the study of artifacts. The application of this material in the classroom is a matter best left to the instructor, but it is advisable that students be allowed considerable freedom rather than be constrained by undue emphasis on detail.

Descriptive Operation

The descriptive operation, as applied to the Coke bottle, would ask the student or team of students to describe the classic bottle (identified in table 12.1 as the "type") in terms of its attributes of shape, symbol markings, structural details, material, color, and the like. There are two objectives to this operation. The methodological objective provides a written and iconic record which can be consulted on other occasions, and the learning objective involves the student, or the scholar-scientist, as a learner of every detail of the object to be studied. In this exercise the

TABLE 12.1
Classification of Coca-Cola Bottles

		DIAGNOSTIC ATTRIBUTES	REMARKS
FAMILY		(1) "Coca-Cola" trademark and (2) Shape	6½, 10, 12, 16, 26 oz. returnables. Before 1957 beverage available only in 6 oz. bottles.
TYPES		Above plus (1) "6" or "6½" fl. ozs. or (2) height 7¾ inches	Green glass in America, clear glass for foreign markets (except Japan)
VARIANTS	Sub-Types	Above plus All-B B&P, or All-P	
A 1915	Sub-Types	Pronounced bulge	Prototype, designed by A. Samuelson, Terre Haute, Ind., U.S. patent No. 48160. One surviving example illustrated in *The Coca-Cola Bottler*, June, 1967, (pg. 102).
B 1916-23	All-Blown	"Bottle Pat'd Nov. 1915"	Slimmed down to accommodate standard bottle filling equipment. Protected by first patent. Mold no., Mfr's mark and year appear either on heel or hobble.
C 1923-37	All-Blown	"Bottle Pat'd Dec. 25, 1923"	U.S. design patent No. 63657.
D 1937-51	All-Blown	"Bottle Pat. D-105529"	Empty weight of bottle 14.01 oz., capacity 207.0 c.c. Bottle pat. March 24, 1937. Year-Mfr's Mark-Mold Number confined (?) to hobble.
E 1951-59	6 ozs.	(1) "Min contents" "6-Fl. ozs" and (2) "In U.S. Patent Office"	Common law rights protection with expiration of patent. Mfr's Mark moved to base, leaving year-mold number on hobble, e.g. "53-21"
F 1957-65	6½ ozs.	"6½ Fl. ozs."	Empty weight 13.80 oz., cap. 202.8 c.c. Second shape ever registered as a trademark (1960), protected while it identifies the product. Other trademarks: "Coca-Cola" (1893), "Coke" (1945).
G 1958-60	Blown & Painted	"Coke" not on throat	Transitional. Bottler's town ceases to appear on G, H, I.: re-appears on J. and K. Registration dimple appears. Empty Wt. 13.65 oz., Cap. 202.1 c.c.
H 1958-60	Blown & Painted	"Coke" on throat	Transitional. Painted labels appeared in 1956 but writer has seen none dated earlier than 1958.
I 1961-62	All-Painted	"Coke" on throat	
J 1963-65	All-Painted	(1) "Coke" on one panel & (2) "6½ oz" on one panel	Bottler's town re-appears on base of some bottles. Empty Wt. 13.26 oz., cap. 205.0 c.c.
K 1965-	All-Painted	"6½ oz" on both panels	Mfr's Marks: © Chattanooga Glass Co.: Ⓘ Owen-Illinois; LG Liberty Glass Co.: L. Laurens Glass Works: ⚓ Anchor Hocking.

learning objective is to develop an awareness of the diverse attributional character of objects.

Believers of the efficacy of words may find the attempt to describe the shape of the bottle a humbling experience. Metaphors have been used, but these are dated: "hobble-skirt"—so called because of the design of the dresses worn when the classic bottle was introduced—"Mae West," and "hourglass." Hence, line drawings are essential and to these a nomenclature of visible attributes should be assigned. Some of these attributes will be generic in that they are expressive of the functional form that we call "bottle" involving the use of such terms as "mouth," "lip," "neck," and so on. There may be collectives of attributes that indicate sections of the bottle, such as "top zone," "middle zone," or "front" and "back." Some attributes are peculiar to the Coca-Cola bottle itself, specifically the shape or design, the signatures "Coca-Cola" and "Coke" (all trademarked), and the ribs. Some attributes, such as material, color, and weight, cannot be visualized iconically, though they must be a part of any proper description. Signs of wear should be noted if they occur. (In the bottlers' lexicon a "bum" is a bottle that can be safely refilled, but that looks disreputable; a "scuffie" is a bum that is scuffed; and a "crock" is a bum with a chipped bottom.)

During this first operation, students may be given one bottle or one example from each of the subtypes designated in table 12.1. The latter choice will raise questions about differences that are to be dealt with in the classificatory operation.

Classification

The difference between description and classification is that the former treats each object as an entity—almost as if each were unique—whereas classification segregates objects on the basis of dissimilar attributes. An assumption at the outset of the classificatory operation is that there is a historical or functional relationship among the objects being classified, so that differences in attributes can be explained in terms of changed behavior or altered conditions, usually as they have taken place over a period of years.

There are two methodological objectives to classification: first, as suggested above, to reveal relationships that are real and not categorical (for example, billiard balls and tomatoes as "round, smooth" objects); and, second, to provide a future reference against which freshly uncovered specimens may be compared and identified or otherwise accounted for. The classification for the classic Coke bottle serves both objectives by indicating relationships among the subtypes and their variants and by providing a model for the identification of bottles. Like most classifications, this one is subject to modification or further refinement.

As for the learning objectives to this exercise, there are three that should be mentioned. The first is that while all objects consist of a variety of attributes, some of these attributes are diagnostic in that they identify groups or differentiate one group from another. Hence the attributes jointly diagnostic of the family are the

Coca-Cola signature and the shape of the bottle. By contrast, glass is not an attribute common to all Coca-Cola bottles.

A second learning objective might show the distinction between relative chronology and absolute chronology. It is possible to arrange the three subtypes and/or variants E through K in the sequence in which they were introduced, using internal evidence and the senses (including common sense) as means for proposing, for example, that blown and painted (B&P) bottles fall between all-blown (A–B) and all-painted (A–P) bottles. Deciding whether or not A–B bottles came before A–P bottles might be answered in two ways. One way is inconclusive, though it would probably lead to a correct choice in the case of the Coke bottle: this would see the development of the bottle proceeding from simple to more complex attributes, which would suggest a relative chronology of A–B, B&P, A–P.

The second way involves the use of frequencies of occurrence, the principle being that earlier specimens will be those that are found in fewer numbers. Since all of the classic Coke bottles carry the date of manufacture, it is possible to establish the absolute chronology and the durations of variants by examining a random sample of bottles and correlating dates with the variants. Sufficient numbers of variants E through K survive to make this frequency analysis possible wherever Coke bottles are found. Earlier variants (A through D) must be identified largely through written and pictorial materials, such as, for example, U.S. patents and advertisements which illustrate these early variants being used at times given by the date of publication.[3]

A third learning objective might indicate the ways in which the systematic analyses of objects are capable of generating information or new knowledge. The frequency approach, just cited, helps to verify what would otherwise be a highly theoretical classification; the fact that Coke bottles can be dated allows us to visualize the development of the Coke bottle and to raise questions about the possible human motivations or economic principles that lie behind the changes. For example, the sequence and durations of the manufacture of variant bottles indicates that while the Coca-Cola Company introduced variants one after another, there was considerable overlapping in the durations of manufacture, so that during the years 1958–60 there were four variants being manufactured. These overlapping durations notwithstanding, the "drift" from blown to painted bottles is apparent. The implications of this "drift" suggest that some sort of evolutionary principle may have been operative in the changes that have occurred in the Coke bottles of the last ten years or so.

Interpretative Operation

Interpretation is the culminating objective, since it addresses itself to the broad question, what possible meanings can be derived from the products of our labors?

For some scholars and scientists the objectives of description and classification constitute legitimate ends in their own right. Classification, they might assert, is itself a form of interpretation, albeit a form that imposes conditions upon any attempt to depart radically from recorded data. Others view interpretation as both an opportunity and a responsibility for the informed imagination to depart, if necessary, from facts to levels of generalization that may not be entirely supported by the evidence at hand. Whether the interpretation is modest or daring, a step or a leap from the bottom to the unknown, will depend upon the nature of the product and the materials that are being dealt with, the criteria of that accepted by the profession involved, and the personal abilities and inclinations of the interpreter. The following examples of analysis represent three (undefined) levels of generalization.

History

The beverage Coca-Cola was invented and first sold in Atlanta, Georgia, in 1886, by a pharmacist, John S. Pemberton.[4] Six years later the business was incorporated as "The Coca-Cola Company," and a year later, in 1893, the signature "Coca-Cola" was registered in the United States Patent Office. Almost from its inception the company adopted an aggressive policy aimed at winning public favor: by 1901 the advertising budget reached $100,000, a sum increased tenfold with the next ten years.

Coca-Cola was first bottled in 1894; between that year and 1915 the beverage was sold in straight-sided bottles of varying colors and designs. To protect their product from imitators, in 1916 the company adopted and patented a design devised the year before by Alexander Samuelson, an employee of the Root Glass Company, of Terre Haute, Indiana. Except for the slimming-down of the initial design and changes in the labeling characteristics, the basic form of the classic bottle has remained essentially unaltered since its introduction more than fifty years ago.

Presently there are three registered trademarks: "Coca-Cola" (since 1893), "Coke" (since 1945), and the design of the bottle (since 1960)—the last being previously protected by a succession of design patents and common law rights. The bottle was the second container to be trademarked (the first was the Haig and Haig "pinch bottle" in 1958).

The bottle is manufactured by six glass companies in approximately twenty-seven factories in the United States. Foreign bottlers obtain their bottles from manufacturers in countries of origin with labels in many languages. Nearly 6.6 billion Coke bottles were manufactured between 1916 and 1960 in the United States alone, and by 1966 the beverage was being sold in 132 countries and territories around the world.

America's pop artists, those flamboyant recorders of the commonplace, singled out the Coke bottle as one of their earliest subjects. Perhaps the first "pop" depiction of the bottle was Robert Rauschenberg's "Coca-Cola Plan," a sculptural construction of 1958 incorporating three bottles. Among other early treatments was Andy Warhol's large canvas illustrating 210 Coke bottles.[5] The remarkable form of the bottle, which Raymond Loewy has called the "most perfectly designed package today,'' and its unparalleled success as a commercial and cultural symbol are mingled in a still-life painting which associates the bottle and an egg. The sacred and the profane are confounded by these juxtapositions, in which the mysteries of art are appropriated by the dumb clutter of everyday life.

The Coke bottle is probably the most widely recognized commercial product in the world. Only one person out of 400 was unable to identify a picture of the bottle in a product recognition study undertaken for a pen manufacturer in 1949.[6] The bottle is one of the few truly participatory objects in the United States and in much of the rest of the world. Presidents drink Coca-Cola and so do sharecroppers; usage cuts across nationalities, social and occupational classes, age groups, and sexes. The bottle, unlike most other objects which might be regarded as symbols *par excellence* of American culture, is singularly free of anxiety-producing associations. It is regarded with affection by generations of Americans brought up in gasoline stations, boot camps, and drug stores, and it has been known to evoke pangs of nostalgia when Americans gather in the cafes of Europe and Asia.

Evolutionary Change

Evolution in the biological world has been applied to the civilizations and institutions of the human world. The extra-Darwinian use of evolutionary thought has been largely metaphorical—a means of visualizing the human story as a succession of periods following one another according to some presumed necessary developmental logic. Previous civilizations seem to have passed through periods of youth, maturity, and decay, but is this due to the preconceptions of historians or is it rather an expression of some profound law governing the development of human societies? Institutions and their products may provide evidence that can be more readily observed than the larger society of which they are a part.

An evolution of a sort has taken place with the Coca Cola bottle beginning in 1955, when the company introduced bottles that were partially painted. The older all-blown bottle, which had seen service since 1916, remained in production while the company determined the public's response to the greater visibility provided by the white label against the brown beverage. Between 1955 and 1965 the company introduced six variant bottles in succession, each variant introducing a new attribute (see table 12.1). What is interesting—and perhaps significant—is the progression in which a new attribute in an earlier variant became an old attribute in a later variant, so that each variant since 1955 has linked old-new attributes.

Do these linked attributes indicate the operation of some evolutionary principle? One might say that each change in the Coke bottle was the result of some overall corporate plan, and that the underlying decisions were arbitrary. But corporate decisions are predicated upon the future success of the product in the marketplace. When the product cannot adapt to changing patterns of buying habits, it will fail or become obsolete—the artifactual equivalent of extinction in the natural world.

In the 1950s the Coca-Cola Company was not expanding its sales to the satisfaction of its directors.[7] Other beverage producers were responding to an affluent consumer market that was willing to buy new varieties of flavors in a range of sizes. The Coca-Cola Company met the competitive challenge by adding four sizes of bottles and the metal can to the established classic bottle. (The nonreturnable bottles are another, more recent, development.)

The old workhorse bottle must have presented a problem: How could it be modified without damaging its demonstrated effectiveness as a seller of Coca-Cola? The answer was a gradual change of the bottle over a ten-year period, retaining the familiar all-blown bottle down to 1965 and introducing, between 1955 and 1965, a series of painted bottles whose modifications would become familiar and hence acceptable to the public. Raymond Loewy presented the dilemma facing corporate planners and industrial designers when he wrote that the "consumer is influenced in his choice of styling by two opposing factors: (a) attraction to the new and (b) resistance to the unfamiliar." [8] That a degree of stability has been achieved after a decade of change is indicated by the fact that variant K has been the only classic bottle in production since 1966.

Other questions that invite interpretation are: What are the sensuous (touch, sight, and so on) and psychological qualities that contribute to the effectiveness of the Coke bottle? How might archaeologists of a future millenium use the bottle in reconstructing the events and forces of the twentieth century? What kinds of ritualized behavior accompany the drinking of Coca-Cola from bottles? Compare the changing historic roles of the Christian cross, the American flag, and the Coca-Cola sign in the non-Western nations of the world.

Several points might be noted in conclusion. While words are not a substitute for first-hand experience, they are the most efficient means of organizing and communicating a part of that experience to oneself and to others. Dr. Johnson's remark, quoted earlier, should be pondered in much the same spirit of humility with which it was written: words and things *are* different, but this is not to say that we must therefore choose between a life of pure conception or of unmediated experiences, a proposition that seems to underlie much of the thinking of those who criticize, with justice, the traditional emphasis or reliance in education upon responses that begin and end with words, seldom consulting the world of the senses as a point of departure.

The second and third points are related, and they are formulated as questions. Are there common modes of perceiving and organizing evidence in artifacts? The Coca-Cola bottle is exceptional only because it provides opportunities for carrying out so many of the procedures that are part of the analyses of such diverse things as prehistoric pottery, candlesticks, and domestic architecture. Finally, do museums, as repositories of things and of these skills and knowledge which make these things understandable, have a legitimate role to play by clarifying, both for themselves and others, how objects may be used to inform the mind, but without burdening it with information which will be useless or forgotten a few years hence?

Part IV

Statements of Practice

The historian should consider looking at artifacts to be so much a part of his trade that he will, over the years, develop a keen critical sense regarding the authenticity and significance of the artifacts and restorations that he sees. To be used effectively, the artifacts must mean something to the historian directly, not once removed through the mind and eye of a curator.
—Eugene Ferguson, *Technology in Early America*

If I could do it, I'd do nothing at all here. It would be photographs; the rest would be fragments of cloth, bits of cotton, lumps of earth, records of speech, pieces of wood and iron, phials of odors, plates of food, and of excrement.
—James Agee and Walker Evans, *Let Us Now Praise Famous Men*

13

Death's Head, Cherub, Urn and Willow

James Deetz
Edwin S. Dethlefsen

Introduction

*Of all the branches of knowledge that use material culture as data, archaeology
probably has enjoyed the closest identification, in both the scholarly community
and the public mind, with artifacts. The stereotype of bearded scholars wearing
pith helmets and digging up Egyptian tombs, Roman cities, or North American
Indian mounds in search of mummies, statuary, or pottery shards persists, for
better or worse, in the popular imagination about the field. Some would relegate
archaeology to being a mere tool, a method of retrieving physical data, usually by
excavation and often employing the assistance of paleontologists, botanists, soil
specialists, and geologists in order to identify, date, and classify such material
remains of prehistory, that is, human history prior to the use of writing.*

*Current archaeologists, represented here by James Deetz and Edwin S.
Dethlefsen, both professors of anthropology, take a wider view of their craft. They
define archaeologists as "anthropologists who usually excavate the material
remains of past cultures, and through the study of such evidence attempt to
re-create the history of man from his earliest past and to determine the nature of
cultural systems at different times and places around the world." [1]*

*In the article that follows, several dimensions of this definition are further
explored. For example, in using seventeenth- and eighteenth-century New England
gravestones as what might be termed "above-ground archaeological evidence,"
Deetz and Dethlefsen suggest that the research of the archaeologist need not be
limited to prehistorical material culture or only to that which is buried. In their
demonstration of this point, they offer a sample analysis of what is now called
historical archaeology. Scholars who do historical archaeology investigate past
human cultures that have left behind both material culture remains and written
records. Since the pioneering work of the historical archaeologists, other subfields*

of the discipline have emerged to analyze American material culture by specific type of site (such as underwater archaeology and landscape archaeology) or by specific type of artifact (such as industrial archaeology and commercial archaeology). These approaches to material culture studies are illustrated by several later chapters in this anthology.

This Deetz-Dethlefsen cameo analysis has become a classic study, graphically portraying the fundamental techniques—dating, seriation, diffusion, typology, and style characterization—that the working archaeologist uses every day. Although the article below is a case-study in methodological control (exact knowledge of an artifact as located in space, fixed in time, and with certain physical properties of form), it is not a study of technique solely for the sake of technique. Rather, as the authors put it, "the objective is to sharpen our understanding of cultural process and cultural change." Hence several sweeping questions are put to the accumulated physical evidence, which, in addition to several thousand gravestones, also includes verbal data such as probate records, newspapers, and epitaphs on the grave markers. The authors ask: Where does innovation in a society's material culture first begin? How is cultural change diffused in a society? What can be the expected style characteristics in urban communities versus rural villages?

Finally, Deetz and Dethlefsen provide an introduction to a type of artifact (mortuary art) that has been the subject of several material culture monographs as well as two important conferences at the Dublin Seminar on New England Folklife since the article appeared in American Antiquity 31 (April 1966): 502–510, and Natural History 76 (1967). Funerary artifacts, particularly when studied for what they reveal about social and economic status, the relationship of religious beliefs and artistic expression, and the cultural values of individuals otherwise anonymous in the traditional historical record, have become the domain of the demographer, the folklorist, and the art historian, as well as the archaeologist and the cultural historian.

James Deetz, a past president of the Society for Historical Archaeology, has taught anthropology at Brown University, University of California at Santa Barbara, and William and Mary College. For many years the assistant director of Plimoth Plantation at Plymouth, Massachusetts, he pioneered in the application of innovative material culture research to historical museum site interpretation. At least two of his several books should be on every material cultural students book shelf: Invitation to Archaeology (1967) and In Small Things Forgotten: The Archaeology of Early American Life (1977). Edwin S. Dethlefsen teaches archaeology at William and Mary College in Virginia. He wrote the Anthropology Curriculum Study Project (1965–1970) for the American Anthropology Association and is also the author of Patterns in Human History (1968) and History as Cultural Change (1970). His special material culture interests include underwater and historical archaeology.

Enter almost any cemetery in eastern Massachusetts that was in use during the seventeenth and eighteenth centuries. Inspect the stones and the designs carved at their tops, and you will discover that three motifs are present. These motifs have distinctive periods of popularity, each replacing the other in a sequence that is repeated time and time again in all cemeteries between Worcester and the Atlantic, and from New Hampshire to Cape Cod.

The earliest of the three is a winged death's head, with blank eyes and a grinning visage. Earlier versions are quite ornate, but as time passes, they become less elaborate. Sometime during the eighteenth century—the time varied according to location—the grim death's head designs were replaced, more or less quickly, by winged cherubs. This design also went through a gradual simplification of form with time. By the late 1700s or early 1800s, again depending on where you are observing, the cherubs were replaced by stones decorated with a willow tree over-hanging a pedestaled urn. If the cemetery you are visiting is in a rural area, the chances are quite good that you will also find other designs, which may even completely replace one or more of the three primary designs at certain periods. If you were to search cemeteries in the same area, you would find that these other designs have a much more local distribution. In and around Boston, however, only the three primary designs would be present.

If you were to prepare a graph showing how the designs changed in popularity through time, the finished product might look something like three battleships viewed from above, the lower one with the bow showing, the center one in full view, and the third visible only in the stern. This shape, frequently called a "battleship-shaped" curve, is thought by archaeologists to typify the popularity career of any cultural trait across time. Such curves can be prepared from controlled data taken from the Stoneham cemetery, north of Boston, where the style sequence is typical of the area around this eighteenth-century urban center of eastern Massachusetts.

It is appropriate here to interrupt and pose the question: Why would an archaeologist study gravestones from a historic period?

Whether archaeology can be considered a science in the strict sense of the word is much debated. One of the hallmarks of scientific method is the use of controls in experimentation that enable the investigator to calibrate his results. Since archaeology deals largely with the unrecorded past, the problem of rigorous control is a difficult one. Much of modern archaeological method and theory has been developed in contexts that lack the necessary controls for precise checking of accuracy and predictive value. For this reason, any set of archaeological data in which such controls are available is potentially of great importance to the development and testing of explanatory models, which can then be used in uncontrolled contexts.

For a number of reasons, colonial New England grave markers may be unique in providing the archaeologist with a laboratory situation in which to measure cultural change in time and space and relate such measurements to the main body of archaeological method. All archaeological data—artifacts, structures, and sites—can be said to possess three inherent dimensions. A clay pot, for example, has a location in space. Its date of manufacture and use is fixed in time, and it has certain physical attributes of form. In a sense, much of archaeological method is concerned with the nature and causes of variation along these dimensions, as shown by excavated remains of past cultures.

The spatial aspect of gravestones is constant. We know from historical sources that nearly all of the stones in New England cemeteries of this period were produced locally, probably no more than fifteen or twenty miles away from their resting places; an insignificant number of them came from long distances. This pattern is so reliable that it is possible to detect those few stones in every cemetery that were made at a more remote town. Once placed over the dead, the stones were unlikely to have been moved, except perhaps within the cemetery limits.

Needless to say, the dimension of time is neatly and tightly controlled. Every stone bears the date of death of the individual whose grave it marks, and most stones were erected shortly after death. Like the spatial regularity, this temporal precision makes it possible to single out most of the stones that were erected at some later date.

Control over the formal dimension of gravestone data derives from our knowledge of the carvers, who, in many instances, are known by name and period of production, and who, even if anonymous, can be identified by their product with the help of spatial and temporal control. Thus, in most cases stones of similar type can be seen to be the product of a single person, and they reflect his ideas regarding their proper form.

Furthermore, it is known that the carvers of the stones were not full-time specialists, but rather they were workers at other trades who made stones for the immediate population as they were needed. We are dealing, then, with ''folk'' products, as is often the case in prehistoric archaeology.

Other cultural dimensions can also be controlled in the gravestone data with equal precision, and with the addition of these, the full power of these artifacts as controls becomes apparent: probate research often tells the price of individual stones, and status indication occurs frequently on the stones, as well as the age of each individual. Since death is related to religion, formal variations in the written material can be analyzed to see how they reflect religious variations. Epitaphs provide a unique literary and psychological dimension. Spatial distributions can be measured against political divisions. In short, the full historical background of the seventeenth, eighteenth, and nineteenth centuries permits both primary and secondary control of the material, and with the resulting precision, explanations became quite reliable.

With such controls available to the archaeologist, the pattern of change in colonial gravestone design and style can be used with great effect to sharpen our understanding of cultural process in general.

To return to the battleship-shaped curves, what does this mean in terms of cultural change? Why should death's heads be popular at all, and what cultural factors were responsible for their disappearance and the subsequent rise of the cherub design? The most obvious answer is found in the ecclesiastical history of New England. The period of decline of death's heads coincided with the decline of orthodox Puritanism. In the late-seventeenth century, Puritanism was universal in the area, and so were death's head gravestones. The early part of the eighteenth century saw the beginnings of change in orthodoxy, culminating in the great awakenings of the mid-century. In his recent, excellent book on the symbolism of New England gravestones, *Graven Images*, Allan Ludwig points out that the ''iconophobic'' Puritans found the carving of gravestones a compromise. While the use of cherubs might have verged on heresy, since they were heavenly beings whose portrayal might have led to idolatry, the use of a more mortal and neutral symbol—a death's head—would have served as a graphic reminder of death and resurrection.

Given the more liberal views concerning symbolism and personal involvement preached by Jonathan Edwards and others later in the eighteenth century, the idolatrous and heretical aspects of cherubs would have been more fitting to express the sentiment of the period.

It is at this point that available literary controls become valuable. The epitaph on each stone begins by describing the state of the deceased: ''Here lies'' or ''Here lies buried'' being typical early examples. Slowly these were replaced by ''Here lies (buried) the body (corruptible, what was mortal) of.'' This slightly, but significantly, different statement might well reflect a more explicit tendency to stress that only a part of the deceased remains, while the soul, the incorruptible or immortal portion, has gone to its eternal reward. Cherubs reflect a stress on resurrection, while death's heads emphasize the mortality of man. The epitaphs that appear on the bottoms of many stones also add credence to this explanation of change in form over time. Early epitaphs, with death's head designs, stress either decay and life's brevity:

> My Youthful mates both small and great
> Come here and you may see
> An awful sight, which is a type
> Of which you soon must be.

Or there may be a Calvinistic emphasis on hard work and exemplary behavior on the part of the predestined: ''He was a useful man in his generation, a lover of learning, a faithful servant of Harvard College above forty years.'' On the other hand, epitaphs with cherub stones tend to stress resurrection and later heavenly reward:

> Here cease thy tears, suppress thy fruitless mourn.
> His soul—the immortal part—has upward flown.
> On wings he soars his rapid way
> To yon bright regions of eternal day.

The final change seen in gravestone style is the radical shift to the urn-and-willow design. It is usually accompanied by a change in stone shape; while earlier stones have a round-shouldered outline, the later stones have square shoulders. "Here lies the body of" is replaced by "In memory of" or "Sacred to the memory of," quite different from all earlier forms. The earlier stones are markers, designating the location of the deceased or at least a portion of him. In contrast, "In memory of" is simply a memorial statement, and stones of this later type could logically be erected elsewhere and still make sense. In fact, many of the late urn-and-willow stones are cenotaphs, erected to commemorate those actually buried elsewhere, as far away as Africa, Batavia, and in one case—in the Kingston, Massachusetts, cemetery—"drowned at sea, lat. 39 degrees N., long. 70 degrees W." The cultural changes that accompanied the shift to urn-and-willow designs are seen in the rise of less emotional, more intellectual religions, such as Unitarianism and Methodism. Epitaphs changed with design and in the early nineteenth century tended more to sentiment combined with eulogy.

This sequence of change did not occur in a vacuum, unrelated to any cultural change elsewhere; indeed, the sequence of three major types also took place in England, the cultural parent of the Massachusetts colony, but about a half century earlier. Thus cherubs became modal by the beginning of the Georgian period (1715), and urns and willows made their appearance, as a part of the neoclassical tradition, in the 1760s. In fact, the entire urn-and-willow pattern was a part of the larger Greek revival, which might explain the squared shoulders on the stones—a severer classical outline.

Thus far we have been discussing formal change through time and some of the fundamental causes. We have seen that New England was changing in harmony with England, with an expectable time interval separating the sequences. But we have not identified the relationship of all of this to archaeological method.

The battleship-shaped curve assumption is basic to many considerations of cultural process in general and to such dating methods as seriation. Seriation is a method whereby archaeological sites are arranged in relative chronological order based on the popularity of the different types of artifacts found in them. The approach assumes that any cultural item, be it a style of pottery or a way of making an arrowhead, had a particular popularity period, and as it grew and waned in popularity, its prevalence as time passed can be represented graphically by a single peaked curve. Small beginnings grew to a high frequency of occurrence, followed in turn by a gradual disappearance. If such an assumption is true, it follows that a series of sites can be arranged so that all artifact types within them form single peaked curves of popularity over time. Such an arrangement is chronological and tells the archaeologist how his sites relate to one another in time.

By plotting style sequences in this manner in a number of cemeteries we find that the assumption, not previously measured with such a degree of precision, is a sound one: styles do form single peaked popularity curves through time. By adding the control of the spatial to the form–time pattern explained above, we gain a number of understandings regarding diffusion—the spread of ideas through time and space and how this, in turn, affected internal change in style. In looking now at the three dimensions, we will see that all of the secondary cultural controls become even more important.

The style sequence of death's head, cherub, and urn-and-willow design is to be found in almost every cemetery in eastern Massachusetts. However, when we inspect the time at which each change took place and the degree of overlap between styles from cemetery to cemetery, it becomes apparent that this sequence was occurring at a widely varying rate from place to place. The earliest occurrence of cherubs was in the Boston-Cambridge area, where they began to appear as early as the end of the seventeenth century. Occasional early cherubs might be found in more distant rural cemeteries, but in every case we find them to have been carved in the Boston area and to be rare imports from there. The farther we move away from the Boston center, the later locally manufactured cherubs make their appearance in numbers. The rate at which the cherub style spread outward has even been approximately measured and shown to be about a mile per year. It is not common in archaeology to make such precise measurements of diffusion rate—the usual measurements are cruder, such as hundreds of miles in millenniums.

We can view Boston and, more significantly, nearby Cambridge, as the focus of emphasis of Puritan religion with its accompanying values and inquire what factors might have contributed to the initial appearance of cherubs and the change in religious values in this central area. We have noted that the change had already been accomplished in England by the early-eighteenth century, so that when the first cherubs began to appear in numbers in Cambridge, they were already the standard modal style in England. While cherubs occurred in Boston, they never made a major impression, and as many death's heads as cherubs were replaced by the urn-and-willow influx.

On the other hand, in Cambridge cherubs made an early start and attained a respectable frequency by the late-eighteenth century. Although they never attained a full 100 percent level there, as they did in most rural areas, they did at least enjoy a simple majority. When the cherub stones in Cambridge are inspected more closely, we find that roughly 70 percent of them mark the graves of high-status individuals: college presidents, graduates of Harvard, governors and their families, high church officials, and in one case, even a "Gentleman from London." From what we know of innovation in culture, it is often the more cosmopolitan, urban stratum of society that brings in new ideas, to be followed later by the folk stratum. If this is true, then the differences between Boston and Cambridge indicate a more liberal element within the population of Cambridge, reflected in the greater frequency of cherub stones there. This is probably the case, with the influence of the Harvard intellectual community being reflected in the cemetery. It would appear that even in the early-eighteenth century, the university was a place for innovation and liberal thinking.

Cambridge intellectuals were more likely to be responsive to English styles, feelings, and tastes, and this could well be what we are seeing in the high number of cherub stones marking high-status graves.

Introduced into Cambridge and Boston by a distinct social class, the cherub design slowly began its diffusion into the surrounding countryside. Carvers in towns farther removed from Cambridge and Boston—as far as fourteen miles west in Concord—began to change their gravestone styles away from the popular death's head as early as the 1730s, but fifty miles to the south, in Plymouth, styles did not change until the 1750s and 1760s and then in a somewhat different cultural context. We find, however, that the farther the cemetery was from Boston, and the later the cherubs began to be locally manufactured, the more rapidly they reached a high level of popularity. The pattern is one of a long period of coexistence between cherubs and death's heads in the Boston center, and an increasingly more rapid eclipsing of death's heads by cherubs in direct proportion to distance, with a much shorter period of overlap. One explanation is that in towns farther removed from the diffusion center, enforcement of Puritan ethics and values was lessened, and resistance to change was not so strong. Furthermore, revivalism and the modification of orthodox Puritanism was widespread from the late 1730s through the 1760s in rural New England, although this movement never penetrated Boston. Such activity certainly must have conditioned the rural populace for a change to new designs.

We have, then, a picture of the introduction of a change in the highly specific aspect of mortuary art, an aspect reflecting much of the culture producing it. We see the subsequent spread of this idea, through space and time, as a function of social class and religious values. Now we are in a position to examine internal change in form through time, while maintaining relatively tight control on the spatial dimension.

One significant result of the use of gravestone data, with its accompanying controls, is the insight it provides in matters of stylistic evolution. The product of a single carver can be studied over a long period of time, and the change in his patterns considered as they reflect both ongoing culture change and his particular manner of handling design elements. The spatial axis extending outward from Boston shows not only systematic change in major style replacement rates but also a striking pattern of difference in style change. We find that in many cases the farther removed we become from Boston, the more rapid and radical is change within a given single design. This has been observed in at least five separate cases involving a number of the styles of more local distribution; we can inspect one of these cases closely and attempt to determine some of the processes and causes of stylistic evolution.

The design in question is found in Plymouth County, centering on the town of Plympton. Its development spans a period of some seventy years, and the changes effected from beginning to end are truly profound. Death's heads occurred in rural Plymouth County, as they did elsewhere in the late-seventeenth century. However, in the opening decade of the eighteenth century, the carver(s) in Plympton made certain basic changes in the general death's head motif.[2] The first step in this modification involved the reduction of the lower portion of the face, and the addition of a heart-shaped element between nose and teeth. The resulting pattern was one with a heartlike mouth, with the teeth shrunken to a simple band along the bottom. The teeth soon disappear entirely, leaving the heart as the sole mouth element. This change was rapidly followed by a curious change in the feathering of the wings.

While early examples show all feather ends as regular scallops crossing the lines separating individual feathers, shortly after the first changes in the face were made, every other row of feather ends had their direction of curvature reversed. The resulting design produces the effect of undulating lines radiating from the head, almost suggesting hair, at right angles to curved lines that still mark the feather separation. These two changes, in face and wing form, occupy a period of 35 years from 1710 through 1745. During the later 1740s this development, which had so far been a single sequence, split into two branches, each the result of further modification of wings. In the first case, the arcs marking feather separations were omitted, leaving only the undulating radial lines. Rapid change then took place leading to a face surmounted by wavy and, later, quite curly hair. The heart mouth was omitted. We have dubbed this style "Medusa." In the second case, the separating lines were retained, and the undulating lines removed; the result in this case was a face with multiple halos. At times, space between these halos was filled with spiral elements, giving the appearance of hair, or the halos were omitted entirely. The heart-shaped mouth was retained in this case and modified into a T-shaped element.

Both of these styles enjoyed great popularity in the 1750s and 1760s, and had slightly different spatial distributions, suggesting that they might have been the work of two carvers, both modifying the earlier heart-mouthed design in different ways. Yet a third related design also appeared in the 1740s, this time with tightly curled hair, conventional wings, and a face similar to the other two. Although this third design seems to be a more direct derivative of the earlier death's head motif, it is clearly inspired in part by the Medusa and multiple-halo designs. This tight-haired style has a markedly different spatial distribution, occurring to the west of the other two, but overlapping them in a part of its range. Of the three, only the Medusa lasted into the 1770s, and in doing so presents us with something of an engima. The final form, clearly evolved from the earlier types, is quite simple. It has a specific association with small children and has never been found marking the grave of an adult and rarely of a child over age five.

The carver of the fully developed Medusa was probably Ebenezer Soule of Plympton; a definitive sample of his style is found in the Plympton cemetery. Normal Medusas, except for the late, simple ones marking children's graves, disappeared abruptly in the late 1760s. In 1769, and lasting until the 1780s, stones identical to Soule's Medusas, including the simple, late ones, appeared in granite around Hinsdale, New Hampshire. Fortunately, a local history has identified the carver of some of these stones as "Ebenezer Soule, late of Plympton." This alone is of great interest, but if Soule did move to Hinsdale in 1769, who carved the later children's stones in Plymouth County? As yet, no answer is known.

This development raises two interesting considerations. First, we see that a style, the Medusa, which had been used for the general populace, ended its existence restricted to small children. This pattern has been observed elsewhere, with children's burials being marked by designs that were somewhat more popular earlier in time. In other words, children are a stylistically conservative element in the population of a cemetery. While no clear answer can be given to this problem, it may well be that small children, not having developed a strong, personal impact on the society, would not be thought of in quite the same way as adults and would have their graves marked with more conservative, less explicitly descriptive stones.

The second problem raised by the Medusas is their reappearance in Hinsdale. If, as archaeologists, we were confronted with the degree of style similarity seen between Hinsdale and Plympton in mortuary art, might we not infer a much greater influence than a single individual arriving in the community? After all, mortuary art would be about the only distinctively variable element in material culture over eighteenth-century New England, and such a close parallel could well be said to represent a migration from Plympton to Hinsdale. One man did move.

Placing this striking case of stylistic evolution in the broader context of culture change and style change in eastern Massachusetts, we find that it is paralleled by other internal modifications of death's head designs in other remote rural areas. The closer we move toward Boston, the less change takes place within the death's head design, and in Boston proper, death's heads from 1810 are not that different from those from 1710. Yet 1710 death's heads in Plympton and elsewhere had changed so radically by 1750 that it is doubtful that we could supply the derivation of one from the other in the absence of such an excellently dated set of intermediate forms. This difference in rate of change can be explained by referring back to the long, parallel courses of development of both death's head and cherub in the diffusion area's Boston center. However, culture change in the area of religion, marked by a shift of emphasis from mortality to immortality, probably generated a desire for less realistic and less grim designs on stones. Given this basic change in religious attitudes, what were the alternatives facing carvers in Boston as opposed to the Ebenezer Soules of rural New England? In Boston it was simply a matter of carving more cherub stones and fewer death's head stones; neither had to be altered to suit the new tastes. The choice between cherub and death's head in Boston has been interpreted as ultimately a social one, and if there was a folk culture component within Boston, there was nothing but folk culture in the more democratic, less-stratified rural areas. With no one to introduce cherubs and to call for them with regularity in the country, carvers set to work modifying the only thing they had— the death's head. The more remote the community, the later the local cherubs appeared, diffusing from Boston, and the more likely the tendency to rework the common folk symbol of skull and wings. Thus we get Medusas and haloed T-mouthed faces populating the cemeteries of Plymouth County until cherubs finally appeared. Even then, the waning popularity of the death's head in this area might be more the result of Soule's exit than their unsatisfactory appearance compared to the new cherubs.

Only a few applications of gravestone design analysis have been detailed here. There is a large and important demographic dimension to these data; since precise date of death is given, as well as age at death, patterns of mortality and life expectancy through time and space can be detailed. The results of this work, in turn, will add a biological dimension of style to the cultural one described above. Studies of diffusion rate and its relationship to dating by seriation will be continued. Relationships between political units—countries, townships, and colonies—and style spheres will be investigated to determine how such units affect the distribution of a carver's products. Finally, a happy by-product will be the preservation on film of over 25,000 gravestones, a vital consideration in view of the slow but steady deterioration these informative artifacts are undergoing.

Aside from the value of this work to archaeology and anthropology in general, one final comment must be made. Compared to the usual field work experienced by the archaeologist, with all of its dust and heavy shoveling under a hot sun, this type of archaeology certainly is most attractive. All of the artifacts are on top of the ground, the sites are close to civilization, and almost all cemeteries have lovely, shady trees.

14

Meaning in Artifacts: Hall Furnishings in Victorian America

Kenneth L. Ames

Introduction

After archaeology, art history ranks among the earliest disciplines to develop and refine tools for the study of American material culture. Traditional art historians, however, have tended to concentrate their energies primarily upon the singular art object–the painting, the sculpture, or the drawing–created by a known artist working in an established aesthetic tradition and a recognizable artistic vocabulary. Anyone who examines the scholarship found in journals such as American Art, The Connoisseur, or Antiques will recognize that this orientation has been a standard approach to the study of American fine, decorative, and applied arts for several decades.

Kenneth Ames, who is as talented as any scholar currently classifying styles and types, identifying artistic conceits and correspondences, and tracing foreign cognates and antecedents, was trained as an art historian. The approach he offers below, however, presses his colleagues to take a different view of American material culture, particularly that of the decorative arts. To begin with, he insists that art history research should be located in the broader context of cultural history and, where appropriate, such research should borrow relevant models and methods from the social sciences. Furthermore, Ames argues that all material culture historians need to widen their scope of historical inquiry beyond the artifactual evidence of the socio-economic elite. We must give greater attention to the material culture of the lower-, middle-, and upper-middle classes, such as the nineteenth-century hall stands, hall chairs, and card receivers that he proposes to examine.

In addition to calling for greater populism in material culture study, Ames seconds a point raised by James Deetz and one that will be reiterated by several authors throughout this anthology: *methodological rigor and analytical models must be applied in any artifact research that aspires to proceed beyond the idiosyncratic and impressionistic. In his own essay, he builds a hybrid model largely atop that which was first formulated by George Kubler, a fellow art historian, who, in an important book which all material culture students should know, The Shape of Time, divides the pool of artifacts into formal sequences composed of prime objects and their replications. The Ames paradigm of a "horizontal constellation" also owes a debt to the archaeologists, particularly those who employ the polar concepts of tradition and horizon as explanatory principles in their work with artifacts. In fact, his delineation of factory-made, mass-produced material culture evidence ("artifacts used by the upper-middle class in urban and urban-oriented areas of the North in the second-half of the nineteenth-century") follows the Deetz-Dethlefsen triparite prerequisite (an artifact having location in time and space and possessing the physical properties of form) for methodological control.*

After a detailed methodological prolegomenon on material culture methodology and resources, Ames turns to the objects themselves, which is where all artifact study truly begins. To provide a necessary architectural context for the domestic artifacts that he wishes to interpret, he first discusses two hall types, their spatial dimensions, and residential function: the hall-as-passage and the hall-as-living-space. Then follow analyses of three basic hall furnishings—the hall stand, the hall chairs, and the card receiver. In what might be called an anatomy lesson in a unique Victorian furniture form—the hall stand appears to be a nineteenth-century invention having no discernible antecedent—Ames carefully dissects the hall stand's multiple components, revealing their functional and symbolic significance. The other two hall furnishings receive similar in-depth study.

The reader should watch in particular for Ames's efforts to uncover wider social, cultural, and even psychological meaning in artifacts beyond what their utilitarian functions alone would indicate. In so doing he follows an important historiographical tradition in material culture studies that has its roots in Thorstein Veblen and Henry Adams as well as in the American studies scholarship of Alan Trachtenberg and Leo Marx. Besides pushing his research on into the speculative and the hypothetical (but always identifying it when so doing), he urges the material culturist to use, in addition to "all the conventional tools of his trade," his "intuition and his own subjective feelings."

For several years Kenneth L. Ames edited the Decorative Arts Newletter and currently serves on the editorial board of Winterthur Portfolio: A Journal of American Material Culture and as its book review editor. He wrote "Grand Rapids Furniture at the Time of the Centennial," Winterthur Portfolio 10 (1975): 23-50, and "Material Culture as Nonverbal Communication: A Historical Case-Study," Journal of American Culture 3 (Winter 1980): 619–641; and in 1977 brought out his own revisionist interpretation of American folk art in a

monograph, Beyond Necessity: Art in the Folk Tradition (Winterthur, Del.:
Winterthur Museum, 1977). The following article first appeared in Journal of
Interdisciplinary History 9 (Summer 1978): 19–46.

Most people agree that Independence Hall, the Statue of Liberty, and the Brooklyn Bridge are important. Unique and heroic artifacts known to millions, they can be viewed as material culture counterparts of great individuals like George Washington, Abraham Lincoln, and Thomas Edison. There is probably less agreement about the significance of Victorian hall stands, hall chairs, and card receivers. Yet the commonplace artifacts of everyday life mirror a society's values as accurately as its great monuments.[1] This article extends our understanding of Victorian America by analyzing hall furnishings typical of that era. By examining artifacts such as these one can gain insights into the past not readily accessible by conventional verbal approaches.

Hall furnishings have usually been outside the scope of historical inquiry. So have the majority of their users. Today, however, many historians are looking at ordinary people rather than traditional heroes and asking new sets of questions. By concentrating less on the unique and more on the typical they hope to compile an account of the past which is more responsive to contemporary needs. Reflecting both this changing orientation of history and the growing intellectual prestige of the social sciences, material culture studies are becoming more varied, rigorous, and suggestive.[2] Once dominated by historians of art and technology, the field is being invaded by scholars from many different disciplines. Students of folk and popular material culture are beginning to explore categories of objects usually ignored in their search for fuller understanding of the culture and values of people who lived apart from elite society. Anthropologists, psychologists, sociologists, educators, and philosophers are studying material culture for what it reveals about the social and psychological realities of the past and present and for insights into the processes of cognition and communication. The diversity of questions being asked and the variety of disciplines generating them indicate that material culture is currently perceived as a new frontier for scholarship likely to yield particularly rich data about what Howard Gardner calls man's systems for making, perceiving, and feeling.[3]

The student of material culture requires some basis for isolating groups of artifacts closely enough related to be discussed intelligibly yet limited enough in number to be encompassed mentally. For reducing artifacts to manageable groups, classifications based on form, function, material, date, school or maker, or style are frequently employed. More subtle models may incorporate several of these factors. George Kubler suggests dividing the pool of artifacts into formal sequences composed of prime objects and their replications. Some archaeologists employ the polar concepts of tradition and horizon. Because both models involve form, function, style, and duration, they may be synthesized. One can, then, designate as traditional objects those that belong to long formal sequences and are produced with minimal change over considerable time. Horizonal objects belong to short formal sequences and are produced for only a brief while before being eliminated or substantially altered. One can also speak of horizonal constellations or clusters of objects in interlocking sequences. As with celestial constellations, artifact constellations yield a larger picture when read as a whole. Horizonal constellations serve as indices of attitudes, values, and patterns of behavior of relatively limited duration.[4]

Hall furnishings in Victorian America form a horizonal constellation. Hall stands, hall chairs, and card receivers became popular around the middle of the nineteenth century, declined by the early years of this century, and are largely obsolete today. Although they survive in museums and in private hands across the country, the culture that produced them, the people who first used them, and the meanings they once had have faded, died, or been forgotten. By studying these objects, one can locate and analyze certain features of the Victorian age. Because these furnishings were commonplace, they can be useful for working toward a definition of Victorian culture and for documenting subdivisions within that culture.[5] Furthermore, it is appropriate to investigate objects that were prominent parts of Victorian everyday life precisely because the Victorians themselves were fascinated with material culture. By studying the things that surrounded them we can not only better comprehend their physical environment but come closer to understanding their mentality as well.[6]

The emphasis of this article is on artifacts used by the upper-middle class in urban and urban-oriented areas of the North in the second half of the nineteenth century. The objects are factory-made, mass-produced examples of Victorian popular culture of the sort found in the more expensive homes in cities and in houses of the villa class in towns and suburbs. The North was selected because of its relative homogeneity; it was dominated and unified by a Yankee culture formulated on the east coast and carried westward to the Mississippi River and beyond. The geographical configuration of this Yankee culture can be seen with remarkable clarity on maps recording urban growth, industrialization, and rail transportation. These maps indicate that the South was, as it remains, a distinctive subculture; for that reason it is not dealt with here. Lastly, the time span treated was dictated by the objects themselves. The discussion that follows includes observations on the nature and availability of materials for research on household artifacts, and hall furnishings in particular, analysis of three major types of hall furnishings, and suggestions for their interpretation.[7]

It may seem like putting the cart before the horse to discuss research materials before the objects themselves, but the nature of the resources has a significant bearing on how one approaches the objects and also explains some of the difficulties encountered in trying to interpret them.

The ideal situation for a scholar interested in the nature and meaning of the hall and its furnishings in Victorian America would be to discover a large number of halls distributed over time, space, and social class, with all original artifacts wholly intact, fully documented, and accompanied by extensive written records of conscious as well as subconscious responses to the space and its objects. In fact, resources are scattered and of varying value. Written documents are among the least useful, at least at the outset, because considerable prior knowledge of the artifacts is necessary to make sense of them. Conventional records like wills, inventories, bills, and receipts list furnishings and place a dollar value on individual pieces but, until large numbers of such documents are tabulated and the results correlated, few conclusions can be drawn.[8]

Literature constitutes an exceptionally rich resource for the study of cultural history. However, it may be rather more fruitfully seen as a manifestation parallel to material culture, responding to or recording related cultural tendencies in a different medium, than as a direct path to the interpretation of the material world. Most of the occasional specific references to objects which appear in novels—"'on one occasion, when my brother was visiting me, his overcoat was taken from the hatstand in the hall,'' or " 'Then I must wait til she returns,' and Ben quietly placed his hat on the hatstand''—do little more than confirm the existence of the objects and describe their most obvious functions. Sometimes authors go further and record the mood of a space in some detail, as John Hay did.[9] Although occasional passages may be illuminating, finding them is not easy; investigating literature is an inefficient way to learn about artifacts of the past. Even when lucid verbal accounts are uncovered, they must always be weighed against other forms of evidence.[10]

Combinations of verbal and pictorial materials occur in architectural and home furnishing books but these, too, are of limited value. Even Andrew Jackson Downing's *Architecture of Country Houses* (1850), notable in so many ways, is of little use for studying hall furnishings. It contains nearly 150 illustrations of furniture appropriate for mid-nineteenth-century homes, but only six are of hall pieces and the discussion of them is minimal. Samuel Sloan's *Homestead Architecture* (1861 and 1867), another major volume of this genre, illustrates no hall furniture and contains only one deprecating reference.[11]

Beginning in the late 1870s, a flurry of books appeared expressing design reform sentiments formulated in England a decade earlier. These works illustrated and discussed halls and their furnishings, but the views that they set forth belonged to a vocal, if growing, minority with new attitudes toward style, the home, and furnishings. These publications are related to a distinct phase in the history of Victorian furnishings of which more will be said later. Here it is sufficient to note that this phase was characterized by a degree of verbal activity absent in the previous phase. Although the latter made its primary appeal through the artifacts themselves, the reform phase relied heavily on rhetoric. As a result, the written testimony is strongly biased in favor of the reform movement and against its immediate antecedents.[12] A typical book, *A Domestic Cyclopoedia of Practical Information* (1877), demonstrates the strong Anglophile stance of this reform phase and its manner of proselytizing for furniture still relatively unknown. Another work from the same year, Clarence Cook's *The House Beautiful*, disparages most mass-produced furnishings in favor of antiques and pieces in the English reform style sensitively combined. Books such as these are valuable as long as their crusading purpose is understood. American historians of the decorative arts, however, have often accepted these polemics at face value without attempting to view the arguments in their original social context. They have also failed to acknowledge that reform sentiments and artifacts belonged only to a small segment of a larger American society which, although unified in a general sense, was nevertheless highly pluralistic in object preference, as it remains today.[13] The reformers represented neither the only point of view nor, in the 1870s, the dominant one. In a rough analogy we could say that their publications reflect conventional Victorian hall furnishings about as accurately as today's professional architectural journals do suburban tract housing.

From these verbal and published sources we still have little idea of the appearance or placement of the most typical objects in Victorian halls, especially for the period before 1880. Here more strictly pictorial materials, paintings, prints, photographs, and trade catalogs, can be helpful. Painted or printed views of American interiors survive in considerable number, but many are nostalgic, mythologizing images of rural life rather than reliable records of the real appearance of middle- or upper-middle-class interiors in the cities and suburbs. Within the class of presumably reliable interior views, paintings or prints showing the hall are scarce. The long, narrow, dark space was difficult to delineate and beyond the recording capabilities of the early camera. Photographs of halls grew more common in the last two decades of the century when the performance of the camera and the space of the hall were both altered, the latter under the impact of the English reform movement mentioned before.[14]

For pictorial records of individual objects, trade catalogs are the most valuable resource. They survive in great numbers from the late 1860s. Hall furniture, lighting, card receivers, cards, wall and floor materials, hardware, and nearly every other element of furnishing needed for the hall or any other room in the house can be found lithographed or sometimes photographed. Trade catalogs are important for providing incontrovertible evidence of objects in production or available on order. They can be used by scholars seeking answers to a variety of questions: How long were certain articles made? Were they manufactured in one location, a few places, or nationwide? How did design and cost change over time? How and to what extent were certain styles reflected in given classes of objects? How was price reflected in the design and construction of the object? How were production and marketing organized within a given industry? Trade catalogs can also be of great help in identifying and dating extant artifacts. Perhaps most significant of all, they can provide a scholar with more images of thoroughly documented artifacts of certain kinds than he could hope to gather in years of scouring museums, historical societies, and private collections.[15]

The drawback of trade catalogs is that the images are only reminders of the objects. To appreciate scale, volume, color, and surface, one must turn to the objects themselves, which is where all artifact study should begin. Working directly with objects is a difficult task, however, and the historian should be willing to use all the conventional tools of his trade, including intuition and his own subjective feelings. But, as John Demos noted in *A Little Commonwealth*, it is not easy to judge the meanings of objects in people's lives or how they felt about a certain artifact. Not only did those meanings and feelings go unrecorded, but they often existed below the level of consciousness. This article, then, can serve to point out to scholars the nature of and problems attached to the various kinds of documents relevant to the study of artifacts. And if it is not an account which resolves major historical problems or contradictions, it may at least be useful, to paraphrase Willie Lee Rose's goal for *A Documentary History of Slavery in North America*, in helping historians to think about ways hall furnishings or other categories of artifacts may profitably be introduced into their own studies.[16]

To understand hall furniture one needs to know something about the hall, for this space and its relationship to other spaces in the home had an influence on the objects placed within it. Domestic building in America is more notable for continuity than lack of it. A few basic ideas, altered occasionally by ideological, economic, or other factors, underlie the spatial organization of most homes. Thus it is possible to separate middle- and upper-middle-class homes of the nineteenth century into two types on the basis of the form of hall employed. The first chronologically was a relatively narrow passage leading from the outside of the house to its interior spaces. Up to about 1880 this was the dominant mode. It was based on late Renaissance ideas introduced to this country in the eighteenth century with the Georgian style. Although the fact is frequently obscured by an overlay of complicated ornament or a degree of asymmetry, Georgian concepts of spatial organization were perpetuated in Victorian houses; some nineteenth-century plans are nearly identical to eighteenth-century examples. A characteristic feature of these houses of the Georgian-Victorian continuum was the use of a hall as a passage.[17]

The other type of hall was a passage expanded into a large living space. It derived from medieval great halls and the multifunction rooms of pre-Georgian dwellings in colonial America. This type, associated with the reform movement, was widely published and illustrated in the last quarter of the century, and became a prominent feature of many architect-designed homes. These two hall alternatives can be related to two very different models for the domestic structure in the nineteenth century. The first is the home as a palace; the second the home as a hereditary estate or an old homestead. The emphasis here is on the pre-reform model of the home as a palace and the hall as a passage.[18]

A typical upper-middle-class house plan illustrates the characteristics of this concept of hall. The space was usually six to eight feet wide and twelve to twenty feet long, or considerably longer if it ran all the way from the front of the house to the back. Its chief architectural embellishments were the framed doorways to parlor, drawing room, library room and the stair and its ornamented newel post. No communal activity took place in the hall; its shape, dimensions, and placement emphasized its function as both a connector and separator of rooms. In most homes of this class, one did not enter directly from the outside into one of the formal rooms but into the hall instead. Although it was possible to move from some rooms to others without entering the hall, it was also possible to enter each room from the hall without passing through any other, thus preserving privacy and the specialized function of each space. By this arrangement social peers of the homeowner could visit in the formal spaces of the home, while social inferiors remained in the hall or were directed elsewhere and kept from intruding upon the family or its guests.[19]

The hall just described might be identified more accurately as a front hall. Many homes also had a back hall, which was sometimes an extension of the front hall, sometimes another smaller corridor adjacent to it. It was not necessarily a discrete space; in some cases, its function was incorporated within another room, such as the kitchen. To divide the front hall from the back and formal space from functional there was usually some real or symbolic barrier—a door, lower ceiling, narrower passage, or change in wall or floor materials or finish. There was also a rear stair, usually narrower and steeper than the front stair and free of architectural pretense. This creation of separate and unequal halls and stairs reflects the segregation of ceremonial and utilitarian functions within the home and the division of nineteenth-century society into the two nations described by Benjamin Disraeli. This same inclination toward stratification is seen in the way the plans of upper-middle-class homes are conceptually divisible into two units. The first, larger than the other, is the formal or ceremonial portion of the house. Behind it, to fulfill the vulgar requirements that make the former possible, is the service section of kitchen, pantry, and laundry room. The significant difference in the way the two areas were conceived is reflected in their decorative treatment. The front section was architecture as John Ruskin understood it; the rear was only building. Designs for facades appeared in architectural books in great numbers, but backs were rarely shown, for the front belonged to ceremony and the rear to utility. The front stair was for dramatic descent to meet family and guests; the back stair for servants carrying slop buckets and dirty laundry. Today, when household servants are unknown to most Americans living in the North, it is easy to forget the social realities of the nineteenth century. Victorian homes document a way of life which has largely disappeared.[20]

In these homes, the front hall was usually too small for much furniture. It sometimes contained a table, stand, or pedestal, and two chairs or a settee or both. In most cases it contained at least a hallstand. The hallstand is a nineteenth-century invention. Unlike most furniture of that age, it has no clearly discernible antecedents. The hallstand appeared around the time of Victoria's accession and its life cycle parallels the course of the Victorian way of life in America. After the middle of the century it grew more popular and became the focus of considerable design attention. The form reached its greatest prominence in the 1870s, then declined in scale and importance, undergoing significant alteration in the late-nineteenth and early-twentieth century and largely passing out of production by 1920.[21]

The appearance of the hallstand in the late 1870s can be seen in various sales catalogs, such as that of the firm of Nelson, Matter, and Co. of Grand Rapids, Michigan, noted for producing quality furniture for the middle- and upper-middle-class markets.[22] A sampling of hallstands indicates that although there was considerable diversity in the details of design, a high degree of consistency prevailed in the overall concept of the object. Four functional components were generally repeated: (1) provisions for umbrellas; (2) hooks or pegs for hats and coats; (3) a looking glass; and (4) a small table, often with a drawer and a marble top. Each of these is conceptually separable from the others but the synthesis of the four (or sometimes only the first three) into an architecturally conceived whole is what constitutes a hallstand: the nineteenth-century innovation consists of combining these elements in precisely this manner.

The provisions for umbrellas normally follow a similar arrangement. Crook-shaped or arm-like devices were mounted on each side of the stand at a height of about twenty-five to thirty inches above the floor. These held the upper ends of the umbrellas. In the base of the hallstand were usually one or two dished receptacles. Their function was twofold: to terminate the implied cylinders in which the umbrellas were placed, and to catch and contain water that might drip from them. Cast iron pans were the most common material for these. Some less expensive hallstands had thin sheet metal boxes, but expensive hallstands, particularly those built as part of the woodwork, had concave marble slabs. Regardless of material, all served the same utilitarian functions of protecting the floor and carpet and keeping the umbrellas accessible.

That such an impressive piece of furniture should be designed for umbrellas indicates something about the status of the latter which, from the vantage point of the twentieth century, might be called the insignia of the Victorian age. The umbrella has a long, eventful history which has been recorded by several artifact historians. It was well known in antiquity in both the Orient and the Occident, but its modern history stems from contacts between the East and West during the Renaissance. It came by sea to Portugal and by land to Italy, spreading from there to other areas. At the outset, the umbrella was associated with high status; servants held them over their masters when they walked in public. By the eighteenth century the umbrella and a related form, the parasol, had become relatively common; they were depicted frequently in paintings and prints of that period and mentioned in written documents. The parasol served largely a cosmetic function by protecting female skin from the harsh rays of the sun; although its use spread through many levels of society, it remained the mark of a woman of leisure. The umbrella performed a more utilitarian function and was carried by men only after the middle of the eighteenth century. Perhaps because the very wealthy owned carriages to protect them from the weather, carrying one's own umbrella came to be associated with lesser affluence and republican sentiments. In the nineteenth century it became a bourgeois attribute, a portable emblem of respectability, and its prominence reflects a culture dominated by middle-class values.[23]

The second set of functional components of the hallstand, the provisions for hat and coats, reiterates the nineteenth-century emphasis on attire and appearance. The peak of popularity for the hallstand coincides with that of the top hat, which in its most extreme form became the "stove-pipe" hat of Lincoln and his generation. James Laver has argued that the top hat was what we would call *macho* today, an assertion of masculinity most extreme at the time of greatest role differentiation between the sexes. Its gradual decline he associated with that of male-dominated society.[24]

Hats and coats were usually hung on turned wooden pegs on less expensive hallstands and on small bronzed or gilt metal hooks on more costly pieces. These rarely projected more than six or eight inches from the surface of the hallstand and were generally only six or eight in number and were arranged symmetrically around the mirror. The relatively few attachments for hats, coats, cloaks, or other outer garments, make it clear that the hallstand was not intended as open storage. Only a limited number of objects could be placed on it; examination of old photographs may help in determining the rules governing the selection. Some homes had storage closets near the hall; some had closets behind the stair, easily accessible from the hall, yet they still had a hallstand in the front hall.[25] When large numbers of people came, to a party, for instance, coats were placed on the beds in the chambers, as they are today. Therefore, there were reasons other than storage for placing these garments on the hallstand. We will suggest what these reasons might be after discussing the two other functional components.

The third element, the mirror, emphasizes again the Victorian fixation with personal appearance, but it has other ramifications as well. Mirrors were a Victorian convention. They appeared where they still do in twentieth-century interiors, on walls in bedrooms and dressing rooms, on chests of drawers, dressing tables, and wardrobes, and adjacent to facilities for washing and shaving. They also appeared, however, on hallstands, *étagères*, cabinets, and sideboards, over mantels, and extending from floor to ceiling between pairs of windows in formal rooms. The functions of glass were not limited to the obvious utilitarian goal of reflecting an image. Behind the glass in parlors and halls of the 1870s lay the example of the *Galerie des Glaces* at Versailles of two centuries earlier. Plate glass was still expensive in the nineteenth century, and its prominent display was a sign of wealth and, as Thorstein Veblen argued, high social standing. Glass was significant, too, for its ability to reflect forms and light and so expand and illuminate a space. Large glasses were normally on axis with lighting fixtures so that illumination was increased. The mirror also caused certain visual effects which people enjoyed. When a glass is viewed from an angle, it reflects segments of the interior which change as the viewer moves, a kinetic phenomenon exploited as a novelty a few years ago on the art scene but once commonplace in Victorian interiors.[26] The glass in the hallstand was also a mirror in the ordinary sense, a dressing glass in front of which to adjust clothing or hair, brush off dust, or otherwise prepare either to leave the house or to enter one of the formal rooms.

The last component of the hallstand, the table, was optional and not included in less expensive examples. It was a convenient resting place for packages, books, gloves, or other small objects. In some instances a decorative object was placed on it; in others it held a card receiver. The drawer was also a place for a variety of small objects, including brushes and whiskbrooms for cleaning garments. The presence of the table can further be explained as providing an occasion for the perpetuation of the "marble-mania" characteristic of the age. The use of marble tops on tables and case pieces is an instance of what Siegfried Giedion called the devaluation of symbols.[27] Marble tops, used in antiquity, were revived during the Renaissance for use on luxury pieces of furniture. By the nineteenth century, what had been confined to the very wealthy became commonplace, as the vast number of surviving examples indicates. Although marble was heavier, more expensive, and more dangerous to fragile objects than wood, it was very popular. It is possible that the marble on hallstands might have helped stabilize the great weight of the mirror, but there were other less expensive ways of achieving this end. It is more likely that this marble, like the clearly disfunctional pieces on sideboards, chests of drawers, dressing cases, washstands, cabinets, tables, and stands, was largely a matter of conspicuous consumption.

All four functional components were combined into a single object by people now as forgotten as any of America's minorities. Indeed, there is no need to turn to what is called folk art to find unsung artisans in the American past; they worked for American industry in the nineteenth century. Their charge was not to express themselves in an uninhibited personal manner but to create a saleable product much like others available at the same time. Surviving artifacts and illustrations in trade catalogs show how these unknown people produced scores of varied designs, yet adhered to shared notions about symmetry, placement of the functional components, projection into space, and consumption of wall area. Because of the limited space of the hall, the components were combined in a spatially efficient way. Hallstands rarely project far into the space of the hall, usually only twelve or fifteen inches. But if practical considerations inhibited the consumption of space, there were no such strictures on the use of area. Most hallstands spread expansively along the wall to creat a major focal point in the hall and indicate their own significance. In fact, the large size of the hallstand is the most obvious clue that it was intended to represent more than the mere total of its utilitarian functions. The Victorians must have felt that the purposes of the hallstand and the concepts and feelings associated with it were important to their lives, for they enshrined them in grandeur.

People do not make objects large if they wish to hide them, and hallstands are usually large. The smallest, usually of cast iron rather than wood, are normally about the height of an adult. The wooden examples are more often between six and a half and eight feet tall and some of the most costly are ten feet. This great size was not inexpensive; the hallstand rarely appeared in lower-class homes. It served, then, as a tool for social differentiation, since its mere possession was a mark of some social standing. The willingness of people to pay significant sums for hallstands, and the obvious expenditure of energy on the design, construction, and finish of the objects, all reaffirm their significance.[28]

The placement of the functional and decorative features of the object is of consequence. The former are placed in a balanced and symmetrical arrangement, augmented and emphasized by the latter, which confer importance and elevate the status of the object. The recurring symmetry has already been mentioned and deserves a few words. Symmetry is such a common feature of manmade objects that it may seem inconsequential, yet one also can argue that it is this very persistence that gives it importance. As common as it is, symmetry has nevertheless not been adequately explained. One of the usual arguments is that man makes symmetrical objects because he is himself symmetrical. Others have argued that symmetry is restful and mentally satisfying, fulfilling the search of the mind for equilibrium. Symmetry is also a way creative man can demonstrate control of his tools and material. A form created once may be an accident; its exact duplication is not likely to be.[29]

The ornamentation of the hallstand suggests that the piece met more than utilitarian necessity. Much of the wooden frame and all the veneer panels, paterae, pilasters, and other applied and incised decoration are functionally superficial, the more so in the more expensive examples. The glass is usually larger than needed and the sections above it are in every case beyond physical need. This top part of the hallstand performs an honorific function in direct relationship to the cost of the object. The ornament of the upper section is also honorific in another less direct, more symbolic way. Most of these examples are capped by an architectural element—an arch, a pediment, a cartouche, or some combination of these devices. Each has a long tradition of playing a status-conferring role in architectural contexts and may have retained a residuum of this meaning in the nineteenth century. It is also worth observing that the architectural quality of these pieces of furniture, the more expensive examples especially, calls to mind the facades of temples, churches, and other monumental and meaning-laden architecture, again suggesting that there was more significance in these objects than their utilitarian functions would indicate.[30]

A final argument for the importance to the Victorians of the hallstand and the activities associated with it is the critical matter of placement. The hallstand stood prominently in the front hall, immediately visible upon entering the house. If people believed that "the hall determines the first impression on entering the house," and that in some cases it might be advisable to economize elsewhere in order to create a good effect there, they must have depended heavily on the hallstand to help achieve the effect that they sought.[31] The hallstand was the major piece of furniture in the hall and one of the most important visual elements. Visitors could not avoid seeing it, nor could they avoid seeing the hats, coats, canes, or umbrellas on it. Today we use closets to keep garments out of sight because they violate our sense of propriety. A century ago, halls were furnished with immense, unavoidable wooden objects which loomed prominently in the semidarkness of the hall and were decked out with articles of personal costume. For some, the scale and stern design were awesome and intimidating; for others, there was a more approachable, human quality about the piece. To all, the hallstand conveyed something of the spirit or mood of the household and was useful as well. It helped with details of grooming. It communicated nonverbally about who was or was not at home by the objects on or missing from the hallstand. It ceremonialized the coming and going, the entry and exit of the members of the household and their guests. And it served as a setting, a theatrical backdrop for the ritual of card leaving, which also took place in the hall.

Clarence Cook, an Anglophile writer of the 1870s, called hallstands "ugly things made of tiresome walnut." [32] Although he rejected its form, he did not reject the hallstand's function. An illustration in his book shows the functions discussed previously performed by objects—a wall mirror with four clothes hooks in its frame and a separate wooden bench—which are nearly devoid of the conspicuous consumption and symbolic meaning suggested above. [33] Yet the image of the mirror with a cloak and top hat hanging from it and the caption—"She'll be down in a minute, sir"—are potent reminders of physical and social realities, including, once again, the harsh fact of a servant class. They also indicate how artifacts were deliberately used in the nineteenth century as props for the drama of life. The self-conscious quality evident here and the suggestions of an emotional response to artifacts based on the functions that they perform and the associations connected with them remind us that hallstands are a creation of the age of Romanticism. The concept of Romanticism is employed by historians of the arts and literature but often ignored by others. Like all such broad terms, it has to be used with caution, but the attitudes and values conventionally associated with it help us understand the creation of the hallstand, for those elements of the object defined as beyond necessity— and in fact, the entire object itself—worked to appeal to the senses and the emotions. It may seem a superficial job of labelling to call the hallstand a product of the Romantic age, but precisely because that term is usually limited to the so-called fine arts, it is important to recognize its relevance to another class of artifacts.

The other usual objects of furniture in the hall were for seating. The wealthy sometimes had leather upholstered settees and matching chairs. The typical middle-class hall seat of the 1870s had certain characteristic features. First, there was the unupholstered plank seat, which was otherwise unknown in the formal rooms of the middle-class home. The plank seat was normally hinged so that it could be raised to give access to a shallow compartment underneath for gloves, brushes, and other small items. Front legs were usually turned, stretchers were rare, and the backs were elaborate and expansive so that, like hallstands, they commanded and controlled considerable wall area. The design of the chairs indicates that they were not intended for prolonged sitting, at least not for members of the household or their social peers, for the qualities that they embodied were visual appeal and utility, not comfort. The plank seat was employed in lieu of upholstery because it would not be ruined by contact with wet or soiled outer garments, because it contributed to the stern, somewhat intimidating grandeur of the hall, and possibly because it was uncomfortable. Peers or superiors were shown into one of the formal rooms of the home. The people kept waiting in the hall were socially inferior to the residents of the house, like the "messenger-boys, book-agents . . . census-man and . . . bereaved lady who offers us soap" condescendingly listed by Cook, who went on to argue that "as visitors of this class are the only ones who will sit in the hall, considerations of comfort may be allowed to yield to picturesqueness. . . ." When hall chairs were used by people of higher status, they served only as perching places for pulling on overshoes or some similar chore. This utilitarian purpose, however, seems to have been secondary to their potential for social and psychological manipulation.[34]

The last important part of this horizonal constellation of hall furnishings was a card receiver. Like the other objects discussed, the card receiver is also an obsolete form, intimately tied to a ritual of card leaving little practiced today. Its early history is obscure, but it was much in vogue by the time of the Civil War. On the grandest scale, card receivers were elaborate cast metal stands, often made in France, which rested directly on the floor. More typical was a smaller model, ranging from a few inches to over a foot in height, which was placed on a table or stand. In all cases, the concept of the card receiver was of a dish or tray on a stand which stabilized it and gave it prominence.

From card receivers one turns logically to the cards themselves and the ritual of calling. Again, it is difficult to fix the point at which cards or the ceremony first became part of middle-class life in the last century. The phenomenon probably derives from royal examples of earlier times, for the dual purpose of preserving social status and distinctions and ritualizing interactions recalls courtly protocol for audiences or interviews. As with so many other adaptations of earlier conventions, certain alterations were made in the nineteenth century which we now think of as typical of that era.

The entire card system was well codified by the middle of the last century and remained largely intact well into the twentieth. The card ritual fitted neatly into the patterns of conspicuous consumption outlined by Veblen, for the task of leaving cards fell to the woman of the household. If she were at all genteel, she was presumed to have the time to devote to this activity. The card ritual, then, was evidence of conspicuous leisure and an instance of nonproductive, if gracious, labor.[35]

It is always difficult to know how much credence to give to the normative arguments of etiquette books. In the case of the ritual of the cards, the existence of the props or tools—hallstand, card receivers, and cards—lends support to the testimony of those books. And since there is general agreement about most aspects of card leaving from the earliest books up to those of only a few years ago, we can assume that many who used cards did so in the same way.[36]

Most of the etiquette books stressed the importance of leaving cards. "Leaving cards is one of the most important of social observances, as it is the groundwork or nucleus in society of all acquaintanceship. . . ." Card leaving was a way of entering society, of designating changes in status or address, of issuing invitations and responding to them, of sending sentiments of happiness or condolence, and, in general, of carrying on all the communication associated with social life. Not to participate in this ritual, with its strict rules, was to risk being considered what was termed ill-bred, a euphemism for lower class.[37]

It was important that cards be left in person. Some books equivocated on this point and indicated that cards could be sent with a messenger or by post. Others took a hard line and maintained that it was a breach of etiquette to do anything but deliver them oneself. Certainly it was in violation of the concept of conspicuous leisure not to deliver them, for to mail them or send them with a servant suggested that one had household responsibilities or an activity one valued higher. Related to emphasis upon leisure was the requirement that cards be left between three and five o'clock in the afternoon. Since these were normal business hours, it is clear that men could not be expected to leave cards. They were at work to support these women of conspicuous leisure.

The card ritual was part of a larger ritual of calling. In this framework, we might speak of primary calling and secondary calling or perhaps human interaction and artifact interaction. When individuals were not present, their cards were their surrogates. Since husbands did not normally accompany their wives when they paid calls, the wife left her husband's card where she visited. If the lady of the house being visited was at home, the guest left two of her husband's cards, one for the lady visited and the other for her husband. She did not leave her own card, for it would be redundant since she had already seen the lady of the house.

If a woman were paying calls and the woman she intended to visit was not home, she left three cards, one of her own and two of her husband's. The latter were to be distributed as before, but her card would be left for the mistress of the house; "a lady leaves a card for a lady only." This cult of protecting the virtue of matrons extended to that of maidens too, for in some circles it was not considered appropriate for a young lady to have visiting cards of her own. Her name was printed beneath that of her mother on the latter's card. The use of "Miss" on a card was reserved for older unmarried women.[38] With this situation, we come closer to the more formalistic aspects of a ritual which was in many ways a social perpetual motion machine which, once set going among equals, could not with propriety be stopped unless one party moved away. In the case of social unequals it could be halted when the superior ignored the inferior. When there was no intention to visit, a woman merely handed three cards to a servant, who presumably placed them in the card receiver, the contents of which were later sorted and evaluated. Whatever the intention of the individual—to pay a visit or only a surrogate visit by way of the card, a kind of social code of Hammurabi obtained—a card for a card, a call for a call, and the person visited or called on was obliged to reciprocate.

Rules were also spelled out about how and when people of different social status might interact. Calling or only leaving a card signified different degrees of intimacy. Among social equals, the law cited before was normally in operation. In cases of obvious social distinction, the situation was different. If a woman of higher social position returned a card with a call, it was considered a compliment. If the opposite took place, it was brash and presumptive.

The use of cards and servants as barriers was extensive in the last century. For example, a man wishing to make the acquaintance of a young woman could arrange to have his card left at her home by a female friend. If the young woman had no interest in meeting him, the solution was simple; his card was not noticed. Similarly, an intended visit could be reduced to the level of a call through the expedient of having the servant announce that one was "not at home."

Today much of this activity takes place in business rather than private life. Telephone calls are our cards and secretaries the servants who announce that the important person is at a meeting or cannot be reached. Yet even if some aspects of these rituals survive today, contemporary American society no longer cherishes the same values the Victorians did nor expresses itself in the same way. The Victorians believed in the ceremony of daily life as a way of attaining elegance and personal nobility. Their world emphasized social competition and the artifacts that they made were often designed as tools for that activity. Yet there was more behind hall furnishings of the nineteenth century than conspicuous consumption and invidious comparison, for the emphasis on personal possessions—hats, coats, umbrellas, and cards—suggests a sentimental or emotional attachment to objects of the kind commemorated in well-known songs and poems like "The Old Arm Chair," "The Old Oaken Bucket," and most of all, "Home, Sweet Home." [39]

If the people who owned the objects we have been discussing could vigorously defend social station and privilege, they could also be moved by associations and relationships with their friends and relatives.[40] The objects that they placed in their halls reflected not only these competing facets of the Victorian personality but the very nature of the hall itself. For it was a space which was neither wholly interior nor exterior but a sheltered testing zone which some passed through with ease and others never went beyond.

15

The "Industrial Revolution" in the Home: Household Technology and Social Change in the Twentieth Century

Ruth Schwartz Cowan

Introduction

In an issue of Technology and Culture, the quarterly journal of the American Society for the History of Technology, Robert Heilbroner raised the question: "Do Machines Make History?" [1] This perennial inquiry of historians of technology—still another group of material culture researchers—focuses the investigation of Ruth Schwartz Cowan, for she is intrigued by the relationship between technological change and societal change. Is it primarily technology that influences the way we live? Or is it principally our changing social values that prompt alterations or innovations in our technology? Which determines which?

In order to probe this problem of historical causality, Cowan looks closely at the origins of many objects that most of us have had in our homes all our lives: central-heating furnaces, indoor-bathroom facilities, and household appliances of all types. What happened, she asks, to middle-class American women when the implements with which they did their everyday household work changed? Did the technological change in household appliances, for instance, have any effect upon the structure of American households, upon the ideologies that governed the behavior of American women, or upon the functions that families needed to perform? By deliberately limiting herself to one genre of artifactual evidence reflecting only one form of technological change affecting one aspect of family life in only one of the many social classes of families that might have been considered, she sets up a well-defined case study to analyze, not so much what E. M. Fleming calls the five properties of artifacts (history, material, construction, design, and function), but rather the cultural ramifications of heretofore largely neglected material culture evidence. Moreover, Cowan seeks to link artifact study with two emerging subfields of social history, the history of women and the history of the family, two areas of contemporary research where exciting material culture study is being done particularly because of the paucity of extensive written records and the abundance of artifactual data in historic house museums, local historical societies, and of course, in many attics and basements of private homes.

The electrification and mechanization of the American household in at least four activities—laundering, heating (both for cooking and for human comfort), cleaning, and food preparation and long-term storage—amount to nothing less than a genuine industrial revolution rarely noticed except for scholars such as Siegfried Giedion in his classic survey, Mechanization Takes Command (1948). Cowan, who acknowledges and uses Giedion's earlier research, insists that the change, for example, from the laundry tub to the washing machine is no less profound than the change from the hand loom to the power loom; that the change from pumping water to turning on a faucet is no less destructive of traditional habits than the change from manual to electric calculating. Like John Schlebecker in his essay on agricultural implements (chapter five), Cowan presses the material culture student to attempt to measure and assess such household tools in terms of overall efficiency, energy expenditure, and time required to perform certain tasks done with the new technology as compared to the old.

The first half of this article traces what might be called the internal history of the major innovations in the four areas of household work just noted; here the analysis borrows a great deal from sociological methodology, particularly the work of scholars such as Robert S. Lynd, Helen M. Lynd, and Lee Rainwater. Cowan also tests a traditional functionalist model that sociologists have used to explain the impact of industrial technology upon family life. Her examination of evidence that is documentary (social surveys and government statistics), artifactual, (interior house designs and domestic utensils), and graphic (pictorial advertisements), finds the functionalist model inadequate as a persuasive interpretation of this aspect of social history. As a revisionist, she employs a type of evidence frequently neglected by traditional historians and historians of technology—the modern advertisement in its multiple forms. For, along with other important two-dimensional documents, such as trade catalogs and mail-order catalogs, advertisements are resources that students of American material culture cannot afford to overlook in seeking to understand the artifact in its total cultural context.

Ultimately Cowan argues that advertisers in the early twentieth century, particularly the 1920s, acted as ''ideologues'' by encouraging specific social changes that were both cause and consequence of innovations in household technology. Taking into consideration historical factors such as the decline in the number of domestic servants, increased child-care requirements, and the expanded

*consumption of economic goods, she thus ends her case study with a hypothesis
that deserves further investigation by other material culturists working with
domestic artifacts.*

*Ruth Schwartz Cowan has continued to explore this topic in a paper, "Two
Washes in the Morning and a Bridge Party at Night: The American Housewife
between the Wars," Women Studies 3 (1976): 147–172. She has also written
"Francis Galton's Statistical Ideas: The Influence of Eugenics," Isis (December
1972). An associate professor of history at the State University of New York at
Stony Brook, she first delivered the article that follows as a presentation at the
Society for the History of Technology annual meeting in 1973. It is reprinted here
from Technology and Culture 17 (January 1976): 1–23.*

When we think about the interaction between technology and society, we tend
to think in fairly grandiose terms: massive computers invading the workplace,
railroad tracks cutting through vast wildernesses, or armies of women and children
toiling in the mills. These grand visions have blinded us to an important and rather
peculiar technological revolution which has been going on right under our noses: the
technological revolution in the home. This revolution has transformed the conduct
of our daily lives but in somewhat unexpected ways. The industrialization of the
home was a process very different from the industrialization of other means of
production, and the impact of that process was neither what we have been led to
believe it was nor what students of the other industrial revolutions would have
been led to predict.

Some years ago sociologists of the functionalist school formulated an explanation of the impact of industrial technology on the modern family. Although that
explanation was not empirically verified, it has become almost universally
accepted.[2] Despite some differences in emphasis, the basic tenets of the traditional
interpretation can be roughly summarized as follows:

Before industrialization the family was the basic social unit. Most families
were rural, large, and self-sustaining; they produced and processed almost everything that was needed for their own support and for trading in the marketplace,
while at the same time performing a host of other functions ranging from mutual
protection to entertainment. In these preindustrial families women (adult women,
that is) had a lot to do, and their time was almost entirely absorbed by household
tasks. Under industrialization the family is much less important. The household is
no longer the focus of production; production for the marketplace and production
for sustenance have been removed to other locations. Families are smaller and they
are urban rather than rural. The number of social functions they perform is much
reduced until almost all that remains is consumption, socialization of small children, and tension management. As their functions diminished, families became
atomized; the social bonds that had held them together were loosened. In these

postindustrial families women have very little to do, and the tasks with which they fill their time have lost the social utility that they once possessed. Modern women are in trouble, the analysis goes, because modern families are in trouble; and modern families are in trouble because industrial technology has either eliminated or eased almost all their former functions, but modern ideologies have not kept pace with the change. The results of this time lag are several: some women suffer from role anxiety, others land in the divorce courts, some enter the labor market, and others take to burning their brassieres and demanding liberation.

This sociological analysis is a cultural artifact of vast importance. Many Americans believe that it is true and act upon that belief in various ways: some hope to reestablish family solidarity by relearning lost productive crafts, such as baking bread, tending a vegetable garden; others dismiss the women's liberation movement as "simply a bunch of affluent housewives who have nothing better to do with their time." As disparate as they may seem, these reactions have a common ideological source—the standard sociological analysis of the impact of technological change on family life.

As a theory, this functionalist approach has much to recommend it, but at present we have very little evidence to back it up. Family history is an infant discipline, and what evidence it has produced in recent years does not lend credence to the standard view.[3] Phillippe Ariès has shown, for example, that in France the ideal of the small nuclear family predates industrialization by more than a century.[4] Historical demographers working on data from English and French families have been surprised to find that most families were quite small and that several generations did not ordinarily reside together; the extended family, which is supposed to have been the rule in preindustrial societies, did not occur in colonial New England either.[5] Rural English families routinely employed domestic servants, and even very small English villages had their butchers, bakers, and candlestick makers; all these persons must have eased some of the chores that would otherwise have been the housewife's burden.[6] Preindustrial housewives no doubt had much with which to occupy their time, but we may have reason to wonder whether there was quite as much pressure on them as sociological orthodoxy has led us to suppose. The large rural family that was sufficient unto itself back there on the prairies may have been limited to the prairies—or it may never have existed at all (except, that is, in the reveries of sociologists).

Even if all the empirical evidence were to mesh with the functionalist theory, the theory would still have problems, because its logical structure is rather weak. Comparing the average farm family in 1750 (assuming that you knew what that family was like) with the average urban family in 1950 in order to discover the significant social changes that had occurred is an exercise rather like comparing apples with oranges; the differences between the fruits may have nothing to do with the differences in their evolution. Transferring the analogy to the case at hand, what we really need to know is the difference, say, between an urban laboring family of 1750 and an urban laboring family 100 and then 200 years later, or the difference between the rural nonfarm middle classes in all three centuries, or the difference between the urban rich yesterday and today. Surely in each of these cases the analyses will look very different from what we have been led to expect. As a guess, we might find that for the urban laboring families the changes have been precisely the opposite of what the model predicted; that is, their family structure is much firmer today than it was in centuries past. Similarly, for the rural nonfarm middle class the results might be equally surprising; we might find that married women of that class rarely did any housework at all in 1890 because they had farm girls as servants, whereas in 1950 they bore the full brunt of the work themselves. I could go on, but the point is, I hope, clear: in order to verify or falsify the functionalist theory, it will be necessary to know more than we presently do about the impact of industrialization on families of similar classes and geographical locations.

With this problem in mind, I have, for the purposes of this initial study, deliberately limited myself to one kind of technological change affecting one aspect of family life in only one of the many social classes of families that might have been considered. What happened, I asked, to middle-class American women when the implements with which they did their everyday household work changed? Did the technological change in household appliances have any effect upon the structure of American households, upon the ideologies that governed the behavior of American women, or upon the functions that families needed to perform? Middle-class American women were defined as actual or potential readers of the better-quality women's magazines, such as the *Ladies' Home Journal, American Home, Parents' Magazine, Good Housekeeping*, and *McCall's*.[7] Nonfictional material (articles and advertisements) in those magazines was used as a partial indicator of some of the technological and social changes that were occurring.

The *Ladies' Home Journal* has been in continuous publication since 1886. A casual survey of the nonfiction in the journal yields the immediate impression that that decade between the end of World War I and the beginning of the depression witnessed the most drastic changes in patterns of household work. Statistical data bear out this impression. Before 1918, for example, illustrations of homes lit by gaslight could still be found in the journal; by 1928 gaslight had disappeared. In 1917 only one-quarter (24.3 percent) of the dwellings in the United States had been electrified, but in 1920 this figure had doubled (47.4 percent for rural nonfarm and urban dwellings), and by 1930 it had risen to 84.8 percent.[8] If electrification had meant simply the change from gas or oil lamps to electric lights, the changes in the housewife's routines might not have been very great (except for eliminating the chore of cleaning and filling oil lamps); but changes in lighting were the least of the changes that electrification implied. Small electric appliances followed quickly on the heels of the electric light, and some of those augured much more profound changes in the housewife's routine.

Ironing, for example, had traditionally been one of the most dreadful household chores, especially in warm weather when the kitchen stove had to be kept hot for the better part of the day; irons were heavy and they had to be returned to the stove frequently to be reheated. Electric irons eased a good part of this burden.[9] They were relatively inexpensive and very quickly replaced their predecessors; advertisements for electric irons first began to appear in the ladies' magazines after World War I, and by the end of the decade the old flatiron had disappeared; by 1929 a survey of a hundred Ford employees revealed that ninety-eight of them had the new electric irons in their homes.[10]

Data on the diffusion of electric washing machines are somewhat harder to come by; but it is clear from the advertisements in the magazines, particularly advertisements for laundry soap, that by the middle of the 1920s those machines could be found in a significant number of homes. The washing machine is depicted just about as frequently as the laundry tub by the middle of the 1920s; in 1929, forty-nine out of those one hundred Ford workers had the machines in their homes. The washing machines did not drastically reduce the time that had to be spent on household laundry, as they did not go through their cycles automatically and did not spin dry; the housewife had to stand guard, stopping and starting the machine at appropriate times, adding soap, sometimes attaching the drain pipes and putting the clothes through the wringer manually. The machines did, however, reduce a good part of the drudgery that once had been associated with washday, and this was a matter of no small consequence.[11] Soap powders appeared on the market in the early 1920s, thus eliminating the need to scrape and boil bars of laundry soap.[12] By the end of the 1920s, Blue Monday must have been considerably less blue for some housewives—and probably considerably less "Monday," for with an electric iron, a washing machine, and a hot water heater, there was no reason to limit the washing to just one day of the week.

Like the routines of washing the laundry, the routines of personal hygiene must have been transformed for many households during the 1920s, the years of the bathroom mania.[13] More and more bathrooms were built in older homes, and new homes began to include them as a matter of course. Before World War I, most bathroom fixtures (tubs, sinks, and toilets) were made out of porcelain, by hand; each bathroom was custom-made for the house in which it was installed. After the war, industrialization descended upon the bathroom industry; cast iron enamelware went into mass production and fittings were standardized. In 1921 the dollar value of the production of enameled sanitary fixtures was $2.4 million, the same as it had been in 1915. By 1923, just two years later, that figure had doubled to $4.8 million; it rose again, to $5.1 million, in 1925.[14] The first recessed, double-shell cast iron enameled bathtub was put on the market in the early 1920s. A decade later the standard American bathroom had achieved its standard American form: the recessed tub, plus tiled floors and walls, brass plumbing, a single-unit toilet, an enameled sink, and a medicine chest, all set into a small room which was very often five feet square.[15] The bathroom evolved more quickly than any other room of the house; its standardized form was accomplished in just over a decade.

Along with bathrooms came modernized systems for heating hot water: 61 percent of the homes in Zanesville, Ohio, had indoor plumbing with centrally heated water by 1926, and 83 percent of the homes valued over $2,000 in Muncie, Indiana, had hot and cold running water by 1935.[16] These figures may not be typical of small American cities (or even large American cities) at those times, but they do jibe with the impression that one gets from the magazines; after 1918, references to hot water heated on the kitchen range, either for laundering or for bathing, become increasingly difficult to find.

Similarly, during the 1920s many homes were outfitted with central heating; in Muncie most of the homes of the business class had basement heating in 1924; by 1935 Federal Emergency Relief Administration data for the city indicated that only 22.4 percent of the dwellings valued over $2,000 were still heated by a kitchen stove.[17] What all these changes meant in terms of new habits for the average housewife is somewhat hard to calculate; changes there must have been, but it is difficult to know whether those changes produced an overall saving of labor and/or time. Some chores were eliminated—hauling water, heating water on the stove, and maintaining the kitchen fire—but other chores were added, most notably the chore of keeping yet another room scrupulously clean.

It is not, however, difficult to be certain about the changing habits that were associated with the new American kitchen, a kitchen from which the coal stove had disappeared. In Muncie in 1924, cooking with gas was done in two out of three homes; in 1935 only 5 percent of the homes valued over $2,000 still had coal or wood stoves for cooking.[18] After 1918 advertisements for coal and wood stoves disappeared from the *Ladies' Home Journal*; stove manufacturers purveyed only their gas, oil, or electric models. Articles giving advice to homemakers on how to deal with the trials and tribulations of starting, stoking, and maintaining a coal or a wood fire also disappeared. Thus it seems a safe assumption that most middle-class homes had switched to the new method of cooking by the time the depression began. The change in routine that was predicated on the change from coal or wood to gas or oil was profound; aside from the elimination of such chores as loading the fuel and removing the ashes, the new stoves were much easier to light, maintain, and regulate (even when they did not have thermostats, as the earliest models did not).[19] Kitchens were, in addition, much easier to clean when they did not have coal dust regularly tracked through them; one writer in the *Ladies' Home Journal* estimated that kitchen cleaning was reduced by one-half when coal stoves were eliminated.[20]

Along with new stoves came new foodstuffs and new dietary habits. Canned foods had been on the market since the middle of the nineteenth century, but they did not become an appreciable part of the standard middle-class diet until the 1920s, if the recipes given in cookbooks and in women's magazines are a reliable guide. By 1918 the variety of foods available in cans had been considerably expanded from the peas, corn, and succotash of the nineteenth century; an American housewife with sufficient means could have purchased almost any fruit or vegetable and quite a surprising array of ready-made meals in a can—from Heinz's spaghetti in meat sauce to Purity Cross's lobster à la Newburg. By the middle of the 1920s home canning was becoming a lost art. Canning recipes were relegated to the back pages of the women's magazines; the business-class wives of Muncie reported that, while their mothers had once spent the better part of the summer and fall canning, they themselves rarely put up anything, except an occasional jelly or batch of tomatoes.[21] In part this was also due to changes in the technology of marketing food; increased use of refrigerated railroad cars during this period meant that fresh fruits and vegetables were in the markets all year round at reasonable prices.[22] By the early 1920s, convenience foods were also appearing on American tables: cold breakfast cereals, pancake mixes, bouillon cubes, and packaged desserts could be found. Wartime shortages accustomed Americans to eating much lighter meals than they had previously been wont to do; and as fewer family members were taking all their meals at home (businessmen started to eat lunch in restaurants downtown, and factories and schools began installing cafeterias), there was simply less cooking to be done, and what there was of it was easier to do.[23]

Many of the changes just described—from hand power to electric power, from coal and wood to gas and oil as fuels for cooking, from one-room heating to central heating, from pumping water to running water—are enormous technological changes. Changes of a similar dimension, either in the fundamental technology of an industry, in the diffusion of that technology, or in the routines of workers, would have long since been labeled an "industrial revolution." The change from the laundry tub to the washing machine is no less profound than the change from the hand loom to the power loom; the change from pumping water to turning on a water faucet is no less destructive of traditional habits than the change from manual to electric calculating. It seems odd to speak of an "industrial revolution" connected with housework, odd because we are talking about the technology of such homely things, and odd because we are not accustomed to thinking of housewives as a labor force or of housework as an economic commodity, but despite this oddity, I think the term is altogether appropriate.

In this case other questions come immediately to mind, questions that we do not hesitate to ask, say, about textile workers in Britain in the early-nineteenth century, but we have never thought to ask about housewives in America in the twentieth century. What happened to this particular work force when the technology of its work was revolutionized? Did structural changes occur? Were new jobs created for which new skills were required? Can we discern new ideologies that influenced the behavior of the workers?

The answer to all of these questions, surprisingly enough, seems to be yes. There were marked structural changes in the work force, changes that increased the work load and the job description of the workers that remained. New jobs were created for which new skills were required; these jobs were not physically burdensome, but they may have taken up as much time as the jobs they had replaced. New ideologies were also created, ideologies which reinforced new behavioral patterns, patterns that we might not have been led to expect if we had followed the sociologists' model to the letter. Middle-class housewives, the women who must have first felt the impact of the new household technology, were not flocking into the divorce courts or the labor market or the forums of political protest in the years immediately after the revolution in their work. What they were doing was sterilizing baby bottles, shepherding their children to dancing classes and music lessons, planning nutritious meals, shopping for new clothes, studying child psychology, and hand stitching color-coordinated curtains—chores (and others like them) for which the standard sociological model has apparently not provided.

The significant change in the structure of the household labor force was the disappearance of paid and unpaid servants (unmarried daughters, maiden aunts, and grandparents fall in the latter category) as household workers and the imposition of the entire job on the housewife herself. Leaving aside for a moment the question of which was cause and which effect (did the disappearance of the servant create a demand for the new technology, or did the new technology make the servant obsolete?), the phenomenon itself is relatively easy to document. Before World War I, when illustrators in the women's magazines depicted women doing housework, the women were very often servants. When the lady of the house was drawn, she was often the person being served, or she was supervising the serving, or she was adding an elegant finishing touch to the work. Nursemaids diapered babies, seamstresses pinned up hems, waitresses served meals, laundresses did the wash, and cooks did the cooking. By the end of the 1920s, the servants had disappeared from those illustrations; all those jobs were being done by housewives—elegantly manicured and coiffed, to be sure, but housewives nonetheless.

If we are tempted to suppose that illustrations in advertisements are not a reliable indicator of structural changes of this sort, we can corroborate the changes in other ways. Apparently, the illustrators really did know whereof they drew. Statistically the number of persons throughout the country employed in household service dropped from 1,851,000 in 1910 to 1,411,000 in 1920, while the number of households enumerated in the census rose from 20.3 million to 24.4 million.[24] In Indiana the ratio of households to servants increased from 13.5/1 in 1890 to 30.5/1 in 1920, and in the country as a whole the number of paid domestic servants per 1,000 population dropped from 98.9 in 1900 to 58.0 in 1920.[25] The business-class housewives of Muncie reported that they employed approximately one-half as many woman-hours of domestic service as their mothers had done.[26]

In case we are tempted to doubt these statistics (and indeed statistics about household labor are particularly unreliable, as the labor is often transient, part-time, or simply unreported), we can turn to articles on the servant problem, the disappearance of unpaid family workers, the design of kitchens, and to architectural drawings for houses. All of this evidence reiterates the same point: qualified servants were difficult to find; their wages had risen and their numbers fallen; houses were being designed without maid's rooms; daughters and unmarried aunts were finding jobs downtown; and kitchens were being designed for housewives, not for servants.[27] The first home with a kitchen that was not an entirely separate room was designed by Frank Lloyd Wright in 1934.[28] In 1937 Emily Post invented a new character for her etiquette books: Mrs. Three-in-One, the woman who is her own cook, waitress, and hostess.[29] There must have been many new Mrs. Three-in-Ones abroad in the land during the 1920s.

As the number of household assistants declined, the number of household tasks increased. The middle-class housewife was expected to demonstrate competence at several tasks that previously had not been in her purview or had not existed at all. Child care is the most obvious example. The average housewife had fewer children than her mother had had, but she was expected to do things for her children that her mother would never have dreamed of doing: prepare their special infant formulas, sterilize their bottles, weigh them every day, see to it that they ate nutritionally balanced meals, keep them isolated and confined when they had even the slightest illness, consult with their teachers frequently, and chauffeur them to dancing lessons, music lessons, and evening parties.[30] There was very little Freudianism in this new attitude toward child care: mothers were not spending more time and effort on their children because they feared the psychological trauma of separation, but because competent nursemaids could not be found, and the new theories of child care required constant attention from well-informed persons, persons who were willing and able to read about the latest discoveries in nutrition, the control of contagious diseases, or the techniques of behavioral psychology. These persons simply had to be their mothers.

Consumption of economic goods provides another example of the housewife's expanded job description; like child care, the new tasks associated with consumption were not necessarily physically burdensome, but they were time consuming, and they required the acquisition of new skills.[31] Home economists and the editors of women's magazines tried to teach housewives to spend their money wisely. The present generation of housewives, it was argued, had been reared by mothers who did not ordinarily shop for things like clothing, bed linens, or towels; consequently modern housewives did not know how to shop and would have to be taught. Furthermore, their mothers had not been accustomed to the wide variety of goods that were now available in the modern marketplace; the new housewives had to be taught not just to be consumers, but to be informed consumers.[32] Several contemporary observers believed that shopping and shopping wisely were occupying increasing amounts of housewives' time.[33]

Several of these contemporary observers also believed that standards of household care changed during the decade of the 1920s.[34] The discovery of the "household germ" led to almost fetishistic concern about the cleanliness of the home. The amount of frequency of laundering probably increased, as bed linen and underwear were changed more often, children's clothes were made increasingly out of washable fabrics, and men's shirts no longer had replaceable collars and cuffs.[35] Unfortunately, all these changes in standards are difficult to document, being changes in the things that people regard as so insignificant as to be unworthy of comment; the improvement in standards seems a likely possibility, but not something that can be proved.

In any event, we do have various time studies which demonstrate somewhat surprisingly that housewives with conveniences were spending just as much time on household duties as were housewives without them or, to put it another way, housework, like so many other types of work, expands to fill the time available. A study comparing the time spent per week in housework by 288 farm families and 154 town families in Oregon in 1928 revealed 61 hours spent by farm wives and 63.4 hours by town wives; in 1929 a U.S. Department of Agriculture study of families in various states produced almost identical results.[36] Surely if the standard sociological model were valid, housewives in towns, where presumably the benefits of specialization and electrifications were most likely to be available, should have been spending far less time at their work than their rural sisters. However, just after World War II, economists at Bryn Mawr College reported the same phenomenon: 60.55 hours spent by farm housewives, 78.35 hours by women in small cities, 80.57 hours by women in large ones, precisely the reverse of the results that were expected.[37] A recent survey of time studies conducted between 1920 and 1970 concludes that the time spent on housework by nonemployed housewives has remained remarkably constant throughout the period.[38] All these results point in the same direction: mechanization of the household meant that time expended on some jobs decreased, but also that new jobs were substituted, and in some cases, notably laundering, time expenditures for old jobs increased because of higher standards. The advantages of mechanization may be somewhat more dubious than they seem at first glance.

As the job of the housewife changed, the connected ideologies also changed; there was a clearly perceptible difference in the attitudes that women brought to housework before and after World War I. Before the war, the trials of doing housework in a servantless home were discussed, and they were regarded as just that—trials, necessary chores that had to be got through until a qualified servant could be found. After the war housework changed; it was no longer a trial and a chore but something quite different—an emotional "trip." Laundering was not just laundering, but an expression of love; the housewife who truly loved her family would protect them from the embarrassment of tattletale gray. Feeding the family was not just feeding the family but a way to express the housewife's artistic inclinations and a way to encourage feelings of family loyalty and affection. Diapering the baby was not just diapering but a time to build the baby's sense of security and love for the mother. Cleaning the bathroom sink was not just cleaning but an exercise of protective maternal instincts, providing a way for the housewife to keep her family safe from disease. Tasks of this emotional magnitude could not possibly be delegated to servants, even assuming that qualified servants could be found.

Women who failed at these new household tasks were bound to feel guilt about their failure. If I had to choose one word to characterize the temper of the women's magazines during the 1920s, it would be "guilt." Readers of the better-quality women's magazines are portrayed as feeling guilty a good lot of the time, and when they are not guilty they are embarrassed: guilty if their infants have not gained enough weight, embarrassed if their drains are clogged, guilty if their children go to school in soiled clothes, guilty if all the germs behind the bathroom sink are not eradicated, guilty if they fail to notice the first signs of an oncoming cold, embarrassed if accused of having body odor, guilty if their sons go to school without good breakfasts, guilty if their daughters are unpopular because of old-fashioned, or unironed, or—heaven forbid—dirty dresses. In earlier times women were made to feel guilty if they abandoned their children or were too free with their affections. In the years after World War I, American women were made to feel guilty about sending their children to school in scuffed shoes. Between the two kinds of guilt there is a world of difference.[39]

Let us return for a moment to the sociological model with which this essay began. The model predicts that changing patterns of household work will be correlated with at least two striking indicators of social change: the divorce rate and the rate of married women's labor force participants. That correlation may indeed exist, but it certainly is not reflected in the women's magazines of the 1920s and 1930s: divorce and full-time paid employment were not part of the life-style or the life pattern of the middle-class housewife as she was idealized in her magazines.

There were social changes attendant upon the introduction of modern technology into the home, but they were not the changes that the traditional functionalist model predicts; on this point a close analysis of the statistical data corroborates the impression conveyed in the magazines. The divorce rate was indeed rising during the years between the wars, but it was not rising nearly so fast for the middle and upper classes (who had, presumably, easier access to the new technology) as it was for the lower classes. By almost every gauge of socioeconomic status—income, prestige of husband's work, and education—the divorce rate is higher for persons lower on the socioeconomic scale, and this is a phenomenon that has been constant over time.[40]

The supposed connection between improved household technology and married women's labor force participation seems just as dubious and on the same grounds. The single socioeconomic factor which correlates most strongly (in cross-sectional studies) with married women's employment is husband's income, and the correlation is strongly negative; the higher his income, the less likely it will be that she is working.[41] Women's labor force participation increased during the 1920s, but this increase was due to the influx of single women into the force. Married women's participation increased slightly during those years, but that increase was largely in factory labor, precisely the kind of work that middle-class women (who were, again, much more likely to have labor-saving devices at home) were least likely to do.[42] If there were a necessary connection between the improvement of household technology and either of these two social indicators, we would expect the data to be precisely the reverse of what in fact has occurred: women in the higher social classes should have fewer functions at home and should therefore be more (rather than less) likely to seek paid employment or divorce.

Thus for middle-class American housewives between the wars, the social changes that we can document are not the social changes that the functionalist model predicts; rather than changes in divorce or patterns of paid employment, we find changes in the structure of the work force, in its skills, and in its ideology. These social changes were concomitant with a series of technological changes in the equipment that was used to do the work. What is the relationship between these two series of phenomena? Is it possible to demonstrate causality or the direction of that causality? Was the decline in the number of households employing servants a cause or an effect of the mechanization of those households? Both are, after all, equally possible. The declining supply of household servants, as well as their rising wages, may have stimulated a demand for new appliances at the same time that the acquisition of new appliances may have made householders less inclined to employ the laborers who were on the market. Are there any techniques available to the historian to help us answer these questions?

In order to establish causality, we need to find a connecting link between the two sets of phenomena, a mechanism that, in real life, could have made the causality work. In this case a connecting link, an intervening agent between the social and the technological changes, comes immediately to mind: the advertiser—by which term I mean a combination of the manufacturer of the new goods, the advertising agent who promoted the goods, and the periodical that published the promotion. All the new devices and new foodstuffs that were being offered to American households were being manufactured and marketed by large companies which had considerable amounts of capital invested in their production: General Electric, Procter and Gamble, General Foods, Lever Brothers, Frigidaire, Campbell's, Del Monte, American Can, and Atlantic and Pacific Tea. These were all well-established firms by the time the household revolution began, and they were all in a position to pay for national advertising campaigns to promote their new products and services. And pay they did; one reason for the expanding size and number of women's magazines in the 1920s was, no doubt, the expansion in revenues from available advertisers.[43]

Those national advertising campaigns were likely to have been powerful stimulators of the social changes that occurred in the household labor force; the advertisers probably did not initiate the changes, but they certainly encouraged them. Most of the advertising campaigns manifestly worked, so they must have touched upon areas of real concern for American housewives. Appliance ads specifically suggested that the acquisition of one gadget or another would make it possible to fire the maid, spend more time with the children, or have the afternoon free for shopping.[44] Similarly, many advertisements played upon the embarrassment and guilt which were now associated with household work. Ralston, Cream of Wheat, and Ovaltine were not themselves responsible for the compulsive practice of weighing infants and children repeatedly (after every meal for newborns, every day in infancy, every week later on), but the manufacturers certainly did not stint on capitalizing upon the guilt that women apparently felt if their offspring did not gain the required amounts of weight.[45] Yet again, many of the earliest attempts to spread "wise" consumer practices were undertaken by large corporations and the magazines that desired their advertising: mail-order shopping guides, "product-testing" services, pseudo-informative pamphlets, and other such promotional devices were all techniques for urging the housewife to buy new things under the guise of training her in her role as a skilled consumer.[46]

Thus the advertisers could well be called the "ideologues" of the 1920s, encouraging certain very specific social changes, as ideologues are wont to do. Not surprisingly, the changes that occurred were precisely the ones that would gladden the hearts and fatten the purses of the advertisers; fewer household servants meant a greater demand for labor and timesaving devices; more household tasks for women meant more and more specialized products that they would need to buy; more guilt and embarrassment about their failure to succeed at their work meant a greater likelihood that they would buy the products that were intended to minimize that failure. Happy, full-time housewives in intact families spend a lot of money to maintain their households; divorced women and working women do not. The advertisers may not have created the image of the ideal American housewife that dominated the 1920s, the woman who cheerfully and skillfully set about making everyone in her family perfectly happy and perfectly healthy, but they certainly helped to perpetuate it.

The role of the advertiser as a connecting link between social change and technological change is at this juncture simply a hypothesis, with nothing much more to recommend it than an argument from plausibility. Further research may serve to test the hypothesis, but testing it may not settle the question of which was cause and which effect, if that question can ever be settled definitively in historical work. What seems most likely in this case, as in so many others, is that cause and effect are not separable and that there is a dynamic interaction between the social changes that married women were experiencing and the technological changes that were occurring in their homes. Viewed this way, the disappearance of competent servants becomes one of the factors that stimulated the mechanization of homes, and this mechanization of homes becomes a factor (though by no means the only one) in the disappearance of servants. Similarly, the emotionalization of housework becomes both cause and effect of the mechanization of that work; and the expansion of time spent on new tasks becomes both cause and effect of the introduction of time-saving devices. For example, the social pressure to spend more time in child care may have led to a decision to purchase the devices; once purchased, the devices could indeed have been used to save time, although often they were not.

If one holds the question of causality in abeyance, the example of household work still has some useful lessons to teach about the general problem of technology and social change. The standard sociological model for the impact of modern technology on family life clearly needs some revision; at least for middle-class nonrural American families in the twentieth century, the social changes were not the ones that the standard model predicts. In these families the functions of at least one member, the housewife, have increased rather than decreased, and the dissolution of family life has not in fact occurred.

Our standard notions about what happens to a work force under the pressure of technological change may also need revision. When industries become mechanized and rationalized, we expect certain general changes in the work force to occur: its structure becomes more highly differentiated, individual workers become more specialized, managerial functions increase, and the emotional context of the work disappears. On all four counts our expectations are reversed with regard to household work. The work force became less rather than more differentiated as domestic servants, unmarried daughters, maiden aunts, and grandparents left the household and as chores which had once been performed by commercial agencies (such as laundries, delivery services, and milkmen) were delegated to the housewife. The individual workers also became less specialized; the new housewife was now responsible for every aspect of life in her household, from scrubbing the bathroom floor to keeping abreast of the latest literature in child psychology.

The housewife is just about the only unspecialized worker left in America—a veritable Jane-of-all-trades at a time when the Jacks-of-all-trades have disappeared. As her work became generalized the housewife was also proletarianized: formerly she was ideally the manager of several other subordinate workers; now she was idealized as the manager and the worker combined. Her managerial functions have not entirely disappeared, but they have certainly diminished and have been replaced by simple manual labor. The middle-class, fairly well-educated housewife ceased to be a personnel manager and became, instead, a chauffeur, charwoman, and short-order cook. The implications of this phenomenon, the proletarianization of a work force that had previously seen itself as predominantly managerial, deserve to be explored at greater length than is possible here, because I suspect that they will explain certain aspects of the women's liberation movement of the 1960s and 1970s which have previously eluded explanation: why, for example, the movement's greatest strength lies in social and economic groups who seem, on the surface at least, to need it least: women who are white, well-educated, and middle-class.

Finally, instead of desensitizing the emotions that were connected with household work, the industrial revolution in the home seems to have heightened the emotional context of the work, until a woman's sense of self-worth became a function of her success at arranging bits of fruit to form a clown's face in a gelatin salad. That pervasive social illness, which Betty Friedan characterized as "the problem that has no name," arose not among workers who found that their labor brought no emotional satisfaction, but among workers who found that their work was invested with emotional weight far out of proportion to its own inherent value: "How long," a friend of mine is fond of asking, "can we continue to believe that we will have orgasms while waxing the kitchen floor?"

16

Building in Wood in the Eastern United States: A Time-Place Perspective

Fred Kniffen
Henry Glassie

Introduction

No artifact is of more importance to the settlement geographer and the historian of vernacular building than the domestic residence. When fully interpreted, the type, form, and uses of houses tell us a great deal, not only about the physical locale and technology of their place and era, but also about the sources and dates of their builder or renovator, the contacts and influences he experienced, his ethnic or racial affiliations, and—possibly—also his class, occupation, and religion.

American houses, as they developed out of three major cultural hearths (southern New England, the mid-Atlantic colonies, and the Chesapeake Bay region) roughly between 1790 and 1850, were largely European in origin. Most early American vernacular building therefore reflected primordial notions about house morphology underlying folk architecture throughout Great Britain and northern Europe. Until folklife scholars and cultural geographers such as Fred Kniffen began systematic studies of American folk building techniques—see his seminal articles "Louisiana House Types" and "Folk Housing: Key to Diffusion," in Annals of the Association of American Geographers 26 (1936) and 55 (1965)—most architectural scholarship dealt with more pretentious structures built in a "high" or "academic" style (a specialized house form designed and constructed by a builder following a pattern book or an architect working within a recognizable artistic vocabulary such as the Greek revival or the Romanesque). Moreover, the studies of vernacular building construction methods that had been done had not been synthesized, nor had a systematic typology, defined by generic groups and precise nomenclature, been formulated.

Fred Kniffen and Henry Glassie's position paper first appeared in The

Geographical Review 56 (1966): 40–66 and sought to rectify these deficiencies. It also demonstrated the contributions that folklife scholarship has made to American material culture research once folklorists came to study folk objects with the same zeal they had traditionally exhibited with regard to researching folk music, dance, and written and oral literature.

In their attempt to trace the construction evolution of three methods of building in wood (framing, vertically timbered walls, and horizontally timbered walls), Kniffen and Glassie devote the bulk of their attention to the last two building types. Combining the comprehensive knowledge of the published literature on folk housing in this country (done largely by folklorists) and especially in Europe, where folk architecture has been studied longer and more thoroughly, the authors show how a single design feature—in this case, the different techniques used to join horizontal members at a building's corners—can become the crucial clue for the identification, classification, and interpretation of a huge corpus of material culture. While this aspect of their argument may appear overdetailed and technical, it is the type of careful quantitative research that simply must be done in order to formulate the necessary taxonomies required for accurate artifact interpretation. Once a typology of construction methods has been established, the plotting of area distribution of the material culture data is done by means of diffusion maps.

Throughout these two processes of material culture study (establishing an accurate typology and mapping its geographical diffusion), antecedents for most of the building methods discovered are traced as far back as the Neolithic Era, quickly dispelling the myth that there were any major indigenous developments or local borrowing from the Indians in the majority of American building before the innovation of balloon-framing in the Midwest in the 1840s. Nor was the horizontal log construction with true corner-timbering that came to characterize the American frontier a New World adaptation to the environment. Nor was it a Scandinavian introduction as has so often been claimed; rather, Kniffen and Glassie argue, it was introduced into America by the Pennsylvania Germans and carried by them and by the Scotch-Irish in all directions from southeastern Pennsylvania. Not long after its introduction in America, the log cabin became an artifact of amazing symbolic import in American cultural history. This development, partially surveyed by C. A. Weslager in *The Log Cabin in America* (1969) needs further study, as does the log cabin's manifestations in popular material culture, such as Lincoln Log toys and colonial cabin architecture of the 1920s.

Kniffen and Glassie also propose an outline of opportunities for further study at their article's conclusion. They call for additional research on the cultural meaning of the several methods of timber construction, on their association with different groups of peoples, on their place in the westward movement, and on their relative importance during the change from frontier to settled community. This research agenda has, in part, been taken up by their own subsequent research. Fred Kniffen, a professor of geography and anthropology at Louisiana

State University, published "On Corner-Timbering," Pioneer America 1 (January 1969). His widespread influence over American cultural geography and folklife research can be partially gauged by the festschrift, H. J. Walker and W. F. Haag, eds., Man and Cultural Heritage: Papers in Honor of Fred B. Kniffen (1974).

Henry Glassie, a Kniffen protege and now a professor of folklore and folklife at the University of Pennsylvania, has become one of the major theoreticians and practitioners of American material culture studies. His seminal research, heavily indebted to cultural anthropology, structuralism, and folkways scholarship, has appeared in two landmark books: Pattern in Material Folk Culture of the Eastern United States (1968) and Folk Housing in Middle Virginia: A Structural Analysis of Historic Artifacts (1975) and in numerous articles. "Meaningful Things and Appropriate Myths: The Artifact's Place in American Studies," Prospects: An Annual of American Cultural Studies, 3 (1977) is a shorter statement of his methodological and philosophical orientation on artifact study.

If the geography of settlement is ever to reach its full potential as the interpretable record of the historical events and cultural processes imprinted on the land, the components of settlements of all kinds must be systematically reduced to types and quantities before they are set against the revealing vagaries of reality.

It is the purpose of this study to examine a basic aspect of settlements—the methods of constructing buildings of wood. In the timber-rich eastern United States other materials in common use in Europe declined in importance as the frontier moved westward. New Englanders never built extensively in anything but wood, and the stone construction of eastern Pennsylvania and the brick of Tidewater Virginia disappeared rapidly away from these nuclear areas.[1]

European America has known three general methods of building in wood: with framed walls, with walls of closely set vertical timbers, and with walls of horizontal timbers. Framing, typologically the youngest, begins with a skeletal structure of horizontal, vertical, and diagonal squared timbers, which is then covered in one of several ways. In this study framing is given less emphasis because it is already amply and expertly documented. It is the older building with timbers or logs, round or faced, vertical or horizontal, about which there is a lack of accurate information and little agreement on concept and nomenclature, and it is here that this study aspires to make its major contribution. However, with respect to areal distribution, framing is of course of equal or even greater concern.

This article is the first part of an undertaking to describe and interpret the first settlements resulting from the westward movement out of established seaboard nuclei, roughly between 1790 and 1850, or between the opening of the trans-Appalachian West and the invasion of the grasslands. We propose to consider, in order, methods of building construction, types of buildings, fences and fencing practices, field forms and agricultural practices, and other aspects of settlements. In treating methods of construction no initial time limit can be set, for their antecedents reach back at least to the European Neolithic.

The procedure consists in the synthesizing of published materials with the results of extensive field observation. All too frequently there are no ready-made generic groupings. Every effort has been made to discover and adapt existing concepts and terms, and to reconcile conflicting usages. Definitions and nomenclature are proposed where they are nonexistent.

A strong emphasis on folk practices will be evident throughout. This is because they better serve the ultimate purposes of the undertaking to find origins and to trace diffusions and changes. Folkways are comparatively the simplest and most direct expression of fundamental needs and urges. They conform to type with a minimum of individual deviation and thus attest to the innate conservatism of their practitioners. They are often areally, even when not numerically, dominant. Further, folk practices with respect to material things have been badly neglected in comparison with, say, traditional music and tales. Architects have largely disregarded the simpler folk methods and forms of construction in favor of more sophisticated methods and more pretentious structures. Finally, the new attack on rural poverty will surely accelerate the destruction of unchronicled folk structures and practices to the point where their record is beyond recovery.

Fully aware of the inability of two persons to familiarize themselves with all the details of building in wood, we proffer an open invitation to correct and extend the observations and conclusions of this presentation.

Antecedents of American Construction in Wood

It seems safe to assert that no significant method of wood construction employed in America before 1850 was developed here. Techniques were modified and even perverted, but their European ancestry is certain. Seventeenth-century Europe provided half-timbering;[2] weatherboarding over heavy frame; vertical log, paling, and plank construction; and horizontal logs, planks, and timbers with various corner joinings. The wattle-daub and thatched huts, and even the more primitive "wigwams" of branches, rushes, and turf that appeared early in Massachusetts had their counterparts in contemporary England.[3]

Frame Construction

Framing is so old in Europe that it became the dominant method of building in the English seaboard settlements. It is typologically more advanced than the vertical construction from which it is derived. The frames were built of very heavy timbers with a safety factor far in excess of any possible demand. This is a major reason why so many of the older houses have survived. It was not until about 1830 that so-called balloon framing was devised, using much smaller and lighter timbers set closely together. Balloon framing for dwellings began to be important only after 1850; barns continued to be heavily framed well into the twentieth century.

To the extent, then, that wood was used in the English and Dutch seaboard colonies, framing was almost the sole method of construction. Except in the upland South and its culturally dominated periphery, frame construction was transmitted westward and became the near-universal form, quickly replacing the pioneer log house. The significant changes were from heavy to balloon framing and, much earlier, from half-timbering, to an almost exclusive sheathing and weatherboarding.

Half-Timbering

Half-timbering—a heavy framing of squared timbers with a filling, or nogging, between them—was part of the cultural heritage of most Europeans in America at the time of the Revolution. Half-timbering was practiced in Britain, France, and Germany, and northward into southern Sweden, to mention only the important source areas. The nogging was sometimes brick, sometimes clay clinging to rods, or "cats," set vertically or horizontally between the timbers. Occasionally the filling was stone, or plastered wattle or lath. This skeletal construction eliminated the need for a large amount of lumber, presumably a reason for its wide use in Europe.

Half-timbering was common in the early seaboard settlements, but the timbers were frequently covered with siding, a not unexpected consequence of an abundance of cheap wood, just as the Old World thatch roof gave way to wooden shingles. Eventually the use of nogging was discontinued (but not, as has sometimes been suggested, exclusively because of the low lime content of American clays). This stage of constructional evolution was practiced by early New England settlers who came from heavily wooded southeastern England,[4] the one area where heavy framing was clapboarded without the use of nogging.

Although surviving examples of half-timbering are fairly common in the easternmost states, notably in Virginia and in German areas of Pennsylvania, the method was not carried westward to any great extent. However, nineteenth-century German immigrants from Europe introduced half-timbering in Ohio, Wisconsin, Missouri, and Texas, and perhaps elsewhere,[5] and the French in the Mississippi Valley have continued the practice virtually to the present.[6] Vestiges of half-timbering are occasionally seen in brick nogging within the light balloon framing of the latter nineteenth century.

Vertical Posts, Planks, and Timbers

Building with closely set vertical members is so widespread and so varied in detail as to suggest that any common origin must lie in a remote European concept. Indeed, vertical post construction seems to have originated in the Near East in the

Neolithic and to have spread across Europe as a major element in the Neolithic complex. By the late Neolithic, it was a dominant form of construction in all of Europe except the far north, the western Mediterranean, and the Atlantic area of England, in the last two of which stone was of greater importance. Initially, the posts were driven into the ground a foot or so apart, and the spaces between them were woven in wattle or filled with clay and straw. During the late Neolithic, in the area of Jutland, the posts were set without interstices for added warmth, perhaps through influence from the palisades known throughout Europe. This type of close-set vertical timber construction spread slowly; it did not reach Russia until the third century before Christ and England until Anglo-Saxon time.[7]

Vertical construction survives in an old Saxon church in Essex,[8] composed of vertical half logs between sill and plate, tongued and grooved on adjoining edges to produce a tight fit. Numerous examples of vertical construction have been noted in France, especially in Normandy.[9] Construction using vertical logs and timbers is cited for early New England,[10] and the medieval "puncheoning"—wattle-daub on upright posts—for Virginia.[11] The use of vertical oak planking to provide structural support in place of studding, which extended into the nineteenth century, has been traced from England.[12] Vertical board-and-batten construction has been postulated for Spanish Florida,[13] and Spanish records show that settlers in St. Augustine built houses "palisado" style before 1597.[14] Another example of vertical log construction is a twentieth-century Scandinavian barn in Wisconsin.[15]

But it was the French in America who employed vertical construction most extensively. *Poteaux en terre* or *pieux en terre* (a variant term is *pièces en terre*) was the earliest method used throughout the great arc of French colonial settlement extending from Acadia westward to the Great Lakes and southward to the lower Mississippi Valley.[16] *Poteaux en terre* consisted of close-set vertical posts tamped into a trench, *pieux en terre* of sharp stakes driven into the ground; the interstices, about as wide as the diameter of a post, were filled with clay and grass or with stones and mortar, sometimes plastered over or even covered with planks. Charles E. Peterson distinguishes *poteaux* as squared above ground, *pieux* as round posts.[17] Here again usage has varied with time and place.

A variant, one might say an improvement, is the placement of the vertical members *sur sole* (on a sill) rather than *en terre*; from pictures, the old courthouse at Cahokia, Illinois, appears to be a surviving example. The old term surely was *poteaux sur sole*, employed concurrently with *poteau en terre* and *colombage*,[18] a term used at least on the upper Mississippi and in Canada to designate half-timbering. The two *poteaux* terms, then, referred to closely set, unbraced vertical timbers, *colombage* to more widely spaced, normally braced, vertical, squared timbers, the spaces between filled with various materials. At least two writers have used *poteaux sur sole* to designate horizontal construction,[19] which is surely a perversion, even if it is popular modern usage.

In French America, only among the Mississippi and Great Lakes settlements did vertical construction long remain popular. In Canada it gave way generally to horizontal timber construction or stone, and George-Marie Butel-Dumont records the change to brick or half-brick and half-wood (half-timber) structures in New Orleans in the early eighteenth century.[20] In rural Louisiana *poteaux en terre* persisted well into the nineteenth century. To this day *pieux en terre* remains faintly alive in Louisiana in the form of a tight paling yard fence, *barrière en pieux debouts*, in the original form of which cypress palings are driven into the ground.

In the attempt to account for the prevalence of vertical construction among the French in America it has been suggested that it was inspired by Indian vertical post stockades or palisades and buildings or was borrowed from the Gulf Coast Spaniards. Neither suggestion seems tenable in view of the fact that the earliest form of construction in French Canada was *poteaux en terre*,[21] which was introduced into Louisiana by the French Canadian Pierre le Moyne Iberville.[22] Moreover, since conclusive evidence indicates that vertical post construction of palisades and buildings reaches back to the European Neolithic, it would seem unnecessary to seek further for explanation of its American incidence. It is in keeping with the evidence to assume, for the present, that a method of construction which was very old and largely vestigial in western Europe experienced a brief rejuvenation in timber-rich colonial America.

Horizontal Logs, Timbers, and Planks

Construction in which the individual members are placed horizontally, close together, and one above the other has been used nearly everywhere in the New World. It appeared most widely in the upland South and only slightly less so in the timber houses of French Canada. Every form of horizontal construction employed in America has ample European precedent, and again it is unnecessary to invoke either local borrowing from the Indians or independent invention.

The fundamental distinction is the manner in which the horizontal members are joined at the corners. The variety of techniques employed is considerable. A basic difference distinguishes two all-inclusive groups: the utilization or nonutilization of corner posts or supports to which the horizontal timbers are attached. To the second group belongs the method commonly used in American log houses, in which the timbers are so notched at the ends that they become immovable when locked to the timbers above and below. In some marginal areas, however, the original and effective type of corner-timbering has deteriorated to the point where the timbers no longer lock and must be secured by some other means.

All horizontal construction may be descriptively classed as having either even tiers or alternating tiers. In the first group the timbers of the corresponding tiers of the four walls lie even with one another; in the second the timbers in one wall lie half a thickness above or below those of the corresponding tiers in the adjoining walls. This latter relative position is inherent in all "true" corner timbering.

There are several methods of providing corner support for even-tiered horizontal timbers. One consists of a vertical post with continuous grooves from top to bottom, into which the tapered ends of the horizontal logs are dropped. In another the vertical post is mortised to receive the tenoned ends of the horizontal pieces. A third uses four posts driven into the ground at each corner (''Canuck'' style), so arranged that the horizontal timbers are held in place. A possibly related form is a ''hog trough'' of heavy planks, the apex set into the corner, the wings abutting the ends of the horizontal logs, to which they are spiked or pegged.

The support of horizontal timbers by corner posts is an old form of construction in Europe. It was apparently carried across much of the continent from Silesia by the Lausitz urnfield culture in the late Bronze Age.[23] Examples persist in southern Sweden,[24] in the Alps, and probably elsewhere. In French America horizontal timber construction came early but was later than *poteaux en terre* to be widely practiced.[25] *Pièce sur pièce*, as the method is commonly called,[26] was used, at least sparingly, throughout French America. Although it has been impossible to localize the European source of *pièce sur pièce* construction as carried by the French to America, its ancient appearance in Europe and its present-day survival there militate against an independent New World origin.

Pièce sur pièce was the prevailing method of wood construction in early French Canada. The old Hudson's Bay Company buildings and remote police posts are overwhelmingly of this type. The American practice of notching the ends of the logs has invaded Canada, in some parts fairly recently,[27] but it has by no means displaced the older method, which is still very much alive. One of the merits of the Candian method is that construction with corner (and intermediate) posts, unlike the American corner-timbering, permits the use of short logs and at the same time puts no restrictions on the size of the building.[28]

Horizontal construction with corner posts has generously invaded the areas of the United States peripheral to Canada—New England, New York, the Upper Lakes region, and the northern Great Plains states.[29] It occurs also in areas as remote from Canada as Pennsylvania, Virginia, and Tennessee, in these last surely a direct importation from Europe by Germans. Also non-French in origin, and hence evidence of the once-widespread European practice, are timbers tenoned into corner posts, found in seventeenth-century garrison houses of the New England frontier.[30] There are rather frequent later references to this method of construction for northern New England.

Types of Corner-Timbering

There are several methods without corner posts, all of European origin, in which horizontal timbers are notched and fitted in alternating tiers in a manner to lock them continuously from bottom to top. In what might be termed ''false'' corner-timbering, the tiers are even and the interlocking, if present, is restricted to one tier. False corner-timbering had appeared in the New England garrison houses by the middle of the seventeenth century,[31] not long after the arrival of the log-using

Swedes on the Delaware. Although later examples might suggest by their nature and location a stimulus diffusion from the areas of true corner-timbering to the south, false corner-timbering is more likely to have originated as a product of English carpentry than as an indirect inspiration from Swedish settlers. From New England false corner-timbering spread through upstate New York and as far west as Michigan, but it never attained any great areal or numerical importance.

In the eastern United States six methods of producing a truly corner-timbered joint are employed: saddle notching, V notching, diamond notching, full dovetailing, half dovetailing, and square notching.[32] In all but the last each log is locked into the ones above and below it, and the necessity of nailing or pegging is eliminated.

Saddle notching is the simplest method and is usually used on logs left in the round. For the corner to be tight the logs must extend somewhat beyond the plane of the wall, and the application of siding is difficult. Although in modern rustic cabins and in frontier structures the end of the log may extend a foot or more beyond the plane of the wall, in traditional American practice the end rarely extends more than a few inches. There are three forms of saddle notching: double notching, in which the notches are on both sides of the log; and single notching, in which the notch may be either on the top or on the bottom.

The V notch seems to have developed directly from the saddle notch on the bottom of the log only. Instead of being rounded, the notch is cut sharply in a V, into which the chamfered head of the lower log fits. If the log is left in the round, the crown is pear-shaped; if the log is hewn, the crown is shaped like the gable end of a house—indeed, it is often referred to as "roof topping." In V notching the ends of the log are cut off flush; the square or box corner thus produced permits the addition of board siding or, rarely, brick veneer.

In the diamond notch both the top and the bottom of the end of the log are chamfered to produce a diamond-shaped crown. Diamond notching, which bears a superficial and probably accidental similarity in the shape of the crown to some Scandinavian types, seems to have been developed from V notching.[33]

Full dovetailing is the most complicated of the methods commonly used in American corner-timbering and the most difficult to execute. It effectively locks the logs in both directions, produces a box corner, slopes downward on every face (so that water drains out), and is employed both on hewn and, though rarely, on round logs. The dovetail is familiar to every joiner of timber, yet many who could apply it in framing a house did not use it when corner-timbering logs. For example, in New England dovetailing was used in the early garrison houses but was seldom, if ever, used in the log construction of ordinary houses.[34] Elsewhere, in areas of log construction, dovetailing was applied to all kinds of buildings.

In half dovetailing, also known to all woodworkers, the head of the notch slopes upward but the bottom is flat. It is, in effect, half of a V notch, yet it seems to have been developed from a full dovetail. The top angle of a full-dovetail notch is more acute than the bottom angle, and the bottom angle was easily straightened to produce the half dovetail, which is no less effective than the full dovetail but much easier to make.

The square notch is simple and familiar as a tenon to a woodworker. It lacks the structure to lock the logs, a deficiency sometimes remedied by drilling and pegging through two squares or more. The square notch degenerated in different areas from both the V notch and the half dovetail. The two forms are distinguishable by the shape of the log: the V notch and its derivative square notch are found on logs square or rectangular in section (that is, about eight by twelve inches); the half dovetail and its derivative square notch are usually found on planked logs (that is, logs hewn to some six inches in thickness and about fourteen to thirty-six inches in width).

What is probably a variant of the square notch is the half notch. It is only occasionally used exclusively but frequently appears with the square notch as a means of adjusting the position of a particular timber.[35]

No other method of corner-timbering has significant distribution in the eastern United States, but odd methods are occasionally encountered, especially in the areas settled relatively recently by Scandinavians and Finns. One such is the double-notch joint, named by Sigurd Erixon as the form most commonly used in Sweden.[36] In the United States it is encountered commonly in the Upper Lakes states and in Hollywood movie sets ranging in locale from Wounded Knee, South Dakota, to Charleston, South Carolina. A popular brand of toy logs is of this type. In both the movies and in the toys the use is an unfortunate and unnecessary violation of the verities of time and place.

The double-notch joint seems to have been widely distributed in Europe at one time; outside Fennoscandia surviving examples are known in the Spreewald, near Berlin, in Poland, in Switzerland, and in southwestern France. Its more recent popularity in northern Europe was apparently not matched in the source areas, for it did not have an effective early introduction into America.

Distribution and development of corner-timbering. Horizontal log construction employing true corner-timbering originated in the Mesolithic with the Maglemosian culture,[37] which was centered in Denmark, southern Sweden, and northern Germany. By the Bronze Age horizontal logs had replaced vertical posts as the commonest method of construction from France to Russia and from Norway to Czechoslovakia.[38] Prehistoric horizontal log construction was universally characterized by round logs notched on the top or on both sides, a foot or more from the end of the log.

Horizontal log construction was not part of the cultural equipment of the Dutch, English, or French emigrants to the New World,[39] since it had receded during the early medieval period into the wooded mountainous sections of an area bounded on the west by an arc reaching from Scandinavia through Germany into the Alps, and possibly into the Pyrenees. The Swedes who settled on the Delaware in

1638 were the first to employ horizontal log construction in what is now the eastern United States. The log work of Scandinavia was similar to that found throughout Europe in the Bronze Age: the logs were generally left in the round; the notches were on the top or both sides of the log about a foot from the end, producing a characteristic overhang; and each log was grooved along the entire length of its bottom to fit tightly with the log below it. Although log houses were certainly built in New Sweden, references to them are strangely few. The first mention of log houses outside New Sweden is in 1669 for Maryland and in 1680 for North Carolina,[40] but there is no evidence that the houses were truly corner-timbered or that they were inspired by Swedish sources. The Swedes had little contact with their English neighbors, and their log work did not spread beyond New Sweden; in fact, they soon abandoned it for stone and brick.[41] Even their normally conservative religious architecture was English or American rather than Swedish.[42]

Beginning in the late-seventeenth century and reaching a peak in the early-eighteenth century, great numbers of Scotch-Irish and Germans arrived in Pennsylvania and settled just west of the English.[43] The Pennsylvania Germans used horizontal log construction of the type which they had known in Europe and which may still be found there, particularly in Bohemia, Moravia, and Silesia.[44] The previously stone- or mud-using Scotch-Irish quickly adopted Pennsylvania German log construction, primarily because of its practicality in timber-rich America. Pennsylvania German log work, and subsequent American log work, were characterized by logs notched near the end, a method that eliminated the overhang and produced a box corner. Spaces between the logs were filled—"chinked"—with clay, stones, poles, or shingles. The logs were usually squared, split and faced, or planked. Logs were hewn for a variety of reasons. A large log could be handled more easily when reduced in size, and a large round log took up interior space and produced an irregular wall that was hard to use. Primarily, however, hewn logs were thought to produce a tighter building, more finished in appearance.

In the German areas of southeastern Pennsylvania, three forms of corner timbering are found: saddle notching, V notching, and full dovetailing. In the saddle notching, in contrast with that of prehistoric Germany and modern Scandinavia, the notch is usually only on the bottom of the log, and as close to the end as possible. Saddle notching was used primarily for barns and other outbuildings, and for temporary structures, which were less carefully constructed than houses. Pennsylvania German houses and the better-built barns and outbuildings were either V notched or, less often, full dovetailed.

The Pennsylvania German forms of corner-timbering were carried from southeastern Pennsylvania in all directions by the Germans and the Scotch-Irish. The earliest movement, beginning about 1732, led into central Maryland and the valley of Virginia. All three corner-timbering forms may be found in the northern Shenandoah Valley, but during the movement east into the Blue Ridge and south through the valley of Virginia, V notching came to predominate to the virtual exclusion of the other forms. Although barns and outbuildings were often constructed as carefully as houses in the valley and Blue Ridge of Virginia, the corner-timbering was frequently of lower quality than that used in houses, and occasionally the logs were left in the round.

The English east of the Blue Ridge received the concept of horizontal log construction more by diffusion than by direct migration. Although they employed the Pennsylvania German handling of the logs, they developed new corner-timbering types from V notching instead of reproducing it. The square notch is the commonest form of corner-timbering east of the Blue Ridge, particularly in the Virginia Piedmont, where also a few buildings use the half notch exclusively. The diamond notch is found only rarely outside the general area of the North Carolina-Virginia border from the Tidewater to the Piedmont. The saddle notch is commonly found east of the Blue Ridge and well into the Tidewater, but it is restricted to smaller outbuildings; the Tidewater English retained rived cypress shakes or clapboards over timber framing as the prevailing method of folk construction.

The movement from eastern Pennsylvania down the western Appalachian valleys began later than that down the valley of Virginia, yet the same three forms of corner-timbering—saddle notching, V notching, and full dovetailing—may be found in the Alleghenies along the northern section of the Virginia-West Virginia border. In this area, where half dovetailing, which was probably brought to America from Europe as a dormant aspect of full dovetailing, first became commonly employed, are farms where the houses are full dovetail and the out-buildings half dovetail; farther south in the Alleghenies, however, into southeastern West Virginia and Kentucky and adjacent Virginia, and down the Cumberlands, half dovetailing predominates on buildings of all kinds, though a few have V notching, and numerous outbuildings and barns have saddle notching.

The two Appalachian streams, one coming down the valley of Virginia bordering the Blue Ridge and the other down the Allegheny front, met in southwestern Virginia, northwestern North Carolina, and northeastern Tennessee, and here saddle notching, V notching, and half dovetailing all commonly appear, even on the same building. In this southern Appalachian region, corresponding roughly to the early settlement areas of Watauga, Holston, and Nolichucky, half dovetailing came to prevail on houses and on carefully made barns and outbuildings, and saddle notching, usually with the notch only on the bottom but occasionally with the notch only on the top, became dominant on temporary cabins, or "pole shacks," and on less carefully made barns and outbuildings. However, V notching was still used, rarely on houses but frequently on barns. In the southwestern Appalachian region half dovetailing degenerated into square notching as V notching had done in the Virginia Piedmont.

Saddle notching, V notching, square notching, and half dovetailing, the last strongly predominant, were carried through the Tennessee Valley, and thence southeast into Georgia, south into Alabama, southwest into Mississippi and Louisiana, and west into Arkansas and Missouri. Although the log work of the mountainous areas of Arkansas and Missouri is comparable in quality with that of the Tennessee Valley, in the Deep South the quality declined with distance. Here, where horizontal log construction is still very much alive, saddle notching is strongly dominant on barns and outbuildings, and square notching and half dovetailing are frequently encountered on older houses. In some southern areas where the pines were so small that they could not be used if hewn, the logs were split, and the half-round section was used with the flat side facing inward. Half-round logs usually were half-dovetailed but sometimes were square-notched or notched only on the bottom to produce a semi-lunate crown approximating the full dovetail.

A stream of log construction in which half dovetailing greatly predominated but square notching, saddle notching, and V notching were also employed flowed northward through the Tennessee Valley and central Kentucky into southern Illinois, Indiana, and Ohio, where it encountered a stream in which V notching was strongly dominant moving westward from Pennsylvania.

Only the northward flow of Pennsylvania corner-timbering into the westward-moving New England stream was largely ineffectual. Here it encountered false corner-timbering and the conceptually different French method of setting horizontal timbers into corner posts and was overlain by more-recent exotic, but excellent, log construction techniques introduced from Fennoscandia directly into the Great Lakes region. The predominance of the simpler methods of corner-timbering—square and saddle notching—over V notching and dovetailing in the northern tier of states tends to support the conclusion that the migrating New Englanders, like the English of the Tidewater, regarded log construction as so temporary as to be unworthy of the skills they undoubtedly possessed as workers in wood.

The horizontal log construction with true corner-timbering that came to characterize the American frontier was, then, not a New World adaptation to environment, nor was it a Scandinavian introduction; rather, it was introduced by the Pennsylvania Germans and carried by them and by the Scotch-Irish in all directions from southeastern Pennsylvania.

For completeness, "stovewood" construction, found most abundantly in Wisconsin but also in Michigan and Quebec, should be mentioned.[45] In some half-timber structures stovewood-length logs form the nogging. In others they are laid horizontally in lime mortar to form unbraced walls. Barns, sheds, two-story buildings, and lumbermen's shanties with stovewood construction have all been observed.

Summary

In the American westward expansion between 1790 and 1850, wood became even more important as a building material than it had been on the seaboard. Nevertheless, every significant method of construction employed had its European antecedents. In the exuberance fostered by an endless supply of wood, construction methods were revived that were no more than vestigial in much of western Europe, if indeed they were even traditional. This is true of construction using closely set vertical or horizontal timbers.

During the early colonial period, wood-saving half-timbering, then widely practiced in western Europe, was fairly common. It died out rapidly in favor of siding over the framing and thus was insignificant in the westward movement. Only the Louisiana French held steadfastly to half-timbering. In this and other respects construction practices in the French pockets stood in strong contrast with those of incoming, frontier Americans. These had no equivalent of the French *poteaux en terre*, *poteaux sur sole*, and *pièce sur pièce*. In complement, the French rarely adopted American log construction.

In the New England stream, the heavily framed clapboarded house was dominant until the substitution of light balloon framing in the latter half of the nineteenth century. This was true also of the western projection of the middle Atlantic states and of that of the tidewater South. Where their influences prevailed, the log house was regarded as a temporary structure to be replaced by traditional forms as soon as circumstances permitted. Only in the upland South was log construction the accepted practice.

Great changes have taken place in the construction, materials, and forms of buildings since 1850. Still, a survey of farm housing published in 1939 revealed that some 97 percent of the rural dwellings sampled were built of wood (frame, 93.2 percent; log, 3.7 percent); 1.8 percent of brick; 0.5 percent of stone; 0.4 percent of earth; and 0.4 percent of concrete.[46] Thus, true to the tradition strengthened during the westward movement, wood was the overwhelmingly dominant building material, at least for the humbler dwellings.

Log houses, though of course far fewer than in 1850, conformed in their relative abundance to the old pattern. From the seaboard westward along the New England route log houses were few. This was true also of New Jersey (for some reason Pennsylvania and New York were not sampled) and the tidewater counties of the South. Percentages climbed sharply in the upland South, even into the southern parts of Ohio, Indiana, and Illinois. In Halifax County, Virginia, well out in the Piedmont, the percentage of rural log dwellings rose to 42. In the more recent "frontier" sections of the Upper Lakes and the wooded West log construction was well represented.[47]

The next stage of our work should shed greater light on the cultural meaning of the several methods of timber construction, on their associations with different groups of peoples, on their place in the westward movement, and on their relative importance during the change from frontier to settled community. The first step will be to relate specific methods of wood construction to specific types and forms of folk housing. It should then be possible to match the idealized results of a systematic approach against the revealing vagaries of reality.

17

The Service Station in America:
The Evolution of a Vernacular Form

Bruce A. Lohof

Introduction

Just as cultural geographers and folklife scholars have labored to include folk housing as a significant topic of material culture research, another cadre of researchers has insisted that machine-made, mass-produced, urban-centered artifacts of modern America should also receive attention as important cultural data. The latter investigators often identify themselves as industrial archaeologists, popular culturists, historians of technology, or commercial archaeologists; they are usually concerned, as is the article that follows, with those ubiquitous artifacts that heretofore fell below the traditional level of cultural investigation and therefore passed unnoticed by most historians.

Applying John Kouwenhoven's paradigm of an American "vernacular tradition" (a national material culture consistently characterized by economy, simplicity, and flexibility) to the American service station, Bruce Lohof offers a case study that incorporates the perspectives of the symbolist, functionalist and, to a limited extent, the structuralist approaches to material culture analysis. Using the several thousand service stations designed and built by the Marathon Oil Company in ten western and southern states as his data base, Lohof first argues "these stations are symbolic of a contemporary, motorized people, for in a very literal sense they pump the lifeblood of their mobile society." Such symbolism, notes the author, has also been celebrated by contemporary pop artists such as Edward Ruscha in paintings such as Standard Service Station, Amarillo, Texas. As a historian of technology, Lohof is quick to recognize that the construction of a typical service station in his sample is but another variation on Eli Whitney's concept of interchangeable parts. In this case, the parts are standardized modular building units, which, as the service station form evolves over time, are arranged

251

horizontally and vertically in order to produce a multiplicity of station types from only a small repertoire of modules.

Lohof implies that a guiding force behind such changes is Louis Sullivan's principle that form follows function. In arriving at this conclusion. Lohof performs a structuralist analysis of the extant Marathon stations much as Henry Glassie has done in his Folk Housing in Middle Virginia (1977). Working with floor plans, photography, and the surviving service stations, Lohof sought to discover the controlling structuralist principles in all the service stations he examined. His analysis yielded two main principles: first, the use of the square or, in its three-dimensional form, the cube, as the universal design unit; and, second, the concept of modularity as the distinguishing characteristic of the architectural competence of the station designers. The principles prevail in the earliest "porcelain box" types of stations and endure into Marathon's most recent and supposedly "newest" designs, such as the "Colonial," the "R-75," the "Alpine," and the "Kettering." With the Kettering, Lohof graphically demonstrates the variety of configurations available within any single artifact type, thereby illustrating to the beginning student a key facet of structuralist methodology.

The following essay also suggests other modern material culture evidence that might be profitably studied via the structuralist approach. Lohof proposes we consider shopping centers, tract houses, fast-food franchises, and everything else that clamors for attention along roadside America. He is persuaded that such artifacts provide the researcher with a novel laboratory wherein to test American material culture's acclaimed "vernacular tradition," a tradition that is "by design seldom aesthetically pure, by intention never unique, and by custom beneath the level of cultural scrutiny."

In addition to the following study, which first appeared in Industrial Archaeology 11 (Spring 1974): 1–13, Bruce Lohof's scholarship on other artifacts of the vernacular tradition and structuralism have appeared in the Journal of Popular Culture, particularly his insightful article, "Morphology of the Modern Fable," Journal of Popular Culture 8 (1974–1975): 15–27.

🦅

In their book *American Skyline*, the urbanists Christopher Tunnard and Henry Hope Reed argued that the form of a people's architecture is a clue to a people's character. Thus it was fitting, they said, that the skyline of seventeenth-century Boston should be dominated by church spires, even as twentieth-century New York is a forest of commercial towers. What more concrete way was there to symbolize the evolution of a nation's ethos from religion to business? [1]

If this be fair, however, the proper study of modern, industrialized, and mobile societies should examine not only the stately skyscraper, but the lowly filling station. After all, in the United States alone (which is the nation I know best) eighty million motor cars annually consume sixty-five billion gallons of gasoline, fuel purchased at one or another of the quarter-million service stations which punctuate the landscape. These stations are symbolic of a contemporary, motorized people, for in a very literal sense they pump the lifeblood of their mobile society. Little wonder, then, that service stations should be celebrated in pop art by Edward Ruscha and others. Little wonder, also, that a major American petroleum company, in its promotional material, should state as a major premise that "service stations are uniquely essential to our modern way of life." [2] Little wonder, finally, that the service station—at first glance a mere shell whose function is its only significance— should have developed an important and instructive, though largely ignored, architectural form.

This article is based upon a scrutiny of the service stations which have been designed and built by the Marathon Oil Company. Marathon is a major American retailer of petroleum products, ranking near the top one hundred largest industrial corporations in the United States.[3] Its 3,600 service stations, located in six midwestern and four southern states, are typical of the architecture throughout the industry and across the continent. They are, in brief, a convenient sample of the whole. But what does the sample say about the whole? And what does the whole say about the culture?

The Marathon Oil Company and its corporate predecessor, the Ohio Oil Company, developed three standardized service station types between 1933, the year in which it entered the retail market, and the close of World War II. The smallest of these, descriptively called the "Metal Portable Service Station," was a metal-and-glass shell with a porcelain enamel interior and a concrete floor. Usually 12 x 18 feet, the type contained a waiting room, rest rooms, and perhaps a small storage area. Metal Portable Service Station, the company's first effort at standardized architectural design, was never successful. It had been conceived for prefabrication on a mass scale, but fewer than five of the type were actually constructed. It was portable, and, therefore, able to follow the dictates of the marketplace, but none was ever moved. It had euphemistically been called a *service* station, but was more properly thought of as a *filling* station, the pumping of gasoline being its only function.

For all these reasons—the last being the most important, given the demand for general automotive service as well as simple refueling—Metal Portable Service Station died, leaving as survivors two remaining prewar designs with less descriptive names, "Standard Service Station No. 2" and "Standard Service Station No. 3." A shadow of the first type remained, however. Both Standard Service Station No. 2 and Standard Service Station No. 3 consisted of a customer area containing a waiting room, rest rooms, and a storage room, and one or more service areas— sheds for lubrication, washing, and other automotive maintenance activities— appended to the customer area. The former, of course, was a functional vestige of the Metal Portable Service Station. In Standard Service Station No. 2 it was a hexagonal structure 18 feet in diameter. In Standard Service Station No. 3 it was an indented rectangle, 14 x 24 feet. In both cases the service areas were rectangular structures, first 12 x 24 feet and later 14 x 24 feet.

Although none of these designs survived World War II, each of them, particularly the second and third, is properly seen as a prototype of all their Marathon successors, because each precisely embodies the specifications of what John Kouwenhoven would call a few years later the "vernacular tradition." Indeed, one cannot view these buildings without recalling the characteristics of the tradition: "economy, simplicity, and flexibility." [4] What better way to describe either these early structures or those which would follow?

Each of the types, from the Metal Portable Service Station to designs currently in use, was conceived with inexpensive replication as the goal. Perhaps a hundred or more individuals of each type were built with no major alteration of design. Moreover, each type was designed for easy and inexpensive maintenance. Concrete floors, metal walls, and, later, concrete block walls and porcelain enamel—a material that would become synonymous with architecture of this variety—were the components from which these structures were built.

"Economy of line, lightness, strength, and freedom from meaningless ornament," words which Kouwenhoven used in describing Donald McKay's nineteenth-century clipper ships, describe twentieth-century service stations as well.[5] The contemporary Eames chair, or more precisely the ersatz form thereof which would eventually decorate bus terminals and airports, was a completely complemental form of interior decoration. Only the garish two-story hexagon of Standard Service Station No. 2 stands as an exception to the rule of simplicity.[6]

Each of the types was an invention in the broadest sense, an architectural contrivance which could be placed down wherever a retail petroleum outlet was needed. Most important, each was conceived to be a series of modules—basic structural elements which could be horizontally "stacked" to produce a multiplicity of station types with only a small repertoire of modules. A given module, or bay, to use the industry's term, could, as we have already seen, be designed to function as a sales or service area. Later modules were designed to serve as storage rooms, vending areas, small restaurants, and the like. Bays could be mixed or matched, "stacked high" or "stacked low" (using many modules or few), depending upon the class and size of station one desired. In short, by the end of World War II the service station became a variation on Ely Whitney's theme of interchangeable parts.[7]

The vernacular flavor of these prewar types carried quite visibly into the "porcelain boxes" which were so characteristic of the postwar decades. Witness, for instance, the "Four-Bay Standard," a type which Marathon built on a limited scale between 1947 and 1949.[8] A nation relieved by the armistice and the subsequent termination of fuel rationing, and looking forward to growth and prosperity in the automotive industries, could take the Four-Bay Standard as a fitting symbol. Part filling station, part service center, part store, the type consisted of four rectangular modules, each 14 x 28 feet, standing in an **I** configuration. The evolution from prewar types is clear. Emphasizing service but also sales, the Four-Bay Standard had two service modules and two sales modules. The latter pair were partitioned into a foyer, waiting room, sales area (what the industry called a TBA area—tires, batteries, and accessories), office, and rest rooms.

Even a cursory comparison of the Four-Bay Standard and its prewar predecessors shows it to be something of an extravagance. The interior appointments included brick floors and ceramic tile walls. Exteriors consisted of glass and white porcelain enamel. In size alone, the type was two or three times larger than the Standard Service Station No. 3. Indeed, its extravagance led to its demise. By 1950, the Four-Bay Standard had been replaced by more popular and economical types.

These more basic porcelain boxes, though now gone the way of the Four-Bay Standard, are perhaps the most familiar form of service station architecture. It was their image, for instance, which Edward Ruscha captured in *Standard Service Station, Amarillo, Texas*. Marathon built more than 600 such stations between 1948 and 1969, many of which are still in operation. Among them was the "Three-Bay Standard." Nearly 400 of the type were built. Each was an **I** of three modules, one sales area and two service bays, with modules measuring 14 x 28 feet. Porcelain enamel pilasters separated the modules from each other, while the roof line, an attribute which would undergo significant change through the decades, was a simple slab.

Similar in appearance to the Three-Bay Standard, the "Standard Modified" was characterized by a deeper service module, an addition of a minor module at the rear of the building, and deeper pilasters between the major modules.[9] Eleven individuals of the type were constructed during the 1950s.

"Facade Modified" represented another difference. Only ten were built, most of them in 1962. Moreover, in the particulars of its floorplan, the Facade Modified is indistinguishable from the Standard Modified. The type was distinctive, however, because its innovative roof line—a crown-shaped self-illuminated facade—replaced the slab look of earlier structures.

Another variation was the "Rear Bay." During the 1960s, fifty-one of this type were built. Its distinctive feature was the rearrangement of the traditional **I** into a **V** configuration. By placing the sales module lengthwise and positioning the service bays behind the sales module, designers were able to remove the service bays, often the scene of grime and noise, from the front of the structure, giving the station a more pleasant image. Minor changes were also made. The modules grew slightly in size, and small patios were appended to the ends of the sales bay. In decor and motif, however, the type followed patterns established earlier.

The "Facade Brow" was a further modification. Structurally identical to both the Standard Modified and the Facade Modified, this type drew its distinctiveness from its decoration. The self-illuminated crown roof line was extended along either side and down to the base of the building, giving it an "eyebrow" appearance.

Another change was "Facade Vending." Though fewer than twenty of these were built, the type is an interesting example of flexibility through interchangeability. The unsightly service area, reduced to a single bay, was, as in Rear Bay, relegated to the rear of the building. The front, in turn, was given over to a sales area and a larger room which could function as a vending area or even a small restaurant. Outside, little changed. Porcelain enamel pilasters rose to support a crown-facade roof line.

The Marathon Oil Company built the last of these types in 1969. Of course, many remain in operation. Moreover, porcelain boxes continue to be constructed by other oil companies and continue, as Ruscha illustrates so graphically, to dominate the national consciousness. In a more generic sense, the "boxes" appear everywhere, metamorphosed into hot dog stands, doughnut shops, car washes, hamburger huts, pizzerias, and other houses of America-the-franchised. To perceive the American roadside without them is difficult indeed.

To the structuralist, all of this is the height of logic. Porcelain box service stations, as well as their counterparts in, for example, the food industry, are merely the reaction of a vernacular tradition to an expanding mobility. They are the soul of economy, simplicity, and flexibility, the architectural extension of Whitney's interchangeability of parts. "Form follows function," Louis Sullivan said, and the minions of anonymous gas station architects took him more literally than he ever cared to take himself.

In more recent years, however, various forces have conspired to replace the porcelain box with newer and more aesthetically pleasing architectural forms. In part, these forces have been political; municipalities have become increasingly determined that service stations and other such structures will harmonize with the neighborhoods they serve. In part, too, they have been economic; oil retailers, in the attempt to stay abreast or ahead of each other, have made stylistic changes which, taken *en masse*, constitute an industry-wide epidemic of architectural innovation. With few exceptions, oil companies are currently building station types consistent with both the demands of local governments and the dictates of the marketplace.

Marathon, for its part, has created four "design" types, a term which industry architects often use to distinguish these buildings from the older "boxes." These newer types are discussed below.

"Colonial" was a style which actually made its debut in 1962 and went into major production in the late 1960s.[10] It takes its name from its ruling motif. A brick veneer exterior, columns and pilasters, hipped and gabled roof, and cupola and weathervane are contrived to lend an eighteenth-century aura to an intrinsically twentieth-century structure.

"Route 75" was so named because individuals of the type appear along the main thoroughfare linking the midwest, Marathon's basic market, with Florida. Route 75 is a brick-and-glass structure with large sales and vending areas and a relatively small service area. The configuration is sensible, given the interstate traveller's greater need for fuel and snacks than for lubrication or repairs.

"Kettering" was named after Kettering, Ohio, the site of the original prototype.

First built in 1967, Kettering quickly became the company's most popular design type. More than 300 have been built, each with its distinctive bay front and cathedral ceiling on the sales area and its crown-facade roof line, reminiscent of the porcelain box, over the service bays.

Finally, there was "Alpine," a type which, like Colonial, took its name from its motif. The A-frame roof line, glass-and-wood exterior, wood-panelled interior, and geographic location—nine of the ten Alpine types extant in 1973 were in Michigan—result in a recognizable image.[11]

Each of the types produced by Marathon has nicely fulfilled the demands made upon the whole design generation of service stations. Each is aesthetically pleasing, particularly when contrasted to its ancestors. Each, therefore, has met the specifications of municipal governments as well as the requirements of the marketplace. In aesthetic terms, then, much is new.

In structural terms, however, little has changed. Consider, for instance, the floor plans of Colonial and the older Standard Modified. In the newer type, the sales module is extended slightly in front, an accommodation to the motif's columns-and-pilasters treatment. Otherwise, Colonial and Standard Modified share an identical structural configuration. In single file stand a sales module (partitioned into a waiting room), an office/storage area, rest rooms, and two or more service bays of equally familiar description. As before, a minor module, the vestigial trash enclosure, stands in the rear. Colonial, in short, is really Standard Modified in eighteenth-century costume. Indeed, Marathon has celebrated the bloodline by renovating many of its porcelain boxes through the application of a colonial motif. So skillful is the renovation and, more to the point, so structurally oldstyle is the genuine Colonial, that the untrained eye seldom detects the porcelain box behind the costume.

Consequently, Route 75 bears a resemblance to the older Facade Vending. Both types emphasize sales and vending at the expense of service. Both, therefore, relegate a single service bay to the rear of the structure, freeing the front for sales and vending functions.

Finally, there is the Kettering and the Alpine, the latter being built on the Kettering floor plan. The plan of the type appears, at first glance, to represent a departure from the modular scheme of things. In fact, say Marathon's architects, it is not. In creating the Kettering, the designers began with the Standard Modified, turned the service module 90 degrees, enlarged the module by pushing back the rear wall and by bulging the front wall into a bay window, and altered the placement of doors on the service bays to provide for side entrance, thereby hiding the noisome service area behind an attractive wall of bricks and shrubbery.

Marathon's design stations are interesting because they are exemplary of the entire industry's response to the repeal of the porcelain box. More important, however, they are interesting because they clearly illustrate the durability of the vernacular tradition. They illustrate the enduring utility of modular design, whether the corporate trademark be a Linco lighthouse or a colonial cupola. Here in the design types, no less than before, a small repertoire of modules can be stacked in a variety of configurations to produce a variety of types.

The concept of modularity, seen first in its survival from generation to generation, and second in its enduring utility from type to type within a generation, is perhaps most graphically illustrated by the variety of configurations available within a single type. Kettering's basic configuration, for example, is set, but true to the dictates of the vernacular tradition, it is flexible, and its modules can therefore be stacked in a variety of ways, depending upon the dictates of its location or the whims of its owners. Even these possibilities are not exhaustive. Larger stations are built merely by adding additional service bays. Compatible configurations can be combined to give a sales module flanked on one side by a pair of service bays, on the other by a small restaurant or store. Nor, it need hardly be said, is this unique to Kettering. Similar configurations can be drawn from virtually every station ever built by the Marathon Oil Company.

The vernacular tradition is by design seldom aesthetically pure, by intention never unique, and by custom beneath the level of cultural scrutiny.[12] Yet its members are all around us in the form of franchised eateries, tract houses, and service stations. The service station, surely the most symbolic of the membership, is also the most instructive. It speaks, obviously, of the intrinsic economy, simplicity, and flexibility of the tradition. But the important lessons, as always, are social and historical. The service station, in this higher sense, is an index of its culture. Its evolution and growth—from hopeful but naive Metal Portable Service Station to imperious, postwar Four-Bay Standard, to the latest design structure—is a lecture on the growth of mechanization and mobility. Finally, its enduring modularity discloses the fact that, in industrial cultures, roadside shrines, like everything else, consist of interchangeable parts.

18

An Indiana Subsistence Craftsman

Willard B. Moore

Introduction

Until recently, a large number of the artifacts produced in most societies were the result of folk crafts—production methods in which one could observe the operation of tradition with a special clarity. Such craft techniques (e.g., basketmaking, weaving, chairmaking) were passed down within a family for many generations or were transmitted by the apprentice system wherein a boy learning the craft served for as long as seven years under a master craftsman. Only in the nineteenth century did the older, traditional system of transmitting the skills and knowledge of a craft begin to be supplanted by formalized training in schools and by printed manuals and books.

In analyzing a twentieth-century southern Indiana farmer and part-time craftsman, Willard Moore addresses the major issues that continually fascinate material culturists working specifically with folk crafts. To begin with, Moore attempts to establish the persistence of tradition within the craftsman's work and life. How, where, and from whom did the craftsman learn his craft? Like other folklorists using the interpretive model of performance theory, Moore also wishes to know what role individual creativity played in the craftsman's work. How did personal taste, aesthetics, and individual innovation affect the crafting of folk artifacts?

In order to explore these fundamental questions, Moore studied a single individual and some of his craft products, which included gambrel sticks, corn knives, foot adzes, half-soled sledge runners, and wheelbarrows—an assortment of material culture data that might be called "the vernacular's vernacular." The author recognizes such artifacts as "the less spectacular but always important tools and implements, hand-made by the traditional farmer, and necessary for survival on the land." He uses this physical evidence, in conjunction with the research techniques of field observation and interviewing to provide us with a case-study of a particular type of artifact producer: the subsistence craftsman. By Moore's definition, such a craftsman is a nonspecialist, generally not well known throughout the community for his skills, and usually working only part-time in the various traditional folk crafts.

As will be evident from the recorded dialogue with his subject, the author was particularly anxious to get a fix on the various components of "the creative act" involved in material culture production. Recognizing that topography and environment as well as religious and ethnic preferences are factors in such production, Moore also raises two additional issues that need be considered. He asks, for example, what role did macro- and micro-economic changes (especially their pace and mode) play in a craftsman's community, and what role did such changes play in his craft production at different stages of his career? In addition to having us consider the impact of real but rather impersonal economic forces, Moore insists that all material culture study should be ultimately grounded in the personal, creative experience of individuals. Here questions of childhood experiences, personal fancy, parental images, and, of course, the individual's perception of the folk tradition in which he works are all necessary inquiries to make of the worker and his work. In Moore's estimate, "a true understanding of the craft cannot be attained without intensive personal interviews and some grasp of the craftsman's background, his development and his values within his personal world."

Moore's essay first appeared in Pioneer America: The Journal of Historic American Material Culture 8 (July 1976): 107–118 and is reprinted here from that quarterly publication of the Pioneer America Society. The former director of education at the Conner Prairie Pioneer Settlement in Indiana and the director of the Minnesota Folklore Project in Minnesota, Willard Moore has also written on techniques for using artifacts in history teaching: "Folklife Museums: Resource Sites for Teaching," Indiana English Journal 11 (Winter 1976–1977): 3–10, as well as coedited a Museum Studies Reader: An Anthology of Journal Articles On Open Air Museums in America (Indianapolis: Indiana Committee on the Humanities, 1978).

The purpose of this study is to document some of the skills of one southern Indiana farmer-craftsman and to analyze some of the influencing factors in his performance in that creative capacity. As currently studied by folklore scholars, the craftsman is usually skilled, working within a tradition, and making objects for consumer use primarily by hand and primarily alone.[1] Today, we are able to study the work and aesthetics of basketmakers, potters, ropemakers, and fence and hurdle makers. But there are, I would argue, some individuals who are constantly making and repairing artifacts for immediate personal or local use who are not working at this job full time and are not well known throughout the community for their skills.[2]

The reasons for this are many, but first we must look into the matter of the persistence of folk tradition in material culture. Henry Glassie suggests that the main factors are tradition itself, topography and environment, immigration, and various religious or ethnic preferences or limitations.[3] Certainly economic change must be added to this list as well as the pace and mode by which the part-time craftsman and his locale adapt to change.

Behind many of these data lie the personality and capabilities, both real and potential, of the craftsman himself. We seldom are offered the chance to look at a craftsman's work and the ideas and values behind the work as well. A notable exception is the work of Michael Owen Jones on Kentucky chairmakers,[4] as well as briefer articles, such as Howard W. Marshall's analysis of a basketmaker from "Little Dixie" in Missouri.[5] Both Jones and Marshall take note of the economic headwall which inhibits their respective craftsmen, influences their work, and threatens to terminate their present mode of expression and livelihood.

Technological change, mass production, mail order houses, and bulk commodity sales (more or less in that order) have, in some cases, helped certain aspects of the traditional craftsman's work, but by-and-large they have cast a shadow over his product and his worth to the community. But the craftsman who is also farmer, stock raiser, or locally employed factory hand or railroad laborer can, with good reason and result, continue his work within a smaller circle of use but with a sustained level of satisfaction with the craft itself. Such a man is Paul Rampley, aged seventy-seven, resident of Indian Creek Township in Monroe County, Indiana.

Personal Background

Paul Rampley was born in 1897 in Switz City, Greene County, Indiana. Before he was ten years old, his parents divorced and Paul went to live with his grandfather, who cared for him until he was a teenager and able to support himself. Paul attended a local school through grade eight and then got into one job or trade after another, usually having to do with handcrafted items.

Rampley, I learned, never stayed at any of these jobs for very long. His excellent memory and engaging style of recounting events and experiences, while outside the focus of this study, is worth noting. He can sit for hours and tell of his days in the Switz City blacksmith shop, his brief tutoring by Walter Holmes in a neighboring wagon maker's shop, and one exciting summer on the threshing circuit "out west" in the vicinity of Pierpont, South Dakota, in 1914.[6] But Rampley's overriding preference was the railroad. His first experience on a road gang came at age fourteen but lasted only a few months—long enough to know he liked it. He was fired when the foreman learned his true age. He had odd jobs with the railroad from then on, working at a forge, cutting ties, doing various repairs on both track and machinery. He also worked in foundries and in quarries on a seasonal basis, but without any technical skills, Rampley was more or less at the mercy of the prevailing economic situation.

Rampley never moved out of southern Indiana. In the depression of the 1930s, he moved onto a forty-acre, marginal farm on Evans Road, relocated the dwelling and rebuilt it from local and original materials. One log, dated 1837, was reshaped and used in the construction of the two-room house with lean-to that stands on Evans Road today.[7] Paul also constructed a large, double-crib barn, covering the structure with clapboards he had riven himself with froe and mallet or froe club. He has rebuilt fireplaces and chimneys, wells (hand-dug in the early nineteenth century and lined with stone), and he has built Indiana-style stone walls and made many of the tools for these and more commonplace labors. As Warren Roberts notes, every farmer had to be something of a craftsman himself just to stay in business.[8].He repaired harness, plow and wagon, and constructed fences and smaller items of many materials. While most studies seek to document the specialized craftsman, this paper will examine some of the less spectacular but always important tools and implements, hand-made by the traditional farmer, and necessary for his survival on the land.

Paul Rampley's personal situation has contributed to his use of traditional crafts in the home and in the farm work. First, he is not well-off financially. He lives comfortably and enjoys good health, but there are no frills in his life. His wife cans and freezes most of what they grow in the garden each summer. Though he shares his persimmon trees with friends and neighbors, he cannot afford to entertain. Given his education, training, and job potential over the years, it is logical that Rampley would avoid the retail store whenever possible in favor of what he can make himself. The interesting and primary point here is that he uses traditional methods to fashion his needs; he does not resort to scavenging, pirating parts from here or there, or using many secondhand items bought at sales.

A second factor in Rampley's adherence to tradition is his physical isolation and reluctance to go to town. To Rampley's way of thinking, it is quicker, easier and "more fun" to fashion the needed article himself. This brings us to a third and very important consideration in the study of an individual craftsman: personal taste, aesthetics, and the creative drive.

Given the proper training and a context in which to use that training Rampley might have become a successful and highly creative craftsman. Instead, he was constantly diverted by day-labor jobs to earn his keep and support his small family. The wielding of his skills in the creative act was relegated to sporadic, practical accommodation and, later, when time allowed, to the level of a hobby. Or, as Rampley himself phrased it:

Well, now, I gotta have somethin' to do! But when I need somethin' like that thar wheelbarra or that knife or whatever, well, I just leave off and make it. Like that! But I allus did that before, you know. Didn't have much time for fancy—you know—stuff I didn't really need.

Allus made what I needed 'stid a-buyin' it. [Pause] But, oh hell, I'm just playin' now. [Laughs]

I questioned Rampley about the things he makes and the reason behind his efforts. He cited need as a primary factor but always attributed his ideas to his grandfather, John Henry Gheen, and to the various craftsmen with whom he worked for brief periods in his youth.

Anybody can be a blacksmith. Don't take no brains to speak of. I always loved to work with my hands. Ruther do it than anything. Worked all day in a smithy and made all kinds of things. But anybody can do it!

What about these other things? The way you made the handle for the foot adz or the wheelbarrow? Or, that other . . . the calf harness to keep it from sucking?

Well, sure that stuff is awful useful. A man can't get by without that kind of doing. My grandpappy showed me most of that stuff. He'd let me watch him and I learned just lots from him. He had a barrow just like that one I made.

From fifteen months' acquaintance and many conversations, I have gleaned some notion of why Rampley goes on with his work. He loves fitting his skills and sometimes creative ingenuity to the daily needs. He conservatively maintains the "old ways," not out of romantic nostalgia, but because he personally prefers a particular life style. So, for example, Rampley and his wife do not use indoor plumbing but prefer to maintain an outhouse. Rampley testifies:

If we have an indoor privy, she'd [his wife] be a-sprayin' with that dope [deodorizer] and that just takes the skin offen the inside o' my nose! I hate that stuff worse'n anythin'. So we just use the privy. It's a lot better and the air is better out there by a lot. I'd say. Wouldn't you?

Childhood experiences, economic status, and parental images are contributing influences to the maintenance of tradition in Rampley's productivity. But what is tradition and what does it have to do with the life of the individual who adheres to it?

H. G. Barnett links the study of tradition to a study of change and attitudes toward the status quo.[9] James Fernandez, in a more recent work, discusses metaphor as movement within "quality space," a culturally determined, abstractive range of behavior through which individuals move (or "improve") as they partici- pate in tradition.[10] While Fernandez's concept works well with closed societies and religious behavior, it is hard to imagine a farmer who attempts straight furrows or a woman who eschews store-bought sugar as "moving up some abstract ladders" of values and self-worth. One might rather picture a bird aloft, maintaining altitude and direction within a matrix of forces—gravity, wind, and individual motivation. One might posit this image upon Rampley's work: man in a complex society, resisting here and there in terms of his personal image and motives. Motive has much to do with meaning, and structuralists in anthropology and literary criticism have attempted to show that meaning too is linked with individual identity attained as a synthesis of what one is not and what one may have been.[11] One might find similar syntheses in the meeting of man and the material (e.g., the farmer and the unplowed field or the raw material from which he fashions some tool) as well as man and the social forces which demand change and the concomitant problem of the Unknown.

It is my contention, then, that Rampley's personal identity is threatened by the complex, the impersonal, and the prepackaged commodities of modern America. He finds self-worth and meaning in the synthesis of his own efforts and natural resources. Not that he reveres them; far from it. He grows trees to be cut down and shaped into implements and furniture. His measurement of self is imposing himself upon the natural state of things and manipulating the materials. The finished product must be the result of personal involvement, without public, legal restriction, modification, or compromise. This attitude is apparent in his diet as it is in his political posture or religious behavior.

The Crafts of Necessity

One of the most necessary implements for the southern Indiana farmer is a gambrel stick. With it he hangs his hogs for the late autumn butchering. The simplest implement in Rampley's repertoire is such a device which he calls "a gamblin' stick." He made his from oak but also suggests hickory and "lind" or basswood would do. He has also seen and made gambrel irons from scrap iron in a blacksmith's shop, and fashioning the piece is simply a matter of heating it and wrapping it around the horn of the anvil and shaping the points on either end. Rampley noted that the ring to accommodate the clevis or supporting mechanism may be fashioned above or below the arch.

In use, the gambrel stick may be set atop a flattened (and preferably notched) beam which in turn is supported by crossed beams. The far end of the top beam may be conveniently poked under a shed or back porch for security. In the absence of a gambrel stick, the butcher may use a singletree. Whether by gambrel or singletree, the suspended hog is ready for the farmer's knife when the first frost comes.[12]

Several other devices are used by the Indiana farmer. Rampley's grandfather had mentioned to him once that an iron "drag" would be useful for retrieving well buckets which had broken loose from the rope. Rampley made one and keeps it among his tools. A second item is the clevis (mentioned above in use with the gambrel iron), an all-around useful device for securing chains from lumber, towing vehicles with a cable, or closing two pieces of reluctant materials which must be joined. The clevis may be fashioned with the main ring parallel or at right angle to the other two rings as the situation requires. Rampley's remark on this was "I'd rather just do it myself. It takes longer to get set up and go into town and pay out money for a clevis than I can do it myself. Just stoke up the fire and go to it!"

Another indication of Rampley's adherence to tradition is his corn knife. Today, Rampley still cuts and "shocks" his corn for gradual use through the autumn and winter. The knife was fashioned from a discarded scythe blade. He threaded the narrow end and secured it within a wooden handle by afixing a hexagonal nut to the end and tamping the bolt-end with a hammer.

Rampley is now past the age at which he might work extensively with a foot adz, yet he was able and eager to show me its use for a few minutes. Knowing that I am left-handed, he handed me the tool and asked me to use it. He watched with a smile as I struggled to accommodate this ''right-handed'' tool to my grip. Then he showed me how to remove the bowed handle and reinsert it for smooth use on ''the other side.''

Shaping the handle is one more traditional skill which Rampley demonstrates. ''There's two ways I can fix up a handle like that. One way and the way I did this 'un is to just put the wood between two bricks and lay some weight across it.'' I asked: How long did you leave it there? ''Oh, it depends. Gotta watch it.'' Do you boil it first, or soak it?

Nah! Just lay it out thar. Now the other way is to just leave it in the sun. Leave it out but just show the middle. Keep the ends kivered up and in the shade like. That way the sun just hits the middle and it draws it.[13]

Foot adz handles are best made of ash wood, which tends to absorb the blows and not telegraph them into the worker's hands. Rampley demonstrated the proper stance for using an adz: the right hand grasps the handle about one-third way from the head, resting the bottom of the forearm against the top of the right thigh. The balance of the tool is secured with the left hand at the butt of the handle. Short chopping strokes are made, first straight down and then parallel to the surface of the beam. The worker straddles the working area and moves backward as the work is done. Rampley explained that this method was followed in reworking a barn floor, for example. The traditional approach to hewing rough timber is to use first the broad ax and then the adz.

One of the most practical and ancient items found on a southern Indiana or Kentucky hill farm is the sledge. Sturdily constructed and usually equipped with heavy ''bobs'' (partial runners which can often be steered) or runners, the sledge can move heavy loads in winter or be used in hilly terrain to move heavy stones, lumber, or produce downhill with minimum effort. Rampley has made iron runners for his sledges and showed me one pair that lies rusting behind his workshop. Such runners could be fashioned by any blacksmith. But Rampley's grandfather did not always use iron runners. To save money and perhaps other assets, Gheen used split ash saplings to make what he called a ''half-sole'' which was fastened to the runner with a clevis and wooden pins.

You just take that clevis and tighten 'er up and clamp that half-sole to the front end of the runner, and you always use the narrer end up front; the thick end goes at the rear. You wouldn't think it, but the rear end of the sled gets the heavy wear and wears out first. And then you set your pins. Right here where the half-sole comes around you put your pin in straight. Right in. But the others you oughta set like this [at an angle]. So's they don't come out. And if'n you want 'er real tight, you set 'em with a teeny wedge just at the end of the pin. Not a big 'un; just enough to drive 'er apart once she goes in. Then she'll never come out'n thar!

The ash saplings are put on "green" and thereby "take to the runner" or season in their places. Rampley added, later, that the saplings must have the bark removed before applying to the runners.

The use of ash saplings for a half-sole carries over to another vehicle of farm transport and the final implement in this study: the wheelbarrow. The wheelbarrow may be a fairly recent mode of farm transport and its distribution is probably limited to those areas of fairly level terrain on which simple paths and relatively short distances allow its full use. The data I have gathered show that wheelbarrows are well suited to urban and semi-urban transport (short distance carrying) and to farms on which buildings are located relatively close to one another, Paul Rampley, in his practical wisdom, agreed: "Well, you couldn't use that thing on a hill. You got to have a level piece of land. A farm like this 'un.'' What was your grandfather's place like?

Well, it was level too. He just used it from the barn to carry out manure to the garden where he dumped it. Or, from the barn to the orchard and back. I see'd him bring in a great big load of wood from the woodlot or stones or feed or whatever. 'Long as it wa'n't too far.

It is now, of course, impossible to ascertain how and why Gheen built his wheelbarrows as he did. He may have concocted his own version of what was beginning to be offered by the retailers and factories of that era. He may have borrowed from tradition and adapted the size and shape of his barrow to his own purposes.[14] The point of interest for the researcher is probably the wheel: how it is made, installed, and kept operative.[15]

Early wooden wheels were solid masses, rotating on a fixed axle, and tended to wobble.[16] Paul Rampley knew this when I asked about it and offered the following description of how his grandfather shaped the wheel for the wheelbarrow:

He just knew that if you left that wheel all one piece—all one thickness, it wouldn't hold straight. She'd wear out too fast or just fall over like that [demonstrates with his hand]. So what he did was to make a wheel out of a thick piece of timber. I reckon she was about four inches thick to start. Then he . . . You know what a grindstone is, set up on a frame? Well, sir, he just took out the stone and set that wheel in there and he took his drawknife or a spoke shave or somethin' and turned the wheel and hewed her down! He got her down to about two inches [at the edges] and had that four inches in the middle [of the wheel] for the axle. That made it set up all right. Kept 'er steady.

Did he put an iron rim on it as you did?

No. He put on a half-sole, just like on the sledge. He just took some ash [sapling] and put 'er on there with pins. Same as I told you.

How did he join the ends? Did he overlap or what?

No, he just cut 'em on the bias. Now on my wheel it was different. I didn't have no heavy lumber around so I built it up and put the rim on 'er. And I lapped the ends of that 'un. I used one-sixteenth-inch iron on the rim and set it with rivets.[17]

Both Rampley and his grandfather fitted the wheel to the axle and to the barrow shafts in the same manner. A brace was fitted to the bottom of the shafts at the front end and the turning mechanism installed. The wheel is held in place by horizontal cleats mounted on the axle, and the axle itself is mounted with hand-carved knobs outside the shafts. Friction was avoided by the insertion periodically of a lubricant around the axle inside the barrow shafts. In both cases, a piece of bacon rind was the lubricant and it was replaced as needed by loosening the braces along the bottom of the shafts.

Rampley's preference for simple, easily modified or easily fashioned materials is a statement about thrift and ingenuity. A simpler method of mounting a wheel is demonstrated in the Indiana University Museum wheelbarrow. This method requires but simple smithing and bolting, but the result is probably not as stable nor as permanent. Rampley's is certainly a better product than the model cited by Rolfe Cobleigh, who seems to be totally unaware of the stability problem.[18]

The mail order catalogues at the turn of the century offered wheelbarrows of "japanned metal" and seasoned hardwoods. Rampley's barrow was more or less built from available scraps from his wood pile, but he has his preferences and he states the reasons for them:

The shafts here are just white poplar and that's not as good as yellow [poplar]. Yellow poplar's best. It colors better and doesn't get that streaked look. Them sides is sycamore and red oak. The half-sole, if I had one on there, would have to be green ash. Either green or I'd have to soak it some. Maybe would anyway. And the bark 'd have to come off too, you know. But poplar, now poplar . . . yellow poplar is best over-all for this kind of thing. It's strong wood.

While strength is an important factor in the making of any wheelbarrow, Rampley is also intent upon making the implement "look right" even though he could not afford to meet this standard in the barrow he built on his grandfather's model. Still, Rampley's approach to constructing his barrow was simple. He used no measured drawings; he merely sketched out what he intended on board and worked things through in his head. One problem baffled him and he sought help from a neighbor:

I couldn't for the life of me remember what the ratio would be for a twenty-one-inch wheel. I had to go over and see George Brasheer, down the road here, and ask him. I said, "George, do you know the ratio for a twenty-one-inch wheel?" And he said, "Why, sure I do! It's nineteen and a quarter inches!" So there I had it and that's what I did.

What tools did you need for the job? "Just the ones I have here. I used a draw knife on them shafts. That wheel I just cut out rough with a hand saw and filled it some." [19]

The dimensions of Rampley's wheelbarrow are interesting. Whereas the Indiana University specimen has a bed three feet long and thirty inches wide, Rampley's is but twenty-seven inches long but twenty-nine inches wide. His purpose here was to accommodate a wide load, and he even placed the cleats or the sideboards inside so that the sideboards would rest on the very edge of the bed. The slots in the headboard hold the sideboards steady. The Indiana University barrow uses an iron loop across the headboard to accommodate the sideboards.

In general, we may say that Rampley has made maximum use of available materials without depending upon the community for iron work, factory-made wheels and axles, and the like. His sole requirement outside his workshop was the bolts for areas of extreme stress in the barrow.

It is my conclusion that it is the independence of Rampley's approach to craftsmanship which marks his skill. Had he made the wheelbarrow at an earlier point in his life, when he had ready access to a forge, he would undoubtedly have used more ironwork and the resulting product would have been different. As it was, Rampley's barrow is the result of working with what is at hand within the confines of a tradition specifically determined by his life.[20]

Subsistence craftsmen are the nonspecialists in the traditional expressive arts. Their products are necessarily practical though often imbued with a particular aesthetic quality which varies within ethnic, regional, and even personal standards. These standards are determined as much by social forces as by environmental and economic factors. A true understanding of the craft cannot be attained without intensive personal interviews and some grasp of the craftsman's background, his development, and his values within his personal world.

19

Monuments and Myths:
Three American Arches

Joseph F. Trimmer

Introduction

"To describe a nation's monuments," writes Joseph Trimmer, "is to describe its values." American authors writing in both the fictive and the factual modes have often used American things to symbolize American beliefs. Recall, for instance, William Dean Howells proclaiming the Great Corliss steam engine of the 1876 Philadelphia Centennial Exposition as the mechanical embodiment of American technological prowess, or Henry Adams wondering about the consequences of that prowess by juxtaposing the dynamo and the virgin in order to dramatize a tension between technics and civilization.

In modern scholarship, particularly within the discipline of American Studies, a "myth and symbol school" has endeavored to explore the cultural, social, and psychological meanings of American artifacts at various levels of individual and group consciousness. This historiographical tradition begins with Henry N. Smith, Virgin Land: The American West As Symbol and Myth (1955) and extends forward through works such as Leo Marx's The Machine in the Garden: Technology and the Pastoral Ideal in America (1967) and Alan Tractenberg, The Brooklyn Bridge, Fact and Symbol (1972).

Trimmer's brief but provocative exegesis of three American artifacts—the natural bridge over Cedar Creek, Virginia; the stainless-steel Gateway Arch in St. Louis; and the ubiquitous neon McDonald arch of highway civilization, Anywhere, U.S.A.—should be included as another example of this approach to artifact study. As such it is a methodology heavily indebted to the techniques of literary studies in at least two respects: first, for its sensitivity to thinking about physical objects in terms of their acting as symbols, conceits, metaphors, or analogs; second, for its close attention to what contemporaries say, especially

*what they say in written form, about objects. In Trimmer's analysis, one notices
that he quickly bolsters his own cultural musing about how an artifact reveals the
depths or heights of the American character with one of the classic texts of
American cultural history, such as Thomas Jefferson's Notes on the State of
Virginia or Frederick Jackson Turner's The Significance of the Frontier in
American History.*

*The literary scholar has a tendency to use artifacts primarily as memorable
images for evoking perceptive cultural criticism or as heuristic devices for the
teaching and ordering of cultural history. In the Trimmer analysis, the reader is
confronted with three forms of an architectural element (arches), executed in three
types of building material (stone, steel, and neon), constructed during three
periods of American history (admittedly the last two artifacts are practically
coterminous). These trinities are interconnected in a pedagogical schema
for synthesizing and summarizing a large slice of American cultural history from a
small number of carefully chosen American artifacts. The technique prompts one
to think of other artifacts that might be compared for the cultural freight they tend
to carry, for example, the comparative material culture of the world's fairs of
Philadelphia (1876), Chicago (1893), or New York City (1939).*

*In a spirit similar to Craig Gilborn's use of the Coke bottle and Bruce
Lohoff's study of the gasoline station, Trimmer wants the definition of historic
American material culture to include even the most contemporary of objects. He
has expanded his research on McDonald's artifacts in an essay, "Enter the
Wizard," The World of Ronald McDonald, ed. Marshall Fishwick (1977), a
useful compilation of assorted pieces, some dealing with the material culture of
the American fast-food industry. Joseph F. Trimmer has also written Black
American Literature (1971), A Casebook on Ralph Ellison's Invisible Man (1972),
and American Oblique: Writing About the American Experience (1976). A
professor of English and American Studies at Ball State University, Muncie,
Indiana, Trimmer initially published the following essay in English News (March
1976): 1, 6–7.*

🦅

When the poet Hart Crane was looking for a symbol to express his mythic
sense of the complexity of American life, he selected that colossal "curveship," the
Brooklyn Bridge. Spanning a portion of the sea, connecting land to land, supporting
the endless flow of humanity above the constant tides of the harbor, the bridge
loomed in Crane's imagination as the archetypal American monument. In form, it
suggested the symbolic completion of the American search for fulfillment. In function, it provided a way of crossing over obstacles to begin the quest.

The mythic meanings Crane saw in the "inviolate curve" of the bridge are also
visible in many of the other monumental structures in our land. The size and variety
of these wonders certainly confirm our national myth about the bigness and unique-

ness of American life. Each of our natural, historic, and commercial monuments seems to embody a slightly different version of that myth. Thus, to describe three of them—arches of limestone, steel, and neon—is to disclose the changing character of that myth which has given direction and meaning to our lives.

One early version of the myth spoke of America as God's promised land: the beneficent Deity had revealed a new garden where a new Adam and Eve, if they were faithful and obedient, could regain paradise. The abundant fertility of this new world, replete with its majestic forests, rivers, and mountains, testified to God's grandeur. But the more dramatic features of our landscape, such as Niagara Falls, the Grand Canyon, and the marvels at Yellowstone, were special evidence of His abiding presence in our destiny.

No monument speaks of our admiration for the glorious works of the Creator better than the Natural Bridge of Virginia. The Monocan Indians called it "The Bridge of God" because, according to legend, the tribe had once been trapped at the edge of a mighty chasm by the hostile Shawnees and Powhatans, and when the frightened people called on the Great Spirit for deliverance, the bridge miraculously appeared.

The scientific explanation of the formation of the bridge is no less a tribute to God's wonder-working powers. Sometime in prehistory, little Cedar Creek, in making its way out of the mountains and down to the James River, formed a high waterfall, the summit of which was probably level with the top of the bridge. The creek cut away slowly at the soft limestone beneath the summit, eventually trenching a chasm some two hundred feet deep. The arch of the bridge withstood this erosion and now spans a canyon that scientists estimate is several million years old.

Here was ample evidence that God had been preparing a place for us. Long before the arrival of Columbus, long before the birth of the culture that produced Columbus, Cedar Creek had been working on God's bridge in the new garden. By comparison, the wonders of the ancient world, the pyramids of Egypt, the Great Wall of China, and the imposing cathedrals of Europe seemed inconsequential and ephemeral, the momentary works of humankind. Because the bridge was God's creation, it inspired not only a sense of the Divinity's majesty and power, but gave the new gardeners a sense of their proper place in the scheme of Nature. As Thomas Jefferson mused in *Notes on the State of Virginia*, "It is impossible for the emotions arising from the sublime to be felt beyond what they are here; so beautiful an arch, so elevated, so light, and springing as it were up to Heaven, the rapture of the spectator is really indescribable."

What was first worshipped as a gift from the Creator was soon reduced to the status of a natural resource, an object to be bought, sold, and visited. Jefferson's rapture at the glorious thing God had made did not prevent him from purchasing it from an earthly king, George III, two years before the war for American independence. Jefferson traveled often to visit and survey his monument, and in 1803 he built a two-room cabin on the site to accommodate visitors.

Indeed there were others who were interested in the bridge. Some years before Jefferson's purchase, a youthful George Washington had mapped the property for Lord Fairfax. Apparently George was also confused about the rightful "owner" of the bridge because he climbed some twenty-three feet up the southeast wall to inscribe his initials.

From a contemporary perspective, Jefferson's instinct for tourism and Washington's impulse for graffiti are early indications of what had since happened to our reverence for natural monuments and the God-centered myth they once embodied. The arch that sprang to Heaven now functions as a minor link in U.S. Highway 11. As they view "The Bridge of God" from below, visitors may still register a sense of religious awe, but the current owners do not rely on the bridge's natural beauty for inspiration.

Every evening tourists are treated to an elaborate pageant involving a colorful light display, musical accompaniment, and dramatic readings from Genesis. The conversion of God's arch into a proscenium arch tells much about the altered place the modern mind assigns itself in the universal order: it presumes not only to own God's monument but also attempts to recreate it. The original "Proprietor" may still be the recipient of praise, but His majesty is recognized only through modern, technical magic. Perhaps some prophecy of God's displacement from our national myth can be seen in the tracings Cedar Creek made on the stone of the bridge; exactly above on the highest spring of the arch appears the figure of a gigantic spread eagle in the pose it now assumes on the American coat of arms.

It is easy to see how the process of civilizing our continent caused the new Adam and Eve to fall gradually from grace. Clearing the land, building a home, and harvesting crops gave the once faithful gardeners an exaggerated sense of themselves as king of God's kingdom. The national myth that once focused on the beneficent Creator now focused instead on those who explored and developed the garden. The change in focus also occasioned a change in locale. The vast new territories that Thomas Jefferson purchased in 1803 from another earthly king, Napoleon I, beckoned as the new promised land, and thousands of Americans journeyed west to claim the bounty the new myth ordained was theirs.

Ninety years later, at a meeting of the American Historical Association in Chicago, Frederick Jackson Turner read a paper entitled "The Significance of the Frontier in American History." Turner argued that the western experience had determined the shape of the American character. By necessity, the solitary characters in the frontier drama—the scout, the trapper, the miner, the rancher, and particularly the yeoman farmer—developed a dedication to the virtues of self-reliance and the pragmatics of democracy, which are identified as our two most laudable national traits.

Turner also pointed out that the availability of free land in the western territories had provided a safety valve for the pressure-packed urban centers on the eastern seaboard. The safety valve was no longer functional, Turner argued, because the frontier no longer existed. Most of the promised land had been settled, plowed, and fenced. The open land that remained was either too expensive or too infertile to satisfy many dreamers of the western dream. Although many Americans continued to believe in that dream, Turner and others pondered the fate of the heroic gardeners when they discovered the garden had been posted with "no vacancy" signs.

The Gateway Arch, located on the western bank of the Mississippi River in downtown St. Louis, commemorates both the myth and the reality of the frontier experience. St. Louis is certainly an appropriate location for such a monument because it was once the most prominent embarkation point for those journeying into the new territories. As they moved out of the gloom of eastern forests and on to vast midwestern prairies that led to and beyond the river dividing our land, early travelers must have experienced a dramatic sense of expanded vision and opportunity. The six-hundred-and-thirty-foot stainless steel arch that now marks the beginning of the West is a spectacular portal through which to glimpse imaginatively the land that once flowed with milk and honey. This radiant land cannot be seen with the eye, however, because it exists only in memory. The arch, like the horizon, encloses an imaginary domain that moves forever backward as we advance upon it.

Forty-two years after Turner announced that the frontier was a subject to be discussed by historians, a small plot of land on the western bank of the Mississippi was designated the Jefferson National Expansion Memorial. Twelve years later, in 1947, a national competition was held to select a design for an appropriate monument for the Memorial. In 1965, Eero Saarinen's inverted catenary curve, built from more than five thousand tons of steel and twelve thousand tons of concrete, was completed on the river site. Sometime in 1976 a Museum of Westward Expansion will be constructed beneath the shadow of the arch.

These details remind us that the monumental arch was built seventy-five years after the myth it commemorated had already ceased to function in our daily lives. The Gateway Arch does not open upon frontier land but upon the football land of Busch Stadium, where local teams battle the "Cowboys" and the "Redskins." The arch is not even functional. As it sits shimmering in the light of the dying day, it is strangely out of place beside the mighty bridges that cross the Mississippi. Like the myth it memorializes, the arch is beautiful and useless.

Visitors may travel within the structure in a contraption reminiscent of a ferris wheel to an observation deck at the apex of the arch. The small windows there provide a thirty-mile view to the west. But tourists have to imagine what their ancestors saw instead of the present sprawl of downtown and suburban St. Louis. Soon the visitors take the ride back to the ground, victims of a western journey that has gone nowhere.

While the myth commemorated by the Gateway Arch may exist only in the museum being built at its base, the myth embodied in the "St. Louis Arch" speaks of present realities. Localizing the name of the arch radically alters its mythic identity. If the Gateway Arch symbolizes the possibility of escape from the imprisonment of the city, then the St. Louis arch stands for the attractive glitter of urban life.

Throughout our national history the frontier myth and the city myth have offered alternative paths of self-fulfillment. The frontier promises the ideals of individuality, contentment, and continuity, while the city promises the ideals of cooperation, prosperity, and mobility. Toward the end of the last century, many people of the middle border, frustrated by the failure of the frontier promise, journeyed eastward to explore the possibilities of city life. Ironically, the arch in the Expansion Memorial has encouraged this latter journey: if one can no longer journey westward from the arch in search of a dream, one can, at least, journey westward from the arch in search of entertainment. Indeed, only three other monuments of human manufacture, the two Disneylands and Lenin's tomb, can boast more visitors each year.

In the past decade, local pride in the arch has initiated a renaissance of boosterism. A host of urban redevelopment projects, such as the Mercantile Complex, the Civic Trust Building, and the General American Life Building, now compete with the arch for dominance of St. Louis's symbolic skyline. The construction of these commercial monuments suggests that perhaps the chief characters in the American drama have never been the faithful gardeners or the heroes of the frontier. The lead has always been played by the energetic people of business, and, like the play's other heroes, they have their own myth and monumental arch.

In the late 1940s, Ray Kroc, a former musician, radio executive, real estate agent, and Lily-Tulip Cup salesman, was working as the exclusive representative for a new invention, a milk shake "multimixer" machine. A small hamburger restaurant in San Bernardino, California, owned by two McDonald brothers, attracted Kroc's attention because it had installed eight of his multimixers. Impressed by the profits of the fast food business, Kroc tried to convince the brothers to open restaurants in other locations. When the brothers indicated that they were satisfied with the size of their present operation, Kroc negotiated a ninety-nine-year contract to represent them. On April 15, 1955, Kroc opened his first McDonald's, complete with identifying "golden arches," in the Chicago suburb of Des Plaines, Illinois. In July of the same year, Kroc granted his first license for a McDonald's franchise in Fresno, California. When the company celebrated its twentieth anniversary in 1975, it had grown from these modest beginnings into a multi-billion-dollar international corporation.

The McDonald's story is, of course, a rather spectacular version of the American success myth. The dream of success exists in one form or another in all our American myths, but it is most often identified with the world of commerce and a particular philosophy of work. That philosophy preaches that success will come to all who believe in the American economy, who work diligently without complaint, and who possess the ability to see and seize opportunity.

Like the myth's more famous heroes, Andrew Carnegie and Henry Ford, Kroc believed in, demonstrated, and proselytized the work ethic. In what the company now refers to as its "Pioneer Days," Kroc worked side by side with the crew in each new franchise. He constantly proclaimed the virtues of efficiency and persistence represented in the company's early symbol, a chef with a hamburger-shaped face named "Speedee."

Eventually Kroc opened his own educational institution, Hamburger University, in Elk Grove, Illinois, to indoctrinate prospective managers in the philosophy of the McDonald's system. That philosophy can best be summed up by the framed declaration that hangs on the wall in the office of each franchise manager:

Press On

Nothing in the world can
take the place of persistence.
Talent will not;
nothing is more common
than unsuccessful men
with talent. Genius will
not; unrewarded genius
is almost a proverb.
Education alone will not;
the world is full of
educated derelicts.
Persistence and
determination alone are
omnipotent.
—Calvin Coolidge

This dedication to the nobility and omnipotence of work would not seem, by itself, to explain McDonald's phenomenal success. Even the decision to specialize in a humble meat and potatoes product does not distinguish McDonald's from thousands of other joints that sell burgers and fries across America. Perhaps some explanation of McDonald's unique position in our culture can be gleaned from an analysis of the subtle and even subliminal symbolism of the activity that take place beneath the arches of neon.

Kroc's decision to open his first McDonald's in Des Plaines was no accident, for he realized early that the future of his operation was connected to the automobile culture of the suburbs. Careful scouting of potential locations with respect to traffic and shopping patterns usually determined that a restaurant should be placed on the edge of town in that elongated commercial district known as "the strip." The two single arches, which in the 1950s functioned as part of the restaurant's structure, towered above the clutter of gas station signs. Another single arch stood at the entrance to a gargantuan parking lot and proclaimed how many millions of fifteen-cent hamburgers had already been sold.

Yet the high visibility of the arches, the easy access to parking, the proof of millions of satisfied customers, even the low cost and high eatability of the food were not as important to customer loyalty as the speed and efficiency with which the food was dispensed. There were no gum-snapping carhops, no pulsating juke boxes, and no booths filled with rowdy teenagers who had time but little money to spend. One merely walked to the window, uttered the cryptic code "2–1–and a coke," and as if by magic a bag of goodies appeared.

Inside the fishbowl of glass, one could see the white-shirted crew attending to the elaborate gadgetry of the stainless steel assembly line. For sixteen hours a day, seven days a week, the work continued at a frantic pace while some chimerical calculator tabulated the number of burgers sold. The customer, impressed by the wondrous precision of the machines and the tireless energy of the crew, returned to the car, ate quickly, and drove off to attend to business.

The intensity of this testimonial to the American work ethic is somewhat abated, however, by the individual worker's loss of identity. It is the crew rather than the chef, the corporation rather than Kroc, which dominated this picture. Indeed, the golden arches attest to the victory of national standardization over individual achievement. Corporate management develops the menu items, the machinery to dispense them, and the promotional campaigns to sell them. The individual franchise owner invests capital (the initial investment required today is about $100,000), agrees to a corporate service charge of 3 percent of gross volume, and submits to a managerial indoctrination at Hamburger University. With the individual franchise grossing close to $700,000 a year and national sales advancing toward an annual average of $2 billion, it became obvious that in McDonald's version of the American success myth the corporation had become the hero.

By the early 1960s, McDonald's had become so successful that it could afford to refashion its national image. The modifications in the McDonald's monument are mythic. Whereas the early restaurants had stressed the reality of work, the new restaurants promoted the fantasy of leisure. Certainly the replacement of Speedee, the chef, with Ronald McDonald, the clown, epitomized this change. But there were other alterations to suggest that the new McDonald's environment was to be viewed as a home (a haven from work) rather than a factory (a replica of the assembly line).

The major architectural change was to replace the glass and steel design of the walk-up window with the brick and wood design of the sit-down dining room. The lofty structural arches were replaced by a modest mansard roof; a decorative double arch, crossed in the shape of an M, replaced the single arch at the entrance to the parking lot.

Inside, the white-shirted crew was replaced by a blue-shirted corps of high school and college kids. The national advertising campaigns assured children that McDonald's was as fascinating as Oz and parents that McDonald's was "your kind of place," a place to treat the family. McDonald's also began to encourage holders of their franchises to become visible in community affairs. At the national level, the corporation committed itself to charity drives such as the Jerry Lewis Telethon for Muscular Dystrophy. The mythic message seemed to be that the products of successful labor were fun and occasional philanthropy.

In our time, we probably feel most comfortable with this last version of our national myth. We would rather worship the American way of life than God. We have no need for the freedom of the frontier when the interstate highway system provides for efficient and extensive travel. We do not even need work: our labor unions negotiate a shorter week, and our legislators guarantee an annual income. But what we do want is someone to tell us how to use our money and our leisure to acquire the sense of fulfillment that still eludes us. The monumental M suggests that we can discover that fulfillment only in the diverting fantasies of McDonald's land.

If Hart Crane were writing poetry today, he could hardly find a better monument than this M to express the new complexities of America's manic quest. Appearing ubiquitously around every corner, recognized by American children before they can speak their first word, calling up musical jingles in the heads of thousands, the double arches proclaim that we have completed the search for the good life ("It's close by, right on your way") only to discover that its realization has brought disillusionment. In trying to get up and get away, we have encountered not the bigness or uniqueness of American life but its eternal sameness. The last arch reveals that instead of getting the break promised by our national myth, we have all been included in the count of the billions sold.

20

Chicago through a Camera Lens: An Essay on Photography as History

Glen E. Holt

Introduction

Photography's potential as historical evidence was recognized almost immediately after the medium's invention. Oliver Wendell Holmes, for example, urged historians to collect and preserve photographs as vital visual records of change for their future counterparts. Holmes, a zealous promoter of the historical significance of nineteenth-century stereograph photography, considered such images "matchless pieces of information, descriptions of things, scenes and persons infinitely more vivid than words." Eventually he hoped that photography might reproduce the entire contemporary world, reducing all objects, events, and experiences to thin film images.

Holmes's grandiose aspirations for a complete visual archive of the present (and thus, ultimately, the past) understandably was an impossibility from the start. His injunctions to historians to use the photographic record, flawed and incomplete though it is, nevertheless continues to be reiterated with increasing persuasion and methodological sophistication. Glen Holt's survey of the value of visual material culture for doing urban history cogently summarizes several recurring themes in using photography as history.

Holt focuses on Chicago, arguing that in its extant photography one can see represented every major type of photograph, photographic process, and photographer from the introduction of the daguerreotype to the city to the work of amateur photographers in the Chicagoland-In-Pictures Project begun in 1947. In advocating this threefold approach to photography as a product, as a process, and as the work of photographers, he also alerts us to the numerous problems a researcher must anticipate while investigating the visual record. For example, there is the constant dilemma of the incomplete record; that is, few or no surviving photographs of certain urban places (such as backyards and slum neighborhoods), certain people (vagrants or transient laborers), and certain activities (urban violence and events at night or indoors, for instance). Thus we have much more visual evidence of the public city than we do of the private city.

In his review of the photographic types that depict urban life, Holt also reminds the material culture student that the vast majority of photographs were made for hire; most images now in archives, libraries, and historical societies were first produced as commercial products, deliberately designed for real estate promoters, architectural firms, municipal governments, advertisers, and individual clients. Even so-called "reform photography," claiming to represent accurately "how the other half lives," had its biases and distortions.

Surprisingly, Holt sees little use for the amateur snapshot, perhaps the most prolific of all American photograph genres, in elucidating city activity of family life. Much more valuable, he claims, are panoramas, architectural views, stereographs, and aerial views.

Holt's rapid survey of the photographic record of a single representative city, of course, raises many questions with which both urban historians and photographic historians still grapple, such as: What role did amateurs like Charles Clark (whom Holt discusses at length) play in shaping a city's visual portrait? Might it be useful to compare the entire collective visual image of one nineteenth-century city like Chicago with that of one of its midwestern rivals such as Cincinnati or St. Louis? How might photography be vital to a scholar wishing to write an interdisciplinary urban history that would consider city planning, land use, ecology, transportation networks, and housing stock?

Well-versed in urban and cultural geography, Glen Holt has frequently pressed fellow historians to give serious consideration to the spatial dimensions of past urban activities. Examples of this orientation are his article "Changing Perceptions of Urban Pathology in Cities," in Cities in American History (1972) and his reader, St. Louis: A Documentary Anthology (1977). Photography provides a major evidential component of Harold Meyer and Richard Wade, Chicago: Growth of a Metropolis (1968), a model study on which Holt worked as the photographic historian. In his most recent book, Chicago Neighborhoods (1979), coauthored with Dominic Pacyga, photographs play a major role as they will in a social history of the city that he is presently researching and which will be titled The People of Chicago. The essay that follows first appeared in Chicago History 1 (Spring 1971): 158–169.

🦅

In April 1839, Samuel F. B. Morse, the inventor of the telegraph, wrote to an American magazine from France that he had seen the ultimate in photographic reproduction. The new image was called a daguerreotype by its inventor, Louis Daguerre. In his letter Morse extolled the Frenchman's method which duplicated details from nature in an "exquisite minuteness of . . . delineation which no painting or engraving ever approached." In September 1839, the scientific details of Daguerre's process were published in the United States. Within months, hundreds of mechanics, blacksmiths, and self-taught scientists mastered the necessary techniques and opened studios. The age of commercial image makers had begun.

Daguerreotypists were primarily portrait makers, and almost all of the estimated fifteen to twenty million images they produced by 1857 were portraits of people. Chicago had its contributors to this number. The first daguerreotypists came to the city in 1845. In the city directory of 1857–58, thirteen daguerreotype studios are listed.

After 1854, at least two of these Chicago studios added another platemaking technique. This form, called the ambrotype, different from the daguerreotype principally in being an image on glass rather than on metal. Throughout America in late 1855 and in 1856 the ambrotype surpassed the daguerreotype in popularity.

The paper print method of recording images on light sensitive paper was introduced into America in 1839, the same year as the daguerreotype. Initially, however, paper print photographs took longer to record than either ambrotypes or daguerreotypes. Consequently, the paper print was not a competitive image-producing technique until about 1856. By the next year, two Chicago studios were advertising portraits in daguerreotype, ambrotype, and by paper print. The last proved its superiority before 1860. Once its recording speed was hastened, it had two advantages over the other two techniques: it offered a wider range of gray-black tones, although without the daguerreotype's sharpness, and, more important, it was cheaper.

While portrait making was the livelihood of early professional cameramen, they did record images of cities. In the late 1840s, daguerreotypists in a few large urban centers captured street scenes and full scale panoramic views of mid-century skylines. If Chicago had such early portraits, they have not survived. The remaining daguerreotypes and ambrotypes of this city show only a few individual houses, a well-kept residential street, a hotel, the remains of a burned-out home, and the Sturges and Buckingham grain elevators at the mouth of the Chicago River.

A body of work by one early Chicago photographer, Alexander Hesler, does remain, although his pictorial legacy begins a decade later than visual records in some other cities. At the Crystal Palace Exposition of 1853, Alexander Hesler won the title of "the leading daguerreotypist in the country," when he took first place in the viewmakers' competition. Hesler moved his studio from Galena to Chicago in the early 1850s and began making portraits of the renowned and obscure of the lakeside city.

By 1856, Hesler had the technical skill to make paper print photographs. In the next half-decade he left his studio many times to turn his camera on Chicago, in the process portraying his consciousness of the dynamic changes of the period. Old Fort Dearborn, Chicago's decaying relic from a previous era, was due for demolition in 1857, and Hesler captured a view of its palisaded interior, mirroring it against the

Lake House, a gleaming new four-story hotel, a symbol of the city's surging growth. He contrasted the white-marble facade of the Marine Building with neighboring balloon-frame business structures. In a grand culmination in 1858, he set his camera atop the Court House and took an eleven-shot panorama which provides the most complete visual record of the city at that time.

The urge of photographers like Hesler to record difficult city views appears to have been tied up with their conception of themselves as artists. While they were unbound by any broad artistic theory, the best of the daguerreotypists and other early photographers took great pride in their work. They derided their unskilled competitors who made only cheap portraits as "blue-bosom boys," an epithet publicizing their tendency to gray out white shirtfronts in their images. This sense of artistic purpose was heightened, too, by a movement within American painting. The art world had long advocated "reality" as one characteristic of good painting, and the daguerreotypist and early photographer could portray the detailed image of reality better than any painter or lithographer. These early photographic artists, to prove their ability, turned their cameras on the most complex subjects they could find, and the cities where they maintained their studios often provided the most accessible and intricate subjects for their visual experiments.

Hesler's photographs and the surviving ones by his contemporaries in other cities are a precious heritage. Like most historical artifacts, they lend themselves to many misconceptions. Certainly the images provide the viewer with a heightened sense of reality of the physical appearance of the city, especially when they are compared with the frequently romanticized lithographs and paintings of the same subjects. But one should be aware of what the early photographs do not show. Photography at the time could not catch motion, so most photographers worked in the early morning before the city was awake, placing their cameras on high points or in wide public streets to make the best use of natural light and, if people were to be included, posing them in place. In Chicago the physical character of a city moving from clapboard storefronts to marbled business facades is recorded, but images of the bustle of street life, the routine of the factory, and the manifestations of poverty do not exist. These inherent biases cannot be overcome except through the imaginative reading of contemporaneous verbal descriptions. Without this nonvisual corrective, early photography provides an unrealistic portrayal of the city.

In 1859, studio photographers began to use another French innovation, the carte-de-visite camera, a four-lensed affair which could record quadruple images simultaneously or in rapid succession. When the single negative plate was printed and backed, it resulted in four 2½ inch by 4 inch photographs mounted on stiff cardboard. The cost for a dozen or so of these clear little images was no more than the price of a single good daguerreotype. A British writer explained the new process. "The price," he wrote, "enables all the better middle class to have their portraits; and by the system of exchange, forty of their friends . . . for two guineas [about $12.00]!"

While the lower price encouraged the exchange of cartes-de-visite, the accumulation of more than a few of them created a storage problem: there was always a danger that a loose photograph would slip behind a drawer or become mixed with a pile of papers slated for disposal. Enterprising photographers had an answer for this problem. They sold albums specially designed to hold and display the little photographs.

Carte-de-visite photographers were quick to see another possibility as well. If clients had extra spaces in their portrait albums devoted to friends and relatives, they might also collect views of familiar streets or buildings which had meaning in their lives. Moreover, in an age without photographs in daily newspapers, there was a demand for cheap images of both significant men and important and unusual events. In Chicago, photographers responded with cartes-de-visite of celebrities like Stephen A. Douglas and Abraham Lincoln. They also carried their cameras into the streets and parks of the city, making images of the Chamber of Commerce, Court House, Camp Douglas, the various railroad depots, and other well-known public buildings. Views of churches abound. In addition, businessmen contracted to have pictorial advertising cards made up for their potential customers. A dealer in baseball goods, for example, had a view of the Chicago team of 1871 printed with his company advertisement on the back, and an auctioneer and commission merchant pictured his new place of business just after the fire of 1871. Businessmen handed such cards to customers or distributed them free in public places. The photographers sold cartes-de-visite of celebrities, disasters, and city views at their studios, capturing the impulse buyer who came for a sitting, and (if we can believe an occasional label) marketed them at city news agencies, probably on a consignment basis. Placed in family albums, these views were preserved into the twentieth century.

Concomitant with the increased popularity of the cartes-de-visite, a new kind of photograph, one concentrating entirely on places and things, was being taken. Since men had begun painting pictures, they had attempted to make things appear three-dimensional. As early as 1838, artists endeavored to draw two identical pictures that could be viewed simultaneously through a binocular lens arrangement, to create the illusion of depth. But so accurate a representation—setting the perspective of two drawings an average of two and a half inches apart—was nearly impossible. However, a binocular camera could achieve the feat with no difficulty. In the late 1850s, American photographers began taking thousands of double-viewed "stereographs." In 1859, production of an inexpensive stereoscopic viewer was announced, and the stereographic revolution was underway.

At about the same time that the binocular vision stereoscope was developed, negatives became sufficiently sensitive so that many moving forms were "perfectly rendered, although the exposure was but the imperceptible fraction of a second." With this new capacity, stereograph makers found the city an ideal subject, and for seventy years they set their binocular lenses on innumerable urban scenes.

Chicago stereograph makers catered to potential customers with views of busy downtown streets. To these were added pictures of the city's distinctive structures and scenic attractions: the Water Tower, the Palmer House, Field, Leiter and

Company, the homes of the wealthy, and formal plantings in the city's major parks. Scenes made at special events—expositions, fairs, and parades—also were put on sale soon after they occurred. Finally, the disasters which beset the city were duly recorded and marketed. A month after the great fire of 1871, for example, *Anthony's Photographic Bulletin* advised its readers that "the latest novelty in American stereographic views is a series from Chicago, which avidly portrays the nature and extent of the recent disaster and its effects on the different buildings." Several such fire series were made, often with views on both sides of the mount; on the one side was a "before" photo from the late 1860s, on the reverse an "after" view taken from an identical perspective.

Street scenes filled with variety and detail, symbols of an ambitious city, important celebrations, calamities, and occasionally an advertising view are the categories into which all but a few existent Chicago-oriented cartes-de-visite and stereographs fit. The similarity in subject matter is no coincidence. Quite often the two types of photographs were made by the same company which marketed identical views on both the viewing formats.

For Chicago at least, more stereographs are extant than are cartes-de-visite. Two factors explain this phenomenon. First, more stereographs were produced over a longer time. Cartes-de-visite of Chicago began about 1861 and ended about 1871 or 1872. Stereographs of the city began about 1866, with new views produced until the early 1930s. Second, the popularity of stereographs increased their possibility for survival. City view companies like Chicago-based John Carbutt took stereographic views, sold them locally and advertised them nationally, either under the Carbutt label or to be marketed by companies in other cities under their names. By 1875, a stereoscope owner could purchase views of Chicago by mail, or in local book stores, news agencies, and department stores. In the end, so many millions of the views were produced and so many thousands of people collected them that their chance for survival to our own time was increased, a result of their cheapness and mass availability.

As in the case of daguerreotypes, ambrotypes, and early photographs, mid-twentieth-century viewers must realize that extant cartes-de-visite and stereographs have limitations. Card and view makers were interested in selling to a mass audience, and most buyers appear to have been "respectable" families who could afford a parlor nicety. Therefore, while views were often "exotic," they were never offensive. A set of city views might include an ethnic shopping district, but the slum homes of the city's poorest residents were not included. Fashionable residences, especially those of well-known people, were marketed; the interior of a sweat shop employing children was not considered appropriate. The daguerreotypist and early photographer took city views to prove themselves as artists; the cartes-de-visite and stereograph makers provided a visual traveler's guide to the public city, marketing views which were of wide public interest.

Photography has always had its amateur practitioners, those who experimented with the techniques of image making or who made pictorial records for their own amusement rather than as a source of income. High costs and the necessity for advanced technical knowledge kept the number of amateurs small until the 1860s. After the introduction of the stereoscope, technical evolution of cameras and developing techniques was rapid. Portability was the initial attraction. By the mid-1880s, several different kinds of "detective cameras," which could be held and in some cases concealed in the hand, were already being marketed.

In 1888, George Eastman, an amateur himself, introduced his simplified box camera, which provided potential users with reliability and freedom from technical concern. ("You press the button, we do the rest," was the advertising slogan he used to popularize the Kodak.) Eastman loaded the box camera at the factory with a roll of flexible "American film" which he had invented. The user then could record one hundred 2½ inch square photographs. When the roll was completed, the purchaser sent the camera back to Eastman who developed the film and reloaded the camera, all for a single modest fee. By 1889, Eastman had perfected a developing technique by which steady-handed amateurs could process their own film. The age of the "snapshot" had arrived.

Most amateur snapshots, unfortunately, do little to illuminate city history. The stereographic viewmaker photographed urban subjects in the belief they would interest others; the amateur aimed his camera at more narrowly personal subjects like his house, family, friends, and garden, or subjects of immediate interest such as a scenic view which fitted his momentary mood, a peculiarity of nature, or a disaster he witnessed. Moreover, if an amateur took a historically important photograph, its chances for survival were small. Both the thin inexpensive film and the cheap "drugstore finish" of these photographs tended to fade rapidly, curl, and crack, eventually deteriorating into brittle scraps.

Not all amateurs were casual dilettantes, however. A few of them, for one reason or another, took time to learn correct field and darkroom techniques, used professional equipment, and broke out of the usual narrow subject limits. Some of these gifted amateurs aimed their cameras at the city with both a sense of history and an attempt at artful portrayal.

One such Chicago amateur was Charles R. Clark. By profession he was a commission merchant, by avocation a pictorial historian of the city and a camera enthusiast. Clark began taking photographs of the city about 1898. But his pictorial interest in Chicago extended to an earlier time. To portray this period, he copied older photographs and engravings. The final result was a collection of over a thousand pictures, a three-album visual overview of the city between 1873 and 1916, with Clark's own photographs covering the last nineteen years.

Throughout his photographing and collecting, Clark demonstrated an acute awareness of Chicago's dynamic development and his own sense of being part of the city's historically significant events. He aimed his camera at streets and parks, took closeups of leaders and important visitors to the city, climbed atop buildings to capture panoramic views, and set up his camera in available downtown open space to catch the shape of the city's skyline. Clark is the most important early gifted amateur of Chicago city photography. While his photographs end before America's entrance into World War I, his tradition does not. It continues into the 1970s in the Chicagoland-in-Pictures project with the Chicago Historical Society, which has elicited from gifted amateurs some nineteen thousand photographs of Chicago and urban-related subjects since 1947.

A few years before George Eastman first marketed his Kodak, a new generation of commercial photographers began to take pictures of the American city. Using the latest technological innovations, these professional cameramen recorded the rapid building of new steel-beamed skyscrapers, the expansion of the city's high-class residential sections, and the erection of the mass production industrial plants throughout the last quarter of the nineteenth and the initial decades of the twentieth century. They contracted with architectural firms to portray their latest and highest buildings, with real estate men who were promoting new suburbs, and with civic groups detailing promotions and tour guides. In the process, they built up a stock of city photographs which they made into view-books and, later, picture postcards which were sold in bookstores, at newsstands and special events, and in some cases, by door-to-door peddlers.

John W. Taylor was the most prolific of such photographers with headquarters in Chicago. Taylor began photographing the city in 1886; his last extant view appears to have been made in 1916. An indication of the scope of Taylor's operations can be found in his advertisements. In February 1887, he informed readers of the *Inland Architect* that he had for sale views of Chicago, Minneapolis, and St. Paul, the price being eighteen dollars for fifty eight-by-ten-inch unmounted photographs. The next month he announced that purchasers might select from a thousand architectural photographs from all parts of the United States. By 1892, Taylor was boasting a collection of photographs titled the ''American Architectural Photographic Series, a constantly growing collection of photographs representing the progressive architecture of American cities.'' Included in the series were some six thousand views of buildings, architectural details, interiors, park landscaping, and general street scenes from fifty cities. Twelve eight-by-ten-inch views could be purchased for six dollars.

One of Taylor's contemporaries was also of special significance in Chicago's photographic history. George R. Lawrence opened his first studio on Chicago's Sixty-third Street in 1896. He moved to a Loop studio five years later. In 1893, Lawrence began experiments to find a practical method of taking interior pictures with a photographic flash. By 1895 he had perfected the technique sufficiently to have earned the title of ''the father of flashlight photography'' from one of his biographers. This innovation had a strong impact on city photography. Practical flashlighting and hand-held cameras created the potential for portrayal of the interior dimension of urban life in home, office, and factory, which before had been difficult, if not impossible, to obtain.

By the turn of the century, Lawrence had proven his ability as a photographic innovator, including among his creations the world's largest camera, which weighed 1,400 pounds, and under the operation of fifteen men produced a negative measuring eight feet by four feet. At this point in his career he began to explore the possibilities of making aerial views. In this quest he joined countless nineteenth-century lithographers who popularized the aerial perspective with their "bird's-eye view"—photographers who sought out high buildings or points at the city's edge from which to record panoramic views. One adventuresome Boston photographer, in 1860, loaded his camera and himself into a wicker basket under a captive balloon and then, hovering in the sky, recorded the first aerial photograph of a city. Lawrence's search took him through a series of experiments with captive balloons, extension ladders, and a guy-wired telescoping tower. Eventually he achieved the capacity to make aerial photographs from as high as two thousand feet with a kite arrangement by which the cameraman never left the ground. Lawrence used his aerial equipment for many panoramic photographs in the Chicago metropolitan area. Subjects include the Stock Yards (1901), the American Derby in Washington Park (1902), the University of Chicago (1907), International Harvester Company's McCormick Works (1907), and United States Steel's Gary Works (1908).

The camera work of commercial photographers like J. W. Taylor adds later but not significantly different views of the city from those of the stereograph makers of previous decades. While the overall quality is generally better, the commercial view still features the public city, its variety and unique symbols and architecture, as well as its celebrations and calamities. If the shape of the subject matter is still the same, so too are the omissions. The poor, blacks, low-priced housing, and slums—the "other side" of the city—is seldom seen.

Lawrence's work represents the practical beginnings of a more youthful heritage. While aerial photography was not widely used until World War I, Lawrence's panoramas illustrated earlier the potentials of the view from above the metropolis. Once this giant's eye view of the city was achieved, it had immediate users, especially among urban planners. Transportation engineers employed it to establish bus routings; urban geographers found it invaluable for delimiting the functional boundaries of the metropolis; and urban ecologists utilized it to mark out the limits of the city's "natural areas." The danger, of course, was that planners would use only this over-simplified statement of the complex interrelationships taking place on the earth below and then make their city plans from this larger perspective. The necessity still existed to plan the city from the street photographer's view up rather than from an aerial abstraction looking down.

In the late 1880s, after years of experiments, an inexpensive method of reprinting photographs in books, magazines, and newspapers was developed. This reprinting capacity plus the availability of fast film, portable cameras, and later, flashlighting, made modern news photography possible. Cameramen who practiced this art went into the homes and streets of the city to record "newsworthy" events. By their nature, such photographs illustrated important urban developments, exposed dramatic occurrences, or pictured the odd and bizarre.

Chicago's visual history is far richer because of the work of the news photographer, especially in the early decades of the twentieth century. In 1960, the Chicago Historical Society acquired the *Chicago Daily News* glass negative collection, numbering over 100,000 items and covering the years between 1902 and 1934. To attempt to classify all the photographs in this collection would be impossible, but it does contain an irreplaceable visual history of the city. Real estate developments received pictorial attention as an indication of the city's growth, and major changes in the city's architecture were often recorded from ground breaking to dedication. Feature story assignments brought photographs of ethnic neighborhoods, portrayals of park usage in each season, illustrations of the newest highway and street construction, and examples of automobile congestion and inadequate parking taken as part of campaigns for new safety measures and stricter regulation.

Reform photographers also began examining the city in the 1890s. Amateurs and professionals alike realized the power of the visual image as a weapon of exposé and a tool for stirring sympathy and action. Settlement workers, investigative newspapermen, and environmental reformers all turned their cameras on the city. Their photographs showed life in slum neighborhoods and immigrant ghettoes, in many cases for the first time. Reform photographers moved into shanty-towns, dark alley dwellings, and slum rooms to capture on film the visual story of how the "other half" lived. The reformers also made their photographs into stereopticon transparencies and with a magic lantern projected them before church groups and social organizations in campaigns to win good will and financial support. Enlarged and backed with heavy pasteboard, such photographs also became the main attractions at public exhibits advocating housing reform, improved garbage collection, and other neighborhood improvements.

Chicago reform photographers have left behind a small but significant collection illustrating the life of the city's poor around the turn of the century. While reform photographs constitute a smaller number proportionately in Chicago than they do in some other cities, those which survive offer a powerful corrective for the work of those who become overly nostalgic about the conditions of life for the urban poor in the not too distant past.

Commercial photographers generally built the image of the city, recorded its achievement and diversity, and gave notice of its retail and industrial strength. News photographers went where the dramatic and hence newsworthy was occurring, and only a small part of their total work was directed toward portraying the life of the poor. Reform photographers, however, took pictures with a different perspective. Their aim was to show the worst side of the city, its grinding poverty, its foul living conditions, and its chamber-of-horrors effect on the people caught in the slums. Slums had been part of the city since its earliest days; reform photographers dramatized the conditions of those who lived there.

Chicago was examined through the viewfinder many times between 1845 and the early 1930s. The photographic record which remains has severe limitations: technology, which has minimized movement and curtailed the taking of photographs in bad weather and at night; the personal interest of the photographer, which in most cases has meant concentration on the public city, rather than on residential neighborhoods; the bias of the photographer, who may have consciously aimed his camera or "cropped" his print to produce a picture that perhaps falsely conveyed more than it recorded; and finally, the "fecklessness of historical preservation," which often, quite by accident, produces the salvaging of one photograph and the destruction of another. Within these limitations, Chicago's photographic legacy is rich. We should look to it carefully for insights into our urban heritage and keys to understanding the metropolis in our own time.

21

Embellishing a Life of Labor: An Interpretation of the Material Culture of American Working-Class Homes, 1885–1915

Lizabeth A. Cohen

Introduction

In the past two decades, American social historians, influenced partially by French proponents of the Annales school, by British economic historians such as E. P. Thompson and, in part, by American scholars such as Herbert Gutman and James Henretta, have sought to document and to comprehend the entire historical compass of working-class culture. For example, they have endeavored to widen the conventional parameters of traditional labor history (e.g., unionization, strikes, the personalities of labor leaders, political action by labor groups) to include the day-to-day experience (child-rearing, family life, social interaction with others, personal values and aspirations) of skilled and unskilled working men and women. Lizabeth Cohen is such a historian, a student of the social rather than the strictly political and occupational lives of American working people in the past. In this essay, she provides a historical understanding of "the values and social identities of workers," and she does so by examining the revealing choices made by such workers "in the process of ordering their personal environments."

Cohen's effective use of home furnishings and domestic spaces (often depicted in family albums and other forms of historical photography) is novel, in that, while social historians have pursued the elusive lives of working people, most have concentrated their research on the workplace rather than the homeplace; few have seen workers' domestic settings, and the material culture within them, as important sources. Cohen does, and along with using myriads of other evidence (popular magazines, home decoration manuals, diaries, notebooks, architectural journals, autobiographies), she has sought out what she calls "the material values'' (i.e., "preferences in the selection and arrangement of objects of material culture'') through a three-part approach to her subject.

In a careful comparative study, Cohen first traces the development of interior styles among the middle class during the period from 1885 to 1915, especially probing the ways in which aesthetic trends such as the Colonial Revival and the Arts and Crafts movement reflected middle-class attitudes. Here, her essay bears comparison with Ken Ames's article (chapter 14) on hall furnishings in Victorian America. Second, she examines efforts by reformers and institutions (especially settlement houses) to influence the tastes of workers toward these middle-class norms. Finally, Cohen analyzes working-class homes—specific rooms and their contents: kitchens, parlors, and bedrooms—in the light of workers' experiences and values and in relation to middle-class society.

Upon her quest for the historical meaning of the consumption preferences of workers, Cohen brings to bear the work of contemporary sociologists and fellow social historians and uses several techniques of material culture research. For example, she prompts us to be sensitive to the ways in which material acculturation can be traced when individuals with a largely preindustrial small-town or village background are confronted with the artifactual largesse of a mass society such as emerged in early twentieth-century America (her discussion of "parlorization" in the working-class home particularly illustrates this point). In the treatment of "spreading the middle-class message" via public relations and private promoters, the author presents a useful example of the principle of diffusion at work, wherein is woven the impact of nativism, anti-industrialism, and xenophobia as factors in this cultural process. We have a parallel instance of the similar role that advertising (whether done by individual advocates or corporate admen) plays in material culture in Ruth Schwartz Cowan's analysis (chapter 15) of the promotion of household appliances among the middle class. Finally, like a good cultural anthropologist, Cohen seeks patterns in her data—patterns of sociability and patterns of social identity.

What is the import of the patterns she finds in the material culture she has examined? We are urged to rethink one of our traditional views of immigrant and ethnic history. While workers brought distinctive cultural heritages to the selection of furnishings for their urban-American homes, Cohen finds that the visual and verbal evidence shows much less variety in material preferences than our usual concept of ethnic enclaves has lead us to expect. Rather than striking ethnic differences in domestic artifacts, Cohen finds patterns of homogenization. A common background before moving to American cities, limits to the preferred and affordable merchandise available for purchase, plus mixed ethnic worker communities, seem to have encouraged a surprisingly consistent American working-class material ethos distinctive from that of the middle class. Thus, while workers did not use their domestic material culture to distinguish themselves among themselves, they did recognize its marked difference from another social class. This difference, Cohen recognizes, has another dimension and one that *should be always remembered in artifact research; that is, people, then as now, can view the same objects with opposite perceptions. In the case of the Cohen study, we learn that, while middle-class people viewed the appearance of working-class homes and their furnishings as unsanitary, tasteless, and un-American, workers in fact felt that their new material world represented acculturation to American urban ways.*

Lizabeth Cohen's involvement with material culture data as social history evidence dates from her appointment to the Education Department staff at Old Sturbridge Village, Massachusetts. There she wrote an important essay, "Reading a Room: A Primer to the Personage Parlor," appearing in the outdoor museum village's Rural Visitor in 1975. Following her innovative work at Old Sturbridge, she took a post with Stamford-Cameron Historic House affiliated with the Oakland Museum in California. She is currently a doctoral candidate in American social history at the University of California at Berkeley. Her essay here is reprinted from the Journal of American Culture, 3:4 (Winter 1980): 752–775.

The material life of American urban workers from 1885 to 1915, as revealed in patterns of home furnishings and organizations of domestic space, provides a new way of understanding the historical development of working-class culture. While in recent years historians have pursued the often elusive lives of working people, they have almost totally ignored domestic settings, and the material culture within them, as sources. Instead, historical investigation has focused on the workplace and local community. Only a few sociologists have examined home environments for evidence of the values and social identities of workers.[1]

Historians have examined working-class homes primarily in the context of the Progressive Era housing reform movement. The keen interest that these early twentieth-century social reformers displayed in workers' home environment, however, should alert us to the significance of the home, the most private and independent world of the worker, in expressing the working-class family's social identity and interaction with middle-class culture.

Studies of the material culture of the working-class home have much to contribute to our understanding of workers' experience beyond the outlines sketched by social historians who have quantified occupations and family events such as births, marriages, and deaths. Although workers were often constrained in their household activities and consumption by low incomes and scarcity in housing options, they still made revealing choices in the process of ordering their personal environments.

This essay explores developments in the consumption preferences of urban working-class families from 1885 to 1915 and interprets ways in which these choices reflected workers' social identity. My investigation places working-class homes in the context of the material standards of the larger society in which the workers lived. Only a comparison between working-class and middle-class homes can elucidate the degree to which working-class material culture was distinctive or part of a larger cultural system.

During the period from 1885 to 1915, new people joined the ranks of the American working class as industry expanded.[2] Foreign-born workers as well as those born in America commonly shared the experience of having recently left rural, small-town settings for the urban industrial workplace. This study examines the homes both immigrant and native-born American workers made within the city environment.

I will first trace the development of interior styles among the middle class during this period, probing particularly ways in which aesthetic trends reflected middle-class social attitudes. While the middle class was by no means a clear-cut group with uniform tastes, still its trend-setters and reflectors, such as popular magazines and home-decoration advice books, articulated a consistent set of standards. Second, I will examine efforts by reformers and institutions to influence the tastes of workers toward these middle-class norms. Finally, I will analyze working-class homes in the light of workers' experiences and values and in relation to middle-class society.

Herbert Gutman urged at the close of his seminal essay on the integration of preindustrial peoples into nineteenth- and early twentieth-century America that "much remains to be learned about the transition of native and foreign-born American men and women to industrial society, and how that transition affected such persons and the society in which they entered." [3] The study of the material life of American working people as expressed in consumption patterns and the arrangement of domestic interiors may offer some new insights toward that goal. Workers who left no private written records may speak to us through the artifacts of their homes.

The Changing Look of the Middle-Class Home

American homes from the 1840s through the 1880s mirrored the nation's transformation from an agricultural to an industrial society. Just as industrialization affected people and places in the country in different ways and at various rates, so, too, homes reflected an individual's or a family's degree of integration into the industrial economy. Location, occupation, and financial status all affected the quantity and quality of consumption. The middle classes, with a status and an income often attributable to an expanded economy and the mechanized means of production, were the most enthusiastic purchasers of mass-produced objects for their homes.[4] Meanwhile, technologically advanced products were less abundant in the houses of those who lived more self-sufficient economic lives.

The home served as an accurate indicator of one's relationship to the industrial economy, not by accident, but as a result of the Victorians' contradictory attitude toward economic and technological change. Enthusiasm for, as well as anxiety toward, industrialization provoked both an appetite for new products and a need to incorporate them carefully into private life. At the same time that new kinds of objects transformed the home, the Victorians loudly proclaimed the sanctity of the family refuge in a menacing, changing world. As John Ruskin wrote:

This is the true nature of home—it is the place of peace; the shelter, not only from injury, but from all terror, doubt, and division. In so far as it is not this, it is not home; so far as the anxieties of the outer life penetrate into it, and the inconsistently-minded, unloved, or hostile society of the outer world is allowed by either husband or wife to cross the threshold, it ceases to be a home.[5]

The home embodied a contradiction as both the arena for and the refuge from technological penetration. Insofar as people could tolerate this contradictory domestic environment, the home provided a setting for gradual adaptation to a technological and commercial world.

The parlor best represented this accommodation to industrial life. As the room reserved for greeting and entertaining those beyond the family circle, the parlor permitted controlled interaction with the outside world. Similarly, a typical parlor overflowed with store-bought, mass-produced objects, carefully arranged by family members: wall-to-wall carpeting enclosed by papered and bordered walls and ceilings; upholstered furniture topped with antimacassars; shawl-draped center tables displaying carefully arranged souvenir albums and alabaster sculptures; shelves and small stands overloaded with bric-a-brac and purchased mementos. Technology made much of this decor possible: carpeting, wallpaper, and textiles were ever cheaper and more elaborate, and the invention of the spiral spring encouraged the mass distribution of upholstered furniture. Artificial covering of surfaces and structural frames thus replaced the painted walls and floors and the hardwood furniture of an earlier era.[6]

After about 1885, popular magazines, home decoration manuals, and architectural journals revealed a gradual but dramatic rejection of the cluttered spaces of the Victorian home in favor of two stylistic trends unified around a common concern for traditional American symbols. The Colonial Revival and the Arts and Crafts Movement both sought an American aesthetic to replace European-inspired and technologically sophisticated styles. In the early twentieth century, an up-to-date middle-class family almost anywhere in America most likely lived in a Colonial Revival house, perhaps along newly extended trolley lines, or in a craftsman-style bungalow, often in a recently developed housing tract.[7]

The Colonial Revival had its debut at the Philadelphia Centennial Exposition in 1876, amid the salute to American technological progress; the style reached full maturity in the 1920s, with the opening of the American Wing of the Metropolitan Museum of Art in New York and the restoration of Williamsburg.[8] Middle-class Americans encountered the Colonial Revival style more intimately, however, not at these public sites, but within their own homes and neighborhoods. Just as house construction had dominated colonial American building, the domestic setting most engaged the attention of the revival style. While for some people Colonial Revival meant "accurately" recreating early American interiors replete with spinning wheels and antique furniture, for most middle-class Americans, adoption entailed purchasing new, usually mass-produced items in the colonial style, such as a house or parlor set.

The Arts and Crafts movement, also referred to at the time as the "Craftsman" or "Mission" style, evolved concurrently with the Colonial Revival. Exteriors and interiors boasted natural materials such as wood, shingles, and greenery, exposed structural elements and surfaces, and open, flexible spaces. Elbert Hubbard's Roycraft Industries, Henry L. Wilson's Bungalow House Plan business, and similar firms popularized on a mass level the unique work of such artists as furniture-maker Gustav Stickley and architects Greene and Greene.

This Craftsman style, justified in contradictory terms, met varied pressures of the day. On the one hand, the style depended on technological innovations in heating, lighting, and window glass, and was merchandised as a solution to the household problems of dust, germs and inefficiency.[9] On the other hand, the Arts and Crafts movement invoked and sought to replicate such traditional American symbols as the farmhouse and its furnishings. In the Hingham, Massachusetts, Arts and Crafts Society, as elsewhere in the country,

bits of old needlework and embroidery were brought down from dusty attics for admiration and imitation. Chairs and tables, of exquisite design and honest purpose, took the place of flimsy and overdecorated furniture.[10]

Middle-class people's attraction to the Colonial Revival and Arts and Crafts movement corresponded to prevailing social attitudes, particularly toward workers and immigrants. Nativism, anti-industrialism, and a propensity toward environmental solutions for social problems were values incorporated into the new aesthetic. Patriotic organizations, such as the Daughters of the American Revolution and the National Society of Colonial Dames, both formed in the early 1890s, frequently encouraged the preservation of colonial artifacts and buildings. Architects and client congregations found in the Colonial Revival an appropriate architecture for Protestant churches to replace the Catholic-associated Gothic style. Founders of the Society for the Preservation of New England Antiquities blamed immigrant residents for the destruction of historical areas like Boston's North End. Outspoken xenophobes like Henry Ford, Abbott Lawrence Lowell and Henry Cabot Lodge were important patrons of the preservation and Colonial Revival movements.[11]

The Arts and Crafts style satisfied the anti-industrial instincts of many middle-class Americans. Montgomery Schuyler, organizer of an arts and crafts production studio outside Philadelphia, argued that this new style was not only wholesome, but it revived the accomplishment of the colonial craftsman, "an educated and thinking being" who loved his work without demanding a wage or labor union membership.[12] Instruction manuals for making mission furniture at home encouraged the demechanization of furniture-making. Earlier, middle-class Victorians had handled ambivalence toward industrialism by monitoring, while increasing, their interaction with industrial products within the home. Now, the next generation was employing technological advances to restrain and deny the extent to which industrialism affected private life.

Supporters of the Craftsman and Colonial Revival styles had confidence in the moral effect of this new physical environment. Stickley's *Craftsman Magazine* declared in a 1903 issue:

Luxurious surroundings . . . suggest and induce idleness. Complex forms and costly materials have an influence upon life which tells a sad story in history. On the other hand, chasteness and restraint in form, simple, but artistic materials are equally expressive of the character of the people who use them.[13] The new domestic ideal represented a search for a truly American environment; in Stickley's words, "American homes exclusively for American needs." [14]

Spreading the Middle-Class Message

Progressive Era reformers seized upon this new American domestic aesthetic, contributing to its popularity and using it to assist in their campaigns to "uplift," "modernize," and "Americanize." Though social reform efforts in this period were broad in scope, a surprising range of reformers made use of the new styles as they sought to transform people's home environments in order to promote social improvement and cultural homogeneity. Often behind their pleas for cleaner, simpler, more sanitary homes for working people lay a desire to encourage more middle-class American environments. In a twist that would have shocked any colonial farmer, the "early American look" became linked with a dust-, germ-, and disease-free scientific ideal. Reformers and associated organizations made efforts to influence workers in their homes, their neighborhoods, and their workplaces through promulgating domestic models; elsewhere, workers encountered these new middle-class style standards more indirectly.

Both public institutions and privately funded organizations conveyed the new aesthetic to working-class girls within model classrooms created for housekeeping instruction. By the 1890s, particularly in urban areas, domestic science classes in public schools promoted ideal domestic environments. Similarly, settlement houses in workers' neighborhoods fostered middle-class home standards through "Housekeeping Centers."

In a guide to planning housekeeping centers (*Housekeeping Notes: How To Furnish and Keep House in a Tenement Flat: A Series of Lessons Prepared for Use in the Association of Practical Housekeeping Centers of New York*), reformer Mabel Kittredge perfectly stated the new aesthetic. The section "Suitable Furnishing for a Model Housekeeping Flat or Home for Five People" recommended wood-stained and uncluttered furniture surfaces, iron beds with mattresses, and un-upholstered chairs. Walls must be painted, not papered; floors should be oak-stained; window seats must be built in for storage; shelves should replace bulky sideboards ("the latter being too large for an ordinary tenement room; cheap sideboards are also very ugly"); screens should provide privacy in bedrooms; a few good pictures should grace the walls, but only in the living room.[15] One settlement worker who gave domestic science instruction observed, "The purpose in our work is to help those in our classes to learn what is the true American home ideal, and then do what we can to make it possible for them to realize it for themselves." [16]

Settlement workers further promoted middle-class styles through the appearance of the house itself. Furnishing the settlement house interior became a self-conscious process for its residents. In a letter to her sister, a young Jane Addams exclaimed,

Madame Mason gave us an elegant old oak side-board . . . and we indulged in a set of heavy leather-covered chairs and a 16-foot cut oak table. Our antique oak book case and my writing desk completes it.[17]

Edith Barrows, a settlement worker in Boston's South End House, recorded in her diary, "The pretty green sitting-room with its crackling fire and gay rugs and simple early American furniture is a good setting for all that transpires. I find that it has a spiritual and, I think, almost a physical reaction in the neighborhood." [18] Settlement workers hoped that community patrons would incorporate the styles observed at the house into the furnishing of their own homes.

Industries were also involved in the business of setting standards for workers' homes through company housing, welfare programs, and the creation of domestic-like spaces in the factory. Companies sought to communicate middle-class values through housing provided for workers. Frequently, individual entrances, even in multiple or attached dwellings, sought to reinforce nuclear family privacy.[19] Interiors promoted the specialization of rooms in an effort to discourage the taking in of boarders and to enforce a middle-class pattern of living revolving around parlor, kitchen, dining room, and bedrooms.

Some companies offered employees welfare programs which also affirmed middle-class domestic standards. Amoskeag Mills's employee benefits, for example, included a textile club (established to compete with ethnic organizations) a textile school, a cooking school, and a home nursing service.[20]

Within the factory, workers were frequently treated to domestic-like environments deliberately planned along middle-class aesthetic lines. Employee lounges and lunchrooms were an innovation in the early twentieth century and frequently provided models for light, airy rooms with hardwood floors and simple furniture. Thus, McCormick Harvesting Machine Company hired a social worker to survey factories nationwide and recommend proper facilities for recreation, education, luncheon, and lounge, which they proceeded to install.[21]

In the minds of the reformers, simple, mission-style furniture and colonial objects, associated with the agrarian world of the preindustrial craftsman, seemed the obvious—and most appropriate—material arrangement for all Americans, particularly for industrial workers newly arrived from rural areas. And they tried with a vengeance to impose it.

Despite the missionary zeal of middle-class reformers, however, they did not succeed very well in communicating new standards for domestic interiors to workers. In part, they were responsible for their own failure through ineffective organizational techniques and flawed programs.[22] Yet these shortcomings notwithstanding, workers seem to have actively rejected the means and messages of the reformers.

Although working-class people patronized settlement houses, employee lounges, and other model environments, many did so on their own terms, partaking of the recreational facilities and resources without taking the social message to heart.[23]

Some working-class people did make objections known directly to the reformers. Miss Jane E. Robbin, M.D., reported that, during her first year at the College Settlement, another resident encountered a patient on a home visit who said "that she had had her breakfast, that she did not want anything, and that she did not like strange people poking around in her bureau drawer anyway." [24] Others used more tact in rejecting the attentions of reformers. A Boston settlement worker recalled response to a circulating collection of photographs of famous paintings:

South End House had a loan collection of photographs of paintings which were given to the House to use in acquainting our friends with great works of art. These were sent from tenement to tenement to stay for a period of time and then removed while others took their place. The "Holy Pictures," as all of the Madonnas were called, were always mildly welcomed, but the lack of color made them unattractive, and the "unholy" pictures were usually tucked away to await the visitor's return. Some of our earliest calls became very informal . . . when the visitor joined the whole family in a hunt, often ending by finding us all on our knees when the missing photographs were drawn from beneath the bed or bureau.[25]

More than working-class rejection of middle-class tastes, however, separated the worlds of the worker and the reformer. Workers' homes themselves hold the key to the nature and sources of their material preferences, apparently at odds with those held by the middle class. This conflict of value systems was powerfully perceived by a young participant in settlement house programs when she was faced with furnishing her own home at marriage.

We had many opportunities to talk quite naturally of some of the problems of home-making and house-furnishing [wrote Esther Barrows]. . . . The lack of plush and stuffed furniture [in our house] was a surprise to many, whose first thought would have been just that. One of our club girls who was about to be married sat down to discuss the matter in relation to her own new home. She seemed convinced by all the arguments brought forward to prove its undesirability from the point of view of hygiene and cleanliness. Months afterward she invited us to her home, much later than would have seemed natural, and as she greeted us rather fearfully she said, "Here it is, but you must remember you have had your plush days." Her small living room was overfilled by the inevitable "parlor set," while plush curtains hung at the windows and on either side of the door. The lesson learned by us from this incident was never to be forgotten.[26]

A commitment to a classless America, achievable through educational and environmental solutions to social problems, blinded settlement workers like Esther Barrows to the strength of workers' own culture. Reformers had little conception of how deeply rooted these material values were in working-class life.[27]

The Working Class Becomes "At Home" in Urban America

A lack of opportunities in both housing and neighborhood selection marked the living conditions of workers in this period. Whether home was an urban slum or a model tenement block, a mill town shack settlement or company housing, families frequently lived in substandard housing far below the quality that middle-class residents enjoyed, and had few alternative options. Furthermore, workers found themselves forced into low-rent districts separated from middle-class residential neighborhoods. Proximity to other working-class people of similar job and income status typified workers' experience more than the ethnic isolation we commonly associate with working-class life. Often, ethnic enclaves were no more than islands of a few blocks within a working-class community.[28] Limitations of housing choices, however, may have encouraged workers to value interior spaces even more.

Within these working-class neighborhoods and homes, workers expressed a distinctive set of material values. An examination of attitudes toward home ownership, space allocation within the house or flat, the covering of the structural shell (floors, walls, and windows), furniture selection, and decorative details illuminates the meanings that workers attached to the artifacts of their homes.

The view that workers should own their homes provided a rare convergence of opinion between reformers and working people, though each group advocated home ownership for different reasons. Some reformers felt that a home-owning working class would be more dependable and less revolutionary, and thus America would be "preserved" as a classless society. Others hoped that meeting mortgage payments in America might discourage immigrants from sending money home, and hence stem the tide of further immigration.[29] In short, reformers saw home ownership as a strategy for directing worker ambition along acceptable middle-class lines.

Workers, on the other hand, sought to purchase homes for reasons more consistent with their previous cultural experience than with American middle-class values.[30] In Russia, even poor Jews often had owned the rooms in which they lived.[31] Jews in many cases left Eastern Europe in response to Tsarist regulations prohibiting their ownership of property and interfering in their livelihoods as artisans, merchants, and businessmen.[32] Emigration to America was a way of resisting "peasantizing" forces for these people. Recent work on Italian immigrants has shown that they likewise came to America hoping to preserve their traditional society and to resist efforts at making them laborers.[33] They viewed a sojourn in the United States as a way of subsidizing the purchase of a home upon return to Italy.[34] Many Italians both in Europe and America sacrificed in order to leave their children a legacy of land, which supports David Riesman's theory that preindustrial families trained and encouraged their children to "succeed them" rather than to "succeed" by rising in the social system.[35] In America, owning a home allowed Italians to uphold traditional community ties by renting apartments to their relatives or paesani, and in less urban areas, to grow the fresh vegetables necessary to maintain a traditional diet.[36] Furthermore, Slavic immigrants, peasants without property in the old country, eagerly sought homes in America to satisfy longstanding ambitions.[37] Native American workers, moreover, descended from a tradition that equated private property ownership with full citizenship and promised all deserving, hard-working persons a piece of land. Thus, working-class people of many backgrounds sent mother and children to work, took in boarders, made the home a workshop, and sacrificed proper diet in order to save and buy a house, compromises too severe to substantiate some historians' claims that workers were merely pursuing upward social mobility toward middle-class goals.[38]

Once workers occupied purchased homes or rented flats, their attitudes toward the utilization of interior space diverged markedly from those of the middle class. Reformers advocated a careful allocation of domestic space to create sharp divisions between public and family interactions and to separate family members from one another within the house. Reformers often blamed working-class people for contributing to unnecessary overcrowding and violations of privacy by huddling in the kitchen, for example, while other rooms were left vacant.[39]

While the middle classes were better equipped with, and could more easily afford, housewide heating and lighting than the working classes, a difference of attitudes toward home living was more at issue. Many people from rural backgrounds were used to sharing a bedroom—and sometimes even a bed—with other family members.[40] And for those working people whose homes were also their workplaces, the middle-class thought of the home as an environment detached from the economic world was particularly inappropriate. Jewish, Irish, Italian, and Slavic women frequently took in boarders and laundry, did homework, and assisted in family stores often adjoining their living quarters. For former farmers and self-employed artisans and merchants, this integration of home and work seemed normal.[41] Among southern Italian women, doing tenement homework in groups sustained "*cortile*" (shared housekeeping) relationships endangered in the American environment of more isolated homes.[42]

The reformer ideal of the kitchen as an efficient laboratory servicing other parts of the house found little acceptance among workers. Even when workers had a parlor, they often preferred to socialize in their kitchens. Mary Antin fondly recalled frequent visits in East Boston in her married sister's kitchen, where after-dinner dishes were washed:

Frieda took out her sewing, and I took a book; and the lamp was between us, shining on the table, on the large brown roses on the wall, on the green and brown diamonds of the oil cloth on the floor . . . on the shining stove in the corner. It was such a pleasant kitchen—such a cosy, friendly room—that when Frieda and I were left alone I was perfectly happy just to sit there. Frieda had a beautiful parlor, with plush chairs and a velvet carpet and gilt picture frames; but we preferred the homely, homelike kitchen.[43]

When investigators surveyed working-class people for their housing preferences in 1920, most still rejected small kitchens or kitchenettes in favor of ones large enough for dining.[44] Workers kept their old-world hearths burning bright in their new American homes.[45]

Reformers applauded all attempts by workers to create parlors in their homes. They viewed such spaces as evidence of civilization, self-respect, and assumption of middle-class standards.[46] A home with a parlor was more likely, they felt, to instill the middle-class image of the family as an emotional, sentimental unit. Margaret Byington's investigation of Homestead workers' homes reflected this bias:

It has been said that the first evidence of the growth of the social instinct in any family is the desire to have a parlor. In Homestead this ambition has in many cases been attained. Not every family, it is true, can afford one, yet among my English-speaking acquaintances even the six families, each of whom lived in three rooms, attempted to have at least the semblance of a room devoted to sociability.[47]

Worker interest in creating parlor space at home varied, though often it correlated with occupational status. People who did little income-producing work at home, such as Jews and native-born Americans, most often established sitting rooms. Among Italians and Slavs, where men frequently had low-status jobs and women brought work into the home, the combination living room/kitchen, so similar to their European homes, survived the longest. When George Kracha left the Homestead steel mills and established his own butcher business, his home soon reflected his change in status in a way that his neighbors all recognized:

They still lived in Cherry Alley and much as they had always lived, though Elena no longer kept boarders. . . . Kracha had bought new furniture, and the room adjoining the kitchen, where the girls had slept, was now a parlor. Its chief glories were a tasseled couch, a matching chair with an ingenious footrest that slid out like a drawer from inside the chair itself, and an immense oil lamp suspended from the ceiling by gilt chains. The lampshade was made of pieces of colored glass leaded together like a church window; it seemed to fill the room and was one of the most impressive objects Cherry Lane had ever seen. On the walls were colored lithographs in elaborate gilt frames of the Holy Family and of the Virgin with a dagger through her exposed heart. Drying ribbons of Easter palm were stuck behind them. On the floor was flowered oilcloth.[48]

Kracha's adoption of a parlor, however, did not entail acceptance of middle-class modes of furnishing. Rather, his parlor presented an elaborate collage of traditional and technological symbols.

Nevertheless, reformers were not mistaken in recognizing a relationship between the presence of a parlor and some acculturation to middle-class ways. The expression of sentiment toward family and community through consumption involved in "parlorization" could indicate a favorable nod to middle-class values. For many workers, though, their usage of kitchen and parlor still respected long-established patterns of sociability. As Mary Antin's comment indicated, people with parlors did not necessarily abandon a preference for the kitchen. Likewise, workers' parlors frequently doubled as sleeping rooms at night.[49] Often when workers accommodated middle-class concepts of space in their homes, they imbued them with different social expectations. For example, Byington noted that even when a native-born American worker in Homestead had a dining room, "it did not live up to its name."

In five-room houses we find an anomaly known as the "dining room." Though a full set of dining room furniture, sideboard, table and dining chairs, are usually in evidence, they are rarely used at meals. The family sewing is frequently done there, the machine standing in the corner of the window; and sometimes, too, the ironing, to escape the heat of the kitchen; but rarely is the room used for breakfast, dinner, or supper. The kitchen is the important room of the house.[50]

Whereas the middle-class home provided a setting for a wide range of complex interactions related to work, family, and community, and therefore required distinctions between private and public space, workers conceived of home as a private realm, distinct from the public world. Because workers only invited close friends and family inside, the kitchen provided an appropriate setting for most exchange. Relationships with more distant acquaintances took place in the neighborhood—on the street or within shops, saloons, or churches. The transference of these traditional patterns of socializing from an intimate preindustrial community to the city had the impact of increasing the isolation of the working-class home. It is not surprising, therefore, that historians have noted that among many immigrant groups, the American home became a haven as it had never been in the old world.[51]

When addressing working-class people, reformers justified the new aesthetic primarily in terms of cleanliness; specifically, they promoted a simple house shell free of "dust-collecting" carpets, drapes, and wallpaper. For most working-class people, however, these decorative treatments were signs of taste and status that they hated to forsake. In almost all European rural societies, as in comparable places in America, only upper-class people had carpets and curtains.[52] Workers embraced the accessibility of these products in urban America with delight.[53] In her autobiography, Mary Antin significantly remarked, "We had *achieved* a carpet since Chelsea days."[54] Given alien and institutional-looking housing facades, curtained windows were often a family's only way to make a personal statement to the world passing by.[55] Wallpaper—the worst demon of all to reformers—was for workers a privilege possible with prosperity and a relief from otherwise dull home walls. The behavior of one family occupying company housing which prohibited wallpaper near U.S. Steel's Gary, Indiana, plant spoke for many others;

"If you'll give us the colors we want, Sophie will do the painting herself." This, broken up into foreign-sounding English, ended the parley with the company decorator. . . . And in the "box" occupied by her family, she had her way. Outside, it remained like all the rest in the row, but indoors, with stencil designs, such as she had learned to make at school, she painted the walls with borders at the top and panels running down to the floor.[56]

This young girl replicated in paint the borders and backgrounds of wallpaper design; though learned in school, this longstanding form of rural folk art satisfied the aesthetic tastes and status needs of her family.

Workers' selection of furniture perhaps best demonstrates their struggle to satisfy both traditional and new expectations with products available on the mass market. The middle-class preference for colonial-inspired, natural wood furniture, built-ins, and antiseptic iron bedsteads satisfied neither of these needs.

As indicated earlier by Mabel Kittredge's despair in her *Housekeeping Notes* at "cheap" and "ugly" sideboards, workers valued case pieces like bureaus, chiffoniers, and buffets. This preference evolved out of a long tradition of dowry chests and precious wardrobes, often the only substantial furniture in rural homes. Workers, however, did not necessarily consider their acquisition of such furnishings in urban America a conscious perpetuation of traditional material values. An uncomprehending settlement worker noted that

There were the Dipskis, who displayed a buffet among other new possessions, and on the top of it rested a large cut-glass punch bowl. Mrs. Dipski said proudly, "And so I become American," as she waved her hand toward the huge piece of furniture, which took an inordinately large place in her small room.[57]

While reformers counseled against unhealthy wood bed frames as vermin-infested and expensive, featherbedding for causing overheating of the body, and fancy linens as unsanitary, working-class people sought to bring all three items into their homes.[58] Byington found a "high puffy bed with one feather tick to sleep on and another to cover" typical of native American homes in Homestead.[59] An observer in Lawrence, Massachusetts, in 1912 described the interior of an Italian millworker's home as boasting "pleasant vistas of spotless beds rising high to enormous heights and crowned with crochet-edged pillows." [60]

Immigrants carried featherbedding with them on the long trek to America more frequently than any other single item.[61] Antin recalled her Russian neighbor's warnings before the family departed for the United States:

"In America they sleep on hard mattresses, even in winter. Haveh Mirel, Yachne the dressmaker's daughter, who emigrated to New York two years ago, wrote her mother that she got up from childbed with sore sides, because she had no featherbed." [62]

Jews, Italians, Slavs, and most other groups shared a native experience which prized featherbedding and viewed "the bed"—unveiled at marriage—as an emotional symbol of future family happiness.[63] The bed was the dominant feature of most peasant homes, often overpowering all other furniture, which usually was very minimal. Elizabeth Hasonovitz nostalgically remembered her mother in Russia, "bending over a boxful of goose feathers, separating the down, preparing pillows for her daughters' future homes." [64] Italian marriage rituals prescribed that the bride's trousseau would provide hand-sewn, heavily embroidered linens along with the marital bed. Pride often produced beds so high that a stool was needed to climb into them.[65] At least for Italians, the bed played a part in the rituals of death, as well. While in Italian villages an elaborate funeral bed commonly was carried into the public square, in America, Italian families laid out their dead ceremoniously at home.[66] The embellished bed, then, was an important family symbol of birth, marriage, and death, not an object to abandon easily.

We have seen throughout this essay that workers' homes were crowded with plush, upholstered furniture, a taste which may have emerged out of valuing fluffy, elaborately decorated beds. As the parlor appeared on the home scene, workers brought traditional bed-associated standards to their newly acquired and prized possessions. Well aware of this working-class market for Victorian-style furniture, Grand Rapids furniture factories produced their cheapest lines in styles no longer fashionable among middle-class consumers.[67]

Since domestic reformers were promoting a simpler aesthetic at the turn of the century, they denounced workers' taste for ornamentation. Photographs of working-class homes nevertheless reveal the persistence of abundant images on the walls (if only cheap prints, torn-out magazine illustrations, and free merchant calendars, objects on tabletops, and layering in fabric and fancy paper of surface areas such as mantels, furniture, and cabinet shelves.

The fabric valance which appears in almost every photograph of a working-class interior demonstrates how a traditional symbol took on new applications in the American environment of industrial textile manufacture. In cultures such as the Italian, for example, where people treasured the elaborate bed, they adorned it with as much decorative detailing as possible. In fact, it was often the only object warranting such art and expense in the home. A visitor to Sicily in 1905 shared with his travelogue readers a peek into a typical home, where

you are greeted by a bed, good enough for a person with a thousand a year, of full double width, with ends of handsomely carved walnut wood or massive brass. The counterpane, which sweeps down to the floor, is either hand-knitted, of enormous weight, or made of strips of linen joined together with valuable lace, over which is thrown the yellow quilt so handy for decoration. The show pillows are even finer, being smaller.[68]

Under this spread, women fastened a piece of embroidered linen in a deep frill to cover any part of the bed's frame that might show. Even when families could afford attractive, wood-frame bedsteads, they still used this "*turnialettu*," or valance, its original purpose forgotten.[69] In America, where fabric was cheap, the valance of gathered fabric found even more applications, adorning every possible surface and exposed area; in the 1930s Phyllis Williams even discovered valances over washing machines in second-generation Italian-American homes.[70] Fabric was draped and decoratively placed in a multitude of other ways, as well. A French-Canadian woman who ran a boardinghouse for shoe-factory workers in Lynn thus adorned the inexpensive craftsman-style Morris chairs in her cluttered parlor with "inappropriate" antimacassars, an affront to any Arts and Crafts devotee.

While workers brought distinctive cultural heritages to bear on the furnishing of their urban-American homes, much less variety in material preferences resulted than one might have expected. Common preindustrial small-town experience, limits to the preferred and affordable merchandise available for purchase, and mixed ethnic worker communities seem to have encouraged a surprisingly consistent American working-class material ethos that was distinct from that of the middle class. The speed with which a particular working-class family forged a material transition to industrial life depended on numerous factors, among them the intent and length of the family's stay in urban America, prior economic and social experience, and financial resources.

Once workers achieved a certain basic level of economic stability, their homes began to reflect this distinctive material ethos. While working-class people at the time may not have viewed their choices in reified terms, their set of preferences seems not arbitrary but a recurrent, symbolic pattern; not a simple emulation of middle-class Victorian standards with a time lag due to delayed prosperity, but rather a creative compromise forged in making a transition between two very different social and economic worlds. This working-class ethos of material values, inspired by rural values and reinforced within the urban neighborhood, departed in almost every way from aesthetics favored by the middle class and promoted by the domestic reformers. Ironically, while middle-class people viewed the appearance of working-class homes as unsanitary, tasteless, and un-American, workers in fact felt that their new material world represented acculturation to American urban ways. Through the purchase of mass-produced objects, they struggled to come to terms with this industrial society.

Material acculturation occurred as an individual or a family made peace between traditional and new-world needs. While many workers must have realized that their home decor differed from the styles promoted by the middle class, they still felt that they had adapted to their new environment and had advanced far beyond their former conditions. While the middle-class person and the reformer could not see it, the working-class home steeped in comfort and covers stood as a symbol of being at home in industrial America.

At the turn of the century, the homes of both the middle class and the working class reflected the transitions in their respective social experience. On the one hand, middle-class people rejected Victorian decor for a simpler, more "American" aesthetic, which they tried to impose on workers. On the other hand, the working class found in the ornate Victorian furnishing style an appropriate transition to industrial life. The "Victorian solution" was not an inevitable stage that working people had to pass through, but a circumstance of needs finding available products. Furniture in the Victorian style persisted even as the Colonial Revival and Arts and

Crafts movements dominated middle-class tastes. The old style well suited workers' rural-based material values, while satisfying their desire to adapt to mass-produced goods, just as it had served for the middle class several generations earlier. The contrast in middle-class and working-class tastes in this period suggests that working-class culture indeed had an integrity of its own.

Further historical research may explain the recent findings of sociologists studying contemporary working-class material life. Lee Rainwater and David Coplovitz, for example, have discovered distinctive patterns in working-class domestic values: a preference for plush and new furnishings over used ones; a taste for modern products, such as appliances; the valuing of the interior over the exterior appearance of the house; and a common conception of home as a private haven for the working-class family.[71] While these sociologists do not attempt to explain the historical development of material choices, connections to workers' homes in the period from 1885 to 1915 are striking and warrant investigation.

The decades discussed in this essay, when waves of new workers were integrated into an expanding industrial society, may have served as the formative stage for the development of a working-class culture. We have seen how the transitional interior created by workers during this period, as they adjusted to twentieth-century American life, satisfied some ambivalence toward the urban, industrial world. Within this material compromise, traditional cultural values and new consumer benefits could coexist. If workers' homes throughout the twentieth century continued to reflect the attributes of this initial transition, as Rainwater's and Coplovitz's studies tentatively suggest, we may have evidence that contradictions still lie at the core of the American working-class identity. Workers may have reified and passed down this transitional style, or a contradictory attitude toward industrial society may continue to inform their domestic selections. In either case, working-class material values have emerged through both resistance and adaptation to the social environment and have remained distinct from those of the middle class. The chief legacy of this contradiction may be a worker population that, on the one hand, boasts a unique and discernible material culture; and, on the other hand, does not identify itself forthrightly as a working class.

22

Immaterial Material Culture:
The Implications of
Experimental Research for Folklife Museums

Jay A. Anderson

Introduction

A criticism frequently made of historians by natural and physical scientists is that the historical method falters when investigators of the past seek to replicate the actual events of the past with any degree of controlled observation and scientific precision. Jay Anderson and a small cadre of other material culture researchers in fields such as folklife, historical archaeology, vernacular building, and the history of technology have challenged this assumption in both theory and practice. Anderson, a folklife scholar with particular training and research interests in American foodways, describes here an approach to artifactual data variously called "imitative archaelogy," "experimental ethnography," or, most commonly, "experimental archaeology."

Following the example of European folk museum research programs such as the Lejre Historical-Archaeological Research Center in Denmark and the Butser Hill Project in Hampshire (England), American experimental archaeologists have usually had two principal objectives: first, to devise methods of testing theories of past cultural behavior, especially technological processes involving the use of tools; and second, to obtain data not readily available from more traditional artifact analyses and historical sources. Robert Coles, an archaeologist extensively quoted by Anderson, has outlined what implementing this twofold research strategy has meant in practice: analyzing the scope of the experiment beforehand, thereby keeping the number of variable factors to a minimum; using only historically accurate materials and methods; limiting modern technology so as not

*to interfere with the experiment's results; documenting the process carefully
enough so that it could be repeated later by another researcher; improvising new
methods if feasible; assessing the experiment in terms of its reliability; and never
claiming absolute proof, just the degree of probability that the process is indeed
historically accurate. In America, such experimentation has been applied to a wide
variety of material culture data: seventeenth-century beer-brewing methods,
eighteenth-century plant and animal husbandry; and nineteenth-century farming
practices and technological efficiency. The laboratories for these experiments have
usually been folk museums and living history farms where, Anderson maintains, a
major purpose is to understand fully the material collections of museums and other
repositories and then communicate that knowledge to scholars and to museum
visitors.*

*In accomplishing this task, experimental archaeologists tend to emphasize an
environmentalist or functionalist approach to material culture. Anderson, however,
makes strong claims for the humanistic dimensions of this technique, an approach
which he considers a combination of "the methods of historic and scientific
research." For example, he argues that in addition to "correcting our perception
of the past, experimental archaeology can also teach us much about contemporary
post-industrial cultural behavior and the mental and physical distance we have put
between our forefathers and ourselves." By citing examples from sites such as
Plimoth Plantation (Massachusetts) and Living History Farms (Iowa), where he
has previously worked, he suggests that such institutions, when engaged in
experimental archaeology, act not only as "repositories for the material culture of the
past but also as catalysts for questioning one's own culture." Museums employing
experimental archaeology "have the potential to become powerful mediums for
encouraging in visitors the habit of disciplined self-analysis."*

*Jay Anderson, currently a professor of folklore and folklife at Western
Kentucky University, first presented this essay at a meeting of the American
Folklore Society; later it was published in Keystone Folklore 21 (1976–1977):
1–11, from which it is reprinted here. In addition to his interest in folklife
museums as material culture evidence, as seen in "Outdoor Museums as Popular
Culture" in Twentieth-Century Popular Culture in Museums, Archives and
Libraries, edited by F. Schroeder (Bowling Green, Ohio: Bowling Green
University Press, 1981), his major research has been on American foodways,
promulgated in articles such as "Ethnic Foodways and Diet" in the Harvard
Encyclopedia of American Ethnic Groups, edited by Stephan Thernstorm
(Cambridge, Mass.: Harvard University Press, 1980); "An Introduction to
Kentucky Foodways" in Kentucky Hospitality, edited by D. C. Cooper
(Lexington, Ky.: University of Kentucky Press, 1976); with James Deetz, "The
Ethnogastronomy of Thanksgiving," Saturday Review (December 1972); and
"Scholarship on Contemporary American Folk Foodways," Ethnologia Europaea
5 (1971).*

Folklife museums and centers are playing an increasing role in preserving and interpreting our nation's cultural history.[1] Colonial Williamsburg, Old Sturbridge Village, Mystic Seaport, and Greenfield Village, for example, host millions of visitors annually and have become significant tourist attractions and educational centers serving both a national and regional audience. In addition to these four giants, there are at least 3,500 smaller regional cultural history museums in operation.[2] A good number of these, such as Plimoth Plantation, the Farmers' Museum in Cooperstown, New York, and Living History Farms in Des Moines, Iowa, number their visitors and students in the hundreds of thousands. Many Americans are looking to museums, especially open-air folklife museums like these, for their images of how their counterparts once lived.[3] Visitors, it seems, have accepted Henry Ford's dictum: "By looking at things people used and that show the way they lived, a better and truer impression can be gained than could be had in a month of reading." [4]

Unfortunately, the images presented at many museums are bowdlerized, with an emphasis on elitist culture.[5] Critics of cultural history museums, frequently museum professionals themselves, clearly understand this fault and the need for greater accuracy in research and interpretation.[6] They have identified many of the problems that inhibit a realistic presentation of the realities of life in the past, especially the failure to understand fully and to communicate the cultural contexts within which historical artifacts—Henry Ford's "things"—functioned. Since museums are essentially institutions which collect "things" and make sense of them to visitors, this is strong criticism indeed.[7] Without an appreciation for the cultural frame of reference of artifacts, a museum's material culture becomes for visitors and students alike simply "immaterial," lacking significant relevance to serve as a bridge to better relate past and present realities. Central questions that must be asked of any artifact—milk dish or hoe, long house or barn—are too frequently ignored or glossed over: How was this used? What process was it a part of? Was it valued? How can it be exhibited so as to reasonably convey an impression of the setting and system in which this object lived?

The subject of this paper is a method of material culture research and interpretation which should, if used carefully, help answer more successfully these crucial questions. This method is now generally called "experimental archaeology," although the more inclusive designation "experimental ethnography" perhaps describes it more accurately.[8]

Initially, experimental archaeology was developed as a means of practically testing theories of past cultural behavior, especially technological processes involving the use of tools, and obtaining data not readily available from more traditional artifactual analysis and historical sources. The resulting data could then be used to formulate new theories about historic economic and sociocultural systems. Because the researcher sought to "imitate" or "replicate" the original process as nearly as possible, the method has also been called "imitative" archaeology or ethnography. Folklorists and folklife researchers familiar with Kenneth Goldstein's induced natural context will readily note the similarity between the two methods. Goldstein, working with living cultures, suggests the induction of a natural context in which a true folkloric performance could be sustained and studied,[9] while experimental ethnographers seek to recreate a reasonable facsimile of a limited historical milieu and then use it as a historic laboratory for carrying out circumscribed experiments. The goals of theory testing and data generation are the same for both methods.

The history of experimental archaeology has been summarized by Robert Asher and elaborated by John Coles.[10] Examples described by Asher and Coles include imitative experiments with prehistoric and historic forest clearing, crop planting, harvesting and storage, ploughing, cooking, house building and usage (including natural and accidental destruction), construction of earthworks and roads, boat building and voyaging, stone and woodworking, manufacturing of weapons and musical instruments, antler craft, metal processing, leather and textile production, pottery, paint, paper manufacture, and animal and plant breeding. Given its due is the most spectacular and publicized experiment to date, the Kon Tiki expedition, in which Thor Heyerdahl sought to prove that people could have sailed the 4,000 miles between South America and the Polynesian Islands, transplanting themselves and their culture before 1100 A.D.[11] Heyerdahl did not claim that they actually *did* make the voyage, he only proposed to generate new data that could prove that such a voyage was feasible and therefore must be considered as evidence in all further considerations of the cultural history of the Pacific and South America. His experiment attained its goal. Many other experimental research projects, more modest in scope, have contributed similarly useful data on theories relating to past cultural behavior.

Asher and Coles, after evaluating a number of such projects, suggest a series of procedural rules applicable to all experiments that will aid the scholar in achieving valid data. For example, Coles reviews eight basic rules that he notes are "observed in most experiments, although they may be unacknowledged as such, because they are basically common sense." [12] These include analyzing the scope of the experiment beforehand, thereby keeping the number of variable factors to a minimum; using only historically accurate materials and methods; limiting modern technology so as not to interfere with the experiment's results; documenting the process carefully enough so that it could be repeated later by another researcher; improvising new methods if feasible; assessing the experiment in terms of its reliability; and never claiming absolute proof, just the degree of probability that the process is indeed historically accurate. For as Coles cautions, experimental archaeology or ethnography does not prove anything. It is "a tool by which some of the basic economic activities of ancient man, those concerned with subsistence and technology, can be assessed for their development and competence." [13]

Recently, many of the most innovative experimental research projects have been undertaken at European folklife museums by research educational and folk museum staff people. Two, especially, are worth careful regard: the Lejre Historical-Archaeological Research and Educational Center, 30 miles west of Copenhagen, Denmark, and the Butser Hill project, near Petersfield, Hampshire, about 75 miles southwest of London.

Lejre, the world's first center for experimental archaeology and ethnography, has since 1964 been the setting for a wide variety of extremely careful experiments in preindustrial Danish technology and folklife. Under the direction of Has-Ole Hansen, the center's staff has sought to "reinvent and perpetuate" traditional processes using accurate reproductions of historic material culture. They have been conducting tests with upright warp-weighted looms, textiles, and tailoring, pottery making, pit and kiln baked earthenware, bog iron smelting and forging, neolithic and medieval housing and usage, animal and plant breeding, slash-and-burn agriculture, ploughing and field preparing, food processing, preservation and storage, tool construction, saddle and horse gear, and household and domestic activities. Hansen is cautious when making claims about the ultimate significance of experimental research, and he prefers to say that its chief value is in augmenting archaeological and anthropological sources by testing theories suggested by them. But he also notes its educational potential: "The idea behind this work is that besides yielding valuable experimental information, these reconstructions have great value for modern man's impression of the living environments in which his ancestors should be imagined as living in through the ages." [14] Hansen warns that the method's usefulness as an interpretive medium can easily be undermined if the results of the experiments are not arrived at scientifically and are not capable of being verified through duplicate tests. Recently, experimentation at Lejre has included tests not only of neolithic Danish culture, but of medieval and recent peasant economic systems, for example, flax production and linen processing and the interior arrangements and working of seventeenth-, eighteenth- and nineteenth-century farmhouses. The high standard of previous experimentation has been maintained for these studies in historic archaeology despite increasing pressure to exploit the center more fully for large numbers of tourists and students interested in Danish folklife.

The Butser Hill Project, under the direction of Peter Reynolds, a classical scholar and archaeologist, has been sponsored since 1964 by the Ancient Agriculture Research Committee of the British Association and the Council for British Archaeology. Located in a 525-acre county park, it is divided into two sites: a 57-acre Iron Age farm serves as a historic laboratory for experimental research and a smaller, similar farm nearby is open to students and the general public as an open-air museum. On the basis of experiments by Reynolds and his staff on the folklife of Roman Britain, new theories have been postulated on neolithic population, settlement patterns, land use, agriculture, food storage, vernacular architecture, and other aspects of culture. Many of these suppositions, quietly advanced in *Farming in the Iron Age* conflict with the popular stereotypes of pre-medieval England. [15] For example, because of new data yielded by experiments with plows and wicker caches, Reynolds suggests that far more land was under cultivation far earlier, that grain storage pits had been perfected to preserve the additional wheat, oats, barley and vetches grown, that the rural population was considerably larger than previously believed, and that the Romans invaded Britain because it was a potential breadbasket for their empire. Such theorizing on the basis of experimental research and the reevaluation of historical sources is forcing a complete reconsideration of British folklife and cultural history. Reynolds, like Hansen, is cautious: "Perhaps the story of Iron Age farming as told in this book [*Farming in the Iron Age*] is almost right, perhaps it is largely wrong. As more excavations take place and more evidence is discovered we shall need to revise the story in places. In ten years' time we may even have to rewrite the whole story." [16]

Reynolds and his colleagues have not had the level of financial support that would allow them to follow Lejre's lead and undertake research on more recent folklife problems, such as medieval and post-medieval heavy plows or grain yields before and after the introduction of the eighteenth-century crop rotation systems. Assistance may come in the near future when the British public realizes the educational and symbolic value of the project to the nation. As Keith Spence pointed out in a *Country Life* article:

When Butser gets under way, its combination of accessibility and technical interest should give vast number of people an entirely new idea of what "Ancient Britain" was really like. When Julius Caesar sailed across the Channel in 55 B.C. he was not confronted merely by parties of capering woad-painted savages. The Celtic farmers of the Iron Ages were skilled operators, admittedly not concentered in towns, but with farming techniques of a high order. And the crowds who will flock to Butser from the cities at weekends will, perhaps subconsciously, feel a kinship with their ancestors who tilled the chalk downs 2,000 years ago. [17]

The pioneering work being done by Hansen and Reynolds has been paralleled in America by Errett Callahan of the Department of Anthropology, Virginia Commonwealth University. His *The Old Rag Report: A Practical Guide to Living Archaeology* (1973), *Experimental Archaeological Papers (APE)* (1974), *Living Archaeology: Projects in Subsistence Living* (1975), and three volumes of *Living Archaeology Newsletter* (1973–1975) constitute the most thorough introduction in English to the potential of experimental projects and the problems of implementing research programs. [18] Callahan's recommendations are based on his experience directing three projects, each consisting of a variety of specific experiments with tool manufacture, architecture, foodways, and daily living. Callahan summarized his approach in 1975:

There exists in archaeology the problems of interpreting the archaeological record. This record consists for the most part of artifacts, objects used by people for obtaining and/or maintaining their cultural and/or biological objectives. An artifact would therefore seem to reflect at least a part of a person's behavior in response to a need. . . . With the advent of W. W. Taylor's treatise, "A Study of Archaeology" in 1948, archaeologists began looking at the archaeological record in a newer and more comprehensive light than before. This new outlook, the "new archaeology" as it has come to be known, called for more creative and comprehensive ways of viewing the archaeological record. . . . Foremost among the objectives of the new trend was the need to view archaeological sites and components as wholes, as interacting systems and subsystems, rather than as isolated islands of culture. . . . It is our contention that only by recreating as closely as we are able, the original environmental and behavioral conditions, can we reduce the skewing of data to a minimum. Of course we will never be able to recreate *exactly* all facets of a tool's creation and utilization or of a people's life-style because of non-evident cultural influences that have vanished without a trace. We may be able to reconstruct prehistorical political, religious, or social behavior with much accuracy in most cases. . . . This recreation is no less than essential to the accurate interpretation of the archaeological record. Such a recreation is a major aim of subsistence projects in experimental archaeology.[19]

So far, there is no American counterpart of Lejre, where extensive research of the standard achieved by Hansen, Reynolds, and Callahan could be carried out and interpreted to the general public. Experimental research has been carried out and interpreted at a number of open air museums, notably Plimoth Plantation in Plymouth, Massachusetts, and the Colonial Pennsylvania Plantation outside Philadelphia. At Plimoth, Roger Welsch and I conducted a limited experiment in traditional brewing in the spring of 1972 before and after the folk museum opened to the public. We were able to thereby first use the folk museum as an accurate historic laboratory and then, once our experiments were completed, to interpret folk brewing utensils and processes to interested visitors.[20] Later in 1972, I undertook a series of experiments in Plimoth on food procurement, processing a preparation following the basic rules which Coles would be recommending the following year.[21] Similar tests were also instituted at the Colonial Pennsylvania Plantation from 1974 to 1976. Supervised by the Plantation research director, Don Callender, Jr., these experiments included the traditional reconstruction and use of a spring house, eighteenth-century farming, monitoring of trash pits and energy used in agricultural activities, such as rail splitting and hoe weeding, and the building and functioning of a 1770s wooden mold board plow.[22] These experiments at Plimoth and the Colonial Pennsylvania Plantation confirmed for those involved the conclusion already reached in Europe: folk museums need to develop experimental research projects to understand fully the original functions of the collections and to communicate accurately to visitors historic environmental contexts and technological processes. The basic research and general interpretive potential of the method for American institutions was recommended at the symposium, "Experimental Research and Living History," held in Philadelphia, January 1976, as part of the annual meeting of the Society for Historic Archaeology.

Since then, four other reasons for embarking on experimental projects have come into mind. Experimental research, in addition to correcting our picture of the past (as Reynolds' work at Butser Hill has shown), can also teach us much about contemporary post-industrial cultural behavior and the mental and physical distance we have put between our forebears and ourselves. This lesson was brought home to Roger Welsch and me during our brewing experiments at Plimoth Plantation in

1972. We had anticipated that living and working in an early-seventeenth-century village would be enlightening, and it was. What we had not expected was the stupifying effects of being confined within the narrow, drab (to us) village in a small one-room hut for even a short period of time.[23] After a week of sleeping on an itchy straw-filled mattress, of being chilled to the marrow by damp nor'easters off Cape Cod Bay, and of unremitting physical work punctuated by meals of boiled salt fish and sour beer, we were worn down in body and mind. It was obvious that neither of us were prepared either mentally or physically for seventeenth-century colonial living. Our conversations turned increasingly from the brewing experiments we had undertaken to how the realities of life had changed in 350 years.

Exactly the same point was made by Errett Callahan's students in 1974. Cut off from all twentieth-century contact, they found that the sudden comparison of prehistoric mid-Atlantic Woodland Indian life with their own modern one heightened their own cultural self-consciousness, often raising more questions about folklife than giving answers about precontact Indian cultures. Obviously, open-air folklife museums can serve not only as repositories for the material culture of the past but also as catalysts for questioning one's own culture. They have the potential to become powerful mediums for encouraging in visitors the habit of disciplined cultural self-analysis. Too often folklorists are rightfully accused of being at best antiquarians interested in "folksy" survivals, of living in the never-never land of the "good old days," and beckoning visitors to folk museums to leave the cares of the modern world behind and stroll into a simpler, quieter past. Experimental research projects can help us re-evaluate the validity of our knowledge of the folklife of particular regions and periods through personal experience and use this experience as a stimulus to question the assumptions of our modern culture today and in the future. The folk museum can and should become an effective medium for humanistic education.

Another value of experimental research is to help us evaluate our own ethnographic methods. For example, Roger Welsch and I had both done extensive work on folk brewing processes before we conducted our experimental research at Plimoth. We felt we had a clear idea of the technology involved in making small beer in Jacobean England and early New England. Only when we actually tried to simulate these processes in an accurate historic context did we realize the extent of our (and other scholars') ignorance. In even the best of recipes from primary sources, basic steps were omitted. Experimental research with historic technological processes rapidly indicated the data that cannot be obtained from the traditional written material and oral sources. Fortunately, it is precisely this kind of data that experimentation generates. However, Hansen cautions,

It is imperative that every single experiment should be observed and recorded to such a degree that it is possible for another researcher, without performing an extensive trial series, to use these results as a foundation for further research. . . . The need for the detailed recording of work processes might be surprising to some people: "But can't these work processes be obtained through still living traditions?'' The answer, unfortunately, is no. Very little of the information in ethnographical studies is sufficiently detailed to be used as work descriptions and as the basis for initiation of the work. Therefore, every notation about an almost extinct work process, a disappearing house-building technique, and other preindustrial skills, should be recorded from the viewpoint of the possibility of future imitation. . . . Imitative experiments may make an essential contribution to general anthropological research: the development of a way [of] describing [how] the work process [must be done] so that the process could be repeated not only by the observer but also by someone unfamiliar with the original work.[24]

A third reason for beginning an experimental program in a folk museum is the method's educational value. It can be an effective means of teaching how history's artifacts were once used. For example, once the researcher has carried out a series of experiments with natural dyes and rediscovers the materials and processes which give a duplicate of the color found in a piece of historic cloth, the experiment could be demonstrated for students, allowing them to encounter the same problems, account for the same variables, and arrive at the same conclusion. The goal of this exercise would be to allow the students to learn by experience not only the principles behind a historic process but also the methods of historic and scientific research. The emphasis is on historiography as well as history. The strength of this approach is obvious. The point of view taken is a questioning, modest one: What don't we know about the work and the lives of our ancestors? How shall we find out? Learning to answer questions by step-by-step experimentation is recognized by educational psychologists as one of the best ways to master and retain material. The practice can be carried over into other disciplines and real life situations. Such learning is experimental. It involves all the senses and leaves a deeper impression on the memory. By rediscovering how to make a simple tool, such as a broom, by trial and error following a sketchy word description gleaned from an oral history source or old ''receipt'' book, will have a deeper effect on the student than watching a documentary film or reading a Foxfire-like description of the craft.

Finally, experimental research may help to create what Alvin Toffler calls ''enclaves of the past,'' specialized centers of living which will ''increase the chances that someone will be there to pick up the pieces in case of massive calamity.'' He writes that

Such communities not only should not be derided, they should be subsidized by the larger society as a form of mental and social insurance. In times of extremely rapid change, it is possible for the larger society to make some irreversible, catastrophic error. Imagine, for instance, the widespread diffusion a food additive that accidentally turns out to have Thalidomide-like effects. One can conceive of accidents capable of sterilizing or even killing a whole population.[25]

For example, at Living History Farms, Iowa's open air agricultural museum, we face this challenge daily. Here, outside Des Moines on a 550-acre tract bounded by interstate highways, industrial parks, and suburban developments, we are recreating two accurate central Iowa farmsteads, circa 1840 and 1900. These "historic laboratories" serve as the setting for many of the experiments and educational programs described in the paper. However, we are also developing a "farm of the future," embodying many of the brightest new ideas from the various agricultural colleges at nearby Iowa State University. Our prototype, as well as many of the ideas underlying it, relies on the expectation of a continued supply of inexpensive energy. We naturally worry about a Toffleresque catastrophe, possibly a sudden elimination of conventional energy sources before newer reservoirs (solar, thermal, and wind) are rendered easily usable for farming. Perhaps the "farm of the future" will draw more heavily on our 1840s subsistence homestead with its twelve acres worked intensively and our 1900s farm with its root cellar, storage cave, and windmill than we had previously planned.

In conclusion, experimental archaeology or ethnography has already played an important research and educational role in European folklife museums and historical centers. Its potential as a supplement to other more conventional research has already been demonstrated. Some parallel work has been undertaken in America with modest success. I hope folklife researchers in this country will examine more carefully the experience of European and American scholars and museum professionals using this method and consider initiating pilot programs in folk museums and living history centers here with a goal of developing their potential as historic laboratories. The study and interpretation of material culture can, using experimental techniques, have a very "material" effect on our society and culture. There will be problems,[26] but the potential results certainly justify the effort.

23

In Praise of Archaeology: Le Projet du Garbage

William L. Rathje

Introduction

Ethnoarchaeologists like William Rathje take very seriously the truth behind the old saw "What you eat is what you are." Actually, Rathje would paraphrase that formula to read "What you have not eaten, but have thrown away, is what you are." Archaeological investigations of prehistorical and historical excavations of trash pits, dumps, privies, and other midden sites have long recognized the value of garbage as material culture evidence. In a novel research project, Rathje, along with colleagues and students at the University of Arizona, applied the theories and methods of this branch of traditional archaeological research to a modern context; that is, to quantifiable refuse collected in selected household units in Tucson, Arizona, over a three-year period (1973–1976).

Beginning with the premise that "material culture is not merely a reflection of human behavior, [but] material culture is a part of human behavior," Rathje argues that researchers need to probe those critical "points where theories of how people will act and how material culture will work give way to real events—observable interactions between people and things." The commonplace and usually unobserved interaction between people and their foodstuffs, particularly their behavior when discarding such food as waste, is one such critical nexus deserving careful material culture study.

Rathje's own pilot study, which follows, is particularly sensitive to the problems of bias in historical data of all types. Previous research (traditional social science interview-survey techniques) on the relation of food waste to price inflation has yielded the conclusion that such interview responses are always subject to questions concerning whether they represent what people do, what they think they do, or what they want an interviewer to think they do. Faced with such

316

*methodological difficulties, Rathje decided to investigate the garbage, "the
quantifiable result of what people actually did."*

*Quantification figures prominently in this project report, not only in
percentages of "straight waste" and "plate scrapings" that the research team
formulated but also in statistical data extracted from census tracts, price indexes,
and governmental bureau reports. In his advocacy of securing a statistically
significant data sample in any form of social science material culture study,
Rathje's work parallels similar claims by James Deetz, Edwin Dethlefsen, Henry
Glassie, and Bruce A. Lohof. As will be seen, his interest in using modern
material culture studies in ongoing, contemporary communities to test
archaeological theories (such as the concept of "stress") and models (such as the
concept of "efficiency") developed by archaeologists working on earlier societies
supports the related claims that Robert Ascher will make for "tin-can
archaeology" in chapter twenty-four. Finally, much like Jay Anderson's hope for
experimental archaeology's possible contribution to agrarian America's quest for
an inexpensive energy source, Rathje hopes that his research will have an impact
on responsible social scientists and government planners as well as the general
populace who can learn about their behavior by the things they have thrown away.
While Rathje does not demand this course of all who investigate American
artifacts, he does argue that "modern material culture studies can provide unique
perspectives into the nature of our own society which can make the techniques and
theories of archaeology immediately useful."*

*In addition to this report, which originally appeared as "Le Projet du
Garbage," in Historical Archaeology and the Importance of Material Things,
edited by Leland Ferguson (Columbia, S.C.: Society for Historical Archaeology,
1977), pp. 36–42, William L. Rathje has also written "The Garbage Project: A
New Way of Looking at the Problems of Archaeology," Archaeology 27 (1974):
236–241. He has coauthored, with W. W. Hughes, "The Garbage Project as a
Nonreactive Approach: Garbage In . . . Garbage Out?" in Manpower Research
and Advisory Services, Technical Report 2 (Washington, D.C.: Smithsonian
Institution, 1975): 151–167. Rathje teaches in the Department of Anthropology
at the University of Arizona.*

Since man first met the pebble tool, his own creations have been his most
important means of coping with his environment. Problem after problem has been
met with a material solution. Technological innovation has been heaped upon technological innovation until man is now completely enmeshed in a material network
of his own making. To study any aspect of man's behavior anywhere is to study his
position in that network.

This truism has rarely been taken seriously in the study of modern behavioral
systems. The analysts and manipulators of our society are basically split between

those who study what people say they do and sometimes how they actually behave in controlled environments, and those who invent, study, and modify material things. Too often when a problem involving the interaction between people and objects arises, the solutions follow two separate courses: one based on inventing or modifying things without careful consideration of related behavior; the other based on attempts to describe and modify the ideas and actions of people without much thought to the nature of associated objects. The two courses join to a degree in some product development and market research endeavors of private business. Neither can be effective alone, as can be seen in the sea of urban renewal disasters awash in our cities.

An area where knowledge needs to be accrued in our society is at the point where theories of how people will act and how material culture will work give way to real events—observable interactions between people and things. Such a contribution does not seem to be forthcoming from modern social scientists who often overlook material culture, perhaps because they have too many people to talk to. It may, however, be brought forth out of a discipline which derived from an interest in the relics of the past. Archaeology, because of the historical accident that all the people it wants to study are dead, has been forced into looking at material things in the context of their relation to behavior. Archaeologists have begun to discover that material culture is not merely a reflection of human behavior; material culture is a part of human behavior.

Can archaeologists, trained to study the interaction of people and their material networks in the past, contribute significantly to needed studies of our present society?

Archaeology pioneer Emil Haury likes to tell his audiences, "If you want to know what is really going on in a community, look at its garbage." The University of Arizona's Garbage Project has taken Haury at his word to provide one example of the way archaeologists can attempt to contribute new insights to the understanding of contemporary problems. In addition to this goal, the Garbage Project, in the tradition of ethnoarchaeology, seeks to test the methods and theories of prehistorians in a familiar on-going society. To implement these goals, for the past three years the Garbage Project has been analyzing quantifiable refuse collected in household units in Tucson, Arizona, to describe the social correlates of modern urban resource management.[1]

The general response to the possibility of the Garbage Project significantly contributing to modern social studies can be summed up in an evaluation given by one large and prestigious funding foundation:

The Foundation devotes its efforts to supporting social science research on problems in our society. I regret to inform you that the analysis of household refuse does not fall within the scope of our current funding program. We support research only.

Despite this kind of reaction, the student volunteers and staff of the Garbage Project have remained convinced that archaeology can contribute to knowledge of our society. The preliminary project study of the effect of inflation on food waste has strengthened that conviction.

The current spiraling cost of food for American consumers requires a concerted effort to evaluate practices which are wasteful of food resources at the household level. Little is known about household-level food discard in America or anywhere else, although discarded food has been called the world's greatest unutilized food resource. If household food discard could be even partially salvaged, it would free food resources with the potential of saving lives abroad and dollars in rising prices for consumers at home.

Too often Americans try to solve their problems by concentrating all their efforts on the development of new technological innovations. Alternative approaches, however, are needed to supplement technological research. To get to the real roots of the problem of household level resource discard, the social corre-lates of food waste must be identified and studied in different contexts. This is not a simple task.

The limitations of traditional interview-survey techniques present problems for gathering accurate data on household level food discard behavior in the United States. The concept of "food waste" is fraught with moral implications. Few Americans like to admit that they unnecessarily discard food, and mere participation in a study of waste behavior is sure to bias results. As a consequence, only a few food discard studies have been attempted. For example, in the late 1950s, the U.S. Department of Agriculture undertook some small studies of household food discard using records of weighed food discard kept by volunteer respondents.[2] They used small nonrepresentative samples, and the authors noted that the behavior of the respondents was changed by participation in the study. What is needed, then, is a means of estimating food discard which is nonreactive, which does not affect the behavior of the subjects.[3]

The Garbage Project has developed a new approach to the study of food discard.[4] For the past two years in Tucson, Arizona, the project has been recording the quantifiable remnants of food consumption and discard in household trash from sample census tracts stratified by United States census and other income and ethni-city data. The advantage of analyzing household refuse is obvious. Interview data are always subject to questions concerning whether they represent what people do, what they think they do, or what they want an interviewer to think they do. In contrast, garbage is the quantifiable result of what people actually did.

Now that the problem and method are outlined, the challenge becomes not only to analyze a meaningful current behavioral situation, but to do it in the context of further pursuing an archaeological concern which has a significant time-depth. The concept of "stress" is a common term in archaeology today and has been applied to almost every situation of relatively long-term, large-scale change. With food discard data it may be possible to test its utility on today's rapid economic and behavioral fluctuations.

Archaeological models suggest that at the level of a whole behavioral system, stress creates changes in actions by selecting from all available patterns of behavior those which initially meet new problems most effectively. On an individual level, since changes in behavior are required to adopt the successful patterns, archaeological stress models imply that variety will increase for most of the system's separable constituents while the transition is occurring. Thus, it will be proposed here that at an individual level there are two major phases in change due to stress: heightened variety in individual activities during initial stress, followed in time by generally decreased variety in individual activities as stress abates or as people successfully adapt to it and begin to routinize their actions.

Perhaps the most interesting conclusion of archaeological studies of reaction to stress in the past is that, in the long run, changes in behavior which may be consciously aimed toward homeostasis, or stabilizing past patterns, often end in changes which do the reverse and create the unexpected.[5] Does the same irony of counter-productive reactions hold true over the short term?—for example, during changes in individual behavior in the initial phases of stress? This question has ramifications which are relevant to the current level of food waste in America.

A simple efficiency model of today's behavior would suggest that under economic stress, people would discard less food. An alternate implication can be derived from the stress hypotheses in archaeology. Variety can be defined in this case in terms of the number of different kinds and quantities of items a family buys in a defined period. As people under the economic stress of rapidly rising prices change from habits which are no longer affordable to new and unfamiliar forms of purchasing behavior, variety may increase. This variety in household input is likely to create increased food discard. For example, new forms of bulk buying may lead to improper storage resulting in spoilage and bulk discard. Unfamiliar foods and recipes may produce unfamiliar results and unfamiliar discards. This suggests that a first reaction to increases in economic stress will be increased discard of food. Further, it may be suggested that as stress levels off or abates, people will be able to routinize their successful experiments or return to old patterns. As a result, variety and food discard will be diminished.

The alternate efficiency and stress expectations can be tentatively tested with garbage data. These data, in fact, can provide two independent tests: one involving beef, the other using most other foods. This distinction can be made on the basis of differential price rises associated with these foods between 1973 and 1974.

In the spring of 1973, when garbage food waste data were first being systematically recorded, there was a highly publicized "beef crisis." Beef was in short supply and prices seemed exorbitant. During the spring of 1974 beef was easy to obtain and prices were only slightly higher. Thus, based on the "efficiency" expectation, beef waste should be low during 1973 and perhaps higher in 1974. The archaeological stress model predicts the opposite: high beef waste during the 1973 shortage, lower waste during the 1974 glut.

To evaluate these propositions, food input and waste data were recorded from the refuse of 226 households collected from 18 census tracts largely during February through June in 1973 and 392 households collected from 19 census tracts from February through June in 1974. Refuse from randomly selected households within sample census tracts was picked up by Tucson Sanitation Division foremen and labeled only by tract to protect anonymity. Analysis was conducted at the Sanitation Division Maintenance Yard by student volunteers under the supervision of a field director. Food input data were derived from packaging and therefore did not include items like some fresh vegetables which come in unmarked wrappers. Food discard was defined as food remains that would have once been edible and was recorded by weight. No bone, separable fat, eggshells, peels, skins (except potato peels), rinds, tops, and so on were included in the category.[6]

Garbage disposals, meals eaten away from home, feeding of leftover food to household pets, fireplaces, compost piles, and recycling of containers, all introduce biases into the data acquired from the trash can. However, these biases all operate in one direction: they decrease the amount of refuse. Thus, garbage data can confidently be interpreted as representing minimum levels of household food use and waste. On this basis, population segments can be compared and changes over time observed.

Food discard was classified into two categories: straight waste was a significant quantity of an item (for example, a whole uncooked steak, half a loaf of bread, or half a can of fruit); hard-to-save plate scrapings represented edible food in quantities of less than one ounce or unidentifiable remains of cooked dishes. Assuming that straight waste is easier to minimize than are plate scrapings, a test of the alternate models can be made in terms of rates of straight waste. The archaeology stress model, for example, expects that high waste should correlate with initial attempts to react to rising prices; that low waste should correlate, generally, with stable or decreasing prices; that there would be higher straight waste of beef in 1973 than in 1974; that there would be lower straight waste of other foods in 1973 than in 1974.

The Division of Economic and Business Research at the University of Arizona reported that in Tucson the cost of putting food on the table was, on the average, 10 percent higher in the spring of 1974 than in the spring of 1973. Garbage Project data for the same time periods indicate that although total food discard remained fairly constant at around 9 percent of food input, the percentage of food discard as plate scrapings decreased as the percentage of discard in the form of straight waste climbed from 55 percent of food discard in 1973 to over 60 percent in 1974. In some census tracts straight waste jumped from around 50 percent of food discard to over 80 percent.

It has been assumed here that straight waste may be more easily avoidable through conscious effort than is the type of food discard classified as plate scrapings. If this assumption is correct, the trend toward increasing straight waste as a proportion of total food discard in Garbage Project sample households represents a trend toward greater inefficiency in utilization of food resources, even during a period of increasing food prices and economic stress.

Waste levels of most foods follow this trend. For example, although fruit and vegetable prices were on an average of 18.5 percent higher in the spring of 1973, straight waste of fruits and vegetables did not decrease; in fact, straight waste actually increased from 16.5 percent of household input of fruits and vegetables to 18.5 percent of household input. The overall household input of fresh fruits and vegetables decreased by 19 percent between the spring of 1973 and the spring of 1974. Nevertheless, the cost of fresh fruit and vegetable straight waste, based on extrapolating from Garbage Project households to Tucson's 110,000 households, was probably $73,000 higher in the spring of 1974 over the spring of 1973.

The costs and straight waste of beef show almost the opposite trend of other foods. On the average, beef prices were up only 5 percent in the spring of 1974 over prices in the spring of 1973. In fact, during the month of April 1974, beef prices were 3 percent lower than beef prices a year earlier, and in May they were almost identical. As a result, it is somewhat surprising that in 1973 weighed beef waste in sample households was 9 percent of beef input; in 1974 it was only 3 percent. The waste of beef was, therefore, almost three times higher in sampled households in 1973, during the shortage, than in 1974 during a time of a more plentiful beef supply. Using actual quantities of wasted beef and extrapolating from our sample households to Tucson, $762,000 less beef was probably wasted in the spring of 1973 than in the spring of 1974.

Thus, on the basis of Garbage Project data, straight waste seems to be, at least in the short run, correlated with the direction of price changes. It may be provisionally concluded that as prices go up for specific commodities, straight waste for those commodities goes up; and as prices level off, waste levels off or decreases.

As neat as this conclusion seems, in any single-dimension study there are many muddling factors. For example, the decrease in beef waste and an overall decrease in total food intake more than compensated financially for the increases in the straight waste of other items. As a result, reactions to stress in food cost culminated in a decrease of more than $500,000 in the cost of straight waste in the spring of 1974 over the spring of 1973. The question of the multivariate relation of beef and other food prices and the cost of waste to inflation still remains open; however, many implications and further questions can be drawn from the preliminary Garbage Project results which tend to support archaeological stress models.

Using 1970 United States census and other data, social correlates can be related to food waste at the census tract level. Straight waste proved highest, between 70 percent and 85 percent of food waste, among census tracts with no households, or under 20 percent of the households, below the poverty level. Straight waste was much lower, between 50 percent and 70 percent of food discard, in census tracts where over 20 percent of the households were below the poverty level. The 1973–1974 increase in straight food waste was less dramatic in the census tracts with many poor households, and, in fact, in some of these tracts straight waste decreased. One implication of this, from an archaeological standpoint, is that for the low-income census tracts, economic stress is nothing new and that few new purchasing and preparation endeavors result from increases in this type of stress.

This leads to another important point. For most census tracts, total evidence of household input of food was down in 1974 from 1973 levels. However, there were no significant changes in input patterns for census tracts with no poor households. But there were changes for households in census tracts where more than 20 percent of the households were below the poverty level. Their input of high protein foods decreased dramatically (meat, fish, poultry, eggs, cheese, and nuts), in some tracts by over 30 percent. Again the implication is that poorer neighborhoods, where economic stress has been a constant factor, can do little to adjust to increases, except to cut down on expensive foods, like meat, fish, or poultry.

As in other archaeological studies, there are always a few surprises. One was provided by a cluster of census tracts in which 20 percent to 40 percent of the households were below the poverty level and over 65 percent of the residents were Mexican-Americans. Food input remained at 1973 levels and straight waste decreased from 75 percent to 56 percent of all food waste. This same census tract cluster also exhibited a larger input of total food per household than any other population segment, a finding which is not surprising because of a relatively large household size in this subgroup. Thus the population segment which was apparently becoming more efficient in terms of waste behavior was also managing a proportionally large share of the food resources. The specific implications here are unclear, except to identify this as an important group to study further. Through this kind of analysis it might be possible to identify behaviors, and their sociocultural correlates, which result in more or less efficiency of food use at the household level; such information would be valuable for policy and program formulation and for a public faced with spiraling prices.

Finally, just as a sidelight, a further correlate to stress can be mentioned. There was only one product whose consumption dramatically increased between 1973 and 1974. Alcoholic beverages in 1974 made up between 15 percent and 25 percent, by volume, of all the food and beverages consumed in sample households. It is interesting to note that ''efficient'' tract clusters seem to imbibe the most beer at home.

Although the above data and inferences are oversimplified and highly speculative, they lay the groundwork for significant hypotheses which need rigorous testing, evaluation, and expansion in the future. This contribution is based on the fact that the Garbage Project has succeeded, in a very preliminary form, in producing the only quantifiable data available on some of the social correlates of food waste and the relation of food waste to economic stress.[7] However, for current problems a project's success cannot just be measured by its proposed results, but has to be measured also by the interest shown in the results by responsible social scientists and governmental planners and by the distribution of the results to the people who can learn about their behavior from them.

The Garbage Project received some interest from scholars and considerable publicity from the press, but much of that coverage was based on viewing garbage analysis as an academic "freak of the week" exhibit. Thus image is an important asset for the project to draw attention to its real contributions, and recently these contributions have been taken more seriously. On January 23, 1975, the Garbage Project reached millions of American households as the subject of a report on the NBC Nightly News. The project has also provided the data for consumer education articles and notes in high-circulation magazines like *Harper's* and *McCall's* and in more specialized publications like *Consumerisms*. Project results were even the subject of posters printed by the Stop and Shop grocery store chain. Finally, the Garbage Project staff is scheduled to testify before Senator George McGovern's Senate Select Committee on Nutrition and Human Needs.

The goal of this paper is not to demand that all archaeologists attempt to be relevant or concerned with studying the relation between modern material culture and behavior. Its only aim is to attempt to show what archaeologists can potentially extract from modern material culture studies.

First, modern material culture studies in ongoing societies can be used to test archaeological theories and methods. Even though material change, law-like propositions and most other archaeological hypotheses should be as testable today as in the past; the same should be true of archaeological methods in sampling and analysis. Second, modern material culture studies can provide unique new perspectives into the nature of our own society which can make the techniques and theories of archaeology immediately useful.

For over a century, archaeologists have been pushing back the frontiers of time-depth in the relation between behavior and material culture. In the past few years, early man specialists have stretched this interaction back to two million B.C., while historic archaeology and ethnoarchaeology have made contributions to the other end of the time frame. Now it is possible to use an archaeological perspective to study the present as it unfolds, thus defining archaeology as a discipline studying the relation between people and their possessions at all times and in all places.

The procurement, use or consumption, and discard of material things is as much a part of human behavior as speech. Through the study of these activities and their remnants, archaeologists can relate us to our ancestors in the past and bridge the gap from the first tool-makers to our own garbage cans.

24

Tin*Can Archaeology

Robert Ascher

Introduction

In the past decade, historical archaeology has been especially prominent in its contributions to American material culture studies. As this article demonstrates, scholars in this research field have sought to extract information from objects, (e.g., pottery, pollen, soils, building fragments) that would result in greater knowledge about past human behavior. Robert Ascher proposes that this approach of traditional archaeology also be extended to include what he calls "the archaeology of recent times" via a perspective he labels "tin*can archaeology." Such a research strategy, he maintains, would investigate modern material culture data as diverse as Craig Gilborn's Coca-Cola bottles and Bruce Lohof's gasoline service stations.

In a spirit akin to John Kouwenhoven's opening manifesto in Part II, Ascher's concluding mandate here in Part IV restates a perennial claim of the material culture theorician: visual data deserves parity with verbal data in historical research. Actually Ascher puts the case more strongly. Citing a melange of human artifacts first described by James Agee and Walker Evans in *Let Us Now Praise Famous Men (1939)*, Ascher notes "all of these pins, bones and buttons are more interesting than word descriptions or even pictorial representations." While arguing for the primacy of the artifact as a pregnant historical resource in depicting certain segments of the past, Ascher also recognizes a major liability of material culture data: the limited or pure chance survival of all artifacts.

As will be apparent, Ascher reiterates several themes found in earlier anthology authors, such as Ruth Cowan's concern for the technological "hardware of culture," the interests of Henry Glassie, Fred B. Kniffen, and Peirce Lewis in the spatial diffusion of artifacts over the American landscape, as well as Joseph

Trimmer's claims for the symbolic meanings of material culture. Finally, Ascher's use of the interpretations of Siegfried Giedion and Daniel Boorstin suggest his concern to move material culture research from mere exercises in description and analysis to the "complex cultural interpretation of the changing relationship of man and the man-made environment."

Several other aspects of Ascher's tin*can archaeology deserve special mention. For instance, in his use of (and contribution to) Norman Daly's artifactual recreation in The Civilization of Llhuros (1972), he reminds the material culture student of other playful, imaginary worlds that have been created by anthropologists, archaeologists, architects, painters, and novelists to prompt reflection (or laughter) upon the symbiotic relation of the way man makes things and the way things make man. Here, for example, one might recall the similar use of artifacts by Robert Nathan in The Weans (1960), by Michael Rynkiewich and James Spradley in The Nacirema (1975), or by David Macaulay in The Motel of the Mysteries (1979).

Mention of a man-made twentieth-century landscape feature such as a motel suggests Ascher's proposal that practitioners of tin*can archaeology should be alert for what he calls "superartifacts," objects such as the automobile, the common nail, or the Coke bottle. Why are such items to be considered superartifacts? Because, argues Ascher, they yield a special insight into the intellectual world of the people of a particular historical time in a way unmatched by any other object of the same period.

While Ascher would have the material culture researcher seek out single superartifacts, an approach reminiscent of the fact-and-symbol model of Alan Tractenberg's The Brooklyn Bridge, he also advocates a democratization of material culture data, methodology, and personnel. In the spirit of the new social history, he urges researchers to "uncover the history of the inarticulate," particularly in its urban context. Thus a final objective of tin*can archaeology is "archaeology in the megapolis."

A historical archaeologist whose earliest published research dealt with the Indian civilization living at Zuma Creek, California, some four thousand years ago ("A Prehistoric Population Estimate Using Midden Analysis and Two Population Models," Bobbs-Merrill Reprints in Anthropology, Number A4 [1962]), Ascher has done material culture studies on other native American sites, including "American Indian Civilization in New York," Man in the Northeast 5 (1973): 55–60. With C. H. Fairbanks, he has also studied black slave compounds in the American South, "Excavation of a Slave Cabin: Georgia, U.S.A.," Historical Archaeology 5 (1971): 3–17. His more contemporary artifact analyses include, in addition to the article reprinted below from Historical Archaeology 8 (1974): 1–16, an essay, "How to Build a Time Capsule," Journal of Popular Culture 8 (Fall 1974): 241–253. Robert Ascher teaches in the Department of Anthropology at Cornell University.

Before them, surrounded by ferns and palm trees, white and pow-
dery in the silent morning light, was an enormous Spanish galleon.
Tilted slightly to the starboard, it had hanging from its intact masts the
dirty rags of its sails in the midst of its rigging, which was adorned with
orchids. The hull, covered with an armor of petrified barnacles and soft
moss, was finally fastened into the surface of the stones. The whole
structure seemed to occupy its own space, one of solitude and oblivion,
protected from the vices of time and the habits of birds.
—Gabriel Garcia Marquez, *One Hundred Years of Solitude*

Now that I was free to explore Rio on foot, I began looking about
for some lingering vestige of adventure. I was to find one, eventually, in
the course of an archaeological excursion to the far side of the bay. On
the swampy beach where the motor-boat had deposited our party I
suddenly saw an old rusted hulk. Doubtless it did not date back to the
sixteenth century; but it introduced the element of historical perspective
into a region otherwise unequipped to illustrate the passage of time. The
clouds hung low and fine rain had fallen continuously since daybreak.
—Claude Lévi-Strauss, *Tristes Tropiques*

Archaeology as a Way of Seeing

On January 28, 1754, Horace Walpole, the fourth Earl of Orford, wrote to a
friend in Florence to acknowledge the arrival of a portrait of the beautiful Bianca
Capello. In the course of his letter, Walpole coined the word "serendipity."
Walpole told his correspondent that he will understand the new word by knowing
how it was derived. And he goes on to write:

I once read a silly fairy tale, called The Three Princes of Serendip: As their highnesses
travelled, they were always making discoveries, by accident and sagacity, of things which
they were not in quest of: for instance, one of them discovered that a mule blind of the right
eye had travelled the same road lately, because the grass was eaten only on the left side,
where it was worse than the right—now do you understand serendipity? [1]

In the more than two centuries since this letter was posted, serendipity has been
variously applied. Accidental inventions, such as the discovery of a soap that floats,
is given as a case in point. Recently, the term was applied to computer art as a
by-product of the use of computing machines.[2] The word persists and its application
spreads, I believe, because it places a label on a crucial, recurrent experience. Here
I use the word to cover the case in which archaeology, on the way to achieving its
main goal, stumbled upon a way of seeing. To understand how this happened, we
need to retrace some early steps.

Archaeology developed along several more or less independent lines. One line can be linked to interest in the Classical world that started with the Renaissance. Another had its beginnings in curiosity about the inhabitants of the New World. A third line, associated with the coming of evolutionary thought in mid-nineteenth-century Europe, sought material evidence for man's origin. Each of these lines, and others, started with asking urgent questions. Some of the questions were answered dramatically. Take, for example, answers to the question of man's antiquity. By 1900 it was shown that there existed a close three-part association as follows: (1) the bones of extinct animals and (2) the bones of men were found in (3) deposits of soil and rock that were very ancient. This done, it was no longer possible to accept dating based upon Biblical calculations which had placed man's origin on the order of 5,000 years ago. Instead of being specially created, man joined the rest of nature.

There is still work to be done along traditional lines. Gaps remain. There are periods of time about which we know too little, and the meaning of some of the findings are not grasped. Approaches were introduced in the 1960s in an attempt to dress archaeology in new garments,[3] but these have been outdated by the counter culture's general criticism of science dogma.[4] In speaking about music, John Cage said: "It is pleasant if you happen to hear Beethoven or Chopin or whatever, but it is not urgent to do so any more." [5] The same can be said of traditional or redressed archaeology.

Now in the pursuit of answers to specific questions, archaeologists adapted from other disciplines, or invented on their own, a multitude of ways to extract information from objects such as pottery, pollen, rocks, and the potassium in soils. For example, I once wanted to know how many people lived at Zuma Creek in California some 4,000 years ago.[6] From excavation, it appeared that shellfish was a major part of the diet. I first determined how much energy was available to the population from shellfish during a limited time period. I then estimated the percentage of energy that was available from other sources. The answer to the question "how many people lived here? " befitting the data is not one value, but falls within limits. I calculated the variable number of people that could survive over a variable period of time. This example is one of literally thousands that could be cited. The point is this: the contribution of traditional archaeology was first to the solution of issues in human history; in addition, and as a by-product, a way of seeing emerged that centered upon extracting information from objects. Almost any kind of object was found to yield information about humans, no matter how uncompromising it appeared at first. Serendipity.

This way of knowing about the remote past can now, if we choose, be applied to the near present. Without intending it, archaeologists found that it is possible to read pieces of pottery like so many words in a book. If old pottery can be read, we should, in theory, be able to read objects that surround us without regard to their age. Let us say that wrecked automobiles are good to study for insights into twentieth-century America just as shipwrecks under the Mediterranean help us to know about the second century B.C.

With this background, the title of the paper can be discussed. Few things are as representative of recent times as tin cans. Although they came into use around 1800, it was not until one hundred years later that the problems of their manufacture were solved. The history of the tin can thus parallels the period in the West of full mechanization. The essential principle of mechanization is "replacing motion for motion the activity of the hand." [7] It is, in fact, this which firmly sets apart the archaeology of recent times. Stone tools and ceramic jugs were made by hands in a folk tradition which changed slowly; tin cans and automobile tires are made by machines and belong to popular culture which generally changes rapidly. The import of this shift extends far beyond the materials and machines themselves. They are different worlds. "In their aggregate, the humble objects," writes Giedion, "have shaken our mode of living to its very roots. Modest things of daily life, they accumulate into forces acting upon whomever moves within the orbit of our civilization." [8] The ubiquitous tin can is shorthand for the processes at work in our contemporary culture.

Art and Archaeology

Tin*can archaeology seems to be a natural kinsman of the arts as they developed in the twentieth century. Let us explore a few of these bonds.

One bond has to do with the idea of chance. Opinions differ on why painters devised such techniques for introducing chance as allowing paint to find its way unaided from the top to the bottom of the canvas. It is claimed that chance in art is intended as a blow against the machine.[9] Alternately, it has been proposed that chance in art "derives from the new quantum-mechanical theories of physics, and the recognition of the importance of random processes in biology." [10] Whatever interpretation is put upon it, we are now accustomed to chance built into modern dance, sculpture, painting, and music.

Some of the artists concerned with chance have done things that to varying degrees are closely related to archaeology. In fact, in some cases artists interested in chance have seen an archaeological connection. In his *Anecdoted Topography of Chance*, Daniel Spoerri takes the items that happened to be gathered on a table in his room and details the history of the objects in themselves and the objects to each other. A map of the table showing the distribution of the items is provided. The objects are mostly modest objects used by everyone; they include a match, a spoon, a bent nail, and some coins. There are also natural things; for example, eggshells and salt, and other phenomena more difficult to classify, such as cigarette burns. Of his work, Spoerri says:

> I have set out here to see what the objects on a section of this table might suggest to me . . . the way Sherlock Holmes, starting with a single object, could solve a crime; or historians, after centuries, were able to reconstitute a whole epoch from the most famous fixation in history, Pompeii.[11]

Spoerri's approach is analytic in that each thing on the table is numbered and discussed by itself; but he does not stop there. The items are interwoven and gradually a complex pattern emerges. The collection becomes more than a list of artifacts. An archaeological site is not very different from Spoerri's table; both are accidental arrangements. For the tin can period, information beyond the items permits the discovery of order in the arrangements. Spoerri's accomplishment is an unintentional model for the analysis of chance arrangements and as such it challenges the archaeologist to find order.

Another instructive creation is the civilization of Llhuros.[12] This place was constructed by chance by my colleague Norman Daly from objects he had found. The artifacts from Llhuros include well-doctored orange juice squeezers, stove pipes, and styrofoam that had once held a dismantled Honda motorcycle. When the artifacts of Llhuros, with appropriate period designations (early, middle, late, and so forth), were first exhibited, many people who viewed them were more than half-convinced that it existed as a once-inhabited civilization. Daly had in fact invented a civilization based upon reconstructed "real" civilizations that fill museum cases. He made, that is, a myth upon a myth.[13] This in itself should provide some moments of thought about the meaning of relic displays.

This leads to another bond: blurring of the fact-fancy, subjective-objective dichotomy. The separation, according to Lynn White, was drawn sharply by Descartes three hundred years ago and has been with us ever since. Attributes such as mass, extension, and motion are "objective," while colors, textures, sounds, and eventually all the most vividly human experiences and values are declared "subjective" and in some way "unreal." [14] With some exceptions, until recently the division was clear and certainly held sway in universities. An exception is in the novel where, as William Van O'Conner tells us, "the real," the "factual," and the "true" are inevitably caught up in the author's private vision.[15] I believe that the arts are forcing us to see that the dichotomy is not universal.

The archaeological connection to the objective-subjective theme is most obvious in the documentary. In the movies, the term was introduced by John Greirson to describe Robert Flahertey's *Moana*, an account of the daily life of a Polynesian boy.[16] In filming a documentary, one does not know what to expect and thus a script may consist of a series of anticipated impressions. For example, the script for an early documentary about a railroad station consisted, in part, of these notations: "Whistles. Steam. Waves from mother . . . Paper bags, half-eaten sandwiches, a bunch of withered flowers, a crumpled paper boat." [17] Today, the documentary approach is used in movies that are not fact but that are based on fact. In such movies it is sometimes hard to tell what is or is not "true."

Documentary can also describe written "fiction," such as Norman Mailer's *Armies of the Night* and "nonfiction," especially *Let Us Now Praise Famous Men* by James Agee (writer) and Walker Evans (photographer). The latter is about three tenant farming families during the great depression. Here, at length, is a typical Agee sentence:

There in the chilly and small dust which is beneath porches, the subtle funnels of doodlebugs whose teasing, of a broomstraw, is one of the patient absorptions of kneeling childhood, dead twigs of living, swept from the urgent tree, signs and relics: bent nails, withered and knobbed with rust; a bone button, its two eyes torn to one; the pierced back of an alarm clock, greasy to the touch: a torn fragment of pictured print; an emptied and flattened twenty-gauge shotgun shell, its metal green, lettering still visible; the white tin eyelet of a summer shoe; and thinly scattered, the dessicated and the still soft excrement of hens, who stroll and dab and stand, shimmying, stabbing at their lices, and stroll out again into the sun as vacantly as they departed it. And other things as well.[18]

Agee's good friend, Robert Fitzgerald, tells us that Agee "was after the truth, the truth about specific events or things, and the truth about his own impressions and feelings." Reading Agee, one cannot help being impressed by his camera eye attention to detail. In addition to nonfiction, Agee wrote novels and short stories, and he reviewed movies. Fitzgerald stresses that Agee was influenced by documentary movies "by which the craft of the cameraman could show forth unsuspected lineaments of the actual." [19] I think that all of this is apparent in the sample of writing above.

Documentary in any media has come to mean the "creative treatment of actuality." [20] This would be a fine definition for the method of tin*can archaeology. If it does not suit your taste, if it seems to be "unscientific," please recall that archaeological data are concrete results of human happenings gathered in one place more or less by chance. All of these pins, bones, and buttons are more interesting than word descriptions or even pictorial representation. More often than not the immediacy of the data is protected under glass or buried in jargon. Theoretical discussions of archaeology never let on that artifacts are visual and tactile rather than abstract experiences. The dismal uniformity of the scientific paper into which form archaeology is invariably cast purports to be noncommittal, objective, and cool. It is also often so contrived as to be inadequate to express the ideas that fit the truth of the situation.

Archaeology of the Inarticulate

The Satyricon is mysterious first and foremost because it is fragmentary. But its fragmentariness is, in a certain sense, symbolic—of the fragmentariness of the ancient world as it appears to us today.
                                        —Federico Fellini, talking about his movie *Satyricon*

History does not exist: all that exists is debris—scattered, mutilated, very fragmentary— left by vanished ages. Each historian knows that by his own labors in scrutiny of the rubbish heaps, he arrives at more and more understanding of what happened in the past.
                                        —Lynn White, Jr., *Dynamo and Virgin Reconsidered*

If archaeology of the recent past were just another "new" approach, it would not be worth my writing this or your reading it. Its importance is found in connection with a major change that is going to take place in the restudy of America's past.

As Jesse Lemisch points out, "The history of the powerless, the inarticulate, the poor has not yet begun to be written because they have been treated no more fairly by historians than they have been treated by their contemporaries." [21] One of my favorite examples in support of Lemisch is this characterization:

> Frontier life was marked by a deplorable amount of outright criminality. Some of the scum of society swirled out to the border. Men developed ungovernable tempers, and had a taste for settling their quarrels with fists and pistols. [22]

This appears in a book on American history that was reprinted, with corrections, at least in 1942, 1943, 1950, and 1960. Even grade "C" western movies of the 1940s did better; no person in them fits the faceless nonperson of the text.

Those who want an American history that is more than the lives and times of the Great White Men search for diaries, letters, reminiscences, legal records, and other forms of writing. There is some recognition that the nonwritten documentation is of value in the study of what the rest of America, outside of politics, was doing. But even those with the laudable purpose of bringing others into history books tend to underestimate nonwritten sources.

It is from another subset of historians that we glimpse concern with the "hardware of culture." These men and women are basically interested in technology. Perhaps their most noted spokesman is Lynn White, Jr., who says, bluntly: "The greatest single defect in most historical scholarship is the greater preoccupation with written records than with other kinds of evidence. . . . We shall continue to have a badly distorted view of the last sixteen centuries until this myopia is corrected." [23] Another historian of technology, Roger Burlingame, calls the preoccupation with writing the "curious obsession of historians." [24] For those who pay attention, historians of technology have produced convincing demonstrations of how simple inventions, such as the button, have affected the course of migration or how the varied rooftops of European houses can be read in terms of environmental history. [25]

Now there is little overlap between those who are concerned with the inarticulate and those who are interested in the hardware of culture. In tin-can archaeology, however, the two approaches meet. To varying degrees, with the degree of variation itself being important, those who did not write or who were not written about left in their wake tons of personal material objects. For the archaeologist, access to the people of the recent past is through the products of technology. Here are some archaeological examples: an investigation of the workshops of the Walnut Street Prison (1755–1835), Philadelphia; a study of the surfmen who patrolled the beaches along Cape Cod on the lookout for ships in danger; a comparative study of the living conditions of a group of Chinese and European immigrants building a railroad; and excavation of a cabin that provided shelter for a white trader and an Indian woman. [26] There are also some studies of the houses occupied by American blacks after slavery, such as "Josh," "Casey," and "Black Lucy." [27] For each of these cases there are some written records, but without the artifacts the most that would be known is a name on a pay roster or on a deed to property.

The largest group of inarticulate Americans were slaves. Indeed, in many states it was a punishable crime to teach a slave to read or write. As is well known, some slaves did manage to write about their experiences. I have worked in the excavation of a slave cabin. In an attempt to apply the documentary film (or tape) method, first-person narratives were used to organize the archaeological findings. As we wrote in our report:

> Our presentation includes a soundtrack and pictures. The soundtrack is composed from eyewitness accounts, slave narratives, and other sources. You are encouraged to sound out the words; the soundtrack selections are based on their auditory value and on their connection with the archaeological findings. The organization follows a modular plan; each module begins with a soundtrack and ends at the start of the next soundtrack. You are invited to reassemble the components to best suit yourself. Artifacts are three dimensional: they are visual and tactile and sometimes they smell and make noise. Word pictures and drawings offer limited help.[28]

I stressed that the narratives were not drawn from the experience of the slaves in the excavated cabin, but from men and women who were thrust into similar circumstances.

Superartifacts, Time, and Space

For several days the thon and his assistant studied the library itself, the files, the monastery's records apart from the Memorabilia—as if by determining the validity of the oyster, they might establish the possibility of the pearl. Brother Kornhoer discovered the thon's assistant on his knees in the entrance of the refectory, and for a moment he entertained the impression that the fellow was performing some special devotion before the image of Mary above the door, but a rattle of tools put an end to the illusion. The assistant laid a carpenter's level across the entranceway and measured the concave depression worn in the floor stones by centuries of monastic sandals.

"We're looking for ways of determining dates," he told Kornhoer when questioned. "This seems like a good place to establish a standard for rate of wear, since the traffic's easy to estimate. Three meals per man per day since the stones were laid."

Kornhoer could not help being impressed by their thoroughness; the activity mystified him. "The abbey's architectural records are complete," he said. "They can tell you exactly when each building and wing was added. Why not save your time?"

The man glanced up innocently. "My master has a saying: 'Nazol is without speech, and therefore never lies.' "

—Walter M. Miller, Jr., *A Canticle for Leibowitz*

Artifacts surround us as if we were in a forest. When studied in a chance context, for example, under the floor boards of a cabin, we consider the interrelations of the found objects. But artifacts reach beyond a particular situation and connect with the same or similar things from other places and times. We now consider aspects of the man-made environment that reach beyond a particular setting.

Archaeological space is often idealized as a three-dimensional layer cake. In this model, a civilization literally sits on top of a previous one. In America of the recent past, however, archaeological space is shaped differently. A model showing a two-dimensional surface is more apt: imagine a spilled glass of liquid rather than a layer cake. I take this notion from the historian, Daniel Boorstin, who put it this way:

The nine cities of Troy, each built on the ruins of its predecessor, were accumulated over millennia, from the Stone Age till Roman times. Pompeii was buried by volcanic eruption. . . .

In America, the archaeology of fast-moving men in a nearly empty continent was spread plain and thin on the surface. Its peculiar product was the abandoned place (the "ghost town") rather than the buried place. Its characteristic relics were things left by choice before they were used up. Because her space was much more plentiful than time, the American past was displayed across the landscape.[29]

An example that fits Boorstin's idea is the Hector Backbone in the Finger Lake region of upstate New York. Here, after genocide, the land was made available in homestead plots for white settlement. But the soil was poor, the rain unpredictable, the hills were too steep, and the growing season was short. The people left for somewhere else. There were few white people in Hector at the start of the nineteenth century; there were 2,000 people by 1880; after that peak, the population fell sharply. No one lives there today. In the 1930s the federal government purchased the land of the few people who stayed. I did an archaeological survey of the 13,000 acres that comprise the Hector Backbone in 1974. There are foundations of schools, mills, and barns. But as Boorstin predicts, the remains occupy a thin, spread-out section of ground.

The important thing about archaeological time is not the calendar date of an object. What counts most is relative position in a time sequence and rate of change. In the case of Stonehenge it is essential to know, for example, if a group of stones showing a particular symmetry was erected before or after another group of stones showing a different symmetry. In the case of the Coca-Cola bottle, we know when the classic "hobble skirt" bottle was introduced, but significance resides in the fact that it has scarcely changed since then. The changeless Coke bottle is unusual for objects in the tin-can period. I recently showed a radio vacuum tube to twenty people all in their late teens. One person knew what it was. In traditional archaeology, it is assumed that change in man-made objects is slow and more or less continuous. But to understand the last few centuries, the exact opposite should be assumed. From the perspective of change in the content of culture, what happened twenty years ago is as far away as something that happened 200 years ago, if the change during the twenty-year period equals the change during the 200-year period. In sociological terms, this is future shock.

In short, for the past few centuries in America, the content of culture is spread thinly in space and it is quickly paced in time. These are seen fitting together, for example, in the study of American roadscapes. The Oregon Trail over which passed the prairie schooners on the trip west is still visible in aerial photographs. The photographs show how the trail was changed as "the later migrants picked a better way or as changes in local conditions made relocations possible." [30] Eventually, part of the trail was covered with hardtop. The connection from the nineteenth to the twentieth century is clear in the development of shopping plazas, new places to live, and in the single most obvious American superartifact, namely the automobile. In the midst of change, the grand American archaeological site is becoming. Automobile graveyards line the roadscape and dot the countryside, and the individually built, owned, and managed motor or tourist courts that were built in the fifteen years before the start of World War II are now part of our past. [31]

The automobile was just called a superartifact. Intuitively, those who live in motorscapes know that a car cannot be viewed simply as a material object whose characteristics change and whose numbers increase. Its production, dissemination, and uses intersect with other material and nonmaterial aspects of culture. Objects become superartifacts for different reasons. Another superartifact is Stonehenge on the Salisbury plain in southeastern England. It is a superartifact because, upon analysis, it yields insights into the intellectual world of neolithic peoples in a way unmatched by any other structure of the same period. Through knowledge of Stonehenge, we understand hundreds of related structures in western Europe. [32] Superartifacts do not need to be expensive or unique. Given what Bernard Fontana tells us about the iron nail, it also fits my category of superartifact. He writes:

> It is not hyperbole to say that today and for at least a hundred years past the United States has literally been held together with nails. Try to imagine our culture without them . . . As interesting as the study of unique and exotic artifacts may be, it is not a study that will tell us most about an entire society. [33]

In any excavated site after 1830, nails are ubiquitous. Slivers of glass are also very common. In modern times, the bottle that holds Coca-Cola sends more vibrations than nails, and I admit it too as a superartifact. The Coke bottle lends itself to formal analysis; this, in fact, has been brilliantly accomplished by Craig Gilborn. He deliberately employs the operations of traditional archaeology (description, classification, and interpretation) and his results reveal systematic drifts through time in the properties of the bottle which were not known to the manufacturer. [34] An ideal time capsule would contain all the superartifacts of a particular civilization, but in practice the choice of these items is very difficult. [35]

Journey to the City Street

I enjoy taking pictures of prehistoric archaeological sites. Whenever I do so, I make certain that powerlines and other signs of modern life are out of focus. The intrusion of contemporary clues ruins my sense of propriety; archaeology (I tell myself) happens in the open country. For other people their heritage is over the ocean, and if they do archaeology, it has to be in some distant place. In this concluding section, we turn to the archaeology of urban America, and suggest that the above notions are strictly limiting.

Some American cities have been lived in for centuries. Still, they do not approach the layer cake model for the classic shape of an archaeological site. In America, cities spread out until they make contact with other spreading cities. Furthermore, entire neighborhoods are torn down and cleared away before they are built over. Yet, in some cases, research is possible. A case in point is D. W. Ingersoll's study of Puddle Dock.[36] This neighborhood in Portsmouth, New Hampshire, was founded in 1630. At first, it was a place for family dwellings, then it became a commercial district, still later is housed immigrants in tenement buildings, and finally it became a slum. The archaeologist pieced together aspects of absentee landlordism, waste disposal, land use patterns, and slum genesis to produce an urban neighborhood archaeology. Other archaeology has been done at several sites in the New York-Philadelphia megalopolis.[37]

In his "Archaeology in Megapolis," Bert Salwen notes that urban archaeology includes interest in structures that are still standing. Ellis Island Immigration Station in New York Harbor is an example. For fifty years, the island was the chief portal for immigrants. A few years ago, when I worked there, the buildings were standing but they were abandoned and decaying. The main processing center, where millions of people received their first impressions of America, is an immense hall: the roof, stripped by thieves of salable copper, leaks badly; the peeling walls reveal layers of paint, and the Kafkaesque rat-infested corridors and rooms that line the main hall are filled with objects left behind: printed cards in many languages used in literacy tests, sea-going trunks, baby shoes, winter coats, wicker desks, and railroad tickets to destinations out of New York City. By the mid-1950s, there were too few immigrants arriving by sea to justify maintaining so large a complex, but there were objections to tearing it down. After congressional deliberations, Ellis Island was turned over to the National Park System. Since then, decades have passed and little is done about one of America's major archaeological sites. The public cannot visit it.

The urgency of archaeology will appear when its study leads to insight or at least to an awareness of the world around us. You probably live in a city, or will live in one soon as population density continues to increase. In urban environments, seeing the sidewalk can be an interesting archaeological experience. Robert Sommer says this about it:

> The sidewalk is the least appreciated element of the urban scene. Children become aware of every crack and change of texture as they play marbles and hopscotch, pitch pennies, ride bicycles, and roller skate through neighborhood streets. But adults use sidewalks simply as traffic arteries and look at them, if at all, mainly to see what to avoid—unmarked holes, lumps of chewing gum, dog droppings, piles of refuse, and broken glass.[38]

Sommer is interested in the more permanent impressions left in the sidewalk by chance. From a footprint left in wet cement, he tries to find the height, weight, and gender of the subject, and from immature leaves similarly embedded he entertains hypotheses such as street-widening programs, and death by city smog. Independently, the city street became the subject for the art of Mark Boyle.[39] He began by randomly choosing pieces of street in the Shepherds Bush section of London and making exact replicas of the street and the stuff that lay in it and upon it. Boyle's streets were hung on museum walls. Contemplate the contrasting effects of contemporary city streets hung on museum walls close to Roman archaeological remains hung on the walls of adjacent museums.

Admittedly, it is a way from these exercises in seeing to the analytic work needed to understand the complex transformations in the interrelations of man and the man-made environment. But it is a place to start.

Part V

Statement of the Field

The message for today's humanistic researchers of material culture is that they should be concerned with prescription as well as description, with analysis as well as observation, and with advancement of concepts as well as calls of neglect.
—Simon J. Bronner, ''Chain Carvers in Southern Indiana''

History does not exist; all that exists is debris—scattered, multilated, very fragmentary—left by vanished ages. Each historian knows that by his own labors in the scrutiny of the rubbish heaps, he arrives at more and more understanding of what happened in the past.
—Lynn White, Jr., *Dynamo and Virgin Reconsidered*

25

Material Culture Studies in America: A Selective Bibliographical Essay

Thomas J. Schlereth

Even the neophyte bibliographer quickly realizes the Sisyphean nature of his task, no matter how specialized his topic. Not only are there some published studies that inevitably elude his most comprehensive dragnet, but there are also important new titles that immediately appear as soon as he sends his work to press. The bibliography, no matter what its disciplinary focus, remains the one genre of scholarly writing doomed never to be truly *au courant*.

Despite these inherent limitations, bibliographies nevertheless serve many purposes. For the beginning student they provide an overview of a field, a sense of its emphases and divisions, and, perhaps most important of all, a reference guide as to where to look for more information on particular topics. For the advanced researcher, a comprehensive bibliography in a subject area can suggest further "needs and opportunities for study" as do two classics in material culture studies: one in the history of early American art, Walter Muir Whitehill, *The Arts in Early American History* (Chapel Hill: University of North Carolina Press, 1965), the other in early American technological history, Brooke Hindle, *Technology in Early America* (Chapel Hill: University of North Carolina Press, 1966).

In this selective bibliography, I have tried to serve both the beginning student and the advanced scholar. In so doing, however, I have imposed several restrictions on my subject. For example, I have largely excluded journal articles and periodical literature from my survey of current research. Although American material culture studies have numerous interconnections with similar work in various countries abroad, I have also focused this bibliography primarily on scholarship done on the American context by American scholars. Hence, essays such as Alexander Fenton, "Material Culture as an Aid to Local History Studies in Scotland," *Journal of the Folklore Institute* 2 (1965): 326–339, and A. Viires, "On the Method of Studying the Material Culture of European Peoples," *Ethnologia Europaea* 9 (1977): 35–41, would be double exceptions to these caveats.

I have also tried not to repeat discussing the majority of the books that I have cited in my long introductory essay to this volume. I consider that essay a historiography as well as a history; its text and notes contain extensive bibliographical information and should be consulted as a companion to this essay.

Bibliographical Surveys

To date, the material culture studies movement has produced only a handful of published bibliographies that make some attempt to appraise the scholarship of this multi-disciplinary field. Harold Skramstad's brief summary of "American Things: Neglected Material Culture" (*American Studies International* 10 [Spring 1972]: 11–22) was one of the first such surveys; it was followed by Sharon Y. Eubanks, *A Bibliography of Books, Pamphlets, and Films Listed in the Living Historical Farms Bulletin from December 1970 through May 1976* (Washington: Association for Living Historical Farms and Agricultural Museums, 1976); Patrick H. Butler III, "Material Culture as a Resource in Local History: A Bibliography," *The Newberry Papers in Family and Community History*, No. 77–2 (1977), pp. 1–24; Simon J. Bronner, "From Neglect To Concept: An Introduction to the Study of Material Aspects of American Folk Culture," *Folklore Forum* 12 (1979): 117–132; Steven K. Hamp, "Special Bibliography/Meaning in Material Culture: Bibliographic References towards an Analytical Approach to Artifacts," *Living Historical Farms Bulletin* 4 (May 1980): 9–13; and Ormond Loomis, *Sources on Folk Musems and Living History Farms* (Bloomington, Ind.: Folklore Forum Bibliographic and Special Series, 1977). My *Artifacts and the American Past* (Nashville: American Association for State and Local History, 1980) has a strong bibliographic flavor, particularly concerning current material culture research on graphics, historic sites, and landscapes. Frederick L. Roth, Jr., and Merrilyn Rogers O'Connell, eds., *A Bibliography on Historical Organization Practices*. Vol. 4: *Documentation of Collections* (Nashville: American Association for State and Local History, 1979) contains annotated bibliographical references to material culture research organized under headings such as "Artifact Collections," "Decorative Arts Collections," "Fine Arts Collections," and "Folk Arts and Crafts Collections."

General and Specialized Anthologies

Other students of American artifacts have collected material research into compendiums that attempt to provide an overview of the field. Beginning with Lucius Ellsworth and Maureen O'Brien, eds., *Material Culture: Historical Agen-*

cies and the Historian (Philadelphia: Reprint Book Service, 1969) we now have similar collections such as Ian M. G. Quimby, ed., *Material Culture and the Study of American Life* (New York: Norton, 1978); Barbara Riley, ed., *Canada's Material History: A Forum* (Ottawa: National Museum of Man, 1979); and Richard A. Gould and Michael B. Schiffer, eds., *Modern Material Culture: The Archaeology of Us* (New York: Academic Press, 1981).

Paralleling these general anthologies are several useful collections of material culture research in the many specific disciplines that comprise the field. For example, in anthropology one should consult Miles Richardson, *The Human Mirror: Material and Spatial Images of Man* (Baton Rouge: Louisiana State University Press, 1974); in folklife, Simon J. Bronner, *American Material Culture and Folklife: A Symposium* (Cooperstown, N.Y.: Cooperstown Graduate Association, 1982); and Don Yoder, *American Folklife* (Austin: University of Texas Press, 1972); in historical archaeology, see Leland Ferguson, *Historical Archaeology and the Importance of Material Things* (Columbia, S.C.: Society for Historical Archaeology, 1977); Robert L. Schuyler, *Historical Archaeology: A Guide to Substantive and Theoretical Contributions* (Farmingdale, N.Y.: Baywood, 1978); M. B. Schiffer, *Advances in Archaeological Method and Theory*, (New York: Academic Press, 1980); Mark P. Leone, ed., *Contemporary Archaeology: A Guide to Theory and Contributions* (Carbondale: Southern Illinois University Press, 1972); and James Deetz, *Man's Imprint from the Past: Readings in the Methods of Archaeology* (Boston: Little, Brown, 1971).

Two valuable collections on humankind's interaction with the material culture of the built environment are H. M. Proshausky, W. H. Ittleson, and L. G. Rivlin, eds., *Environmental Psychology* (New York: Holt, Rinehart and Winston, 1970), a monumental compendium of sixty-five reprinted papers, as well as J. H. Sims and D. D. Baumann, eds., *Human Behavior and the Environment* (Chicago: Maaroa, 1974). Of course, technology has played a significant role in environmental studies of American material culture and that theme can be found in a wide assortment of specialized anthologies in the history of American technology: Brooke Hindle, *America's Wooden Age: Aspects of Its Early Technology*, (Tarrytown, N.Y.: Sleepy Hollow Restorations, 1975); Brooke Hindle, ed., *Material Culture of the Wooden Age* (Tarrytown, N.Y.: Sleepy Hollow Restorations, 1981); Edwin T. Layton, ed., *Technology and Social Change in America* (New York: Harper and Row, 1973); and Carroll W. Pursell, ed., *Readings in Technology and American Life*, (New York: Oxford University Press, 1969); and Carroll W. Pursell, ed., *Technology in America: A History of Ideas and Individuals* (Cambridge, Mass.: MIT Press, 1981). Ian M. G. Quimby and Polly F. G. Earl, eds., *Technological Innovation and the Decorative Arts* (New York: Norton 1969) provides the researcher with an unusual collection of essays linking two of material culture's often separated disciplines. See also Ian M. G. Quimby and Scott Swank, eds., *Perspectives on American Folk Art* (New York: Norton, 1980).

Specialized Bibliographies

By a happy coincidence, however, the history of technology, and art and decorative arts history possess some of the most extensive bibliographic tools. In the history of technology, this fortuitous state of affairs can be attributed largely to Eugene Ferguson, *Bibliography of the History of Technology* (Cambridge, Mass.: MIT Press, 1968), a monumental work that remains the *summa* in the field. For many years, Eugene Ferguson was responsible for the annual bibliography published in *Technology and Culture*, and this yearly feature should be consulted whenever one wishes to survey the field's scholarship of the last decade. Of immense bibliographic use to the colonial historian is Brooke Hindle's previously cited *Technology in Early America* with its invaluable "Directory of Artifact Collections" compiled by Lucius F. Ellsworth. The purpose of Ellsworth's directory was to locate and "describe the types of objects, including accurate models of artifacts, a researcher could expect to find in several representative public and company collections in the United States, and to list additional museums, historical sites, and historical societies which have similar holdings" (p. 102). Unfortunately, American material culture studies can boast of very few similar research tools in the disciplines other than art history.

American art history, however, can be researched through a growing shelf of reference works. In addition to Whitehill, *The Arts in Early American History*, there is now Bernard Karpel, ed., *The Arts in America: A Bibliography*, 4 vols. (Washington: Smithsonian Institution Press, 1979), which includes bibliographies on American architecture, sculpture, design, painting, graphic arts, photography, and film. In this context, other valuable resources are old standards, such as *Art Index* (1929–) and the *Avery Index To Architectural Periodicals*, 15 vols., (1973). It should also be noted that Karpel, *The Arts in America*, pp. U6–U538, also contains a section titled "Visual Resources: A Survey of Pictorial Materials on Americana Available for Study and Purchase in Institutions of the United States."

In the decorative arts, there is Donald Ehresmann, *Applied and Decorative Arts: A Bibliographic Guide to Basic Reference Works, Histories and Handbooks* (Littleton, Colo.: Libraries Unlimited, 1977), while in American architecture, consult David Sokol, *American Architecture and Art: A Guide to Information Sources* (Detroit: Gale Research, 1976).

Bibliographies in American folk art and folklife are uneven. Simon J. Bronner, *Bibliography of American Folk and Vernacular Art* (Bloomington, Ind.: Folklore Publications Group Monograph Series, 1980), is superb in every way: comprehensive, accurate, well-organized, and annotated; whereas Robert Wildhaber, "Folklife Bibliography," *New York Folklife Quarterly* 21 (1965): 259–302 needs to be updated. A useful survey of early American folk art is Beatrice Rumford, "Uncommon Art of the Common People: A Review of Trends in the Collecting and Exhibiting of American Folk Art," in *Perspectives on American Folk Art*, eds. Ian M. G. Quimby and Scott T. Swank (New York: Norton, 1980), pp. 13–53. In order to find the most current surveys of scholarship on vernacular housing (a frequent interest of folklife researchers), one should examine the quarterly bibliographies that Dell Upton has published as part of the *Vernacular Architecture Newsletter*. Another valuable compendium of material specifically on folk architecture is Howard Wight Marshall, *American Folk Architecture: A Selected Bibliography* (Washington: Publications of the American Folklife Center, 1981). Similar listings for new work in general architectural history can be found in the "New Books and Articles" section of the Society of Architectural Historians *SAH Newsletter*.

Material culturists needing background material on general American culture history will profit from the detailed bibliographical essays that accompany each volume of Daniel Boorstin's trilogy on *The Americans* (New York: Random House, 1965–1973). The three-volume *Handbook of Popular Culture* edited by Thomas Inge (Westport, Conn.: Greenwood, 1982) contains valuable bibliographies of research using toys, foodways, photography, popular architecture, and automobiles as material culture evidence. Also of use is the special issue, "Focus on Material Culture," in the *Journal of American Culture* (Winter 1980) edited by Edith Mayo. The student of American artifacts should also be aware of Frederick L. Rath, Jr., and Merrilyn Rodgers O'Connell, *Guide To Historic Preservation, Historical Agencies, and Museum Practices: A Selective Bibliography* (Cooperstown: New York State Historical Association, 1966) and of the extensive bibliographies that are found in each issue of the *Living Historical Farms Bulletin*.

John A. Jakle's *Past Landscapes: A Bibliography for Historic Preservationists Selected from the Literature of Historical Geography* (Monticello, Ill.: Council of Planning Libraries, 1974) is one avenue into the literature of historical and cultural geography; Fred B. Kniffen's "Material Culture in the Geographic Interpretation of the Landscape," *The Human Mirror*, ed. Miles Richardson (Baton Rouge: Louisiana State University Press, 1974) is another. In this context, it is also worth consulting Marvin W. Mikesell, "Tradition and Innovation In Cultural Geography," *Annals of the Association of American Geographers* 68 (March 1978): 1–16; Marvin W. Mikesell, "Geographic Perspectives in Anthropology," ibid., 57 (1967): 617–634; and Douglas R. McManis, *Historical Geography of the United States: A Bibliography* (Ypsilanti, Mich., 1965).

Journals and Newsletters

Any serious worker in American material culture studies must be a conscientious reader of several journals in diverse sub-fields and especially a variety of newsletters in more specialized areas. An introductory list includes:

American Anthropologist. American Anthropological Association, Washington (1888–), quarterly

American Antiquity. Society for American Archaeology, University of Kansas (1935–), quarterly

American Quarterly. American Studies Association, Philadelphia (1949–   ), quarterly
American Walpole Society Notebook. American Walpole Society (1910–   ), randomly
Antiques (The Magazine of Antiques). New York (1922–   ), monthly
Aperture: The Quarterly of Fine Photography. Millerton, N.Y. (1952–   ), quarterly
APT Bulletin. Association for Preservation Technology, Ottawa (1969–   ), quarterly
Architectural Forum. Whitney Publications, New York (1917–1973), ten issues annually
Architectural Review. Boston (1876–   )
Archives of American Art Journal. Archives of American Art (1960–   ), quarterly; previously *Archives Quarterly Bulletin*
Art in America. Marion, Ohio (1913–   ), bimonthly
Art Journal. College Art Association of America (1917–   ), quarterly
Association of American Geographers Annals, Association of American Geographers, Washington (1911–   ), quarterly
Association of Historians of American Art Newsletter. City University of New York (1979–   ), three issues annually
Burlington Magazine. London (1903–   ), monthly
Chronicle of the Early American Industries Association. (1947–   ), quarterly
Clarion, America's Folk Magazine. Museum of American Folk Art, New York (1971–   ), quarterly
Classical America. Boston, randomly
Connoisseur. London (1901–   ), nine issues annually
Cooperstown Graduate Association Proceedings. Cooperstown, N.Y. (1978–   ), randomly
Decorative Arts Newsletter. Decorative Arts Society of the Society of Architectural Historians (1975–   ), quarterly
Dress: Journal of the Costume Society of America. The Costume Institute, New York (1975–   ), annually
Early American Industries Association Chronicle. Albany, N.Y. (1933–   ), quarterly
Environmental Review. Society for Environmental History, Duquesne University (1973–   ), semi-annually
Folklife. Society for Folklife Studies (1956–   ), annually; published under the title *Gwerin* (1956–1961)
Folklore Forum. Bloomington, Ind. (1968–   ), three issues annually
Furniture History. London, (1970–   ), annually
Geographical Review. American Geographical Society, New York (1916–   ), quarterly
Historical Archaeology. Society for Historical Archaeology, California, Penn. (1967–   ), annually
History News. American Association for State and Local History (1954–   ), monthly
IA: The Journal of the Society for Industrial Archaeology. Boston (1976–   ), annually
Industrial Archeology. Devon, England (1964–   ), quarterly
Isis. History of Science Society, Philadelphia (1912–   ), five issues annually
Journal of American Culture. Popular Culture Association, Bowling Green, Ohio (1978–   ), quarterly
Journal of American Folklore. American Folklore Society, Washington (1888–   ), quarterly
Journal of American Institute of Architects. American Institute of Architects, Washington (1913–   ), thirteen issues annually
Journal of Cultural Geography. Bowling Green, Ohio (1980–   ), quarterly

Journal of Early Southern Decorative Arts. Museum of Early Southern Decorative Arts, Winston-Salem, N.C. (1975–), quarterly

Journal of Glass Studies. Corning Museum of Glass, Corning, N.Y. (1959–), annually

Journal of Interdisciplinary History. Cambridge, Mass. (1970–), quarterly

Journal of Popular Culture. Popular Culture Association, Bowling Green, Ohio (1967–), quarterly

Journal of the Society of Architectural Historians. Philadelphia (1941–), quarterly

Keystone Folklore. Pennsylvania Folklore Society, Philadelphia (1956–), quarterly

Landscape. Berkeley, Calif. (1952–), three issues annually

Landscape Architecture. American Society of Landscape Architects, Louisville, Ky., (1910–), bi-monthly

Living History Farms Bulletin. Association of Living History Farms and Agricultural Museums, Washington (1975–), bi-monthly

Material History Bulletin. National Museum of Man, Ottawa, Canada (1971–), semi-annually

Museum News. American Association of Museums, Washington (1924–), bi-monthly

New York Folklore Quarterly. New York Folklore Society, Buffalo, N.Y. (1975–), semi-annually

Nineteenth Century. Victorian Society of America, Philadelphia, (1975–), quarterly

Old-Time New England. Society for the Preservation of New England Antiquities, Boston (1910–), quarterly

Pennsylvania Folklife. Pennsylvania Folklife Society, Lancaster (1949–), quarterly

Pioneer America: The Journal of Historic American Material Culture. Pioneer American Society, Georgia State University (1969–), semi-annually

Prospects: An Annual of American Cultural Studies. New York (1975–), annually

Smithsonian Studies in History and Technology. Washington (1969–), randomly; replaced *Contributions to the Museum of History and Technology* (1959–1968)

Studies in the Anthropology of Visual Communications. Temple University (1973–), three issues annually

Southern Exposure. Institute For Southern Studies, Chapel Hill, N.C. (1973–), quarterly

Studies in Traditional American Crafts. Madison County Historical Society, Madison County, N.Y. (1979–), annually

Technology and Culture. Society for History of Technology, University of Chicago Press (1960–), quarterly

Winterthur Portfolio: A Journal of American Material Culture. Winterthur Museum, Winterthur, Del. (1964–1978), annually; University of Chicago Press (1979–), three issues annually.

Dissertations and Exhibition Catalogs

At present there are no published resources that enable the material researcher to gain easy and comprehensive access to two of the field's important scholarly formats: masters' theses and doctoral dissertations, and museum exhibition catalogs. In neither case do we have a comprehensive, cumulative index to all previous work in these two components of the field.

One can patiently consult University Microfilms, *Dissertation Abstracts* (Ann Arbor, Mich: University Microfilms, annually) in order to seek out past Ph.D. research in any of the dozen or so disciplinary approaches (e.g., art history, cultural geography, and historical archaeology) that comprise the field. But there is no way one can quickly assess the totality of Ph.D. material culture research in any given year or decade. None of the finding aids dealing with Ph.D. scholarship in this country contain a separate category for material culture studies. Hence, knowledge of valuable studies like George McDaniel, "Preserving the People's History: Traditional Black Material Culture in Nineteenth- and Twentieth-Century Southern Maryland" (Ph.D. dissertation, Duke University, 1979) and Simon J. Bronner, "Chain Carvers in Southern Indiana: A Behavioristic Study in Material Culture" (Ph.D. dissertation, Indiana University, 1981) is never adequately disseminated within the scholarly community interested in such research.

An even greater problem exists with regard to the promulgation of masters' theses done on material culture topics since there is no research tool analogous to *Dissertation Abstracts* for master's-level research except in a few disciplines. Ever since interdisciplinary material culture training was institutionalized in the mid-1950s, a large portion of the advanced study in the field has been done for the master's degree. While places such as the Winterthur Museum, the Eleutherian Mills-Hagely Program, the New York State Historical Association, and George Washington University have kept records of their graduate students and their thesis topics, this information has never been collected into a single sourcebook containing abstracts of each thesis's subject matter, methodology, and interlibrary loan access. Art history and the history of technology, however, are exceptions to this general problem. Bernard Karpel's "List of Theses and Dissertations in the Visual Arts," *Arts in America,* 3: T30–T1352, is an outgrowth of the Index of Dissertations and Theses in American Art originally begun at the University of Delaware. The journal *Technology and Culture* annually publishes a "Current Bibliography in the History of Technology" that includes dissertations.

Unlike advanced degree research, museum exhibit catalogs are published. While a few journals in the field (e.g., *Decorative Arts Newsletter*, *Technology and Culture*, and *Winterthur Portfolio*) have begun to publish scholarly reviews of such publications, the material culture researcher must largely depend on his own professional contracts and frequent trips to the bookstores of the country's major museums and historical agencies if he wants to keep current with this mode of material culture publication. Again, there is no single reference work that, say, annually publishes a descriptive analysis of that year's catalogs, indexing them by subject, methodology, and region. Thus there is no regular way the scholar can learn of innovative catalog publications noted earlier by material culturists such as Kenneth Ames, John Vlach, Robert Trent, Howard Wight Marshall, Barbara Ward, or Herbert Hemphill. One can, however, get some idea of previous publications by patiently going through Paul Wasserman and Esther Herman, eds., *Catalog of Museum Publications and Media*, 2nd. ed. (Detroit: Gale Research, 1980).

Representative Works

To date, no one has compiled and published a brief, selective bibliography of what might be termed major works of modern American material culture scholarship. I have in mind a selective list designed to assist the beginning student in recognizing some of the outstanding intellectual achievements in the field. Since many colleagues who teach American material culture studies have been kind enough to share their unpublished course syllabi and bibliographies with me over the years, I have prepared a list of titles many of us consider required reading for the serious student of the subject. I have sequenced them in no particular order other than alphabetical, first listing general studies that, while not specifically concerned with American material culture, are landmarks in the field because of their theoretical or methodological contributions to research involving artifactual data. The second listing contains a pesonal selection of some important books of American material culture scholarship.

General Studies

Alexander, Clifford. *Notes on the Synthesis of Form*. Cambridge, Mass.: Harvard University Press, 1964.

Ariès, Philippe. *Centuries of Childhood: A Social History of Family Life*. Translated by Robert Baldick. New York: Random House, 1962.

――――. *Western Attitudes toward Death: From the Middle Ages to the Present*. Translated by Patricia M. Ranum. Baltimore: The Johns Hopkins University Press, 1974.

Armstrong, Robert R. *The Affecting Presence: An Essay in Humanistic Anthropology*. Urbana: University of Illinois Press, 1971.

Bachelard, Gaston. *The Poetics of Space*. Translated by Maria Julas. New York: Orion, 1964.

Barthes, Roland. *Mythologies*. Translated by Annette Lavers. New York: Hill and Wang, 1972.

Bloch, Marc. *French Rural History: An Essay on Its Basic Characteristics*. Translated by Janet Sondheimer. Berkeley: University of California Press, 1966.

Boas, Franz. *Primitive Art*. New York: Dover, 1955.

Bogatyrev, Petr. *The Functions of Folk Costume in Moravian Slovakia*. Translated by Richard G. Crum. The Hague: Mouton, 1971.

Braudel, Fernand. *Capitalism and Material Life, 1400–1800*. Translated by Miriam Kochar. New York: Harper and Row, 1974.

Brunskill, R. W. *Illustrated Handbook of Vernacular Architecture*. London: Faber and Faber, 1970.

Childe, Gordon Vere. *Man Makes Himself*. New York: New American Library, 1951.

Collier, John, Jr. *Visual Anthropology: Photography as a Research Method*. New York: Holt, Rinehart and Winston, 1967.

Evans, G. Ewart. *Ask the Fellow Who Cut the Hay*. London: Faber and Faber, 1956.

Geertz, Clifford, ed. *Myth, Symbol, and Culture*. New York: Norton, 1974.

Giedeon, Siegfried. *Mechanization Takes Command: A Contribution to Anonymous History*. New York: Oxford University Press, 1948.

————. *Space, Time and Architecture*. Cambridge, Mass.: Harvard University Press, 1967.

Haddon, Alfred C. *Evaluation in Arts As Illustrated by the Life-Histories of Designs*. London: W. Scott, 1895.

Hall, Edward T. *The Hidden Dimension*. Garden City: Doubleday, 1966.

Harris, Marvin. *Cultural Materialism: The Struggle for a Science of Culture*. New York: Random House, 1979.

Herskovits, Melville J. *Man and His Works*. New York: Knopf, 1948.

Hoskins, W. G. *English Landscapes*. London: British Broadcasting Corp., 1973.

Jenkins, Geraint. *The English Farm Wagon: Origins and Structure*. Newton Abbot, Eng.: David and Charles, 1972.

Kluckhohn, Clyde. *Mirror for Man*. New York: McGraw-Hill, 1949.

Kroeber, Alfred E. *Anthropology*. New York: Harcourt, Brace and World, 1948.

Kubler, George. *The Shape of Time: Remarks on the History of Things*. New Haven: Yale University Press, 1962.

Langer, Suzanne K. *Philosophy in a New Key: A Study in the Symbolism of Reason, Rite and Art*. Cambridge, Mass.: Harvard University Press, 1942.

Lévi-Strauss, Claude. *The Savage Mind*. Chicago: University of Chicago Press, 1966.

————. *The Raw and the Cooked*. Translated by John Weightman and Doreen Weightman. New York: Harper and Row, 1969.

————. *Structural Anthropology*. Translated by Claire Jacobson and Brooke Grunfest Shoepf. Garden City: Doubleday, 1967.

Lynch, Kevin. *What Time is this Place?* Cambridge, Mass.: MIT Press, 1972.

Mumford, Lewis. *Art and Technics*. New York: Columbia University Press, 1952.

Murdock, George P., Chellan S. Ford, and Alfred E. Hudson. *Outline of Cultural Materials*. New Haven: Yale University Press, 1945.

Norberg-Schulz, Christian. *Intentions in Architecture*. Cambridge, Mass.: MIT Press, 1968.

————. *Existence, Space and Architecture*. New York: Praeger, 1971.

Panofsky, Edwin. *Studies in Iconology: Humanistic Themes in the Art of the Renaissance*. New York: Oxford University Press, 1939.

————. *Gothic Architecture and Scholasticism*. New York: Meridian, 1957.

Pye, David. *The Nature of Design*. New York: Reinhold, 1964.

————. *The Nature and Art of Workmanship*. London: Cambridge Unviersity Press, 1968.

Rapoport, Amos. *House Form and Culture*. Englewood Cliffs: Prentice-Hall, 1969.

Read, Herbert. *Icon and Idea: The Function of Art in the Development of Human Consciousness*. New York: Schocken, 1967.

Smith, Cyril Stanley. *From Art to Science: Seventy-two Objects Illustrating the Nature of Discovery*. Cambridge, Mass.: MIT Press, 1980.

Taylor, Walter W. *A Study of Archaeology*. Carbondale: Southern Illinois University Press, 1967.

White, Leslie A. *The Science of Culture: A Study of Man and Civilization*. New York: Farrar, Strauss and Giroux, 1969.

————. *The Evolution of Culture: The Development of Civilization to the Fall of Rome*. New York: McGraw-Hill, 1959.

White, Lynn, Jr. *Medieval Technology and Social Change*. Oxford, Eng.: Clarendon Press, 1962.

American Works

Adams, Henry. *The Education of Henry Adams*. Boston: Houghton Mifflin, 1918.
Ames, Kenneth. *Beyond Necessity: Art in the Folk Tradition*. Winterthur, Del.: Winterthur Museum, 1977.
Banham, Reynor. *Los Angeles: The Architecture of Four Ecologies*. New York: Harper and Row, 1971.
Benes, Peter. *Masks of Orthodoxy: Folk Gravestone Carving in Plymouth County, Massachusetts, 1689–1805*. Amherst: University of Massachusetts Press, 1977.
Boorstin, Daniel. *The Americans: The Colonial Experience*. New York: Random House, 1958.
———. *The Americans: The National Experience*. New York: Random House, 1965.
———. *The Americans: The Democratic Experience*. New York: Random House, 1973.
Burlingame, Roger. *The March of the Iron Men: A Social History of Union through Invention*. New York: Scribner's, 1938.
Condit, Carl. *American Building Materials and Techniques from the First Colonial Settlements to the Present*. Chicago: University of Chicago Press, 1968.
Deetz, James. *An Invitation to Archaeology*. Garden City: Natural History Press, 1967.
———. *In Small Things Forgotten: The Archaeology of Early North American Life*. Garden City: Anchor, 1977.
Demos, John. *A Little Commonwealth: Family Life in the Plymouth Colony*. London: Oxford University Press, 1971.
Ferguson, Leland, ed. *Historical Archaeology and the Importance of Material Things*. Lansing, Mich.: Society for Historical Archaeology, 1977.
Fitchen, John. *The New World Dutch Barn: A Study of Its Characteristics, Its Structural System, and Its Probable Erectional Procedures*. Syracuse, N.Y.: Syracuse University Press, 1968.
Glassie, Henry. *Pattern in the Material Folk Culture of the Eastern United States*. Philadelphia: University of Pennsylvania Press, 1968.
———. *Folk Housing in Middle Virginia: A Structural Analysis of Historic Artifacts*. Knoxville: University of Tennessee Press, 1975.
Goffman, Erving. *The Presentation of Self in Everyday Life*. Garden City: Doubleday, 1959.
Greenough, Horatio. *Form and Function: Remarks on Art, Design and Architecture*. Edited by Harold A. Small. Berkeley: University of California Press, 1966.
Gowans, Alan. *Images of American Living: Four Centuries of Architecture and Furniture as Cultural Expression*. Philadelphia: Lippincott, 1964.
Harris, Neil. *The Artist in American Society: The Formative Years, 1790–1860*. New York: Braziller, 1966.
Hornung, Clarence. *The Treasury of American Design*. New York: Abrams, 1972.
Jackson, J. B. *American Space: The Centennial Years, 1865–1867*. New York: Norton, 1972.
Jones, Michael Owen. *The Hand-Made Object and Its Maker*. Berkeley: University of California Press, 1975.
Kouwenhoven, John. *Made in America: The Arts in Modern Civilization*. Garden City: Doubleday, 1948.
Ludwig, Alan. *Graven Images: New England Stonecarving and Its Symbols, 1650–1815*. Middletown: Wesleyan University Press, 1966.

Lynes, Russell. *The Tastemakers*. New York: Harper, 1954.

Mayer, Harold M. and Richard C. Wade. *Chicago: Growth of a Metropolis*. Chicago: University of Chicago Press, 1969.

Meinig, D. W., ed. *The Interpretation of Ordinary Landscapes*. New York: Oxford University Press, 1979.

Mercer, Henry C. *Ancient Carpenter Tools*. Doylestown, Penn.: Bucks County Historical Society, 1929.

Miller, Lillian B. *Patrons and Patriotism: The Encouragement of the Fine Arts in the United States, 1790–1860*. Chicago: University of Chicago Press, 1966.

Montgomery, Charles F. *American Furniture in the Henry Francis duPont Winterthur Museum: The Federal Period*. New York: Viking, 1966.

Mumford, Lewis. *The Brown Decades: A Study of the Arts in America, 1865–1895*. New York: Harcourt, Brace, 1931.

Nöel Hume, Ivor. *Historical Archaeology*. New York: Knopf, 1969.

————. *Here Lies Virginia: An Archaeologist's View of Colonial Life and History*. New York: Knopf, 1963.

Smith, Merritt Roe. *Harper's Ferry Armory and the New Technology: The Challenge of Change*. Ithaca, N.Y.: Cornell University Press, 1977.

Stokes, I. N. Phelps. *The Iconography of Manhattan Island, 1498–1909*. 6 vols. New York: Dodd, 1915–1928.

Tractenberg, Alan. *The Brooklyn Bridge: Fact and Symbol*. New York: Oxford University Press, 1965.

Veblen, Thorstein. *The Theory of the Leisure Class: An Economic Study of Institutions*. New York: Macmillan, 1912.

Vlach, John Michael. *The Afro-American Tradition in Decorative Arts*. Cleveland: Cleveland Museum of Arts, 1978.

Welsch, Roger L. *Sod Walls: The Story of the Nebraska Sodhouse*. Broken Bow, Nebr.: Purcells, 1968.

Wertenbaker, Thomas. *The Founding of American Civilization: Middle Colonies*. New York: Scribner's, 1938.

————. *The Founding of American Civilization: The Old South*. New York: Scribner's, 1942.

————. *The Founding of American Civilization: Puritan Oligarchy*. New York: Scribner's, 1947.

NOTES

Notes

Preface

1. Lucius F. Ellsworth and Maureen A. O'Brien, *Material Culture: Historical Agencies and the Historian* (Philadelphia: Book Reprint Service, 1969), pp. 2–3.

2. Unlike the Ellsworth-O'Brien focus on historical agencies, I have tried to provide readers with a much more extensive, although introductory, discussion of the methodological approaches, theoretical assumptions, and conceptual models that have influenced material culture scholarship in America over the last century.

3. To propose the term "folklife studies" as a subset of material culture studies will undoubtedly irritate a few veteran scholars and perhaps confuse some beginning researchers. I resort to it as the most generic label under which one could subsume the majority of contemporary scholars who call themselves folklorists and yet also include material culture (e.g., folk art, craft, architecture, foodways, and settlement patterns) as important evidence in their research. Thus, under my category of folklife studies, I think it is feasible to include those who call themselves "folklorists" (such as Henry Glassie), those who prefer the term "folklife scholars" (like Don Yoder), folklorists engaged in what they call "folkloristics" (Michael O. Jones), and those wishing to be identified as researchers working in the "folklife sciences" (like Simon J. Bronner).

This pluralism prevails despite the fact that folklife is one of the few disciplines ever to be officially defined by an act of Congress—American Folklife Preservation Act (P.L. 94–20), H. R. 6673, 94th Cong. (1976), and National Historic Preservation Act Amendments of 1980 (P.L. 96–515), 96th Cong. (1980)—and institutionalized by the federal government in its American Folklife Center at the Library of Congress. For a detailed account of the debates over both terminology and methodology in American folklore-folklife research, see: William K. McNeil, "A History of American Folklore Scholarship before 1908" (Ph.D. dissertation, Indiana University, 1980); Susan Dwyer-Shick, "The American Folklore Society and Folklore Research in America, 1888–1940" (Ph.D. dissertation, University of Pennsylvania, 1979); and Don Yoder, "The Folklife Studies Movement," *Pennsylvania Folklife* 13 (July 1963): 43–56.

4. See, for example, Carroll W. Pursell, Jr., *Readings in Technology and American Life* (New York: Oxford University Press, 1969); Richard M. Dorson, *Folklore and Folklife: An Introduction* (Chicago: University of Chicago Press, 1972); Don Yoder *American Folklife* (Austin: University of Texas Press, 1976); Miles Richardson, *The Human Mirror: Material and Spatial Images of Man* (Baton Rouge: Louisiana State University Press, 1974); Philip Wagner and Marvin W. Mikesell, *Readings in Cultural Geography* (Chicago: University of Chicago Press, 1962); Robert L. Schuyler, *Historical Archaeology: A Guide to Substantive and Theoretical Contributions* (Farmingdale, N.Y.: Baywood, 1978); W. Eugene Kleinbauer, *Modern Perspectives in Western Art History* (New York: Holt, Rinehart and Winston, 1971).

5. Others have convincingly argued this point prior to my own book, Thomas J. Schlereth, *Artifacts*

and the American Past (Nashville, Tenn.: American Association for State and Local History, 1980). See also Murray G. Murphey, "American Civilization as a Civilization," *Emory University Quarterly* 48 (March 1967): 51–52; Richard E. Sykes, "American Studies and the Concept of Culture: A Theory and a Method," *American Quarterly* 15 (Summer 1963): 253–270; Charles T. Lyle, "The Artifact and American History: An Examination of the Use of the Artifact for Historical Evidence" (Masters thesis, University of Delaware, 1971); Louis C. Jones, "Three Eyes on the Past: A New Triangulation for Local Studies," *New York Folklore Quarterly* 12 (1956): 3–13.

6. Simon J. Bronner, "Concepts in the Study of Material Aspects of American Folk Culture," *Folklore Forum* 12 (1979): 165.

7. For example, the influential work of scholars such as George Kubler, Louis C. Jones, Warren Roberts, Ivor-Nöel Hume, Brooke Hindle, Don Yoder, Anthony Garvan, Robert Trent, John Vlach, Leland Ferguson, Mark Leone, Cary Carson, Barbara Carson, Howard Wight Marshall, Alan Gowans, Robert Vogel, John Cotter, J. B. Jackson, C. Malcolm Watkins, Jules D. Prown, Eugene Ferguson, Darwin Kelsey, Charles Hummel, Benno Forman, Scott Swank, Michael Owen Jones, and Harold Skramstad has not been included only because a brief, article-length study by them was unavailable or, if available, it strongly paralleled another essay already selected for the anthology.

8. Two exceptions to this restriction would be scholarship by Steven Beckow, a Canadian, and by David Pye, a native of Great Britain.

9. Leland Ferguson, *Historical Archaeology and the Importance of Material Things* (Columbia, S.C.: Society for Historical Archaeology, 1977), p. 6.

10. Henry David Thoreau, *Journals*, ed. Bradford Torrey and Francis H. Allen (New York: Dover, 1962), March 28, 1859; Henry Glassie, "Eighteenth-Century Cultural Processes in Delaware Valley Folk Building," *Winterthur Portfolio* 7 (1972): 30; and Henry Glassie, "Vernacular Architecture," *Journal of the Society of Architectural Historians* 35 ((December 1976): 293–295.

Chapter One

1. A segment of this essay was first presented as a paper at the International Conference on Material History sponsored by the Canadian government's National Museum of Man, Ottawa, Canada, March 1–3, 1979, and subsequently published, in abbreviated form, in *Material History Bulletin* 8 (1979): 89–98. In the extensive expansion and revision of the essay, I am greatly indebted to E. McClung Fleming, Steven K. Hamp, Barney Finn, Susan Myers, Ann Golvin, Wilcomb Washburn, Kenneth Ames, Claudia Kidwell, John Mannion, Harold Skramstad, Joanna Schneider Zangrando, John Zukowsky, Simon J. Bronner, Bernard Mergen, Michael Owen Jones, Harvey Green, Mark Leone, Brooke Hindle, and Howard Wight Marshall for their helpful critique and generous advice.

2. See Gordon R. Willey and Jeremy A. Sabloff, *A History of American Archaeology* (San Francisco: Freeman, 1974); Don Yoder, "The Folklife Studies Movement," *Pennsylvania Folklife* 13 (July 1963): 43–52; William N. Fenton, "The Advancement of Material Culture Studies in Modern Anthropological Research" in *The Human Mirror: Material and Spatial Images of Man*, ed. Miles Richardson (Baton Rouge: Louisiana State University Press, 1974), pp. 15–36; W. Eugene Kleinbauer, *Modern Perspectives in Western Art History* (New York: Holt, Rinehart and Winston, 1971), pp. 1–65; Howard Wight Marshall, "Folklife and the Rise of American Folk Museums," *Journal of American Folklore* 90 (October-December 1977): 391–413; George H. Daniels, "The Big Questions in the History of Technology," *Technology and Culture* 11 (January 1970): 1–35.

3. Archaeologist and anthropologist James Deetz offers one of the most comprehensive contemporary definitions.

"Culture" is socially transmitted rules for behavior, ways of thinking about and doing things. We inherit our culture from the teachings and examples of our elders and our peers rather than from genes, whether it is the language we speak, the religious beliefs that we subscribe to, or the laws that govern our society. All such behavior is reflected in subtle and important ways in the manner in which we shape our physical world. Material culture is usually considered to be roughly synonymous with artifacts, the vast universe of objects used by mankind to cope with the physical world, to facilitate social intercourse, and to benefit our state of mind. A somewhat broader definition of material culture is useful in emphasizing how profoundly our world is the product of our thoughts, as that sector of our physical environment that we modify through culturally determined behavior. This definition includes all artifacts, from the simplest, such as a common pin, to the most complex, such as an interplanetary space vehicle. But the physical environment includes more than what most definitions of material culture recognize. We can also consider cuts of meat as material culture, since there are many ways to dress an animal; likewise plowed fields and even the horse that pulls the plow, since scientific breeding of livestock involves the conscious modification of an animal's form according to culturally derived ideals. Our body itself is a part of our physical environment, so that such things as parades, dancing, and all aspects of kinesics—human motion—fit within our definition. Nor is the definition limited only to matter in the solid state. Fountains are liquid examples, as are lily ponds, and material that is partly gas includes hot air balloons and neon signs. I have suggested in *Invitation to Archaeology* that even language is a part of material culture, a prime example of it in its gaseous state. Words, after all, are air masses shaped by the speech apparatus according to culturally acquired rules.

James Deetz, *In Small Things Forgotten: The Archaeology of Early North American Life* (New York: Doubleday, 1977), pp. 24–25.

Other definitions of material culture can be found in Ian M. G. Quimby, editorial statement in "Material Culture Is" a promotional brochure for the new series of the *Winterthur Portfolio* (1979); Richard S. Latham, "The Artifact as a Cultural Cipher," in *Who Designs America?* ed. Laurence B. Holland (Garden City: Doubleday, 1966), pp. 257–280; Jules D. Prown, "Material Culture and the Use of Artifacts as Cultural Evidence," *Winterthur Portifolio* 17 (Spring 1982): 1–3; John Chavis, "The Artifact and the Study of History," *Curator* 7 (1964): 156–162; Leland Ferguson, "Historical Archaeology and the Importance of Material Things," in *Historical Archaeology and the Importance of Material Things,* ed. Leland Ferguson (Columbia, S.C.: Society for Historical Archaeology, 1977), pp. 6–7; James Deetz, "Material Culture and Archaeology—What's the Difference?" ibid., pp. 9–12; William L. Rathje "In Praise of Archaeology: Le Projet du Garbage," ibid., p. 37.

4. Melville J. Herskovits, *Cultural Anthropology* (New York: Knopf, 1963), p. 119.

5. Such an analysis might begin with a careful comparative exegesis of various definitions of material culture. Compare: Clark Wissler, "Material Cultures of the North American Indian," *American Anthropologist* 16 (1914): 447–505; H. S. Harrison, "Material Culture," *Encyclopaedia Britannica,* 14th ed. (New York: Encyclopaedia Britannica, 1930); George I. Quimby, "Material Culture," *Encyclopaedia Britannica,* (Chicago: Encyclopaedia Britannica, 1968), and by Clyde Kluckhohn, *et al.,* *Navaho Material Culture* (Cambridge, Mass.: Belknap Press and Harvard University Press, 1971).

6. Ferguson, *Historical Archaeology,* p. 8.

7. Thomas J. Schlereth, "Material Culture Studies in America: Notes toward a Historical Perspective" *Material History Bulletin* 8 (1979): 89–98.

8. E. McClung Fleming, "History 802: The Artifact in American History," unpublished course outline, Winterthur Program in Early American Culture, 1969; Elizabeth B. Wood, "Pots and Pans History: Relating Manuscripts and Printed Sources to the Study of Domestic Art Objects," *The American Archivist* 30 (July 1967): 431–442; David Goldfield, "The Physical City as Artifact and Teaching Tool," *The History Teacher* 8 (August 1975): 535–556; Charles F. Montgomery, "Classics and Collectibles: American Antiques as History and Art," *Art News* (November 1977): 126–136; Kenneth L. Ames, "Meaning in Artifacts: Hall Furnishings in Victorian America," *Journal of Interdisciplinary History* 9 (Summer 1978): 19–46; John Cotter, *Above-Ground Archaeology,* (Washington: Government Printing Office, 1972); Ivor Nöel Hume, *Historical Archaeology* (New York: Knopf, 1968), p. 21; American Association of Museums, *Museum Studies: A Curriculum Guide for Universities and Museums* (Washington: American Association of Museums, 1973).

9. Ferguson, ed., *Historical Archaeology,* pp. 8, 37.

10. Jules D. Prown, "Mind in Matter: An Introduction to Material Culture Theory and Method," p. 2.

11. *Pioneer America's* 1981 board of editorial advisors offers an example of the diversity of fields and fields frequently identified with material culture studies in the United States: folklore, placenames, cultural geography, architectural history, historical geography, social anthropology, crafts, museums, American Studies, local history, and historical archaeology. For the *Portfolio's* editorial manifesto, see *Winterthur Portfolio* (February 1979): p. 1.

12. For example, in the 1979 description of Boston University's American and New England Studies Program, Jane C. Nylander, a curator of textiles and ceramics at Old Sturbridge Village and an adjunct professor of American Studies at the university, is specifically designated as a specialist in eighteenth- and nineteenth-century American material culture. In the *Society for Historical Archaeology Newsletter* 12 (March 1979): 12–13, the University of Pennsylvania's Department of American Civilization also advertised a new teaching position for an assistant professor of American material culture.

The Colorado Historical Society now employs a curator of material culture who administers the "material culture department of the Colorado Historical Society with the responsibility for planning, developing, implementing and supervising programs to aid in the understanding of the cultural and historical heritage of Colorado." *History News* 35 (May 1980): 19.

13. Lucius Ellsworth and Maureen O'Brien, eds., *Material Culture: Historical Agencies and the Historian* (Philadelphia: Book Reprint Service, 1969); Ian M. G. Quimby, ed., *Material Culture and the Study of American Life* (New York: Norton, 1978); Henry Glassie, *Patterns in Material Folk Culture of Eastern United States* (Philadelphia: University of Pennsylvania Press, 1968); "Material Culture: A Conference" sponsored by the Bay State Historical League, Bradford, Massachusetts, June 20–22, 1980; Simon J. Bronner, ed. *American Material Culture and Folklife: A Symposium* (Cooperstown, N.Y.: Cooperstown Graduate Associate Proceedings, 1982); North Carolina Department of Cultural Resources, "The Material Culture of Black History: Problems and Methods," Durham, North Carolina, December 13, 1980.

14. As early as the 1950s, Anthony N. B. Garvan offered a seminar in the University of Pennsylvania's American Civilization Program listed as "The Material Aspects of American Culture." E. M. Fleming notes that he developed his course, "The Artifact in American History," in the Winterthur Museum-University of Delaware program with Garvan's model in mind. Author's interview with E. M. Fleming, August 14, 1977. I am also indebted to E. M. Fleming, "The Study and Interpretation of the Historical Artifacts: A New Profession," unpublished essay, 1965, p. 16.

15. The Center for American Art and Material Culture, *Brochure for Prospective Students* (New Haven: Yale University, 1978); also see Montgomery "Classics and Collectibles," p. 136. On developments at George Washington University and the Smithsonian Institution, I have used Robert H. Walker, "American Studies at the George Washington University," *American Quarterly* 22 (Summer 1970): 528–538; Wilcomb Washburn, "American Studies at the Smithsonian Institution," *American Quarterly* 22 (Summer 1970): 560–570; and profited by a letter of July 19, 1979, from Joanna Schneider Zangando, who held George Washington University's initial fellowship in material culture studies. On April 11–12, 1980, the Graduate American Studies Student Organization at George Washington sponsored a conference, "An American Montage: New Interpretations of Culture Evidence," specifically devoted to "integrating material evidence in the study of culture."

16. Deetz, "Material Culture and Archaeology—What's the Difference?" pp. 11, 66.

17. National Endowment for the Humanities, *American Social History* (Washington: Government Printing Office, 1979); Laurence Vesey, "The 'New' Social History in the Context of American Historical Writing," *Reviews in American History* 7 (March 1979): 1–12.

18. Howard W. Marshall and Richard E. Ahlborn, *Buckaroos in Paradise: Cowboy Life in Northern Nevada* (Washington: Library of Congress, 1980).

19. Warren E. Roberts, "Fieldwork: Recording Material Culture," in *Folklore and Folklife: An Introduction*, ed. Richard Dorson (Chicago: University of Chicago Press, 1972), pp. 431–444.

20. Scott Swank, in his introduction to the published proceedings of the three-day conference on American folk art held at the Winterthur Museum, sees this interdisciplinary emphasis on "the convergence of disciplines as one of the most exciting aspects of material culture study in the 1970s." Ian M. G.

Quimby and Scott Swank, eds., *Perspectives on American Folk Art* (New York: Norton, 1980), p. 10. Swank's point is bolstered by another essay in the proceedings: Johannes Fabian and Ilona Szombati-Fabian, "Folk Art from an Anthropological Perspective," pp. 247–292.

21. John J. Mannion, "Multidisciplinary Dimensions in Material History," *Material History Bulletin* 8 (1979): 21.

22. Examples of such identification and of the expanding currency of material culture studies as an interdisciplinary movement can be found in the course descriptions and syllabi currently filed by scholars (e.g., Joanna Schneider Zangando, David Cohen, Jane Nylander, Leon Siroto, Richard Rabinowitz, and Thomas Schlereth) in the "Faculty Curricular File," American Studies Association, College Hall, University of Pennsylvania, Philadelphia, Penn. Steven Hamp (Department of Education, Henry Ford Museum) and Edwin Dethlefsen (Department of Anthropology, William and Mary College) have also shared with me their course syllabi on American material culture.

23. European scholarship, however, has been much more cooperative and collaborative. Team projects, rather than isolated researchers, have fostered impressive outdoor folk museums, such as the Skansen of Arthur Hazelius and the Welsh Folk Museum of Iorwerth Peate, elaborate folklife research centers, like the Leire Historical-Archaeological Research Center in Denmark and Butser Hill Project in Hampshire England, and monumental folk material culture atlases, including the *Atlas over Svensk Folkkultur* and the *Atlas der schweizerischen Volkskunde*. For additional details of these directions in European material culture research, see Robert Wildhaber, "Folk Atlas Mapping," and J. Geraint Jenkins, "The Use of Artifacts and Folk Art in the Folk Museum," in *Folklore and Folklife*, ed. Dorson, pp. 479–496 and pp. 497–516.

24. George A. Kubler, "The Arts: Fine and Plain," in *Perspectives on American Folk Art*, ed. Quimby and Swank, pp. 235–246. Pertinent here, from the perspective of the social sciences, is Leland Ferguson's introductory essay in *Historical Archaeology and the Importance of Material Things*, ed. Ferguson, pp. 5–8.

25. Historian Michael Kammen has done a quick overview of this cultural phenomenon; see Michael Kammen, "In Search of America," *Historic Preservation*, 32 (September/October 1980): 30–37.

26. Neil Harris, "Museums, Merchandising, and Popular Taste: The Struggle for Influence," in *Material Culture and the Study of American Life*, edited by Ian M. G. Quimby (New York: Norton, 1978): pp. 141–149. Writing of American world fairs, in the same work (p. 179), Harris claims: "Their design, development and production required the systematic organization and assemblage of material culture into a new and complex artifact which in turn affected not only popular taste but Americans' perceptions of their society."

27. See Charles B. Hosmer, *Presence of the Past: A History of the Preservation Movement in the United States before Williamsburg* (New York: Putnam, 1965) and Charles B. Hosmer, *Preservation Comes of Age*, 2 vols. (Charlottesville: University Press of Virginia, 1981). David E. Finley, *History of the National Trust for Historic Preservation, 1947–1963* (Washington: National Trust for Historic Preservation, 1965); Elizabeth Mulloy, *History of the National Trust for Historical Preservation, 1963–1973* (Washington, D.C.: Preservation Press, 1976); and William E. Cline, *Historic Preservation Literature, 1969–1977: Selected References* (Monticello, Ill.: Council of Planning Librarians, 1978).

28. No comprehensive, analytical cultural history of the American collector (other than art collectors) exists at present. Some ideas as to his or her role can be gleaned from Douglas Rigby and Elizabeth Rigby, *Lock, Stock and Barrel: The Story of Collecting* (Philadelphia: Lippincott, 1944).

29. To date, the Americana movement has only been studied piecemeal. In the museum world, for instance, historical studies have been primarily on art museums. See Nathaniel Burt, *A Social History of the American Art Museum* (Boston: Little, Brown, 1977); and Daniel M. Fox, *Engines of Culture: Philanthropy and Art Museums* (Madison: Wisconsin State Historical Society, 1963). Only Neil Harris, "The Gilded Age Revisited: Boston and the Museum Movement," *American Quarterly* 14 (Winter 1962): 545–566, and Helen L. Horowitz, *Culture and the City* (Lexington: University of Kentucky Press, 1976) have attempted social-cultural analyses. Historical societies have received some attention; see

David D. Van Tassel, *Recording America's Past: An Interpretation of the Development of Historical Societies in America, 1607–1884* (Chicago: University of Chicago Press, 1960); William T. Alderson, "The American Association for State and Local History," *The Western Historical Quarterly* 1 (April 1970): 175–182; Anne Farnam, "The Essex Institute of Salem," *Nineteenth Century* 5 (Summer 1979): 76–81; and Russell W. Fridley, "Critical Choices for Minnesota Historical Society," *Minnesota History* 46 (Winter 1978): 130–146.

30. The majority of scholarship that surveys American material culture studies has been largely bibliographic in intent and format; see, for instance, Harold K. Skramstad, "American Things: Neglected Material Culture," *American Studies International* 10 (Spring 1972): 11–22; Thomas J. Schlereth, "The City as Artifact," *American Historical Association Newsletter*, 15 (February 1977): 7–9; Patrick H. Butler, "Material Culture as a Resource in Local History: A Bibliography," *The Newberry Papers in Family and Community History*, 77–2 (January 1977): 1–23; Simon J. Bronner, "Concepts In the Study of Material Aspects of American Folk Culture," *Folklore Forum* 12 (1979): 133–172.

31. E. McClung Fleming, "The Study and Interpretation of the Historical Artifact: A New Profession," unpublished paper presented to Fellows in American Studies, Philadelphia, 1965, pp. 2–7.

32. My historical division into stages of development shares a considerable affinity with a periodization scheme conceptualized by Gordon R. Willey and Jeremy A. Sabloff in their historical assessment of the development of American archaeological strategies and methods, Gordon R. Willey and Jeremy A. Sabloff, *A History of American Archaeology* (San Francisco: Freeman, 1974), pp. 16–21. My schema also has parallels with a chronology suggested by Edith Mayo's introductory essay to the special section, "Focus on Material Culture," *Journal of American Culture* 4 (Winter 1980): 597. She proposes that since the early-twentieth century, "the general thrusts in material culture approaches have been: (1) a descriptive phrase, from the 1920s to the 1950s, where emphasis was placed on describing the objects in a collection; (2) the use of objects as supplementary to documentary evidence, that is, objects appearing as "footnotes" or corroborative evidence to an already-existing historical thesis derived from written sources (in the 1950s); (3) the use of objects as important documents in conveying historical information about the past (in the 1960s); (4) the perception of cultural values reflected in the objects (the 1970s)."

33. Harold K. Skramstad, Jr., "Interpreting Material Culture: A View From the Other Side of the Glass," in *Material Culture and the Study of American Life*, ed. Quimby, p. 176. Charles Coleman Sellers, *Mr. Peale's Museum: Charles Willson Peale and the First Popular Museum of Natural Science and Art* (New York: Norton, 1980). Also see Daniel Boorstin, *The Lost World of Thomas Jefferson* (Boston: Beacon, 1948), pp. 19–21.

34. Frank H. Sommer, "John F. Watson: First Historian of the Decorative Arts," *Antiques* 83 (March 1963): 300–303; Richard H. Saunders, "Collecting American Decorative Arts in New England," *Antiques* 109 (May 1976): 996–1003, 110, 754–763.

35. Alan Gowans, *Images of American Living: Four Centuries of Architecture and Furniture as Cultural Expression* (Philadelphia: Lippincott, 1964), p. xiii; Deetz, *In Small Things Forgotten*, pp. 29–30; Alma S. Wittlin, *Museums: In Search of a Useable Future* (Cambridge, Mass.: MIT Press, 1970), pp. 51–53.

36. Sellers, *Mr. Peale's Museum*, p. 2.

37. Wilcomb E. Washburn, "Joseph Henry's Conception of the Purpose of the Smithsonian Institution," in *A Cabinet of Curiosities: Five Episodes in the Evolution of American Museums* (Charlottesville: The University Press of Virginia, 1967), pp. 106–166.

38. Also see William J. Rhees, ed., *The Smithsonian Institution: Documents Relating to its Origin and History, 1835–1899*, 2 vols. (Washington: Smithsonian Institution, 1901); and Michael J. Lacey, "The Mysteries of Earth-Making Dissolve: A Study of Washington's Intellectual Community and the Origins of American Environmentalism in the Late Nineteenth Century" (Ph.D. dissertation, George Washington University, 1979).

39. Kenneth Ames, "Folk Art: The Challenge and the Promise," in *Perspectives on American Folk Art*, ed. Quimby and Swank, p. 295.

40. Ames goes on to argue (in "Folk Art: Challenge and Promise," pp. 295–296): "Centripetal

patterns generally yield safe and relatively predictable results which offend or surprise few people because they avoid substantive issues. Centripetal patterns are generally predicated on the acceptance of the status quo; major questions are either considered to have been settled or assumed to be the responsibility of someone else or some other field.''

41. In this country, historical societies begin with the Massachusetts Historical Society in 1791. A list of historical societies with the dates of their founding is included in John Spencer Bassett, ''Later Historians,'' in *The Cambridge History of American Literature* (New York: Cambridge University Press: 1917–1921), 3:172–173; see also, J. Franklin Jameson, *History of Historical Societies* (Savannah, Ga.: Morning News Print, 1914).

42. Dianne Pilgrim, ''Inherited from the Past: The American Period Room,'' *American Art Journal* 10 (1978): 6; J. B. Jackson, *American Space: The Centennial Years* (New York: Norton, 1972), pp. 231–240; Elizabeth Stillinger, *The Antiquers* (New York: Knopf, 1980), pp. 17–22; also see Robert Trent, *Pilgrim Century Furniture: An Historical Survey* (New Haven, Conn.: Yale University Press, 1948), p. 7.

43. Rodris Roth, ''The Colonial Revival and 'Centennial Furniture,' '' *Art Quarterly* 27 (1964): 57–82; John Maass, *The Glorious Enterprise: The Centennial Exhibition of 1876 and H. J. Schwarzmann, Architect-in-Chief* (Watkins Glen, N.Y.: American Life Foundation, 1973); Robert Post, ed., *1876: A Centennial Exhibition* (Washington: Smithsonian Institution, 1976), pp. 11–23, 189–206.

44. Compare Vincent J. Scully, Jr., ''Queen Anne and Colonial Revival, 1869–1876,'' in *The Shingle Style* (New Haven: Yale University Press, 1955), pp. 9–33 and Maass, *Glorious Enterprise*, pp. 84–92.

45. William Rhodes, *The Colonial Revival* (New York: Garland, 1977), pp. 48–52.

46. Oliver W. Larkin, ''Samuel McIntire and the Arts of Post-Colonial America,'' *Samuel McIntire: A Bicentennial Symposium, 1757–1957*, ed. Benjamin W. Labaree (Salem, Mass.: Essex Institute, 1957), pp. 99–109; and Holger Cahill, ''Introduction'' in *The Index of American Design*, ed. Erwin O. Christensen (New York: Macmillan, 1950), pp. ix–xvii.

47. James Ackerman, ''Art History in America,'' in *Art and Archaeology*, ed. James Ackerman and Rhys Carpenter (Englewood Cliffs: Prentice-Hall, 1963), pp. 187–195; Erwin Panofsky, ''Three Decades of Art History in the United States,'' in *The Cultural Migration: The European Scholar in America*, ed. Franz L. Neumann et al. (Philadelphia: University of Pennsylvania Press, 1953), pp. 82–111.

48. See, for instance, Wissler, ''Material Cultures of the North American Indians,'' *American Anthropologist*, 16 (1914): 447–505.

49. Fenton, ''Advancement of Material Culture Studies,'' pp. 20–21.

50. David Burg, *Chicago's White City of 1893* (Lexington: University of Kentucky Press, 1976), pp. 180–234; Reid Badger, *The Great American Fair: The World's Columbian Exposition and American Culture* (Chicago: Nelson-Hall, 1979), pp. 103–107, 119–129.

51. Anne Hollingsworth Wharton, ''Colonial and Revolutionary Objects,'' *Report of the Committee on Awards of the Columbian Commission* (Washington: Government Printing Office, 1901), 1:167–186.

52. Katharine H. Rich, ''Beacon,'' *Old-Time New England* 66 (1976): 42–60; Charles B. Hosmer, Jr., ''William Sumner Appleton,'' in *Presence of the Past* (New York: Putnam, 1965), pp. 237–259.

53. W. Stull Holt, ''The Idea of Scientific History in America,'' *Journal of the History of Ideas* 1 (June 1940): 359–360; David Ricardi, ''Popular History and Scholarly History,'' *History News* 35 (September/October 1980): 38–39.

54. John Higham, Leonard Krieger, and Felix Gilbert, *History: The Development of Historical Studies in the United States* (Englewood Cliffs: Prentice-Hall, 1965), pp. 3–4, 15–16.

55. Robert W. DeForest quoted in Metropolitan Museum of Art, *Addresses at the Opening of the American Wing* (New York: Metropolitan Museum of Art, 1925), p. 20; see also Edward H. Hall, *The Hudson-Fulton Celebration, 1909* (Albany, N.Y.: J. B. Lyon, 1910).

56. Montgomery, ''Classics and Collectibles,'' pp. 127–128; Wendy J. Kaplan, ''R. H. Halsey: An Ideology of American Decorative Arts'' (Master's thesis, University of Delaware-Winterthur Museum, 1980), p. 20.

57. Henry W. Kent, ''The Walpole Society, 1910–1935,'' in *The Twenty-Fifth Anniversary Meet-*

ing of the Walpole Society (Boston: Walpole Society, 1935), pp. 16–19; also consult *The Walpole Society Notebook*, published since 1910. Instances of Walpoleans who donated their collections to museums include Charles Hitchcock Tyler (Museum of Fine Arts, Boston); George Dudley Seymour (Connecticut Historical Society); William B. Goodwin (Wadsworth Atheneum); Russell Hawes Kettell (Concord Antiquarian Society); Henry N. Flynt (Historic Deerfield); and Henry Francis duPont (Winterthur Museum). The first major private collection of American decorative arts to be given an American museum was that of Charles L. Pendleton (1849–1904). His bequest was to The Rhode Island School of Design.

58. The full impact of the American Wing on historic America material culture remains to be assessed. Contemporary estimates can be found in R. T. H. Halsey, *Handbook of the American Wing* (New York: Metropolitan Museum of Art, 1924); and R. T. Halsey, *Addresses on the Occasion of the Opening of the American Wing* (New York: Metropolitan Museum of Art, 1924). For the influence of the Essex Institute period rooms on the Metropolitan Museum's similar exhibits, see R. T. H. Halsey, "Early American Rooms in the Museum," *Bulletin of the Metropolitan Museum of Art* 17 (November 1922): 6; and Pilgrim, "American Period Rooms," p. 7. Charles P. Wilcomb's still earlier use of artifacts in interior room settings has been analyzed in James Deetz, "A Sense of Another World: History Museums and Cultural Change," *Museum News* 58 (May/June, 1980): 42–43 and Melinda Young Frye, "Pioneers In American Museums: Charles P. Wilcomb," *Museum News* 55 (May/June: 1977): 55–60.

59. Wendy A. Cooper, *In Praise of America: American Decorative Arts, 1650–1830: Fifty Years of Discovery since the 1929 Girl Scouts Loan Exhibition* (New York: Knopf, 1980), pp. 4–13.

60. Wendell Garrett, "Henry Ford the Collector," in *A Home For Our Heritage: The Building and Growth of Greenfield Village and Henry Ford Museum, 1929–1979*, ed. Geoffrey C. Upward (Dearborn: The Henry Ford Museum Press, 1979), p. viii; also see William Greenleaf, *From these Beginnings: The Early Philanthropies of Henry and Edsel Ford, 1911–1936* (Detroit: Wayne State University Press, 1964), pp. 71–100.

61. Roderick Nash, "Henry Ford, Symbol for an Age," in *The Nervous Generation, 1917–1930* (Chicago: Rand McNally, 1970), pp. 153–163.

62. Frank Caddy, "Foreword" in *Home for Our Heritage*, ed. Upword, pp. x–xi.

63. Richard W. E. Perrin argues that the first American outdoor history museum, established at Decorah, Iowa, in 1922 predates both Greenfield Village and Williamsburg. Richard W. E. Perrin, *Outdoor Museums* (Milwaukee: Milwaukee Public Museum, 1975), pp. 29–60.

64. On early historical archaeology in Williamsburg, Virginia, consult Ivor Nöel Hume, *Here Lies Virginia: An Archaeologist's View of Colonial Life and History* (New York: Knopf, 1963); for a sampling of subsequent research, see John Cotter and J. Paul Hudson, *New Discoveries at Jamestown* (Washington: National Park Service, 1957); *Archeological Excavations at the Jamestown Colonial National Historical Park and Jamestown Historical Site, Virginia* (Washington: National Park Service, 1958); and Ivon Nöel-Hume, *A Guide to Colonial Artifacts* (New York: Knopf, 1972).

65. On the architectural restoration of Williamsburg, see William G. Perry, "Notes on the Architecture," *Architectural Record* 78 (December 1935): 367–77; and Colonial Williamsburg, *Official Guidebook and Map* (Williamsburg, Va., 1970), pp. xii–xix.

66. Fenton, "Advancement of Material Culture Studies," pp. 17–21; William C. Sturtevant, "Does Anthropology Need Museums? " *Proceedings of the Biological Society of Washington* 89 (1969): 630–639.

67. Alice Morse Earle, *Home Life in Colonial Days* (New York: Macmillan, 1898); Henry C. Mercer, *Ancient Carpenters' Tools* (Doyleston, Penn.: Bucks County Historical Society, 1920); Luke V. Lockwood, *Colonial Furniture in America* (New York: Scribner's, 1913); Fiske Kimball, *Domestic Architecture of the American Colonies and of the Early Republic* (New York: Scribner's, 1922); John H. Morgan, *Life Portraits of Washington and Their Replicas* (Lancaster, Penn.: Lancaster Press, 1931) I. N. Phelps Stokes, *The Iconography of Manhattan Island, 1498–1909*, 6 vols., (New York: Dodd, 1915–1928); Wallace Nutting, *Furniture of the Pilgrim Century, 1620–1720* (Farmington, Mass.: Old American Company, 1924). Henry C. Mercer's contribution to material culture studies, particularly in the area

of tools, is the subject of a thesis: Donna G. Rosenstein, "Historic Human Tools: Henry Chapman Mercer and His Collection, 1897–1930" (M.A. thesis, Winterthur Museum-University of Delaware, 1977); another Winterthur thesis is a good historical survey of regional collecting practices: Richard H. Saunders, "Collecting American Decorative Arts in New England (1873–1876)," *Antiques* 109 (1976): 996–1003; Richard H. Saunders, "Collecting American Decorative Arts in New England, Part II (1876–1910)," ibid. 110 (1977): 754–763.

68. Walter Muir Whitehill, *The Arts in Early American History: Needs and Opportunities for Study* (Chapel Hill: University of North Carolina Press, 1965), p. 146.

69. Cooper, *In Praise of America*, pp. 10, 12.

70. Typical of this attitude was George Sheldon, "Note to Visitors," in *Catalogue of the Collection of Relics in Memorial Hall* (Deerfield, Mass.: Pocumtuch Valley Memorial Association, 1920): "Not a single article is here preserved on account of its artistic qualities. The Collection is founded on purely historical lines and is the direct memorial of the inhabitants of this valley, both Indian and Puritan. . . . Many articles may seem trivial in themselves, but as a part of the whole broad scheme of the projectors the most humble belong here as much as the most notable."

71. Carl Russell, "Relation of Archaeology and History," *Proceedings of the Wisconsin State Historical Society* 57 (1910): 146–152; Carl Russell, "Historic Objects as Sources of History," in *Firearms, Traps and Tools of the Mountain Men*, by Betty W. Russell (New York: Knopf, 1967), pp. 387–401.

72. James Harvey Robinson, *The New History* (New York: Macmillan, 1912), p. 1.

73. Arthur M. Schlesinger, Sr., ed., *History of American Life*, 13 vols. (New York: Macmillan, 1927–1948). James Truslow Adams, *Provincial Society* (New York: Macmillan, 1927). Subsequent volumes in another multi-volume publishing venture (New American Nation series) where one might have expected to find material culture evidence taken seriously, emphasized only traditional intellectual history and high style decorative arts: Russell Nye, *The Cultural Life of the New Nation, 1776–1830* (New York: Harper and Row, 1960); Russell Nye, *Society and Culture in America, 1830–1860* (New York: Harper and Row, 1974); and Louis B. Wright, *The Cultural Life of the American Colonies, 1607–1763* (New York: Harper and Row, 1957).

74. Russell, "Historic Objects as Sources of History," pp. 387–401; Arthur Woodward, "Archeology—The Scrapbook of History," *Regional Review, National Park Service* (August 1938): 8–10; R. F. Lee and C. P. Russell, eds., *Historic Objects: Their Place in Research and Interpretation* (Washington: National Park Service, 1940) [56 pp. mimeographed].

75. Arthur F. Wertheim, "Constance Rourke and the Discovery of American Culture in the 1930s," in *The Study of American Cultures Contemporary Conflicts*, ed. Luther S. Luedtke (Deland, Fla.: Everett/Edwards, 1977), pp. 49–61.

76. Constance Rourke, "Index of American Design," *Magazine of Art* (April 1937): 207–11; Holger Cahill, "Introduction," *Treasury of the Index of American Design* (New York: Harry Abrams: n.d.), pp. xix–xxvii. Also see Charles C. Alexander, *Nationalism in American Thought, 1930–45* (Chicago: Rand McNally, 1969), pp. 72–76; Alfred H. Jones, "The Search for a Useable Past in the New Deal Era," *American Quarterly* 23 (1971): 710–724.

77. Beatrix Rumford, "Uncommon Art of the Common People," *Perspectives on American Folk Art*, ed. Ian M G. Quimby and Scott Swank (New York: Norton, 1980), pp. 15–21.

78. Holger Cahill, *American Folk Art: The Art of the Common Man in America, 1750–1900* (New York: Museum of Modern Art, 1932); Clare Endicott Sears, *Some American Primitives: A Study of New England Faces and Folk Portraits* (Boston: Houghton Mifflin, 1941).

79. See, for example, the descriptive catalog, *Federal Writers' Project Guidebooks* (St. Clair Shores, Mich.: Somerset, 1979).

80. U.S. Department of the Interior, National Park Service, *Historic American Buildings Survey* (Washington: Government Printing Office, 1941); Charles B. Hosmer, "The Broadening View of the Historical Preservation Movement," in Quimby, ed., *Material Culture*, pp. 124–128; Freeman Tilden, *Interpreting Our Heritage* (Chapel Hill: University of North Carolina Press, 1967); Robert G. Garvey

and Terry B. Morton, "The United States Government in Historic Preservation," *Monumentum* 2 (1968): 24–26.

81. Karin Ohrn, *Dorothea Lange and the American Documentary Tradition* (New York: Oxford University Press, 1980), is a superb analysis of a famous Farm Security Administration photographer; the book also serves as a model for treating photographs as historical evidence.

82. In 1939, the centenary of Daguerre's public announcement of his photographic process, the American Historical Association devoted one of the sessions at its national convention to documentary photographs as evidence for the study of cultural history. The principal speakers were Roy Stryker and Paul H. Johnstone. Their analysis at that meeting of nine photographs still remains one model survey of the possibilities and pitfalls of using photography in historical research. Caroline F. Ware, *The Cultural Approach to History* (New York: Columbia University Press, 1940), pp. 324–330.

83. Gene Wise, " 'Paradigm Dramas' in American Studies: A Cultural and Institutional History of the Movement," *American Quarterly* 31 (Bibliographical Issue, 1979): 304–309; Murray G. Murphey, "American Civilization as a Discipline," *Emory University Quarterly* 23 (Spring 1967): 51–52.

84. George Tremaine McDowell, *American Studies* (Minneapolis: University of Minnesota Press, 1948), p. 7.

85. John Kouwenhoven, *American Studies: Words or Things?* (Wilmington, Del.: Wemyss Foundation, 1962). This argument is reprinted in *American Studies in Transition* ed. Marshall W. Fishwick (Philadelphia: University of Pennsylvania Press, 1964) pp. 15–35. Other instances of the ways in which material culture studies have been an important part of American Studies include: pedagogical strategies, see Linda Funk Place, Joanna Schneider Zangrando, James W. Lea, and John Lowell, "The Object as Subject: The Role of Museums and Material Culture Collections in American Studies," *American Quarterly* 26 (1974): 281–294; methodological debates, see John L. Cotter, "Archaeology and Material History: A Personal Approach to the Discovery of the Past," in *The Study of American Cultures/ Contemporary Conflicts*, ed. Luther S. Luedtke (Deland, Fla.: Everett/Edwards, 1977), pp. 77–98; theoretical perspectives, see Henry Glassie, "Meaningful Things and Appropriate Myths: The Artifact's Place in American Studies," in *Prospects: An Annual of American Cultural Studies*, ed. Jack Salzman (New York: Burt Franklin, 1977), pp. 2–49; national conferences, see *Sixth Biennial Convention of the American Studies Association, Program* (1977), pp. 16, 18, 19, 22, 28, 36, 43, 46; and bibliographical literature, see Harold Skramstad, "American Things: A Neglected Material Culture," *American Studies: An International Newsletter* 10 (Spring 1972): 11–22.

86. John Kouwenhoven, *Made In America: The Arts in Modern Civilization* (Garden City: Doubleday, 1948); later editions of the same work appeared as John Kouwenhoven, *The Arts in Modern American Civilization* (New York: Norton, 1967); an abridgement of the Kouwenhoven thesis can be found in John Kouwenhoven, "Democracy, Machines and Vernacular Design," *The Ohio Review: A Journal of the Humanities* 14 (Winter 1973): 4–22.

87. Edgar Richardson, *Washington Allston* (Detroit: Detroit Institute of Arts, 1948); and Oliver Larkin, *Art and Life in America* (New York: Holt, 1948). For the immediate postwar milieu of American art history scholarship, see Kleinbauer, *Modern Pespectives on Western Art History*, pp. 31–36.

88. Kenneth L. Ames, *Beyond Necessity: Art in the Folk Tradition* (New York: Norton: 1977), pp. 13–21.

89. Compare, for example, the discussion between Richard M. Dorson, "A Theory for American Folklore," *Journal of American Folklore* 72 (1959): 197–215; Melville J. Herskovits, "Folklore after a Hundred Years: A Problem in Redefinition," ibid. 59 (1946): 89–100; William R. Bascom, "Folklore and Anthropology," ibid. 63 (1953): 283–290; Richard Weiss, *Volkskunde der Schweiz* (Zurich, 1946), pp. 11–14; and Don Yoder, "The Folklife Studies Movement," *Pennsylvania Folklife* 13 (July 1963): 43–50.

90. "Folklife studies (regional ethnology) is a subject of recent development in the United States," writes Yoder. "Essentially it is the application to the American scene of the European discipline called *folklivsforskning*, or regional ethnology, in Scandinavian lands (particularly in Sweden where the term *folkliv* was coined) and *Volkskunde* in the German-speaking areas of Europe. Folklife studies, or folklife research, has penetrated American academia both directly from the Scandinavian sources and indirectly

from the British Isles, where the term folklife is used for scholarly journals, societies, and university programs." Don Yoder, "Folklife Studies in American Scholarship," in *American Folklife*, ed. Don Yoder (Austin: University of Texas Press, 1976), p. 3.

91. The term "folk-lore" first appeared in the British journal, *The Athenaeum* (August 22, 1846) in a letter by Ambrose Merton (W. J. Thoms); see the *Oxford English Dictionary*, (Oxford, Eng.: Clarenden, 1931), 4:390. On W. J. Thoms and his defense of the originality of the term against changes that it was borrowed from the German, see Duncan Emrich, " 'Folklore': William John Thoms," *California Folklore Quarterly* 5 (1946): 355–374.

92. Such literary emphasis can be briefly traced by comparing Martha W. Beckwith, *Folklore in America: Its Scope and Method* (Poughkeepsie, N.Y.: Vassar College, Folklore Foundation, 1931) with Tristram Coffin and Hennig Cohen, eds., *Folklore in America* (Garden City: Doubleday, 1966); Duncan Emrich, *Folklore on the American Land* (Boston: Little, Brown, 1972); and Richard Dorson, *American Folklore and the Historian* (Chicago: University of Chicago Press, 1971).

93. Stith Thompson, ed., *Four Symposia on Folklore*, (Bloomington, Ind.: Indiana University, 1953); also see Stith Thompson, "Advances in Folklore Studies," in *Anthropology Today: An Encyclopedic Inventory*, ed. A. L. Kroeber (Chicago: University of Chicago Press, 1953), pp. 592–593.

94. A sample of the folklore and folklife student scholarship done at Indiana can be found in the volumes of *Folklore Forum, Indiana Folklore, Folklore Monograph Series, Journal of the Folklore Institute*, and *Folklore Preprint Series;* also see Linda Dégh, Henry Glassie, and Felix J. Oinas, *Folklore Today: A Festschrift for Richard Dorson* (Bloomington, Ind.: Research Center for Language and Semiotic Studies, 1976); also Nikolai Burlakoff and Carl Lindahl, eds., *Folklore on Two Continents: Essays in Honor of Linda Dégh* (Bloomington, Ind.: Trickster Press, 1980); and John Vlach, "Folklore and Museum Artifacts," paper presented at the American Association for State and Local History Folklore and History Conference, New Orleans, September 6, 1980, pp. 2–4.

95. The numerous debts of American folklife scholars to European work can be traced in historiographical surveys such as those by Sigurd Erixon, "European Ethnology in Our Time," *Ethnologia Europaea* 1 (1967): 3–11; Ronald H. Buchanan, "A Decade of Folklife Study," *Ulster Folklife* 10 (1965): 63–75; Ingeborg Weber-Kellermann, *Deutsche Volkskunde zwischen Germanistik und Sozialwissenschaften* (Stuttgart: Metzlersche Verlagsbuchhandlung, 1969); Don Yoder, "The Folklife Studies Movement," *Pennsylvania Folklife* 13 (July 1963): 43–56; and Marshall, "Folklife and the Rise of American Folk Museums," pp. 391–413. The best manual of the subject thus far, although unfortunately not available in English, is Sigfrid Svensson, *Introduktion till Folklivsforskningen* (Stockholm: Natur och Kultur, 1969).

96. Yoder, "Folklife Studies Movement," p. 44, and Yoder, "Folklife Studies in American Scholarship," p. 5.

97. Henry Glassie argued "folklife is beginning to fill the ethnographic void left by American anthropologists who have continued to conduct their research almost exclusively away from home." Henry Glassie, "Introduction," in *Forms Upon the Frontier: Folklife and Folk Art in the United States*, ed. Henry Glassie, Austin Fife, and Alta Fife (Logan: University of Utah Press, 1969), p. 6. For a similar argument, see Henry Glassie, "Structure and Function, Folklore and the Artifact," *Semiotica* 7 (1973): 323.

98. Murray G. Murphey, "American Civilization at Pennsylvania," *American Quarterly* 22 (Summer 1970): 464–488; Marilyn Cohen, "The National Museum of History and Technology of the Smithsonian Institution" (Ph.D. dissertation, George Washington University, 1980).

99. Brooke Hindle, *Technology in Early America: Needs and Opportunities For Study* (Chapel Hill: University of North Carolina Press, 1966), pp. 38–41. For an example of each type, see Henry Howe, *Memoirs of the Most Eminent American Mechanics* (New York: Alexander V. Blake, 1842); *Appleton's Dictionary of Machines, Mechanics, Engine-Work, and Engineering*, 2 vols. (New York: D. Appleton, 1852): Constance McLaughlin Green, *History of Naugatuck, Connecticut* (New Haven, Conn.: Yale University Press, 1948); and John W. Oliver, *History of American Technology* (New York: Ronald, 1956).

100. James M. Swank, *Progressive Pennsylvania* (Philadelphia: Lippincott, 1908) expresses this

overly optimistic view. See also the complaints on the field's "antiquarian chronologies of water mill and steam engines" in Eugene S. Ferguson, "Toward a Discipline of the History of Technology," *Technology and Culture* 15 (January 1974): 13–17.

101. For example, Charles Singer, E. J. Holmyard, and A. R. Hall, eds., *A History of Technology* (Oxford: Oxford University Press, 1954); Thomas K. Bullock, *The Silversmith in Eighteenth Century Williamsburg* (Williamsburg, Va.: Colonial Williamsburg Craft Series, 1956); Henry C. Mercer, *Ancient Carpenters' Tools* (Doylestown, Pa.: Bucks County Historical Society, 1960); Harold L. Peterson, *Arms and Armor in Colonial America* (Harrisburg, Pa.: Stackpole, 1956).

102. John E. Sawyer, "The Social Basis of the American System of Manufacturing," *Journal of Economic History* 14 (1954): 361–379.

103. Compare Hugo Meier, "Technology and Democracy, 1800–1860," *Mississippi Valley Historical Review* 43 (March 1957): 618–640; and Eugene Ferguson, "The American-ness of American Technology," *Technology and Culture* 20 (January 1979): 3–24.

104. Robert S. Woodbury, "The Legend of Eli Whitney and Interchangeable Parts," *Technology and Culture* 1 (Summer 1960): 235–253. *Technology and Culture* is a journal that has been crucial in nurturing historical interpretation based on technological artifacts.

105. George H. Daniels, "The Big Questions in the History of American Technology," *Technology and Culture*, 11 (January 1970): 2–4.

106. W. F. Ogburn, *Social Change with Respect to Culture and Original Nature* (New York: Huebsch, 1922); Patrick Geddes, *Cities in Evolution: An Introduction to the Town Planning Movement and to the Study of Civics* (London: Williams and Norgate, 1915).

107. See Kouwenhoven, *Made In America*; D. L. Burn, "The Genesis of American Engineering Competition, 1850–1870," *Economic History* 2 (1931): 292–311; Daniel Boorstin, *The Americans: The National Experience* (New York: Random House, 1965); and Frank W. Fox, "The Genesis of American Technology," *American Studies* 17 (Fall 1976): 29–48.

108. Eugene S. Ferguson, "Toward a Discipline of the History of Technology," *Technology and Culture* 15 (January: 1974): 14–15; Melvin Kranzberg, "At The Start," *Technology and Culture* 1 (1960): 1.

109. The College Art Association's *Art Bulletin* (1913–); *Journal of the Society of Architectural Historians* (1941–); and the Decorative Arts Chapter's *Decorative Arts Newsletter* (1975–). In 1979, the Decorative Arts chapter changed its name to Decorative Arts Society. On the evolution of the Society of Architectural Historians, see "A.S.A.H. Beginnings: A Report," *Journal of the Society of Architectural Historians*, 1 (January 1941): 20–22.

110. Jay Anderson, "Immaterial Material Culture: The Implications of Experimental Research for Folklife Museums," *Keystone Folklore Quarterly* 21 (1976–1977): 6. Also see James B. Griffin, "The Pursuit of Archaeology in the United States," *American Anthropologist* 61 (1959): 379–388; Douglas Schwartz, "North American Archaeology in Historical Perspective," *Actes du Congres International d'Historie de Sciences* (1968): 311–315; Gordon Wiley and Philip Phillips, "Method and Theory in American Archaeology, II: Historical-Developmental Interpretations," *American Archaeologist* 57 (1955): 723–819; and Gordon R. Wiley and Jeremy A. Sabloff, *A History of American Archaeology* (San Francisco: Freeman, 1974). Walter W. Taylor, *A Study of Archaeology* (Carbondale: Southern Illinois University Press, 1967).

111. U.S. Department of the Interior, National Park Service, *Historic American Buildings Survey* (Washington: Government Printing Office, 1941); Charles B. Hosmer, "The Broadening View of the Historical Preservation Movement," in Quimby, *Material Culture*, pp. 124–128; Freeman Tilden, *Interpreting Our Heritage* (Chapel Hill: University of North Carolina Press, 1967); and Robert G. Garvey and Terry B. Morton, "The United States Government in Historic Preservation," *Monumentum* 2 (1968): 24–26.

112. Louis C. Jones, "Autobiographical Preface," unpublished manuscript, 1980, pp. 16–17. Courses included American arts and crafts, writing local history, teaching state and local history, history in museums, and collecting folklore. In 1949, the seminar emphasized American folk art; in Jones'

estimate it was "the first time a historical society had offered a serious approach to this as yet generally unacknowledged body of American art." Ibid., p. 17. On Jones's important pioneering work in folk material culture, see Louis C. Jones, "The Folklorist Looks at Historians," *Dutchess County Historical Society Yearbook* 23 (1943): 30–33; and Louis C. Jones, "The Triumph of American Folk Art," *Search: A Journal of Scholarly Research* 4 (Fall 1978), unpaginated.

113. Hart M. Nelson, "The Democratization of the Antique: Meanings of Antiques and Dealer's Perceptions of Customers," *Sociological Review* 18 (1970): 407–419. Also useful on this point is W. Lloyd Warner, ed., *Yankee City* (New Haven, Conn.: Yale University Press, 1963), pp. 64–67; Robert Maisel, "Antiques Old and New: Changing Patterns of Middle Class Sumptuary Styles," paper read at the American Sociological Association meeting, Chicago, 1965; and Russell Lynes, *The Taste Makers*, (New York: Harper and Row, 1954), pp. 238–241.

114. Laurence Vail Coleman's extensive research into American museums in the 1930s and 1940s remains the best descriptive historiography to date. See, for example, Laurance Vail Coleman, *Historic House Museums* (Washington: American Association of Museums, 1933); Laurence Vail Coleman, *College and University Museums* (Washington: American Association of Museums, 1942); Laurence Vail Coleman, *Company Museums* (Washington: American Association of Museums, 1943); and Laurence Vail Coleman, *The Museum in America: A Critical Study* (Washington: American Association of Museums, 1948).

115. Abbott Lowell Cummings perceptively identified one of the key cultural implications of the multiplication of historic museum villages in the 1950s and 1960s: "Few changes of the past generation have been so unsettling as the expansion of the American village into a sprawling, impersonal aggregation of buildings—neither city nor town. The impact on people's imaginations by the disappearance of the village can be best measured in the number of restored and reconstructed villages which have sprung into existence in the last few years." Cummings went on to suggest that there were civic lessons to be learned in the museum villages by "those who hope to discover some clue to the problem of how we may keep our own environments from losing completely the sense of unity among people that existed in the early American village." Abbott L. Cummings, "Restoration Villages," *Art in America* 43 (May 1955): 12–13.

116. Louis C. Jones, *The Farmer's Museum* (Cooperstown, N.Y.: New York State Historical Association, 1948).

117. Edward P. Alexander, "Historical Restorations," in *In Support of Clio*, eds. W. Hesseltine and W. McNeil (Madison: State Historical Society of Wisconsin, 1958), pp. 195–214; Frederick L. Rath, Jr., and Merrilyn Rogers O'Connell, "Outdoor Museums," in *Guide to Historic Preservation, Historical Agencies, and Museum Practices: A Selective Bibliography* (Cooperstown, N.Y.: New York State Historical Association, 1970), pp. 29–31.

118. E. McClung Fleming, "Accent on Artist and Artisan: The Winterthur Program in Early American Culture," *American Quarterly* 22 (1970): 593.

119. On the origins of the Cooperstown Graduate Programs, see Bruce Buckley, "New Beginnings and Old Ends: Museums, Folklife and the Cooperstown Graduate Programs" in *American Material Culture and Folklife*, pp. 6–8; Louis C. Jones, "Autobiographical Preface," ibid., pp. 16–17.

120. George Murdock, et al., *Outline of Cultural Materials*, 3rd ed. (New Haven, Conn.: Human Relations Area Files, 1950).

121. Anthony Garvan describes the index and its anticipated application to artifact research in Anthony Garvan, "Historical Depth in Comparative Culture Study," *American Quarterly* 14 (Summer 1962): 260–274.

122. Outside such institutions, the work of the independent collector-writer of material culture topics, especially the provenance of American antiques, continued in the careers and writings of collectors such as Jean Lipman, Howard Lipman, and Nina Fletcher Little.

123. Fleming, "Study and Interpretation of the Historical Artifact," pp. 11–12. Louis C. Jones, "Autobiographical Preface," pp. 4–11; author's interview with Louis C. Jones, June 19, 1980, Cooperstown, New York.

124. See Thomas J. Wertenbaker, "Introduction," in *The Founding of American Civilization: The Middle Colonies* (New York: Scribners, 1938); Thomas J. Wertenbaker, "Introduction," in *The Founding of American Civilization: The Old South* (New York: Scribner's, 1942); Thomas J. Wertenbaker, "Introduction," in *The Founding of American Civilization: The Puritan Oligarchy* (New York: Scribner's, 1947); also see Thomas J. Wertenbaker, "The Archaeology of Colonial Williamsburg," *Annual Report of the Smithsonian Institution for 1953* (Washington: Government Printing Office, 1964).

125. Kouwenhoven, *Made in America*; Louis C. Jones and Agnes Halsey Jones, *New-Found Art of the Young Republic* (Cooperstown, N.Y.: New York State Historical Association, 1960); Alan Gowans, *Images of American Living: Four Centuries of Architecture and Furniture as Cultural Expression* (Philadelphia: Lippincott, 1964); George Kubler, *The Shape of Time: Remarks on the History of Things* (New Haven, Conn.: Yale University Press, 1962); C. Malcom Watkins, *The Cultural History of Marlborough, Virginia* (Washington: Smithsonian Institution Press, 1968); J. B. Jackson, *American Space: The Centennial Years* (New York: Norton, 1972): Charles Montgomery, *American Furniture: The Federal Period* (New York: Viking, 1966).

126. Jens Lund and R. Serge Denisoff, "The Folk Music Revival and the Counter Culture: Contributions and Contradictions," *Journal of American Folklore* 84 (October-December 1970): 394–405. For another perspective of the growth and institutionalization of American folklore study, see John Williams, "Radicalism and Professionalism in Folklore Studies: A Comparative Perspective," *Journal of the Folklore Institute* 11 (March 1975): 211–234. In this context, also consult Philip Gleason, "Our New Age of Romanticism," *America* (October 7, 1967): 372–375; Arthur Bestor, "The Study of American Civilization: Jingoism or Scholarship?" *William and Mary Quarterly* 9 (January 1952): 3–9.

127. Until the twentieth century, historic preservation had been largely the province of women and women's groups such as Ann Pamela Cunningham's Mount Vernon Ladies' Association and the Ladies' Hermitage Association, while the conservation of the American natural landscape had been primarily a masculine avocation led by individuals such as George Perkins Marsh, Frederick Law Olmsted, John Wesley Powell, Gifford Pinchot, and John Muir.

128. John Maass, "Where Architectural Historians Fear to Tread," *Journal of the Society of Architectural Historians* 18 (March 1969): 3–8.

129. Carl Condit, "The Chicago School and the Modern Movement in Architecture," *Art in America* 36 (January 1948): 19–37. The first major work on the skyscraper, however, was Francisco Mujica, *History of the Skyscraper* (Paris, 1929).

130. William A. Pierson, Jr., and Marshall Davidson, eds., *Arts of United States: A Pictorial Survey* (New York: McGraw-Hill, 1960), pp. vii–x.

131. The limited scholarly literature on tourism includes Dean MacCannell, *The Tourist: A New Theory of the Leisure Class* (New York: Schochen, 1976). John E. Rosenow and Gerald L. Palsipher, *Tourism: The Good, the Bad, and the Ugly* (Lincoln, Nebr.: Century Three, 1980), is a popular promotional survey that provides a contemporary estimate of the state of the art.

132. Thomas J. Schlereth, "The 1876 Centennial: A Heuristic Model for Comparative American Studies," *Hayes Historical Journal* 1 (Spring 1977): 201–210.

133. Montgomery, "Classics and Collectibles," p. 134.

134. For a sample of National Endowment for the Humanities-sponsored museum exhibitions, consult staff reports, "Grants For Planning/Implementing Exhibitions" issued periodically by the National Endowment for the Humanities, Washington; on the Smithsonian Institution's role, review *Smithsonian Opportunities for Research and Study in History, Art and Science* (Washington: Smithsonian Institution, 1974). The report, *Program Information and Application Procedures-Fiscal Year 1979*, (Washington: Institute of Museum Services, Department of Health, Education and Welfare, 1979), details the work of the Institute of Museum Services.

135. Ellen C. Hicks, "The AAM After Seventy-Two Years," *Museum News* 56 (May/June 1978): 47–49; William Alderson, "The American Association for State and Local History," *The Western Historical Quarterly* 1 (April 1970): 175–182.

136. W. Wayne Smith, et al., "New Approaches in Teaching Local History" in *The Newberry Papers in Family and Community History*, 78–5 (Chicago: Newberry Library, 1978).

137. Sample single-course offerings include Joanna Schneider Zangrando, "Material Culture in the United States" (Skidmore College); Staff, "Material Aspects of American Civilization" (University of Pennsylvania); Wilcomb Washburn and Bernard Mergen, "Material Aspects of American Civilization" and Lawrence Lankton, "Introduction to Industrial Archaeology and Material Culture" (George Washington University-Smithsonian Institution); Thomas J. Schlereth, "Material Culture in America" (University of Notre Dame).

138. A sampling of this generation's pertinent work includes: Brooke Hindle, *Technology in Early America: Needs and Opportunities for Study* (Chapel Hill: University of North Carolina Press, 1966); Brooke Hindle, *Pursuit of Science in Revolutionary America* (Chapel Hill: University of North Carolina Press, 1956); Deetz, *In Small Things Forgotten*; Charles F. Hummel, *With Hammer in Hand: The Dominy Craftsmen of East Hampton, New York* (Charlottesville: University Press of Virginia, 1968); Carl Condit, *American Building: Materials and Techniques from the First Colonial Settlement to the Present* (Chicago: University of Chicago Press, 1968); Carl Condit, *The Chicago School of Architecture: A History of Commercial and Public Building in the Chicago Area, 1875–1925* (Chicago: University of Chicago Press, 1964); Ivor Noël Hume, *A Guide to the Artifacts of Colonial America* (New York: Knopf, 1970); Ivor Noël Hume, *Historical Archaeology* (New York: Knopf, 1968); Don Yoder, ed., *American Folklife* (Austin: University of Texas Press, 1976); John T. Schlebecker, *Whereby We Live: A History of American Farming, 1607–1972* (Ames: Iowa State University Press, 1975).

139. Representative of this diversified contemporary generation is the work of Kenneth Ames, Henry Glassie, David Orr, Claudia Kidwell, John Kirk, Alan Ludwig, Jay Anderson, Ruth Schwartz Cowan, John Vlach, Robert Trent, Clifford Clark, Craig Gilborn, Jules Prown, Neil Harris, Jay Cantor, Howard Wight Marshall, Barbara Carson, Darwin Kelsey, Mark Leone. Arlene Palmer, Cary Carson, Peter Cousins, Michael Owen Jones, Peter Marzio, William Ferris, Lucius Ellsworth, Steven Hamp, Simon Bronner, and Dell Upton.

140. Steven Hamp, "Meaning in Material Culture: References towards an Analytical Approach to Artifacts," *Living History Farms Bulletin* 9 (May 1980): 9. Author's correspondence with Steven Hamp, March 23, 1980.

141. George Kubler, *The Shape of Time: Remarks on the History of Things* (New Haven: Yale University Press, 1962), Gowans, *Images of American Living*; Anthony N. B. Garvan, "Historical Depth in Comparative Culture Study," *American Quarterly* 14 (Summer 1962): 260–74; Glassie, *Pattern in Material Folk Culture*; Hesseltine, "The Challenge of the Artifact," in *The Present World of History* (Madison, Wis.: American Association For State and Local History, 1959); and E. McClung Fleming, "Early American Decorative Arts as Social Documents," *Mississippi Valley Historical Review* 44 (September 1958): 276–284, appear to be the only major discussions of methodology among American scholars using artifacts as evidence prior to the 1960s.

142. E. McClung Fleming "Artifact Study: A Proposed Model," *Winterthur Portfolio* 9 (June 1974): 153–161, owes a considerable debt to the similar but more circumscribed primer, Charles Montgomery, "Remarks on the Practice and Science of Connoisseurship," *American Walpole Society Notebook* (1961): 7–20. Both are reprinted in Part III of this volume. They can be contrasted with the taxonomical approach of Ronald T. Marchese, "Material Culture and Artifact Classification," *Journal of American Culture* 3 (Winter 1980): 605–617.

143. In 1981, the Society for the North American Cultural Survey was directed by John Rooney, Department of Geography, Oklahoma State University, Stillwater, Oklahoma.

144. Mannion, "Multidisciplinary Dimensions in Material History," p. 24.

145. Walter Muir Whitehill, *Arts in Early America* (Chapel Hill: University of North Carolina Press, 1965), pp. 115–119. Other regional examples of such biographical directories of craftsmen include Rita Susswein Gottesman, *The Arts and Crafts in New York, 1777–1799: Advertisements and News Items from New York City Newspapers* (New York: New York Historical Society, 1954); Walter

Hamilton Van Hoesen, *Craftsmen of New Jersey* (Rutherford, N.J.: Fairleigh Dickenson University Press, 1973); James Craig Hicklin, *The Arts and Crafts in North Carolina, 1699–1840* (Winston-Salem, N.C.: Museum of Early South Decorative Arts, 1966); Alfred Coxe Prime, *The Arts and Crafts in Philadelphia, Maryland, and South Carolina: Gleanings from Newspapers* (Topsfield, Mass.: American Walpole Society, 1929).

146. Gloria L. Main, "Probate Records as a Source for Early American History," *William and Mary Quarterly* (1975): 89–99; Mary C. Beaudry, "Worth Its Weight in Iron: Categories of Material Culture in Early Virginia Probate Inventories," *Quarterly Bulletin of the Archaeological Society of Virginia* 33 (1978); Cary Carson, "Doing History with Material Culture" in *Material Culture and the Study of American Life*, ed. Ian M. G. Quimby (New York: Norton, 1977): pp. 47–64.

147. Lucius F. Ellsworth, "A Directory of Artifact Collections," in *Technology in Early America: Needs and Opportunities For Study* (Chapel Hill: University of North Carolina Press, 1966), pp. 95–126, provides an excellent introductory reference tool for locating technological material culture.

148. Thomas J. Schlereth, "It Wasn't that Simple," *Museum News* 56 (January/February 1978): 36–41. In the case of providing annual bibliographies, the historians of technology are, again, ahead of the pack; see "Annual Current Bibliography" in *Technology and Culture* and Eugene S. Ferguson, *Bibliography of the History of Technology* (Cambridge, Mass.: MIT Press, 1968).

149. Thomas W. Leavitt, "Toward a Standard of Excellence: The Nature and Purpose of Exhibit Reviews," *Technology and Culture* 9 (January 1968): 70–75; E. McClung Fleming, "The Museum Exhibit as a Curatorial Publication," *Museum News* 50 (June 1972): 39–42; Thomas J. Schlereth, "A Perspective on Criticism: Guidelines for History Museum Exhibit Reviews," *History News* 35 (August 1980): 18–19.

150. See, for example, Cooper, *In Praise of America*.

151. Some recent museum catalogs in this rare class are: Kenneth Ames, *Beyond Necessity: Art in the Folk Tradition* (Winterthur, Del.: Winterthur Museum, 1977); Robert Trent, *Hearts and Crowns: Folk Chairs of the Connecticut Coast, 1720–1840, as Viewed in Light of Henri Focillon's Introduction to Arts Populaire* (New Haven, Conn.: Haven Colonial Historical Society, 1977); Barbara Ward, ed., *Silver in American Life: Selections from the Mabel Brady Garvan and Other Collections at Yale University* (New York: American Federation of Arts, 1979); Peter Benes and Phillip D. Zimmerman, *New England Meeting House and Church, 1630–1850* (Boston: Boston University Press, 1979); Herbert W. Hemphill, Jr., *Folk Sculpture, U.S.A.* (Brooklyn, N.Y.: Brooklyn Museum of Art, 1976); Robert St. George, *The Wrought Covenant: Source Materials for the Study of the Craftsmen and Community in Southeastern New England, 1620–1700* (Brockton, Mass.: Brockton Art Center, 1979); John Michael Vlach, *The Afro-American Tradition in the Decorative Arts* (Cleveland: Cleveland Museum of Art, 1978); Howard Wight Marshall, *Buckaroos In Paradise: Cowboy Life in Northern Nevada* (Washington: Library of Congress, 1980); Martha V. Pike and Janice Gray Armstrong, *A Time to Mourn: Expressions of Grief in Nineteenth Century America* (Stony Brook, N.Y.: Museums at Stony Brook, 1980).

152. Michael Kammen, "The Historian's Vocation and the State of the Discipline in the United States," *The Past Before Us: Contemporary Historical Writing in the United States*, Michael Kammen, ed. (Ithaca, N.Y.: Cornell University Press, 1980), p. 34. Commentary on the impact of social history on American historical research is voluminous; a sampling of the more useful accounts includes Laurence Vesey, "The 'New' Social History in the Context of American History," *Reviews in American History* 7 (March 1979): 1–12; Richard R. Beeman, "The New Social History and the Search for 'Community' in Colonial America," *American Quarterly* 29 (1977): 422–443; Lawrence Stone, "History and the Social Sciences in the Twentieth Century," in *The Future of History* ed. Charles F. Deltzell (Baltimore: The Johns Hopkins University Press, 1977), pp. 3–42.

153. John R. Commons, *Trade Unionism and Labor Problems* (Boston: Ginn, 1905); Arthur J. Schlesinger, Sr., *The Rise of the City* (New York: Macmillan, 1937); Theodore C. Blegen, *Grass-Roots History* (Minneapolis: Minnesota Historical Society, 1947); William Greenleaf, *From These Beginnings: The Early Philanthropies of Henry and Edsel Ford, 1911–1936* (Detroit: Wayne State University Press, 1964), p. 85.

154. George G. Iggers, *New Directions in European Historiography* (Middleton, Conn.: Wesleyan University Press, 1975), pp. 166–67; Marius Barbeau, "The Field of European Folk-Lore in America," *Journal of American Folklore* 32 (1919): 185–97; Stone, "History and the Social Science," pp. 11–15.

155. Fernand Braudel, *Capitalism and Material Life: 1400–1800* (London: Weiderfeld and Nicholson, 1973); Philipe Ariès, *Western Attitudes toward Death from Middle Ages to the Present* (Baltimore: The Johns Hopkins University Press, 1974); Robert Forster, "Achievements of the *Annales* School," *Journal of Economic History* 38 (1978): 58–76; Traian Stoianovich, *French Historical Method: The "Annales" Paradigm* (Ithaca, N.Y.: Cornell University Press, 1976).

156. An example of social history's impact can be seen in the 1981 Annual Conference Program for the Association for Living History Farms and Agricultural Museums at Cadiz, Kentucky, April 6–10, featuring such sessions as "Social History and Today's Museum," "Interpreting Social History," "Research Methods for Social History and Their Application to a Living History Site," "Addressing Social History Concerns through Interpretive Media," and "Developing Educational Programs on Social History Issues." A parallel reorientation of disciplinary emphasis appears to be occurring in the multidisciplinary field of American Studies; see Wise, "Paradigm Dramas," pp. 308–331.

157. See *Historical Methods Newsletter* (1967), *History and Theory* (1960), *Journal of Social History* (1967), *Journal of Interdisciplinary History* (1970), *Reviews in American History* (1973), *Social Science History* (1976), and *Review: A Journal of the Fernand Braudel Center for the Study of Economies, Historical Systems, and Civilizations* (1977).

158. See David Hackett Fischer, *Historians' Fallacies: Toward a Logic of Historical Thought* (New York: Harper and Row, 1970); Murray G. Murphey, *Our Knowledge of the Historical Past* (Indianapolis: Bobbs-Merrill, 1973); and Peter D. McClelland, *Causal Explanation and Model Building in History, Economics, and the New Economic History* (Ithaca, N.Y.: Cornell University Press, 1975).

159. See Gene Wise, *American Historical Explanations: A Strategy for Grounded Inquiry* (Homewood, Ill.: Dorsey, 1973); J. Morgan Kousser, "The Agenda for 'Social Science History,' " *Social Science History* 1 (1977): 383–391. See also Cecil F. Tate, *The Search for a Method in American Studies* (Minneapolis: University of Minnesota Press, 1973).

160. For important opening salvos in the debate, however, see Simon J. Bronner, "Concepts in the Study of Material Aspects of American Folk Culture," *Folklore Forum* 12 (1979): 133–172 and Simon J. Bronner, "Toward a Philosophy of Folk Objects: A Praxic Perspective," *Journal of American Culture* (in press); Manion, "Multidisciplinary Dimensions in Material History," pp. 21–26; Kenneth L. Ames, *Beyond Necessity: Art in the Folk Tradition* (Winterthur, Del.: Winterthur Museum, 1977), pp. 11–21; Glassie, "Meaningful Things and Appropriate Myths: The Artifact's Place in American Studies," *Prospects* 3 (1977): 1–50.

161. With modifications, I am greatly indebted to the typologies of Richard Dorson, John Mannion, Kenneth Ames, and Simon J. Bronner for my own heuristic system of cataloging the interpretive positions of current American material culture scholars. Richard Dorson, "Concepts of Folklore and Folklife Studies," in *Folklore and Folklife*, ed. Dorson, pp. 7–47; Mannion, "Multidisciplinary Dimensions in Material History," pp. 21–26; Kenneth Ames, "Folk Art: The Challenge and the Promise," in *Perspectives on American Folk Art*, ed. Quimby and Swank, pp. 297–324; and Bronner, "Concepts in the Study of Material Aspects," pp. 136–165.

162. Warren Roberts, for instance, has employed an environmentalist or historic-geographic approach for many years in his research but recently has also begun to explore the potential of the functionalist and the symbolic perspectives. Allan Ludwig uses both a symbolist and a social history approach in his research on New England gravestones; Cary Carson does material culture research from the perspectives of social history and historical archaeology.

163. In this context, I am indebted to Michael Owen Jones for drawing my attention to the work of Adrienne Kaeppler. Over several years, Kaeppler managed to publish an article which was clearly environmentalist (historic-geographic), one that was functionalist, and one that was structuralist—all using the same data base. See Adrienne Kaeppler, "Preservation and Evolution of Form and Function in Two Types of Tongan Dance," *Polynesian Culture History: Essays in Honor of Kenneth P. Emory*, ed.

Genevieve G. Highland, et al. (Honolulu: Bishop Museum Press, 1967), pp. 503–536; Adrienne Kaeppler, "Tongan Dance: A Study in Cultural Change," *Ethnomusicology* 14 (1970): 266–277; Adrienne Kaeppler, "Folklore as Expressed in the Dance in Tonga," *Journal of American Folklore* 80 (1967): 160–168; Adrienne Kaeppler, "The Structure of Tongan Dance" (Ph.D. dissertation, University of Hawaii, 1967).

164. Thomas J. Schlereth, "Artisans and Craftsmen: A Historical Perspective," in *The Craftsman in Early America* ed. Ian M. Quimby (New York: Norton, 1982).

165. Svetlana Alpers, "Is Art History? " *Daedalus* 106 (Summer 1977): 1–13; Theodore K. Rabb, "The Historian and the Art Historian," *Journal of Interdisciplinary History* 4 (1973): 107–117.

166. John I. Kirk, *American Chairs: Queen Anne and Chippendale* (New York: Knopf, 1972).

167. Ames, "Folk Art," pp. 297–301.

168. For a complete elaboration of Kenneth Ames's position, see Kenneth Ames, *Beyond Necessity: Art in the Folk Tradition* (New York: Norton, 1977); the catalog that accompanied the Winterthur 1977 Folk Art Exhibition at the Brandywine Museum; Ames, "Folk Art." Compare Ames's argument with: John Michael Vlach, "American Folk Art: Questions and Quandries," *Winterthur Portfolio* 15 (Winter 1980): 345–355; Jules Prown, "Style as Evidence," ibid., 15 (Autumn 1980): 197–210; and Simon J. Bronner, "Investigating Identity and Expression in Folk Art," ibid., 16 (Spring 1981): 138–154.

169. Rumford, "Uncommon Art of the Common People," p. 52.

170. Scott Swank, "Introduction," in *Perspectives on American Folk Art*, ed. Quimby and Swank, pp. 4–5; Trent, *Hearts and Crowns*: pp. 2–3.

171. Jules D. Prown, "Style in American Art: 1750–1800," in *American Art, 1750–1800*, ed. Charles F. Montgomery and Patricia E. Kane (Boston: New York Graphic Society, 1976), pp. 32–39; Jules D. Prown, "Mind in Matter: An Introduction to Material Culture Theory and Method," *Winterthur Portfolio* 17 (Spring 1982): 1–19; Jules D. Prown, "Style as Evidence," p. 200.

172. Prown, "Style as Evidence," p. 207.

173. Mary Douglas, "Deciphering a Meal," in *Myth, Symbol, and Culture*, ed. Clifford Geertz (New York: Norton, 1971), pp. 61–82. For a critique of the symbolistic focus in ethnography, see I. C. Jarvie, "On the Limits of Symbolic Interpretation in Anthropology," *Current Anthropology* 17 (1976): 687–701.

174. Alan Trachtenberg, *Brooklyn Bridge: Fact and Symbol* (New York: University Press, 1965), p. vii.

175. A sampling would include Marvin Trachtenberg, *The Statue of Liberty* (New York: Viking, 1976); W. Lloyd Warner, *The Living and the Dead: A Study of the Symbolic Life of Americans* (New Haven, Conn.: Yale University Press, 1959); John Kouwenhoven, *The Beer Can by the Highway* (Garden City: Doubleday, 1961); John F. Kasson, *Civilizing the Machine: Technology and Republican Values in America, 1771–1906* (New York: Oxford University Press, 1976); Robert Venturi, Denise Scott Brown, and Steven Izenour, *Learning from Las Vegas* (Cambridge, Mass.: MIT Press, 1972); Jan Cohn, *The Palace or the Poorhouse: The American House as Cultural Symbol* (East Lansing, Mich.: University of Michigan Press, 1979).

176. Roger A. Fischer, "1896 Campaign Artifacts: A Study in Inferential Reconstruction," *Journal of American Culture* 3 (Winter 1980): 706–721; also see Wilcomb Washburn, "The Great Autumnal Madness," *Quarterly Journal of Speech* 49 (December 1969): 417–431, and Otto Charles Thieme, "Wave High the Red Bandanna: Some Handkerchiefs of the 1888 Presidential Campaign," *Journal of American Culture* 3 (March 1980): 686–705.

177. Edith P. Mayo, "Campaign Appeals to Women," *Journal of American Culture* 3 (March 1980): 722–741; Edith Mayo, "Ladies and Liberation: Icon and Iconoclast in the Women's Movement," in *Icons of America*, ed. Ray B. Browne and Marshal Fishwick (Bowling Green, Ohio: Bowling Green University Press, 1978), pp. 209–227.

178. E. McClung Fleming, "Artifact Study: A Proposed Model," pp. 153–73.

179. E. McClung Fleming, "Symbols in the United States: From Indian Queen to Uncle Sam," in *Frontiers of American Culture*, ed. Ray B. Browne et al. (Lafayette, Ind.: Purdue University Studies,

1968), pp. 1–24; also consult Louis C. Jones, *Outward Signs of Inner Beliefs: Symbols of American Patriotism* (Cooperstown, N.Y.: New York State Historical Association, 1975).

180. Bronner, "Concepts in the Study of Material Aspects," pp. 151–153.

181. Richard M. Dorson, "Concepts of Folklore and Folklife Studies," in *Folklore and Folklife*, pp. 12–13; Kent V. Flannery, "Cultural History vs. Cultural Process: A Debate in American Archaeology," in *Contemporary Archaeology: A Guide to Theory and Contributions* ed. by Mark P. Leone (Carbondale, Ill.: Southern Illinois University Press, 1972), pp. 102–107.

182. Following the thesis of Leslie A. White, *The Evolution of Culture: The Development of Civilization to the Fall of Rome* (New York: McGraw-Hill, 1959), Paul K. Martin also argues this point. Paul K. Martin, "The Revolution in Archaeology," in *Contemporary Archaeology*, ed. Leone, pp. 11–12.

183. Howard Wight Marshall, "Folklife and the Rise of American Folk Museums," *Journal of American Folklore* 90 (1977): 391–413.

184. Norbert Riedl, "Folklore and the Study of Material Aspects of Folk Culture," *Journal of American Folklore* 79 (1966): 557–563; Don Yoder, "Historical Sources for American Foodways: Research and Plans for an American Foodways Archive," *Ethnologia Scandinavia* 2 (1971): 41–55; and Glassie, *Pattern in Material Folk Culture*, pp. 238–239.

185. Henry Glassie, "The Wedderspoon Farm," *New York Folklore Quarterly* 22 (September 1966): 165–187; John T. Schlebecker, "Stockman and Drovers during the Revolution," *Pioneer America Society Proceedings* 2 (1973): 4–15; John T. Schlebecker, *Living Historical Farms: A Walk into the Past* (Washington: Smithsonian Institution, 1968); Ivor Nöel Hume, *Here Lies Virginia: An Archaeologist's View of Colonial Life and History* (New York: Knopf, 1963); John Cotter and J. Paul Hudson, *New Discoveries at Jamestown, the Site of the First Successful English Settlement in America* (Washington, 1957); John Cotter, *Archaeological Excavations at Jamestown* (Ann Arbor: University Microfilms, 1959).

186. Mark P. Leone, "Issues in Anthropological Archaeology," in *Contemporary Archaeology*, ed. Leone, p. 19.

187. Leone, "Issues in Anthropological Archaeology," p. 18.

188. James Deetz, "A Cognitive Historical Model for American Historical Culture," in *Reconstructing Complex Societies*, ed. Charlotte Moore (Cambridge, Mass.: Bulletin of Schools of American Research, 1974), pp. 21–24; Deetz, *In Small Things Forgotten*.

189. James Deetz, "Scientific Humanism and Humanistic Science: A Plea For Paradigmatic Pluralism in Historical Archaeology," unpublished paper, 1981, p. 10.

190. Deetz, "Scientific Humanism," p. 10.

191. Carson, "Doing History with Material Culture," pp. 41–74; Ivor Nöel Hume, "The Way, What and Who of Historical Archaeology," in *Historical Archaeology* (New York: Knopf, 1969), pp. 7–20; Robert L. Schuyler, ed., *Historical Archaeology: A Guide to Substantive and Theoretical Contributions* (Farmingdale, N.Y.: Baywood, 1978)); Bernard L. Fontana, "Artifacts of the Indians of the Southwest," in *Material Culture*, ed. Quimby, pp. 75–108; Mark P. Leone, "Archaeology as the Science of Technology: Mormon Town Plans and Fences," in *Research and Theory in Current Archaeology* ed. Charles Redman (New York: Wiley, 1973), pp. 125–150; and J. C. Harrington, "Archaeology as an Auxiliary Science to American History," *American Anthropologist* 57 (December 1955): 1121–1130.

192. Edwin Dethlefsen, "Material Culture and Human Being: Messages from the Graveyard," paper read at the Joint Conference of the Bay State Historical League and the Association for Gravestone Studies, Bradford College, Bradford, Massachusetts, June 20, 1980, pp. 1–2, 3.

193. Robert L. Schuyler, "Image of America: The Contribution of Historical Archaeology to National Identity," *Southwest Lore* 42 (1977): 27–39.

194. Jared Van Wagenen, *The Golden Age of Home Spun* (Ithaca, N.Y.: Cornell University Press, 1953); Henry Chanlee Forman, *Jamestown and St. Mary's: Buried Cities* (Baltimore: Johns Hopkins Press, 1938). Also see Iorwerth C. Peate, "The Study of Folklife and Its Part in the Defense of

Civilization,'' *Gwerin* 2 (1959): 97–109; Alexander Fenton, ''An Approach to Folklife Studies,'' *Keystone Folklore Quarterly* 12 (1967): 5–12.

195. James E. Vance, *This Scene of Man* (New York: Harper and Row, 1978)); David Ward, *Cities and Immigrants* (New York: Oxford University Press, 1971).

196. Philip L. Wagner and Marvin W. Mikesell, eds., *Readings in Cultural Geography* (Chicago: University of Chicago Press, 1962), p. 23.

197. Peirce Lewis, ''Common Houses, Cultural Spoor,'' *Landscape* 19 (January 1976): 1–22. Henry Glassie, ''Eighteenth-Century Cultural Process in Delaware Valley Folk Building,'' *Winterthur Portfolio* 7 (1972): 29–57. John M. Vlach, ''The Shot-Gun House: An African Legacy,'' *Pioneer America* 8 (January 1976): 47–56; ibid. (April 1976): 57–70. J. B. Jackson, *American Space: The Centennial Years, 1865–1876* (New York: Norton, 1975).

198. On the early history of cultural geography in America, see Marvin W. Mikesell, ''Tradition and Innovation in Cultural Geography,'' *Annals of the Association of American Geographers* 68 (March 1978): 1–16; on Carl O. Sauer, consult John Leighley, ed., *Land and Life: A Selection from the Writings of Carl Ortwin Sauer* (Berkeley: University of California Press, 1963); and on A. L. Kroeber, see A. L. Kroeber, *An Anthropologist Looks at History* (Berkeley: University of California Press, 1963).

199. The influence of Kniffen's theory and practice can be easily seen in H. J. Walker and W. G. Haag, eds., *Man and Cultural Heritage: Papers in Honor of Fred B. Kniffen* (Baton Rouge, La.: Louisiana State University Press, 1974).

200. Fred Kniffen, ''American Cultural Geography and Folklife,'' in *American Folklife*, ed. Yoder, pp. 51–59, 57. .

201. Fred Kniffen, ''Folk Housing: A Key to Diffusion,'' *Annals of the Association of American Geographers* 55 (1965): 549–577; see also Fred Kniffen, ''Louisiana House Types,'' ibid. 26 (1936): 179–193.

202. Glassie, *Pattern in Material Folk Culture*, p. 33.

203. Bronner, ''Concepts in the Study of Material Aspects,'' p. 140.

204. Kniffen, ''American Cultural Geography,'' pp. 60, 63. A survey of other environmentalist positions can be found in Simon J. Bronner, ''Modern Anthropological Trends and Their Folkloristic Relationships,'' *Folk Life* 19 (1981): 66–83.

205. John F. Moe, ''Concepts of Shelter: The Folk Poetics of Space, Change, and Continuity,'' *Journal of Popular Culture* 11 (1977): 219–253.

206. Dorson, ''Concepts of Folklore and Folklife Studies, pp. 20–21; Bronner, ''Concepts in the Study of Material Aspects,'' pp. 145–46. Siegfried Giedeon, *Mechanization Takes Command* (New York: Oxford University Press, 1948); Lynn White, *Medieval Technology and Social Change* (New York: Oxford University Press, 1964); Carl Condit, *The Chicago School of Architecture* (Chicago: University of Chicago Press, 1964). American Studies scholar Gordon Kelly has applied the functionalist perspective to American literature in Gordon Kelly, ''Literature and the Historian,'' *American Quarterly* 26 (May 1974): 141–159.

207. See, for example, Warren Roberts, ''Folk Architecture in Context: The Folk Museum,'' *Pioneer America Society Proceedings* 1 (1973): 34–50.

208. E. N. Anderson, ''On the Folk Art of Landscaping,'' *Western Folklore* 21 (1972): 179–188.

209. For a detailed review of *The Functions of Folk Costume* by Petr Bogatyrev, see Henry Glassie, ''Structure and Function, Folklore and the Artifact,'' *Semiotica* 7 (1973): 313–351. In Henry Glassie, *All Silver and No Brass: An Irish Christmas Mumming* (Dublin: Dolmen, 1976), Glassie proposes several applications of the functionalist perspective.

210. Richard S. Latham, ''The Artifact as Cultural Cipher,'' in *Who Designs America?* ed. Laurence B. Holland (New York: Anchor, 1966), pp. 257–280.

211. Jay Anderson, ''Immaterial Material Culture: The Implications of Experimental Research for Folklife Museums,'' *Keystone Folklore* 21 (1976–1977): 1–13; Robert Asher, ''Experimental Archaeology,'' *American Anthropology* 63 (1961): 793–816; John Coles, *Archaeology by Experiment* (New York: Scribner's, 1973).

212. Thor Heyerdahl, *Kon-Tiki*, translated by F. H. Lyon (New York: Rand McNally, 1950); also see Errett Callahan, *The Old Rag Report: A Practical Guide to Living Archaeology* (Richmond, Va.: Department of Sociology/Anthropology, Virginia Commonwealth University, 1973); and Donald W. Callender, "Reliving the Past: Experimental Archaeology in Pennsylvania," *Archaeology* 29 (1976): 173–178.

213. Claude Lévi-Strauss, "Overture to *Le Cru et le Cuit*," trans. Joseph H. McMahon, in *Structuralism*, ed. Jacques Ehrmann (Garden City: Anchor, 1970), pp. 31–55. Lévi-Strauss's key works include: Claude Lévi-Strauss, *The Raw and the Cooked: Introduction to a Science of Mythology*, tr. John Weightman and Doreen Weightman (New York: Harper and Row, 1969); Claude Lévi-Strauss, *Structural Anthropology*, tr. Claire Jacobson and Brooke Grunfest Shoepf (Garden City: Doubleday, 1967); and Claude Lévi-Strauss, *The Savage Mind* (Chicago: University of Chicago Press, 1966); Barthes's major studies are Roland Barthes, *Elements of Semiology*, translated by Annette Larens and Colin Smith (London: Cape, 1967); and Roland Barthes, *Mythologies*, tr. Annette Larens (New York: Hill and Wang, 1972); whereas Foucault's primary work is Michel Foucault, *The Order of Things: An Archaeology of the Human Sciences* (London: Tavistock, 1970). A bibliographic overview is *Structuralists and Structuralisms: A Selected Bibliography of French Contemporary Thought, 1960–1970* (n.p.: Diacritics, 1971).

214. Useful summaries of the structuralist debate are John G. Blair, "Structuralism, American Studies, and the Humanities," *American Quarterly* 30 (Bibliography Issue, 1978): 261–281; David Pace, "Structuralism in History and the Social Sciences," ibid., pp. 282–297; G. de Rohan-Csermak, "Structural Analysis in Material Culture," in *Man, Language and Society: Contributions to the Sociology of Language*, ed. Samir K. Ghosh (Paris: Moulton, 1972), pp. 190–205.

215. Blair, "Structuralism, American Studies, and the Humanities," p. 261.

216. Roland Barthes, *Writing Degree Zero and Elements of Semiology* (New York: Hill and Wang, 1968).

217. "The Scope of Anthropology," in *Structural Anthology II*, pp. 9–11 and "The Story of Asdiwal," ibid., pp. 146–197.

218. Hayden White, "Structuralism and Popular Culture," *Journal of Popular Culture* 7 (1974): 759–775; R. E. Johnson, Jr., "The Dialogue of Novelty and Repetition: Structure in 'All My Children,' " ibid. 10 (1976): 560–570; Bruce A. Lohof, "A Morphology of the Modern Fable," ibid. 8 (1974–1975): 15–27; Eugene M. Wilson, "Form Changes in Folk Houses," *Geoscience and Man* 5 (1974): 64–71; Bernard Herman, "The Whole Cloth of Ethnography: Time, Performance, and Folk Artifact," in *American Material Culture and Folklore*, ed. Bronner. Glassie, *Folk Housing in Middle Virginia*.

219. Edna Scofield, "'The Evolution and Development of Tennessee Houses," *Journal of the Tennessee Academy of Science* 11 (1936): 229–240; Glassie, *Folk Housing in Middle Virginia*.

220. Scofield, "Evolution and Development of Tennessee Houses," p. 230.

221. Eugene M. Wilson, "Some Similarities between American and European Folk Houses," *Pioneer America* 3 (1971): 8–14; Bronner, "Concepts in the Study of Material Aspects," pp. 155–156.

222. Glassie, *Folk Housing in Middle Virginia*, p. 17.

223. Glassie, *Folk Housing in Middle Virginia*, p. 161.

224. See reviews of Glassie, *Folk Housing in Middle Virginia*, by Harvey Green in *American Quarterly* 32 (Summer 1980): 222–228; and by George McDaniel in *Journal of American Folklore* 91 (1978): 51–53.

225. Michael Owen Jones, "Ask the Chairmaker," unpublished paper presented at American Studies Association National meeting, Boston, October 1977.

226. Michael Owen Jones, "Comment: Folkloristics and Fieldwork," in *American Material Culture and Folklife*, ed. Bronner. Jones argues a similar point in Michael Owen Jones, "L. A. Add-ons and Re-Does: Renovation in Folk Art Study and Architectural Design," in *Perspectives on American Folk Art* ed. Quimby and Swank, pp. 325–364.

227. For example, see Ruth Bunzel, *The Pueblo Potter: A Study of the Creative Imagination in Primitive Art* (New York: Columbia University Press, 1929); and Alan Ludwig, *Graven Images: New*

England Stonecarving and Its Symbols, 1650–1815 (Middletown, Conn.: Wesleyan University Press, 1966).

228. Michael O. Jones, *The Hand-Made Object and Its Maker* (Berkeley: University of California Press, 1975); Michael O. Jones and Robert A. Georges, *People Studying People: The Human Element in Fieldwork* (Berkeley: University of California Press, 1980). See also Elizabeth Mosby Adler, "Direction in the Study of American Folk Art," *New York Folklore* 1 (1975): 40–41; and Michael O. Jones, "Two Directions for Folkloristics in the Study of American Art," *Southern Folklore Quarterly* 32 (1968): 249–259.

229. Jones, *Hand-Made Object and Its Maker*, p. vii; Jones, "L.A. Add-ons and Re-dos," pp. 325–363.

230. Jones, *Hand-Made Object and Its Maker*, pp. vii–viii. To demonstrate the "hand-made" quality of his own book manuscript, Jones had the entire text hand-lettered by David Comstock.

231. On Glassie's quest to "move on through buildings and their architects to the people who lived in them and eventually to a reexamination of cherished and fundamental concepts about humanity," see Henry Glassie, "Vernacular Architecture," *Journal of the Society of Architectural Historians* 35 (December 1976): 293–295; and Henry Glassie, "Delaware Folk Building: *Winterthur Portfolio*, 7 (1972) p. 30.

232. See Thomas Adler, "Personal Experience and the Artifact: Musical Instruments, Tools, and the Experience of Control," in *American Material Culture and Folk Art*, ed. Bronner; Simon J. Bronner, "We Live What I Paint and I Paint What I See: A Mennonite Artist in Northern Indiana," *Indiana Folklore* 12 (1979): 5–17; Simon J. Bronner, "Investigating Identity and Expression in Folk Art," *Winterthur Portfolio* 16 (1981): 65–84; Simon J. Bronner, "Chain-Carvers in Southern Indiana: A Behavioristic Study in Material Culture" (Ph.D. dissertation, Indiana University, 1981); Simon J. Bronner, "The Paradox of Pride and Loathing and Other Problems," *Western Folklore* 40 (1981): 115–124.

233. Edward T. Hall, *The Hidden Dimension* (Garden City: Doubleday, 1966); Edward T. Hall, *The Silent Language* (Garden City: Doubleday, 1959); Edward O. Laumann and James S. Morris, "Living Room Styles and Social Attributes: The Patterning of Material Artifacts in a Modern Urban Community," *Sociology and Social Research* 54 (April, 1970): 321–342. Also see Martin Laba, "Urban Folklore: A Behavioral Approach," *Western Folklore* 38 (1979): 158–169; Michael Lesy, *Wisconsin Death Trip* (New York: Pantheon, 1973); Michael Lesy, *Time-Frames: The Meaning of Family Pictures* (New York: Pantheon, 1979); Robert Akeret, *Photoanalysis: How To Interpret the Hidden Psychological Meaning of Personal and Public Photographs* (New York: Peter Wydem, 1973).

234. Michael Owen Jones, "Bibliographic and Reference Tools: Toward a Behavioral History," unpublished paper, presented at the American Association for State and Local History Folklore and Local History Conference, New Orleans, September 4–6, 1980.

235. M. O. Jones, "Bibliographic and Reference Tools," pp. 7–9.

236. For a summary statement of these subfields and their emergence in the American Studies movement, see Wise, "Paradigm Dramas," pp. 322–324.

237. G. Ewart Evans, *Ask the Fellows Who Cut the Hay* (London: Farber, 1956); James Spradley, *You Owe Yourself a Drunk: An Ethnography of Urban Nomads* (Boston: Little, Brown, 1970); Richard Horwitz, *Anthropology toward History: Culture and Work in a 19th-Century Maine Town* (Middletown, Conn.: Wesleyan University Press, 1978).

238. Thomas Adler, following Edmund Husserl, summarized the phenomenological position as applied to folk artifacts as follows:

> We are beginning to get a pretty good idea of the distribution of folk houses on the land, and we can all mostly agree how baskets were made, how bread was baked, and how quilts are put together. We are now in need of some perspectives that can help us to elicit and to generalize about the traditional meanings that underlie and are embedded in traditional artifacts. The hardest core of meanings to get at may be those that arise directly from the phenomenal stream, from the actual experiences a person has with an object.

The study of such experiences necessarily involves the taking of an internalized view. In conducting a phenomenological investigation an analyst sets aside the referential knowledge he already has and momentarily divests himself of his memories of an object, recognizing crucial distinctions to be made between direct experiential knowledge, the memories of experience, and referred knowledge to others. Whether or not historical and personal knowledge can actually be set aside is a moot point; phenomenologists make the attempt, because experiences are by their very nature things of the here-and-now. All we have, experientially speaking, is the present, and each moment of our experience is filled, in part, by material presences that are loci of denotational and connotational meaning. If we can create an appropriate language in which to speak of the ways we all experience artifacts, we may be able to commence an unambiguous discussion of the significance of objects, as well as of their distribution and construction.

(Thomas Adler, "Personal Experience and the Artifact: Musical Instruments, Tools, and the Experience of Control," in *American Material Culture and Folklore*, ed. Bronner, pp. 1–2, typescript copy.)

For discussions òf phenomenology's relation's to time in history, see Edmund Husserl, *Cartesian Meditations: An Introduction to Phenomenology*, trans. Dorian Carins (The Hague: Nijhoff, 1960), pp. 33–43; Donald M. Lowe, "Intentionality and the Method of History," in *Phenomenology and the Social Sciences*, ed. Maurice Natanson (Evanston, Ill.: Northwestern University Press, 1973), pp. 11–14; C. D. Keys, "Art and Temporality," *Research in Phenomenology* 1 (1971), pp. 63–73.

239. Dell Upton, "Toward a Performance Theory of Vernacular Architecture: Early Tidewater Virginia as a Case Study," *Folklore Forum* 12 (1979): 173–195; Adler, "Personal Experience and the Artifact," pp. 1–2.

240. Adler, "Personal Experience and the Artifact," p. 13.

241. Bronner, "Concepts in the Study of Material Aspects," p. 160.

242. Bronner, "Toward a Philosophy of Folk Objects," personal correspondence with Bronner, March 23, 1981.

243. Bronner, "Toward a Philosophy of Folk Objects," pp. 7–8; for further discussion of this point, see Janet L. Dolgin, David S. Kemnitzer, and David M. Schneider, "As People Express Their Lives, So They Are . . . , " in *Symbolic Anthropology*, ed. Janet L. Dolgin, David S. Kemnitzer, and David M. Schneider (New York: Columbia University Press, 1977), pp. 3–44.

244. David M. Potter, "The Quest for the National Character," in *The Reconstruction of American History*, ed. John Higham (New York: Harper and Row: 1962), pp. 197–220.

245. Anthropologist Ralph Linton has written one of the most trenchant satires of those who make excessive claims for an "American exceptionalism" in material culture study; see Ralph Linton, "One-Hundred Per-Cent Americanism," *American Mercury* 40 (1937): 427–429.

246. An example of a European scholar with an articulate ideological orientation is Sergei Aleksandrovic Tokarev, a Russian ethnographer; see Sergei Aleksandrovic Tokarev, "Toward a Methodology for Ethnographic Study of Material Culture," *Ethnologia Europea* 6 (1970): 163–178 [in German]; it was translated into English and appears in *American Material Culture and Folklife*, ed. Bronner.

247. Ronald Radosh, "The Rise of a Marxist Historian: An Interview with Eugene Genovese," *Change* 10 (November 1978): 31–35.

248. *Radical History Review* 21 (Fall 1979) is of particular use to material culture students because it is devoted to research on the spatial dimension of history. For two ideological critiques of American material culture exhibition practices, see Carol Duncan and Alan Wallach, "The Museum of Modern Art as Late Capitalist Ritual: An Iconographic Analysis," *Marxist Perspectives* (Winter 1978): 28–51; and Rudolf Baranik et al., *An Anti-Catalog* (New York: Catalog Committee, 1977). See also David Noble, *America By Design: Science, Technology and Corporate Capitalism* (New York: Oxford University Press, 1977).

249. Langdon Winner, "Do Artifacts Have Politics? " *Daedalus* 109 (1980): 121–136.

250. Horace Bushnell, "The Age of Homespun," and "The Day of Roads," in *Work and Play*, by Horace Bushnell (New York: Scribner's, 1964), pp. 374–408, 409–445, strike me as one of the earliest

uses of artifacts as representatives of the national spirit. For a brief estimate of Gowans's similar proclivity in *Images of American Living*, see Harold Skramstad, "American Things: A Neglected Material Culture," in *American Studies: Topics and Sources*, ed. Robert Walker (Westport, Conn.: Greenwood, 1976), pp. 185–193.

251. Lewis Mumford, "Authoritarian and Democratic Technics," *Technology and Culture* 5 (1964): 1–8.

252. Kouwenhoven, *Made In America*, p. 15.

253. J. C. Furnas, *The Americans: A Social History of the United States, 1587–1914* (New York: Putnam, 1969); J. C. Furnas, *Great Times: An Informal Social History of the United States, 1914–1929* (New York: Putnam, 1974); J. C. Furnas, *Stormy Weather: Crosslights on the Nineteen Thirties: An Informal Social History of the United States* (New York: Putnam, 1977); Gilman M. Ostrander, *American Civilization in the First Machine Age, 1890–1940: A Cultural History of America's First Age of Technological Revolution and "Rule by the Young"* (New York: Harper and Row, 1972); Christopher Tunnard and Henry Hope Reed, *American Skyline* (New York: New American Library, 1956); Elting E. Morison, *From Know-How to Nowhere: The Development of American Technology* (Oxford, Eng.: Blackwell, 1974).

254. Samples of typical American Studies scholarship in quest of the national character include: David Potter, *People of Plenty: Economic Abundance and the American Character* (Chicago: University of Chicago Press, 1954); Elting E. Morison, ed. *The American Style: Essays in Value and Performance* (New York: Harper, 1958); Max Lerner, *America as a Civilization: Life and Thought in the United States Today* (New York: Simon and Schuster, 1957); and Ralph Barton Perry, *Characteristically American* (Freeport, N.Y.: Books for Libraries, 1949).

255. Alan Gowans, *Images of American Living: Four Centuries of Architecture and Furniture as Cultural Expression* (Philadelphia: Lippincott, 1964), p. xv.

256. Skramstad, "American Things," pp. 14–15.

257. Daniel J. Boorstin, *The Americans: The Democratic Experience* (New York: Random House, 1973), p. 389.

258. Daniel J. Boorstin, *The Republic of Technology* (New York: Harper and Row, 1978), p. 7.

259. For critical analyses of the Boorstin corpus, see J. R. Pole, "Daniel J. Boorstin," in *Paths to the American Past*, ed. J. R. Pole (New York: Oxford University Press, 1979), pp. 299–334; John P. Diggins, "The Perils of Naturalism: Some Reflections on Daniel J. Boorstin's Approach to American History," *American Quarterly* 23 (1971): 153–180; Robert V. Bruce, "Packaging the Past: The Boorstin Experience," *Journal of Interdisciplinary History* 6 (Winter 1976): 507–511.

260. Philippe Ariès, *Centuries of Childhood: A Social History of Family Life*, trans. Robert Baldick (New York: Knopf, 1962); Fernand Braudel, *Capitalism and Material Life*, trans. Miriam Kochan (New York: Harper and Row, 1975). Other works in the Braudelian mode include Rudolph Bell, *Fate and Honor, Family and Village: Demographic and Cultural Change in Rural Italy since 1880* (Chicago: University of Chicago Press, 1979); and Immanuel Wallerstein, *The Modern World-System: Capitalist Agriculture and the Origins of the European World Economy in the Sixteenth Century* (New York: Academic, 1974). A new journal, *Review: A Journal of the Fernand Braudel Center for the Study of Economies, Historical Systems, and Civilizations*, suggests the continuing interest in the approach.

261. Recognizing the orientation of social history, the American Association for State and Local History concentrated its five week-long "Current Trends in American History" seminars, 1980–81, for museum and historical agency personnel on American social history.

262. Thompson, *The Rise of the English Working Class*, pp. 10–13; Laurence Vesey, "The 'New' Social History in the Context of American Historical Writing," *Reviews in American History* 7 (March 1979): 4–5.

263. John Demos, *A Little Commonwealth: Family Life in Plymouth Colony* (New York: Oxford University Press: 1970), pp. vii–xvi.

264. Ariès, *Centuries of Childhood*, pp. 50–61.

265. Demos, *Little Commonwealth*, pp. 57–58.

266. Cary Carson, "From the Bottom Up: Zero-Base Research for Social History at Williamsburg," *History News* 35 (January 1980): 7–9.

267. *Vernacular Architecture Newsletter* sponsored by the Vernacular Architecture Forum and edited by Dell Upton, Department of American Studies, George Washington University, Washington.

268. Ames, "Meaning in Artifacts," pp. 33–56; Clifford E. Clark, Jr., "Domestic Architecture as an Index to Social History: The Romantic Revival and the Cult of Domesticity in America, 1840–1870," *Journal of Interdisciplinary History* 7 (Summer 1976): 33–56; Harvey Green, "The Problem of Time in Nineteenth Century America," in *Time to Mourn*, ed. Pike Armstrong, pp. 31–38.

269. Gwendolyn Wright, *Moralism and the Model Home: Domestic Architecture and Cultural Conflict in Chicago, 1873–1913* (Chicago: University of Chicago Press, 1980); Dolores Hayden, *Seven American Utopias: The Architecture of Communitarian Socialism, 1790–1975* (Cambridge, Mass.: MIT Press, 1976); Martha Moore Trescott, ed., *Dynamos and Virgins Revisited: Women and Technological Change in History* (Metuchen, N.J.: Scarecrow, 1979).

270. Thomas A. Zaniello, "American Gravestones: An Annotated Bibliography," *Folklore Forum* 9 (1976): 115–137.

271. Peter Benes, *Masks of Orthodoxy: Folk Gravestone Carving in Plymouth County, Massachusetts, 1689–1805* (Amherst, Mass.: University of Massachusetts Press, 1977); David Stannard, *The Puritan Way of Death: A Study in Religion, Culture and Social Change* (New York: Oxford University Press, 1977). See also the collection of articles by other social historians on the topic in David Stannard, ed., *Death in America* (Philadelphia: University of Pennsylvania Press, 1975). Anita Schorsch, ed., *Mourning Becomes America: Mourning Art in the New Nation* (New Jersey: Main Street Press, 1976); and Pike and Armstrong, eds., *A Time to Mourn*.

272. David Hackett Fisher, *Growing Old in America* (NY: Oxford University Press: 1977).

273. See Bernard Mergen, "Work and Play," *American Quarterly* 32 (Fall 1980): 453–463; Bernard Mergen, "The Discovery of Children's Play," ibid. 27 (October 1975): 399–420; and Bernard Mergen, "Games and Toys," in *Handbook of American Popular Culture*, ed. Thomas Inge (Westport, Conn.: Greenwood, 1980); Carroll W. Pursell, Jr., "Toys, Technology and Sex Roles in America, 1920–1940" in *Virgins and Dynamos Revisited:* ed. M. M. Trescott, pp. 252–267.

274. Jay Anderson, "Food and Folklore: A Special Issue," *Keystone Folklore Quarterly* 16 (1971): 153–214; Charles Camp, "Food in American Culture: A Bibliographic Essay," *Journal of American Culture* 2 (1979): 559–570; Don Yoder, "Folk Cookery" in *Folklore and Folklife*, ed., Dorson, pp. 325–350; Howard Wight Marshall, "Meat Preservation on the Farm in Missouri's 'Little Dixie,' " *Journal of American Folklore* 92 (October-December 1979): 400–417; Michael Owen Jones, Bruce Giuliano, and Robert Krell, eds., "Foodways and Eating Habits: Directions for Research" [special issue], *Western Folklore* 40 (1980).

275. William R. Rathje, "In Praise of Archaeology, Le Projet du Garbage" in *Historical Archaeology and the Importance of Material Things*, pp. 36–42. Also see George R. Stewart, *Not So Rich as You Think* (Boston: Houghton Mifflin, 1968), which has several pithy essas on American garbage, junk, factory effluents, and other waste as neglected material culture.

276. David Brody, "Labor History in the 1970s: Toward a History of the American Worker," in *The Past Before Us*, ed. Kammen, pp. 252, 266–267. For Gutman's influential perspective, see Herbert Gutman, "Work, Culture, and Society in Industrializing America," *American Historical Review* 78 (1973): 531–587.

277. Jean-Pierre Hardy, "Un Projet de Recherche sur les Artisans du Quebec,' " *CMA Gazette* 11 (1978): 26–34; Bruce Laurie, Theodore Hershberg, and George Alter, "Immigrants and Industry: The Philadelphia Experience, 1850–1880," *Journal of Social History* 9 (1975): 219–248.

278. On Lynn, consult Paul Faler, "Cultural Aspects of the Industrial Revolution: Lynn, Massachusetts, Shoemakers and Industrial Morality, 1826–1860," *Labor History* 15 (1974): 367–394; Alan Dawley, *Class and Community: The Industrial Revolution in Lynn* (Cambridge, Mass.: Harvard Uni-

versity Press, 1976). Tamara K. Hareven and Randolph Langenbach, *Amoskeag: Life and Work in the American Factory City* (New York: Pantheon, 1978). The Amoskeag study was also the subject of a photography exhibition mounted by the Currier Gallery of Art in New Hampshire.

279. Stokes, *Iconography of Manhattan Island;* see also D. W. Meinig, *The Interpretation of Ordinary Landscapes* (New York: Oxford University Press, 1979); John Reps, *Cities of the American West: A History of Frontier Urban Planning* (Princeton, N.J.: Princeton University Press, 1979); David Goldfield, "Living History: The Physical City as Artifact and Teaching Tool," *History Teacher* 8 (1975): 535–556. Other bibliographic leads can be found in Thomas J. Schlereth, "Above-Ground Archaeology," in *Artifacts and The American Past* (Nashville: American Association for State and Local History, 1980), pp. 184–203; Simon J. Bronner, "Material Folk Cultural Research in the Modern City," in *American Material Culture and Folklife.*

280. William Ferris, ed., *Afro-American Folk Art and Crafts* (Boston: Hall, 1981); John Michael Vlach, *The Afro-American Tradition in Decorative Arts* (Cleveland: Cleveland Museum of Art, 1978); Charles H. Fairbanks, "The Kingsley Slave Cabins in Duval County Florida, 1968," *Conference on Historic Site Archaeology Papers* 7 (1972): 62–93; *Archaeological Perspectives of Ethnicity in America: Afro-American and Asian American Culture History,* ed. Robert L. Schuyler (Farmingdale, N.Y.: Baywood, 1980). Also see Rodney Barfield, "North Carolina Black Material Culture: A Research Opportunity," *North Carolina Folklore Journal* 27 (November 1979): 61–66.

281. Margaret Hobbie, comp., *Museums, Sites, and Collections of Germanic Culture in North America* (Westport, Conn.: Greenwood, 1980); Charles Von Ravenswaay, *The Arts and Architecture of German Settlements in Missouri: A Survey of a Vanishing Culture* (Columbia, Mo.: University of Missouri Press, 1977).

282. Roberta S. Greenwood, *3500 Years on One City Block,* Buenaventura Mission Plaza Project Archaeological Report, Vol. 1 (Ventura, Calif.: City of Buenaventura, Redevelopment Agency, 1975); and Roberta S. Greenwood, *The Changing Faces of Main Street,* Buenaventura Mission Plaza Project Archaeological Report, Vol. 2 (Ventura, Calif.: City of Buenaventura, Redevelopment Agency, 1976).

283. For example, see Peter O. Wacker, "Dutch Material Culture in New Jersey," *Journal of Popular Culture* 11 (1978): 948–958, Don Yoder, "A Note on the Study of Sectarian Culture," in *American Material Culture and Folklife;* ed. Bronner; C. Fred Blake, "Graffiti and Racial Insults: The Archaeology of Ethnic Relations in Hawaii," in *Modern Material Culture: The Archaeology of Us,* ed. Richard A. Gould and Michael B. Schiffer (New York: Academic, 1981), pp. 87–100; Simon Bronner, Alan Cicala, and Stephen Stern, *Creative Ethnicity* (Detroit: Wayne State University Press, 1981); Yvonne R. Lockwood, "The Sauna: An Expression of Finnish-American Identity," *Western Folklore* 36 (1977): 71–84; Cotton Mather and Matti Kaups, "The Finnish Sauna: A Cultural Index to Settlement," *Annals of the Association of American Geographers* 53 (1963): 497–504.

284. Kenneth L. Ames, "Meaning in Artifacts," p. 20.

285. Take, for instance, the new groups that have sprung up recently to study nineteenth-century material culture. The Victorian Society in America had its beginnings in Margot Gayle's Greenwich Village kitchen in 1968. In the decade since then American scholars, collectors, and museums have "discovered" the artifactual record of the nineteenth century with an exuberance and bravado not unlike the era itself. Journals, such as *Nineteenth Century,* begun in 1975, publishing houses, like American Life Foundation, newsletters, including *American Life Foundation News,* and societies devoted to artifacts indigenous to the period, such as the Friends of Cast-Iron Architecture and the Society for Historical Photography, are all intensely serious about the collection, documentation, and interpretation of Victorian America. See also Ralph Kovel and Terry Kovel, *Specialized and General Publications for the Collector* (Beachwood, Ohio, 1978).

286. Chester H. Liebs, "Remember Our Not-So-Distant Past?" *Historic Preservation* 30 (January/ March 1978): 30–35; Bruce A. Lohof, "The Service Station in America: The Evolution of a Vernacular Form," *Industrial Archaeology* (Spring 1974): 1–13; Robert Heide and John Gilman, *Dime-Store Dream Parade, Popular Culture, 1925–1955* (New York: Dutton, 1979); Warren J. Belasco, "The Origins of

the Roadside Strip, 1900–1940,'' paper presented at the annual meeting of the Organization of American Historians, New Orleans, April 13, 1979.

287. Fred Kniffen, "On Corner-Timbering," *Pioneer America* 1 (January 1969): 1.

288. See Carroll Smith-Rosenberg, "The New Woman and the New History," *Feminist Studies* 3 (1975): 185–198. Gene Wise has parallel remarks on pluralism in both the American studies movement and the material culture movement; see Wise, "Paradigm Dramas," pp. 332–333.

289. Representative museum exhibitions in this category include "Plain and Elegant, Rich and Common, Documented County Furniture," New Hampshire Historical Society, Concord, N.H., 1978; "American Folk Art from the Traditional to the Naive," Cleveland Museum of Art, 1978; "Bo' Jou, Neejee! Profiles of Canadian Art," Renwick Gallery, Washington, 1979; "At Home: Domestic Life in the Post-Centennial Era, 1876–1920," State Historical Society of Wisconsin, Madison, 1976; and "The Afro-American Decorative Arts," Cleveland Museum of Art, 1978.

290. Fred E. Schroeder, "The Democratic Yard and Garden," in *Outlaw Aesthetics: Arts and the Public Mind* (Bowling Green, Ohio: Bowling Green University Popular Press, 1977), pp. 94–122; and Thomas J. Schlereth, "Plants Past: A Historian's Use of Vegetation as Material Culture Evidence," *Environmental Review* 4 (Fall 1980): 20–28.

291. On the continual neglect by historians of material culture evidence, see Charles T. Lyle, "The Historian's Attitude toward the Artifact" (M.A. thesis, Winterthur Museum-University of Delaware, 1972); on Fleming's call for a new profession of material culturists, see E. M. Fleming, "The University and the Museum: Needs and Opportunities for Cooperation," *Museologist* 111 (June 1969): 10–18.

292. The Winterthur Museum's 1979 three-day conference was called "The Craftsman in Early America"; its 1981 meeting was "The Colonial Revival In America." One valuable outcome of a 1978 conference held at Connor Prairie's Living History museum was Ormond Loomis and Willard B. Moore, eds., *Museum Studies Reader: An Anthology of Journal Articles on Open Air Museums in America* (Indianapolis: Indiana Committee for Humanities, 1978). On December 13, 1980, the Archives and History division of the North Carolina Department of Natural Resources sponsored a symposium in Durham, N.C., titled "The Material Culture of Black History: Problems and Methods."

293. No mention of American material culture studies is made in either Charles F. Delzell, *The Future of History* (Nashville, Tenn.: Vanderbilt University Press, 1977), Kammen, *The Past before Us*, or Richard E. Beringer, *Historical Analysis: Contemporary Approaches to Clio's Craft* (New York: Wiley, 1978).

294. Roger Burlingame, "The Hardware of Culture," *Technology and Culture* 1 (1959): 11–19.

295. John Fitchen, *The New World Dutch Barn: A Study of Its Characteristics, Its Structural System, and Its Probable Erectional Procedures* (Syracuse, N.Y.: Syracuse University Press, 1968) is based solely on material culture evidence.

296. Roger Welsch, *Sod Walls: The Story of The Nebraska Sodhouse* (Broken Bow, Nebr.: Purrells, 1968); Edwin A. Battison, "Eli Whitney and the Milling Machine," *Smithsonian Magazine of History* (1966); E. McClung Fleming, "Early American Decorative Arts as Social Documents," *Mississippi Valley Historical Review*, 44:2 (1958): 276–284.

297. Fred B. Kniffen, "Material Culture in the Geographic Interpretation of the Landscape," in *The Human Mirror*, ed M. Richardson: pp. 252–267.

298. Deetz, *In Small Things Forgotten*, pp. 28–45; Merritt Roe Smith, *Harper's Ferry Armory and the New Technology: The Challenge of Change* (Ithaca, N.Y.: Cornell University Press, 1977); Robert A. Howard, "Interchangeable Parts Re-Examined: The Private Sector of the American Arms Industry on the Eve of the Civil War," *Technology and Culture* 19 (1978): 633–649.

299. Howard Wight Marshall, *Folk Architecture in Little Dixie: A Regional Culture in Missouri* (Columbia: University of Missouri Press, 1981), p. 17.

300. Brooke Hindle, "How Much Is a Piece of the True Cross Worth?" in *Material Culture and the Study of American Life*, ed. Quimby, p. 20.

Chapter Three

1. John Chavis, "The Artifact and the Study of History," *Curator* 7 (1964): 156–162; Holman Swinney, "The Artifact as a Historical Source," paper presented to the Second Annual Idaho History Conference, Caldwell, Idaho, 1965; and Charles T. Lyle, "The Artifact and American History," (Master's thesis, University of Delaware-Winterthur Museum, 1970).

2. For a complete discussion of the technique of internal-external criticism, see Louis Gottschalk, *Understanding History: A Primer of Historical Method* (New York: Knopf, 1950), pp. 118–171.

Chapter Four

1. The Smithsonian Institution has important collections of campaign memorabilia from 1800 up to, and including, the campaign of 1960, in which television played such a key role. An attempt to capture the significance of a portion of this material has been made in Wilcomb E. Washburn, "The Great Autumnal Madness: Political Symbolism in Mid-Nineteenth-Century America," *Quarterly Journal of Speech* 49 (December 1963): 417–431.

Chapter Five

1. This observation may be a direct quote of a remark made by Andrew Jewell, Keeper of the Museum of English Rural Life, Reading, England, in the summer of 1973. Anyhow, the idea was his.

2. Edward C. Kendall, "John Deere's Steel Plow," *Contributions from the Museum of History and Technology* (Washington: U.S. National Museum Bulletin 218, 1959), pp. 15–25.

3. Roland H. Bainton, *The Medieval Church* (Princeton: Van Nostrand, 1962), pp. 25, 79; and Wilcomb E. Washburn, ed., *Proceedings of the Vinland Map Conference* (Chicago: University of Chicago Press, 1971).

4. Edwin Battison observes, "But merely seeing the stove doesn't reveal the smoke labyrinth that was its undoing. The later, so-called Franklin, is only an iron fireplace." When possible, the object should be used.

5. Peter Paul Haring, Cotton Pickers, U.S. Patent 1176891, issued March 28, 1916. See also: James T. Allen, *Digest of Agricultural Implements Patented in the United States from A.D. 1789 to July 1881*, 2 vols. (New York: J. C. von Arx, 1886); and U.S. Patent Office, *Subject-Matter Index of Patents for Inventions from 1790 to 1873, Inclusive*, 3 vols. (Washington: Government Printing Office, 1874).

6. Based on conversations or visits: Albert Eskerose, Nordiska Museet, Stockholm, July 12, 1967; Edwin Battison, Smithsonian Institution, February 1974; Stensjo, Sweden; Lejre Denmark; Skansen, Stockholm, Sweden; Frilandsmuseet, Lingby, Denmark; Farmer's Museum, Stowmarket, England; Living History Farms, Des Moines, Iowa; Old Sturbridge Village Farm, Sturbridge, Mass.; Stonefield Village, Cassville, Wisc.; Museum of English Rural Life, Reading, England; and Plimoth Plantation, Plymouth, Mass. See also John T. Schlebecker, "Curatorial Agriculture," *Agricultural History* 44 (Januray 1972): 95–103.

7. W. R. Paton, *Polybius, the Histories* (New York: Putnam, 1932), 2:79, 135, 139–143; A. D. Godley, trans., *Herodotus* (Cambridge, Mass.: Harvard University Press, 1960), I. vii–xvi. 19; 2–4. xvii. See also Ronald Latham, *The Travels of Marco Polo* (London: Folio Society, 1968), pp. 14–16; for careful distinction between what was seen and what was told of, see p. 256.

8. Dylan Thomas, *A Child's Christmas in Wales* (New York: New Directions, 1959).

9. Most of this is based on observations of farm-implement collections in various museums where the types of implements can be compared, but only by visiting the different museums. I particularly studied the collections at the Smithsonian Institution and at the Farmer's Museum at Hadley, Mass., and for the same general period, the collections at the Museum of English Rural Life, Reading, England,

and the Farmer's Museum at Stowmarket, Suffolk, England. Implement advertisements in America, and wills and estate inventories support this general view.

10. "Goucher and Wylie, Cutlers, at the Sign of the Cythe and Sickle, in Fourth-Street, the fourth Door from Market-street, Philadelphia, have prepared a large Quantity of Grass and Cradling Scythes and Sickles, for the ensuing Harvest . . ." *Pennsylvania Gazette*, May 18, 1774, p. 4.

11. Wayne D. Rasmussen, *Readings in the History of American Agriculture* (Urbana: University of Illinois Press, 1960), p. 67.

12. All sorts of farm implements are mentioned in support of the general theme in the following: Kenneth Beeson, Jr., "Indigo Production in the Eighteenth Century," *Hispanic American Historical Review* 44 (May 1964): 214–218; Joseph Doddridge, *Notes on the Settlement and Indian Wars: Of the Western Parts of Virginia and Pennsylvania from 1763 to 1783 . . .* (Pittsburgh, Pa.: Ritenour and Lindsey, 1912), p. 319; John Drayton, *View of South Carolina, As Respects Her Natural and Civil Concerns* (Charleston, S.C.: W. P. Young, 1802); S. G. Griffin, *A History of the Town of Keene* (Keene, N.H.: Sentinel Printing, 1904), p. 314; Lewis C. Gray, *History of Agriculture in the Southern United States to 1860*, 2 vols. (Washington: Carnegie Institution of Washington, 1933); Patrick M'Robert, *A Tour through Part of the North Provinces of America: Being a Series of Letters Wrote on the Spot, in the Year 1774 & 1775* (Edinburgh: The Author, 1776), p. 47; *Pennsylvania Gazette*, 1774, passim; Rasmussen, *Readings in the History of American Agriculture*, p. 79; Robert A. Rutland, *The Papers of George Mason, 1725–1792*, vol. 1 (Chapel Hill: University of North Carolina Press, 1970); *Virginia Gazette*, 1774–1776, passim; Curtis P. Nettels, *The Emergence of a National Economy, 1775–1815* (New York: Holt, Rinehart, and Winston, 1962.

13. Axel Steensberg, "Some Recent Danish Experiments in Neolithic Agriculture," *Agricultural History Review* 5 (1957): 66–73, exhibits several discoveries made by working.

14. "Journal of Joseph Joslin, Jr. of South Killingsly, A Teamster in the Continental Service, March 1777-August 1778," *Collections of the Connecticut Historical Society* 7 (Hartford: Connecticut Historical Society, 1899): 297–369; and Christopher Ward, *War of the Revolution* (New York: Macmillan, 1952), 1:127.

15. Darwin P. Kelsey, "Outdoor Museums and Historical Agriculture," *Agricultural History* 46 (January 1972): 105–127.

16. Bill Mauldin, *Up Front* (New York: World Publishing, 1945), p. 165.

Chapter Seven

1. John Ruskin, *The Stones of Venice* (London: Smith, Elder, 1853) 2:162, 169.

2. Holger Rasmussen, ed., *Dansk Folkemuseum and Frilandsmuseet* (Copenhagen: Nationalmuseet, 1966), pp. 7–11.

3. For William Morris, his friends and times, these readily available books are valuable: Paul Thompson, *The Work of William Morris* (New York: Viking, 1967); Asa Briggs, ed., *William Morris: Selected Writings and Designs* (Baltimore: Penguin, 1962); William Gaunt, *The Pre-Raphaelite Dream* (New York: Schocken, 1966); Robert Furneaux Jordan, *Victorian Architecture* (Baltimore: Penguin, 1966); John Gloag, *Victorian Tastes* (London: Adam and Charles Black, 1962).

4. For examples, see *Palliser's New Cottage Homes and Details* (New York: Palliser, Palliser, 1887), p. 1, pls. 7, 39; *Shoppell's Modern Houses* 1 (January 1886): 1–2, 30, 63, 64.

5. Thomas Hart Benton is treated briefly in Michael Owen Jones, "Two Directions for Folkloristics in the Study of American Art," *Southern Folklore Quarterly* 32 (September 1968): 249–259.

6. For the exhibit, see Allen Eaton and Lucinda Crile, *Rural Handicrafts in the United States*, Miscellaneous Publication 610 (Washington: U.S. Department of Agriculture and Russell Sage Foundation, 1946), pp. 8–21. Eaton wrote two major books on crafts, each including information on both folk and revivalistic crafts: Allen Eaton, *Handicrafts of the Southern Highlands* (New York: Russell Sage Foundation, 1937); and Allen Eaton, *Handicrafts of New England* (New York: Harper and Brothers, 1949).

7. Holger Cahill, *American Folk Art: The Art of the Common Man in America, 1750–1900* (New York: Museum of Modern Art, 1932.)

8. H. J. Hansen, ed., *European Folk Art in Europe and the Americas* (New York: McGraw-Hill 1968), p. 7.

9. These are the adjectives of most of the contributors to "What is American Folk Art? A Symposium," *Antiques* 57 (May 1950): 355–362.

10. The result of "Country Furniture: A Symposium," ibid., 93 (March 1968): 342–377, were similar to those of the earlier symposium on "folk art." Another statement produced at the same time is in Eric de Jonge, "Country Furniture, So-Called," *The Delaware Antiques Show* (Wilmington: Wilmington Medical Center, 1968), pp. 75–85.

11. Compare H. G. Barnett, *Innovation: The Basis of Cultural Change* (New York: McGraw-Hill, 1953), pp. 318–321.

12. Claude Lévi-Strauss, *The Savage Mind* (Chicago: University of Chicago Press, 1969), pp. 16–22.

13. Arthur Hayden, *Chats on Cottage and Farmhouse Furniture* (London: Ernest Benn, 1950), pp. 107, 109–110, 131. Originally printed in 1921.

14. More sophisticated art historians carefully distinguish between folk art, popular ("amateur") art, and fine art; see E. P. Richardson, *A Short History of Painting in America* (New York: Crowell, 1963), pp. 4–6; James Thomas Flexner, *Nineteenth Century American Painting* (New York: Putnam's, 1970), chap. 6.

15. Mark Twain, *Adventures of Huckleberry Finn* (New York: Charles I. Webster, 1885), chap. 17.

16. Cahill, *American Folk Art*, pp. 11, 18, pls. 79–108; Agnes Halsey Jones and Louis C. Jones, *New-Found Folk Art of the Young Republic* (Cooperstown: New York State Historical Association, 1960), pp. 7–8, 16, fig. 17; Peter C. Welsh, *American Folk Art: The Art and Spirit of a People* (Washington: Smithsonian Institution, 1965), figs. 1, 9, 21; Mary Black and Jean Lipman, *American Folk Painting* (New York: Potter, 1966), pp. 99–100, 119, 121–23. Nina Fletcher Little intelligently avoids the adjective "folk" in Nina Fletcher Little, *Country Art in New England: 1790–1840* (Sturbridge: Old Sturbridge Village, 1965), pp. 22, 34–35, though she allows it in Nina Fletcher Little, *American Folk Art from the Abby Aldrich Rockefeller Folk Art Collection* (Williamsburg: Colonial Williamsburg, 1966), pp. 10, 16–17. Works of art such as these, of course, deserve preservation and study; calling them "folk," which relates them automatically to cultural expressions like fraktur, however, confuses the issue beyond the possibility of meaningful communication.

17. Clement Greenberg, *Art and Culture: Critical Essays* (Boston: Beacon Press, 1969), p. 130. This essay, "Primitive Painting," pp. 129–132, as well as his opening piece, "Avant-Garde and Kitsch," pp. 3–21, show that, while his terminology is unfamiliar to the social scientist, he distinguishes between three kinds of art—folk, kitsch, avant-garde—in a way similar to the folklorist.

18. Joyce Cary, *Art and Reality: Ways of the Creative Process* (Garden City: Doubleday, 1958), pp. 41–43.

19. Leopoldo Castedo, *A History of Latin American Art and Architecture*, trans. and ed. Phyllis Freeman (New York: Praeger, 1969), chap. 16.

20. *Views in America, Great Britain, Switzerland, Turkey, Italy, The Holy Land, Etc.* (New York: J. Milton Emerson, 1852) consists entirely of advertisements and scenic engravings, mostly of pictures by W. H. Bartlett, whose illustrations were widely reproduced as homemade paintings.

21. Joshua Reynolds, *Discourses on Art* (London: Collier-Macmillan, 1969), pp. 42–52.

22. A good early study of the paintings is Sigurd Erixon, "Schwedische Bauern-Malereien," *Vom Wesen der Volkskunst, Jahrbuch für historische Volkskunde* 2 (Berlin: Herbert Studenrauch, 1926): 110–25. An easily accessible source is Iona Plath, *The Decorative Arts of Sweden* (New York: Dover, 1966), chap. 7. Reprint of the 1948 edition.

23. See the stimulating essay, Robert Plant Armstrong, *Forms and Processes of African Sculpture* (Austin: African and Afro-American Research Institute of the University of Texas, 1970), pp. 17–21.

24. Raymond Firth, *Elements of Social Organization* (Boston: Beacon Press, 1963), pp. 163, 173–175.

25. Bernard L. Fontana, William J. Robinson, Charles W. Cormack, and Ernest E. Leavitt, Jr., *Papago Indian Pottery* (Seattle: University of Washington Press, 1962), pp. 81–83.

26. Bernie Wise lives in the vicinity of River Springs, Saint Mary's County, Maryland. I have enjoyed talking with him many times; the interviews discussed here took place in May of 1969. An outstanding local historical book, full of folklife data (including good information on boat types) for this area, is Edwin W. Beitzell, *Life on the Potomac River* (Abel, Md.: Edwin W. Beitzell, 1968).

27. David Pye, *The Nature of Design* (New York: Reinhold, 1967), p. 21; Richard S. Latham, "The Artifact as Cultural Cipher," in *Who Designs America?* ed. Laurence B. Holland (Garden City: Doubleday, 1966), pp. 261–262; James Marston Fitch, "The Future of Architecture," *Journal of Aesthetic Education* 4 (January 1970): 102–103.

28. John Ruskin, *Lectures on Art* (New York: John Wiley, 1888), lecture 4.

29. John O. Livingston, maker of white oak baskets, was seventy-six when I visited him several times in April and May of 1967 at his home near Mount Pleasant, northeast of Dillsburg, York County, Pennsylvania.

30. George Kubler, *The Shape of Time: Remarks on the History of Things* (New Haven: Yale University Press, 1967), pp. 14–16.

31. Francis Bacon, "Of Gardens," *Essays* (London: J. M. Dent, 1947), p. 137.

32. Compare Herbert Read, *Art and Industry* (Bloomington: Indiana University Press, 1964), pp. 22–23.

33. Herbert Cescinsky, *English Furniture from Gothic to Sheraton* (Garden City, N.Y., 1937), p. 1. His dedication and preface are vintage Ruskin and Morris: "There is no greater pleasure, to my mind, than in the appreciation of fine things, necessarily made in an age when time was of little account, and when the craftsman gloried in his work. Modern conditions have killed all this; the refuge is only in the past."

34. Ad Rinehart, "Writings," in *The New Art* ed. Gregory Battcock (New York: Dutton, 1966), pp. 199–209.

35. For Amish dress, See Elmer Lewis Smith, *The Amish People* (New York: Exposition, 1958), pp. 164–171; Calvin George Bachman, *The Old Order Amish of Lancaster County* (Lancaster: Pennsylvania German Society, 1961), pp. 89–95; John A. Hostetler, *Amish Society* (Baltimore: Johns Hopkins University Press, 1963), pp. 134–138, 236–241, 311. The Amish plainness is well set in historic and cultural context by Don Yoder, "Sectarian Costume Research in the United States" in *Forms Upon the Frontier*, eds. Austin Fife, Alta Fife, and Henry Glassie (Logan: Utah State University Press, 1969), pp. 41–75.

36. Paul Klee, *Pedagogical Sketchbook*, trans. Sibyl Moholy-Nagy (New York: Praeger, 1965); pp. 22–23.

37. These patterns are described in Franz Boas, *Primitive Art* (New York: Dover, 1955), chap. 2.

38. See John Maas, *The Gingerbread Age* (New York: Bramhall House, 1957), chaps. 3–6.

39. All of the central hall house types—Georgian, Georgian I, and dogtrot houses, the New England central chimney houses and their derivatives, and the English, Dutch, northern basement, Pennsylvania, double-crib, single-crib, and transverse-crib barns—that is, all of the common barn types and most of the common house types of the eastern United States—can be represented in plan and facade by *dAb*. In house types there are several exceptions, though many of these are fragmentary representations, *dA*, or examples of the simplified *db* pattern, in which there is no element to mark the separation of mirrored halves (as in the Pennsylvania farmhouse, the double-pen houses, and Creole houses of the south). These types are pictured and described in Henry Glassie, *Pattern in the Material Folk Culture of the Eastern United States* (Philadelphia: University of Pennsylvania Press, 1969).

For the art of the Kentucky rifle, see John G. W. Dillin, *The Kentucky Rifle* (York: George Shumway, Trimmer, 1959); Henry J. Kauffman, *The Pennsylvania-Kentucky Rifle* (Harrisburg:

Stackpole, 1960); Joe Kindig, Jr., *Thoughts on the Kentucky Rifle in its Golden Age* (York: Trimmer, 1960).

41. John B. Brendel is the recipient of generations of Pennsylvania Dutch wisdom. A middle-aged highway worker, he lives in Reinholds, Lancaster County, Pennsylvania, where I visited him regularly between 1967 and 1970. John talked often and perceptively about folk belief and barn stars; he told me about the pentangle or "hexafoos" on the evening of May 4, 1967.

42. The digression on the pentangle takes place early in the tale. See Gordon Hall Gerould, trans. *Beowulf and Sir Gawain and the Green Knight* (New York: Ronald Press, 1935), pp. 148–50.

43. See José E. Espinosa, *Saints in the Valleys* (Albuquerque: University of New Mexico Press, 1967).

44. See B. F. Skinner, "Creating the Creative Artist," in *On the Future of Art*, ed. Edward F. Fry (New York: Viking, 1970), pp. 61–75.

45. Kasimir Malevich, "Suprematism," in *Modern Artists on Art*, ed. Robert L. Herbert (Englewood Cliffs: Prentice-Hall, 1964), p. 97.

46. For sgraffito, see L. M. Solon, *The Art of the Old English Potter* (New York: D. Appleton, 1886), pp. 82–83; Edwin Atlee Barber, *Tulip Ware of the Pennsylvania-German Potters* (Philadelphia: Philadelphia Museum and School of Industrial Art, 1903); John Spargo, *Early American Pottery and China* (Garden City: Garden City, 1926), chap. 6; Erich Meyer-Heisig, *Deutsche Bauerntöpferei* (Munich: Prestel, 1955).

Chapter Nine

1. Benno M. Foreman, ed., "Selected Readings in the Decorative Arts," unpublished anthology, Education Division, Winterthur Museum, 1976, sect. 15.

Chapter Ten

1. E. McClung Fleming, "The Period Room as a Curatorial Publication," *Museum News* 50 (June 1972): 39–43; Thomas W. Leavitt, "Toward a Standard of Excellence," *Technology and Culture* 9 (1968): 70–75; Thomas J. Schlereth, "It Wasn't that Simple," *Museum News* 36 (January-February 1978): 36–44.

2. The word "culture," as used in this paper, can be defined as "that complex whole which includes artifacts, beliefs, art, all the other habits acquired by man as a member of society, and all products of human activity as determined by these habits." Clyde Kluckhohn and W. H. Kelly, "The Concept of Culture," in *The Science of Man in the World Crisis*, ed. R. Linton (New York: Columbia University Press, 1945), pp. 78–106; see also A. L. Kroeber and Clyde Kluckhohn, *Culture: A Critical Review of Concepts and Definitions* (New York: Vintage, 1963). The word "artifact," as used in this paper, can be defined as "a product of human workmanship," *Webster's New Collegiate Dictionary* (1959), or "anything made by man at any time," Ivor Nöel Hume, *A Guide to Artifacts of Colonial America* (New York: Knopf, 1970), p. 4.

3. Kenneth Clark, *Civilisation: A Personal View* (London: British Broadcasting Corporation, 1969), p. 1.

4. Leslie A. White, *The Science of Culture* (New York: Farrar, Straus and Giroux, 1969), pp. 364–365. The term material culture, as used in this paper, can be defined as the totality of artifacts in a culture. See Melville J. Herskovits, *Cultural Anthropology* (New York: Knopf, 1963), p. 119.

5. For one of the few other models suggested, see Craig Gilborn, "Pop Pedagogy: Looking at the Coke Bottle," *Museum News* 47 (December 1968): 12–18. See below, chapter twelve.

6. Oscar Handlin, ed., *Harvard Guide to American History* (Cambridge, Mass.: Belknap, 1955), pp. 22–25.

7. See, for example, R. Peter Mooz, "An Art Historian's View: A Commentary on Style in Country Art," in *Country Cabinetwork and Simple City Furniture*, ed. John D. Morse (Charlottesville: Univer-

sity Press of Virginia, 1970). Erwin Panofsky uses the term "iconographical analysis," as distinguished from "iconological interpretation," for the extended identification of the influence of style centers. Erwin Panofsky, *Meaning in the Visual Arts* (Garden City: Doubleday, 1955), pp. 35–40.

8. For example, see Charles F. Montgomery, *American Furniture: The Federal Period* (New York: Viking, 1966), p. 229; Alan Gowans, *Images of American Living* (Philadelphia: Lippincott, 1964), pp. 69, 97.

9. Montgomery, *American Furniture*, pp. 48–49.

10. For three examples of functional analysis dealing with the utility function, see Rodris C. Roth, "Tea Drinking in Eighteenth Century America: Its Etiquette and Equipage," *Contributions from the Museum of History and Technology* (Washington: Smithsonian Institution, 1961); Frank H. Sommer III, "The Functions of American Church Plate," in *Spanish, French, and English Traditions in the Colonial Silver of North America* (Winterthur, Del.: Henry Francis du Pont Winterthur Museum, 1969); Charles F. Hummel, *With Hammer in Hand: The Dominy Craftsmen of East Hampton, New York* (Charlottesville: University Press of Virginia, 1968). A good example of an analysis of the function of the artifact as a culture symbol is Alan Trachtenberg, *Brooklyn Bridge: Fact and Symbol* (New York: Oxford University Press, 1965). For a treatment of artifacts as agents of cultural change, see Marshall McLuhan, *Understanding Media: The Extensions of Man* (New York: McGraw-Hill, 1965).

11. See Bruce R. Buckley, "A Folklorist Looks at the Traditional Craftsman," in *Country Cabinetwork and Simple City Furniture*, ed. John D. Morse (Charlottesville: University Press of Virginia, 1970), pp. 265–276.

12. For an example of a design chronology, see Margaret Burke, "Massachusetts High Chests, 1710–1780: Regional Characteristics and a Chronology of Design" (unpublished seminar report, University of Delaware, 1972). For examples of typology and seriation, see Gilborn, "Pop Pedagogy"; James Deetz and Edwin Dethlefson, "Death's Head, Cherub, Urn, and Willow," *Natural History* 76 (March 1967): 28–37; James Deetz, *Invitation to Archaeology* (Garden City: Natural History Press, 1967), pp. 26–33. For examples of statistical analysis, see Anthony N. B. Garvan, "American Church Silver: A Statistical Study," in *Spanish, French, and English Traditions*, pp. 73–104; Barbara G. Teller, "Ceramics in Providence, 1730–1800: An Inventory Survey," *Antiques* 94 (October 1968): 570–577.

13. James J. F. Deetz, "Ceramics from Plymouth, 1620–1835: The Archaeological Evidence," in *Ceramics in America*, ed. Ian M. G. Quimby (Charlottesville: University Press of Virginia, 1973), p. 15.

14. Geoge A. Kubler, "Time's Perfection and Colonial Art," in *Spanish, French, and English Traditions*, pp. 8–9.

15. For an attempt to trace parallel patterns in architecture, painting, sculpture, literature, and music, see Frederick B. Artz, *From the Renaissance to Romanticism* (Chicago: University of Chicago Press, 1962); Panofsky, *Meaning in the Visual Arts*, p. 39.

16. Richard E. Sykes, "American Studies and the Concept of Culture: A Theory and Method," *American Quarterly* 15 (Summer 1963, supplement): 263–270; Garvan, "American Church Silver"; Garvan, "The New England Porringer: An Index of Custom," in *Smithsonian Annual Report* (Washington: Government Printing Office, 1958), pp. 543–552; Edward J. Nygren, "Edward Winslow's Sugar Boxes: Colonial Echoes of Courtly Love," *Yale University Art Gallery Bulletin* 33 (Autumn 1971): 39–52; Teller, "Ceramics in Providence"; Henry Glassie, "Architecture as Cognitive Process" (public lecture, Brown University, December 1971); Gowans, *Images of American Living*, pp. 206–209; Deetz and Dethlefson, "Death's Head, Cherub, Urn, and Willow"; Edwin Dethlefson and James Deetz, "Death's Head, Cherub, Urn and Willow Trees: Experimental Archaeology in Colonial Cemeteries," *American Antiquity* 31 (November 1966): 502–510.

17. Deetz, "Ceramics from Plymouth"; Edward O. Lanmann and James S. House, "Living Room Styles and Social Attributes: The Patterning of Material Artifacts in a Modern Urban Community," *Sociology and Social Research* 54 (April 1970): 321–343; Gowans, *Images of American Living*, pp. 173–178.

18. Edgar Kaufman, *An Exhibition for Modern Living* (Detroit: Detroit Institute of Arts, 1949), p. 40; Handlin, ed. *Harvard Guide to American History*, pp. 61–63; see E. McClung Fleming, "Early

American Decorative Arts as Social Documents," *Mississippi Valley Historical Review* 45 (September 1958): 276–284. For an example of historians' use of artifacts as evidence, see John Demos, *A Little Commonwealth: Family Life in Plymouth County* (New York: Oxford University Press, 1970), pp. 36–51.

19. For a discussion of this problem, see William B. Hesseltine, "The Challenge of the Artifact," *The Present World of History* (Madison, Wisc.: American Association for State and Local History, 1959), pp. 64–70; Fleming, "Early American Decorative Arts as Social Documents"; John Chavis, "The Artifact and the Study of History," *Curator* 7 (1964): 156–162.

Chapter Eleven

1. Mae Thielgaard Watts, *Reading the Landscape: An Adventure in Ecology* (New York: Macmillan, 1957).

2. Grady Clay, *Close-up: How to Read the American City* (New York: Praeger, 1973).

3. Henry Glassie, *Pattern in the Material Folk Culture of the Eastern United States* (Philadelphia: University of Pennsylvania Press, 1971); and Fred Kniffen, "Folk Housing: Key to Diffusion," *Annals of the Association of American Geographers* 55 (1965): 549–577.

4. David Lowenthal, "The American Scene," *Geographical Review* 58 (1968): 61–88; and John Frazer Hart, *The Look of the Land* (Englewood Cliffs: Prentice Hall, 1974).

5. George Stewart, *US 40: Cross Section of the United States of America* (Boston: Houghton Mifflin, 1953).

6. Alan Gowans, *Images of American Living: Four Centuries of Architecture and Furniture as Cultural Expression* (Philadelphia: Lippincott, 1964); and Reyner Banham, *Los Angeles: The Architecture of the Four Ecologies* (New York: Harper & Row, 1971).

7. Pierre Dansereau, "The Barefoot Scientist," *Colorado Quarterly* 12 (1962): 101–115; Pierre Dansereau, "New Zealand Revisited," *Garden Journal* 12 (1962): 1–6; and J. Hoover Mackin, "Concept of the Graded River," *Bulletin of the Geological Society of America* (1948): 463–512.

8. Peirce Lewis, "Common Houses, Cultural Spoor," *Landscape* (1975): 1–22.

9. Russell Lynes, *The Tastemakers* (New York: Grosset and Dunlap, 1949).

10. David McCullough, *The Great Bridge: The Epic Story of the Building of the Brooklyn Bridge* (New York: Simon and Schuster, 1972); and David Plowden, *Bridges: The Spans of North America* (New York: Viking, 1974).

11. Tom Wolfe, *The Kandy-Kolored Tangerine-Flake Streamline Baby* (New York: Farrar, Straus, and Giroux, 1965).

12. *Ulrich's International Periodicals Directory* (1975).

13. Melvin E. Hecht, "The Decline of the Grass Lawn Tradition in Tucson," *Landscape* 19 (1975): 3–10.

14. David Lowenthal, "The American Way of History," *Columbia University Forum* 9 (1966): 27–32; David Lowenthal, "Past Time, Present Place: Landscape and Memory," *Geographical Review* 65 (1975): 1–36; Peirce Lewis, "The Future of the Past: Our Clouded View of Historical Preservation," *Pioneer America* 7 (1975): 1–20.

15. Donald E. Meinig, "Environmental Appreciation: Localities as a Humane Art," *Western Humanities Review* 25 (1971): 1–11.

Chapter Twelve

1. "Words and Machines: The Denial of Experience," *Museum News* 47 (September 1968): 28–29.

2. See, for example, Irving Rouse, "The Strategy of Culture History," in *Anthropology Today* (Chicago: University of Chicago Press, 1958), pp. 57–76.

3. See, for example, *Saturday Evening Post*, July 9, 1932 and August 28, 1937 (variant C), and July 30, 1938 and July 24, 1943 (variant D).

4. The single most complete source of historical information is the fiftieth anniversary issue of *The Coca-Cola Bottler* 51 (April 1959).

5. "Portrait of a Product," *Art in America* 52 (April 1964): 94–95.

6. E. J. Kahn, *The Big Drink* (New York: Random House, 1960), pp. 155–156.

7. Jack B. Weiner, *Dun's Review* 88 (October 1966): 280.

8. Raymond Loewy, *Never Leave Well Enough Alone* (New York: Simon and Schuster, 1951), 279. See also Robert W. Sarnoff, "Anatomy of a New Trademark," *Saturday Review* 51 (April 13, 1968): 91.

Chapter Thirteen

1. James Deetz, *Invitation to Archaeology* (Garden City: Natural History Press, 1967), p. 3.

2. Photographs of gravestones illustrating these changes can be found in James Deetz and Edwin S. Dethlefsen, "Death's Head, Cherub, Urn and Willow," *Natural History* 76 (1967): 12–13.

Chapter Fourteen

1. Among America's best known artifacts, Independence Hall is widely illustrated, especially in studies of colonial architecture and history; the Brooklyn Bridge and the Statue of Liberty are the subjects of recent monographs: Alan Trachtenberg, *Brooklyn Bridge, Fact and Symbol* (New York: Oxford University Press, 1965); Marvin Trachtenberg, *The Statue of Liberty* (New York: Viking Press, 1976). For a defense of monuments, see Theo Crosby, *The Necessary Movement: Its Future in the Civilized City* (Greenwich, Conn.: New York Graphic Society, 1970).

2. For succinct comments on elitism in history and the need to use artifacts, see Henry Glassie, *Folk Housing in Middle Virginia* (Knoxville: University of Tennessee Press, 1975), pp. 8–12. Comments on the impact of sociology appear in Dwight Macdonald, *Against the American Grain* (New York: Random House, 1962).

3. Most art historians still seem constrained to work only with those artifacts defined as art. Their unwillingness to go beyond this artificial barrier makes it unlikely that art history, among the earliest disciplines to develop and refine tools for the study of material culture, will make further significant contribution to artifact study. For appraisals of art history practices and paradigms, see James S. Ackerman and Rhys Carpenter, *Art and Archaeology* (Englewood Cliffs: Prentice-Hall, 1963), pp. 196–229; W. Eugene Kleinbauer, *Modern Perspectives in Western Art History: An Anthology of 20th-Century Writings on the Visual Arts* (New York: Holt, Rinehart and Winston, 1971), pp. 1–105; Michael Owen Jones, *The Hand Made Object and Its Maker* (Berkeley: University of California Press, 1975). For observations on the usefulness of art to historians, see Theodore K. Rabb, "The Historian and the Art Historian," *Journal of Interdisciplinary History* 4 (1973): 107–117. On folk material culture, see Kenneth L. Ames, *Beyond Necessity: Art in The Folk Tradition* (Winterthur, Del.: Winterthur Museum, 1977); Henry Glassie, *Folk Housing;* Henry Glassie, *Pattern in the Material Folk Culture of the Eastern United States* (Philadelphia: University of Pennsylvania Press, 1969); Jones, *Hand Made Objects;* Robert F. Trent, *Hearts and Crowns* (New Haven: Yale University Press, 1977). Works suggesting avenues to understanding artifacts from social or psychological perspectives include Edward T. Hall, *The Hidden Dimension* (Garden City: Doubleday, 1966); Edward T. Hall, *The Silent Language* (Garden City: Doubleday, 1973); Albert E. Scheflen, *How Behavior Means* (New York: Gordon and Breach, 1973); Robert Sommer, *Personal Space: The Behavioral Basis of Design* (Englewood Cliffs: Prentice-Hall, 1969). Cognition and communication are discussed in Howard Gardner, *The Arts and Human Development: A Psychological Study of the Artistic Process* (New York: Wiley, 1973); D. E. Berlyne, *Aesthetics*

and Psychobiology (New York: Appleton-Century-Crofts, 1971); David Perkins and Barbara Leondar, eds., *The Arts and Cognition* (Baltimore: Johns Hopkins University Press, 1977).

4. George Kubler, *The Shape of Time: Remarks on the History of Things* (New Haven: Yale University Press, 1962). In archaeological use, tradition refers to phenomena of relatively long temporal duration but narrow geographic range. Horizon is the opposite: broad geographic range but limited temporal duration. See Gordon R. Willey and Philip Phillips, *Method and Theory in American Archaeology* (Chicago: University of Chicago Press, 1958), pp. 11–43.

5. By plotting the life spans of objects like hall furnishings and many others as well, and then looking for correlations in functions, design elements, materials, and other measurable phenomena, we may be able to see (literally, perhaps) the extent of Victorianism. One way to extract elements that might be quantified and seriated is through structuralism. For some general comments on its application to objects, see James Deetz, *Invitation to Archaeology* (Garden City: Natural History Press, 1967), pp. 83–101. For an example, see Glassie, *Folk Housing.*

6. The Victorian fascination with the material world can be noted first and most impressively in the rich physical remains of that era. This fascination was institutionalized with the world fairs held from 1851 onward. Some of the period's most perceptive authors, among them Karl Marx, Thorstein Veblen, and Mark Twain, wrote in response to contemporary enthusiasm for what Lewis Mumford called "the goods life." Lewis Mumford, *Technics and Civilization* (New York: Harcourt, Brace, 1934), p. 105.

7. The generalizations about Victorian culture are from Daniel Walker Howe, "American Victorianism as a Culture," *American Quarterly* 27 (1975): 507–532. For the geographical aspect, see David Ward, *Cities and Immigrants: A Geography of Change in Nineteenth-Century America* (New York: Oxford University Press, 1971), pp. 11–49.

8. Quantitative studies of earlier periods include Barbara Carson and Cary Carson, "Styles and Standards of Living in Southern Maryland, 1670–1752," paper delivered to the Southern Historical Association, 1976; Susan Prendergast, "Fabric Furnishings Used in Philadelphia Homes, 1700–1775," (M.A. thesis, University of Delaware, 1977).

9. Horatio Alger, *The Store Boy or the Fortunes of Ben Barclay,* in *Strive and Succeed* (New York: Holt, Rinehart and Winston, 1967), pp. 114, 155; John Hay, *The Bread-Winner: A Social Study* (New York: Harper and Brothers, 1884).

10. Nor do artifacts normally provide a useful approach to literature. The two realms are distinct and often very different aspects of human creativity. Older attempts at synthesis include two books, Wylie Sypher, *Four Stages of Renaissance Style: Transformations in Art and Literature* (Garden City: Doubleday, 1955); and Wylie Sypher, *Rococo to Cubism in Art and Literature* (New York: Random House, 1960). A more recent attempt to find correspondences in the arts is David Burrows, "Style in Culture: Vivaldi, Zeno, and Ricci," *Journal of Interdisciplinary History* 4 (1973): 1–24. A somewhat different approach is used by Gaston Bachelard, *The Poetics of Space,* trans. Maria Solas (Boston: Beacon Press, 1969).

11. Andrew Jackson Downing, *The Architecture of Country Houses* (New York: Da Capo, 1968), pp. 441–442, 459–460; Samuel Sloan, *Homestead Architecture,* 2nd. ed. (Philadelphia: J. B. Lippincott, 1867), p. 328.

12. In art historical parlance, this phenomenon is usually referred to as the arts and crafts movement and seen as the beginning of modern design. See Nikolaus Pevsner, *Pioneers of Modern Design: William Morris to Walter Gropius,* rev. ed. (Harmondsworth, Eng.: Penguin, 1964); Gillian Naylor, *The Arts and Crafts Movement: A Study of Its Sources, Ideals, and Influence on Design Theory* (Cambridge, Mass.: MIT Press, 1971). Succinct analyses of the social aspects of this movement appear by Robert W. Winter, "The Arts and Crafts Movement as a Social Movement," and Carl E. Schorske, "Observations on Style and Society in the Arts and Crafts Movement," in *Aspects of the Arts and Crafts Movement in America, Record of the Art Museum, Princeton University* 34 (1975): 36–40 and 41–42, respectively.

13. Todd S. Goodholme, ed., *A Domestic Cyclopaedia of Practical Information* (New York: H. Holt, 1877): Clarence Cook, *The House Beautiful: Essays on Bed, and Table, Stools and Candlesticks* (New York: Scribner, Armstrong, 1877); Robert Judson Clark, ed., *The Arts and Crafts Movement*

in America, 1876–1916 (Princeton: Princeton University Press, 1972); Mary Jean Smith Madigan, "The Influence of Charles Locke Eastlake on American Furniture Manufacture, 1870–1890" *Winterthur Portfolio* 10 (1975): 1–22. The difficulty of sorting ideology from reality is constantly faced by historians who deal with verbal, especially literary, sources. Compare, for example, the interpretation of the nineteenth-century home in Kirk Jeffrey, "The Family as Utopian Retreat from the City," *Soundings* 55 (1972): 21–41, with that in Thorstein Veblen, *The Theory of the Leisure Class: An Economic Study of Institutions* (New York: Macmillan, 1912).

The question of cultural heterogeneity or homogeneity is related to the ideology of the melting pot, debunked in recent years. See Nathan Glazer and Daniel Patrick Moynihan, *Beyond the Melting Pot: The Negroes, Puerto Ricans, Jews, Italians, and Irish of New York City* (Cambridge, Mass.: MIT Press, 1963); Charles Keil, *Urban Blues* (Chicago: University of Chicago Press, 1966).

14. Important collections of photographs of nineteenth-century interiors have been assembled in William Seale, *The Tasteful Interlude: American Interiors through the Camera's Eye, 1860–1917* (New York: Praeger, 1975); George Talbot, *At Home: Domestic Life in the Post-Centennial Era, 1876–1920* (Madison: University of Wisconsin Press, 1977). Halls of the wealthy, usually bearing the impress of the English reform taste, appear frequently in *Artistic Houses* (New York: B. Blom, 1971). The photograph has recently come into its own as a collectible artifact, as art, and as a tool for historians. Two recent controversial but compelling historical studies emphasizing photographs are by Michael Lesy, *Wisconsin Death Trip* (New York: Pantheon, 1973); and *Real Life: Louisville in the Twenties* (New York: Pantheon, 1976).

15. Extensive collections of nineteenth-century trade catalogs of household furnishings can be found at the following institutions: Chicago Historical Society; Eleutherian Mills Historical Library (Greenville, Del.); Henry Ford Museum (Dearborn, Mich.); Metropolitan Museum of Art (New York); National Museum of History and Technology (Washington); Margaret Woodbury Strong Museum (Rochester, N.Y.); and Winterthur Museum (Winterthur, Del.). Most state libraries and larger historical societies also have holdings in this area. Although out of date, the best introduction to trade catalog holdings in America is Lawrence B. Romaine, *A Guide to American Trade Catalogs, 1744–1900* (New York: Bowker, 1960).

16. For comments on subjective history and scientific measurement, see Glassie, *Folk Housing*, pp. 41–42; Peter L. Berger, *Invitation to Sociology* (Garden City: Doubleday, 1963), p. 141. John Demos, *A Little Commonwealth: Family Life in Plymouth Colony* (New York: Oxford University Press, 1970), pp. 20–23. Willie Lee Rose, ed., *A Documentary History of Slavery in North America* (New York: Oxford University Press, 1976), p. 3.

17. On eighteenth-century house plans, see George B. Tatum, *Philadelphia Georgian: The City House of Samuel Powel and Some of Its Eighteenth-Century Neighbors* (Middletown, Conn.: Wesleyan University Press, 1976), pp. 55–61.

18. Vincent J. Scully, Jr., *The Shingle Style and the Stick Style: Architectural Theory and Design from Richardson to the Origins of Wright*, rev. ed. (New Haven: Yale University Press, 1971), pp. 3–7. Hundreds of house plans can be found in the many nineteenth-century architectural manuals aimed at the lay public. For an extensive listing of these, see Henry Russell Hitchcock, *American Architectural Books* (Minneapolis: University of Minnesota Press, 1962). A brief bibliography of twentieth-century titles on domestic architecture is in Clifford E. Clark, Jr., "Domestic Architecture as an Index to Social History: The Romantic Revival and the Cult of Domesticity in America, 1840–1870," *Journal of Interdisciplinary History* 7 (1976): 34. Clark's article might be read in conjunction with this one, for it presents the ideology behind the architecture, its style, and its form. A more cynical view might be that the elaborate religious and moral arguments Clark records disguised middle-class emulation of the upper class, as compellingly described in Veblen, *Theory of the Leisure Class*. One might add to Clark's comments on specialization of household spaces that such division was already typical in the homes of the wealthy in the eighteenth century, where the services were often located in outbuildings symmetrically deployed around the main block of the house.

19. In some more costly homes the hall was preceded by a vestibule, which can be considered as an

insulating area. The vestibule also heightened the sense of drama of moving into the house by adding another stage to the process.

20. A discussion of front and back zones is skillfully developed in Erving Goffman, *The Presentation of Self in Everyday Life* (Garden City: Doubleday, 1959). Benjamin Disraeli, *Sybil: or The Two Nations*, 3 vols. (London: Henry Colburn, 1850). Evidence of stratification in types of domestic structures is found in Downing, *Architecture of Country Houses*, p. 257, where he argues that a cottage is appropriate for a family with no more than two servants, but three or more servants entitle one to a villa. Much of Downing's approach can be traced to John Claudius London, *An Encyclopaedia of Cottage, Farm, and Villa Architecture and Furniture* (London: Longman, Rees, Orme, Brown, Green, and Longman, 1833). Comments on Downing's debt to Loudon appear in J. Stewart Johnson's introduction to Andrew Jackson Downing, *Architecture of Country Houses* (New York: Dover, 1969), pp. ix–x. John Ruskin, *The Seven Lamps of Architecture* (New York: Cassell, 1909), pp. 13–16.

21. Comments about hallstands appear in John Claudius Loudon, *Loudon Furniture Designs from the Encyclopedia of Cottage, Farm, and Villa Architecture and Furniture, 1839* (East Ardsley, Eng.: S. R., 1970), pp. 56–57; Thomas Webster, *An Encyclopaedia of Domestic Economy* (New York; Harper and Brothers, 1845), pp. 287–288; *The Repository of Arts, Literature, Fashion, etc.*, 2nd. ser. 14 (1822); Charles Montgomery, *American Furniture: The Federal Period in the Henry Francis du Pont Winterthur Museum* (New York: Viking, 1966), p. 435; Henry Havard, *Dictionnaire de l'Ameublement et de la Décoration* (Paris, Libraries-imprimeries rénies, 1887–1890), 4:515–518. Despite its prominence and extensive production, the hallstand has not held much appeal for enthusiasts of elegant furniture: "As a piece of furniture it was seldom designed; it merely occurred." John Gloag, *A Short Dictionary of Furniture* (New York: Holt, Rinehart, and Winston, 1965), p. 282. On the 1870s as the visual high point of Victorian style, see the provocative concept of picturesque eclecticism in C. L. V. Meeks, *The Railroad Station: An Architectural History* (New Haven: Yale University Press, 1956), pp. 1–25.

22. For more on Grand Rapids furniture on the 1870s, see Kenneth L. Ames, "Grand Rapids Furniture at the Time of the Centennial," *Winterthur Portfolio* 10 (1975): 23–50.

23. On umbrellas, see Louis Octave Uzanne, *Les Ornements de la Femme* (Paris: Libraries-imprimeries réunies, 1892); A. Varron, "The Umbrella," *Ciba Review* 42 (1942): 1510–1548; T. S. Crawford, *A History of the Umbrella* (Newton Abbot, Eng.: David and Charles, 1970). Canes were also placed on hall stands. For a classic analysis of this object in nineteenth-century society, see Veblen, *Theory of the Leisure Class*, p. 265. There is a notable distinction between the connotations of the umbrella and the cane or walking stick. In nineteenth-century imagery, the umbrella was often associated with the country parson, the cane with the dandy or rake.

24. James Laver, *Modesty in Dress: An Inquiry into the Fundamentals of Fashion* (Boston: Houghton-Mifflin, 1969), pp. 121–123.

25. Closets were known in eighteenth-century halls, often also under the stair.

26. *Glass: History, Manufacture and its Universal Application* (Pittsburgh, 1923), p. 21; Sloan, *Homestead Architecture*, p. 321; Veblen, *Theory of the Leisure Class*, pp. 33–40. The use of similar visual effects is found most notably in the work of Michelangelo Pistoletto. See Edward Lucie-Smith, *Late Modern: The Visual Arts Since 1945* (New York: Praeger 1969), p. 132; Aldo Pellegrini, trans. Robin Carson, *New Tendencies in Art* (New York: Crown, 1966), pp. 244, 247.

27. Siegfried Giedion, *Mechanization Takes Command* (New York: Oxford University Press, 1948), pp. 329–332.

28. It was possible to purchase the various components of the hallstand individually and in this case the units themselves were small; cast iron umbrella stands and wooden hat and coat racks with mirrors designed to be hung on the wall are the most common. These were less expensive than the combination models discussed here.

29. Ray Faulkner and Edwin Ziegfield, *Art Today*, 5th ed. (New York: Holt, Rinehart, and Winston, 1969), pp. 373–375; Glassie, *Folk Housing*, pp. 170–175; Henry Glassie, "Folk Art," *Folklore and Folklife, an Introduction*, ed. Richard Mercer Dorson (Chicago: University of Chicago Press, 1972), pp. 272–279.

30. An important aspect of meaning in artifacts is style. The social function of style has yet to be suitably analyzed; see Hanna Deinhard, "Reflections on Art History and Sociology of Art," *Art Journal* 35 (1975): 30. A summary of some of the theories about the style of the later nineteenth century is in James D. Kornwolf, "High Victorian Gothic; or the Dilemma of Style in Modern Architecture," *Journal of the Society of Architectural Historians* 34 (1975): 34–47. For comments on the neo-grec style of 1870s hallstands, see Kenneth L. Ames, "What is the *neo-grec*?" *Nineteenth Century* 2 (1976): 12–21; Kenneth L. Ames, "Sitting in (*neo-grec*) Style," *Nineteenth Century*, 2, (1976): 50–58. For hall stands in the Gothic style, see Katherine S. Howe and David B. Warren, *The Gothic Revival Style in America, 1830–1870* (Houston: Museum of Fine Arts, 1976), pp. 59–60. Studies of the meanings of these architectural elements and related forms include Karl Lehmann, "The Dome of Heaven," *Modern Perspectives*, ed. Kleinbauer, pp. 227–270; Earl Baldwin Smith, *The Dome, a Study in the History of Ideas* (Princeton: Princeton University Press, 1950); John Summerson, *Heavenly Mansions and Other Essays on Architecture* (New York: Norton, 1963), pp. 1–28.

31. Goodholme, *Domestic Cyclopaedia*, 223.

32. Cook, *House Beautiful*, p. 31. Todd S. Goodholme agrees: "Probably the worst possible step is to buy the stereotyped hat and umbrella rack. No matter how elaborate, they are always the same thing over again, and generally very ugly." Goodholme, *Domestic Cyclopaedia*, p. 223.

33. If the ideology surrounding domestic architecture around the middle of the century deserves to be called a reform movement (Clark, "Domestic Architecture as an Index to Social History"), it needs to be reconciled with the reform movement of the 1870s. Perhaps the best way to see these two manifestations is as stages of the same movement. Despite Clifford Clark's claims, I see little evidence that the mid-century ideology had a marked effect on material culture. I would agree that the publications of the earlier period helped to set the stage for the reform movement, which left a much stronger imprint on the artifactual world. Both stages are part of the transition from palace to old homestead.

34. Plank seat chairs were inexpensive but durable forms of seating, normally used by the poor or in utilitarian contexts where upholstery was not appropriate. Unlike hallstands, hall chairs can be traced to the early-eighteenth century in England and have Continental cognates and antecedents. They were especially used in the great Palladian houses of the eighteenth century and occasionally were adorned with a family crest. The history of this form may suggest that it was another attribute of the wealthy democratized, but to an undemocratic purpose. The quotation is from Cook, *House Beautiful*, p. 33.

35. Veblen, *Theory of the Leisure Class*, pp. 41–60; Abba Goold Woolson, *Woman in American Society* (Boston: Roberts Brothers, 1873).

36. The rules for card etiquette can be found in the following volumes, among others: Mrs. E. B. Duffey, *The Ladies' and Gentlemen's Etiquette: A Complete Manual of the Manners and Dress of American Society* (Philadelphia: Porter and Coates, 1877), pp. 50–62, 174–177; John A. Ruth, comp., *Decorum: A Practical Treatise on Etiquette and Dress of the Best American Society* (Chicago: J. A. Ruth, 1877), pp. 70–90; George D. Carroll, *Diamonds from Brilliant Minds: Gems of Poesy, Quotations, and Proverbs* (New York, Dempsey and Carroll, 1881), books V and VI. For a survey of these books, see Arthur M. Schlesinger, *Learning How to Behave: A Historical Study of American Etiquette Books* (New York: Macmillan, 1947).

37. Carroll, *Diamonds from Brilliant Minds*, 5:3. On the social uses of etiquette, see Berger, *Invitation to Sociology*, 140.

38. Carroll, *Diamonds from Brilliant Minds*, 5:7. There is some disagreement in these works about the appropriate use of "Miss."

39. The card ritual may still be practiced in some circles. Sophie C. Hadida, *Manners for Millions* (New York: Barnes and Noble, 1956), pp. 85–87, begins her section on cards by noting, "When you call at a private home and the door is opened by a maid, ask for the person whom you wish to see. If the home is conducted with style, the maid extends her card tray." She went on to note that "in simple homes where there is no attempt at formality, the maid may have no card receiver." It is not likely that many of the millions referred to in the title lived in homes with maids in 1959. Howe, "American Victorianism as a Culture," p. 522.

40. On what is called segregated consciousness, see Berger, *Invitation to Sociology*, p. 108.

Chapter Fifteen

1. Robert Heilbroner, "Do Machines Make History? " *Technology and Culture* 8 (1967): 335–345.

2. For some classic statements of the standard view, see W. F. Ogburn and M. F. Nimkoff, *Technology and the Changing Family* (Cambridge, Mass.: Riverside, 1955); Robert F. Winch, *The Modern Family* (New York: Holt, 1952); and William J. Goode, *The Family* (Englewood Cliffs: Prentice-Hall, 1964).

3. This point is made by Peter Laslett, "The Comparative History of Household and Family," in *The American Family in Social Historical Perspective*, ed. Michael Gordon (New York: St. Martin's, 1973), pp. 28–29.

4. Phillippe Ariès, *Centuries of Childhood: A Social History of Family Life* (New York: Random House, 1962).

5. See Laslett, "Comparative History of Household and Family," pp. 20–24; and Philip J. Greven, "Family Structure in Seventeenth Century Andover, Massachusetts," *William and Mary Quarterly* 23 (1966): 234–256.

6. Peter Laslett, *The World We Have Lost* (New York: Scribner's, 1965).

7. For purposes of historical inquiry, this definition of middle-class status corresponds to a sociological reality, although it is not, admittedly, very rigorous. Our contemporary experience confirms that there are class differences reflected in magazines, and this situation seems to have existed in the past as well. On this issue, see Robert S. Lynd and Helen M. Lynd, *Middletown: A Study in Contemporary American Culture* (New York: Harcourt, Brace and World, 1929), pp. 240–244, where the marked difference in magazines subscribed to by the business-class wives as opposed to the working-class wives is discussed; Salme Steinberg, "Reformer in the Marketplace: E. W. Bok and *The Ladies Home Journal*" (Ph.D. dissertation, Johns Hopkins University, 1973), where the conscious attempt of the publisher to attract a middle-class audience is discussed; and Lee Rainwater, Richard P. Coleman, and Gerald Handel, *Workingman's Wife: Her Personality, World and Life Style* (New York: Oceana, 1959), which was commissioned by the publisher of working-class women's magazines in an attempt to understand the attitudinal differences between working-class and middle-class women.

8. *Historical Statistics of the United States: Colonial Times to 1957* (Washington: Government Printing Office, 1960), p. 510.

9. The gas iron, which was available to women whose homes were supplied with natural gas, was an earlier improvement on the old-fashioned flatiron, but this kind of iron is so rarely mentioned in the sources that I used for this survey that I am unable to determine the extent of its diffusion.

10. Hazel Kyrk, *Economic Problems of the Family* (New York, Harper, 1933), p. 368, reporting a study in the *Monthly Labor Review* 30 (1930): 1209–1252.

11. Although this point seems intuitively obvious, there is some evidence that it may not be true. Studies of energy expenditure during housework have indicated that by far the greatest effort is expended in hauling and lifting the wet wash, tasks which were not eliminated by the introduction of washing machines. In addition, if the introduction of the machines served to increase the total amount of wash that was done by the housewife, this would tend to cancel the energy-saving effects of the machines themselves.

12. Rinso was the first granulated soap; it came on the market in 1918. Lux Flakes had been available since 1906; however, it was not intended to be a general laundry product but rather one for laundering delicate fabrics. "Lever Brothers," *Fortune* 26 (November 1940): 95.

13. I take this account, and the term, from Lynd and Lynd, *Middletown* p. 97. Obviously, there were many American homes that had bathrooms before the 1920s, particularly urban row houses, and I have found no way of determining whether the increases of the 1920s were more marked than in previous

decades. The rural situation was quite different from the urban; the President's Conference on Home Building and Home Ownership reported that in the late 1920s, 71 percent of the urban families surveyed had bathrooms, but only 33 percent of the rural families did. John M. Gries and James Ford, eds., *Homemaking, Home Furnishing and Information Services*, President's Conference on Home Building and Home Ownership, (Washington, 1932), 10:13.

14. The data above come from Siegfried Giedion, *Mechanization Takes Command* (New York: Oxford University Press, 1948), pp. 685–703.

15. For a description of the standard bathroom, see Helen Sprackling, "The Modern Bathroom," *Parents' Magazine* 8 (February 1933): 25.

16. *Zanesville, Ohio and Thirty-six Other American Cities* (New York, 1927), p. 65. Also see Robert S. Lynd and Helen M. Lynd, *Middletown in Transition* (New York: Harcourt, Brace and World, 1937), p. 537. Middletown is Muncie, Indiana.

17. Lynd and Lynd, *Middletown*, p. 96; and Lynd and Lynd, *Middletown in Transition*, p. 539.

18. Lynd and Lynd, *Middletown*, p. 98; and Lynd and Lynd, *Middletown in Transition*, p. 562.

19. On the advantages of the new stoves, see Fannie Merritt Farmer, *Boston Cooking School Cookbook* (Boston: Little, Brown, 1916), pp. 15–20; and Russell Lynes, *The Domesticated Americans* (New York: Harper, 1963), pp. 119–120.

20. "How to Save Coal While Cooking," *Ladies' Home Journal* 25 (January 1908): 44.

21. Lynd and Lynd, *Middletown*, p. 156.

22. Lynd and Lynd, *Middletown*, p. 156; see also "Safeway Stores," *Fortune* 26 (October 1940): 60.

23. Lynd and Lynd, *Middletown*, pp. 134–135, 153–154.

24. *Historical Statistics*, pp. 16, 77.

25. For Indiana data, see Lynd and Lynd, *Middletown*, p. 169. For national data, see David L. Kaplan and M. Claire Casey, *Occupational Trends in the United States, 1900–1950*, U.S. Bureau of the Census Working Paper No. 5 (Washington: Department of Commerce, 1958), table 6. The extreme drop in numbers of servants between 1910 and 1920 also lends credence to the notion that this demographic factor stimulated the industrial revolution in housework.

26. Lynd and Lynd, *Middletown*, p. 169.

27. On the disappearance of maiden aunts, unmarried daughters, and grandparents, see Lynd and Lynd, *Middletown*, pp. 25, 99, 110; Edward Bok, "Editorial," *American Home* 1 (October 1928): 15; "How to Buy Life Insurance," *Ladies' Home Journal* 45 (March 1928): 35. The house plans appeared every month in *American Home*, which began publication in 1928. On kitchen design, see Giedion, *Mechanization Takes Command*, pp. 603–621; "Editorial," *Ladies' Home Journal* 45 (April 1928): 36; advertisement for Hoosier kitchen cabinets, *Ladies' Home Journal* 45 (April 1928): 117. Articles on servant problems include "The Vanishing Servant Girl," *Ladies' Home Journal* 35 (May 1918): 48; "Housework, Then and Now," *American Home* 8 (June 1932): 128; "The Servant Problem," *Fortune* 24 (March 1938): 80–84; and *Report of the YWCA Commission on Domestic Service* (Los Angeles, 1915).

28. Giedion, *Mechanization Takes Command*, p. 619. Frank Lloyd Wright's new kitchen was installed in the Malcolm Willey House, Minneapolis.

29. Emily Post, *Etiquette: The Blue Book of Social Usage*, 5th ed. rev. (New York: Funk and Wagnall's, 1937), p. 823.

30. This analysis is based upon various child-care articles that appeared during the period in the *Ladies' Home Journal, American Home,* and *Parents' Magazine*. See also Lynd and Lynd, *Middletown*, pp. 131–152.

31. John Kenneth Galbraith has remarked upon the advent of woman as consumer in John Kenneth Galbraith, *Economics and the Public Purpose* (Boston: Houghton Mifflin, 1973), pp. 29–37.

32. There was a sharp reduction in the number of patterns for home sewing offered by the women's magazines during the 1920s; the patterns were replaced by articles on "what is available in the shops this

season." On consumer education see, for example, "How to Buy Towels," *Ladies' Home Journal* 45 (February 1928): 134; "Buying Table Linen," *Ladies' Home Journal* 45 (March 1928): 43; and "When the Bride Goes Shopping," *American Home* 1 (January 1928): 370.

33. See, for example, Lynd and Lynd, *Middletown*, pp. 176, 196; and Margaret G. Reid, *Economics of Household Production* (New York: Wiley, 1934), pp. 209–215.

34. See Reid, *Economics of Household Production*, pp. 64–68; and Kyrk, *Economic Problems of the Family*, p. 98.

35. See advertisement for the Cleanliness Institute: "Self-respect Thrives on Soap and Water," *Ladies' Home Journal* 45 (February 1928): 107. On changing bed linen, see "When the Bride Goes Shopping," *American Home* 1 (January 1928): 370. On laundering children's clothes, see, "Making a Layette," *Ladies' Home Journal* 45 (January 1928): 20; and Josephine Baker, "The Youngest Generation," *Ladies' Home Journal* 45 (March 1928): 185.

36. As reported in Kyrk, *Economic Problems of the Family*, p. 51.

37. Bryn Mawr College, Carola Woerishoffer Graduate Department of Sociology and Social Research, *Women during the War and After* (Philadelphia: Curtis, 1945); and Ethel Goldwater, "Woman's Place," *Commentary* 4 (December 1947): 578–585.

38. JoAnn Vanek, "Keeping Busy: Time Spent in Housework, United States, 1920–1970" (Ph.D. dissertation, University of Michigan, 1973). Vanek reports an average of 53 hours per week over the whole period. This figure is significantly lower than the figures reported above, because each time study of housework has been done on a different basis, including different activities under the aegis of housework, and using different methods of reporting time expenditures. The Bryn Mawr and Oregon studies are useful for the comparative figures that they report internally, but they cannot easily be compared with each other.

39. This analysis is based upon my reading of the middle-class women's magazines between 1918 and 1930. For detailed documentation, see Ruth Schwartz Cowan, "Two Washes in the Morning and a Bridge Party at Night: The American Housewife between the Wars," *Women's Studies* 3 (1976): 147–172. It is quite possible that the appearance of guilt as a strong element in advertising is more the result of new techniques developed by the advertising industry than the result of attitudinal changes in the audience, a possibility that I had not considered when doing the initial research for this paper. See A. Michael McMahon, "An American Courtship: Psychologists and Advertising Theory in the Progressive Era," *American Studies* 13 (1972): 5–18.

40. For a summary of the literature on differential divorce rates, see Winch, *The Modern Family*, p. 706; and William J. Goode, *After Divorce* (Glenco, Ill.: Free Press, 1956), p. 44. The earliest papers demonstrating this differential rate appeared in 1927, 1935, and 1939.

41. For a summary of the literature on married women's labor force participation, see Juanita Kreps, *Sex in the Marketplace: American Women at Work* (Baltimore: Johns Hopkins Press, 1971), pp. 19–24.

42. Valerie Kincaid Oppenheimer, *The Female Labor Force in the United States: Demographic and Economic Factors Governing Growth and Changing Composition*, Population Monograph Series, No. 5 (Berkeley: Institute of International Studies, University of California, 1970), pp. 1–15; and Lynd and Lynd, *Middletown*, pp. 124–127.

43. On the expanding size, number, and influence of women's magazines during the 1920s, see Lynd and Lynd, *Middletown*, pp. 150, 240–244.

44. See, for example, the advertising campaigns of General Electric and Hotpoint from 1918 through the rest of the decade of the 1920s; both campaigns stressed the likelihood that electric appliances would become a thrifty replacement for domestic servants.

45. The practice of carefully observing children's weight was initiated by medical authorities, national and local governments, and social welfare agencies, as part of the campaign to improve child health which began about the time of World War I.

46. These practices were ubiquitous. *American Home*, for example, which was published by Doubleday, assisted its advertisers by publishing a list of informative pamphlets that readers could obtain; devoting half a page to an index of its advertisers; specifically naming manufacturer's and list

prices in articles about products and services; alloting almost one-quarter of the magazine to a mail-order shopping guide which was not (at least ostensibly) paid advertisement; and, as part of its editorial policy, urging its readers to buy new goods.

Chapter Sixteen

1. The brick- and stone-using Dutch on the Hudson are not considered here because they were insignificant as a cultural source.

2. The term "half-timbering" is employed here in the full realization that its use is discouraged by architectural historians as misleading and confusing. However, we know of no substitute term to apply to heavy framing, commonly with horizontal, vertical, and diagonal squared members spaced as much as several feet apart, and with the interstices filled with various materials.

3. Fiske Kimball, *Domestic Architecture of the American Colonies and of the Early Republic* (New York: Scribner's, 1922), p. 4.

4. Martin Shaw Briggs, *The Homes of the Pilgrim Fathers in England and America (1620–1685)* (London: Oxford University Press, 1932), p. 56.

5. For illustrations of half-timbering in Wisconsin, see Richard W. E. Perrin, "Historic Wisconsin Buildings: A Survey of Pioneer Architecture, 1835–1870," *Milwaukee Public Museum Publication in History* 4 (1962): 14–25. Zoar, Ohio, has a number of examples of German half-timbering and so have the German settlements between San Antonio and Austin, Texas, though in the examples observed there the half-timbering was hidden by siding.

6. French half-timbering in Louisiana uses both brick and clay cats as nogging. The brick nogging is refered to as *briquette entre poteaux*, the clay simply as *bousillage*. Plastered brick nogging appears in New Orleans, but more rural *bousillage* is now invariably weatherboarded except, occasionally, for the front wall, which is protected by a broad roof overhang. Here the *bousillage* may be whitewashed and the wood framing left exposed, or the whole may be plastered over. This old practice explains the frequent appearance today of small rural frame houses with only the fronts painted white or whitewashed. The clay-wrapped rods, or "rabbits," of Louisana *bousillage* are horizontally set, whereas in Europe they are more commonly vertical.

7. Siegfried J. de Laet, *The Low Countries*, trans. J. A. E. Nenquin (London: Thames and Hudson, 1958), pp. 62–88; Marija Gimbutas, *The Balts* (New York, 1963), pp. 103–104.

8. Briggs, *Homes of the Pilgrim Fathers*, pp. 56–57. Recent research indicates that the vertical logs were originally set in the ground and that the sill was introduced to preserve them. See Herbert L. Edlin, *Woodland Crafts in Britain: An Account of the Traditional Uses of Trees and Timbers in the British Countryside* (London: Batsford, 1949), p. 137.

9. See Antonio di Nardo, *Farm Houses, Small Chateaux and Country Churches in France* (Cleveland: Jansen, 1924), pp. 18, 75, and 82. Note that in contrast with half-timbering, the vertical members are close together and lack diagonal or horizontal bracing.

10. Kimball, *Domestic Architecture of the American Colonies*, p. 6.

11. Henry Chandlee Forman, *Virginia Architecture in the Seventeenth Century* (Williamsburg, Va.: Virginia 350th Anniversary Celebration Corporation, 1957), p. 30.

12. Kimball, *Domestic Architecture of the American Colonies*, p. 6. See also the description of "plank-frame" houses in Connecticut as early as 1690 in John Frederick Kelly, *Early Domestic Architecture of Connecticut* (New Haven: Yale University Press, 1924), pp. 40–41.

13. "Evolution of the Oldest House," *Notes in Anthropology*, Department of Anthropology, Florida State University, Tallahassee 7 (1962): 7.

14. Henry C. Mercer, "The Origin of Log Houses in the United States," *Collection of Papers Read before the Bucks County Historical Society*, vol. 5, p. 572.

15. Perrin, "Historic Wisconsin Buildings," p. 12.

16. See, for example, [George-Marie Butel-] Dumont, *Memories historiques sur la Louisiane*, 2

vols. (Paris, 1753), 1:50, 2:50; and (for Quebec) Reuben Gold Thwaites, ed., *The Jesuit Relations and Allied Documents*, 73 vols. (Cleveland: Burrows, 1896–1901), 7:281.

17. Charles E. Peterson, "Early Ste. Genevieve and Its Architecture," *Missouri Historical Review* 35 (1940–1941): 207–232; reference on p. 217.

18. Rexford Newcomb, *Architecture of the Old Northwest Territory* (Chicago: University of Chicago Press, 1950), p. 21. In modern French, *colombage* refers to frame construction.

19. Richard W. Hale, Jr., "The French Side of the 'Log Cabin Myth,' " *Proceedings Massachusetts Historical Society* 72 (1957–1960): 118–125; and Marius Barbeau, "The House That Mac Built," *The Beaver: A Magazine of the North*, Outfit 276 (December 1945): 10–13.

20. Dumont, *Memories historiques sur la Louisiane*, 2:50.

21. In addition to Thwaites, *Jesuit Relations* see Richard Colebrook Harris, "A Geography of the Seigneurial System in Canada during the French Regime," (Ph.D. dissertation, University of Wisconsin, 1964), pp. 147, 278.

22. See Dumont, *Memories historiques sur la Louisiane*, 2:7.

23. V. Gordon Childe, *The Bronze Age* (Cambridge, Eng.: University Press, 1930), pp. 206–208.

24. Sigurd Erixon, "The North-European Technique of Corner Timbering," *Folkliv* (1937): 13–60, fig. 25 and plate XIV.

25. Harris, "Geography of the Seigneurial System," pp. 147, 278.

26. Hale, "French Side of the 'Log Cabin Myth,' " p. 121, cites the use of *pièce sur pièce* for the "notch and saddle" construction that found its way into Canada from the United States. Again, this may be a modern usage, but it is a perversion of the term used for corner-post construction before American notching was introduced into Canada, probably about 1740. See Mercer, "Origin of Log Houses in the United States," p. 571. Incidentally, Mercer's citation for 1727 clarifies a misunderstanding sometimes expressed that Canadian French laws opposed the use of timber for construction in towns where stone was available. Surely this measure was directed against the fire hazard inherent in closely set wooden buildings, rather than against log or timber construction as such.

27. Mercer, "The Origin of Log Houses in the United States," p. 571, refers in his citation for 1664 to a church constructed of "round wood dovetailed at the corners," which sounds much like an American-style structure. Dovetailing, however, was known to every joiner; the logs may have been dovetailed into a corner post. If this was a case of alternating tiers and true corner-timbering, it must have been an isolated freak.

28. A limit to the size of a corner-timbered building is imposed by the very weight of the timber and by the tapering of tree trunks to an unusable disparity in dimension between the two ends; twenty-four to thirty-six feet has been advanced as the average maximum practicable length. There is no widely practiced means of enlarging a corner-timbered house except by adding a story; for the logs are not commonly spliced, and building a new structure poses the problem how to connect it with the old.

29. Philip W. Sultz, "From Sagebrush to Hay and Back Again," *American West* (1964): 20–30, shows a number of pictures of buildings, chiefly, one may surmise, in western Wyoming. On pages 26, 27, and 30 are shown respectively a house, a jail, and a church, all of which appear to have corner-post construction. The other buildings illustrated are corner-timbered.

30. Stuart Bartlett, "Garrison Houses along the New England Frontier," *Pencil Points* 14 (1933): 253–268; reference on p. 255.

31. Bartlett, "Garrison Houses along the New England Frontier," p. 254.

32. The nomenclature proposed by Erixon, "North-European Technique of Corner Timbering," p. 14, for the constituent parts of corner-timbering is used here.

33. In support of his theory that the American log cabin is of Swedish origin, Henry C. Mercer states that the "notch and chamfer" (V notch) corner-timbering is Scandinavian. Mercer, "Origin of Log Houses in the United States," p. 582. Further, the log house in America as pictured in many books and labeled seventeenth-century Swedish is roughly V-notched and has wide, chinked interstices. See, for example, Ernest Pickering, *The Homes of America* (New York, 1951], p. 9, fig. P–1. However, Mercer quotes Dutch visitors who, traveling in 1679–1680, contrasted the English frame house with the Swedish

log house in which the logs are notched a foot from the end. Mercer, "Origin of Log Houses in the United States," pp. 577–579. Two things are learned from this description: first, by 1680, only five years before large numbers of Germans began arriving in eastern Pennsylvania, the English colonists had not adopted Swedish construction, second, authentic seventeenth-century Swedish log houses were corner-timbered like those found today in Sweden and not like those in America labeled seventeenth-century Swedish. Mercer states also (p. 579) that he knows of no definitely Swedish or seventeenth-century log houses that were extant in America in the early twentieth century. It seems, therefore, that the so-called seventeenth-century Swedish houses in America are more recent than that and, although conceivably built by Swedes, reflect Pennsylvania German log-construction techniques rather than Swedish.

34. Bartlett, "Garrison Houses along the New England Frontier," p. 255.

35. Our attempt to compile a synonymy of terms for corner-timbering has yielded nothing worthwhile. The only usage that might conceivably prove confusing is the apparent employment of "halved" for our "square" notch in Mercer, "Origin of Log Houses in the United States," p. 80.

36. Erixon, "North-European Technique of Corner Timbering," p. 30.

37. Karl Schuchhardt, *Vorgeschichte von Deutschland* (Berlin, 1934), p. 29.

38. Childe, *Bronze Age*, p. 206; Gimbutas, *The Balts*, p. 74.

39. C. F. Innocent, *The Development of English Building Construction* (Cambridge, Eng.: University Press, 1916), p. 109, finds no evidence that log construction was ever practiced in England. Pierre Deffontaines, *Les hommes et leurs travaux dans les pays de la moyenne Garonne* (Lille, 1932), plate 26, shows what is unquestionably corner-timbering in an old abandoned structure in southwestern France, but this seems to possess no significance with respect to French practice in America.

40. Kimball, *Domestic Architecture of the American Colonies*, p. 7.

41. C. A. Weslager, "Log Structures in New Sweden during the Seventeenth Century," *Delaware History* 5 (1952–1953): 77–95; reference on p. 92.

42. Thomas Jefferson Wertenbaker, *The Founding of American Civilization: The Middle Colonies* (New York: Scribner's, 1938), p. 241.

43. The Scotch-Irish were primarily Lowland Scots who had emigrated to Ulster. The Pennsylvania Germans, also known as the Pennsylvania Dutch, were primarily from the Rhenish Palatinate and Switzerland, but were also from Bohemia, Silesia, Moravia, Württemberg, and Hesse.

44. Moravian log work is much like that introduced by the Germans into Pennsylvania. See *Ethnographica* III–IV (1962). Polish log work, on the other hand, more nearly resembles Swedish practice. See H. Grisebach, *Das polnische Bauernhaus*, Beiträge zur polnischen Landeskunde, ser. B, vol. 3 (Berlin: Gea-Verlag, 1917). It now begins to appear that the primary source of log construction in America not only was not Swedish, but neither was it Rhenish German or Swiss. More likely conveyers were the Germans who came from Moravia, Bohemia, and Silesia. To this day it is the local tradition that the Schwenkfelders who arrived from Silesia in 1734 brought V notching to Pennsylvania.

45. Richard W. E. Perrin, "Wisconsin 'Stovewood' Walls: Ingenious Forms of Early Log Construction," *Wisconsin Magazine of History*, 46 (1962–1963): 215–219.

46. "The Farm-Housing Survey," *U.S. Department of Agriculture Miscellaneous Publications* No. 323 (1939), table 2.

47. The figures are 48.8 percent for Albany County, Wyoming, and 25.4 percent for San Miguel County, New Mexico, but the New Mexican log house is possibly not entirely of Anglo-American provenance.

Chapter Seventeen

1. Christopher Tunnard and Henry Hope Reed, *American Skyline: The Growth and Form of Our Cities and Towns* (Boston: Houghton Mifflin, 1955), pp. 15–31.

2. "Your Community Service Station," a pamphlet published by the Marathon Oil Company, Findlay, Ohio, n.d.

3. "The Fortune Directory of the 500 Largest Industrial Corporations," *Fortune* 85 (May 1972): 188.

4. John A. Kouwenhoven, *Made in America: The Arts in Modern Civilization* (Garden City: Doubleday, 1948), p. 41. Though Kouwenhoven did not allude to service stations as an example of the vernacular, he defined the tradition (on p. 15) in terms wholly compatible with them: the art of a people who "found themselves living under democratic institutions in an expanding machine economy."

5. Kouwenhoven, *Made in America*, pp. 32–33.

6. Even the hexagon is explicable. The Marathon Oil Company was formed through the acquisition of various smaller firms, notably the Lincoln Oil Company and the Ohio Oil Company. Each of these forerunners brought commercial trademarks to the merger, Lincoln Oil its lighthouse and Ohio Oil its hexagon. Standard Service Station No. 2's elaborate service module was the unhappy marriage of those two motifs.

7. Compare Kouwenhoven, *Made in America*, pp. 41–42.

8. Five of the Four-Bay Standards were built in 1947, two in 1948, and one in 1949.

9. The minor module, which made its first appearance with Standard Modified as an unroofed concrete block enclosure for the storage of unsightly trash, was later roofed and turned into a dry storage area.

10. Twenty-nine of the type were built between 1962 and 1966. During the next four years another 122 were built. Colonial was still in construction in 1973.

11. Interview with Marathon Oil Company designer Jack Morehart, May 30, 1972.

12. See, for instance, John Maass, "Where Architectural Historians Fear to Trade," *Journal of the Society of Architectural Historians* 28 (March 1969): 3–8.

Chapter Eighteen

1. This definition is suggested by Warren Roberts. A full survey of the field of folk crafts is available in his chapter on that subject in Richard Dorson, ed., *Folklore and Folk Life: An Introduction* (Chicago: University of Chicago Press, 1972).

2. Dorson, *Folklore and Folk Life*, p. 246. For a careful review of folk crafts in the British Isles, see J. Geraint Jenkins, *Traditional Country Craftsmen* (New York: Praeger, 1965).

3. Henry Glassie, *Pattern in the Material Folk Culture of the Eastern United States* (Philadelphia: University of Pennsylvania Press, 1968), pp. 187–188. The entire problem of functionalism, involving questions of the persistence of tradition versus the abandonment of tradition in favor of mass-produced items, is worthy of investigation. To this end, see Warren Roberts, "Function in Folk Architecture," *Folklore Forum* 66 (1971): 10–13.

4. Michael Owen Jones, "Chairmaking in Appalachia" (Ph.D. dissertation, Indiana University, 1970). Jones recently published his research in a somewhat shorter form in Michael Owen Jones, *The Handmade Object and Its Maker* (Berkeley: University of California Press, 1975).

5. Howard Wight Marshall, "Mr. Westfall's Baskets: Traditional Craftsmanship in Northcentral Missouri," *Mid-South Folklore* 11 (1974): 43–60. Other good examples of this kind of scholarship can be found in recent issues of *Indiana Folklore*. See, for example, Sylvia Ann Grider, "Howard Taylor, Cane Maker and Handle Shaver," *Indiana Folklore* 7 (1974): 5–25.

6. Paul Rampley's account of his days in the threshing field are colorful and filled with valuable details from life in that time and place. He also, at times, can tell a variety of stories, including variants of "The Miraculous Hunt," AT 1890.

7. Today this farm is owned by Lee Sterrenberg, a professor of English at Indiana University. Rampley has moved to a smaller farm about one-half mile west of the old place.

8. Roberts, "Folk Crafts," in Dorson, ed., *Folklore and Folklife*, p. 246.

9. H. G. Barnett, *Innovation: The Basis of Cultural Change* (New York: McGraw-Hill, 1953).

10. James Fernandez, "The Mission in Expressive Culture," *Current Anthropology* 15 (1974): 119–133.

11. See, for example, Kenneth Burke, *A Grammar of Motives* (Berkeley: University of California Press, 1945). Burke and French anthropologist Claude Lévi-Strauss have both contributed to the study of material culture. For an excellent example, see Henry Glassie, ''The Variation of Concepts within Tradition: Barn Building in Otsego County, New York,'' *Geoscience and Man* 5 (1974): 117–235; also, see Henry Glassie, *Folk Housing in Middle Virginia* (Knoxville: University of Tennessee Press, 1975), pp. 41–42.

12. The details of hog butchering can be found in Frank G. Ashbrook, *Butchering, Processing and Preservation of Meat* (New York: Van Nostrand, 1955), pp. 59–60. A similar meat hanging device is offered in Gordon Winter, *A Country Camera* (London: Routledge and Kegan-Paul, 1966), which documents British hog killing techniques.

13. This is not an example of contagious magic as one might find among believers in the phase of the moon on cutting and laying timber.

14. For a brief comment on the distribution of wheelbarrow usage, see ''Notes and News,'' *Antiquity* 10 (1936): 463. Details on the kind of wheelbarrows available through mail order houses can be found in *Montgomery Ward and Company Catalogue and Buyers' Guide No. 57, Spring and Summer, 1895* (New York: Dover, 1969), p. 407; and *Sears, Roebuck and Company Catalogues* (1929–1939). There is a fair amount of literature on the development of the wheelbarrow in various cultures. Most of the work has been done by cultural geographers and anthropologists with the usual attention to function and the ususal inattention to details concerning the people who make and use the implements. Apparently, one of the earliest scholars to study the wheelbarrow was Cyril Fox, and among his publications is Cyril Fox, ''Sleds, Carts and Waggons,'' *Antiquity* 5 (1931): 185–199. The work of I. F. Grant in the Scottish Highlands includes notes from eighteenth-century travelers and their observations of local modes of transportation. See I. F. Grant, *Highland Folk Ways* (London: Routledge and Kegan-Paul, 1961), pp. 281–283. The studies of folklife scholar J. Geraint Jenkins are well known. See J. Geraint Jenkins, *The English Farm Wagon: Origins and Structures* (Surrey: University of Reading, 1961); and J. Geraint Jenkins, *Traditional Country Craftsmen* (London: Routledge and Kegan-Paul, 1965). Janos Kodolanyi, *A Neprajzi Muzeum, 1963–64* (Budapest, 1965) presents a collection of museum artifacts among which wheelbarrows are included. Other ethnographic studies include R. H. Lane, ''Waggons and their Ancestors,'' *Antiquity* 9 (1935): 140–150; and Eric J. Simpson, ''Farm Carts and Wagons of the Orkney Islands,'' *Scottish Studies* 7 (1963): 154–159. Eric Sloane, *Diary of an Early American Boy: Noah Blake, 1805* (New York: Random House, 1965), p. 58, suggests the progression of the wheelbarrow's development from hand-drawn ''hand barrows'' to ''sledgebarrows'' to ''wheelbarrows.'' An example of research in the far East by a Soviet ethnographer is V. S. Starikov, ''Kvoprosam proisxozdenie i razvitie tradicionyx sredstv perevedenija severnyx kitajcev,'' *Kyl' tura narodov zarubeznoj azii* (Leningrad: Akademii nauk, 1973), pp. 37–40. Other studies ot rarm transport include George B. Thompson, ''Some Primitive Forms of Farm Transport Used in Northern Ireland,'' *Ulster Folklife* 1 (1955): 32–36; and Gordon Winter, *A Country Camera, 1844—1914* (London: Routledge and Kegan-Paul, 1966). Also, E. O. Lormier, ''Note on the Wheelbarrow of Hunza,'' *Antiquity* 10 (1936): 464–465; Axel Steensberg, ''Tools and Man,'' in *Man and his Habitat*, eds. R. H. Buchanan, E. Jones, and D. McCourt (London: Routledge and Kegan-Paul, 1971). An unusual manual of how to ''make do'' with odds and ends, including instruction for wheelbarrow making, is Rolfe Cobleigh, *Handy Farm Tools and How to Make Them* (New York: Orange Judd, 1913), pp. 239–240.

15. Lorimer, ''Note on the Wheelbarrow of Hunza,'' p. 464, suggests that in at least one culture the wheelbarrow developed subsequent to the innovation of the runged ladder. This may be true in some cases, but the point of actual development probably came about when man substituted a wheel at the point of contact of a sledge with the ground. As such, early wheelbarrows tended to have a small wheel, usually of solid wood and located at the ends of two parallel shafts. This type is primitive and has a low mechanical advantage, placing some weight on the wheel but a good deal more on the shoulders of the operator. More modern types show a more stable wheel design and the relocation of the wheel under the center of the load. In this type the operator's main job is steering.

16. On p. 464 of ''Note on the Wheelbarrow,'' Lorimer comments that ''The wheel does not rotate on its axis, but the axis itself rotates in the two holes in the side of the poles. The jarring of the somewhat

irregular and wobbly wheel against the sides is mitigated by two wicker rings (about the size of wooden curtain rings) threaded on the axis at each side of the wheel. Since the distances to be traversed (in Hunza culture) are slight, at most a few yards, the crudeness of the barrow, and the friction of the axis in its sockets, are of little moment.''

17. Rampley did indeed use two rivets to join the lapped ends of the iron rim, but the iron rim is, in turn, held to the wooden wheel with lag screws which make the wheelbarrow difficult to use on any smooth, hard-surfaced area. Obviously, Rampley never considered operating the barrow anywhere but in fields or on gravel paths.

18. Cobleigh, *Handy Farm Tools*, p. 240.

19. Checking with Rampley later, I found that the wheel was approximately twenty inches in diameter before the rim was applied, and the rim was fashioned just a quarter inch short of the wheel's circumference. The wheel, when finished, was fitted with the cold, uncut iron rim, two inches wide. Rampley tightened the rim over the wheel with a chain and measured the required circumference. Then the wheel was placed on an open barrel top, the rim was heated in a fire in the open yard, and, when heated, placed on the wheel and doused with cold water. Some details of "ironing a wheel" are included in J. G. Hoistrom, *Drake's Modern Blacksmithing and Horseshoeing* (New York: Drake, 1972).

20. In April 1976, Rampley's wheelbarrow was purchased by Conner Prairie Pioneer Settlement, an open air museum in Noblesville, Indiana. It is now part of the museum's collection of artifacts and is being studied as a possible model of early nineteenth century wheelbarrows. Obviously, Rampley's use of circle-sawn lumber and lag screws are inappropriate for this earlier period. An earlier wheelbarrow type belonging to the Plimoth Plantation Museum in Plymouth, Massachusetts, is supposedly an accurate reproduction of a seventeenth century vehicle. The wheelbarrow has a solid wooden wheel similar to the one attributed by Rampley to John Henry Gheen. It rotates on a fixed axel lubricated with animal fat. In general, Rampley's wheelbarrow resembles modern types in its profile, shaft design, and width. It is in the construction of the wheel and the wheel-support mechanism that Rampley's wheelbarrow resembles earlier American and European models.

Chapter Twenty-One

1. See Lee Rainwater, *Workingman's Wife: Her Personality, World and Life Style* (New York: Oceana Publications, Inc., 1959); Lee Rainwater, "Fear and the House as Haven in the Lower Class," *Journal of the American Institute of Planners* 32 (January 1966): 23–31; Denis Chapman, *The Home and Social Status* (London: Routledge and Kegan Paul, 1955); Marc Fried, *The World of the Urban Working Class* (Cambridge, Mass.: Harvard University Press, 1973); Michael Young and Peter Wilmott, *The Symmetrical Family: A Study of Work and Leisure in the London Region* (London: Routledge and Kegan Paul, 1973).

2. All historians who study the working class struggle with ways to define it. While I am convinced the experience is complex, I will adopt a simple definition for the purposes of this essay and use *working class* to refer to skilled and unskilled workers. This essay will explore the extent to which people in the manual trades developed a distinctive material culture.

3. Herbert Gutman, *Work, Culture and Society in Industrializing America* (New York: Vintage Books, 1977), pp. 3–78.

4. Siegfried Gideon, *Mechanization Takes Command* (New York: Norton, 1969), p. 365.

5. John Ruskin, "Of Queen's Gardens," *Sesame and Lilies* (1864; New York: Metropolitan Publishing, 1871), quoted in Gwendolyn Wright, "Making the Model Home: Domestic Architecture and Cultural Conflict in Chicago, 1873–1913," Ph.D. dissertation, University of California at Berkeley, 1978, p. 21.

6. Gideon, *Mechanization*, p.384.

7. See Sam Bass Warner, *Streetcar Suburbs* (Cambridge, Mass.: Harvard University Press, 1962) and photographs of newly developed areas in almost every town or city in America during this period.

8. John Rhoads, *The Colonial Review* (New York: Garland Publishing, 1977).

9. Barbara Ehrenreich and Deirdre English, "The Manufacture of Housework," *Socialist Revolution* 26 (October-December 1975): 5–40.

10. C. Chester Lane, "Hingham Arts and Crafts," in Rhoads, *Colonial Review*, p. 367. Even though American Arts and Crafts designers like Stickley were inspired by William Morris's English Arts and Crafts Movement, their debt to that source did not receive much attention in America. Stickley conveniently equated the American colonial experience with the medieval heritage being revived by the British.

11. Rhoads, *Colonial Revival*, p. 416; p. 207; p. 517; p. 524. See also Barbara Solomon, *Ancestors and Immigrants* (Cambridge, Mass.: Harvard University Press, 1956).

12. Rhoads, *Colonial Revival*, p. 390.

13. *The Craftsman Magazine* (July 1903) in Rhoads, *Colonial Review*, p. 285; also pp. 412, 834.

14. Gustav Stickley, "Made in America," in Rhoads, *Colonial Revival*, p. 488.

15. Mabel Kittredge, *Housekeeping Notes* (Boston: Whitcomb and Barrows, 1911), pp. 1–13.

16. College Settlements Association, *Annual Report 1902* (New York: 1902), p. 3.

17. Jane Addams to Sara Alice Addams Haldeman, September 13, 1889. Jane Addams Papers Project, Hull House, Chicago, Illinois.

18. Esther Barrows, *Neighbors All: A Settlement Notebook* (Boston: Houghton Mifflin, 1929), p. 37.

19. Roy Lubove, *The Progressive and the Slums: Tenement House Reform in New York City, 1890—1917* (Pittsburgh: University of Pittsburgh Press, 1962), p. 163.

20. Tamara Hareven and Randolph Langenbach, *Amoskeag: Life and Work in an American Factory City* (New York: Pantheon, 1978).

21. Gerd Korman, *Industrialization, Immigrants and Americanization* (Madison: University of Wisconsin Press, 1967), p. 88.

22. See Maxine Seller, "The Education of the Immigrant Woman, 1900 to 1935," *Journal of Urban History* 4 (May 1978); John Daniels, *Americanization via the Neighborhood* (New York: Harper, 1920); Sophonisbia Breckinridge, *New Homes for Old* (New York: Harper, 1921).

23. Herbert Gans, *The Urban Villagers* (New York: The Free Press, 1962), pp. 152–1.

24. Jane E. Robbins, M.D., "The First Year at the College Settlement," *The Survey*, 27 (February 24, 1912), 1801.

25. Barrows, *Neighbors All*, pp. 7–8.

26. Barrows, *Neighbors All*, pp. 40–41.

27. Here and elsewhere in the paper, *material values* refers to preferences in the selection and arrangement of objects of material culture.

28. See Stephen Thernstrom and Peter R. Knights, "Men in Motion," *Journal of Interdisciplinary History* (Autumn 1970): 7–35; Humbert S. Nelli, *Italians in Chicago, 1880–1930* (New York: Oxford University Press, 1970); Madelon Powers, "Faces along the Bar: The Saloon in Working-Class Life, 1890–1920," Ph.D. dissertation, University of California, Berkeley, California, 1979. Madelon Powers has found that neighborhood saloons drew together mixed ethnic groups living in the same residential areas.

29. Rhoads, *Colonial Revival*, p. 716; Lubove, *Progressives*, pp. 23–24.

30. James Henretta, "The Study of Social Mobility," *Labor History* 18 (Spring 1977): 165–178.

31. Philip Cowen, *Memories of an American Jew* (New York: International Press, 1932), p. 231.

32. See Moses Rischin, *The Promised City* (Cambridge, Mass.: Harvard University Press, 1962), p. 22; Eli Ginzberg and Hyman Berman, eds., *The American Worker in the Twentieth Century: A History Through Autobiographies* (New York: The Free Press, 1963), p. 12.

33. John Briggs, *An Italian Passage: Italians in Three American Cities, 1890–1930* (New Haven: Yale University Press, 1978).

34. Pascal D'Angelo, *Son of Italy* (New York: Macmillan, 1924), p. 50.

35. David Riesman, *The Lonely Crowd: A Study of the Changing American Character* (New Haven:

Yale University Press, 1950), pp. 17–18, 40, in James Henretta, "Families and Farms: *Mentalite* in Pre-Industrial America," *William and Mary Quarterly* 35 (January 1978): 30.

36. Phyllis Williams, *South Italian Folkways in Europe and America* (New Haven: Yale University Press, 1938), p. 50.

37. Peter Roberts, *The Anthracite Coal Communities* (New York: Macmillan, 1904), p. 43.

38. For sacrifices made toward buying a house, see Stephen Thernstrom, *Poverty and Progress* (New York: Atheneum, 1971); John Modell, "Patterns of Consumption, Acculturation and Family Income Strategies in Late Nineteenth-Century America," in Tamara Harevan and Maris Vinovskis, *Family and Population in Nineteenth-Century America* (Princeton, N.J.: Princeton University Press, 1978), pp. 206–240; Virginia Yans-McLaughlin, *Family and Community: Italian Immigrants in Buffalo, 1880–1930* (Ithaca, N.Y.: Cornell University Press, 1977).

39. Edith Abbott and Sophonisba Breckinridge, *The Tenements of Chicago, 1908–1935* (Chicago: University of Chicago Press, 1936), pp. 263–264.

40. D'Angelo, *Son of Italy*, p. 5.

41. See Sydelle Kramer and Jenny Masur, eds., *Jewish Grandmothers* (Boston: Beacon Press, 1976); Mary Antin, *Promised Land* (Boston: Houghton Mifflin, 1912; Sentry Edition, 1969).

42. Donna Gabaccia, "Housing and Household Work in Sicily and New York, 1890," Ph.D. dissertation, University of Michigan, Ann Arbor, Michigan, p. 18.

43. Anton, *Promised Land*, p. 337.

44. Morris Knowles, *Industrial Housing* (New York: McGraw-Hill, 1920), p. 295.

45. Donald Cole, *Immigrant City: Lawrence, Massachusetts, 1845–1921* (Chapel Hill, N.C.: University of North Carolina Press, 1963), p. 107.

46. Robert Woods, *The City Wilderness* (1898; New York: Arno Press, 1970), p. 102.

47. Margaret Byington, *Homestead: The Households of a Mill Town* (New York: Russell Sage Foundation, 1910), p. 55.

48. Thomas Bell, *Out of This Furnace* (Boston: Little, Brown, 1941), p. 62.

49. See Rose Cohen, *Out of the Shadow* (New York: 1918), 196–197 in Judith Smith, "Our Own Kind," *Radical History Review* 17 (Spring 1978): 113; William Elsing, "Life in New York Tenement Houses," in Robert Woods, *Poor in Great Cities* (New York: Scribner's Sons, 1895), p. 50.

50. Byington, *Homestead*, p. 56.

51. Williams, *South Italian Folkways*, p. 17; Yans-McLaughlin, *Italians in Buffalo*, p. 223; Nelli, *Chicago Italians*, p. 6.

52. Inventory research at Old Sturbridge Village on western Massachusetts homes, 1790 to 1840, revealed a similar pattern; carpets and curtains were rare and precious.

53. Carlo Bianco, *The Two Rosetos* (Bloomington, Ind.: Indiana University Press, 1974), p. 14; Williams, *South Italian Folkways*, p. 43.

54. Antin, *Promised Land*, p. 274. (Emphasis is mine.)

55. Robert Roberts, *The Classic Slum* (London: Penguin, 1971), p. 33.

56. Graham Taylor, *Satellite Cities* (1915; New York: Arno Press, 1970), p. 194.

57. Barrows, *Neighbors All*, p. 70.

58. *Reports of President's Home Commission* (Washington: Government Printing Office, 1909), p. 117.

59. Byington, *Homestead*, in Ginzberg, *American Worker*, p. 46.

60. Cole, *Immigrant City*, p. 107.

61. See Thomas Wheeler, ed., *The Immigrant Experience* (New York: Dial Press, 1971; London: Penguin, 1977), pp. 20, 155; Cowen, *Memories of an American Jew*, p. 233.

62. Antin, *Promised Land*, p. 164.

63. Williams, *South Italian Folkways*, p. 86.

64. Elizabeth Hasonovitz, *One of Them* (Boston: Houghton Mifflin, 1918), p. 6.

65. Williams, *South Italian Folkways*, p.42.

66. Bianco, *Two Rosetos*, p. 124.

67. Kenneth Ames, "Grand Rapids Furniture at the Time of the Centennial," *Winterthur Portfolio* 10 (1975): 42.

68. Douglas Sladen and Norma Latimer, *Queer Things about Sicily* (London: Anthony Treherene, 1905), p. 85.

69. Williams, *South Italian Folkways*, pp. 42–43.

70. Williams, *South Italian Folkways*, p. 47.

71. Rainwater, *Workingman's Wife*; Rainwater, "House as Haven"; David Coplovitz, "The Problem of the Blue-Collar Consumer," in Arthur Shostak and William Gomberg, eds., *Blue-Collar World: Studies of the American Worker* (Englewood Cliffs, N.J.: Prentice Hall, 1964).

Chapter Twenty-two

1. I am using the definition of folklife commonly used in Europe and recently put forth by Ward Goodenough: "Folklife refers to the study of one's own national cultural heritage." Ward Goodenough, "Folklife Study and Social Change," in *American Folklife*, ed. Don Yoder (Austin: University of Texas Press, 1976), p. 20.

2. Ellis G. Burcaw, *Introduction to Museum Work* (Nashville: American Association for State and Local History, 1976), pp. 26–27.

3. Holly Sidford, "Stepping into History," *Museum News* 53 (1974): 30–34.

4. David Lowenthal, "The American Way of History," *Columbia University Forum* (Summer 1966): 27.

5. Lowenthal, "American Way of History," pp. 27–32; James Marston Fitch, "Uses of the Artistic Past," in *American Folklife*, ed. Don Yoder (Austin: University of Texas Press, 1976), pp. 45–46.

6. Robert D. Ronsheim, "Is the Past Dead? " *Museum News* 53 (1974): 16–19.

7. J. Geraint Jenkins, "The Use of Artifacts and Folk Art in the Folk Museums," in *Folklore and Folklife: An Introduction*, ed. Richard Dorson (Chicago: University of Chicago Press, 1972), pp. 502, 508.

8. Robert Asher, "Experimental Archaeology," *American Anthropoligist* 63 (1961): 793–816; John Coles, *Archaeology by Experiment* (New York: Scribner's, 1973).

9. Kenneth S. Goldstein, "The Induced Natural Context: An Ethnographic Folklore Field Technique," in *Essays in the Verbal and Visual Arts*, ed. June Helm (Seattle: University of Washington Press, 1967).

10. Asher, "Experimental Archaeology"; Coles, *Archaeology by Experiment*.

11. Thor Heyerdahl, *Kon-Tiki*, trans. X. F. H. Lyon (New York: Rand McNally, 1950).

12. Coles, *Archaeology by Experiment*, p. 15.

13. Coles, *Archaeology by Experiment*, p. 18.

14. Hans-Ole Hansen, *Some Main Trends in the Development of the Lejre Center* (Lejre, Denmark: Lejre Center, 1973), p. 7.

15. Peter J. Reynolds, *Farming in the Iron Age* (Cambridge, Eng.: Cambridge University Press, 1976).

16. Reynolds, *Farming in the Iron Age*, p. 4.

17. Keith Spence, "The Iron Age Brought to Life," *Country Life* 17 (September 1970): 693.

18. Errett Callahan, *The Old Rag Report: A Practical Guide to Living Archaeology* (Richmond: Department of Sociology/Anthropology, Virginia Commonwealth University, 1973); Errett Callahan, ed., *Experimental Archaeological Papers (APE)* (Richmond: Department of Sociology/Anthropology, Virginia Commonwealth University, 1974); Errett Callahan, *Living Archaeology: Projects in Subsistence Living* (Richmond: Department of Sociology/Anthropology, Virginia Commonwealth University, 1975).

19. Callahan, *Living Archaeology*, pp. 2–3.

20. Roger Welsch, "Very Didactic Stimulation," *American History Teacher* (Spring 1974): 356–357.

21. Jay Anderson, "Foodways Programs on Living Historical Farms" and Roger Welsch, "Sowbelly and Seedbanks," in *Association for Living Historical Farms and Agricultural Museums Annual* 1 (1975): 21–23 and 23–26.

22. Donald W. Callender, "Reliving the Past: Experimental Archaeology in Pennsylvania," *Archaeology* 29 (1976): 173–177.

23. Welsch, "Very Didactic Stimulation," pp. 357–358.

24. Hansen, *Some Main Trends in the Development of the Lejre Center*, pp. 11–12.

25. Alvin Toffler, *Future Shock* (New York: Bantam, 1971), pp. 390–391.

26. Jay Anderson, "On the Horns of a Dilemma: Research, Interpretation, and Fund Raising in Folk Museums," *Association for Living Historical Farms and Agricultural Museums Annual* 2 (1976).

Chapter Twenty-three

1. William L. Rathje, "The Garbage Project: A New Way of Looking at the Problems of Archaeology," *Archaeology* 27 (1974): 236–241; W. L. Rathje and W. W. Hughes, "The Garbage Project as a Nonreactive Approach: Garbage in . . . Garbage Out? " in *Perspectives on Attitude Assessment: Surveys and Alternatives*, ed. H. W. Sinaiko and L. A. Broedling, Manpowr Research and Advisory Services, Technical Report No. 2 (Washington: Smithsonian Institution, 1975).

2. S. F. Adelson, E. Asp, and I. Noble, "Household Records of Foods Used and Discarded," *Journal of the American Dietetic Association* 39 (1961): 578–584; S. F. Adelson, I. Delaney, C. Miller, and I. Noble, "Discard of Edible Food in Households," *Journal of Home Economics* 55 (1963): 633–638.

3. Eugene J. Webb, Donald T. Campbell, Richard D. Schwarts, and Lee Sechrest, *Unobtrusive Measures: Nonreactive Research in the Social Sciences* (Chicago: Rand McNally, 1966).

4. G. G. Harrison, W. L. Rathje, and W. W. Hughes, "Socioeconomic Correlates of Food Consumption and Waste Behavior: The Garbage Project," paper presented at the American Public Health Association meeting, 1974.

5. K. V. Flannery, "The Cultural Evolution of Civilization," *Annual Review of Ecology and Systematics* 3 (1968): 399–426; M. Gibson, "Violation of Fallow and Engineered Disaster in Mesopotamian Civilization" S. W. Lees, "The State's Use of Irrigation in Changing Peasant Society," in *Irrigation's Impact on Society*, ed. M. Gibson and T. Downing, Anthropological Papers No. 25 (Tucson: University of Arizona Press, 1974), pp. 7–20 and 123–128.

6. Harrison, Rathje, and Hughes, "Socioeconomic Correlates of Food Consumption"; G. G. Harrison, W. L. Rathje, and W. W. Hughes, "Food Waste Behavior in an Urban Population," *Journal of Nutritional Education* 7 (1975): 13–16.

7. Harrison, Rathje, and Hughes, "Socioeconomic Correlates of Food Consumption."

Chapter Twenty-four

1. T. G. Remer, *Serendipity and the Three Princes* (Norman: University of Oklahoma Press, 1965), p. 6.

2. J. Reichardt, *Cybernetic Serendipity* (New York: Praeger, 1969).

3. K. V. Flannery, "Cultural History versus Cultural Process: A Debate in American Archaeology," *Scientific American* 217 (1967): 119–122.

4. T. R. Blackburn, "Sensuous-Intellectual Complementarity in Science," *Science* 172 (1971): 10003–10007.

5. John Cage, *Silence* (Cambridge, Mass.: MIT Press, 1971), p. 70.

6. Robert Ascher, "A Prehistoric Population Estimate Using Midden Analysis and Two Population Models," Bobbs-Merrill Reprints in Anthropology No. A4 (Indianapolis: Bobbs-Merrill, 1962).

7. Siegfried Giedion, *Mechanization Takes Command* (New York: Norton, 1969), p. 147.

8. Giedion, *Mechanization Takes Command*, p. 3.

9. V. Papanek, *Design for the Real World* (Westminster, Md.: Pantheon, 1971), p. 41.

10. C. H. Waddington, *Behind Appearance* (Cambridge, Mass.: MIT Press, 1970), p. 159.

11. Daniel Spoerri, *An Anecdoted Topography of Chance* (New York: Something Else Press, 1966), p. xv.

12. Norman Daly, ed., *The Civilization of Llhuros* (Ithaca: A D. White Museum, 1972).

13. Robert Ascher, "Look for the Red Layer under the Blacktop Parking Lot in the Shopping Plaza," in *Civilization of Llhuros*, ed. Daly, p. 55.

14. Lynn White, Jr., *Dynamo and Virgin Reconsidered* (Cambridge, Mass.: MIT Press, 1968), p. 60.

15. William Van O'Connor, "The Novel and the 'Truth' about America." in *Studies in American Culture*, ed. J. K. Kwait and M. C. Turner (Minneapolis: University of Minnesota Press, 1960), p. 82.

16. W. H. Baddeley, *Documentary Film Production* (New York: Focal Press, 1969), p. 9.

17. Baddeley, *Documentary Film Production*, p.24.

18. James Agee and Walker Evans, *Let Us Now Praise Famous Men* (New York: Ballantine, 1969), p. 134.

19. Robert Fitzgerald, "A Memoir," in *The Collected Short Prose of James Agee*, ed. Robert Fitzgerald (New York: Ballantine, 1970), p. 29.

20. P. Rotha, *Documentary Film* (New York: Communication Art Books, 1969), p. 70.

21. Jesse Lemisch, "The American Revolution Seen from the Bottom Up," in *Towards a New Past: Dissenting Essays in American History*, ed. Barton J. Bernstein (London: Catto and Windus, 1970), p. 29.

22. Allan Nevins, *The United States* (Oxford, Eng.: Clarendon, 1960), p. 71.

23. Lynn White, Jr., "Introduction: The Reticences of the Middle Ages," in R. Berger, *Scientific Methods in Medieval Archaeology* (Berkeley: University of California Press, 1970), p. 3.

24. Roger Burlingame, "The Hardware of Culture," *Technology and Technology* 1 (1959): 14.

25. M. T. Watts, "Reading the Rooflines of Europe," in *The Subversive Science*, ed. P. Sheppard and D. McKinley (Boston: Houghton, Mifflin, 1971).

26. J. Cotter, "Walnut Street Prison," *Society for Historical Archaeology Newsletter* 6 (1973): 12; R. Roberts, *Imprisoned Tongues* (Manchester, Eng.: Manchester University Press, 1968); E. Lenik, "The Truro Halfway House, Cape Cod, Massachusetts," *Historical Archaeology* 6 (1972): 77–86; A. Briggs, "Announcement of a Report in Railroad Construction Camps," *Society for Historical Archaeology Newsletter* 4 (1971): 15–16; D. F. Morse and P. A. Morse, "The Brake Site: A Possible Early-Nineteenth-Century Log Cabin in Stewart County, Tennessee," *Florida Anthropologist* 17: 165–176.

27. C. A. Weslager, "The Excavation of a (Colonial) Log Cabin, Near Wilmington, Delaware," *Bulletin of the Archaeological Society of Delaware* 6 (1954); C. T. Snow, "Excavation at Casey's House," Archaeological Research Report, National Park Service, mimeographed, 1969; A. K. Bullen and R. P. Bullen, "Black Lucy's Garden," *Bulletin of the Massachusetts Archaeological Society* 6 (1945): 17–28.

28. Robert Ascher and C. H. Fairbanks, "Excavation of a Slave Cabin: Georgia, U.S.A.," *Historical Archaeology* 5 (1971): 3–17.

29. Daniel J. Boorstin, *The Americans: The National Experience* (New York: Random House, 1965), pp. 92–93.

30. T. Morley, "The Independence Road to Fort Laramie: By Aerial Photograph," *Plains Anthropologist* 6 (1961): 242–251.

31. Robert Ascher, "American Indian Civilization in New York," *Man in the Northeast* 5 (1973): 55–60.

32. R. J. C. Atkinson, *Stonehenge* (London: Hamish Hamilton, 1956); and F. Hoyle, "Speculations on Stonehenge," *Antiquity* 46 (1966): 262–276.

33. Bernard Fontana, et al., "Johnny Ward's Ranch," *Kiva* 28 (1962): 62.

34. C. Gilborn, "Pop Pedagogy," *Museum News*, 47 (1968): 16.

35. R. Ascher, "How to Build a Time Capsule," *Journal of Popular Culture* (1974).

36. D. W. Ingersoll, "Problems in Urban Historical Archaeology," paper presented at the Northeastern Anthropological Association, April 8, 1971.

37. E. A. M. Gell, "Preliminary Report on the Excavation of Two Privies under Old City Hall, Independence National Historical Park, Philadelphia," *Bulletin of the Philadelphia Anthropological Society* 20 (1969): 3–15.

38. Robert Somer, "Where Did You Go? What Did You Find? Fossils.," *Natural History* (May 1973): 9.

39. Mark Boyle, *Journey to the Surface of the Earth* (Boston: Boston Books and Art Publishers, 1970).

INDEX

Above-ground archaeology, 195
Access: as requirement of design, 158–159
Adams, George Burton, 13
Adams, Henry, 269
Adams, Henry Baxter, 13
Adams, James Truslow, 18
Addams, Jane, 296
Adler, Thomas, 62–63
Advertising: as historical evidence, 180;
    household appliances, 223, 227, 228, 234,
    235; use of photographs, 282, 283
Adz, 265
Aerial photography, 286
Aesthetics: folk art, 134–135; in evaluation, 168;
    of service stations, 257; folk crafts, 262–268
Agee, James, 194, 330–331
Aging of artifacts, 152
Agricultural history, 107
Agriculture: tools, 107–108, 111, 112–113;
    experimental ethnography, 310–315
Alcoholic beverages, 323
Ambrotype, 280
American Architectural Photographic Series, 285
American Association for State and Local
    History, 31, 73
American Association of Museums, 31
American Folklife Center, 3–4, 33
American Folklore Society, 22
American Heritage, 30
American Historical Association, 13, 73, 165
American Indians. *See* Native Americans
American Museum, 9
American Perspectives (symposium), 86
American Quarterly, 20
American Studies, 20–21, 27, 64, 66, 79–92,
    170, 269
American Studies Association, 20
American Walpole Society, 15
American Wing, Metropolitan Museum of Art,
    15, 293

Americana, 6
Americana movement, 5–6, 29–31
Americanization, 49, 295
Ames, Kenneth, 10, 40, 41–43, 72, 206–208
Amish, 136
Amoskeag Mills, 296
Ancient Agriculture Research Committee of the
    British Association, 310
Anderson, E. N., 54
Anderson, Jay, 54, 306–307
Annales d'historie économique et social, 36
Annales school, 36–37, 68
Anthony's Photographic Bulletin, 283
Anthropology, 116, 118
Antin, Mary, 299, 301, 302
Antiquarian, 100
Antique forums, 26
Antiques, 17
Appalachian region, 248
Appearance: of an artifact, 145, 160–161
Appleton, William Sumner, 13
Appliances, 222–236
Appraisal, 152
Archaeology: historical, 25–26, 47–50; artifact
    study, 164; gravestones, 195–205; and modern
    society, 318–320, 324, 325, 328–337
Arches, 269–277
Architectural historians, 11, 16–17, 21, 30, 182
Architecture: revivalism, 128; Pennsylvania
    German, 131; revival decoration, 138;
    Georgian homes, 212–213; vernacular houses,
    237–250; service stations, 253–258; arches,
    269–277; fast-food restaurants, 276; and
    photographic record, 278–288; middle-class
    homes, 293–294; church, 294
Ariès, Philippe, 36–37, 68, 224–225
Arrangement: as applied to design, 154–161
Art, 126, 129, 134
Art history, 11–12, 16–17, 41–43, 164, 185, 206
Art Nouveau, 128

409

E
169.1
M416
1982

Material culture studies in America /
compiled and edited, with
introductions and bibliography, by
Thomas J. Schlereth. -- Nashville,
Tenn. : American Association for
State and Local History, c1982.
xvi 419 p. ; 24 cm.

Includes bibliographical references
and index.
ISBN 0-910050-61-9. -- ISBN 0-
910050-67-8 (pbk.)

1. Material culture--United States--Study and
teaching--Addresses, essays, lectures. 2.
Material culture--United States--Addresses,
essays, lectures. 3. Archaeology and history--
(Cont'd on next card)

MUNION ME   830311   830309 CStoC
C001082   KW /JW   A*   83-B2042
                            82-8812